INSIDERS' GUIDE® TO

AUSTIN

SEVENTH EDITION

CAM ROSSIE & HILARY HYLTON

INSIDERS' GUIDE

GUILFORD, CONNECTICUT
AN IMPRINT OF GLOBE PEQUOT PRESS

All the information in this guidebook is subject to change. We recommend that you call ahead to obtain current information before traveling.

To buy books in quantity for corporate use or incentives, call **(800) 962-0973** or e-mail **premiums@GlobePequot.com**.

INSIDERS' GUIDE ®

Editor: Amy Lyons
Project Editor: Heather Santiago
Layout Artist: Kevin Mak
Text Design: Sheryl Kober
Maps: XNR Productions, Inc. © Morris Book Publishing, LLC

ISSN 1533-5216
ISBN 978-0-7627-6466-2

Printed in the United States of America
10 9 8 7 6 5 4 3 2 1

CONTENTS

CONTENTS

Directory of Maps

ABOUT THE AUTHORS

Cam Rossie is a journalist and freelance writer who started her professional career while still a university student, working as a reporter, copy editor, and editor for daily and weekly newspapers in the Midwest. A former domestic and foreign correspondent for the Associated Press news service, she has had news and feature articles published in newspapers throughout the United States and abroad. Her career with the AP began in Nebraska and later took her to New Mexico, Texas, and New York. She then was chosen to open a new AP bureau in Northern Mexico. From her base of operations in Monterrey, Cam covered the US–Mexico border from coast to coast, as well as other regions of Mexico and Central America. She is fluent in Spanish and is an accomplished public speaker who has lectured on journalism issues in the United States and Mexico.

An international journalism scholarship took her to Caracas, Venezuela, for nearly two years, sparking an interest in world cultures that remains to this day. In addition to living and working many years in Mexico and South America, Cam also lived for several years in Europe, where she wrote on education issues. While not at home in Austin, she travels throughout the United States and the world. Her passion for globe-trotting has taken her to more than 30 countries in Europe, Africa, the Middle East, and Central and South America. Her daughter, Quint Simon, was born in Mexico and has grown up as a third culture kid. This is Cam's seventh edition of *Insiders' Guide to Austin*.

Hilary Hylton is a freelance writer and author whose work covers a variety of topics, including business, social issues, personalities, government, politics, cuisine, and travel. Her work has been published in regional, national, and international publications.

Hilary has lived in Austin since 1977, watching it grow and change. She has written about many aspects of life in Austin—its food, politics, lifestyles, and business—for both Texas and national publications. Hilary is a freelance reporter for *Time* magazine. Her magazine articles also have appeared in major city, business, lifestyle, and airline magazines—features on food, travel, business, and political personalities. Prior to freelancing, she worked as a journalist for several Florida and Texas newspapers. Her work was honored with a number of awards, including Texas Star Reporter by the Austin Headliners' Club. Hilary is also the author of a guidebook, *Texas Monthly's Mexico: A Completely Up-to-Date Guide to an Extraordinary Country*. Hilary is married to Peter Silva, an award-winning photographer represented by Zuma Press. They have two Australian shepherds, siblings Ben and Pepper, and several cats who serve as substitute livestock for the dogs. Hilary's personal interests include reading history, armchair travel, gardening, cooking, and collecting cookbooks—interests all nurtured by Austin's vibrant offerings.

ACKNOWLEDGMENTS

One of the perks of working on *Insiders' Guide to Austin* is the opportunity to talk with so many of the fascinating people whose drive and creative energy help make our city so vibrant. Through their eyes I always discover new dimensions of Austin and grow to appreciate the singularity of this region even more than before. Thanks to everyone who took the time to offer their particular Insider information for this seventh edition. I am most appreciative of the editors and staff at Globe Pequot Press who labor most diligently to make this book happen, and I would like especially to acknowledge my coauthor on this project, Hilary Hylton, an excellent journalist and friend and a true Austin Insider. Of course I am eternally grateful for my daughter, Quint Simon, who always provides pearls of wisdom and outstanding moral support.

—Cam Rossie

Every time we venture forth for even the most mundane daily task we spot something new in Austin. This is an organic city that is ever-changing, making it exciting to live in and visit, but difficult to pin down sometimes in an ordered, guidebook-friendly fashion. A funky rundown storefront can morph into a hip cafe, a bungalow can become a boutique, and a warehouse can find new life as a gallery, making a city drive for even the longest of longtime residents a series of double takes and head turns. Downtown is a veritable wonderland of discoveries for those of us who have lived here for decades, a place that has captured the city's modern, young vibe. Old neighborhoods are a wonderful mix of longtime family businesses like Mexican bakeries and old plumbing supply shops, sitting side-by-side with gypsy food trailer courts, urban garden shops, and sewing studios.

There is an old saying here: "I wasn't born in Texas, but I got here as fast I could." That's the way we feel about Austin and revisiting the city through this latest edition reinforces that sentiment. Keeping track of those changes means relying on a wealth of resources, friends, neighbors, and those Austinites we interact with every day—the butcher, the baker, and the barista. Thanks to my coauthor, Cam, whose enthusiasm and professionalism are unmatched; and thanks to my husband, Peter Silva, whose insights into our hometown are invaluable.

—Hilary Hylton

Greater Austin

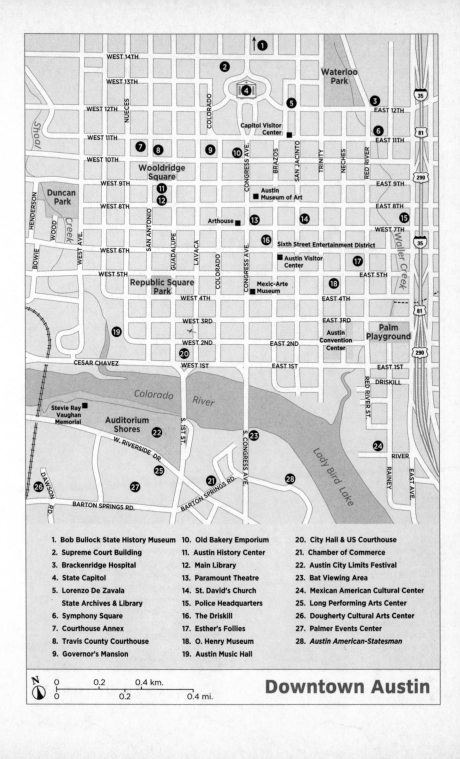

Downtown Austin

1. Bob Bullock State History Museum
2. Supreme Court Building
3. Brackenridge Hospital
4. State Capitol
5. Lorenzo De Zavala State Archives & Library
6. Symphony Square
7. Courthouse Annex
8. Travis County Courthouse
9. Governor's Mansion
10. Old Bakery Emporium
11. Austin History Center
12. Main Library
13. Paramount Theatre
14. St. David's Church
15. Police Headquarters
16. The Driskill
17. Esther's Follies
18. O. Henry Museum
19. Austin Music Hall
20. City Hall & US Courthouse
21. Chamber of Commerce
22. Austin City Limits Festival
23. Bat Viewing Area
24. Mexican American Cultural Center
25. Long Performing Arts Center
26. Dougherty Cultural Arts Center
27. Palmer Events Center
28. *Austin American-Statesman*

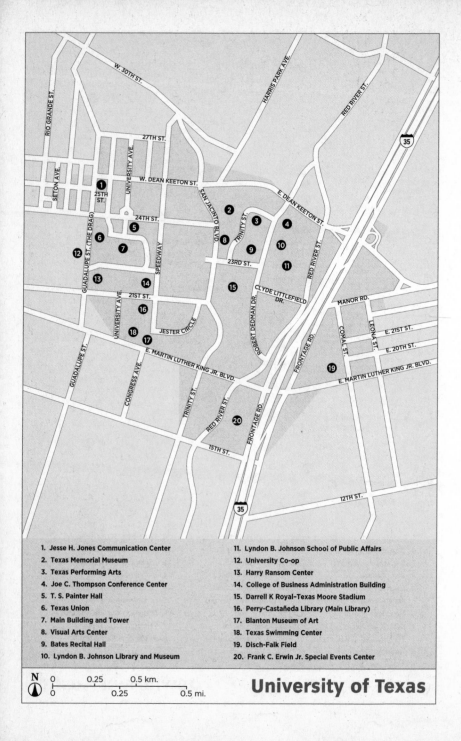

1. Jesse H. Jones Communication Center
2. Texas Memorial Museum
3. Texas Performing Arts
4. Joe C. Thompson Conference Center
5. T. S. Painter Hall
6. Texas Union
7. Main Building and Tower
8. Visual Arts Center
9. Bates Recital Hall
10. Lyndon B. Johnson Library and Museum

11. Lyndon B. Johnson School of Public Affairs
12. University Co-op
13. Harry Ransom Center
14. College of Business Administration Building
15. Darrell K Royal–Texas Moore Stadium
16. Perry-Castañeda Library (Main Library)
17. Blanton Museum of Art
18. Texas Swimming Center
19. Disch-Falk Field
20. Frank C. Erwin Jr. Special Events Center

N

| 0 | 0.25 | 0.5 km. |
| 0 | 0.25 | 0.5 mi. |

University of Texas

INTRODUCTION

Austin! Just the name evokes so many images. Music. High-tech. Universities. Government. Movies. Research. The hills. The lakes. The springs. Independence! Opportunity! Austin is all those things and much more, as you'll soon discover.

Riding on nothing more than beauty, its perch on the edge of a wild frontier, and the determination of its citizens, Austin became the capital of the Republic and then of the state of Texas, a vast territory that reaches from the Mexican border almost halfway to Canada. Like other Texans, Austinites who shaped this region developed a kinship with the land and with one another. To be a Texan is a definite distinction. To add Austinite—now that's the shine on the star.

Like many other Austinites, we are not natives, although Austin is one city that quickly becomes your own, no matter where you've lived before. The familiar bumper sticker "I wasn't born in Texas, but I got here as soon as I could" goes double for Austin. We're speaking from experience when we give these words of caution, especially for you who've come for just a visit: Austin sneaks up on you unexpectedly, like a sudden shower on a hot summer day. It will capture your heart as quickly as a dry field blossoms into wildflowers. Once you've gotten swept up in the energy of this city or given in to our peaceful pastimes, it's hard to leave. Austin is clever that way. It's old, and it's new, and every minute it's got something different to offer you. That's part of the Austin mystique.

Perhaps you've come to see for yourself what it is about Austin that causes people to perk up when they hear the name. We hope you'll find this guide useful in that regard. Within these pages we've shared our ideas about the people and places, the sounds and the scenery that contribute to Austin's unique style. We've sought to give you a deeper understanding of who we are by telling you where Austin has been and where it's headed as this booming region endeavors to define its future and preserve its acclaimed quality of life.

It's hard to argue with the national magazines that have rated Austin among the top cities for living and conducting business. Citing Austin's "emergence as a hotbed for high-tech startup firms," the prestigious *Fortune* magazine has listed Austin as "The Best City for Business in North America." "Austin has always been the sort of town where the '60s never really died, where creativity was encouraged, and free spirits were nurtured," *Fortune* praised. In his 2002 book *The Rise of the Creative Class*, economist and author Richard Florida lists Austin as the "No. 2 Creative Hot Spot" in the nation. Indeed, Austinites are warmhearted, outgoing people who tolerate about anything but encroachment on our stunning natural environment or challenge to our way of life. Our music scene is so hot that we call ourselves "The Live Music Capital of the World." Our vibrant film industry, which includes local actors and directors who are making it big, is luring more and more internationally known stars and directors to Austin. At any given time there are a dozen or more stage productions to enjoy as well as art museums and galleries to visit and poetry readings to attend. Our countless sports enthusiasts, the bikers, boaters, runners, golfers, and swimmers, keep Austin humming with their passion.

The University of Texas contributes much more than character and economic drive. UT, along with our other colleges and universities, draws leading scholars and researchers to Austin and offers our students and the public countless educational opportunities and chances to hear world-renowned speakers. Our bookstores and libraries are abuzz day and night. It's no surprise, then, that Austin is considered a literary capital as well as the center of our massive state government. Along with thousands of jobs, the vigorous high-tech industry adds another dimension to Austin's intellectual community. The reward in living and working in Austin comes in knowing that no matter what challenges the day brings, there is a fascinating, fun, beautiful, easygoing city right outside the door.

Austin's amazing ability to combine that vitality—that feeling that anything is possible here—with a sense of tranquility is among its greatest attributes. There's plenty of space to get away: lying on the beach at Lake Travis, strolling along a wooded trail, flying a kite atop breathtaking Mount Bonnell, taking a cool dip in Barton Springs, picnicking at the park, exploring the natural wonders of the Hill Country, canoeing along Lady Bird Lake (formerly Town Lake).

Don't take our word for it, though. Austin is a city that must be experienced firsthand. This book is meant to point you in the right directions. For those of you who've come to live, congratulations, you've chosen well. If you're here as a visitor, enjoy your Austin experience. Like we said, however, beware of its captivating charm.

HOW TO USE THIS BOOK

Whether you're planning to stay in Austin for a night, a fortnight, or the rest of your life, this book will guide you to, and through, the best the Capital City has to offer in more than two dozen areas of interest. *Insiders' Guide to Austin* is arranged by categories that appeal to both tourists and newcomers and can be useful whether you've just arrived or are only contemplating a visit or a move to Austin. Longtime residents may even discover a new thing or two about our city.

Our challenge in writing this book was to provide solid information and arrange it suitably so that you can map out a tour of Austin according to your own interests. It's up to you whether you take in these pages in one big gulp or choose to savor them slowly, chapter by chapter, as you make your way around town. Whatever your style, *Insiders' Guide to Austin* is meant to be used and used again as you delve deeper into the treasures of our Capital City. More than anything, we've designed this book to answer that age-old question: Where can I go to find . . . ?

Within these pages you'll encounter detailed descriptions of many of our most popular restaurants, attractions, hotels and motels, bed-and-breakfasts, and resorts as well as extensive listings of great places to shop and fun things to do with the kids. The chapter devoted to The Music Scene was a must, as you'll see, and we've dedicated another to Austin Nightlife. We've described our dynamic Literary Scene and given you an introduction to Austin's great Arts community. Nature lovers and outdoor types will discover the best that Austin has to offer in the Parks & Recreation chapter. Within all chapters, you will find frequent cross-references and even, for the sake of convenience, some cross-listings.

For a wealth of information on our diverse periodicals, and radio and television stations, we've included a chapter on Media. Newcomers will want to take special note of the blue-tabbed pages at the back of the book, where they'll find the **Living Here** appendix with chapters on Relocation, The Senior Scene, and Health Care & Wellness. The Schools & Child Care chapter includes information on private schools and all 10 public school districts in and around Austin, including those in our neighboring communities.

Because much of the subject matter begs to be included in more than one chapter, we've noted where to look in the book for further information on a particular topic. Austin is loaded with resources, and we regret that we could not include every choice available in each chapter. We have, however, provided a solid foundation for you in all our categories and have pointed out additional resource materials that may provide more information.

Throughout this book you'll find **Insider's Tips** (indicated by an **i**), which offer quick insights, and **Close-ups,** which provide in-depth information on topics that are particularly interesting, unusual, or distinct. You'll also find listings accompanied by the ✳ symbol—these are our top picks for attractions, restaurants, accommodations, and everything in between that you shouldn't miss while you're in the area. You want the best this region has to offer? Go with our **Insiders' Choice.**

Finding your way around town will probably be the first challenge you face upon arriving in Austin. While Austin does have some great natural and manufactured boundaries, such as the Colorado River and our main highway arteries, the layout can be confusing due to our unique Hill Country terrain and the fact that Austin isn't too keen on east-west thoroughfares. No two people agree exactly on how to divide Austin into geographic regions, especially now that the city has grown so much. (The area that is still referred to today as West Austin, for example, is now in Central Austin, while a new West Austin is, well, farther west.)

Start your tour of Austin by reading our Getting Here, Getting Around chapter. In this chapter we've explained the boundaries we use in this book to divide the city into 11 regions: Central, South Central, North Central, North, South, East, West, Northeast, Northwest, Southeast, and Southwest. In some chapters we've subdivided these regions even further. In the Hotels and Motels chapter, for instance, you will find an extensive listing for accommodations under the I-35 Corridor heading. Because there are so many Attractions in Central Austin, we've divided that region into Downtown, The University of Texas, and Central Austin.

Refer to the maps we've provided to get started on your Austin adventure.

AREA OVERVIEW

Folks on planes sometimes ask us: "Where do you live?" "Austin, Texas," we say. Nine times out of ten the questioner smiles, sighs, and says, "Lucky you."

Austin gets good press. In the past two decades, the city has been touted as a top place to live by numerous magazines. Perhaps the most overused adjective in all this positive coverage is "laid-back." But it fits. After all, this is a city where you can get by with one or two pairs of pantyhose a year or keep your tie rack in the back of the closet.

As former Mayor Kirk Watson once described Austin to us in an interview, "Austin is a city of boots and suits, hippies and nerds, all in the same boardroom . . . a city that allows almost ironic contradictions—at the same time we boast that we are the Live Music Capital of the World, we also boast we are Silicon Hills."

Laid-back, but on the high-tech cutting edge; cherishing the past, but charting the future. That dichotomy makes Austin an exciting, sometimes challenging place to live. We are embracing the future, yet looking longingly at the past, and, as the former mayor told us, so far each new wave of Austinites thinks they got here just in time to enjoy the real Austin.

Austin is a mecca for musicians and moviemakers, software engineers and hardware wizards, entrepreneurs and investors, artists and artisans, intellectuals and teachers, political activists and environmentalists, and lots of hardworking, everyday Texans who labor to make this city flourish. More than a million people call themselves Austinites these days, but there is still a neighborly feel about Austin and a notion that much of what goes on here is authentic.

As Austin has grown in both population and acreage, the pivotal question has been "How can Austin stay Austin, yet flourish?" The answer, so far, has come from within. Homegrown is the key here—whether it is homegrown businesses such as Dell Computer and Whole Foods Market or homegrown restaurants such as Threadgill's and Jeffrey's, Austin's creative juices flow from the ground up. Franchise and chain operations, national corporations, and international businesses are represented in Austin, and they are growing in number; but, for the most part, they opt to adapt an Austin face, and often are overshadowed when viewed side by side with Austin originals.

This makes Austin a great place to live and to visit. Despite all its attributes, Austin has avoided being labeled a tourist town. Visitors are drawn to Austin not by a single, large attraction, a Disney World or a Fisherman's Wharf, but by the ambience of Austin. Consequently, we also are relatively free of touristy bric-a-brac, restaurants, and other sites that attract only out-of-towners. So whether you're visiting Sixth Street or stopping in for some spicy Tex-Mex food or barbecue, you will find yourself among the locals.

Austin's Many Faces

The population of Austin is diverse and growing more so every year as new residents join the Austin melting pot. According to the US Census Bureau, 12.4 percent of the city's residents are African American, 23 percent Hispanic, and 3 percent Asian. Approximately 7 percent of the city's residents are older than 65. About 9 percent of Austin's residents are foreign-born, and 23 percent speak a language other than English at home.

Founded: 1821 by Stephen F. Austin's colonists and named Waterloo; incorporated as Austin December 27, 1839

Mayor/Governor: Mayor Will Wynn; Governor Rick Perry

Population:
>   Austin: 785,850
>   Austin/Round Rock metropolitan statistical area: 1.7 million
>   Texas: 23.5 million

Area: Austin: 308 square miles
>   Austin/Round Rock metro area: 4,286 square miles

Counties in the Austin area (with major cities and county seats):
>   Travis County (Austin is county seat and state capital)
>   Williamson County (Round Rock; county seat Georgetown)
>   Hays County (county seat San Marcos)
>   Bastrop County (county seat Bastrop)
>   Caldwell County (county seat Lockhart)

Major airports/interstates: Austin-Bergstrom International Airport; I-35, the Nafta Highway, runs through Austin

Nicknames: "Live Music Capital of the World," "Third Coast," and "City of the Violet Crown"

Average temperatures:
>   Mean 68° F
>   Mean low 58° F
>   Mean high 79° F

Average annual precipitation: 33.65 inches

Annual days of sunshine: 200+

Major colleges and universities: University of Texas, Austin Community College, St. Edwards University, Texas State University—San Marcos, Southwestern University Georgetown, Concordia University of Austin, Huston-Tillotson College, Austin Presbyterian Seminary

Major area employers: University of Texas, Dell Computer, City of Austin, Austin Independent School District, Motorola, H-E-B Grocery Company, Seton Healthcare Network, IBM,

Internal Revenue Service, Austin Community College, Advanced Micro Devices, Applied Materials

Famous sons and daughters: (Some native; others, as they say in Texas, got here as fast as they could.) Lyndon Baines Johnson, Lady Bird Johnson, O. Henry, Dabney Coleman, Lou Ann Barton, Charles Umlauf, Michael Dell, Stevie Ray Vaughn, Earl Campbell, J. Frank Dobie, James Michener, Lance Armstrong, Ethan Hawke, Zachary Scott, Molly Ivins, Willie Nelson, Karl Rove, Linda Ellerbe, Ben Crenshaw, Nelly, Joe Ely, Roger Clemens, Tom Kite, Bud Schrake, Ann Richards, Steven Fromholz

Public transportation: Capital Metro operates buses and downtown 'Dillo: buses, light rail from Cedar Park to downtown Austin opened in the fall of 2008.

Driving laws: Speed limits vary according to the size of the street or highway and its location. Generally, interstate speed limits are 70 mph, city freeways are 55 mph or 65 mph, and most neighborhood speed limits are 30 mph. There are hefty fines for drivers who use cell phones in school zones, and Austin levies big fines for texting while driving.

Alcohol laws:
> You must be 21 to purchase wine, beer, or liquor in bars, restaurants, and stores. Blood alcohol level at which one is presumed to be intoxicated is 0.08 percent. Beer and wine may be purchased in grocery and convenience stores 7 days a week. Fortified wines like port cannot be sold on Sunday, and liquor stores are closed on Sunday.
>
> Bars remain open until 2 a.m.

Daily newspapers: *Austin American-Statesman, Daily Texan*

Alternative newspaper: *Austin Chronicle*

Taxes: State sales taxes vary in the Central Texas region but generally range around 8 percent. In the City of Austin the rate is 8.25 percent. Groceries are not taxed. Hotel-motel occupancy tax in Austin is 15 percent.

Chamber of Commerce: Austin Chamber of Commerce, in the Lakeshore Tower building at 210 Barton Springs Rd., Suite 400, Austin, TX 78704; (512) 478-9383; www.austin-chamber.org

Visitor center: Austin Convention and Visitors Bureau, 209 East Sixth St.; (512) 478-0098 or (866) GO-AUSTIN; www.austintexas.org

Time and weather:
> KVUE–TV operates a time and temperature service at (512) 451-2424.
> Fox Channel 7 has a live weather cam at www.fox7.com, and Cable Channel 8 has "weather on the eights" throughout the hour.
> National Weather Service: www.srh.noaa.gov/ewx

The percentage of adults with college degrees stands at 40 percent and two-thirds of the city's residents have some college education. The median income in Austin in 2000 was $42,689, and according to the 2000 census, only 4.5 percent of households received public assistance, ranking 72nd out of those 77 cities. In 2005 the median income was $68,600.

One startling statistic is that the Austin labor force increased 44 percent in the decade from 1980 to 1990, and as the 21st century got under way unemployment rates stood at less than 3 percent, dipping to 1.9 percent in mid-2001 and climbing to just under 6 percent in mid-2003. By the spring of 2008, the rate had dipped again to 3.6 percent. But as the recession hit the country Austin was not immune, although the numbers never climbed as high as outside Texas. In September of 2010, the Austin unemployment rate stood at 7.1 percent. Austin residents are predominantly young, diverse, dynamic, and hardworking; perhaps that is why the Austin lifestyle is characterized by a love for the outdoors and a lively interest in the latest music and art. But there is also a fondness for old Texas traditions; witness the abundance of annual events dedicated to cultural traditions (see our Annual Events & Festivals chapter).

While the past is celebrated, cultural diversity is unfolding at a furious pace in Austin. Restaurants and shops reflecting diverse cultural origins are growing in number. In a city where 25 years ago the choice of restaurants was relatively limited and dominated by Tex-Mex, barbecue, and homestyle cooking, residents and visitors can now choose from a wide variety of cuisines, often presented as "fusion" cuisine by one of the city's hot young chefs. There is a palpable sense of exploration in the air as the city adopts and absorbs a multitude of influences, translating them into an authentic Austin experience.

THE GREAT OUTDOORS

No description of Austin would be complete without an ode to the area's physical surroundings. Forget those cliched Texas movie images you have seen in the Westerns. Austin is a city where trees and plants abound. Live oaks, pecans, cedar elms, and redbuds shade city streets, and city ordinances make it illegal to cut down trees of a certain diameter. Wildflowers, native plants, and grasses provide a year-round palette for both gardeners and Mother Nature as she paints the wild and natural areas of Central Texas.

Anyone who has visited Austin in the spring when the bluebonnets and Indian paintbrushes are in bloom leaves with a much-changed image of Texas. Hill Country pastures cry out for the brush of Monet, while the grassy banks along city freeways and country roads have been painted with a riot of color thanks to the state highway department's wildflower planting program.

The parade of wildflowers continues to bloom through summer and into fall. Every visitor and resident should make a pilgrimage to the Lady Bird Johnson Wildflower Center in Southwest Austin to take in the beauty, learn about native plants, and pay homage to the former First Lady who made saving American wildflowers a personal crusade (see our Attractions chapter).

Other examples of Austin natural wonders include Barton Springs, the spring-fed natural swimming pool that sits in the heart of the city's large downtown greenbelt, Zilker Park (see our Parks & Recreation chapter). Then there are the bats: North America's largest urban colony of Mexican freetail bats lives under the Congress Avenue bridge spring through fall, and their nightly flight in search of bug dinners draws crowds to the shores of Lady Bird Lake in downtown Austin (see our Attractions chapter). To the west of the city are the Highland Lakes, a chain of artificial lakes that stretch more than 150 miles, encompass 56,000 acres of water, and offer 700 miles of shoreline, making up the greatest concentration of fresh water in Texas. A network of lake and state parks, county and city parks, plus nature preserves and greenbelts surround Austin and provide green havens within the city limits (see our Parks & Recreation chapter).

In addition to a beautiful environment, Austinites also enjoy a generally benign climate. There are a few weeks in summer, notably late July and August, when the midday sun can take its toll, but since most buildings and cars in the city are air-conditioned, even those days are bearable. In winter there can be some brief spells of cold weather, but freezes are infrequent and snow is very rare, falling in any measurable amount about once every decade. One local tradition that new residents soon learn is the "plant shuffle"—hauling in all those patio plants that are sensitive to a hard freeze and then hauling them back out again a day or two later, but some winters pass without a single hard freeze.

The so-called "blue norther" is another Texas phenomenon that quickly becomes part of a newcomer's lexicon. These winter cold fronts often can be seen coming as the wind shifts to the north and the clouds are swept from the sky, allowing temperatures to fall into the 40s and 30s. Visitors often are astounded by how quickly the temperature falls, going from 70-something to 40-some-thing literally in minutes—a good reason to carry a sweater in winter.

Spring is usually the rainy season, but Austin also enjoys spring days that border on the sublime, when residents can keep their windows open night and day. The average yearly rainfall is 32 inches, and there are on average 116 clear days, 114 partly cloudy days, 135 cloudy days, and 84 days with measurable rain. While winters are mild, sudden summer thunderstorms can be threatening. The Hill Country is riddled with what appear to be dry creek beds, but after a sudden spring or summer rainfall they quickly become dangerous, as flash floods rage along their paths. Never try to drive across a flooded creek bed, and be aware of weather warnings about lightning storms and infrequent tornadoes.

For much of the year, the weather is benevolent and beautiful, allowing Austinites to spend their leisure time outdoors enjoying the many parks and recreational facilities in the area, perhaps a cup of coffee at an outdoor cafe, or a walk along Lady Bird Lake in the heart of downtown. But when the sun goes down they turn to other activities, enjoying the area's casual dining scene (see our Restaurants chapter) and the abundant nightlife.

THE MUSIC SCENE

Boasting the hottest live music scene in the country, Austin rocks day and night with just about any style of music imaginable: blues, country, jazz, folk, funk, punk, bluegrass, Tejano, rock and roll, alternative, and the savory sounds of our true Texas hybrids. Called a mecca for musical mavericks in 1998 by *Billboard* magazine, Austin is world renowned for its unique brands of original music and for attracting top-notch performers who would

Close-up

Notable Events in Austin History

1730: Spanish explorers establish a temporary mission at Barton Springs.

1821: Stephen F. Austin sends settlers to the banks of the Colorado River.

August 1833: The settlers are attacked by Indians.

March 2, 1836: Texas declares its independence from Mexico.

1838: Mirabeau Lamar, vice president of the Republic of Texas, goes on a buffalo hunt near the Colorado River and declares, "Here should reside the seat of the future empire."

May 1839: A one-story capitol is erected at what is now Colorado and Eighth Streets.

August 1, 1839: The first city lots are sold in the town initially dubbed "Waterloo."

November 1839: Waterloo is renamed Austin in honor of Stephen F. Austin.

December 1840: Jean Pierre Isidore Alphonse Dubois de Saligny builds the French Legation mission, Austin's oldest structure still intact.

February 19, 1846: Texas joins the Union, and Austin is declared the state capital.

February 1861: Austin and Travis County vote against secession from the Union.

1874: The first street lamps are placed along Austin's streets.

1876: David T. Lamme Sr. opens a candy store on Congress Avenue; the company is still in business in Austin.

1881: The city charters the University of Texas, and Tillotson Collegiate and Normal Institution opens to provide higher education to African Americans.

1885: St. Edward's College opens.

1886: The Driskill Hotel opens downtown.

May 16, 1888: The new pink granite capitol opens, replacing the first structure.

1892: Sculptor Elisabet Ney builds Formosa, her home and studio, in Hyde Park.

1894: O. Henry dubs Austin "The City of the Violet Crown" in a story titled "Tictocq."

1895: Thirty-one so-called moonlight towers cast light over the city.

April 7, 1900: Austin Dam collapses; eight die and the city is without power for months.

1918: Andrew Zilker's land, with iconic Barton Springs, becomes a city park.

1920: Austin's population reaches 34,876.

1923: A major oil find in West Texas on land owned by the University of Texas sets the stage for the establishment of a permanent university fund.

October 14, 1930: Robert Mueller Municipal Airport opens.

December 6, 1933: Travis County Beer License No. 01 is issued to Kenneth Threadgill, whose little saloon becomes a major magnet for musicians.

1937: The 27-story UT Tower is built, prompting J. Frank Dobie to ask why, with all the space in Texas, does a building here have to look like one in New York City.

1937: Lyndon Baines Johnson is elected to Congress and supports New Deal programs like electrification of the Hill Country, which helps Austin through the Great Depression.

1941: Mansfield Dam on Lake Travis is completed.

Thanksgiving Day 1952: Launched by Lyndon and Lady Bird Johnson, Central Texas's first television station, KTBC, makes its debut.

1956: The University of Texas is the first major Southern school to admit African-American undergraduates.

1963: Football Coach Darrell Royal leads the UT Longhorns to their first national championship.

November 10, 1964: James M. White opens the legendary Broken Spoke.

April 1, 1966: From his perch in the UT Tower, sniper Charles Whitman shoots, killing 14 and wounding 31, after earlier murdering his mother and wife.

1967: IBM locates in Austin, later followed by Texas Instruments and Motorola.

1968: An African American is elected to the Austin school district; three years later the first African American is elected to the city council. Mexican-American candidates succeed in 1972 and 1975 to the same bodies.

August 7, 1970: The legendary Armadillo World Headquarters opens.

1971: The LBJ Presidential Library opens.

1974: KLRU–TV producer Bill Arhos proposes a new music show, *Austin City Limits;* Willie Nelson stars in the pilot.

July 15, 1975: Clifford Antone opens his first blues club on Sixth Street.

1982: Lady Bird Johnson opens her wildflower research center.

1983: City political and business leaders push successfully for the MCC high-tech consortium to be located in Austin.

1984: Michael Dell starts his computer company and direct flights, "Nerd Birds," are launched between Austin and Silicon Valley.

1994: A seismic shift takes place in state politics as Republicans led by George W. Bush dominate both US Senate seats and most of the state's highest offices and judicial posts.

November 7, 2000: Thousands of supporters and media stand in a cold downpour on Congress Avenue, watching the presidential election gridlock.

October 2004: A record two million yellow "Live strong" bracelets are sold as the legendary cyclist and Austin resident Lance Armstrong rides through the streets of Austin in his annual Ride for the Roses bicycle event, all in support of his cancer-fighting foundation.

March 2005: Austin-born Whole Foods celebrates its 25th anniversary by opening its huge Landmark Store at Sixth and Lamar, just blocks from its first tiny location.

September 2006: Beloved Austin resident, former Governor Ann Richards dies. The Congress Avenue Bridge is renamed in her honor. First Lady Lady Bird Johnson dies a year later. Austinites line Congress Avenue and the highway all the way to LBJ Ranch in Johnson City in her honor.

November 2007: A live oak tree is hoisted atop 360 Condominiums as downtown booms.

June 2008: An arsonist inflicts heavy damage on the Governor's Mansion.

March 2010: Capital Metro opens the 32-mile, $22 million light rail line from Leander in far northwest Austin to downtown.

rather live and play in Austin than bend to the prevailing winds of musical fashion elsewhere. Home to the world's best-known country music outlaw, Willie Nelson, launching stage for the late blues legend Stevie Ray Vaughan, a haven for scores of world-class artists and up-and-comers, Austin is a paradise of live music. Read more about our music haven in The Music Scene chapter, which includes a Close-up on Austin favorites, Willie and Stevie Ray.

THE ARTS

While they haven't earned equal billing with the Live Music Capital of the World, Austin's dynamic arts and literary scenes lend the cultural dimension that makes this city such an inviting place to live. Long known as a haven for artists and intellectuals, more and more talented artists have found inspiration in Austin over the past few decades. Today Austin offers more than 250 theater productions a year, including national touring shows and an excellent variety of local productions. There are numerous annual arts and music events throughout the year, including the SXSW (South-By-Southwest) music and media conference in spring and the Texas Book Festival in fall (see our Annual Events & Festivals chapter). Our art museums, galleries, and bookstores abound with fresh voices in both the visual and literary arts. The city also is home to the Texas Film Commission, the state agency that has been successful in bringing many movie productions to what is affectionately called "The Third Coast." See our chapters on The Literary Scene and The Arts.

THE UNIVERSITY

Sprawling over 357 acres in the very heart of Central Austin, the University of Texas is an omnipresent force throughout this region. UT's contribution to Austin's economy and to its intellectual, political, and artistic development over the past 115-plus years has helped make Austin the envy of Texas and one of the coolest places in the land to live, work, study, and play. With about 50,000 students, UT gives Austin much of its youthful energy while bolstering its reputation as one of the country's hippest small cities. A breeding ground for intellectuals and a renowned research center, UT is one factor driving Austin's knowledge-intensive economy today. What's more, UT rewards Austinites almost daily by offering a rich variety of artistic, educational, and sporting events.

Although it's not considered one of the country's most beautiful campuses, UT nevertheless is a sight to behold. Towering shade trees, sculptures and fountains by world-class artists, dozens of architectural wonders representing more than a century of development, and the 27-story UT Tower that soars as a landmark for all of Austin give the UT campus its unique flair. UT-Austin, the flagship of the system's 15 campuses spread throughout the state, is a source of pride for all Texans. Read about UT in our Attractions, Spectator Sports, The Arts, and Higher Education chapters and about its libraries in The Literary Scene chapter.

UT's size and importance to the economic development of Central Texas over the past century make UT Austin's most significant institute of higher learning. But our other colleges and universities—St. Edward's University in South Austin, Huston-Tillotson on the east side, Concordia University near UT, Southwestern University north of us in Georgetown, Texas State University south in San Marcos, and Austin Community College's campuses all over the region—combine to give Central Texas its fame as an educational Eden (see our Higher Education chapter).

i Visitors to Austin are captivated by the flora in Central Texas, particularly the abundant wildflowers. The University of Texas Press publishes a wonderful full-color guide called *Texas Wildflowers* by Campbell and Lynn Loughmiller. The book has a foreword by Lady Bird Johnson.

GOVERNMENT

The Austin economy rests on three sectors: higher education, government, and the high-tech industry. The State of Texas employs approximately 50,000 people in the Austin area. As the state capital, the city is headquarters for many state agencies and, of course, the legislature and high courts.

The Texas legislature is convened on the second Tuesday of January in odd-numbered years for a 120-day regular session. Special sessions are occasionally called at other times by the governor. During the biennial session Austin takes on a little different air as hotels and restaurants fill with politicians, their staffs, and lobbyists. But Austin is also a political city year-round, since many legislative staffers live here, along with those agency heads, judges, and state bureaucrats who live, eat, and breathe the political air of the city.

Austin is also known for its active local political scene where the environment and the fight to keep Austin true to itself are always center stage.

HIGH-TECH

The third major pillar of the Austin economy is a relative newcomer. High-tech is now an integral part of the picture, and the three largest private-sector employers in Austin are technology companies— Dell Computer Corp., Motorola Inc., and IBM Corp. The vibrant music industry, a burgeoning film scene, and an up-and-coming multimedia sector have added to the diverse economic picture, giving Austin a much wider economic base and ensuring that it is not as subject to the whims of a single economic sector's ups and downs as it was in the past.

Austin's homegrown computer titan, Dell Computer Corp., along with other Fortune 500 companies that established Central Texas branches in the 1980s and 1990s, brought tens of thousands of jobs to become the driving force behind this region's economy. What's more, it didn't take too long for the Texas spirit of adventure to emerge in a big way in the technology field, and venture capital has played a major role.

Oil wildcatters of earlier decades enhanced Texas's mystique as a hotbed of fiercely independent risk-takers, but a new breed of prospectors is leading Austin today. Armed with computer chips rather than drill bits, Austin's modern wildcatters are gambling on start-up technology companies in computers and especially in software development.

GROWTH ISSUES

Long known as a low-growth region, Austin lived out its unique vision for more than 150 years without much concern for policies in then-far-off Round Rock, Cedar Park, Dripping Springs, and other neighboring communities. But as this booming region expands into one big metropolis, Austin now is faced with developing a plan for the

Close-Up

Texas Pronunciation Guide

"Texas—It's a whole other country!" Turns out the ad slogan used to promote Texas as a tourist destination is right, at least when it comes to the local lingo. Newcomers and visitors to Austin can be confounded by the local eccentricities in language, so we have developed this handy primer:

Balcones (Bal-CONE-niss): A geological fault line that runs north-south through the city. This is just the first of several Spanish names that are not pronounced the way you were taught in high school Spanish.

Boerne (BURN-nee, rhymes with Bert and Ernie): A small town southwest of Austin noted for its dude ranches. Just as many local names have their roots in Mexican culture, many also derive from German settlers.

Bowie (BOO!-ee): As in that buoy in the water. A hero of the Alamo, Jim Bowie gave his name to both a knife and an Austin high school.

Brazos (BRAA-ziss): A Texas river that runs through Waco and the name of a downtown Austin street. All seven major Texas rivers give their names to downtown, north-south streets in Austin; memorize their names and their respective east-west position on the Texas map and you will know how to find them in downtown Austin (see our Getting Here, Getting Around chapter).

Buchanan (Buck-ANN-un): Rhymes with buckin' bronco and is one of the Highland Lakes northwest of Austin.

Buda (BYEW-dah): Rhymes with phew! This is a small town just south of Austin.

Bonnell (Bun-NELL): That's Mount Bonnell, a popular spot to take in a view of Austin (see our Attractions chapter).

Burnet (BURN-it): Rhymes with "durn it." It's an Austin road and a Hill Country town.

Cameron Road (CAM-run): Drop the middle syllable here, and you'll sound okay.

Coupland (COPE-land): As in Aaron Copland, home of the famous Coupland Dance Hall.

Dessau (DESS-aw): Dessau Lane is in North Austin.

Del Valle (Dell Valley): Another Spanish word that has been Texas-ized, Del Valle is a neighborhood southeast of Austin near the airport.

Elgin (ELL-ghin): No gin here (it rhymes with "kin"), or vermouth, just sausages. This small town east of Austin makes a famous German-style sausage.

Gruene (Green): The German word for green and the name of a small town south of Austin known for its antiques shops and artists (see our Day Trips & Weekend Getaways chapter).

Govalle (Go Valley): Another Spanish word corrupted by gringo tongues? Surprise! No, this is derived from a Swedish phrase *go val* meaning "good grazing land," and Swedish settlers gave this name to fertile pastureland east of Austin along the Colorado River. A cabin built there in 1840 by S. M. Swenson, the first Swedish settler in Texas, is now found in the Zilker Park Garden Center (see our Attractions chapter).

Guadalupe (GWA-da-loop): If you can remember Alley Oop, you will quickly get the hang of this street name. The portion of Gwadaloop that runs through the University of Texas campus is known as "The Drag."

Huston (HYOU-stun): As in Sam Houston, and part of the name of Huston-Tillotson College (see our Higher Education chapter).

Jager (YAY-gahr): That's Yeager as in Chuck "The Right Stuff" Yeager and the name of a lane, now a major roadway, in North Austin.

Koenig (KAY-nig): Another German name that was given to a lane in North Austin and another of those "lanes" that is now a major thoroughfare.

Kreuz (Cry-tzz): You don't really have to know how to pronounce this name if you have good sense of smell. Simply start sniffing as you approach Lockhart, and your nose will carry you to the famous barbecue spot (see our Annual Events & Festivals chapter).

Lavaca (La-VAH-cah): One of the few Spanish names pronounced correctly here, it means "the cow" and is he name of a Spanish explorer, an Austin street, and a Texas river.

Llano (LAN-oh): The name means "plains" in Spanish, but historians believe the county and town of the same name northwest of Austin take their name from the Llano River in the plains west of the Hill Country.

Manchaca (MAN-shack): Not only has this Spanish word been given the Texas treatment, but the spelling has been changed as well. Legend says a spring south of Austin was named for Colonel Jose Antonio Menchaca, scion of an old San Antonio family. The "e" was changed to an "a" over the years. The Manchaca community is now part of the growing Austin, but the elementary school there has been named for Menchaca with the original spelling.

Manor (MAY-ner): Forget your "to the manor born" accent when pronouncing the name of this community east of Austin and opt for a down-home twang.

New Braunfels (New BRAWN-fells): This is one of several picturesque Hill Country towns that owe much of their character to German settlers (see our Day Trips chapter).

Pedernales (PUR-der-nal-liss): This "purdy" river runs through the LBJ Ranch near Johnson City (see our Day Trips chapter).

Pflugerville (FLEW-ger-ville): The "p" is silent here, but this booming small town northeast of Austin is not a quiet backwater anymore.

Rio Grande (REE-oh Grand): If it was good enough for John Wayne, then it's good enough for those Austinites who drop the final syllable on the street name here.

San Jacinto (San Jah-SIN-tow): In Spanish it would be "San Hah-seen-toh," but locals opt for the hard "J" here when they pronounce the name of this downtown street.

San Marcos (San MAR-kiss): Round vowels are not the preferred Texas pronunciation, like the name of this college town south of Austin.

future that encompasses all of Central Texas's concerns. Growth has been the No. 1 topic in Austin for the last two decades, and now those once-small, quiet communities like Cedar Park and Dripping Springs are wrestling with the same issue.

Growth has been a double-edged sword for the Austin area. It has brought economic stability and even boom times, but it also has put stress on the environment. It has led to more restaurants, more shops, more donations to the arts, and contributions to the cultural scene, but it also has put pressure on infrastructure and public resources. However, growth also has led to dynamic, creative solutions, has revitalized old neighborhoods, given downtown a new vibrancy, and brought people together in new ways.

AUSTIN OVERLOOK

We called this section Overlook because visitors get many of the grandest views of this city looking down from one of its many hills or from above: the first view of the city from an airplane, a tapestry of lights surrounding two distinctive landmarks, the capitol and the University of Texas tower; a view of the downtown sky line from a scenic lookout point on Capital of Texas Highway west of the city; or the sun shimmering on Lake Travis at sunset, viewed from the deck of a lakeside restaurant; the reflections of the downtown lights in Lady Bird Lake viewed from a high-rise hotel; the view of the city from a picnic site on Mount Bonnell.

Weather Watch

Local weather forecasts are available from a variety of sources, including the websites of four local television stations:

1. KTBC-TV, Channel 7, www.my foxaustin.com
2. KVUE-TV, Channel 24, www.kvue.com
3. KXAN-TV, Channel 36, www.kxan.com
4. KEYE-TV, Channel 42, www.keyetv.com

Time Warner Channel 8, www.news8austin.com, a 24-hour news channel, has weather "on the eights" every hour. The *Austin American-Statesman,* www.statesman.com, and the television stations listed above will send e-mail and cell phone weather alerts to subscribers.

But Austin is not a city to be experienced only from above—or from afar. To get the most of this city, walk among the people and the places that have made Austin what it is today. So many of the places visitors find enjoyable are places the locals love to visit also.

By the time you're ready to leave Austin, if you can tear yourself away, you'll really know what it means when the locals bid you farewell with a "Y'all come back." You might even find yourself responding, "Y'all take care!"

HISTORY

Sam Houston rarely lost a fight. Of all the heroes who struggled for Texas's independence from Mexico, General Houston had been the one to lead the decisive bloody conflict. His troops had captured the ruthless Mexican dictator, General Antonio Lopez de Santa Anna, at the Battle of San Jacinto on April 26, 1836. As commander-in-chief of the Texas Army, he had altered the destiny of a continent.

As a youth he had gone off on his own to live among the Indians and had been accepted as a son by a chief of the Cherokees. His Indian name, Co-lon-neh, meaning "The Raven," would add luster to his legend. Houston had served as governor of Tennessee before striking out for the wilds of Texas. He was among the courageous leaders who had signed the Texas Declaration of Independence at Washington-on-the-Brazos on March 2, 1836, and he had already served a term as the first elected president of the fledgling Republic of Texas. He was the ultimate prototype of the new Texan: tall, independent, fearless, self-assured, every bit the maverick, a hero among heroes.

And he was furious. The year was 1839, and the new president of the Republic, Mirabeau Lamar, was suggesting that Texas's permanent capital be established in the tiny hamlet of Waterloo. The hamlet, on the banks of the Colorado River, sat in the middle of nowhere, perched on the edge of a wild frontier. The US border was 250 arduous miles east at the Sabine River, while the disputed Texas-Mexico boundary stood just half that distance away at the Nueces River. Comanche Indians occupied the hills nearby. Mexican marauders could invade at any time. Besides, Houston had already secured a pledge from the Texas government that the capital would remain, at least until 1840, in the town that bore his own name—or so he thought.

Lamar had other ideas. He envisioned a Texas empire that spread far into the west. Moving the capital to the center of the Republic, he believed, would give Texas a launching point from which to carve out its future. Lamar dreamed of the newly adopted Lone Star flag sailing one day over lands still controlled by Mexico and the Indians.

While camping near Waterloo on an excursion with Texas Rangers the year before, Lamar had awakened to shouts that a buffalo herd had been spotted nearby. He rode out and shot the biggest buffalo some had ever seen. As fate would have it, his prey had been standing right on the corner of what would become the heart of downtown Austin at Congress Avenue near Eighth Street. Lamar recalled the beautiful spot when it came time to assign a commission to select Texas's permanent capital.

THE CAPITAL OF TEXAS

The new capital was to be named Austin in honor of the "Father of Texas," Stephen F. Austin, who less than 20 years before had brought the first Anglo settlers to the territory. Citizens of Houston, Washington-on-the-Brazos, Matagorda, and other Texas towns lobbied hard for the capital. But there was something about Waterloo that drew out the romantic in the roughest of men. According to articles published in the *Austin American-Statesman*, Indian fighter James Jones described the scene in letters to President Lamar in 1839: "We are marching through a beautiful country—its face presents a scene of grandeur and magnificence rarely, if ever witnessed," Jones wrote. "It is the most beautiful and sublime scene. Rome itself with all its famous hills could not surpass the natural scenery of Waterloo."

Equally infatuated, commissioners investigating potential capital sites filed this report: "The imagination of even the romantic will not be disappointed on viewing the valley of the Colorado, and the fertile and gracefully undulating woodlands and luxuriant prairies at a distance from it. The most skeptical will not doubt its healthiness, and the citizen's bosom must swell with honest pride when, standing in the portico of the capitol of this country, he looks abroad upon a region worthy only of being the home of the brave and free."

Waterloo, renamed Austin, got the nod in April 1839. For the next 33 years Austin would have a precarious grip on the seat of government.

Despite objections from Sam Houston and many others who believed it was madness to venture to the very brink of civilization, Lamar moved quickly to establish the new center of government. He dispatched a veteran of the Texas Revolution, Edwin Waller, to lay out the town and begin construction of its public buildings.

"Convinced that delay would give the opposition an opportunity to crystallize, Waller resolved to have Austin ready when Congress convened in November," Austin historian David C. Humphrey wrote in his book, *Austin: An Illustrated History*, "Despite the frenzied pace, Waller planned his infant city in a manner that has pleased its citizens and visitors ever since."

Waller's popularity soared in the town he designed. In January 1840 he won unanimous election as mayor by the town's 187 voters.

As the capitol and other wooden public buildings took shape along Congress Avenue (the capitol was surrounded by stockades to protect it against Indian attack), more and more souls moved to Austin, many to take jobs as public servants in the fledgling government, some to set up private professions and businesses, still others arriving with their owners as slaves. By 1840 Austin's population had grown to 856, according to an informal census taken by a resident, the Reverend Amos Roark. The population, by Roark's count, totaled 711 whites and 145 blacks and included 75 religious people, 35 mechanics, 6 doctors, 4 lawyers, and 20 gamblers.

Sam Houston, still seething over the transfer of power to Austin, made plans to end this wild experiment once and for all. Having been reelected president of the Republic, succeeding Lamar in September 1841, Houston was provided the perfect excuse when invading Mexicans briefly recaptured San Antonio in 1842—causing nearly the whole population of Austin to flee. He ordered the official papers be transferred from Austin to Washington-on-the-Brazos, the site Houston had selected for the interim capital. In what has gone down in history as the "Archive War," however, a group of the remaining Austinites fired a cannon at their Texas brethren, and then chased them into the night to recover the papers. The following day, December 31, 1842, the victors returned the archives to Austin. Sam Houston, ever the rebel, continued to conduct his presidential business at Washington-on-the-Brazos. Austin, with no reason for existence, slipped into decline as Comanche raids grew more frequent.

This was the darkness before the dawn, as it turned out. A constitutional convention held in Austin on July 4, 1845, voted to approve the United States' offer to annex Texas. Austin was again chosen the interim capital, this time of the State of Texas. In a poignant ceremony held at high noon on February 19, 1846, Texas President Anson Jones declared, "The Republic of Texas is no more." While the decadelong experiment in frontier democracy had come to an end, its legacy would live on in generations of proud Texans yet to be born.

THE 28TH STATE

With Texas representing the 28th star on the flag of the United States, Austin's tensions could ease somewhat. The Mexican-American War, fought largely on Mexican soil, settled the international boundary far south of Austin along the Rio Grande with the 1848 Treaty of Guadalupe Hidalgo. By 1850, when Austin won another 20-year term as the state capital, the city claimed just 629 residents. Ten years later, the population had grown to 3,494, nearly a third of them slaves, as the number of government jobs grew and the private sector expanded. While the threat of Indian attack remained strong in the new capital during those years, stalwart

Austinites moved ahead to build a lasting city. Texas's first permanent state capitol was open for business by 1853, and the city's master builder, Abner Cook, completed the Governor's Mansion (which was extensively damaged by fire in 2008) by 1856. The architecturally magnificent Texas Land Office Building, which today is the Capital Complex Visitors Center, was completed by 1857. The future looked bright. Then came the Civil War—and secession.

Sam Houston had envisioned Texas as part of the United States since the early days of the Republic. Now, as the 70-year-old governor of Texas, "Old Sam" denounced the idea of seceding from the Union, despite the incendiary slavery issue and other grievances about states' rights that increasingly angered the South. In the face of growing revolt against the Union, Houston departed the Austin Governor's Mansion and traveled around the state in an attempt to prevent secession. Houston biographer Marquis James reported in *The Raven* that the aging statesman faced an angry mob in Galveston and still would not back down. "Some of you laugh to scorn the idea of bloodshed as the result of secession," Houston told the throng. "But let me tell you what is coming. You may, after the sacrifice of countless millions of treasure and hundreds of thousands of lives, as a bare possibility, win Southern independence, but I doubt it."

In February 1861, Texas voted overwhelmingly to secede. On March 16, the ever-defiant Houston stepped down as governor rather than take the oath of allegiance to the Confederacy. Despite all his former ill-will toward Austin as the capital, Houston must have taken a small degree of pleasure in learning that Austin and Travis County, as well as neighboring Williamson County, also voted against secession at first. As historian Humphrey reported, Austin was a slave city just as Texas was a slave state, but Austinites, like Sam Houston, "opposed efforts to precipitate Texas 'into revolution.'" After war broke out in April, however, most of tolerant Austin accepted the secession and hundreds of local men and boys marched off to battle. Four years later, Houston's dire prediction came true when the South fell.

While Austin had grown by nearly 3,000 people between 1850 and 1860, the war had taken its toll. By 1870, when Union forces (commanded for a time by General George Armstrong Custer) ended a five-year occupation of Austin, the city claimed just 4,428 residents, not even a thousand more than a decade before. A good portion were freed slaves eager to start new lives. Clarksville, still on the west side of town today, became just one of several thriving black communities that grew up during this period (see the Relocation chapter).

Austin was set to take off. But first it had to battle the city of Houston once again. Austin's 20-year term as interim capital had expired, and the issue again was to be put to a vote. The debate raged across the miles as each side volleyed nasty remarks about its opposition. Houston, according to Austinites, was home to "fetid, green-scum-covered bayous," while Austin was called a "bleak, inhospitable rocky waste." In November 1872 Austin won the vote by nearly a 2-to-1 margin over its longtime rival. Four years later, the new state constitution designated Austin the permanent capital. At long last, the issue was settled.

A THRIVING CAPITAL

The years following the Civil War became a time of unprecedented growth for Austin and for Texas as a whole. Despite the enormous suffering brought by the war, the state remained physically undamaged. While much of the South was in shambles, Texas offered huge expanses of open frontier just awaiting settlement. Southern in heritage and yet so Western in character, Texas became the great Southwestern frontier as immigrants poured in. With the coming of the railroad in 1871, Austin surged full steam ahead. The city more than doubled its 1870 population within 10 years, growing to 11,013. The newcomers arrived largely from the South but also from Europe. Germans, more than any other European ethnic group, forged new lives here, but Swedes, English, Irish, Italians, and Poles came too. Congress Avenue and Pecan Street (now Sixth Street) became the commercial and political center of this thriving region.

The Texas Constitution, which encouraged immigration, certainly contributed to the state's, and Austin's, open attitude toward diversity as both American and foreign-born newcomers discovered a warm climate of acceptance. Great homes and commercial buildings designed to last the ages appeared on the landscape. Scholz Garten, a restaurant and beer garden built by German immigrant August Scholz in 1866, would become a popular gathering spot for Austin citizens of all nationalities during these years—and remains so to this day. Allen Hall, the first building west of the Mississippi River dedicated to the higher education of blacks, rose up on Austin's east side at Tillotson College, chartered in 1877 and opened to students by 1881. Austin, meanwhile, rallied for its next important phase.

Back in 1839, President Lamar had gained recognition as the Father of Education when, at his urging, the Congress of the Republic set aside land in each existing county to be used for public education. In Austin a 40-acre site named College Hill had been designated for a university. But Texas in those early days lacked the resources for such a grand scheme, so education had been left to churches and private schools. In 1854 Governor Elisha Pease had signed a bill establishing the Texas Public School System. Now it was time to do something about a university. The Constitution of 1876 called for establishment of "a university of the first class." The location for the University of Texas was to be decided by a vote of the people.

College Hill had been standing by for nearly four decades. But with the location suddenly up for grabs, town leaders throughout the state quickly moved to claim the university as their own. Ten towns, including Waco, Lampasas, Tyler, and Matagorda, vied with Austin for the honor. But Austin had an ace in the hole in a man by the name of Alexander Penn Woolridge, a New Orleans–born, Yale-educated up-and-comer. As head of the Austin campaign, Woolridge, according to Humphrey, flooded Texas with pro-Austin literature, pointing out the city's beauty, healthfulness, central location, and the fact that Austin already had land ready and waiting. East Texas voters went solidly for Tyler, but Austin triumphed, and Woolridge went on to serve Austin in one capacity or another for four decades. A wonderful downtown city park (see the Parks & Recreation chapter) is named for him. On September 15, 1883, townspeople gathered for an inaugural ceremony in the unfinished Main Building on College Hill, right on the original 40-acre site. In 1885 St. Edward's opened as a Catholic college on Austin's southern edge.

Three years later, on May 16, 1888, the youngest son of Sam Houston dedicated the magnificent new Texas State Capitol with the words, "Here glitters a structure that shall stand as a sentinel of eternity to gaze upon the ages." Presiding majestically over the hill looking down Congress Avenue, the capitol was, indeed, a site to behold.

BUILDING A VIABLE ECONOMY

Seat of government. Center of education. The twin economic pillars for Austin's development stood as solidly as the glorious new structures that served as their symbols. Instead of bringing instant wealth to Austin, however, the University of Texas struggled in its early years. In fact, all of Austin struggled to define its economic future. Early dreams of a commercial center ushered in by the railroad failed to materialize as rail lines spread and shippers found other cities more convenient. The Colorado River proved unnavigable, dashing hopes for lucrative barge traffic. Factories were few and far between. Still, Austin remained the seat of political power in Texas. Along with important government jobs came the prestige of catering to the state's most influential men.

Besides, if jobs didn't come from huge factories or meccas of trade, enterprising Austinites would just invent their own. Retailers, lawyers, doctors, journalists, butchers, bakers, and brewers as well as operators of boardinghouses, brothels, and saloons all found work in Austin. Builders certainly didn't lack work. Some of Austin's finest historic buildings today, including the regal hotel built by cattle baron Jesse Driskill, opened in the latter decades of the 19th century. The distinguished neighborhood of Hyde Park in then far North Austin, which touted electric street car service, got its start during this period and became Austin's first suburb (see the Relocation chapter), while celebrated European sculptor Elizabet Ney set about building her elegant Hyde Park studio. A few blocks west of Congress Avenue, a neighborhood of wealthy merchants and bankers rose up. Churches, hospitals, and a courthouse dotted the Austin landscape, along with two grand opera houses that served the growing population's desire for cultural entertainment. Contributing to that scene were locally formed bands as well as the Austin Saengerrunde, a singing society founded by the city's German immigrants in 1879.

By the late 1880s Austin's growing number of professors and students bestowed a scholarly touch on the region, while the presence of the artist Ney and the short-story writer who would later become famous as O. Henry foreshadowed future artistic and literary communities. O. Henry would later give Austin one of its most endearing nicknames, "the City of the Violet Crown," in honor of the purplish cast that emerges over the city at dusk. (Some say the color comes from the cedar pollen in the air.)

"Austin's diverse population grew like the town itself during these years," historian John Edward Weems wrote in the 1989 *Austin American-Statesman* supplement, "Austin 1839–1989." "The diversity helped give the town a degree of tolerance that, however slight at first and however imperfect still today, broadened into an accommodation of people with a remarkable variety of beliefs and lifestyles."

Through it all, dreams of commerce and manufacturing remained strong among some of Austin's leaders. By 1893 Austinites gathered to celebrate the opening of a new million-dollar dam on the Colorado River and the beautiful lake it created. The dam was aimed at producing enough hydroelectric power for both the city and for the manufacturing plants city officials expected would come along to propel Austin to prosperity. Lake McDonald, named for John McDonald, the building contractor-turned-mayor who had championed the dam, quickly became the city's prime recreational center. Accompanied by their dapper escorts, fashionable ladies wearing flower-topped bonnets boarded the great steamers *Ben Hur* and the *Belle of Austin* for relaxing cruises on the lake by day and dances by night. Rowing regattas at the lake attracted sports enthusiasts from around the world. Sunbathers and swimmers relaxed on shore, while the town elite snapped up resort properties along the perimeter.

Despite its increasingly civilized appearance, Austin retained much of its frontier flavor during the last two decades of the 19th century. In 1881 Austinites exhibited a mixture of tolerance and plain common sense by electing Ben Thompson to the job of city marshal. Thompson, considered the best gunfighter in the West by many, was also one of Pecan Street's most notorious gamblers. "During his tenure as marshal, it was claimed that major crime dropped to an all-time low," wrote Larry Willoughby in his book, *Austin: A Historical Portrait*. Unfortunately, the colorful Thompson resigned in 1882 to face murder charges in San Antonio and was killed later in a saloon shoot-out. Well into the 1890s, according to Humphrey, "Cowboys were familiar figures, and horses tied to hitching posts lined dusty Congress Avenue. Along the east side of the Avenue the saloons, cowmen, and gamblers were so thick in the evenings that 'ladies' would not think of walking there."

Austin's red-light district grew into an enterprise during these years. Located west of Congress Avenue and called Guy Town, "it was not at all an unpopular part of town for many men—Austin residents, male visitors, and legislators," reported Weems. "It was said that additional women were brought in when the state government blossomed into full lawmaking activity."

THE 20TH CENTURY

Austin's Wild West spirit didn't disappear overnight, but the coming of the 20th century marked the beginning of its decline. By New Year's Day 1900 Austin's eyes were clearly focused on the future—and progress. Only one small item appeared on the front page of the local paper that day to indicate anything might be awry in the land of opportunity. "Saturday and yesterday some alarmists were busy circulating the report that there were great leaks in the powerhouse, in the dam, in the lake, and everywhere else out at the power and light plant up the river," the article said. "Superintendent Patterson stated that they were without foundation." Austin got busy with its plans for the new century.

Whether those "alarmist" reports were true at the time mattered little just three months later when the skies unleashed a torrent of rain. On April 7, 1900, dreams of turning Austin into a manufacturing center were literally swept away along with the seven-year-old dam in a devastating flood that cost at least eight lives, destroyed everything in its path, and left Austin without power for several months. When Austin overcame the shock enough to take stock of its situation—no big business, no big industry—city leaders determined to make the best of it. Austin's economic future would be built on the twin pillars of education and government the city had fought so hard to win in the past. Besides, they reasoned, Austin was just a beautiful place to live.

Growth and progress were now the name of the game. Wide and stately, yet made of dirt for more than 60 years, Congress Avenue was finally paved with brick in 1905, while a new concrete bridge replaced a rickety iron bridge across the Colorado River at Congress. "By 1910, Austin had its own skyscrapers, the Scarborough and Littlefield buildings. The horseless carriage was no longer considered an intrusion into the lives of 'civilized' people, and as early as 1910 the automobile was an invaluable part of Austin's lifestyle and economy. When the first airplane landed in Austin in 1911, the 20th century had really arrived," wrote Willoughby.

COLOR BARRIERS

While Austinites had always made time for leisure and cultural activities, the coming of the industrial age made those pursuits even easier. Austin's new Majestic Theatre (now the Paramount) opened in 1915, hosting major touring acts from around the country. Two years later the Austin Symphony Orchestra presented its first concert. Human habitation at Barton Springs, the jewel in a town endowed by enormous natural beauty, has been traced back several thousand years, but the arrival of the automobile made trips to this glorious swimming hole easier for "modern" Austinites. In 1917 Colonel A. J. Zilker gave the city hundreds of acres around the springs for use as a park. UT football, first played in 1893, became a popular spectator sport in the 1900s, along with the horse races that thrilled the crowds in Hyde Park. Grand balls attended by the city's most fashionable citizens continued at the elegant Driskill Hotel, while the lovely Hyde Park Pavilion hosted other stylish affairs.

Hyde Park, however, was an exclusively Anglo community; its posh gatherings were barred to Austin's minorities, as was Barton Springs, to name just two. Austin's black citizens, who had enjoyed some acceptance during Reconstruction, were now subjected to segregation and discrimination. As far back as 1885 a group of citizens in one ward had formed an "Anti-Colored Movement" to block the reelection of a black city council member, Humphrey reported. During the first decade of the 1900s, Austin's color barrier became as distinct as in many other cities throughout the South. While the white-robed Ku Klux Klan paraded through Austin streets undeterred, blacks sat in a separate section on streetcars, attended separate schools, drank from separate drinking fountains, and used separate public restrooms—when such facilities could be found. They also increasingly congregated on Austin's east side, away from their Anglo oppressors. Austin's many black professionals—doctors, lawyers, dentists, pastors, as well as business owners—found a racially mixed district to work in but remained excluded from Austin "society." Not until 1950 would the first black student gain admittance to the UT law school—under order from the US Supreme Court.

Austin's small but growing Mexican-American population also faced treatment that would be considered despicable today. Most of the town's Mexicans had been chased out of town during the 1850s, while those who had followed found themselves still considered foreigners despite their birthright. Even worse, some Austinites counted them as enemies because of the Texas Revolution, forgetting that many Mexicans living in the region during the war had fought—and died—for Texas.

By 1910 Austin claimed not quite 30,000 citizens. Houston, already a railroading and shipping center, witnessed huge industrial development following Texas's first great oil strike in the region in 1901. Its population had surged to nearly 79,000 by 1910. Dallas, enjoying success as a center for insurance, banking, commerce, and the cotton trade, had skyrocketed to 92,000 people. Following World War I, Austin's population had increased by just 5,000, while Houston and Dallas soared to 128,000 and 156,000, respectively.

Although not cash rich at the beginning of the Roaring '20s, the University of Texas did own a great deal of land, including two million acres in West Texas, some of it leased to oil speculators. On Monday morning, May 28, 1923, the Santa Rita oil well blew in a gusher of black gold. The Big Lake Oil Field out west would continue to pump riches into the Permanent University Fund for nearly seven decades. Wealthy for the first time in its 40-year history, UT went on a building spree.

THE "ATHENS OF THE WEST"

Now city officials really had something to brag about. Besides the rapidly growing UT, Austin also claimed St. Edward's University on the south side and two black colleges on the east. Austin was indeed becoming the center of culture, learning, and politics that leaders had envisioned. They began touting Austin as the "Athens of the West," and citizens responded by earmarking funds to develop the city. Parks and playgrounds, wide boulevards, and public buildings rose up. Austin's population more than doubled during the 1920s and 1930s, hitting nearly 88,000 by 1940.

UT's spending binge, coupled with an influx of local and federal funds, staved off the worst of the Great Depression for

Austin, according to local historians. One of the city's most treasured landmarks today, the 27-story UT Tower, was among many buildings completed on campus during the 1920s and 1930s. President Roosevelt's New Deal, solidly backed by Austin's ubiquitous new mayor, Tom Miller, brought millions in construction funds to the area through the Works Progress Administration (WPA). Camp Mabry on Austin's west side, home to the Texas Volunteer Guard since 1891, mushroomed with new WPA construction, as did other areas of the city. By late 1936, when *Forbes* magazine reported that Austin was one of the "bright spots in the nation," it appeared the worst of the Depression was over. And yet Miller, along with Austin's newly elected US Representative, Lyndon Johnson, won for Austin the country's first federal housing project, completed in 1939 for the city's rapidly expanding Mexican-American population.

Miller, who would remain at the forefront of Austin business and politics throughout the '30s, '40s, and even well into the '50s, was responsible in many ways for fashioning modern Austin. A liberal among liberal Democrats of the era, Miller was a master politician who worked to gain support from all three sectors of Austin's increasingly tri-racial community. Although he did support racial segregation (not unusual even for liberal Southerners of the era), Miller nonetheless promoted equal civil rights for all.

"Miller was one of those fairly numerous anomalies in the South—the good businessman, the deep Southerner, who also stood strong on behalf of much of Roosevelt's New Deal, and Truman's Fair Deal, civil rights, and the like," according to Anthony M. Orum, author of *Power, Money & the People: The Making of Modern Austin*. Low-income housing

extended to blacks and Mexican-Americans under his reign, while Miller also saw to it that East Austin's black community received basic city services. The lovely Rosewood Park that remains today was commissioned by Miller. His broader vision, however, remained on the city's future growth.

Among Miller's greatest coups was his success—along with LBJ—in getting federal Depression-era funds to complete the Austin Dam (now named in his honor) by 1940. Two years later, construction of the Mansfield Dam that created Lake Travis wrapped up efforts around these parts to bring the unpredictable Colorado River under control.

SHAPING THE FUTURE

On December 7, 1941, the United States went to war. While Austin's youth waged battle on far-off fronts, loved ones remained at home, sharing with the rest of the country in the hardships of scarcity and rationing—and the fear that a knock on the door would mean a son, husband, brother, or even a daughter had paid the ultimate price. In 1943 Congressman Johnson and his wife, University of Texas graduate Lady Bird Johnson, bought small Austin radio station KTBC. Nine years later, on Thanksgiving Day 1952, KTBC became Central Texas's first television station. What more important event could have been chosen as a first broadcast during the heyday of the postwar years? The station aired the football game between arch rivals UT and Texas A&M. UT, of course, prevailed.

According to Humphrey, the seeds of Austin's eventual blossoming as a high-tech mecca were also planted in the 1940s with the creation of the Austin Area Economic Development Foundation. Established in 1948 with C. B. Smith as president, the council "foreshadowed and helped shape what was to come," Humphrey wrote. "Smith's foundation sought to diversify Austin's economy in a manner compatible with its 'way of life.' Research and development laboratories and high technology companies fit the bill."

Austin would also elect its first woman city council member in 1948. Interestingly, Emma Long was not just a female version of the reigning power elite but "an avowed enemy of the city establishment and a champion of the underdog," as Weems described her.

GAINING NEW SENSIBILITIES

Meanwhile, somewhere during the second half of the 1940s, Austin's population hit 100,000 as the city became one of the fastest growing cities in the Southwest. By 1950 the population had reached 132,459. While nowhere near the size of Houston or Dallas, or even San Antonio, Austin had nevertheless turned into a thriving metropolis.

The time to address some long-ignored social injustices had arrived. Heman Marion Sweatt's victorious Supreme Court battle to gain admission to the UT law school in 1950 opened UT's doors to other black graduate students. Six years later, by decree of the UT Board of Regents, the university admitted its first black undergraduates, while Austin's public schools began the excruciatingly slow process of integration. In 1954 UT graduate and social activist Ronnie Dugger debuted the *Texas Observer* in Austin. Within months the small biweekly magazine had established itself as the liberal voice in Texas media, reporting on lynchings in East Texas. (The *Observer* continues its mission as a liberal voice in Texas media to this day.) As the tide for racial equality swelled across the United States, students at UT and the

city's other colleges spearheaded the Austin movement of the 1950s and 1960s.

The movement, however, reached beyond UT and the city's other campuses to extend deep into the community. As a result, Austin experienced nascent political and social enlightenment as established barriers against minorities slowly cracked. Black and Mexican-American communities began taking places in positions of power by the late '60s and into the '70s.

While UT "radical" politics reached back decades, the university boomed during the 1960s as a haven for serious social activists and the hippies who brought their music and their faith in flower power. Austin's antiwar protesters took to the streets throughout the decade as public opinion against the Vietnam War surged. (In May 1970, students led Austin's largest protest of the Vietnam era following the deaths of four students in Ohio during an antiwar demonstration at Kent State University.)

UT enrollment had swelled to more than 25,000 by 1966, although only about half remained on campus for the summer session. The morning of August 1, 1966, dawned like any other hot, lazy summer day in the city. A few hours later, Austin became the site of what was then the largest simultaneous mass murder in American history when a heavily armed 25-year-old UT student and ex-Marine climbed the beloved campus tower and commenced firing. Charles Whitman, who had murdered his mother and his wife the night before, fired round after round at unsuspecting victims below, killing 14 people and wounding 31 more before he was finally shot to death by Austin police. The 19-minute melee would spawn debate across the country over the issue of gun control.

At the epicenter of America's turbulent 1960s stood Lyndon Johnson, the former schoolteacher who had risen to political power from his boyhood home 50 miles southwest of Austin. A century had passed since Sam Houston stared Southern slave owners in the face—and lost. Now another tall Texan was storming the bastion of bigotry. He had already guided two civil rights measures through the Senate and as president was fighting for passage of a landmark Civil Rights act. Angry Southerners rebuked Johnson and Lady Bird at every turn, but the Texas leader prevailed. Johnson signed the Civil Rights Act of 1964 and the Voting Rights Act a year later. Johnson, however, would be judged at the time not for his efforts on behalf of human rights nor for the dozens of education bills and social reform measures he championed, but for drawing the United States further into the mire of the Vietnam War. Battered by public opinion against the war, Johnson chose not to seek reelection in 1968. He and Lady Bird returned home to their Central Texas ranch.

THE UPS & DOWNS

While live music concerts had formed part of the Austin lifestyle since its earliest days, the 1960s would see the city boom with musicians of all kinds. Among UT's growing "folkie" music crowd was a shy freshman named Janis Joplin, who performed first on campus and later at a popular beer joint called Threadgill's. Later came the psychedelic sounds, rock 'n' roll, the blues, and the country rock that would eventually turn Austin into the Live Music Capital of the World.

The '60s brought much more than music and social change, however. Attracted by UT's excellent reputation for research and development and by the city's attractive surroundings, high-tech manufacturers moved in. By the end of the decade, Austin claimed three major technology plants: IBM, Texas Instruments, and Tracor. The high-tech revolution had arrived.

By 1970 Austin's population topped a quarter million. UT had mushroomed to more than 40,000 students. The number of city, county, state, and federal government employees reached into the thousands, and high-tech firms had become the city's largest private employers. The Armadillo World Headquarters opened in 1970 and soon earned a nationwide reputation as a hot live music venue. Austin's cultural explosion during this decade extended into the areas of writing, theater, and visual arts as more and more artists found themselves drawn to the city.

In the summer of 1970, just a couple of months after UT students rallied 25,000 people for a march in protest of the Kent State shootings, a group of UT students gathered to map out a plan for Austin's future. Among the students was Jeffrey Friedman, a law school student who had taken a leadership role in the protest march. Armed with the knowledge that the voting age was about to be lowered from 21 to 18, and realizing that students could register by proclaiming they intended to remain in Austin after graduation, the group determined to register thousands of university students. That accomplished, Friedman and a slate of other liberal candidates decided to challenge the existing power structure.

Friedman, according to Orum, "wanted things to be better in East Austin for the browns and the blacks. He wanted the poor people to have better jobs and better housing. But he also wanted to bring down the forces of the Establishment. He wanted to bring down the rich and the powerful." For his part, Friedman's conservative opponent, Wick Fowler, ran on a platform "that hippies were unfit to hold public office."

While the conservative business sector claimed the majority of seats on the council that year, Friedman won his race to become the first student and youngest council member. Berl Handcox also won election, becoming the first African American to serve on the city council since the 1880s. Five years later Friedman became Austin's youngest mayor in what Orum called "the watershed council election of 1975, in which the majority of those elected were liberals." Among those voted in was John Trevino, Austin's first Mexican-American council member.

TREE HUGGERS UNITE

Apart from the frustration over establishment politics that colored the 1970s, Austin's population explosion became a source of increasing consternation. Longtime residents mourned the good ol' days and expressed fears that Austin's scenic beauty was being bulldozed away to make way for expressways, shopping malls, housing developments, and skyscrapers. The slogan "Keep Austin Weird" became a popular rallying cry during these years. Austin's increasingly powerful environmental protection groups successfully thwarted major development in several environmentally sensitive areas, while helping to keep the protection of Austin's natural endowments on the minds of old-timers and newcomers alike—as well as on the front burner of local politics. Lady Bird Johnson, who divided her time between Austin and her ranch nearby, spearheaded a project to beautify Town Lake (renamed Lady Bird Lake after her death), which led to the planting of thousands of trees as

well as construction of a hike-and-bike trail and gazebos. Austin had indeed changed radically from its days as a small, sleepy town. But of the nearly 94,000 new residents who would move into Austin during the '70s, the majority would still be left breathless by the city's natural appeal—and still are today.

By the mid-1980s nothing appeared to stand in the way of continued growth. The economy boomed as more high-tech industries moved into Central Texas, bringing investment dollars and plenty of jobs. Austinite Michael Dell started his own little computer company in 1984 to add to the high-tech landscape. Housing costs rose, then skyrocketed, as Austin's population continued to expand. Banks made exorbitant loans, with little money down, as real estate speculators and tycoon developers snapped up residential and commercial properties around the region.

Then the bubble burst. Downturns in oil prices—which had already hurt many parts of Texas—contributed to the problem, as did a slump in the technology field, but many economists pointed to the overheated real estate economy as the leading cause of Austin's recession. For a while during the second half of the decade, it appeared that more people were leaving the city than moving in. Real estate prices plummeted, businesses failed, bankruptcies became common, offices closed. By the end of the decade, according to reports, Austin led the country in the percentage of vacant office space and topped all other Texas cities for amount of indebtedness.

THE HIGH-TECH ERA IGNITES

Austin entered 1990 with a gloomy economic forecast. The United States as a whole was in recession, banks remained in turmoil, and another US president who claimed Texas as home, George H. W. Bush, was preparing to declare war on Iraq. Despite earlier indications, however, Austin's population had grown by nearly 120,000 people during the past decade. In 1993 Apple Computer bought 129 acres in neighboring Williamson County for a financial services and customer support site. That same year, Motorola announced plans to build a $1 billion chip plant in Northeast Austin. Meanwhile, young Austinites Richard Linklater and Robert Rodriguez had each made a low-budget, wildly successful film (*Slacker* and *El Mariachi,* respectively) that was to skyrocket them to Hollywood—and help put the Austin film scene on the map. All the while, the beat of Austin music pulsated in every corner of the city.

By the end of the decade, Austin was riding the crest of another wave in growth and development as Central Texas solidified its reputation as one of the country's leading high-tech hubs. Dell Computer had grown to become the city's largest private employer and the world's third-largest maker of personal computers, with more than $12 billion in annual sales. Samsung built a $1.3 billion Austin plant. Computer manufacturers and chip makers, however, formed just part of the scene. Local start-up companies focusing on software development and the Internet also swelled during the '90s.

Along with the economic good times came increasing pressures. Rampant growth became the norm as the city expanded by about 1,500 inhabitants each month throughout the decade. Signs of the changing times were clearly visible everywhere as roads jammed, office space diminished, trees were sacrificed to make way for housing and commercial developments, and school districts scrambled to build new facilities to keep up with expanding enrollment.

As a result, a new phrase entered the Austin lexicon in 1998: "Smart Growth." Aiming to develop a city that grew "smart" as it grew fast, the Austin City Council and then-Mayor Kirk Watson presented a series of initiatives designed to protect the environment and to limit sprawl, especially into environmentally sensitive areas, by encouraging development inside the city. Race relations, often ignored in the past, also climbed on the city agenda as more enlightened leaders sought to bring some sense of community to a city that remained fractured in many respects—despite important strides among Austin's minority racial and ethnic groups over the past 40 years.

SINGING THE BLUES

If Austin ever really needed a reason to party, the dawn of the 21st century provided an excellent excuse. Indeed, on December 31, 1999, an estimated 260,000 revelers packed Austin's "A2K" downtown bash. And why not? These were technological boom times, and the venture capital was flowing as freely as the beer. If the US economy was hot, Austin's was red hot. Jobs were plentiful, high-tech salaries soared, and the stock market skyrocketed. Locally, dot-coms glittered among the investment darlings of the "new" Internet economy, while the region's chip makers were selling their goods as fast and furious as Frito-Lay. To the enormous relief of tormented Austin techies, and the partygoers on Sixth Street, the ominously predicted Y2K bug never even hatched.

By March 2000, Austin officials had signed deals with two computer biggies, software manufacturer Computer Sciences Corp. (CSC) and Intel Corp., to build giant complexes downtown—the heart of Smart Growth territory. These were to be the first in a string of computer companies whose presence in the city center would create a "Downtown Digital District" and thus rejuvenate the entire area. The building boom extended even further as the construction of office towers, posh condominiums, and lofts changed the face of downtown forever.

True, Austin's $600 million annual music industry was feeling a pinch as musicians struggled to find affordable housing and clubs faced escalating costs. Austin already had lost three great music venues: Steamboat, the Electric Lounge, and, perhaps worst of all, Liberty Lunch. The Lunch, an Austin leader in live music for nearly a quarter of a century, was demolished to make room for the pending CSC complex and a proposed new City Hall. The city's poor also suffered. Not only had the number of poor increased, but the gap between the lowest- and highest-paid workers in the private sector had doubled. The basic cost of living increased as demands for goods and services by the area's high-salaried consumers—and the droves of new Central Texas residents— drove prices up. In fact, when census figures came in, the Austin Metropolitan Statistical area, which includes Austin's Travis County as well as neighboring Bastrop, Caldwell, Hays, and Williamson Counties, had burgeoned to nearly 1.25 million people—and still the people poured in.

The stock market rollover of April 14, 2000, caused little more than a sprinkle on the long-running Austin parade. By August another computer biggie, Austin's Vignette Corp., announced plans to spend more than $100 million on its new downtown complex. Meanwhile, the man living in the Austin Governor's Mansion, George W. Bush, had clinched the Republican nomination for president and would by year's end become the third US president from Texas.

A year that had started on such a high note, however, then went flat. By the end of 2001, Austin musicians weren't the only ones singing the blues. The Central Texas economy had witnessed its worst downturn in a decade. The stock market plummeted, consumer confidence vanished, venture capital dried up, the chip industry melted, and many developers pulled the plug on downtown plans. To make matters worse, the entire nation was reeling from the September 11 terrorist attacks. The results of Austin's economic downturn included thousands of workers—especially high-wage earners—laid off, foreclosures on expensive homes and office buildings, shrinking retail sales, school districts scrambling to make ends meet, and cutbacks in state and local government budgets. These were the norm well into 2003. CSC did complete its downtown complex, and several other new public and private buildings now grace the skyline. Fairly or not, however, Intel's abandoned skeleton of a high-rise stood for years as a grim reminder of better days. In 2003 Mayor Will Wynn and the Austin City Council quietly replaced the Smart Growth plan with a far more extensive economic development policy.

For various reasons—among them the city's growing population, reputation as a tech center, increasingly diverse economy, and the fact that high property taxes kept the housing bubble (and subsequent bust) at bay—Austin has weathered the current recession better than many cities across the country. That's not to say the years since 2008 have been rosy for many here; rather that the city as a whole avoided the worst of the recession. In fact, in a June 2010 report, the Brookings Institute's Metropolitan Policy Program placed Austin third on its list of 21 strongest-performing metro areas, while CNNMoney.com noted, "The 'Keep Austin Weird' campaign must have worked, because the Texas capital is among the country's oddball cities that bucked the downturn." On the tech side, meanwhile, Austin scored a major coup in 2010 with the opening of Facebook's first office outside of Palo Alto, CA. The social media giant plans to hire more than 200 workers over the next three years.

THE MUSIC BIZ: COLD BEER & HOT TUNES

Austin luminary Eddie Wilson responds matter-of-factly when asked what launched the spectacular music scene we know today. "Cold beer and cheap pot," he says with a laugh. Wilson, however, humbly neglects to mention his own contributions to Austin's rise as a music mecca. As a founder of the renowned Armadillo World Headquarters in 1970, Wilson helped catapult Austin to the big time.

Of course, the collective talent of the hundreds of artists who have illuminated Austin stages over these many years goes without saying. But Wilson points out, too, that the sizable number of sofas offered to musicians during the '60s and '70s allowed brother and sister performers to find, if not a home, at least a place to bed down.

We're getting way ahead of ourselves, though. Austin's music history goes back much further than the 1960s—all the way back to the dance hall pickers, cowboy crooners, and black blues belters who were making music around Austin long before it had any reputation as a musical mecca.

Some performed as far back as the 1800s, and those who followed in their footsteps, would continue to fill our city with their own sound of music despite the various musical invasions that followed.

Some say Austin's modern music scene started with Travis County Beer License No. 01, issued to one Kenneth Threadgill on December 6, 1933. Threadgill, a singer and yodeler who sold gasoline from the front side of his Gulf service station and bootleg whiskey out the back, stood in line all night to be the first to get a beer license after the county voted to go "wet" following Prohibition. Over the years, this little station evolved into a beer joint and haven for music makers. By the early 1960s the ongoing hootenanny at Threadgill's was attracting University of Texas "folkie" musicians, including a freshman named Janis Joplin, who gathered for the regular Wednesday night jam sessions. "The folkie invasion of Threadgill's was a brave move given the general attitude about hippies, beatniks, and long-haired men among the rednecks of the era," Wilson wrote in his book, *Threadgill's: The Cookbook*. As things turned out, however, Threadgill's was just the test kitchen for this bizarre social concoction. A decade later, the Armadillo would perfect the recipe when it became a melting pot of blue-haired grannies, bikers, rednecks, and hippies. Threadgill's proved that the music, not the costume, mattered most.

As the '60s stoked up, Joplin joined up with a few budding UT musicians to form the Waller Creek Boys, a folk group that could play just about any kind of music the Threadgill's crowd demanded: blues, country, bluegrass, whatever. Other musicians soon began arriving in Austin and finding their way to Threadgill's. Meanwhile, a few joints near UT, including the Jade Room and the New Orleans Club, were making names for themselves by offering Austin's flower children the kind of live music that appealed to them.

UT's hippies may have invaded Austin, but this was still Texas as sure as shootin', and no amount of folk, blues, or rock 'n' roll could wean this town off good old country and western music. In 1964 a young Austinite fresh from service in the Army established a little roadhouse on the southern outskirts of town. The Broken Spoke, as James White would call his restaurant and club, would become a hub for some of the best country bands in Austin and around the country—and remains so to this day.

By 1965 Joplin had split for San Francisco (being voted the ugliest "male" on campus perhaps hastened the move), and Austin was ripe for a band that could turn on the masses. In the fall of '65 a band called the 13th Floor Elevators burst on the scene at a Jade Room performance. Fronted by a young, good-looking singer/guitarist named Roky Erickson, the Elevators would go on to record two magical albums, break into the top 40, and carve a lasting place for themselves in the collective consciousness of Austin music disciples.

Despite Austin's own psychedelic sounds, the blossoming of the counterculture revolution, and the drugs that fueled the movement, Austin at that time was still firmly rooted in Bible Belt mores and morality. By the fall of 1967 "there wasn't a hint of the now-bustling music biz in our town," Spencer Perskin, a member of another notable Austin band of the time, Shiva's Headband, wrote in the *Austin Chronicle* in 1993. "To perform only original material was considered almost outrageous by our musician friends, and there was zero tolerance for

us at the few bars around town [serving beer only at the time]. Only the opening of the Vulcan Gas Company gave us the foothold we would need."

The Vulcan Gas Company, Austin's first musical haunt for hippies, opened in 1967 at 400 Congress Ave., just 10 blocks from the state capitol. The 13th Floor Elevators, Shiva's Headband, and another esteemed Austin band called the Conqueroo all found a home at the Vulcan, while "groundbreaking acts such as the Velvet Underground, Moby Grape, and the Fugs would have bypassed the entire state of Texas if not for the Vulcan," wrote Joe Nick Patoski and Bill Crawford in their book, *Stevie Ray Vaughan: Caught in the Crossfire*. The experiment lasted only three years. The Vulcan closed in 1970. As the new decade dawned, however, Austin was set to explode onto the national music stage.

On August 1, 1970, Armadillo World Headquarters opened as a counterculture concert hall. "We wanted to create an entertainment facility that was different from anything Austin had ever seen," Wilson told the Insiders' Guide. Indeed. Despite early wobblings, the Armadillo succeeded in drawing throngs of fans desperate to hear top touring bands and even more of the original music that was by then the "in" thing. As the music grew better and better and the number of fans multiplied, talented musicians from around the country started appearing at the Armadillo. Other entrepreneurs riding the coattails of the Armadillo's success began opening clubs all over town.

"Through the interest of a curious national press and word-of-mouth communication by touring musicians, Austin gained almost overnight a reputation as one of the most exciting centers of music activity in the country," Austinite Jan Reid wrote in his book, *The Improbable Rise of Redneck Rock.*

Still, the list of ingredients that went into Austin's magical musical brew was far from complete. Willie Nelson's return to his native Texas led the way for a rising tide of young musicians whose music was labeled progressive country, country rock, and redneck rock. A young country rock group led by Marcia Ball, called Freda and the Firedogs, catered to this new breed of music listeners, while Jerry Jeff Walker also settled in. San Antonio native Doug Sahm, who'd found musical success on the West Coast, came home to Texas to leave an indelible mark on the Austin music scene. (A small monument to him was unveiled on "Doug Sahm Hill" near The Long Center in 2010.) Michael Murphey released his album *Cosmic Cowboy Souvenirs* in 1973, which unwittingly gave a name to the musical rebels. With the arrival of these and other "cosmic cowboys," Austin burst on the national scene as the hub of the redneck rock movement.

Suddenly, hippies and rednecks found themselves bonded by a common sound, rock- and blues-infused country and western music. Local radio station KOKE–FM began exalting the new sound, calling it "progressive country." The pickup truck became the preferred mode of transportation, while no self-respecting, long-haired, cowboy-hatted "goat roper" would be caught dead drinking anything but a longneck beer.

"This was a direct reversal of the previous decade's attitudes, when the city's young pacesetters, rebelliously rejecting haircuts while embracing rock, folk, and blues, would have preferred to drink muddy water and sleep in a hollow log rather than betray affinity with their hillbilly cousins," Clifford Endres wrote in his book, *Austin City Limits.*

Before long, however, Willie was on to his next incarnation as a musical outlaw and Austin moved on to new sounds.

The time had come for Austin's music scene to go national. With Willie Nelson as a featured act, Austin's own country music program, *Austin City Limits,* hit the airwaves in the spring of 1975. The program, still airing on Public Broadcasting Stations around the country, features the best-known acts in music today. In the past three and a half decades, *ACL* has taken its place among the city's music legends.

The cosmic cowboys may have dominated the music scene for a good spell during the 1970s, but theirs wasn't the only sound in town. Down at the Broken Spoke, fans of traditional country music found a refuge away from the city's invading hippies. (Austin lore has it that young men with hair longer than their dates' were refused service at the Spoke during these years.)

On other stages, a band that included a young guitarist by the name of Eric Johnson blasted out a radically different tune. The Electromagnets, as the quartet called itself, "generated fan reaction proportional to the volume of its music, gathering an intense, almost worshipful, fan base that seemed to expand with each live date," *Austin American-Statesman* music critic Michael Point wrote in a 1998 article celebrating the re-issue of the Electromagnets self-titled album.

A group of West Texas singer/songwriters also migrated to Austin during the 1970s. Joe Ely, Butch Hancock, and Jimmie Dale Gilmore found Austin audiences receptive to the original music they wanted to make—and stayed to make a contribution. So did a teenage Dallas transplant named Jimmie Vaughan. Vaughan's group, Storm, would be just the beginning of the blues tradition Vaughan would help to inspire in his new hometown. Austin's musical tree, it appeared, was destined to produce many branches.

Yet another Austinite geared up in the '70s to take his place in music history. Clifford Antone, a Port Arthur, Texas, native of Lebanese descent, came to Austin at age 19 to run the family gourmet grocery business. In 1973 the tiny back room of Antone's Imports became the unofficial launching pad for a group of blues artists that included Jimmie Vaughan's little brother, Stevie Ray. Antone opened his first club on Sixth Street on July 15, 1975, featuring such blues greats as Muddy Waters, Albert King, and Sunnyland Slim—in just its first year. Antone's is credited with helping to develop a blues tradition in Austin where none existed before, at least not in the predominantly white area west of I-35.

By the time Armadillo World Headquarters closed in 1980, Austin's status as a "mecca for musical mavericks" had solidified. And there was still more to come.

A star among Austin's rebels during this time was a lanky Texan by the name of Townes Van Zandt. Born in 1944 to a prominent Fort Worth oil family, Van Zandt had rejected the easy life to become a singer/songwriter. The writer of such country hits as "Pancho and Lefty," recorded by Willie Nelson and Merle Haggard, and Emmylou Harris's "If I Needed You," Van Zandt's work would influence a generation of Texas songwriters. Despite his near-constant struggles with alcohol, his recording career spanned more than a quarter of a century. During his many years living and performing in Austin, Van Zandt became one of our city's most revered musicians—and a magnet for

other musical storytellers. In fact, it's been said that he helped establish the "couch circuit" for drifting musicians. "I really, honestly believe Townes was one of the main reasons Austin received a reputation for quality," Jimmie Dale Gilmore told the *Austin American-Statesman* after Van Zandt's death, at age 52, in 1997. Van Zandt had died of a heart attack while recovering from hip surgery in Tennessee. His music lives on, however, and there have been many posthumous releases of his work. In 2010, another artist who has contributed to the Austin music scene, Steve Earle, was awarded a Grammy for Best Contemporary Folk Album for his collection of Townes's songs. The album is simply titled *Townes*.

The Sixth Street music scene, which had taken root in the 1970s, fired up in the 1980s and has since become a dominant district for live music and dancing. Well-established Sixth Street hangouts like Maggie Mae's saw the once-tranquil strip turn into a frenzy of clubs turning out live music seven nights a week, and now the greater downtown area packs in more outstanding live music than anyone could ever experience in a short visit here. Many of Austin's most notable live clubs, including Antone's, La Zona Rosa, and the Continental Club, can all be found in greater downtown. Wilson himself went on to revive the old Threadgill's saloon, turning it into one of Austin's most illustrious restaurants (featuring live music, of course). Threadgill's now touts two Austin locations, including one near the spot of the former Armadillo and appropriately named Threadgill's World Headquarters (see the Restaurants chapter).

Austin's star on the world stage continues to rise as more and more young artists flock to The Live Music Capital of the World yearning to make a name for themselves. In what's been called "the second coming of the outlaw attitude," this century has witnessed a stunning national revival in Texas's unique brand of country music. Hot, hot, hot among the cities showcasing the talents of hometown "Texas Music" artists is Austin. Pat Green, Kevin Fowler, and other young artists are just the latest links in Austin's talent-heavy outlaw chain. Of course the Austin beat goes on in so many other musical realms as well. As Wilson told us, "There are many more quality musicians and 10 times more music in Austin today than there was during the days of the Armadillo." Indeed.

THE BEAUTIFUL & THE SUBLIME

As we progress into the second decade of the 21st century, debates over Austin's future rage on. Yet the city's heart and soul have managed to survive. Ever true to their eccentric roots, Austinites have indeed embraced the "Keep Austin Weird" mentality. The phrase, appearing on bumper stickers, T-shirts, event promos, and even on shot glasses, just about says it all. Austin is not the city some old-timers remember; but then again, the generations before them most likely said the same. For the thousands of newcomers who are seeing it for the first time, however, Austin remains one of the prettiest, most vibrant spots on the planet. Austin's once-forlorn downtown is experiencing a renaissance to become a thriving center for culture and entertainment. Live music pours from clubs all over greater downtown as the Live Music Capital of the World continues to attract the young, the restless, and the talented. UT's influence on the arts has helped spawn entire communities of performing and visual artists, writers, and filmmakers. Austin's enduring youthful spirit and creative energy add a luster that is as much a hallmark of this city as the State Capitol and the UT Tower.

The Texas pioneers who first laid eyes on this "beautiful and sublime scene" 170 years ago could not possibly have envisioned the Austin of today. And yet, in countless ways, Austin remains ever so sublime.

GETTING HERE, GETTING AROUND

Xmarks the spot, and smack dab in the middle of Texas is Austin. There is an old saying in the Lone Star State: "The sun has riz and the sun has set, and I ain't outta Texas yet." That says a lot about traversing the state. Austin is about a three-hour drive south of Dallas, a little less than a three-hour drive west of Houston, and a little more than an hour north of San Antonio. It is about a five-hour drive to Nuevo Laredo, Mexico; a five-hour drive to both the Louisiana and Oklahoma borders; and if you are heading west to New Mexico, plan on taking all day for the eight-hours-plus drive.

I-35, often called the Nafta Highway (a reference to the North American Free Trade Agreement), bisects the state from north to south, running from Laredo on the Mexican border up through the middle of the country to the Canadian border. I-10 runs from the Louisiana border through Houston, south of Austin through San Antonio and on to El Paso. US 290 connects Houston to Austin and then joins I-35 for a short stretch, cuts west through the Oak Hill area of Austin and off into the Hill Country.

Austin is literally deep in the heart of Texas. This chapter provides tips on getting here—and getting around once you have arrived.

OVERVIEW

We have divided Austin into regions in order to help newcomers and visitors find our insider spots. It is likely no two Austinites agree on geographic definitions in a city where growth is an ongoing phenomenon and neighborhoods are constantly being revitalized. But for our purposes, here is a rundown on our regional definitions. Major roadways are illustrated in the map at the beginning of this book:

- **Central Austin:** North of Lady Bird Lake, west of I-35, south of Forty-fifth Street on the east side of MoPac (Loop 1), south of Thirty-fifth Street on the west side of MoPac to Lake Austin.

- **South Central:** South of Lady Bird Lake, west of I-35, north of Ben White Boulevard (US 290 W) and east of MoPac.

- **North Central:** North of Forty-fifth Street, west of I-35, east of MoPac and south of US 183.

- **South:** South of Ben White Boulevard, west of I-35, bounded on the west by Manchaca Road.

- **Southwest:** South of US 290 W through Oak Hill and west of Manchaca Road.

- **West:** West of MoPac and Lake Austin, south of the Colorado River.

- **Northwest:** North of the Colorado River and west of MoPac.

- **North:** North of US 183, bounded by MoPac in the west and I-35 in the east.

- **Northeast:** East of I-35 and north of US 290E.
- **East:** South of US 290 E, east of I-35, and north of Lady Bird Lake.
- **Southeast:** South of Lady Bird Lake and east of I-35.

AIRPORTS/COMMERCIAL

AUSTIN-BERGSTROM INTERNATIONAL AIRPORT
3600 Presidential Blvd.
(512) 530-ABIA: General Information
(512) 530-6358: Travelers with Disabilities
(512) 530-COPS: Airport Police and Lost and Found, 24-hour number
(512) 530-PAGE: Paging, 24-hour number
(512) 530-3300: Parking Information, 24-hour number
www.ci.austin.tx.us/austinairport

Austin was the only city in the United States to embark on a major airport building program as the 20th century drew to a close. In the spring of 1999, the city shut down the municipal airport near downtown Austin, Robert Mueller Municipal Airport, and opened a new international facility in the southeast sector of the city called Austin-Bergstrom International Airport. The airport code remains AUS. The same airlines and rental car companies serve the new $690 million airport, but the facility is much larger with twice as many gates, two runways (as opposed to one) aptly named for two famous Texas politicians, President Lyndon Baines Johnson and Congressman J. J. "Jake" Pickle, and a much larger terminal, named in honor of the late Texas congresswoman Barbara Jordan. Austin-Bergstrom has a two-level access road (one level for arrivals, the other for departures) and a three-level parking garage.

The site of the old airport is being developed as a major, mixed-use town center that will be a total community. Already located there are the Austin Film Society's studios and the Dell Children's Medical Center of Central Texas (see the Health Care chapter). There are plans for other health care facilities, plus the University of Texas will build a research campus onsite. Homes, apartments, shops, cafes and open spaces also are planned. For a preview go to www.muelleraustin.com.

The designers and builders sought to evoke the spirit of Austin at the new facility by including a stage in the terminal for live music performances and Hill Country landscaping by using water elements, rocks, and native plants. The new terminal includes a business center, 16 restaurants and snack shops (some of them operated by local businesses such as Amy's Ice Creams, Book People, and the Salt Lick barbecue), retail shops, and bookstores. The restaurants and snack bars sell food at "street prices," rather than the inflated prices often found at airports. The retail stores feature regional items, including music by Austin musicians and works by local artists and crafters.

The airport also offers guided tours for groups of adults and children (5 years and older). Reservations are necessary; call the program at (512) 530-2242. There is also an outdoor family viewing area (with a parking area and picnic tables) on the west side of Highway 71 East, near the east runway, where one acre has been set aside for visitors to watch planes take off and land.The parking garage next to the terminal provides 2,419 covered short-term public parking spaces on the first and second levels. Car rental returns are located on the third level. There is a close-in surface parking lot (Lot A) near the terminal and several outlying long-term lots (Lots B, C, D, E, and F), providing 7,733 parking spaces. There are also several privately operated offsite parking facilities. Shuttle buses run every seven to 10 minutes and 24 hours a day from the parking lots. Airport shuttles from all surface parking lots pick up at shuttle stops within the lots and discharge departing passengers in front of the terminal on the lower baggage level. Airport parking shuttles pick up arriving passengers outside the lower baggage level in front of the terminal and take them to surface parking lots.

Wheelchair-accessible parking is available free for up to 5 days in the parking garage and up to 10 days in all parking lots. Wheelchair-accessible parking spots are located on the first available row in the garage and near the shuttle stops in all surface parking lots. Shuttle buses are equipped with wheelchair lifts.

i A variety of names were suggested for Austin's new international airport, but city officials decided to stick with the name given to the Air Force base that occupied the site. It was named in honor of Austin's first World War II casualty, Captain J. A. Bergstrom.

Airport Transportation

There is a transportation information desk on the ground floor of the terminal. Passengers arriving and departing from the airport have several options, in addition to rental cars and their own personal automobiles. SuperShuttle provides door-to-door minivan service for a fixed fee for one-way rides. Fees are determined by the zip code of destination or pickup. The shuttles also are available for groups at charter rates. Contact **SuperShuttle** at (512) 258-3826, (800) BLUE-VAN, or make reservations online at www.supershuttle.com. **Capital Metro** also offers local bus service between downtown Austin and the airport, linking to other bus routes in the city. Call (512) 474-1200, (512) 385-5872 (TDD), or (512) 474-1201 (free call from any local telephone booth); or visit www.capmetro.org.

AIRPORTS/GENERAL AVIATION

There are two fixed-base operators at Austin-Bergstrom International Airport. Both provide general aviation terminals, hangars, maintenance, and fuel facilities and access to the adjacent instrumented 9,000-foot runway. They provide 170 spaces, including 50 T-hangar spaces for small aircraft. For general aviation information provided by the airport, visit www.ci.austin.tx.us/austinairport/geninfo.htm.

ATLANTIC AVIATION SERVICES, INC.
4309 General Aviation Ave.
(512) 530-7000
www.atlanticaviation.com

LAKEWAY
115 Flying Scott Rd.
(512) 261-4385
www.3r9.org
Operated by Lakeway Airpark Association, a cooperative, this private facility is nonprofit and unattended. There is a 4,000-foot landing strip open from sunrise to sunset plus self-serve gas facilities. Overnight parking is $5, but that is waived with gas purchase. The landing strip is 15.5 statute miles from Austin. The association reminds pilots there is a noise ordinance in place, plus pilots should watch for the deer grazing near the landing strip.

SIGNATURE FLIGHT SUPPORT
4321 General Aviation Ave.
(512) 530-5451
www.signatureflight.com

AIR CHARTERS

MCRAE AVIATION
4309 General Aviation Ave.
(512) 385-9615
www.mcraeaviation.com
McRae offers jet charters and light cargo service from its location at the general aviation area of Austin-Bergstrom International Airport.

NEW FLIGHT CHARTERS
(800) 732-1653
www.newflightcharters.com
A national charter company servicing the Austin market.

PULSE AVIATION
3600 Presidential Blvd.
(512) 351-4338
www.pulseaviation.com
This charter service has offices on site at ABIA.

STRATOS JET CHARTER SERVICES
(888) 478-7280
www.stratosjets.com
Charter aircraft and seat availability on inbound Austin private flights are offered by this national company.

TRAIN STATIONS

There are several recreational trains for sightseeing in the Austin area. (For more information on recreational trains, see the Attractions chapter.)

AMTRAK
250 North Lamar Blvd.
(512) 476-5684, (800) 872-7245
(reservations)
www.amtrak.com

North/south service is available four times a week on the Amtrak Eagle. Northbound trains leave on Sun, Tues, Wed, and Thurs mornings; southbound on Sun, Wed, Fri, and Sat evenings. The north route goes through Dallas to Chicago, the south route goes to San Antonio. Fares to San Antonio range from $9 to $17, depending on how close to departure time reservations are made; fares to Dallas range from $20 to $40. Children 2 to 15 travel for half price with an adult. East-west service is available from San Antonio; that route connects Los Angeles with Miami.

i The pink granite on the outer walls of the new Austin-Bergstrom International Airport comes from Marble Falls, west of the city, and is the same type of granite used at the State Capitol.

BUS SERVICES

Bus service within the city of Austin is covered in the Public Transportation section.

GREYHOUND
816 East Koenig Lane
(512) 458-4463, (800) 231-2222
www.greyhound.com
The intercity bus station is near Highland Mall, just west of the intersection of US 290 East and I-35. Greyhound offers service to more than 2,500 US cities and the station is open 24 hours a day.

KERRVILLE BUS CO., INC.
(800) 874-3522
www.iridekbc.com
This Texas-grown bus company is also served by the Greyhound station facility (see previous listing). Kerrville serves several Texas cities and small towns.

ROADWAYS

Austin sits at the crossroads of two major highways: I-35 and US 290. That sounds simple, but as visitors and newcomers to Austin quickly discover, the picture gets muddied first by a local propensity for calling highways by names other than the state highway department designations, and second by the absence of any clear east-west routes in the center of the city.

I-35 runs right through the middle of the city, heading south to San Antonio and on to the Mexican border, heading north to Waco, Dallas–Fort Worth, and points north.

US 290 runs from Houston westward to the northeast section of Austin where it is called US 290 East. It merges with I-35, emerging again in South Austin as US 290 West, where it is called Ben White Boulevard.

Highway 71 merges with US 290 West at I-35 through the southern and southwestern section of the city, separating at what locals call the "Y" in Oak Hill. US 290 West heads west to Johnson City, while Highway 71 heads northwest to Bee Cave and the Highland Lakes.

US 183 runs diagonally through the city from northwest (at Cedar Park) to southeast (near the Austin-Bergstrom International Airport). It has numerous names along its route. In the north, US 183 at intervals is called Research Boulevard, Anderson Lane, Ed Bluestein Boulevard, and Bastrop Highway.

The MoPac Expressway, called Loop 1 on all the highway signs, runs north-south through the western environs of the city. The locals just call it MoPac, as we do throughout this book.

Loop 360, or the Capital of Texas Highway, runs north-south through far West Austin. Businesses along this roadway use Capital of Texas Highway in their addresses, but the locals usually call it "360." We use both in this book.

RM 620 is a primarily north-south road that swings around Austin in the Hill Country west of Lake Austin and east of Lake Travis. Usually called just "620," the designation RM means Ranch-to-Market road, a leftover from the days when the state built highways so that farmers and ranchers could bring their goods and cattle to town. Some roads are called RM, while others are FM (Farm-to-Market). In some areas, drivers also will see the designation RR which denotes a Ranch Road, a public roadway through ranchland.

Commute times have become longer as the city has grown, but they pale in comparison with commutes in some of America's larger cities. During morning and evening rush hours (6:30 to around 9 a.m. and 4:30 to 7 p.m.), traffic slows to a crawl on the area's major roadways, notably I-35, MoPac, and US 183. At other times, driving in Austin is relatively easy.

Perhaps the biggest problem in navigating Austin streets is the fact that there is no major east-west freeway in the heart of the city. US 183 has been widened and improved, while in the southern end of the city US 290 West (known as Ben White Boulevard for much of its length) has been widened and turned into a freeway from I-35 to Oak Hill.

As for a midtown freeway, the issue has been a major political football for years as older central city neighborhoods have fought attempts to widen their streets. Another major political battle has been brewing over the increasing use of toll roads. Several new toll roads have opened including TX 45 which runs east from I-35 south of Austin, joining up with TX 130 running north from the airport to Georgetown. TX 45 splits from TX 130 just north of Pflugerville in far northeast Austin and heads west across the northern far suburbs to Cedar Park. TX 133A heads north from Cedar Park and TX 45 to Leander. The far northern portion of MoPac (Loop 1) is also a toll road and takes travelers north to connect with I-35. Tolls are $1 or less, and commuters can buy a TxTag, which allows drivers to fly through tollbooths. The tags issued in Dallas and Houston—Dallas TollTag and Houston's EZTag—also work in the Central Texas area. For information on tags, visit www.txtag.org; for information on toll roads current and planned, visit www.texastollways.com.

CAR RENTAL

Rental car counters are located on the ground floor of the airport terminal, with express service available on the third level of the parking garage immediately north of the terminal. In addition to airport-based rental car agencies, several companies offer rental car services in the city. One growing rental car service in Austin is www.Car2go.com. Approximately 200 of the small, 2-person vehicles are located in the greater downtown area, and members of the program can access them for local trips by reserving online.

PARKING

Downtown parking can be hard to find—many meters allow only 30-minute parking, and 2-hour meters are located several blocks away from Congress Avenue.

There are several parking garages in the downtown area, which are a good place to park if the weather is hot (shade is invaluable in the hot Texas summer) or at night when street parking can be hard to find. Other lots

have attendants, and some have banks of boxes where patrons must deposit their fees. If you don't pay, you will be towed.

Parking around the capitol has improved with the opening of a new visitor parking garage on San Jacinto east of the capitol. There is a large parking garage under the capitol extension, but that is for legislators and their staffs.

Parking meters around the capitol are limited to 2-hour stays, which is a hassle for anyone wanting to spend time touring the building or doing business at one of the many state buildings in the area. The idea behind this implementation is to discourage state workers from using street parking. The electronic meters allow you to pay with a bank-issued debit card. Previously, a 5-minute "grace period" was given before a ticket was issued when your meter ran out, and parking was free on Saturday, but at press time, in light of the economic downturn, those luxuries were on the chopping block as a way to increase the city's revenue.

i Generally, the rule is that the farther away from Congress Avenue you are, the longer the meters will allow you to park.

TAXIS

Taxi cabs line up to serve customers at the western end of the airport terminal. Cabs wait in a holding area at the airport and are dispatched into the pickup lane, which is immediately outside the terminal. Note: There is a $1 surcharge at the airport. Only at very slow times will a passenger have to call for a cab. Austin's taxi services are regulated by the city, which requires companies to operate both smoking and nonsmoking cabs plus wheelchair-accessible vehicles.

The flag-drop charge is $1.75, and each mile is $1.75. The charge from the airport to downtown ranges from around $20 to $30, depending on what part of downtown you need to reach. Taxi service is available throughout the city 24 hours a day, 7 days a week. Taxis cruise downtown, particularly around the capitol area. Response time, especially downtown, is very good. Cabbies accept cash and credit cards. There are even pedicabs (roving bicycle cabbies) downtown detailed in our Nightlife chapter.

AUSTIN CAB
(512) 478-2222
www.austincab.com

LONE STAR CAB
(512) 836-4900
www.lonestarcabaustin.com

YELLOW CAB CO.
(512) 452-9999, (512) 835-7272 (TTY)
www.yellowcabaustin.xohost.com

LIMOUSINES

There are many limousine operators in Austin, and, like taxi cab companies, they are regulated by city ordinances governing safety and business practices. Companies charge hourly rates, starting around $70 for 4 passengers. Most also add service and gratuity charges, usually 15 percent each, and many also charge more during the peak spring prom season and on holidays such as Halloween and New Year's Eve. Sedan limos used for hotel/airport pickups cost around $120 an hour.

The limo business is highly competitive, and there is frequent turnover. Several large chains also operate in Austin. For a comprehensive listing, check the airport website, www.ci.austin.tx.us/austinairport/limoservice.htm.

PUBLIC TRANSPORTATION

CAPITAL METRO
2910 East Fifth St.
(512) 474-1200, (512) 385-5872 (TDD)
www.capmetro.org
One of the easiest ways to navigate the downtown area is to ride the 'Dillo, the free trolley-style buses that cruise the area from early morning to around 10 p.m. Downtown-area bus stops have 'Dillo route maps. A special weekend 'Dillo, Route 470, the "Tour the Town" bus operates from 10 a.m. until 6 p.m. on Sat and from 11 a.m. to 6 p.m. on Sun, stopping at the major cultural and historical attractions downtown. You can ride the route all day long for just $1. The 'Dillos are just one service of the Capital Metro public transportation service, a publicly funded agency that operates buses and shuttle services in the greater Austin area. Most of the major attractions in Austin are located on bus routes, including the museums and live music spots. Capital Metro also operates an airport-to-downtown bus line and Night Owl routes that carry revelers from the Sixth and Congress area to the suburbs.

In 2010, after some delays, Cap Metro launched its light rail service connecting bedroom communities in far northwest Austin to the downtown area. The trains run from Leander to Cedar Park, then past Lakeline Mall, southeast to stations in East Austin and then west along a short route to the Austin Convention Center, just north of Lady Bird Lake and 3 blocks east of Congress Avenue. The service is designed to ferry commuters and runs from just after 5 a.m. to just after 9 a.m. and later from just after 3 p.m. to just before 8 p.m. It is best used in connection with bus services to reach popular sights and attractions. Fares are minimal and tickets can be bought online.

Capital Metro also runs the UT Shuttle, a bus service that takes students back and forth to the campus for 50 cents a ride—the same fare it charges on its regular city bus routes. The suburbs are served by flyers, which are nonstop buses that operate from park-and-ride stops in the outlying areas.

The Capital Metro bus system serves a 500-square-mile area that encompasses the cities of Austin, Cedar Park, Leander, Lago Vista, Jonestown, Pflugerville, Manor, and San Leanna. Capital Metro offers a comprehensive booklet of its policies and schedules that is available at all area H-E-B, Fiesta, Randall's, and Albertson's grocery stores; Ace Cash Express; major shopping malls; and the agency's offices.

Capital Metro's Customer Information Center has operators on duty from 6 a.m. to 10 p.m. Mon through Sat and 7 a.m. to 6 p.m. on Sun. The agency operates a local toll-free number, (800) 474-1201, that allows customers to dial free from any local pay phone.

There are several methods of payment on Capital Metro buses. Ticket books are available at previously listed grocery stores and at the Capital Metro Customer Information Center. Discount passes covering a variety of days from a single unlimited use pass for 1 day to a 31 day pass are available. Passengers must have tickets or exact change to board the bus.

Seniors and mobility-impaired riders may ride free on city buses by obtaining a free ID at the information center. There are discounts for individuals who qualify for Special Transit Services, which provide transportation for those who cannot ride public buses. All city buses have bike racks and are equipped with wheelchair lifts.

The agency provides a variety of programs including park-and-ride services, a car-pooling program called Ridefinders, a special van service for seniors called Easyrider, and other programs tailored to the mobility impaired. Capital Metro often provides free public shuttles at major Austin events and festivals, and visitors and downtown workers can avail themselves of the free 'Dillo service.

BICYCLING

Austin is trying its best to be a bike-friendly city. The city even employs a Bicycle & Pedestrian Program Coordinator, who is charged with formulating a bicycle- and pedestrian-friendly transportation plan. The coordinator may be contacted at www.ci .austin.tx.us/bicycle, by calling (512) 972-9876, or by writing to the **Department of Public Works and Transportation,** City of Austin, P.O. Box 1088, Austin, TX 78767. The city's Bicycle Planning policy is published by the city, and complimentary copies are available at the above address. There is also a downloadable bike map on the city website.

The city currently has approximately 62 miles of roadway with marked bicycle lanes. In the works is the Lance Armstrong Bikeway, named after Austin's famed cyclist who is not the inspiration for the project, but its main planner. The route will take cyclists the 6-mile ride from downtown to the veloway (see the Parks & Recreation chapter). City ordinances also require bicyclists 17 and younger to wear a bicycle helmet. An ordinance to require all bicyclists to wear a helmet was amended after many free-spirited adults complained; however, given the city's busy streets, all riders are advised to wear a helmet in traffic.

We provide more information on recreational biking and cycling, including rentals, in the Austin area in our Parks & Recreation chapter. A great resource website is www.bicycleaustin.com.

There are several organizations in Austin that promote bicycle awareness, commuting, and safety. They include:

THE AUSTIN CYCLING ASSOCIATION
P.O. Box 5993, Austin, TX 78763
www.austincycling.org
A recreational riding club. The website provides a "map my ride" tool.

AUSTIN RIDGE RIDERS
www.austinridgeriders.com
A recreational mountain-biking club.

THE TEXAS BICYCLE COALITION
(512) 476-RIDE
www.biketexas.org
A nonprofit advocacy organization.

THE YELLOW BIKE PROGRAM
(512) 916-3553
www.austinyellowbike.org
A nonprofit group promoting community free-use bicycles, which are painted yellow and left at various locations, notably around the University of Texas campus.

WALKING

There are areas of Austin where walking can be a pleasure, notably Congress Avenue, the Lady Bird Lake Hike and Bike Trail, and in some of the neighborhood parks. There are also several popular Historic Walking Tours in the city. For more information on these opportunities, see the Attractions and Parks & Recreation chapters.

Walking in downtown Austin is a wonderful way to see the city. Visitors should, of course, always exercise caution. Street crime is not a problem in downtown Austin during daylight hours, but do avoid alleyways after dark. Always exhibit caution when using ATMs, and carry purses and wallets in a secure manner. The Austin Police Department operates both horseback patrols and bicycle patrols in the city's parks and downtown streets.

i Bicyclists 17 and younger must wear helmets in the city of Austin on all streets, on bike trails, and in parks. Violation is a Class C misdemeanor punishable with a $20 fine for the first offense and $40 for each subsequent violation.

HORSE-DRAWN CARRIAGES

One of the most romantic ways to tour downtown Austin is in a horse-drawn carriage. Carriages are not permitted on East Sixth Street, and it's likely the horses would not appreciate the sometimes rowdy atmosphere on that stretch of Sixth between Congress Avenue and I-35, anyway.

AUSTIN CARRIAGE TOUR
(512) 243-0044
www.austincarriagetours.com
This service has Belgian and Percheron horses to pull the carriages, which take up positions near the capitol, usually around sunset. Fees are $60 an hour or $30 for a half-hour tour of the downtown area. The drivers are equipped with radios so that they can be summoned to a restaurant, hotel, or nightclub, sometimes for an extra fee if

it is far from the capitol. One pleasant ride is a tour of the Bremond Historic District downtown (see the Attractions chapter) or a waterfront tour along Lady Bird Lake. Hours are Sun through Thurs from just before sunset to around midnight and on Fri and Sat from sunset to around 2 a.m.

DIE GELBE ROSE CARRIAGE
(512) 477-8824
www.austinsdiegelberosecarriage.com
Headquartered near the Radisson Hotel at Cesar Chavez Street and Congress Avenue, this carriage company uses Clydesdale horses but also has one Belgian and one Percheron. Rates are $70 an hour or $45 for a half hour. A popular tour is along Congress Avenue to the capitol. Carriages are available from around sunset to midnight during the week and until 2 a.m. on weekends.

HOTELS & MOTELS

Are you the type of traveler who just wants a comfortable, clean, inexpensive place to fling your bags and rest your body so that you can spend all your time getting to know Austin? Or are you looking for a lodging that caters to your every business need? Do you prefer divided space to conduct private meetings or to give you some breathing room from the kids? Perhaps you're looking for accommodations that reflect the history of Austin and transport you back in time. Is luxury the key to your heart? Whether you're looking for a massage and a sauna, a morning jog along Lady Bird Lake, a view, shopping, or nightlife, you've come to the right place!

While Austin offers plenty of accommodations for the traveler who believes the best surprise is no surprise, there also is an ever-increasing number of rooms for those searching for the unique. If you're wishing to be transported, think of us as "OZ-tin," click your heels, make a reservation, and repeat, "There's no place like Texas."

OVERVIEW

Perhaps the most "Austin" of Austin's grand hotels is the Driskill, the Sixth Street landmark that has been treated to a historically accurate restoration valued in the millions of dollars. Another classic Austin landmark, the long-vacant Stephen F. Austin Hotel, has been restored to splendor and is now part of the luxury InterContinental chain. An exquisite piece of Austin history, the stately Goodall Wooten Mansion, was rescued in 2003 with the opening of the luxury boutique hotel the Mansion at Judges' Hill. A hip hotel on trendy South Congress Avenue is the restored World War II–era Hotel San José. These hotels, and a few others scattered around the city, are Austin through and through. Several of the other major chain hotels have also created a Texas ambience, notably the Four Seasons Hotel, where the lobby bar has become a perfect people-watcher spot. Here, high-tech executives from around the world rub shoulders with

lobbyists and world-famous musicians, actors, and film executives (see the Nightlife chapter). But travelers don't have to shell out big bucks to get a real Austin experience. Some of our locally owned, older motels are truly Austin—and a lot easier on the pocketbook.

While Austin may never see a return to the days when the grand hotel was the center of community activity, hotels are giving residents more and more reasons to check in. As a result, out-of-towners aren't the only ones to benefit from Austin's hotel industry. For weddings and other festivities, meetings, dining, socializing, or getaway weekends, Austinites are discovering the pleasures of our local hotels.

Whether you've come to live in Austin, or only wish you could, there are a few things you should know before making your hotel or motel reservation. If this is your first visit, or you haven't had the pleasure of returning for a while, allow us to orient you to the lay of the land regarding accommodations.

i Austin is a pretty laid-back city when it comes to dress. Shorts, T-shirts, and sandals are the standard uniform for summer and will get you in just about anywhere. Unless you've come for a gala, casual dress for evening is just perfect. While you can plan on it being hot in summer, winter can be trickier. We can have 80-degree days and 20-degree days. Mostly, however, Austin's winters are pretty mild.

The majority of Austin's full-service and luxury hotels are clustered around downtown. However, you'll also find several noteworthy, full-service hotels along the I-35 corridor, up north in the Arboretum and Domain areas, at the airport, and down in Southeast Austin. A high concentration of hotels and motels is found along I-35, the north-south artery that bisects Austin. We've divided I-35 into sections in our geographical listings for those who prefer to stay close to this practical thoroughfare and yet be near their destination. We've also pointed out the best choices among the other hotels and motels scattered around the city. Growth in the Austin hotel-motel industry has exploded since we published our first edition of the *Insiders' Guide to Austin* in 1999. Included in that growth are new— or newly restored—Austin originals. For this seventh edition, we are focusing primarily on those hotels and motels that are truly unique to Austin or have a particular Austin feel for one reason or another. To offer our readers a range of choices, however, we also have included a few of the chain hotels.

Our annual music and film festivals, sessions of the Legislature, University of Texas football weekends, and other big social and sporting events all draw crowds to Austin, so it's especially important to reserve your room well in advance for these times (check the Annual Events & Festivals chapter).

The listings include a dollar-sign code that will give you an idea of the hotel's rate. Taxes are not included in the rates, so when you're calculating the cost of your stay, make sure to add 15 percent. A portion of the tax goes to support the arts in Austin. The rate information has been provided by the hotels themselves and is subject to change. Unless otherwise noted, all the hotels and motels listed accept major credit cards.

Price Code

The following price code is based on the average room rate for one-night double occupancy during peak business. These prices do not include taxes, which in Austin total 15 percent. Please note that prices may change without notice.

$	Less than $80
$$	$80 to $125
$$$	$125 to $170
$$$$	$170 to $225
$$$$$	More than $225

GREATER DOWNTOWN

THE DRISKILL HOTEL $$$$$
604 Brazos St.
(512) 474-5911, (800) 252-9367
www.driskillhotel.com
Cattle baron Jesse Driskill opened his stately hotel in downtown Austin on December 20, 1886, offering guests an architectural wonder and such modern conveniences as steam heat and gas lights. More than

Close-up

Austin's Resorts

The Texas Hill Country west of Austin and the rolling prairie and woodlands east of the city are conducive to outdoor recreation and relaxation. The lakes and waterways, the natural beauty of the hills, the hospitable climate, and Texas hospitality have been combined to create several top-quality resorts that offer a variety of experiences. Three of the four listed here are noted golf resorts, and they are detailed in our Golf chapter. The fourth is a Hill Country spa that offers not only outdoor recreational activities but also all manner of therapies designed to relax both body and spirit.

Barton Creek Conference Resort and Country Club
8212 Barton Club Dr.
(512) 329-4000, (800) 336-6157
www.bartoncreek.com
A topflight resort with four beautiful golf courses designed by the top names in the sport, Barton Creek is on some of the most beautiful land just west of Austin. Barton Creek wends its way through the hills here, creating not only a beautiful setting for golf but also for other activities, including tennis, skeet shooting, jogging on wonderful Hill Country trails, swimming, boating, fishing, and horseback riding. The resort also offers sight-seeing and shopping tours, a spa, and even a Kid's Club where the youngsters can be entertained while Mom and Dad enjoy their own playtime.

The resort has several excellent dining facilities, for both casual meals and special occasions. (It has one of the few restaurants in Austin where a jacket is required.) The resort's spa offers an extensive menu of treatments from facials to salt rubs to aromatic loofah scrubs. There is also a fitness center in the resort complex. The resort maintains recreational facilities, including swimming and tennis, at Barton Creek Lakeside at nearby Lake Travis.

There are a total of 303 rooms at the resort, but despite the size the atmosphere on the 4,000-acre property is private and quiet. The rooms all have views of the golf course or the surrounding Hill Country. The resort offers a number of packages tailored to guests' interests. High season is from Mar to Nov; low season is Dec through Feb. Packages begin at around $270 per person per night in low season and $330 in high season. Room rates vary from around $230 to $1,000 plus for the large suites.

Lake Austin Spa Resort
1705 South Quinlan Park Rd.
(512) 372-7300, (800) 847-5637
www.lakeaustin.com
You can ask the concierge to fix you up for a round of golf. Or perhaps a set or two of tennis. A sailboat ride. A little water-skiing. But why would you? Wouldn't you rather just have another massage? This spa on the shores of Lake Austin aims to capture the essence of Austin and rid you of all those uptight urban ills. Readers of *Condé Nast Traveler* and *Travel + Leisure* magazines have named it one of the Top 10 spas in North America. Lake Austin Spa Resort offers a large variety of spa services by the day or week. A 3-night refresher package is a little more than $1,500 and includes 2 spa

treatments of your choice, fitness classes and programs, a 30-minute personal fitness consultation, meals, and a deluxe private room. The 7-night ultimate pampering program costs approximately $4,500 to $6,500 depending on room choices, and that includes a monogrammed robe.

Just reading the brochures is enough to make you long for a night or two of pampering. How about a Blue Lagoon massage—a body wrap of blue seaweed? Or a Texas two step—someone rubs your toes while you get an herbal face-lift?

The spa also offers special programs throughout the year on diverse topics, including gardening, cooking, and nutrition. Guest speakers from all walks of life are invited to these presentations. One special package is dubbed "A Gathering of Wise Women" and features experts on women's health issues.

If you really want to get more active, in addition to golf and tennis the spa offers a long list of outdoor activities, including watersports on adjacent Lake Travis and hiking in the hills.

Hyatt Regency Lost Pines Resort
575 Hyatt Lost Pines Rd.
(512) 308-1234, (888) 591-1234, (800) 228-9548 (TDD)
www.visitlostpines.com

Just 30 miles southeast of Austin sits a piney woodlands called the "Lost Pines"—lost because these loblolly pines are some 100 miles from East Texas where piney woods are ubiquitous. The area is now home to a luxury resort built by Hyatt. The resort attracts golfers to its topflight Wolfdancer Club (see our Golf chapter); families who enjoy outdoor activities, such as horseback riding; seekers of sybaritic pleasures at the hotel's spa; and even movie stars, who sometimes stay here when filming on location in Central Texas. At Spa Django (the name means "I awake") guests can enjoy spiritual awakening treatments like an "herbal spice percussion scrub" that includes a body wrap and rhythmic Austin music for $250. A full day of "awakening" is $650. The resort also features trails for horseback riding, a water park, several outstanding restaurants and quiet corners that reflect the ranch-style atmosphere. There are 492 guest rooms and suites, with rates beginning at $300.

Lakeway Resort and Spa
101 Lakeway Dr.
(512) 261-6600, (800) LAKEWAY
www.lakewayresortandspa.com

This resort hotel on Lake Travis, west of the city, is a longtime favorite for visitors from around Texas and Mexico. The resort has topflight amenities for golfers and tennis players plus provides the facilities and equipment for a variety of watersports. Prime season is Mar to Nov; "value season" runs from Dec to Feb. The resort offers a variety of packages ranging in price from approximately $200 a couple per night in value season to $280 in prime season.

In addition to golf packages, the resort also offers romantic getaways, "lake escape" packages, and family packages and is a popular spot for catered events, including weddings and family reunions.

a century later, The Driskill adds timeless grandeur to the Sixth Street Historic District, where live music pours from the popular nightclubs and packed restaurants of Austin's most-visited strip. Guests leave all that commotion behind when they step into The Driskill's handsome marble-floored lobby. Each of the hotel's 180 rooms and suites is unique, designed to reflect the exceptional beauty of the 1880s Driskill. Among the multi-room suites at this hotel are the opulent Cattle Baron Suite, the Lyndon and Lady Bird Johnson Presidential Suite and 3 distinctive bridal suites. There's also a sitting room named the Maximilian Room, known for its 8 gold-leaf mirrors called the Empress Carlota mirrors. These French mirrors were a wedding gift from Maximilian, briefly emperor of Mexico, to his bride Carlota. The story goes that these mirrors were discovered in crates in San Antonio in the 1930s. The 2-story side of the hotel is the original hotel and features spacious, alluring rooms with nearly 14-foot ceilings. The tower side was built in the 1920s and has 9 levels, offering guests better views of downtown Austin. Some rooms feature balconies for an even closer perspective on downtown. The ballroom, upper lobby piano bar, and restaurant also accentuate the beauty of a bygone era. The piano bar, which features live music in the evenings, is also home to portraits of some of Austin's leading historical figures, including Stephen F. Austin, the Father of Texas (see the History chapter for more on Stephen F. Austin). A captivating Western sculpture called Widow Maker, by the artist Barvo, adorns this lobby—a must see.

The award-winning gourmet restaurant, the **Driskill Grill,** is open Tues through Sat for dinner, while the meticulously restored

1886 Cafe & Bakery is open 7 days a week for breakfast, lunch, dinner and late-night dining. The Driskill also offers a fully equipped fitness center, as well as an executive business center. There is no parking garage on the premises, but valet parking is offered.

i Don't forget to make The Driskill Hotel part of your walking tour of downtown Austin, even if you're lodging elsewhere. Look for *The Driskill, A Walking Tour* brochures in the hotel lobby, and learn about this historic site.

EXTENDED STAY AMERICA $$
600 Guadalupe St.
(512) 457-9994, (800) 803-3724
www.extendedstayhotels.com
Finding a reasonably priced hotel downtown can be difficult, but this national chain offers mid-priced rooms that can be rented by the night or the week. The rooms are small suites with kitchen facilities and desks, making them ideal for business visitors or families on a budget. The Extended Stay group has several other hotels in the area, including the Homestead Studio Suites and the Crossland Economy Studios. If you're looking for choices in the $$ range, you might check here.

FOUR SEASONS HOTEL $$$$$
98 San Jacinto Blvd.
(512) 478-4500, (800) 332-3442
www.fourseasons.com
It doesn't take many steps past the lobby entrance to know you're in one of Austin's premier hotels. Elegance abounds as you make your way to **TRIO** restaurant and out to the terrace, offering a drop-dead-gorgeous view of Lady Bird Lake and the hotel's

own manicured lawns. The hotel and its 292 exceptionally spacious rooms and suites are designed with a sophisticated flair that is both elegant and relaxing. The amenities and services go on and on: 24-hour room service, twice-daily housekeeping, a heated outdoor pool overlooking Lady Bird Lake, a state-of-the-art health club, full-service spa, complimentary morning newspaper, overnight shoe shine, and 1-hour pressing service. There's even a dock for sunning, splashing your feet in the lake, or doing some kayaking or canoeing. And while you're outside, you can take advantage of the hotel's direct access to Austin's wonderful Hike and Bike Trail. The Four Seasons will even arrange a bicycle if you want.

LA QUINTA INN $$
300 East Eleventh St.
(512) 476-1166
www.laquinta.com

If you want to stay in downtown Austin, but don't need all the amenities of Austin's upscale hotels, it's hard to beat La Quinta Inn. For comfort, location, and comparative price, La Quinta is an excellent choice. It has valet parking only, however, at an extra $13 a day. The 145 rooms and suites are spotless and comfortably sized. Nice touches have been added to spruce up the outdoor walkways, such as flowers and plants. Among the motel's features are free continental breakfast, Internet access, a fitness room, and premium cable channels. The state capitol is just around the corner, Sixth Street is 5 blocks down the road, and the University of Texas is a mile away. During the week, La Quinta's guests are mostly professionals. Weekends tend to draw a college crowd. There are more than 10 other Austin-area locations, including Round Rock and Cedar Park.

THE MANSION AT JUDGES' HILL $$$–$$$$$
1900 Rio Grande St.
(512) 495-1800, (800) 311-1619
www.mansionatjudgeshill.com

Small and ultrachic, the Mansion at Judges' Hill brings one of Austin's historic homes back to splendor—making it, perhaps, even better than during its prime. For more than a century the Goodall Wooten Mansion has stood just a few blocks from the University of Texas in the Judges' Hill neighborhood. But time had taken its toll on this graceful, stone-colonnaded structure. The once-luxurious residence had over the years been used as a dormitory, a sorority house, and finally a drug rehabilitation center. Owner William Gurasich, one of the founders of Austin's well-known GSD&M advertising agency and now a real estate developer, oversaw a complete renovation, paying special attention to the details.

This 48-room luxury hotel and gourmet restaurant features rich colors and textures throughout. The large rooms, some with fireplaces, include antique and custom-made furniture, and each is uniquely designed to reflect a timeless quality. Even the spacious bathrooms are gorgeous. What mansion would be complete without its own private courtyard, library, and covered garage? There are separate rates for the Mansion and the North Wing, the latter being somewhat less expensive.

OMNI AUSTIN HOTEL DOWNTOWN $$$$$
700 San Jacinto Blvd.
(512) 476-3700, (800) 444-6664
www.omnihotels.com

Enormous plate-glass windows supported by steel beams rise from the ground to the towering ceiling in this modern hotel, which features huge abstract paintings and polished granite throughout the atrium-style lobby. Sunlight pours through the tremendous wall of glass and illuminates the sprawling lobby, which is home to **Ancho's,** the hotel restaurant featuring Southwestern cuisine. The lobby bar next to Ancho's also has that airy look and is a nice place to relax and have a drink or a bite. The hotel has 375 guest rooms and suites, all offering superior comfort and a cozy capitol-city feel, with Texas stars scattered here and there throughout the hotel. Guests are treated to the ultimate in comfort in the hotel's large rooms, meeting and convention spaces, and ballroom. The upper floors provide excellent views of downtown Austin and across town. The Omni also offers massage and facial services.

STEPHEN F. AUSTIN HOTEL $$$$$
701 Congress Ave.
(512) 457-8800, (888) 424-6835
www.austin.intercontinental.com
"Austin's Dream Comes True with Brilliant Opening of New Hotel." So read the *Austin American's* front-page headline on May 20, 1924, the day following the grand opening of the Stephen F. Austin Hotel. Three-quarters of a century later, the hotel reopened as one of Austin's finest luxury hotels, while retaining the look and feel of 1920s opulence. A grand staircase of marble and brass beguiles visitors as they enter the lobby and walk up to the Grand Ballroom. The 189 rooms and suites have a truly Texan ambience, with star emblems on some headboards and lots of wrought iron. Facilities include a state-of-the-art fitness center, an indoor swimming pool, a cigar bar, a cafe, and a restaurant for fine dining. Austin and Texas history wafts through the halls and hangs like tapestries

from the walls. Lyndon B. Johnson made this grand hotel his congressional campaign headquarters after World War II, and it seems as if everybody who had a hand in shaping modern Texas walked through its doors at one time or another. In 1984 the *Dallas Morning News* wrote this about the hotel: "To native Austinites and University of Texas Exes, she is known simply as 'the Stephen F.' The name has been adopted for the second story bar which features an outside balcony overlooking Congress Avenue. And if walls could talk, they would relate fascinating tales of oil and cattle deals transacted over breakfast and a handshake, of political intrigue involving state legislators, and of romances begun during World War II." Who knows what tales will be told about the Stephen F. at the end of this century?

SOUTH CENTRAL

✳AUSTIN MOTEL $$–$$$
1220 South Congress Ave.
(512) 441-1157
www.austinmotel.com
Location, history, personality, and price combine to make the family-owned Austin Motel one of the city's most unique lodgings. As Congress Avenue gentrification spreads south of Lady Bird Lake, this motel is in the right spot at the right time, again. The main buildings were built in 1938 on Austin's central thoroughfare and way before the coming of the highway system. With its now classic red and white neon sign, this motel attracted travelers from near and far. When the traffic moved to the highways, so did much of the Austin Motel's business. South Congress, meanwhile, grew into a popular spot for prostitutes and drug dealers. These days South Congress is hip and happening, and the bad influences are long gone.

Today's Austin Motel, like many other businesses along this funky stretch, is attracting visitors who want to get a distinct feel for Austin. This is not a place for guests who like modern, cookie-cutter accommodations. Artists, musicians, and poets seem especially attracted to the Austin Motel's particular flair, as are others who put character before elegance. This motel has 41 rooms for 41 personalities, from small rooms for those who'd rather spend their time out on the town, to spacious executive suites, to rooms overlooking the pool. A small, shaded garden just off the pool provides a great place for guests to gather. **El Sol y La Luna,** the Mexican restaurant next door that is leased from the hotel, is a popular spot for travelers and residents alike (see the Restaurants chapter). This hotel has become so popular with travelers that it asks guests who want a specific date and room to call the hotel directly on the first of the month—3 months in advance! In most cases the hotel requires that weekend reservations include both Fri and Sat nights.

√ **HOTEL SAINT CECILIA**　　**$$$$$**
1112 Academy Dr.
(512) 852-2400
www.hotelstcecilia.com
Travelers looking for luxury, seclusion, and even artistic inspiration in a boutique hotel will find their muse at the Hotel Saint Cecilia. Named for the patron saint of music and poetry, the Saint Cecilia is truly a work of art. The hotel offers 5 guest suites, 6 poolside bungalows, and 3 studios in a private garden retreat in the trendy South Congress district near downtown. The large, multi-room suites are in the main house, an Austin Landmark built in 1888 and featuring New Orleans-style Victorian architecture. Designed by owner Liz Lambert (who also has the Hotel San José listed above), the suites feature vintage furniture and floors of dark woods, rich leathers and velvets, sumptuous wallpapers, and luxurious (uber-pricey) beds from the Swedish company Hästens. At the same time, there's a funky Austin '60s music/art vibe here (each room has a turntable and LPs), accentuated by original paintings, videos, and vintage posters. Suite 5, called the Rock 'n' Roll Room, features an upright piano, a bright yellow rocking chair, red tufted-leather sofa, and an American flag-style curtain. Guests can also choose a suite with a private garden, an outdoor fireplace, or an outdoor shower. Even the minibars are upscale, with choices that include Russian caviar, select cheeses, and organic beers. The sophisticated, ultramodern bathrooms feature Côté Bastide bath products. The Saint Cecilia's beautifully landscaped grounds, iconic neon SOUL sign at the lap pool, and the indoor/outdoor guest lounge are crowning touches on a truly unique design.

√ **HOTEL SAN JOSÉ**　　**$$–$$$$$**
1316 South Congress Ave.
(512) 444-7322, (800) 574-8897
www.sanjosehotel.com
Hip is the word most often used to describe this restored Congress Avenue motel, and it suits not only the San José but also the neighborhood. No wonder it is favored by visiting musicians and artists, since it is just across the street from the famed Continental Club (see the Music Scene chapter) and in the midst of the dynamic South Congress scene (see the Shopping chapter). The hotel was built in 1939 as a "court hotel," the forerunner of the motel, with rooms built around a central courtyard. Forty rooms and suites in assembled bungalows make up the San

José, all decorated in retro-style but with up-to-date conveniences like high-speed Internet service. The courtyards and gardens have been decorated in Texas-style with cactus, aloes and yuccas; gravel pathways; and outdoor seating areas. One public area of the hotel is dedicated to the works of local artists. Prices have increased since the traveling salesmen days, but the hotel offers top-notch services including dry-cleaning, bike rental, access to a music and video library, plus a swimming pool. On the first Thurs (see the Close-up in the Arts chapter), the hotel hosts a live band, while other musical events are held each week on Wed. The popular **Jo's Coffeehouse** is on the premises. The lower-priced rooms at this hotel are for a shared bath.

**HYATT REGENCY
  AUSTIN** $$$$–$$$$$
208 Barton Springs Rd.
(512) 477-1234, (888) 591-1234
www.hyatt.com

A great location is just one of the perks at this luxury, 448-room hotel in downtown Austin. Situated on the south bank of Lady Bird Lake, the Hyatt offers excellent views of downtown and the lake from many of its rooms and outdoor patios. Spring and summer guests get a great spot from which to watch the bats, although the view of the evening spectacle is not good from the lobby lounge or the lower rooms because the bats take off from the opposite side of the Congress Avenue Bridge (see the Attractions chapter). If you want to catch a glimpse of the bats, be sure to request an appropriate room—perhaps one with a balcony—or take the elevator up to the 17th floor and watch from the huge picture window up there. Of course, the hotel also offers all the amenities one would expect in a Hyatt. The Hyatt chain has business-class hotels in the northwest Arboretum area and in north-central Austin. Additionally, it has opened a luxury resort and spa past the airport. See the listing in the Resorts Close-up in this chapter.

i Many locally owned establishments sell T-shirts and gifts with their own logos, and more. At some you can get locally produced CDs, Austin-made salsas, and other items. When you see a gift section, don't just pass it by. It could have the perfect item for yourself or a loved one who didn't get to come to Austin.

√ ✳**KIMBER MODERN** $$$$$
110 The Circle
(512) 912-1046
www.kimbermodern.com

Locally owned, upscale, one-of-a-kind, *and* contemporary, the Kimber Modern adds a new dimension to the Austin hotel scene. While most of our locally owned properties tend to have the funky Austin or restored mansion vibe, the Kimber Modern is uber-sleek, sparkling in its simplicity, and yet almost magically cozy. Its size, just 5 rooms and 2 suites, contributes to the intimate feel, as does the missing front desk (keyless-entry codes are provided when you reserve so you can go straight to your room.) The real standout here, however, is the superbly designed courtyard that anchors the property and serves as an alfresco lobby. Its canopy of Live Oaks (beautifully lighted at night), soothing water fall and comfortable seating groups make you want to drop your bags and sit a spell. Once you do make it to your room you'll find crisp white Egyptian cotton linens, clean lines, original artwork, and a nice assortment of amenities, including a refrigerator and iPod docking station. The hotel also features a glass-walled indoor breakfast room/lounge, where guests are offered a self-serve breakfast of locally baked goods and granola, fresh fruits, yogurt, and such. There's also a happy hour daily. Just a stone's throw from hip South Congress Avenue, the Kimber Modern is near all of downtown Austin's entertainment districts. One note, however, the hotel is built on a slope and is accessed via a flight of stairs only. Owners Kimber Cavendish and spouse Vicki Faust say their hotel is for the "independent urban traveler." We say it's for anyone who wants to get another perspective on creative Austin.

W AUSTIN HOTEL   **$$$$$**
200 Lavaca St.
(512) 542-3600
www.whotels.com

Opened to guests in January 2011, the W Austin is our city's newest luxury hotel. The 37-story high-rise—another addition to the burgeoning Austin skyline—features 251 exquisitely appointed guest rooms and suites offering stunning views of Lady Bird Lake and the downtown skyline. As with the Starwood chain's other W brands in major cities around the world, the Austin property features fine dining in the hotel's signature restaurant, 24-hour in-room dining, state-of-the-art fitness center, beautiful outdoor pool and lounge, the Away Spa, and complimentary chauffeur service. This brand also offers the "Whatever/Whenever" promise, meaning the hotel will get you whatever you want, whenever you want it—as long as it's legal. Birthday party in the sky? No problem. How

about a bath of hot chocolate? They can do that, too.

This might be a chain, but no other property on earth is the new home of *Austin City Limits* music television show, our city's "cultural calling card to the world." (See the Music Scene chapter.) The hotel has an Austin vibe in other respects, too. Much of the music that gives this property such ambience, the food served in the restaurants, and even the art in the rooms hails from our city. Located just north of City Hall in the heart of downtown's Second Street District, the W Austin Hotel is steps away from upscale boutiques, live music venues, outdoor cafes, and fine dining.

SOUTHWEST

THE HEART OF TEXAS MOTEL   **$**
5303 US 290 West
(512) 892-0644
www.heartoftexasmotel.com

This 30-room motel draws a steady stream of regular customers and plenty of newcomers. The attractively decorated, good-size rooms all have microwaves, refrigerators, and coffeemakers. The motel also offers one Jacuzzi-suite room with a king-size 4-poster bed. Other rooms have 2 double beds or a double bed with a sleeper sofa. Upper-level rooms have ceiling fans, a real plus for Austin's long, hot summers. For those who like to spend their spare time outdoors, the Heart of Texas Motel has a putting green, a horseshoe pit, a basketball hoop, and a barbecue grill. On US 290 near the junction with the MoPac Expressway, this motel offers easy access to many parts of town and to Austin-Bergstrom International Airport.

AIRPORT

BEST WESTERN AUSTIN
AIRPORT INN $$
1805 Airport Commerce Dr.
(888) 370-2126
www.bestwestern.com

Opened in late 2010, this fresh Best Western is a nice choice for airline travelers, as it's just a mile north of Austin-Bergstrom Airport and 3 miles from downtown. The comfortable rooms and suites all feature minirefrigerators and microwaves, along with the other basic amenities, including Internet access. The hotel also has an outdoor pool, guest laundry, exercise room, and business center. Guests are offered complimentary airport shuttles and free hot buffet breakfasts.

HILTON AUSTIN AIRPORT $$$$
9515 New Airport Dr.
(512) 385-6767, (800) 774-1500
www.hilton.com

While there are other chain hotels in the Austin-Bergstrom Airport area, this one is the closest—it's on-site. It also is the most "Austin." Housed in the former administration building and officers' headquarters of what was Bergstrom Air Force Base, the round building was affectionately known as "the donut." The hotel offers all the amenities of a full-service hotel, including 262 well-appointed guest rooms, an outdoor swimming pool, state-of-the-art fitness center, jogging trails, a gift shop, lobby bar, and a casual restaurant, **The Creeks.** For that really big party, there's also the Bergstrom Grand Ballroom, which holds up to 800 persons. Located 2 minutes from the passenger terminal, the hotel offers a free airport shuttle. It's 7 miles from downtown Austin and is also located quite conveniently close to the area's high-tech businesses. For those wishing to stay at a full-service Hilton closer to downtown, the high-rise Hilton Austin is at 500 East Fourth Str. The chain also has other more budget-friendly brands around the area, including Hilton Garden Inn, Homewood Suites, and Hampton Inn. For more information, check the Hilton website.

LAKE TRAVIS

MOUNTAIN STAR LODGE $$
3573 RR 620 South
(512) 263-2010, (888) 263-2010
www.mountainstarlodge.com

A great location not far from fabulous Lake Travis and a superb unobstructed view of the Texas Hill Country combine to make the Mountain Star Lodge an excellent choice in accommodations. From its vantage point on RR 620, the main thoroughfare to an abundance of lakeside recreational spots and restaurants, the lodge offers guests easy access to the community of Lakeway and to fishing, boating, skiing, and other outdoor activities. And yet it's just 1 mile north of Highway 71 in Southwest Austin. The 2-story Mountain Star Lodge is locally owned and operated. This lovely building of native limestone offers 40 rooms and suites, each with a private patio or balcony overlooking the large outdoor swimming pool and the vast Canyon Lands Nature Preserve. The rooms, which feature outdoor access and parking just outside, are decorated in an early Texas theme. For traveling families and other groups, the property offers a 3-bedroom guest house. Each morning guests are treated to a complimentary continental breakfast in the large, inviting lobby, which is designed to reflect the look and feel of a mountain lodge. A large fireplace, a soaring wood-beam ceiling, and huge windows that take advantage of that gorgeous view make this a very cozy spot for relaxing, conducting small business conferences, or hosting parties or weddings.

VINTAGE VILLAS $$$
4209 Eck Lane
(512) 266-9333, (800) 267-7623
www.vintagevillas.com
The view of Lake Travis is simply stunning from Vintage Villas' hillside perch. It's no wonder this locally owned 43-room hotel is popular for outdoor weddings, parties and business gatherings. But it also is an excellent, meticulously maintained hotel for those who want to escape the hustle and bustle of the city. Divided into 3 villas, each has its own theme: South Texas (western), Central Texas (Austin/Hill Country), and East Texas (Victorian/antique), and the decor in each unique room reflects the subtle differences between those regions. All of the rooms have a lake view, with patios on the ground floor and balconies on the upper ones, though the view gets better the higher up you are. Each of the villas has its own lounge/common area, while the breakfast room—which serves a reasonably priced hot breakfast buffet daily—is located in the South Villa. Additionally, the rooms all feature minifridges, microwaves, and coffeemakers. One room in each of the villas is a master suite with a kitchen, living area, king-size bed and more generous bath. Many of the rooms have fireplaces. One of the main attractions at this hotel is the great outdoors and the areas for enjoying the lake view. Note, however, that the hotel does not have a beach or direct lake access, though there is lake access for boaters within about 3 miles. The hotel is less than 1½ miles off of RR 620, the main thoroughfare to the lake and the restaurants and clubs in this area. So while the hotel does not serve lunch or dinner, there

are many dining choices close by. For weddings and other gatherings, however, there is an in-house executive chef and reception facilities.

I-35 CORRIDOR—NORTH

Hotels in this area are north of the I-35—US 290 East interchange. Because of the high concentration of hotels and motels along I-35, especially in this area, some of the following hotels are only a few blocks north of those listed under I-35 Corridor—Central lodgings.

HABITAT SUITES HOTEL $$$
500 Highland Mall Blvd.
(512) 467-6000, (800) 535-4663
www.habitatsuites.com
For the environmentally conscious traveler—or anyone who wants beautiful environs—the Habitat Suites Hotel is a miniature Eden in the heart of a bustling commercial area. This 96-suite locally owned property in an apartmentlike setting has received many major industry prizes, including a Keep Austin Beautiful award. Everything from breakfast to bedtime is planned to protect and honor the earth's bounty. The complimentary full-course breakfast buffet includes healthful alternatives—soy milk, tofu *migas*, stone-ground tortillas, and black beans—as well as traditional breakfast dishes. Nontoxic, phosphate-free cleansers are used to maintain the suites and clean the laundry, while the grounds are kept using natural fertilizers and pesticides. Ionizers are used to maintain clean air quality in all the suites, and the hotel uses biodegradable, recycled paper products and returns to the recycling bin all possible items. Habitat is "green" both figuratively and literally. The property is totally surrounded by native foliage and

flowering plants that create a lush, inviting atmosphere, while they require the least amount of water. The hotel staff even grows a variety of fruits, vegetables, and herbs on the property. Habitat's outdoor swimming pool, also enveloped by greenery, uses ionized water and bromine instead of chlorine, better for the environment and for the skin. What's inside is also inviting. The spacious 1- and 2-bedroom suites, all with fully equipped kitchens, are tastefully decorated and include, of course, green plants.

> **i** Following the death of Lady Bird Johnson in 2007, Town Lake was renamed in honor of the former first lady who had done so much to make the lake area the Austin gem it is today. Old habits die hard, however, so don't get confused if you hear us call it Town Lake. Even more confusing, it looks more like a river than a lake. It's the body of water that divides north from south in the downtown area.

HAWTHORN SUITES— CENTRAL $$–$$$
935 La Posada Dr.
(512) 459-3335, (800) 527-1133
www.hawthorn.com

With easy access to downtown and many high-tech industries, and nestled between two of Austin's luxury hotels, Hawthorn Suites can claim a great location as one of its major advantages. But there's much more. Hawthorn's 71 spacious 1- and 2-bedroom suites all have complete kitchens with full-size appliances, and they all feature patios or balconies, and working fireplaces. A collapsible door separates the sleeping area from the living quarters in the 1-bedroom studio unit and on the lower level of the 2-bedroom lofts. For the business traveler, Hawthorn Suites offers a meeting room that can accommodate up to 50 people. A second Hawthorn Suites is located near the airport.

MOTEL 6—AUSTIN NORTH $
9420 North I-35
(512) 339-6161, (800) 4-MOTEL6
www.motel6.com

One of seven Motel 6s for the budget-minded traveler coming to the Austin area, this northern location offers 158 guest rooms on 2 levels. Guests are treated to free HBO, and the motel's outdoor swimming pool is open from May through Sept. There's also a coin-operated laundry. Sixth Street is about 9 miles away, and Austin Bergstrom International Airport is 15 miles southeast. This Motel 6 property offers easy access to I-35, US 183, and US 290. Guests can get wireless Internet for a nominal fee. Call the 800 number above for information on other Austin locations, most of them situated along the I-35 corridor and a newer one in Cedar Park.

I-35 CORRIDOR—CENTRAL

This area of I-35 is defined in our book as the area south of the I-35/US 290 East junction and north of Lady Bird Lake. Hotels in this listing can be found on either side of the Interstate or just a block or two away.

CLUB HOTEL BY DOUBLETREE $$$–$$$$
1617 North I-35
(512) 479-4000, (800) 444-CLUB
www.doubletreehotels.com

DoubleTree's innovative concept has taken the business traveler's hotel to a new level with its Club Hotel. A self-contained business environment—just like the office back home—has been created right off the lobby area for the use of hotel guests. Two private cubicles complete with reference materials and six well-lighted personal work stations create a functional and comfortable work setting. A private conference room in this space would seat 3 or 4 people comfortably. And just a step away guests have access to a copier, a fax machine, and a printer. There is an extra charge for these services. While this area is designed to create an "office-away-from-the-office" setting, the spacious lobby is fashioned to make guests feel as if they are at home. This is all just steps away from **Au Bon Pain–The Bakery Cafe,** the hotel's delica-tessen-style restaurant serving fresh pastries, soups, sandwiches, and more. The limited-service hotel's 152 spacious and immaculate rooms of varying sizes all come equipped with desks, wireless Internet service, and cof-feemakers. The hotel offers many other ame-nities, including an outdoor swimming pool, exercise room, guest laundry facilities, and an evening lounge. A larger meeting room on the premises holds up to 50 people. This hotel is conveniently located just across the Interstate from the University of Texas, down-town Austin, and the Frank Erwin Center. The DoubleTree also has a Guest Suites Hotel on Fifteenth Street downtown.

DAYS INN UNIVERSITY $
3105 North I-35
(512) 478-1631, (800) 329-7466
www.daysinn.com
Days Inn University is a reasonable choice for the traveler on a budget who wants to be close to some of Austin's featured attractions. The motel is near the University of Texas and all its sports stadiums. Its location right next to the Interstate offers easy access to many parts of town, though there could be some traffic noise. Rates are cheaper during the week.

Days Inn operates two other motels in Austin and one in Round Rock. All are on I-35.

HOLIDAY INN—
TOWN LAKE $$$–$$$$
20 North I-35
(512) 472-8211, (800) 593-5676
www.ichotelsgroup.com
This 320-room property was designed to give guests the best possible view of Lady Bird Lake—and what a view it is. (The hotel still lists this as a Town Lake property, even though the name of the lake has changed.) On Austin's central waterway, many of the hotel's sleeping quarters, meeting rooms, common areas, and the outdoor swimming pool provide stunning views of the lake. Large picture windows in the rooms maxi-mize the view. The 14-floor, round "Capitol Tower" portion of this hotel was built in the 1960s, making it one of Austin's oldest full-service hotels. (The newer "Lake Tower" was built in the mid-1980s.) All the facilities are very well maintained, so it's hard to tell when you're in the older part. That, combined with a great location, services, and lower prices than some other full-service proper-ties, make the Holiday Inn comfortable in many aspects. Ask about the hotel's special packages that include tickets to the Austin Children's Museum or Bob Bullock Museum.

I-35 CORRIDOR—SOUTH

The hotels in this area are on I-35 beginning on the south side of Lady Bird Lake and heading south.

CANDLEWOOD SUITES
AUSTIN SOUTH $–$$
4320 I-35 Service St.
(512) 444-8882, (800) 593-5676
www.candlewoodsuites.com

Renovated in 2008–09 and still in sparkling condition, this Candlewood is in an excellent location between the airport and downtown. The extended-stay brand of the Inter-Continental Hotel chain, Candlewoods offer full kitchens, complete with microwaves and 2-burner cooktops. This hotel features 122 suites on 3 floors, as well as a nice-sized fitness center and guest laundry.

> **i** If you're coming to Austin for one of our city's major annual events, like SXSW, the *Austin City Limits* Music Festival, or the Republic of Texas Motorcycle Rally, check the event's web page or the Austin Visitor Center site at www.austintexas.org. Often there are special hotel deals available. Don't dally though, as visitors come from far and wide.

OMNI AUSTIN HOTEL
AT SOUTHPARK $$$–$$$$
4140 Governors Row
(512) 448-2222, (888) 444-6664
www.omnihotels.com
An enticing lobby designed with luxurious dark woods, marble, and subdued lighting greets guests upon arrival at the Omni Austin Southpark, I-35's southernmost full-service hotel in Austin, with access to nearby high-tech giant AMD. A unique and inviting horseshoe-shaped gourmet coffee and cocktail bar beckons visitors to "come, relax, unwind." The 313 rooms and suites in this 14-story hotel are exceptionally large and well-equipped. The upper-level floors on the north side offer the best views of downtown Austin and St. Edward's University. There is also a room here called the Kid's Sensory Suite, which is designed with all the amenities children will love. For those who prefer

the outdoors, the hotel offers 24 rooms with walk-out balconies. We especially like the huge heated outdoor-indoor swimming pool, a wonderfully original concept. The outdoor portion of the pool is surrounded by a large deck and lovely garden area and then wraps around into the fitness center building. The fully equipped fitness center includes a sauna and a hot tub surrounded by tropical foliage—very relaxing. The Omni's **Onion Creek Grille,** popular with both travelers and local residents, serves breakfast, lunch, and dinner beginning at 6:30 a.m. Don't miss the made-to-order pasta bar, open for lunch daily. After a full day of work or sightseeing, the Republic of Texas Bar, designed with a Western flair, is a great place to watch a game on television or socialize. The hotel also is home to the Trinity Spa, which offers massage and facial services.

NORTH

ALOFT AUSTIN AT
THE DOMAIN $$$–$$$$
11601 Domain Dr.
(512) 491-0777
www.starwoodhotels.com
The Starwood Hotel chain has come into Austin in a big way over the past few years. Of the newer Starwoods, which include the W Austin downtown and the Westin Austin at The Domain, this is the most reasonably priced. Like the Westin, the Aloft is in North Austin's trendy Domain development, and both are excellent choices for travelers who want to stay in the area for the shopping, the dining, or the nearby high-tech area. The Aloft, however, is for those who don't need, or simply don't want to pay for, the finest sheets and all the amenities of a full-service Westin or luxury W. Yet its rooms have all the space, comfort, and techie stuff you might

crave, while its sophisticated, contemporary design is very nice on the eyes. Plus, the Aloft has an inviting lounge with pool table, a cafe/snack bar, an airy exercise room, and an outdoor pool. If you want to step up a notch, reservations can also be made at The Domain's Westin hotel through the website.

RENAISSANCE AUSTIN HOTEL $$$$$
9721 Arboretum Blvd.
(512) 343-2626, (800) 468-3571
www.marriott.com
Northwest Austin's luxury hotel, the Renaissance Austin pampers each guest as it caters to nearly every whim and any need. Enter through the lobby into the immense pavilion, the airy indoor courtyard that reaches up 10 stories to the skylight. Here among trees and plants, attractive sculptures, and tremendous dangling mobiles, visitors will find **Banderas-A Texas Bistro** that serves breakfast, lunch, and dinner. The menu features local flavors served tapas style. Across the pavilion is the cleverly named hotel delicatessen and cybercafe, **Austinbytes.** Need a 2 a.m. snack? The hotel also offers 24-hour room service. Swim indoors or outdoors, drop in to the fitness center, or walk next door or across the street to some of Austin's finest shops and a great selection of nearby restaurants. The upscale Domain shopping/dining district is just minutes away by car. The rooms are ample and tasteful and, for those staying on the Hill Country side, afford excellent views of the trees and hillsides. This hotel, owned by Marriott, is the largest of Austin's luxury hotels, with 478 rooms and suites. The Renaissance is one of the farthest hotels from the airport, but its location near the junction of MoPac and US 183 is great for the discriminating traveler who wants to be on the edge of Austin's beautiful Hill Country

and yet have easy access to the high-tech industries in the north and other parts of town. The Marriott chain offers a Courtyard Hotel and Residence Inn in the area as well.

HOSTELS

HOSTELLING INTERNATIONAL $
2200 South Lakeshore Blvd.
(512) 444-2294, (800) 725-2331
www.hi-austin.org
Austin is a mecca for young travelers, especially those fascinated by the city's music scene. Finding a cheap place to stay can be a challenge, but the arrival of Hostelling International on the shores of Lady Bird Lake near the city's Hike and Bike Trail has made Austin affordable for travelers on a budget. There are 39 beds in 4 dormitories in the facility, and beds are assigned at check-in. Guests must show an ID with an address outside the Austin area, and guests who are members of Hostelling International pay a few dollars less for their accommodations. The central location is not far from the city's entertainment area, and the hostel even offers its own live music 2 nights a week. The hostel is located on city and University of Texas bus lines and is an easy walk to banks, grocery stores, and restaurants. There is a kitchen on premises, common areas, Internet access, and a laundry, and the hostel is air-conditioned and heated. Visitors also can rent canoes, kayaks, and bicycles. There are some rules—no alcoholic beverages on-site, no smoking inside, and no sleeping bags. Reservations are recommended and can be made with a credit card or a Hostelling International membership card. Groups of up to 20 persons are accepted.

BED-AND-BREAKFASTS & COUNTRY INNS

For a truly unique Austin experience, spend a night, or longer, in one of our many bed-and-breakfast establishments. The eclectic assortment includes luxury establishments designed to pamper you, restored colonial and Greek Revival homes for stepping back into another era, and plenty of places to just hang out and relax—in town or out by the lake. The common denominator for all our bed-and-breakfasts, however, is the attention to detail paid to each property. The special people who operate these lodgings are, in many cases, sharing their own homes and their lives—not to mention favorite breakfast recipes. Visitors will also find bed-and-breakfasts created for the exclusive use of their guests. There is no better reason to choose a bed-and-breakfast than simply the desire to stay in a one-of-a-kind lodging.

For distinctive special events such as weddings, parties, and business gatherings, several of Austin's bed-and-breakfasts can fulfill all your needs. For that romantic interlude, some offer celebration packages that include champagne and other delights. With all these special services, it's no wonder more and more Austinites are discovering they don't have to leave town to go on vacation.

OVERVIEW

In this chapter you'll find a wide selection of the bed-and-breakfast establishments in Austin. Unless otherwise noted, the inns listed here accept major credit cards. The Americans with Disabilities Act does not require that these lodgings create wheelchair-accessible rooms, although you will find some with that amenity. Smoking is permitted only outdoors at these establishments. Guests should be aware that check-in times and cancellation policies at bed-and-breakfast establishments differ from those at hotels and motels and that some charge a cancellation fee. Please check with the individual establishment regarding those details when you make your reservation. And if you're planning to stay in Austin for a while, be sure to ask about extended-stay rates.

Price Code

Our rate categories are based on a one-night stay for two people throughout the year. Because some bed-and-breakfasts offer a wide range of room sizes and amenities, their rates can vary greatly. In that case we have given you two dollar codes and you will expect to find rates within those spectrums. These rates do not include the 15 percent total Austin tax on lodgings. Nor do they take into account the extended-stay or other special rates available at many establishments. Also be aware that rates can soar during important events in town.

$	Less than $100
$$	$100 to $150
$$$	$150 to $200
$$$$	More than $200

CENTRAL

1110 CARRIAGE
HOUSE INN $$$–$$$$
1110 West Twenty-second 1/2 St.
(512) 472-2333
www.carriagehouseinn.org

This well-established, award-winning B&B is unique in that its 6 guest rooms and suites are housed in 3 different buildings on-site, each with its own special features and most with private entrances. The inn's location—on a quiet street yet minutes from downtown and the UT campus—is another pleasant anomaly. The main house, a beautifully restored 100-year-old colonial structure, is the home of proprietors Tressie and Jim Damron. The 2 lovely guest rooms in this building are upstairs via a private outdoor staircase, which ends at a large deck—perfect for looking down on the gazebo and koi pond below or up at the stars. There's a telescope if you'd like to find Cassiopeia. The rooms here share a kitchen that, like the others at the inn, comes stocked with dishes, crystal, soft drinks, tea, and coffee.

Out back on the property is the Cottage, which houses 2 spacious suites. The Robinson Suite features a living room/kitchen and a separate bedroom highlighted by a queen-size poster bed. A queen-size sleigh bed is the focal point of the bedroom in the Garden Suite, which also has a comfortable living/kitchen area. Unlike the inn's other rooms, however, this suite has no phone—for those who wish to totally withdraw from the real world. Next door is the Guesthouse, a quaint gem made from lava rock from an inactive volcano near here! In addition to

2 well-appointed guest rooms, each with a queen-size bed and private bath, this building features a communal living room with extra half bath, microwave, and coffee and tea service. Each of these rooms also has its own private outdoor seating area. The Guesthouse also is home to the B&B's contemporary Western-style breakfast room, accentuated by individual handmade cedar tables. The real treats, however, are the breakfasts Tressie puts on these tables. Homemade waffles with homemade whipped cream and fresh blueberries, rosemary breakfast tacos, chicken sausage, and homemade scones are among her guests' favorites.

The 1110 Carriage House Inn has received several honors from the industry trade publication *Arrington's Bed & Breakfast Journal,* including being listed among the top 15 most elegant inns in the country. Indeed, the inn is long on attributes. We especially like its many private decks, terraces, and patios—and the large garden itself. Most notable, however, is the warm Texas charm of Tressie herself.

i The owners of Austin's bed-and-breakfast establishments are a wonderfully helpful bunch, so if one of the B&Bs you call is booked, simply ask the innkeeper to refer you to another that suits your tastes and price range.

ADAMS HOUSE $$–$$$
4300 Avenue G
(512) 453-7696
www.theadamshouse.com

Adams House opened for business in 1998. And what a house it is. Historic-preservation architect Gregory Free has restored this 1911 home in historic Hyde Park from top to bottom. He installed stylish gray slate floors in some areas and added a gray wash to the original hardwood floors in others. White woodwork, high ceilings, and wraparound sunrooms on 2 levels give this home a bright and airy look that adds to its beauty. The current owner, Sidney Lock, has added her own special touches, which give this old colonial revival house the look and feel of a classy modern dwelling—even with the many remarkable antiques throughout. Adams House originally was built as a one-story bungalow. W. T. Adams and his family purchased the home in 1922 and added another level in 1931. The home, however, fell on hard times during the second half of the 20th century and was turned into apartments. Now it looks better than ever before. Original paintings, a baby grand piano, and a designer kitchen with granite counters all contribute to its charm. Adams House offers 4 rooms on the second floor, accessible only by stairs, as well as a bungalow, which is a separate house behind the main one.

AUSTIN FOLK HOUSE $$–$$$$
506 West Twenty-second St.
(512) 472-6700, (866) 472-6700
www.austinfolkhouse.com
Some people stay at this great bed-and-breakfast just to enjoy the eclectic collection of folk art on display throughout the house. But don't come to feast your eyes on the art alone. University of Texas grads Sylvia and Chris Mackey have created a classy, Austin-hip inn that invites guests to settle in, relax, and stay awhile. This B&B got its name from the artwork (the collection is from Sylvia's family). The 2-story establishment offers 9 well-appointed rooms, each one quite distinctive. Some are painted in vibrant red or olive tones; others are light and airy. There are sleigh beds, canopy beds, iron beds, and 4-poster beds,

each with a handmade spread that perfectly accentuates the decor. The elegant dining room, another showcase for some intriguing paintings, consists of 5 individual pub tables. Guests also are invited to take their breakfast out to the spacious front porch. The porch, by the way, is a fine hangout any time of the day or night. The kitchen is always open for those who like to make a late-night cup of tea or grab a snack from the fridge.

The Folk House is perfectly located for easy access to downtown or the UT campus, although one trade-off for its central location is a bit of traffic noise. For that, there are soothing sound machines in each room. This B&B also has its own parking lot, a real plus for this neighborhood, and the free 'Dillo people mover stops right across the street. While the establishment does not accept pets, well-behaved children are welcome.

BRAVA HOUSE $$–$$$
1108 Blanco St.
(512) 478-5034, (888) 545-8200
www.bravahouse.com
Blanco Street in downtown Austin is lined with many of Austin's Victorian-era homes, among them Brava House, built in the 1880s and now beautifully restored. The home is within easy walking distance of Austin's central city sights and nightlife. There are 2 guest rooms, 2 suites, and a large apartment, each named for the era the decor suggests. The Van Gogh Room on the first floor off the garden has its own private entrance, a lovely bay window, and a queen-size bed with canopy netting. A beautiful 4-poster bed is the centerpiece of the Moroccan-style Casablanca Room, which also has a sitting area by the large corner picture windows.

Fireplaces in both the parlor and the bedroom and an antique wooden queen bed add touches of romance to the Garbo Suite, which brings to mind the Hollywood of the 1930s. The spacious Fitzgerald Suite, named for F. Scott of course, has a 1920s Art Deco decor. This room is great for families; there's a sleeper sofa in the parlor, as well as a fireplace. The Monroe Suite upstairs is a one-bedroom, fully equipped apartment of about 650 square feet. It features a wood-burning fireplace, full kitchen, and plenty of space in the living room to spread out.

CARRINGTON'S BLUFF $$–$$$
1900 David St.
(512) 479-0638, (888) 290-6090
www.carringtonsbluff.com
A 500-year-old native oak is just one of the many trees that shade the one-acre bluff where this attractive bed-and-breakfast stands. Operated by resident owner Phoebe Williams, this English Country–style home is a real Austin original. The Main House, built in 1877, features 5 guest rooms with elegant king- or queen-size beds, most decorated with floral fabrics and featuring American and English antiques. The large covered porch is a great place to rock and relax while enjoying the view of the garden and gazebo, where many Austin couples have been married. The Writers' Cottage just across the lawn has its own kitchen and living area, as well as 3 additional guest rooms, including one especially large room that holds 2 queen-size beds. This cottage is a great place for family retreats or for those who want to feel like they're off on their own, to work or just to unwind. All the rooms have private bathrooms and come with guest bathrobes, irons and ironing boards, TVs, and telephones.

Carrington's Bluff, part of an original 22-acre homestead of the Republic of Texas, is just above busy Lamar Boulevard, but it's nestled so well amid the lush greenery and flower gardens that it's hard to tell. Guests feel isolated here, even though they're minutes from downtown—and just 7 blocks from the University of Texas. For those who really want to pamper themselves, Phoebe can arrange on-site spa services. She also offers some great special packages, such as candles, flowers and chocolates, and breakfast in bed.

THE INN AT PEARL STREET $$$–$$$$
809 West Martin Luther King Jr. Blvd.
(512) 478-0051, (800) 494-2261
www.innpearl.com
When the Inn at Pearl Street opened in 1995, it immediately earned a reputation as one of Austin's most luxurious bed-and-breakfast establishments and was selected as the year's Designer Showhouse by the Austin Symphony League. The Inn includes 2 properties, the 5-room Victoria House and the 4-room Burton House, as well as 2 free-standing cottages on the grounds. Each of the rooms and many common areas are luxuriously decorated to reflect Old World radiance. Sumptuous designer fabrics and wallpapers throughout this cozy home add the perfect touch to each room. The French Room, for example, features French antique furniture, a stylish 4-poster iron bed, a crystal chandelier, and a claw-foot bath. The European Room exudes the utmost in Old World charm, with its king-size bed, billowy-topped floral chintz draperies, and unique furnishings. The common areas also are a feast for the eyes. The music room is especially attractive, with its ivory-lacquered grand piano, mirrored pedestals, and antique fireplace. The large outdoor deck, surrounded by oak and pecan trees, is perfect for a wedding or a special gathering. This is one place that begs

to be discovered. For that special occasion, make arrangements in advance for the Inn's Twilight Dinner: an elegant 5- or 6-course meal served by candlelight for an extra fee. This bed-and-breakfast is just blocks from the UT campus and close to downtown entertainment of all kinds. Children age 12 and up are invited to stay at this historic inn.

i February through June and September through November are the busiest seasons for Austin's bed-and-breakfasts. We highly recommend making your reservations well in advance, especially if your heart is set on one particular establishment. The limited number of rooms in each inn can fill up quickly, especially during special events in Austin.

STAR OF TEXAS INN $$–$$$$
611 West Twenty-second St.
(512) 472-6700, (866) 472-6700
www.staroftexasinn.com
If stepping back in time is your idea of a perfect getaway, Star of Texas Inn should not be missed. The inn is a beautifully restored neoclassic Victorian structure—and an Austin treasure—having been built in 1897. Star of Texas Inn, managed by the same folks as the Austin Folk House listed above, offers 10 guest rooms, ranging from a simple room with a twin-size bed to the larger and more elegantly decorated rooms with king- and queen-size antique beds. Room number 12 (we'll call it the "red" room) on the second floor not only is one of the property's most beautiful guest rooms but also has private access to the large covered balcony, where guests can sit and unwind after a full day—or night—of Austin excitement. The elegant room number 14, which features a 4-poster

bed and canopy, also has a private door to the balcony and the added advantage of a view of the famous UT Tower (see the Attractions chapter). There also is an attic room that can accommodate a group of 3 or 4 people.

The rest of the house is equally inviting, especially the large, antiques-filled breakfast room, which features individual, elegantly appointed tables, dark wood floors, and artwork depicting the home's era. In addition to the upstairs balcony, this property features a large wraparound porch, a perfect place to while away an Austin afternoon.

i The smaller towns in Central Texas claim a growing number of B&Bs and country inns. Check out the Historic Accommodations of Texas website at www.hat.org for a listing of some of our favorites.

VERDE CAMP $$$–$$$$
1505 Drake Ave.
(512) 850-5150
www.verdecamp.com
If we haven't offered you enough alternatives, locally owned places to stay in Austin, here's another. How about completely renovated and modernized 1930s-era cottages in a quiet neighborhood within walking distance of the South Congress Avenue district? UT alums B.J. and Carrie Heinley bought the property a few years ago after returning to Austin from California. Originally considering a complete demolition, the Heinleys chose the green option (verde is the Spanish word for green) and went with a renovation instead. And what a job they did. Lodgers can chose from among 5 tastefully designed 1-bedroom and two 2-bedroom cottages. All are fully furnished and the kitchens come complete with

pots, pans, and utensils—so no need to pack the kitchen sink! The cottages also feature cable TV, DVD players, and each has a nice deck or patio. The Heinleys also have a couple other cottages in other parts of Austin, so check the website or give them a call if you're wanting to stay elsewhere.

i Who among us isn't interested in saving a buck these days? Sign up for the city of Austin's eNewsletter on the Visitors' tab at www.austintexas .org and select the "travel discounts" option. You'll also be the first to know about special events in the area.

LAKE TRAVIS/HILL COUNTRY VIEWS

LOST PARROT CABINS $$$$
15116 Storm Dr.
(512) 266-8916
www.lostparrotcabins.com
One glance at this property, nestled among the trees in the hills near Lake Travis, and you know this is not your normal bed-and-breakfast. The first impression is the color explosion: 7 individual cabins painted in bright lavenders, neon oranges and lime greens— Fiesta style. And then there are the large outdoor murals reminiscent of San Miguel de Allende and the Mexican artists Frida Kahlo and Diego Rivera, handpainted by local artist Linda LaPierre. If that isn't enough, take a look at the outdoor b.y.o.b. bar/patio/ hot tub area, with its colored lights, Mexican and Guatemalan folk art, and palapa-style tables. And then, standing at the bar, you can look down through the trees upon the crystal-clear swimming pool and large deck area—where musicians occasionally perform And this is the scene before you even step inside the roomy cabins, each one with

its own deck (complete with hammock) and tasteful, Caribbean-inspired decor. Talavera and Saltillo tiles, south-of-the-border textiles, rustic furniture, and handpainted detailing on the walls is the common theme. The comfortable queen-size beds and cozy seating areas, some with futons for extra guests, are *muy* inviting. Proprietors Cat Flood and Cliff Bennett have managed to create an atmosphere that is both romantic and lively.

The 8-acre property is about 20 minutes from downtown Austin off of RR 620. That puts it near the lake (and a free place to launch a boat), as well as several restaurants and clubs—if you can tear yourself away from this adults-only escape. Don't be alarmed when you hit an unpaved section of road as you drive in. The cabins are right around the corner.

i Migas are a specialty item on the breakfast menu of several Austin B&Bs. For those of you not from these parts, migas are sliced corn tortillas fried up with eggs and cheese and, perhaps, onion, chile-peppers, cilantro, tomatoes—or whatever else inspires the chef.

ROBIN'S NEST $$$–$$$$
1007 Stewart Cove
(512) 266-3413
www.robinsnestlaketravis.com
Resident owner Robin Maisel celebrates the great outdoors with this casual, eclectically furnished bed-and-breakfast on a small Lake Travis cove. She has converted 50-year-old fishing cabins, and a brand new house, into a fascinating assortment of guest rooms, making a perfect spot for families traveling with children, couples wanting a little romance, or individuals looking for a peaceful getaway.

Offering 12 guest rooms and suites, plus an option to rent the full 3-bedroom cottage, Robin's Nest aims to please. Those looking for an intimate setting may like the Robin's Perch, which features an antique sleigh bed of burled wood, cozy chairs, and a large covered deck overlooking the lake. A Western theme prevails in the spacious Windy Lindy's Guesthouse: The drapes are hung on antlers, the antique rockers are done in cowhide, and the king-size bed is made of cedar posts. This room is just beautiful. The room, Old Blue Two, has one of the most unique pieces of furniture we've ever seen: an antique table that converts to a love seat.

This waterfront property has a huge front lawn, plenty of patios and decks for enjoying the view, a soft hot tub, and a large dock—a great place to enjoy the sun or to take a cool dip in the lake. While Robin's Nest is secluded, it's not far from the Oasis, one of the most popular partying spots in the area (see the Attractions chapter). The downtown entertainment districts are less than 25 minutes away.

RESTAURANTS

If there is one rule of thumb on the Austin restaurant scene it likely is this: You got a shirt, you got shoes or sandals, you got service! There are only a few restaurants in town (maybe a private club or two) where a tie is required. This is a city where dining is supposed to be fun, not an exercise in tailored torture. But as Austin grows, the question being asked is will things stay this way?

For years, Austin restaurants were often described as "laid-back," but as the number of "upscale" restaurants increases and more and more restaurants are demanding that diners make reservations, there is a fear that Austin's dining scene will lose some of that wonderful casual flavor. But to counter that fear, Austin foodies look at the blossoming of the so-called "gypsy food trailers" in areas like SoCo as evidence of a dynamic culinary scene. One thing is constant—the Austin dining scene is an exciting one where changes can be swift.

Some of the new restaurants are franchises or outlets for a national chain, but many are homegrown. There has been a dramatic increase in the number of Asian restaurants in the city as immigrants from that continent have found a home here. Several long-established local restaurants have opened additional locations, often in the burgeoning northwest and southwest sections of the city. One of the coolest trends has been the emergence of young, dynamic chefs, eager to take advantage of the wide variety of fresh foods in the city and to open up their cafes in what, until now, have been neighborhoods that were not part of the Austin boom, areas like the revived East Eleventh Street in downtown Austin. Plus, there is a willingness of Austin diners to try new things. (See the Close-up, Texas Cuisine, in this chapter.) There is no such thing as "Austin cuisine." But there are certain signature cuisines that do have a connection to Texas culture. Given the fact that Texas once was part of Mexico and Mexican-American life is vibrant and very much a part of the state's cultural weave, it is only natural that Mexico's culinary influence is felt in a number of ways. There's Tex-Mex, Nuevo Tex-Mex, South Texas/Northern Mexico, New Mexican, Interior Mexican, Latin American, and South American. Even on the menus of so-called fine dining restaurants and in the city's bistros you are likely to detect a hint of Mexican or Southwest influence.

OVERVIEW

Clichés abound when it comes to Texas, perhaps because the state has been celebrated and spoofed, caricatured and lauded in movies and books, magazine articles and newspaper stories around the world. So no wonder that when it comes to eating, most people think a typical Texas meal features a big slab of beef and not much else.

But Texas beef (and it is good) is just one tiny part of the true picture, and while this is a place where cattle do roam, the food picture is much more complex and growing more diverse every day. Agribusiness is 12 percent of Texas's gross state product. Texas farmers and ranchers produce rice, citrus, nuts, pears, peaches, apricots, strawberries, blackberries, avocados, chile peppers, onions, spinach, and herbs; they raise pigs, cattle, goats, sheep, turkeys, and fish; and food processors are engaged in developing a multitude of products that tout their Texas origins—everything from axis deer venison to zucchini blossoms.

In addition to a variety of ingredients, the state also draws inspiration from several cultures and countries: Spain and Mexico, of course, and Germany, as evidenced in Hill Country towns like Fredericksburg and New Braunfels (see the Day Trips chapter). African-American cooks have left their mark, and in the east of the state, Cajuns and Creoles have tossed their contributions into the pot. The culture of the Mexican *vaquero* (cowboy) influenced Texas trail riders, and small towns settled by Czechs, Wends, and Alsatians brought new elements into the mix. Waves of immigrants from Italy and the Mediterranean countries have brought their flavors west. More recently, Asian immigrants have left their mark with Chinese, Vietnamese, and Indian cooking introducing new flavors.

With each wave of immigrants, Texas cuisine has grown, and adapted, and old favorites are constantly being re-created. How about shrimp fajitas, pizza topped with chorizo, sushi garnished with goat cheese, chocolate pie with a dash of chile powder?

That said, Tex-Mex is probably the most prevalent and recognizable cuisine. In our listings we have included a variety of Tex-Mex and other Mexican/Latino restaurants in an effort to give readers a good cross section of that multifaceted cuisine. Not all Mexican food is spicy hot. The chile pepper is a staple of the Mexican kitchen, but not all peppers are hot, and many are served in rich sauces, called moles, that blend the pepper with herbs, spices, even chocolate to create multi-nuanced tastes.

Most Austinites have their favorite Mexican restaurant, particularly when it comes to weekend brunch. A popular traditional dish is migas, eggs scrambled with tortilla chips, diced chiles, and tomatoes. Given the city's late nightlife, weekend breakfast is often served into mid-afternoon. During the week, breakfast tacos are the early-morning order of the day, economical and easy to eat—simply flour tortillas stuffed with combinations of eggs, chorizo (sausage), potatoes, bacon, and salsa.

Another star in the Texas culinary pantheon is, of course, barbecue. It's a subject, like religion and politics, that should be discussed carefully and with great consideration for individual beliefs—even the spelling of barbecue promotes debate. Generally speaking, Texas barbecue is slow-cooked with indirect heat over wood coals, often mesquite—a quite delicate-looking tree with a gnarled trunk that is the bane of ranchers since it spreads like a weed and sucks up water. Brisket is the most popular cut of meat to be slow-cooked, and most cooks "marinate" with a dry rub of spices and sometimes herbs. (This is treacherous ground, because already some aficionados are saying, "No! No!")

Barbecue is usually served with pinto beans, potato salad, perhaps coleslaw, certainly sliced raw white onions (or sweet 1015 Texas Onions), pickles, plain old white bread, and barbecue sauce—often the ingredient by which a barbecue joint is judged.

Some of the best barbecue can be found in the small towns of Texas, among them five communities just a short drive from Austin. Most barbecue joints are open all day but close around 6 p.m.—earlier on Sun afternoon. We recommend calling ahead to check on hours of operation. Here are just a few of the most famous and popular joints in the area beyond Austin's city limits; other barbecue cafes within the Austin city limits and environs are included in the restaurant listings in this chapter.

i *Vegetarian Times* magazine named Austin number 2 on its list of "greenest cities" in 2005. For a green view of the Austin dining scene, visit www.vegoutaustin.com.

Lockhart, which touts itself as the barbecue capital of Texas, is home to several barbecue joints. In 2002, with the death of "Smitty" Schmidt, the fabled owner of Kreuz Market, a family feud erupted. Smitty had left the business to his sons and the building to his daughter. The battle even made national headlines and only quieted when the brothers moved **Kreuz Market** to a new building nearby at 619 Colorado St. (512-398-2361; www.kreuzmarket.com), while the founder's daughter started selling barbecue in the original building at 208 South Commerce St. (512-398-9344) under the new label, **Smitty's** (www.smittysmarket.com). A third popular restaurant is **Black's Barbecue,** 215 North Main St. (512-398-2712; www.blacksbbq.com).

Luling, a small town southeast of Austin, is famous for its annual **Watermelon Thump** festival in June (www.watermelonthump.com) and the numerous natural gas rocker wells in town, many of them decorated in folk art style. But barbecue aficionados seek out **Luling City Market** at 633 East Davis St. (830-875-9019; www.lulingcitymarket.com) for its famous barbecue.

Northeast of Austin, the town of Taylor is home to two Texas barbecue legends: **Louie Mueller's** at 206 West Second St. (512-352-6206; www.louiemuellerbarbecue.com), and **Rudy Mikeska's** at 300 West Second St. (512-365-3722; www.mikeska.com).

A fifth Central Texas town, Llano in the Hill Country west of Austin, is home to the "Big Chop," a huge barbecued pork chop that is the highlight on the menu at **Cooper's Old Time Pit Bar-B-Que,** 505 West Dallas (325-247-5713; www.coopersbbq.com). Cooper's also barbecues beef and sausage on its old-fashioned pit and you can order from the website.

One of the most popular items to toss on the barbecue in Central Texas is Elgin sausage, and the original can be found in the small town of the same name just east of Austin. Visitors can watch the sausage being made just as it has been since 1882 and then sit down to a feast at **Elgin Southside Market,** 1212 US 290 (512-281-4650; www.southsidemarket.com). The owners also have opened a second location, **Meyers Elgin Smokehouse,** at 188 US 290 East (512-281-3331).

A word or two about local customs. Smoking is a crime in Austin, as the late Timothy Leary, LSD guru, found out when he lit up in the Austin airport.

Many restaurants are open for major holidays, except Christmas. It is wise to call ahead. Most restaurants do not take reservations except for parties of 6 or more. We have noted where reservations are advised or required. All restaurants listed accept major credit cards, except where noted. More and more restaurants are staying open later to accommodate Austin's penchant for late-night noshing after the movies or theater, but most close at 10 p.m. during the week and 11 p.m. on weekends. Some stay open throughout the afternoon to serve late lunch or afternoon snacks, since many Austin businesspeople, particularly the city's large self-employed population, utilize favorite local restaurants as a conference room or an office away from their home office. We have noted restaurants that stay open beyond the usual hours.

Our restaurant listings are arranged by area of town, starting with central Austin, then South Central and moving south, west, and continuing clockwise around the area. But do not limit your choices to one geographic area, many homegrown favorites have expanded and operate at more than one location, noted in the listings, so browse the entire chapter and check restaurant web links for those additional locations.

Price Code

The price key symbol in each listing gives the range for the cost of a meal for two, an entree and beverage, but not including alcoholic beverages, appetizer, or dessert. Since some restaurants serve three meals a day, or have a wide range of entree prices, the range is noted by the symbols.

$ . . . . **Less than $20**
$$ . . . . **$20 to $40**
$$$ . . . . **$40 to $60**
$$$$ . . . . **More than $60**

CENTRAL

AQUARELLE RESTAURANT
FRANÇAIS $$-$$$
606 Rio Grande St.
(512) 479-8117
www.aquarellerestaurant.com
Austin has seen the proliferation of small boutique restaurants that evoke their European cousins, intimate places where the food is a work of art. The inspiration at this topflight restaurant and wine bar is French with an emphasis on fresh American ingredients. Aquarelle consistently ranks among Austin's best. Dinner only; closed Sun.

ASTI TRATTORIA $$-$$$
408–C East Forty-third St.
(512) 451-1218
www.astiaustin.com
Anyone who is familiar with the Tuscan countryside can't help but see echoes of the Italian landscape in the limestone hills and oak trees of Central Texas. The affinity for things Tuscan doesn't stop there. Rural entrepreneurs producing wine, goat cheese, olive oil, and herbs proliferate in the Hill Country. Emmett and Lisa Fox are longtime fixtures on the Austin culinary scene and key contributors to the successful Texas Hill Country Wine and Food Festival (see the Annual Events & Festivals chapter). They celebrate those Italian inspirations at their neighborhood trattoria in Hyde Park, open Mon through Fri for lunch and dinner, Sat for dinner only. Closed Sun.

AUSTIN LAND AND
CATTLE COMPANY $$$-$$$$
Enfield Shopping Center
1205 North Lamar Blvd.
(512) 472-1813
www.austinlandandcattlecompany.com

Steakhouse—the term usually brings to mind leather banquettes, red walls, and dark wood paneling—but this locally owned steakhouse in a small, quiet shopping center a few blocks from downtown has a lighter touch. The soft, cool palette acts as a foil to the hearty fare found here. Open daily for dinner.

THE BELMONT $$–$$$
305 West Sixth St.
(512) 457-0300
www.thebelmontaustin.com
With its 60s–Las Vegas vibe and sink-into leather banquettes, patrons might expect to see the Rat Pack arrive at this downtown bar and restaurant. The menu echoes the surroundings with steaks and seafood, lighter fare at lunch. There is a late-night bar and patio menu featuring sandwiches and salads. The bar also features live music and movies on Mon. Open for lunch on weekdays, dinner and late-night dining 7 days a week.

BESS BISTRO $$–$$$
500 West Sixth St.
(512) 477-2377
www.bessbistro.com
Some movie stars come to town and fall in love—with Austin that is. Sandra Bullock bought a historic old building, the Stratford Arms, just west of Congress Avenue, and opened a French bistro that gets rave reviews for its traditional fare and comfort food additions like mac and cheese. There is no dress policy, but the website urges patrons "just make an effort" and also asks that cameras be left at home, given the owner's sensitivity to flashbulbs. These days, with camera phones, the original no-camera ban is hard to enforce so Bullock wants her

customers to "please be considerate." Open for lunch and dinner Mon through Sat with late night dining and Sun brunch.

CAFE JOSIE $$–$$$
1200–B West Sixth St.
(512) 322-9226
www.cafejosie.com
This is one of those Austin cafes that lie hidden behind unassuming storefronts and in back of other businesses where creative chefs are exploring the world of cuisine. The emphasis is on Caribbean flavors described as "cuisine of the American tropics" by chef-owner Charles Mayes. The restaurant is tucked behind Portabla, a gourmet food shop (see the Shopping chapter) in the West Sixth Street shopping district, and has a small indoor dining room plus a comfy outdoor patio. Open for lunch Tues through Fri and dinner Tues through Sat.

CARMELO'S $$–$$$
504 East Fifth St.
(512) 477-7497
www.carmelosrestaurant.com
Carmelo's serves large portions of rich Italian-American food with flair and drama inspired by the owner's Sicilian roots. Steak Diane is flambéed tableside, while lobster-stuffed veal is presented with a flourish. The restaurant is housed in an old limestone building that once served as the Depot Hotel. Lunch on weekdays and dinner daily.

**CORAZON AT CASTLE
  HILL CAFE** $$–$$$
1101 West Fifth St.
(512) 476-0728
www.corazonatcastlehill.com
Where's the castle? Where's the hill? Old-timers know that this popular cafe began

as a tiny, tiny restaurant a few blocks north of its current location near the West Sixth Street shopping district. That spot is now occupied by Wink (see below). West of the original tiny restaurant is a well-known landmark, a home on a hill that looks like a castle—hence the name. Castle Hill outgrew its original location but continues to draw crowds. The food here is a delightful mix of Southwestern and Mexican, created by chef/co-owner David Daley. The restaurant is airy and decorated with Oaxacan folk art, a far cry from the tiny, cramped quarters it once occupied. One thing the larger location does share with the old is the air of culinary excitement. Lunch and dinner daily. Reservations recommended on weekends.

CENTRAL MARKET $
4001 North Lamar Blvd.
(512) 206-1020
www.centralmarket.com
Austin's showcase grocery store and top tourist spot (see the Close-up in the Shopping chapter) is a favorite lunch and early dinner spot, particularly among parents and grandparents. The cafe features a varied menu with homestyle food, bistro fare, sandwiches, pizza, and desserts. Dishes are reasonably priced, and customers can either graze or dig into a hearty meal. There is a large indoor dining room, flanked by a wide wooden deck looking out over the greenbelt. Kids can race around outside, dogs can sit in the shade while their owners nosh, and families can enjoy nightly live music concerts featuring a wide variety of musicians. The eateries are open daily from 7 a.m. to 10 p.m.

✳CHEZ NOUS $$-$$$
510 Neches St.
(512) 473-2413
www.cheznousaustin.com
Since 1982, Chez Nous has been serving authentic French bistro fare at this cozy restaurant half a block south of Sixth Street. *Bistro* is a word much bandied about these days, but Chez Nous is as close to the real thing as you can get in Austin, with traditional dishes like oven-roasted chicken and homemade pâtés. There is a menu du jour, daily chef's specials, plus lighter fare including crepes. The bistro is open for lunch and dinner Tues through Fri; dinner only on the weekends.

CIPOLLINA $-$$
1213 West Lynn St.
(512) 477-5211
www.cipollina-austin.com
It looks like a little European sidewalk cafe nestled in the heart of Clarksville (see the Relocation chapter), and it reflects the sensibilities of its owners who also created Jeffrey's, the quintessential Austin fine dining experience across the way. The menu features simple fare, pizzas, salads, small plates, soups, and desserts that can be eaten in-house or taken home or to a picnic. There is an affordable wine menu, also. Open daily for lunch and dinner.

CLAY PIT $$-$$$
1601 Guadalupe St.
(512) 322-5131
www.claypit.com
The Clay Pit occupies a historic stone building not far from the capitol and is a much-praised Indian dining spot, including plaudits from *Bon Appetit* magazine. The owners brought a highly rated chef who had worked at a leading Indian hotel, among

other top spots on his résumé. Both vegetarian and meat dishes are on the menu. Open Mon through Fri for lunch and dinner.

✳DIRTY MARTIN'S PLACE $
2808 Guadalupe St.
(512) 477-3173
www.dirtymartins.com

In this day of image-makers and spin doctors, who would ever name a restaurant "Dirty's"? This is a restaurant that has roots back to the '20s, but the story of the name has been lost in time. Some call this campus-area hamburger joint "Martin's Kumback"—and that is what the sign says—but the majority refer to it as "Dirty's." The fare is fry-cook simple here: hamburgers off the grill with fries and onions, a cold beer or soda, but Dirty's has entered the Internet age with a website and free Wi-Fi so you can Google away while watching the football game on the patio. Dirty's is open daily for lunch and dinner.

DRISKILL GRILL $$$–$$$$
Driskill Hotel
604 Brazos St.
(512) 391-7162
www.driskillgrill.com

The Grill, with its polished wooden walls and soft lighting, is one of the best places in Austin for a special dinner—a place where the setting and the food combine to create a wonderful experience. The Grill has been named one of the top 50 hotel restaurants in the country by *Food & Wine* and is noted for seeking out the highest quality ingredients, employing classic techniques, and adding a touch of Southwestern flavor in an homage to the Driskill Hotel's Texas history. Open for dinner daily.

EDDIE V'S EDGEWATER
GRILLE $$$–$$$$
301 East Fifteenth St.
(512) 472-1860
www.eddiev.com

As the Austin culinary scene has matured, seafood has finally taken pride of place at the table in a number of top dining spots. Eddie V's two locations, one downtown and the other northwest, are the creation of two veterans of the local culinary scene, Larry Foles and Guy Villavaso (Z'Tejas creators), and they have chosen to focus on seafood prepared in classic, simple ways. In addition to an oyster bar, Eddie V's also has a relaxing piano bar. Open daily for dinner.

1886 CAFE AND BAKERY $–$$
116 East Sixth St.
(512) 391-7121
www.1886cafeandbakery.com

Located in the Driskill Hotel, this cafe is famous for its breakfast fare and wonderful baked goods (the website even shares some of the recipes). Breakfast here can be simple and healthy, like granola and fruit, or downright Texas-decadent, like the "Austin Eggs Benedict" with poached eggs and smoked bacon atop jalapeño corn biscuits and topped with chorizo gravy. There are crepes and pancakes, plus muffins and croissants from the bakery. Lunchtime features sandwiches and salads and at night there is bistro fare. The cafe serves breakfast, lunch, and dinner daily, and is open until midnight on Fri and Sat.

EL ARROYO $
1624 West Fifth St.
(512) 474-1222
www.ditch.com

The hallmark of this West Sixth Street–area restaurant, affectionately known as "The

Ditch," a loose translation of its name, is the large sign out front that offers pithy, scathing, and sometimes self-deprecating comments on a daily basis. The restaurant offers standard Tex-Mex fare, and the owner-humorists have been known to cast aspersions on their own culinary efforts, but that does not stop the crowds from coming. Customers love the funky atmosphere, the cheeky waiters, and the lively bar scene featuring "floaters": margaritas topped with liqueurs. El Arroyo is open daily for lunch and dinner.

i Foodies who want to keep up with the latest trends might want to mark their calendars for the Texas Hill Country Wine and Food Festival (see the Annual Events & Festivals chapter). The spring event always attracts some of the top chefs in Texas and the nation.

EL SOL Y LA LUNA $-$$
600 East Sixth St.
(512) 444-7770
www.elsolylalunaaustin.com
What began in an old motel coffee shop in SoCo as a nuevo Mexican cantina, El Sol fast became part of the changing face of South Congress Avenue. It has moved now to the Sixth Street District. A favorite place to have a late breakfast, the menu also features Latin American and Central American dishes, and the restaurant showcases the work of local artists and musicians. Open daily for breakfast, lunch, and dinner.

FINN & PORTER $$
500 East Fourth St.
(512) 493-4900
www.finnandporter.com

Austin's downtown hotels can boast some of the city's best restaurants, not always the case in some areas. Located in the Hilton Hotel, Finn & Porter takes the classic seafood and steak fare to new heights. There are several "trios" on the menu, including one featuring a crab cake, petite filet and lobster, the creations of Christopher Bauer who trained at the Culinary Institute of America. There is also a sushi bar in house and the luxurious, clubby surroundings make the restaurant's bar a popular spot. Open daily for dinner and late night dining at the sushi bar.

FINO $$-$$$
2905 San Gabriel St.
(512) 474-2905
www.astiaustin.com
This sister restaurant to Asti Trattoria, described earlier in this chapter, Fino focuses on other areas of the Mediterranean for its inspiration, including Spain, Greece, and northern Africa. Its location upstairs in a small, brick shopping center gives it a "treehouse" feel and the wrap-around outdoor patio is a favorite spot for enjoying tapas and small plates with a glass of wine. Paella is a menu favorite and Tues patrons get a discount on the dish. Open daily for lunch and dinner. Closed Sun.

FLEMING'S $$-$$$$
320 East Second St.
(512) 457-1500
www.flemingssteakhouse.com
Part of a national chain founded in California and with a heavy presence on the East Coast, Fleming's has opened in a restored warehouse near the convention center and offers prime beef, lamb, veal, and top-quality seafood dishes. The restaurant features an exhibition kitchen in a sophisticated setting. One thoughtful touch is an extensive

wine-by-the-glass menu, 100 offerings that also can be ordered by flight (3 small selections in one serving). Open daily for dinner.

FRANK $
Fourth and Colorado Streets
(512) 494-6916
www.hotdogscoldbeer.com

Hotdogs. Beer. Say no more. But these are dogs like you have never encountered before. Made from antelope, rabbit, pork sausage, and bacon. Try "The Notorious P.I.G." concocted from bacon, pork, and jalapeño and sage sausage. There are also salads and desserts on the menu. Chocolate-covered bacon, anyone? Open for lunch and dinner daily, plus late-night noshing and delivery.

GARRIDOS $–$$$
360 Nueces St.
(512) 320-8226
www.garridosaustin.com

The menu takes inspiration from Chef David Garrido's grandmother, and this inventive chef has taken Tex-Mex to new heights with items like oyster tostados and mahi-mahi mushrooms. There are hearty entrees on the dinner menu including grilled lamp chops and rib eye, and guests have the choice of dining under the stars or in a hip interior dining room. Open daily for dinner, lunch service Tues through Sat, and brunch on Sun.

GUMBO'S $$–$$$$
710 Colorado St.
(512) 480-8053
www.gumbosaustin.com

The trend in Austin usually follows a pattern—a restaurant becomes a hit in downtown Austin and then takes that success to the suburbs. Gumbo's has bucked that trend by first finding success in Round Rock and then moving downtown. The restaurant chose to move into one of the most interesting buildings downtown, the Brown Building. It was built in 1938 by Herman Brown, one of the founders of Brown & Root, the legendary Houston construction company that parlayed its close political ties to President Lyndon B. Johnson and others into worldwide ventures. In 1998 the owners, the LBJ Company (guess which prominent Texas political family owns the company), transformed the building into a loft project. Gumbo's occupies a ground-floor space where it serves up a menu with a Louisiana flair. Open weekdays for lunch, daily for dinner. Closed Sun.

HUT'S HAMBURGERS $
807 West Sixth St.
(512) 472-0693
www.hutsfrankandangies.com

There are 20 types of burgers on the menu here, plus chicken-fried steak, fried chicken, and meat loaf—in a word, all the stuff you want to eat, and you did back when cholesterol was just a gleam in the surgeon general's eye. The daily blue plate specials attract a faithful crowd. The decor here is '50s diner, and the walls are decorated with college sports memorabilia. There is a second location in Southwest Austin in the Westgate shopping center. Hut's is open for lunch and dinner daily.

HYDE PARK BAR & GRILL $–$$
4206 Duval St.
(512) 458-3168
http://hpbng.com

Look for the 2-story giant fork out front and the potato truck parked out back in the historic Hyde Park neighborhood. According to local lore, the grill goes through one and a quarter tons of potatoes a week making its famous spicy, battered fries. But not all the fare is hearty—grilled fish and salads are also offered. The restaurant is open daily for lunch and dinner, with late-night hours on Fri and Sat. It occupies a large, old home in the Hyde Park neighborhood, the historic heart of Austin just north of the university campus.

III FORKS $$$–$$$$
111 Lavaca St.
(512) 474-1776
www.iiiforks.com

With sister restaurants in Dallas and Palm Beach Gardens, no wonder this Second Street District restaurant is described as elegant. The black mahogany and Italian marble decor matches the European flair given to the traditional steakhouse menu. There is a fish market menu also and a huge wine list, plus walk-in wine room. The restaurant's piano bar is very popular. Open for dinner Mon through Sat.

IMPERIA $$–$$$
310 Colorado St.
(512) 472-6770
www.imperia-austin.com

The menu is inspired by Asian flavors and the decor has a luxurious but modern Eastern ambience. Imperia features dim sum and small plates, plus luscious interpretations of classics like Peking Duck. Open for dinner until midnight Mon through Thurs and on Sun; open until 1 a.m. on Fri and Sat.

IRON WORKS BARBECUE $$
100 Red River St.
(512) 478-4855
www.ironworksbbq.com

Home to the Weigl Iron Works for years, this converted workshop just east of the city's convention center is now a popular barbecue spot, particularly during weekday lunch hours. The Weigl family's ironwork can be seen on several buildings around town, including the History Center at 810 Guadalupe St. Diners can sit inside or on an outdoor deck. Lunch and dinner are served daily.

✳JEFFREY'S $$$–$$$$
1204 West Lynn St.
(512) 477-5584
www.jeffreysofaustin.com

This is one of the city's best, and, perhaps, the quintessential Austin restaurant—a longtime favorite of Austinites and the place where President George W. Bush and First Lady Laura Bush loved to take friends when they occupied the Governor's Mansion. Founded in the 1970s by three University of Texas friends (one of them a childhood friend of the First Lady), Jeffrey's was creating topflight cuisine in an unassuming, quiet atmosphere when most Austin restaurants were serving up everyday fare. The restaurant's home is a restored house in Clarksville, one of the city's revered central city neighborhoods (see the Relocation chapter). The founders took over a space occupied by a small wine shop, put up an inconspicuous sign outside and the work of local artists inside, and embarked on a culinary journey that draws on the world's cuisines but has Hill Country roots. A procession of creative chefs has ruled the range here, some going on to spread the Jeffrey's vibe and values to other notable Austin dining spots, but while they each add their own touches to the menu, some items have become signature dishes, like the classic Jeffrey's crispy oysters on yucca root chips with habañero aioli. In addition to a dinner menu fueled by local ingredients and regional flavors, Jeffrey's offers a small plates bar menu. Open nightly except Sun.

KENICHI $$–$$$$
419 Colorado St.
(512) 320-9993
www.kenichiaustin.com
Who would have thought that Austin would ever have a restaurant that attracted the "beautiful people"? Yet that's how one local critic described the clientele when this Japanese-American import from Aspen arrived in Austin. The minimalist setting outside gives way to a high-fashion black-on-black interior. The menu offers beautifully presented sushi, plus American specialties such as steak, lamb, ribs, and seafood for heartier appetites. Dinner daily.

KERBEY LANE CAFE $–$$
3704 Kerbey Lane
(512) 451-1436
www.kerbeylanecafe.com
The original Kerbey Lane Cafe now has four sister restaurants, testimony to the concept that homemade, healthful food is a necessity 24 hours a day. Many of the cafe's dishes are Tex-Mex in origin, but the emphasis is on fresh local ingredients. The menu also features vegan cuisine, burgers, sandwiches, omelets, pancakes, and desserts. You can buy the famous pancake mix online.

LA CONDESA $–$$$
400 West Second St.
(512) 499-0300
www.lacondesaaustin.com
The name derives from Mexico City's hip neighborhood, appropriate since the restaurant is located in Austin's equally hip Second Street District. Serving classic Mexico City

cantina fare with a modern touch, the menu offers ceviches and tasty tacos, plus salads and entrees that take Mexican cuisine to new heights. Duck breast is braised in Shiner beer and the wood-fired carne asada gets accolades from the likes of *Texas Monthly* magazine. Open daily for dinner and on the weekends for lunch.

LAMBERTS $$$–$$$$
401 West Second St.
(512) 494-1500
www.lambertsaustin.com
It had to happen. "Fancy barbecue" is on the menu in this downtown restaurant, the kind of grilled fare we would all like to master on our backyard grills: grilled asparagus, brown sugar, coffee-rubbed brisket, pan-seared French beans, crispy wild boar ribs, and cold-smoked rainbow trout. Lambert's also features live music. Lunch Mon through Fri, weekend brunch and dinner nightly.

LA TRAVIATA
  ITALIAN BISTRO $$–$$$
314 Congress Ave.
(512) 479-8131
www.latraviata.net
Chef Marion Gillcrist, who learned her profession under Stephen Pyles and was the winner of the *Austin Chronicle* Readers' Poll "best female chef" in 2001, opened this small, intimate restaurant determined to produce authentic Italian cuisine. La Traviata, a romantic spot, consistently gets high marks. Open for lunch Mon through Fri and for dinner nightly, except Sun.

MAGNOLIA CAFE $
2304 Lake Austin Blvd.
(512) 478-8645
www.cafe-magnolia.com

Close-up

Austin Cuisine

A cornucopia of available ingredients inspires both the home cook and the state's chefs. If you want to experience a fusion of talent and local produce, check out the work of Tyson Cole at Uchi, Jeff Blank at Hudson's on the Bend, David Garrido formerly with Jeffrey's and now running Garrido's, Stewart Scruggs and Mark Paul at Wink, and Miguel Ravago at Fonda San Miguel. These are just some of the star names in the Austin culinary pantheon, but other top-quality chefs are celebrating homegrown produce and feeding off each other's inspirations in what has become a very dynamic foodie town.

Inspired by Austin's food scene? Consider taking inspiration from some of the city's top chefs and tastemakers. Some of Austin's most creative chefs also offer cooking classes—Hudson's on the Bend and Fonda San Miguel are just two top picks, and Central Market has an on-site cooking school where top Texas talent and visiting stars teach the culinary arts.

Another good way to get the flavor of the Austin food scene is to read books by some of the city's chefs. Miguel Ravago is coauthor of *Fonda San Miguel: Thirty Years of Food and Art*. Jeff Blank has authored *Cooking Fearlessly: Recipes and Adventures from Hudson's on the Bend,* and David Garrido is coauthor of a fun cookbook, *Nuevo Tex-Mex.* Not all the food stars are chefs at Austin's top restaurants. Others create in their own whimsical way, working in small commercial kitchens to produce favorite food products. David Ansel followed a girlfriend (now an ex-girlfriend) to Austin and began delivering homemade soups on his yellow bike to a small group of neighborhood clients, celebrated in his first cookbook, *The Soup Peddler's Slow and Difficult Soups.* From his website, www.souppeddler.com, he now delivers soups and entrees to a large part of the city.

The area's farmers' markets celebrate the city's passion for homegrown food (see the Shopping chapter), and one of the most beloved is Boggy Creek Farm (again, see the Shopping chapter), an organic farm in East Austin that provides fresh produce

This is a homey, comfortable diner where gingerbread pancakes rank as comfort food 24 hours a day, 7 days a week. The cafe is not far from downtown, just west of MoPac, and serves breakfast dishes, sandwiches, even fajitas whenever you want them, no matter the hour. A second location in SoCo.

MANDOLA'S ITALIAN MARKET $
4700 West Guadalupe St.
(512) 419-9700
www.mandolasmarket.com

The creation of Houston restaurateur-turned Hill Country winemaker, Damian Mandola and his wife Trina, this Italian market is a valuable resource for Austin cooks, but it also serves as a family-style cafe serving pizza, panini, antipasto, and salads in a light and airy setting at The Triangle, a mixed-use, town centerlike development just north of the UT campus. Two additional locations have opened in the west and southwest of the city. Open daily for breakfast, lunch, and dinner.

to several Austin restaurants. Be sure to sign up for the farm's e-mail list for not just news of what is ready for the market but also wonderful soul-nourishing tales of what is going on at the farm with the workers and animals who live there; www .boggycreekfarm.com.

Another eccentricity turned leitmotif for the city are the street vendors, dubbed "Airstream Cuisine" by *Food & Wine* magazine. These restored Airstream camping trailers and other "gypsy food trailers" serve as kitchens on wheels, setting up in vacant lots and parking areas in the city's busy nightlife districts. Foodie blogger Tiffany Harelik keeps track of the local scene on www.trailerfooddiaries.blogspot.com. On a much humbler scale—and one that speaks to Austin's multiculti vibe—look for the paleta man (paleta is a Mexican popsicle) plying his trade from his small freezer mounted on his bicycle in the South Central neighborhoods.

The Texas Department of Agriculture helps small producers market their wares and guides consumers to homegrown products, www.gotexan.org. Look for products labeled "Taste of Texas" and you know you are helping a Lone Star farmer, rancher, or food producer. Products marked "Naturally Texas" have been created by the state's cotton, wool, mohair, and leather producers.

Hill Country fare is popular on menus, for example, Pure Luck Goat Cheese is an award-winning favorite; www.purelucktexas.com. There are also herb and lavender farms west of the city, and early summer is a popular time to harvest lavender and buy Hill Country peaches; www.hillcountrylavender.com and www.texaspeaches.com. There is a lavender festival in Blanco every summer; see the Annual Events & Festivals chapter. And then there are the state's wineries, many located in the hills west of Austin. Some visitors look askance when a local offers them a glass of Texas wine, but the established industry has won recognition. Information about the state's wineries can be found at www.agr.state.tx.us/wine. (For information about the Hill Country wine trail, see the Close-up in the Day Trips & Weekend Getaways chapter.)

✳**MANSION AT JUDGES' HILL** $$–$$$
1900 Rio Grande St.
(512) 495-1800
www.mansionatjudgeshill.com
The dining room at this restored mansion not far from the capitol and the University of Texas campus is one of the most sophisticated and refined in Austin. The restaurant echoes the elegant decor of the boutique hotel (see listing in our Hotels & Motels chapter). The mansion has taken the freshest of ingredients—some local, others like lobster and imported foie gras—and created sophisticated dishes that are described as "modern American cuisine with classical French influences."

MANUEL'S $–$$$
310 Congress Ave.
(512) 472-7555
www.manuels.com
The setting is sleek and modern, with black booths, neon signs, and hip jazz music at this downtown restaurant, but the food is light, saucy, and evocative of interior Mexican classics. Chile rellenos are made as they are in

Mexico, stuffed with spicy and fruit-studded meat filling then topped with almond sauce. Fish is served Veracruzano-style with tomatoes and peppers, and enchiladas banderas reflect the red, green, and white of the Mexican flag. Manuel's is open for lunch and dinner and has a jazz brunch on Sun. There is a late-night snack menu. A second location has been opened in Northwest Austin.

MAX'S WINE DIVE $$–$$$
207 San Jacinto St.
(512) 904-0111
www.maxswinedive.com
A Houston transplant that has become a downtown favorite, Max's features an extensive wine list with "gourmet comfort food." How about mac and cheese with truffles accompanied by the best bubbly? Housed in a large industrial space just 2 blocks from Congress, Max's is open from late afternoon until midnight Mon through Wed; Thurs through Sat until 2 a.m. and on Sun opens early for brunch and closes at 10 p.m.

MCCORMICK & SCHMICK'S $$–$$$
401 Congress Ave.
(512) 236-9600
www.mccormickandschmicks.com
Part of a national chain, this seafood restaurant is housed in Frost Bank Tower, a fitting setting for the sophisticated menu that focuses on fresh seafood. Open daily for lunch and dinner.

MOONSHINE $$–$$$$
303 Red River St.
(512) 236-9599
www.moonshinegrill.com
Corn dog shrimp and high-class mac and cheese are just two of the dishes on the menu at Moonshine, where all-American

comfort food is taken to new heights in a setting that is both cozy and historic, a small stone house and carriage house just east of the convention center. Open daily for lunch and dinner, open Sun for brunch.

i   Several of Austin's brew houses offer hearty pub grub fare. If you are hungry for fish 'n' chips or Irish stew, check out our listings in the Nightlife chapter for pub food, tapas, and sports bars with burgers and wings fare. If you are looking for a "hangout"—a place to sip something, nosh, and watch the sunset; or wash those nachos down with margaritas at a bridal shower; perhaps a place where Dad can have a beer while the kids play in a sandbox, check out our Hangouts Close-up in that same chapter.

MOTHER'S CAFE AND GARDEN $–$$
4215 Duval St.
(512) 451-3994
www.motherscafeaustin.com
Vegetarian food with international inspiration is served at this neighborhood cafe. The menu has low-fat and vegan options, and local beers and Texas wines are featured. The cafe is in the heart of the Hyde Park neighborhood and features a large outdoor patio. Open daily for lunch and dinner and serves weekend brunch.

NAU ENFIELD DRUG $
1115 West Lynn St.
(512) 476-1221
An old-fashioned drugstore in the historic Clarksville neighborhood, Nau's serves up sandwiches, burgers, malts, and breakfast dishes daily (see the Attractions chapter).

The atmosphere here is authentic and draws customers from both the neighborhood and downtown to the booths and bar daily for breakfast and lunch.

THE ORIGINAL HOFFBRAU $-$$
613 West Sixth St.
(512) 472-0822
www.originalhoffbrausteaks.com
Since 1934 they have been serving meat off the grill at this West Sixth Street no-frills restaurant. The founder's granddaughter now runs the joint. The decor here has been minimalist before minimalist got a name. The tables are simple orange Formica, and the wall decorations include a print of the Alamo, an old photograph or two, and a proclamation from former state representative Sarah Weddington (attorney in the Roe v. Wade case) praising the joint. In 1934 a T-bone steak was 35 cents, and a bottle of beer was a dime. Prices have risen, but the menu has remained the same—steak or, in a concession to modern times, grilled chicken breast. Salad is extra, but don't expect field greens. On the side there is white bread and saltines. Open weekdays for lunch; early dinner Mon through Sat.

✳PARKSIDE
301 East Sixth St.
(512) 474-9898
www.parkside-austin.com
Chef Sawn Cirkiel's creations get high marks from critics for their hearty flavors and full utilization of the whole animal. Marrow bones and sweetbreads appear on the menu, along with seasonal risottos and homemade ravioli. The restaurant's raw bar is one of the best around with an extensive menu of fresh oysters. Even the bar fare like a fried egg sandwich gets careful attention.

Open daily for happy hour, dinner, and late-night noshing.

ℹ A great way to integrate into the local foodie scene is to join the Dai Due Supper Club. Founded by former Vespaio chef Jesse Griffiths and experienced organic farmer Tamara Mayfield, the club is a roving banquet that offers unique dining experiences often on local farms and always featuring local produce and products. The duo also offers cooking classes and operates a noted butchery that sells its products at local farmers' markets. Visit their website and blog at www.daidueaustin .com or call (512) 769-7261 for details.

P. F. CHANG'S CHINA BISTRO $$-$$$
201 San Jacinto Blvd.
(512) 457-8300
www.pfchangs.com
Chang's, part of a national chain, is popular for both its sophisticated atmosphere and its menu of fresh Chinese dishes. Vegetarians and lovers of spicy food will appreciate the variety on the menu. P. F. Chang's offers a wide selection of wines. There is a second location northwest. Open for lunch and dinner.

ROARING FORK $$-$$$
701 Congress Ave.
(512) 583-0000
www.eddiev.com
The focus at the Southwestern-themed restaurant is on wood-fire cooking to produce those smokey, spicy flavors of the region. Dishes like green chile pork stew, fish tacos, and Dr Pepper-braised short ribs are featured. Open for lunch weekdays, dinner daily.

RUTH'S CHRIS $$$
107 West Sixth St.
(512) 477-RUTH
www.ruthchris.com

When it comes to steakhouses, the national Ruth's Chris chain is noted as one of the best. The restaurant is housed in the historic Scarborough Building, 1 block west of Congress Avenue, and offers valet parking for patrons. The menu features thick-cut steaks simmered in butter made famous by Ruth Fartel, founder of the restaurant chain. Reservations are recommended, particularly when the legislature is in session—in the odd years from Jan to May, except for specially called sessions.

SANTA RITA CANTINA $$
26 Doors, 1206 West Thirty-eighth St.
(512) 419-7482
www.santaritacantina.com

Owner Eddie Bernal has created a mythical culinary saint, Santa Margarita, who looked over the kitchens of South Texas and created a wonderful Tex-Mex cuisine that is a far cry from the standard fare with gloppy yellow cheese and soggy enchiladas that unfortunately passes for the real thing in some restaurants. Bernal gets top marks for his fare. Open from lunch to dinner daily. Brunch on weekends.

SCHOLZ GARTEN $
1607 San Jacinto Blvd.
(512) 474-1958
www.scholzgarten.com

Political junkies regard this old German beer garden as something of a shrine, a place that serves as a favorite watering hole and meeting place for political types, their staffers, and supporters (particularly Democrats). Hillary and Bill Clinton hung out here during their days as workers for the George McGovern presidential campaign. The beer garden is also featured in the 1962 novel about Texas politics, *The Gay Place*, by Billy Lee Brammer. The beer hall, which dates back to 1866, is east of the capitol and is owned by the Austin Saengerrunde, a German-American fraternal organization. The tree-shaded beer garden is a favorite gathering spot for state workers, politicians, and pre- and postgame fans of UT football and basketball. The restaurant features German food and typical American down-home fare: burgers, chicken, sandwiches, Tex-Mex specials, and beer, of course. Scholz's is open for lunch and dinner. Closed Sun.

SERRANO'S CAFE & CANTINA $$
Symphony Square, 1105 Red River St.
(512) 322-9080
www.serranos.com

There are five Serrano's cafes in various regions of the city, but this one has the best setting—in the small historic complex saved by the Austin Symphony (see the Attractions chapter). Tex-Mex plates, grilled meat and chicken, plus fajita platters are popular fare here. Open daily for lunch and dinner.

SHORELINE GRILL $$$$
98 San Jacinto Blvd.
(512) 477-3300
www.shorelinegrill.com

Tucked into a prime location on Lady Bird Lake, just west of the Four Seasons, the Shoreline is known for its sophisticated fish and seafood creations and the great view of the nightly summer evening exodus of Austin's famous bat colony. The best bat viewing is on the restaurant's patio, but seating is first-come, first-served there. Reservations can be made for the indoor rooms. Open daily for lunch and dinner.

STUBB'S BAR-B-Q $–$$
801 Red River St.
(512) 480-8341
www.stubbsaustin.com

The late C. B. Stubblefield is the soul of this restaurant, and his portrait hangs here as homage to his vision of barbecue and home cooking plus the blues. Barbecue—beef, sausage, brisket, chicken, ribs, turkey—is served with old-fashioned potatoes, beans, and greens. (Stubb's barbecue sauce is used in-house and can be found in Austin grocery stores.) In addition to serving lunch and dinner and offering live music nightly except Sun (see The Music Scene chapter), Stubb's also serves a Sun Gospel Brunch with typical Southern breakfast fare and a live gospel band.

i Want to eat out in? Call EatOutIn, (512) 346-9990, www.eatoutin .com, a local delivery company that brings the food of some 20 local restaurants to your door for a fee. The service will fax you a menu, you can ask them to mail you a brochure, or they can brief you on your choices.

SULLIVAN'S $$$–$$$$
300 Colorado St.
(512) 495-6504
www.sullivansteakhouse.com

Just when you think you have Austin figured out as a town where the hallmark is natural and laid-back, you walk into Sullivan's, where the menu is red meat, red meat, red meat, and the atmosphere reeks of confidence and power. Stand in the lobby during the legislative session and you could get a quorum. Chat with the parking valet, and you will hear tales of movie stars and directors who love to eat here. Sullivan's is in the heart of the downtown warehouse district and it touts itself as a "Chicago-style steakhouse." Dinner is served daily.

✳SWEETISH HILL BAKERY $
1120 West Sixth St.
(512) 472-1347
www.sweetishhill.com

The lemon bars are addictive, but since no one can live by sweets alone, Sweetish Hill also serves up a popular breakfast and lunch menu that finds inspiration in several quarters—France, Italy, and just plain wholesome. The bakery is in the middle of the West Sixth Street district and is usually busy all morning and into late afternoon as Austinites move to their own internal clocks, eating breakfast and lunch at their own pace. Food can be enjoyed on the premises, inside or on the small sidewalk cafe area, or it can be packed for an afternoon picnic.

TEXAS CHILI PARLOR $
1409 Lavaca St.
(512) 472-2828

The Texas equivalent of a neighborhood pub, this bar and restaurant attracts a loyal clientele, many of them state workers, attorneys, and political types from the nearby capitol. The ambience is funky bar meets roadhouse. The highlight of the menu is, of course, chili, served at varying degrees of heat and completely without beans (beans are a Yankee aberration). Sandwiches, tacos, and burgers are also on the menu, plus something called a Frito Pie, a Texas original—the recipe begins, "Take one bag of Fritos . . ." Open for lunch and dinner daily.

34TH STREET CAFE $-$$
1005 West. Thirty-fourth St.
(512) 371-3400
www.34thstreetcafe.com

A popular lunch spot for employees in the nearby hospital and doctors' offices, this neighborhood cafe also attracts a neighborhood crowd that enjoys the commitment to fresh fare, featuring organic vegetables from Austin's popular Boggy Creek Farm (see the Shopping chapter). Pastas, grilled seafood, and meats, plus salads are on the menu, plus light Mexican fare and popular Tuscan pizza. The cafe is open for lunch and dinner Mon through Sat, late lunch on Sat.

Redefining Fast Food

Fast food even has an Austin flair. The creators of P. Terry's, the hamburger drive-in at the corner of South Lamar Boulevard and Barton Springs Road (512-473-2217; www.pterrys.com), read *Fast Food Nation* and vowed to create "anti-fast food." Their burgers are all-natural, their potatoes fresh, the veggie burger tasty, and whether you drive up or drop by you can get a free dog biscuit for your sidekick. There are two additional locations now in the city. Leaf (www.leafsalad.com) is a foodie's dream of a salad bar downtown at 419 West Second St. (512-474-5323). Then there is Zen (www.eatzen.com), which has grown from one location to several across the city selling healthy fast noodles and salads, sushi, and teriyaki. One branch is located at 1300 South Congress Ave. (512-444-8081).

TRIO AT THE FOUR SEASONS $$$$
98 San Jacinto Blvd.
(512) 478-4500
www.fourseasons.com/austin

Elegant is the word most critics apply to this hotel restaurant, where the menu is a tribute to the best European traditions touched by Southwestern flair as divined by Chef Elmar Prambs. This is the place for a power lunch, power dinner, or divine brunch. The hotel is a favorite among visiting movie stars, high-tech wunderkinder in town for networking, and politicians and lobbyists. The menu is a wondrous combination of elegant dishes, some of them with Texas connections, bistro fare, and healthy, low-fat choices, all concocted in high style. One of the best and most affordable ways to experience the cafe is to sample brunch at the Four Seasons. Lunch and dinner are served daily, plus a prix fixe brunch. Reservations are recommended.

TRULUCKS $$-$$$
400 Colorado St.
(512) 482-9000
www.trulucks.com

It is all about seafood at Trulucks, which has a second location near the Arboretum in northwest Austin. The ingredients are flown in from both coasts and the Gulf, ensuring high quality. Some dishes have a distinctive Texas touch, like the jalapeño salmon béarnaise. Texas Gulf snapper, another regional star, also is featured on the menu. Trulucks offers valet parking. Open for lunch Mon through Fri and for dinner nightly.

UPPER CRUST BAKERY $
4508 Burnet Rd.
(512) 467-0102
www.theuppercrustbakery.com

The city has several neighborhood bakeries that serve as gathering places for friends and a comfy spot to enjoy a breakfast croissant or midmorning break. In addition to sandwiches, soups, and breads, Upper Crust has a selection of croissants, both sweet and savory, that can be enjoyed while perusing the morning papers. Open daily for breakfast, lunch, and afternoon snacks.

WHOLE FOODS
LANDMARK STORE $-$$$
525 North Lamar Blvd.
(512) 476-1206
www.wholefoods.com

The headquarters of homegrown Whole Foods Market is a veritable movable feast. Much more than a grocery store (see the Close-up in the Shopping chapter), the new landmark store houses a vast array of possibilities for diners from 8 a.m. until closing at 10 p.m. daily. There are several intimate food counters within the store where diners can watch and chat with the cook. There's a cafe with free Wi-Fi, plus a rooftop garden where shoppers can picnic with a view of the city. There are a sandwich bar, pizza and calzone oven, a sushi counter, ethnic food bars, and a favorite spot for the health conscious, the Raw and Living Food counters. Open daily from breakfast to dinner.

✳WINK $$$-$$$$
1014 North Lamar Blvd.
(512) 482-8868
www.winkrestaurant.com

Blink and you might miss Wink, but you would be missing a small jewel of a restaurant that has wowed locals. The small 15-table restaurant is located in an inconspicuous small shopping center. Austin chefs Stewart Scruggs and Mark Paul have created

a popular, if crowded, foodie hotspot. The aim is to create a degustation menu—simply put, several smaller portions to allow diners to sample a variety of delicacies. The chefs and their staff shop daily for the best ingredients they can find. The food is the focus here, and the tiny restaurant bubbles with enthusiasm. Reservations are accepted and recommended, given its size and popularity. Open daily for dinner; closed Sun.

ZOCALO CAFE $-$$
1110 West Lynn St.
(512) 472-TACO
www.zocalocafe.com

This is a "taqueria fresca" in the style of Mexico City, a place where fresh ingredients are used to make a variety of tacos and salads, served along with agua frescas, those fresh fruit drinks popular south of the border, and Mexican sodas and beer. This is an expression of Austin's love for our Mexican neighbors and the menu also includes an homage to Mexican vegetarian dishes, all served in the heart of one of Austin's oldest neighborhoods, Clarksville. Open for lunch and dinner, weekend brunch.

Z'TEJAS GRILL $$-$$$
1110 West Sixth St.
(512) 478-5355
www.ztejas.com

There are three Z'Tejas restaurants in Austin—the original in the West Sixth Street shopping/restaurant district and two in Northwest Austin. Perhaps a visit to the original and one northwest is the best way to get a quick fix on old Austin and new Austin. Both serve much the same menu, but the original Z'Tejas is housed in a converted home where the garage doors can be opened, exposing diners to the elements.

Close-up

A Word about Ice Cream

It's hard to beat a cold cup of ice cream on a balmy night as a fitting end to an evening out. Several Austin small businesses offer "handmade" ice cream. Perhaps the most famous is Amy's, which began as a single store but now has nine outlets and growing and also packs ice cream for sale in local shops and restaurants. There is also an Amy's at Austin's airport. Patrons pick their flavor and toppings and watch as they are hand-beaten to a yummy, creamy, but cold consistency on marble counters. For a complete list of all **Amy's Ice Creams** shops, check out their website, www.amysicecream.com.

All locations are open late; the downtown Sixth Street store is open until 1 a.m. on weekends. Look for the big moving cows on the outer wall of Amy's at 1012 West Sixth St., (512) 480-0673. Other favorite locations are the small, walkup store at 1301 South Congress Ave. and the new Amy's in a remodeled gas station at 5624 Burnet Rd., (512) 538-2697, next door to Amy's production plant. On Sun nights there are "Moooovies" shown on site. The Hyde Park neighborhood in Central Austin is home to the Dolce Vita Gelato and Espresso Bar, 4222 Duval St., (512) 323-2686, www.dolcevitagelato.com. This neighborhood coffee shop and Italian-style gelateria opens early for breakfast and stays open late for gelato.

Dolce Vita also is a great spot for an after-dinner drink, perhaps coffee and a liqueur, or one of the 35 grappas the cafe has on hand. In addition to gelato, the menu includes wonderful tarts with traditional Italian flavors like hazelnut and walnut. The cafe has a small indoor space plus an outdoor area with tables and chairs.

Another addition to the ice cream scene in Austin is **Teo** in the 26 Doors Shopping Center in Central Austin. Teo's features authentic Italian ices and gelatos. The shop, which also houses a small coffee shop featuring Italian beans, opens early—around 6 a.m. on weekdays, a little later on weekends—and stays open until late evening daily except Sun, when the cafe shuts down around 9 p.m. Teo's is located at 1206 West Thirty-eighth St., Suite 1204–B, (512) 451-9555, www.caffeteo.com.

The interior of the West Sixth Street location is decorated in the bright colors of the Southwest, and the outdoor patio serves as a lazy-day refuge just a few blocks from downtown or a place to relax during rush hour and enjoy the restaurant's "appetizer happy hour." The newer locations embrace the Hill Country vibe with limestone walls, fireplaces, and cathedral ceilings. The menu is sometimes described as Santa Fe meets Texas, with a dash of Louisiana thrown in. Don't pass on the restaurant's most famous dessert, Ancho chile fudge pie. Open daily for lunch through dinner, plus Sunday brunch.

SOUTH CENTRAL

ARTZ RIB HOUSE $
2230 South Lamar Blvd.
(512) 442-8283
www.artzribhouse.com
Live music and Texas barbecue are on the menu at this South Austin restaurant, but just to make sure no one feels left out, the

menu also offers vegetarian dishes, including a grilled vegetable platter. There is live music 7 nights a week. The restaurant has both indoor dining and a screened-in porch with ceiling fans. Open daily for lunch and dinner.

BABY ACAPULCO $-$$
1628 Barton Springs Rd.
(512) 474-8774
www.babyacapulco.com
A favorite with young, downtown workers, this restaurant on the Barton Springs strip is usually packed on weekends, especially when the weather conjures up margarita fantasies. The Tex-Mex menu offers the usual fare, including 14 types of enchiladas. The outdoor patio is the heart of the action on balmy days, and inside there is a casual, colorful atmosphere. There are four locations in the city. Open for lunch and dinner daily.

CASA DE LUZ $-$$$
1701 Toomey Rd.
(512) 476-2535
www.casadeluz.org
This is a gathering place where the principles of macrobiotic diets, yoga, tai chi, massage, and music come together in a quiet retreat not far from downtown Austin. The restaurant features macrobiotic and vegan dishes, a raw food bar with sushi, and Mexican food featured on Wed and Indian on Fri. Open daily for breakfast, lunch and dinner. The campus also is home to a culinary arts program, the National Epicurean Academy of Culinary Arts (512-476-2276; www.natural epicurean.com). The students present meals on the second Sun of every month.

CHUY'S $-$$
1728 Barton Springs Rd.
(512) 474-4452
www.chuys.com

Chuy's is perhaps the most famous restaurant on the Barton Springs Road strip and one of the most colorful in Austin. Where else would you find a shrine to Elvis? The decor is a mixture of fantasy and kitsch, with iguanas and lava lamps setting the theme. The food is a mixture of Tex-Mex and New Mexico. When the harvest comes in, New Mexico chiles are grilled out front on a large metal barbecue rig. There are now four Chuy's in Austin, and the lively atmosphere makes them a popular family spot. The restaurant also sponsors a Christmas Parade (see the Annual Events & Festivals chapter). Chuy's is open for lunch and dinner daily.

*CURRA'S GRILL $-$$
614 East Oltorf St.
(512) 444-0012
www.currasgrill.com
Austin abounds in small family restaurants that bring the flavors of Mexico home in a variety of ways. Curra's signature is a variety of authentic salsas. The menu features all-day breakfast tacos, enchiladas and carne guisada, a slow-simmered stew, and other traditional Mexican dishes, including several delicious Yucatecan offerings. Open daily for breakfast, lunch, and dinner, and you can buy the restaurant's tamales online at holiday time.

EL MERCADO RESTAURANT AND
   CANTINA $-$$
1302 South First St.
(512) 447-7445
www.elmercadorestaurant.com
This South Central location is the original of now three El Mercados in Austin. All serve up the same generous proportions of Tex-Mex favorites in a lively, colorful setting. The restaurant is open daily for breakfast, lunch, and dinner.

EL NOPALITO $
2809 South First St.
(512) 326-2026

This typical Mexican cafe near St. Edward's University is popular with the working-class neighbors, students, and foodies who love homemade Mexican food. The small restaurant—its name means "little cactus"—serves breakfast and lunch only. Popular dishes include tacos and migas (eggs scrambled with tomatoes, onions, chiles, and strips of corn tortillas), the homemade flan, and, on weekends, menudo. Touted as a hangover cure, menudo is a tripe and hominy stew that is an acquired taste. No credit cards.

GREEN MESQUITE $-$$
1400 Barton Springs Rd.
(512) 479-0485
www.greenmesquite.com

Texas barbecue and Louisiana Cajun fare are the specialties here. But there are also chicken-fried steaks, hamburgers, and sandwiches. On the Cajun side, the spicy gumbo jambalaya and catfish are favorites. The pies are homemade, and there is live music on weekends. A second location has opened in South Austin. Green Mesquite is open daily for lunch and dinner.

GREEN PASTURES $$$-$$$$
811 West Live Oak Rd.
(512) 444-1888
http://greenpasturesrestaurant.com

In 1945 the Koock family decided to turn their family mansion into a restaurant, and ever since Green Pastures has been a quiet, elegant place to celebrate special events and family gatherings. The mansion was built in 1894 and has been in the Koock family since 1916. Surrounded by a large garden with more than 200 live oak trees, the mansion is hidden away in an everyday South Austin neighborhood. Patrons can begin their dining experience with a glass of milk punch out on the veranda, watch the peacocks stroll on the lawn, and listen to music being played on the restaurant's grand piano. The restaurant serves lunch and dinner daily, but one highlight of the week is the Sunday brunch, when Green Pastures sets a table that astounds both the eye and the palate. Reservations are recommended for brunch and for lunch and dinner on weekends.

i Can't afford to splurge for one of those top flight restaurants? Then head to the Le Cordon Bleu culinary academy, an Austin insider secret where the students serve classical French cuisine at bargain prices. Located in north Austin, the academy serves lunch and dinner at La Ventana, the school's showcase restaurant, 3110 Esperanza Crossing, (512) 339-3850. The menus are featured online at www.chefs.edu/austin.

GÜERO'S TACO BAR $-$$
1412 South Congress Ave.
(512) 447-7688
www.guerostacobar.com

Architectural ingenuity has turned an old feed store on the avenue in SoCo into Güero's, where the food reflects both Tex-Mex and Mexican influences. The interior has been decorated with Mexican tiles, old photographs from the Mexican Revolution, and a picture of former President Bill Clinton, who has eaten here when visiting Austin. Breakfast tacos are a bargain here and are served all day, although the restaurant is not open for breakfast during the week. On weekends Güero's opens early for breakfast, featuring tacos, migas, huevos rancheros, and other popular Tex-Mex favorites. There is usually live music on Sun afternoon.

LA MEXICANA BAKERY $–$$
1924 South First St.
(512) 443-6369

When the owners of the original bakery, La Reyna (named for the picture of the Virgin Mary whose image hangs on a wall of the bakery), retired, they sold the business to one of their longtime bakers, Jesus Becerra, who still gets to work at midnight. The bakery and cafe is in the heart of one of Austin's old Mexican-American neighborhoods, but it's a neighborhood that, like much of Austin, is changing demographically while trying to hold on to its authentic atmosphere. The cafe is a meeting place for neighbors, local politicians, artists, and those who appreciate the homey atmosphere of the long-established South Austin restaurant. More than 70 different kinds of Mexican sweet breads are offered, and the staff will help you learn their names. Coffee and Mexican hot chocolate are good accompaniments. Be sure to take home a bag of Mexican pastries and cookies—the conchas, a sweet bread with a whirled shell design in sugar, are a favorite. But eat them the same day: Mexican pastries have no preservatives and little salt, so they do not stay fresh for long. The cafe is open daily from 6 a.m. to 8:30 p.m.

MATT'S FAMOUS EL RANCHO $$
2613 South Lamar Blvd.
(512) 462-9333
www.mattselrancho.com

In 1952 Matt Martinez opened up the first El Rancho, now operating in a new, large building south of downtown. President Lyndon B. Johnson ate here before he was president, and lots of other Austin notables have come here for a regular Tex-Mex fix. The menu includes all the old faithful standbys: enchiladas, fajitas, tacos, chile rellenos, and grilled shrimp. The hacienda-style restaurant can seat 500, but there is always a line on weekends at peak dining hours. Open for lunch and dinner daily, except Tues.

✳OLIVIA $$–$$$$
2043 South Lamar Blvd.
(512) 804-2700
www.olivia-austin.com

When it opened in 2009, Olivia was named one of the top 10 best new restaurants in the country by *Bon Appetit* magazine and it continues to wow. Like other top Austin eateries, Olivia is located in an unassuming neighborhood, but in a modern building that captures the new South Lamar zeitgeist. From local kobe beef to lamb's tongues, the eclectic menu draws from Texas tradition and locally sourced ingredients. Even the mundane gets the Olivia treatment with a Dandy Don Meredith (Dallas Cowboys fans get the link) Chile Frite Pie or a pickled pigs ear and gouda sandwich on the brunch menu to a veal chop with gnocchi among the dinner offerings. Open daily for dinner, Fri and Sat for lunch, and Sun for brunch.

PAGGI HOUSE $$–$$$
200 Lee Barton Dr.
(512) 473-3700
www.paggihouse.com

This romantic restaurant, nestled in a live oak grove with patio views of Lady Bird Lake, is housed in a historic home dating back to the 1840s. The seasonal gourmet menu features top flight ingredients flown in, such as Hawaiian fish and New Zealand lamb, plus locally produced food products. Open Mon through Sat for dinner, Sun for brunch.

PERLA'S SEAFOOD
& OYSTER BAR $$–$$$$
1400 South Congress Ave.
(512) 291-7300
www.perlasaustin.com

Hailed by *Esquire* magazine as a bright new face on the Austin scene, Perla's clients enjoy an outside patio with a view of SoCo action, plus a lavish oyster bar inside. There is a simply grilled seafood menu, plus unctuous offerings like a Texas bouillabaisse and lobster, chile and cheese grits. Open daily for lunch and dinner, brunch on the weekends.

ROMEO'S $$
1500 Barton Springs Rd.
(512) 476-1090
www.romeosrestaurants.com

From the concrete stone swan planters in front to the plastic grapevines inside, the owners of Romeo's have managed to re-create the kitschy atmosphere of a neighborhood Italian-American cafe with a menu to match. The atmosphere and the prices make this a great date restaurant. Open daily for lunch and dinner plus a Sunday brunch featuring vegetarian and meat frittatas, Italian eggs Benedict, and, of course, migas, the Tex-Mex breakfast must.

SCHLOTZSKY'S MARKETPLACE/BREAD
ALONE BAKERY $
218 South Lamar Blvd.
(512) 476-2867
www.schlotzskys.com

Schlotzsky's is a chain sandwich shop that was founded in Austin and has grown worldwide, including an outpost in Beijing. There are almost two dozen outlets in Austin, but this special branch just south of Lady Bird Lake is notable for its breezy atmosphere, airy architecture, and its on-site partner, Bread Alone Bakery. The famous sandwiches are sold here—the Original is made with special bread (grilled sourdough buns) stuffed with salami, ham, several cheeses, olives, onions, lettuce, and tomato—plus soups, salads, and small pizzas. The bakery offers whole loaves of specialty bread, cakes, cookies, desserts, and coffees. This is a good place to put together lunch or afternoon snacks for an impromptu picnic on the shores of Lady Bird Lake. Open daily for breakfast, lunch, and dinner.

SHADY GROVE $–$$
1624 Barton Springs Rd.
(512) 474-9991
www.theshadygrove.com

This Texas roadhouse–style restaurant takes its name from the pecan grove that shades the patio and the parking lot. There is seating inside, but many patrons prefer to sit outside and enjoy the sort of food served in roadhouses across America back in the days before Interstate highways. Hamburgers are a staple, or try a Frito pie (Fritos topped with chili and cheese). For vegetarians there is a variety of salads and a Hippie Sandwich made with grilled eggplant and other vegetables. The Airstream Chili is hot and named for the Airstream trailer that sits in the garden. During summer, Shady Grove features live music evenings and even movies on the patio. Open daily for lunch and dinner.

SOUTH CONGRESS CAFE $–$$
1600 South Congress Ave.
(512) 447-3905
www.southcongresscafe.com

The fact that this neighborhood cafe offers brunch daily until 4 p.m. says a lot about the SoCo lifestyle. The dishes are lavish and guaranteed to revive after a late night session of music, writing code, or working on that novel. Eggs Benedict, crab cakes, smoked brisket hash, and the mandatory migas are on tap. At night, the cafe specializes in bistro fare and comfort food. Open daily.

TACO XPRESS $
2529 South Lamar Blvd.
(512) 444-0261
www.tacoxpress.com
The bumper stickers in this part of Austin often say "Keep Austin Weird," and funkiness is a point of pride in South Austin. At this—what else—funky cafe the patio features a shrine to Santa Taqueria Austin del Sur, and the menu has literally dozens of taco combos. Owner and chef Maria Corbalon, who is portrayed in a large folksy bust that crowns the restaurant, is noted for her roasted meats, which evoke memories of those tacos savored by travelers in the Yucatan and other regions of Mexico. The cafe is open daily for breakfast and lunch, closes midafternoon on Mon and Sun, and stays open until mid evening on other nights.

THREADGILL'S WORLD
HEADQUARTERS RESTAURANT $$
301 West Riverside Dr.
(512) 472-9304
www.threadgills.com
Eddie Wilson founded the Armadillo World Headquarters (see The Music Scene chapter) and now owns Threadgill's, the two Austin restaurants that cherish home-cooking and celebrate the Austin music scene. The original Threadgill's is in North Austin (see the North section), but this downtown restaurant has carried the Threadgill's banner back to the block where the legendary Armadillo stood. The restaurant celebrates the past by decorating the walls with Armadillo memorabilia. Much larger than the original

Threadgill's, the downtown venue is nevertheless packed, especially at lunchtime. The food here is down-home diner-style with entrees like meat loaf, chicken-fried steak, fried chicken, and sandwiches. There is live music here and a Sunday gospel brunch. Open daily for lunch and dinner.

i Two local writers are indispensable when it comes to understanding vital ingredients in Texas food. The late Jean Andrews, often called the "Pepper Lady," authored a couple of books on the genus *Capsicum* and her text, recipes, and beautiful drawings of peppers are invaluable to food fans and cooks. Another local expert with several books in print is herb and tequila expert Lucinda Hutson.

✳UCHI $$–$$$
801 South Lamar Blvd.
(512) 916-4808
www.uchiaustin.com
Tyson Cole was named one of *Food & Wine*'s best new chefs in 2005, and his restaurant housed in a small home (uchi means "house" in Japanese) has become something of a shrine for visiting foodies. But don't be intimidated by all the accolades. The food is lovingly prepared here in a setting that is so reflective of Austin, a humble, converted South Austin cottage. The sushi is inspired by both tradition and inspiration from other culinary realms—chiles, goat cheese, and other nontraditional ingredients make appearances. Foodies know that Cole took his knives to Kitchen Stadium on the Food Network's *Iron Chef* show where he challenged Masaharu Morimoto, someone he admired, to a battle. Cole did not win, but won praise for his efforts. The website, which is as beautiful as the food, offers a tour of

the menu and the surroundings. Open Mon through Sat for dinner.

✳VESPAIO $$–$$$$
1610 South Congress Ave.
(512) 441-6100
www.austinvespaio.com
This Italian-inspired restaurant in the heart of the hot South Congress Avenue corridor (see the Shopping chapter) represents all that is both good and bad about the Austin restaurant scene these days. The food is inspired, the atmosphere lively, but the wait can be long! A small restaurant, Vespaio rocketed to fame soon after it opened. Created by Chef Alan Lazarus, the menu here allows patrons to dine in a small dining area with a view of the kitchen or to sit in the bar area and simply nosh for an hour or two on a wide selection of antipasti. Many of the dishes reflect Italian classics like Tuscan grilled steak and mussels in wine sauce; others are inspirations that draw on top Texas food products prepared in the Italian manner and in tune with the seasons. Next door is Vespaio's country cousin, Enoteca Vespaio which offers casual meals and take away. Vespaio is open Tues through Sun for dinner.

SOUTH

EL GALLO $–$$
2910 South Congress Ave.
(512) 444-2205
www.elgallorestaurant.com
A popular Tex-Mex eatery that offers servings of enchiladas, tacos, chalupa, and fajitas so generous that no one leaves hungry. The dinner menu also features several dishes that are typical of South Texas cookery, including cabrito (roasted baby goat) and chicken mole, the rich, complex chocolate and chile-based sauce that legend says was created

by nuns in Puebla, Mexico. The restaurant is located in a colorful building across the street from St. Edward's University. Open daily from lunch through dinner.

HABANA $$
2728 South Congress Ave.
(512) 443-4252
www.habana.com
Roast pork, tostones, Cuban sandwiches, mojitos—all the Cuban classics are on the menu here. The restaurant even serves Havana Cola, imported from Florida, this is a pure cane sugar cola that expats yearn for. There is a second location at 709 East Sixth St. (512-443-4252). Open daily for lunch and dinner.

SOUTHWEST

AUSTIN PIZZA GARDEN $–$$
6266 US 290 West
(512) 891-9980
It took 19 years for James Patton to finish the Old Rock Store in Oak Hill; chances are it won't take much more than 19 minutes for you to get your pizza in the restaurant now housed in the historic building. Patton (the local elementary school is named for him) finished the store in 1898. Now Oak Hill is a suburb of Austin, and a major freeway has wiped out many of the small stores that once lined the old highway. But Patton's stone structure is a registered historic building, and even the highway had to shift south to preserve history. The restaurant also offers take-out service. Open daily for lunch and dinner.

CENTRAL MARKET
**   AT WESTGATE** $–$$
4477 South Lamar Blvd., Westgate Mall
(512) 899-4300
www.centralmarket.com

Just as the cafe at the original Central Market (see Central Austin) is a popular spot for family dining, this second location has proved to be a favorite place to take the whole family. The varied menu offers sandwiches, homestyle entrees, gourmet salads, pizza, burgers, soups, and sandwiches, ensuring that everyone in the group will find something to suit his or her fancy. The cafe also opens early for breakfast, and there is free live music on the patio at night. Open daily 7 a.m. to 10 p.m., until 11 p.m. on Fri and Sat.

ESTANCIA CHURRASCIA $$
4894 US 290 West
(512) 892-1225
www.estanciachurrascaria.com
Tucked away on the side of a freeway access road in Sunset Valley (see the Relocation chapter), the outside of this Brazilian steakhouse looks like another limestone-clad restaurant. But inside the atmosphere is South American home-on-the-range, as gaucho-style cuisine with its heavy emphasis on grilled meat is served—beef, lamb, chicken, and pork ribs cooked the way the south of the equator cowboys do it. Open Mon through Sat for lunch and dinner, Sun dinner only.

JACK ALLEN'S KITCHEN $$–$$$
7720 Highway 71 West
(512) 852-8558
www.jackallenskitchen.com
This restaurant in Southwest Austin is just beyond what is locally known as the "Y" because it is where US 290 West and Highway 71 West part company, one heading west to the hills, the other northwest to the lakes. Veteran Chef Jack Gilmore took over what has been a "snakebit" location and has proved as successful as he did in previous

ventures like Z'Tejas. The menu is contemporary American and stresses locally sourced ingredients with Southwest and Louisiana flavors. Locally popular, especially for Sunday brunch. Open daily for lunch and dinner.

NUEVO LEON $–$$
5900 West Slaughter Lane
(512) 288-4550
www.nuevoleoninaustin.com
The menu at this modern neighborhood cafe in the Circle C neighborhood pays homage to the cooking of Northern Mexico and the state of Nuevo Leon. The original "mother" restaurant is located in East Austin. The dishes make it plain that Texas once was part of Old Mexico, and many of the featured items are found on South Texas Mexican cafe menus—beef and vegetable caldo (soup), fajitas, rib-eye steak with ranchero sauce, and a burrito dressed with chili. Open daily for lunch and dinner, open for breakfast Sun.

NUTTY BROWN CAFE AND
AMPHITHEATRE $–$$$
12225 US 290 West
(512) 301-4648
www.nuttybrown.com
One of the hottest growth areas of Austin has been the southwest region and the once-sleepy community of Dripping Springs down the road from what the locals call the Y at Oak Hill. This is a popular family restaurant, especially on the weekends, when there is live music outdoors. The menu features Mexican food, salads, and sandwiches. On Fri night there is a free taco bar, and on Sun morning breakfast is served, which makes it a good stop on the way to a Hill Country day trip. Open daily from lunch through dinner; open earlier on Sun.

*THE SALT LICK $$
RR 1826, Camp Ben McCullough Road, Driftwood
(512) 858-4959
www.saltlickbbq.com

One of the most atmospheric barbecue restaurants in the area, the Salt Lick occupies a rural site about 12 miles south of US 290 West on RR 1826, known as Camp Ben McCullough Road. Set in a Hill Country pasture, the Salt Lick has garnered a worldwide reputation, thanks to its mail-order food shipments, corporate parties by some of Austin's top employers, and coverage in national and international publications. There are picnic tables inside and out, and the place is always busy. In winter a large fireplace inside warms diners. The menu includes brisket, chicken, ribs, sausage, homemade pickles, and peach and berry cobblers. Open daily for lunch and dinner. Reservations are suggested for large groups. The Salt Lick is located in a dry area of Hays County, so no beer, wine, or liquor is served; however, patrons can bring their own alcoholic beverages. No credit cards. There is an ATM machine on site, but watch out for those fees. Get a last minute taste of Salt Lick to go at the Austin airport.

TRATTORIA LISINA $$-$$$$
13308 FM 150 West, Driftwood
(512) 894-3111
www.trattorialisina.com

Damian Mandola (see Mandola's Italian Market under Central Austin) has made Driftwood, near the famous Salt Lick barbecue, a center for his culinary adventures that include a rural trattoria and a winery. The setting is evocative of the Italian countryside given the limestone pastures and gnarled live oak trees of the Hill Country. The menu is classic Italian with pastas, main course meat dishes including osso buco and rabbit, and dessert includes light fruits and cheeses. Open for dinner Tues through Sun, lunch on Sat and Sun.

i Austin abounds with bakeries and food shops where a last-minute picnic can be put together for outdoor (or indoor) munching. Check out the Food/Gourmet/Kitchenware section of our Shopping chapter.

WEST

BACKSTAGE STEAKHOUSE $$
21814 Highway 71 West, Spicewood
(512) 264-2223

Longtime Austin foodies know that Raymond Tatum was the first chef at Jeffrey's, what we describe as the quintessential Austin restaurant. Now he is the conjurer at this relaxed steakhouse west of Austin on the road to the lakes. The food is inspired Texas fare with smoked meats, succulent beef, and seafood touched with the magic of chiles and other favorite Texas ingredients. The patio is a favorite place to dine. Open daily for dinner.

BISTRO 88 $$-$$$
2712 Bee Caves Rd.
(512) 328-8888
http://bistro88.com

Touted as Pacific Rim cuisine with Euro-Asian flair, the menu here is the creation of three partners who have operated top restaurants in Mexico and China. *Austin Chronicle* readers lauded this West Austin restaurant with its sophisticated menu and decor as "The Best New Restaurant in 2000." Dishes include such fusion creations as hot-and-sour seafood gumbo, roast lamb with a curried Asian pasta, mussels with a black bean sauce, plus entrees featuring top-quality seafood and

Texas game. Open for lunch Sun through Fri, dinner daily.

CHINATOWN $$
3300 Bee Caves Rd.
(512) 327-6588
www.chinatownwestlake.com
Among the most popular items on the menu at this West Lake Hills restaurant are several searing dishes, Thai pepper basil shrimp, and jalapeño chicken with black bean sauce—a reflection of the spicy Szechuan-style Chinese cuisine featured at Chinatown. Of course not all the dishes are spicy, but diners with a taste for the fiery can turn up the heat on request. Chinatown is open daily for lunch and dinner.

COUNTY LINE ON THE HILL $$-$$$
6500 Bee Caves Rd.
(512) 327-1742
www.countyline.com
Upscale barbecue is the order of the day at this hillside restaurant. Over the years, the view from the hilltop patio has changed as Austin has grown and homeowners have headed for the hills. One of the highlights of the menu is the smoked prime rib, served with baked potato, coleslaw, and beans. Barbecued ribs, brisket, chicken, sausage, pork, and baby back ribs are available by the plate or by the pound. The restaurant is open for lunch during the week and for dinner daily.

THE EMERALD
RESTAURANT $$$-$$$$
13614 Highway 71 West
(512) 263-2147
www.irishemeraldrestaurant.com
Step inside this Hill Country cottage and you will think you have crossed the threshold of an Irish country cottage. The walls are decorated with shamrock wallpaper, the tablecloths and curtains are lace, and there are cozy nooks and crannies where diners can enjoy an intimate dinner. The Kinsella family, whose matriarch hailed from County Mayo, runs this little Irish gem near Lake Travis. The evening begins here with orders of Irish soda bread and English treacle loaf (made with molasses) served with whipped strawberry butter and goes on from there to embrace roast pork in puff pastry, chateaubriand for two, roast lamb, grilled salmon inspired by Irish and continental influences. The desserts are rich, and Irish coffee is almost an obligatory end to dinner. The Emerald is open daily for dinner.

HILL COUNTRY PASTA HOUSE $$-$$$
3519 RR 620 North
(512) 266-9445
www.hillcountrypasta.com
This Lake Travis–area restaurant offers a variety of pastas and Italian-inspired entrees. The wood-fired oven produces pizza and focaccia, and there are grilled offerings, including steaks. The restaurant is kid-friendly, and crayons come with the menu so that the kiddies can be occupied while parents ruminate on the choices. Because it is close to the lake, many patrons come in after a day of boating or swimming, so the dress code is relaxed. Open daily for lunch and dinner.

i As Austin grows, the list of restaurants is beginning to look like a Russian novel. One way to view the *Cliff's Notes* version is to check in with local food blogs like www.urbanspoon.com and local food blogger www.austinfoodjournal.com where the "locals" give their views and tips.

*HUDSON'S-ON-THE-BEND $$$$
3509 RR 620
(512) 266-1369
www.hudsonsonthebend.com

Chef/owner Jeff Blank and executive chef Becky Barsch Fischer have built a wide-ranging reputation as innovators in Texas cuisine from their base near the shores of Lake Travis. *Condé Nast Traveler* magazine has named it one of the best 50 restaurants in the United States. The restaurant is housed in and around a small Hill Country cottage. On the grounds are a smokehouse and an herb garden that offers a hint of what Hudson's has to offer. Much of the menu is devoted to showcasing exotic game and ingredients—one of the popular appetizers is Diamond Back Rattlesnake Cakes with chipotle cream sauce. Other dishes utilize venison, javelina (a South Texas wild boar), and Axis antelope raised on Hill Country ranches. For the less adventurous there are top-quality steaks, veal, seafood, and pasta dishes. The restaurant's sauces, both savory and sweet, garnered such a devoted following they are now sold on specialty food store shelves and by mail order. (Look for them at Central Market, and look for Central Market in our Shopping chapter.) Diners can eat or wait for a table on a balmy evening in the garden decorated with twinkling lights. Weekends are especially busy, so reservations are recommended. The restaurant is open daily for dinner but closes a little earlier in winter, so it is wise to call ahead. Hudson's also offers cooking classes.

LAS PALOMAS $$
3201 Bee Caves Rd.
(512) 327-9889
www.laspalomasrestaurant.com

Tucked away in the corner of a fairly non-descript strip shopping center, this Mexican restaurant serves delicious interior food in a light, airy setting. Specialties from various Mexican states are featured, including pork pibil, inspired by Yucatecan cuisine, shrimp a la Veracruzana (green olives, tomatoes, and capers), and the much-praised mole poblano, a complex sauce made from chiles, chocolate, spice, and herbs. The restaurant features live Latino trio music on Fri and jazz midweek to add to the ambience. Las Palomas is open for lunch and dinner daily.

RUDY'S BAR-B-Q $-$$$
2451 Capital of Texas Hwy. (Loop 360)
(512) 329-5554
www.rudys.com

You can gas up your car and grab a grocery bag of barbecue at this popular small Texas chain. Rudy's touts itself as serving "the worst barbecue in Texas," but obviously that's a gimmick, judging from the crowd. The gas station is not one of those small-town stations; this is an up-to-date copy that simply reminds patrons that good barbecue originated in small-town country stores. Patrons can eat in or get food to go here and at two other locations in town, and Rudy's opens early to serve breakfast tacos. Open daily for breakfast, lunch, and dinner.

TRES AMIGOS $$
1801 South Loop 360
(Capital of Texas Highway)
(512) 327-1776
www.tresamigos.com

A longtime fixture on the Westlake Hills scene, Tres Amigos serves familiar Tex-Mex favorites such as enchiladas and tacos, fajitas, and Mexican plates. Some of the waitresses have been on the job for years and have watched as families grew up, nourished by the kind of food all Texans hanker for regularly. The setting is a pleasant evocation of Old Mexico and there is a second location in north Austin. Try the homemade mango ice cream. Tres Amigos is open for lunch and dinner daily.

ZOOT $$$–$$$$
11715 Bee Caves Rd.
(512) 477-6535
www.zootrestaurant.com
Gourmet magazine has praised Zoot executive chef John Maxwell for creating some of the "most exciting food" in Austin. Zoot has consistently ranked as one of the city's best restaurants. Originally located just west of MoPac, Zoot has moved west to the hills where it continues to capture the spirit of Austin with its relaxed atmosphere and emphasis on the best ingredients, many of them produced in Texas. The menu changes with the seasons, and a vegetarian entree is usually on the menu, perhaps eggplant prepared osso buco-style. Given the restaurant's size and popularity, reservations are recommended. Open daily for dinner.

NORTHWEST

CHEZ ZEE $$–$$$
5406 Balcones Dr.
(512) 454-2666
www.chez-zee.com
This stylish bistro, with a large outdoor patio, art-studded walls, and a baby grand where customers can work a jigsaw puzzle while listening to cafe music, is a fixture on the Austin scene. The menu features both American and continental specialties, including sandwiches, pastas, salads, and grilled entrees, but it is the breakfast and weekend brunch menus that get rave reviews, particularly the crème brûlée French toast. Brunch is served into midafternoon on weekends, breakfast begins early during the week, and lunch and dinner are served daily, plus there is a late-night dessert menu.

i Austin's Asian food scene has expanded in recent years and one favorite foodie gathering spot is the Chinatown shopping center (10901 North Lamar Blvd.; www.chinatown austin.com) in north Austin. Anchored by a large Asian supermarket, the center also is home to noodle shops, Vietnamese bakeries, Korean grills, and Chinese barbecue spots.

COUNTY LINE ON THE LAKE $$–$$$
5204 FM 2222
(512) 346-3664
www.countyline.com
This Northwest branch of a popular upscale barbecue restaurant (see West Austin) is situated along a creekbed. Diners can wait for a table or enjoy a drink on the outdoor deck under the trees. This is a popular place to bring out-of-town visitors given its Hill Country setting and top flight barbecue. One word of warning: FM 2222 is a wide, winding road that leads to Highland Lakes, making it very busy on weekends. There have been serious accidents here, many involving alcohol; visitors should designate a driver if they plan to drink with dinner. Open daily for lunch and dinner.

HOOVER'S $–$$
13376 Research Blvd.
(512) 335-0300
www.hooverscooking.com
The original Hoover's is in East Austin and this homestyle restaurant is a wonderful example of how a humble neighborhood spot finds a

place in Austin's heart and grows. The menu is described by founder Hoover Alexander as "smoke, fire and icehouse" cooking that has its roots in Central Texas. A fifth generation Texan, Alexander is inspired by his Mexican-American classmates in Catholic school, his grandmother's homestyle cooking, and barbecue bosses of old. Open daily for lunch and dinner; open for breakfast on weekends.

KENOBI $$
10000 Research Blvd.
(512) 241-0119
www.kenobiaustin.com
This Arboretum restaurant (see the Shopping chapter) takes Southwestern flavors and melds them with Asian cuisine all served up amid a decor that evokes the Far East in a stylish way. In addition to sushi, the menu features items like an Asian-marinated rib-eye, a 5-spice pork chop and miso-chipotle chile salmon. Extensive sake menu. Open for lunch and dinner.

MANNY HATTANS
UPTOWN KITCHEN $–$$
Gateway Shopping Center,
9503 Research Blvd.
(512) 794-0088
www.mannyhattans.com
Manny came to Texas to play college football, but decided to open a New York deli where the menu reflected his family's roots. Manny's has now added bistro dishes to the menu, in addition to huge portions of deli fare. Open daily for breakfast, lunch, and dinner, closes mid evening Mon through Thurs.

✳MIRABELLE $$–$$$
8127 Mesa Dr.
(512) 346-7900
www.mirabellerestaurant.com

Don't be fooled by the location; Mirabelle is one of Austin's best restaurants. Located in Northwest Austin, a neighborhood of town-homes and innocuous, small strip shopping centers, Mirabelle consistently ranks as one of Austin's most creative places to dine. The restaurant is the creation of Michael Vilim and Cathe Dailey, two restaurateurs with credits at some of the city's favorite places. Chef David Apthorpe also has been touted in populous polls by the *Austin Chronicle*. The goal of the kitchen here is to take top-quality regional ingredients and concentrate the flavor using time-honored techniques—for example, the espresso-rubbed venison. While the restaurant evokes the name of Provence in its pitches, it also relies on Southwestern touches and emphasizes the role of wine in its cuisine. Open weekdays for lunch, daily for dinner; closed Sun.

NORTH BY NORTHWEST $$–$$$
10010 Capital of Texas Hwy.
(512) 467-6969
www.nxnwbrew.com
This classy brewpub and restaurant was hailed by the locals as a much-needed addition to what some dub the Silicon Hills region of Austin. The building is sleek and modern, with that "Hill Country" look derived from local limestone and lots of natural light. There is a large bar inside, plus a dining area overlooking the brewery rooms where the House beers are concocted. The menu features grilled meats, fish, salads, sandwiches, and wood-fired pizzas. Open daily for lunch through dinner.

SIENA $$$–$$$$
6203 North Capital of Texas Hwy.
(Loop 360)
(512) 349-7667
www.sienarestaurant.com

The goal here was to create a restaurant evocative of grand dining in Italy, notably northern Italy and the Tuscan countryside, and place it at one of Austin's busiest intersections, Loop 360 and RR 2222. Judging from local reviews, Siena has fulfilled that mission. The decor is enough to make patrons imagine they are dining in an Italian villa, and the menu with its extensive wine list enhances that feeling. A popular restaurant, reservations are recommended. Open Mon through Sat for lunch and nightly for dinner.

NORTH CENTRAL

BLUE STAR CAFETERIA $
4800 Burnet Rd.
(512) 454-STAR (7827)
www.bluestarcafeteria.com
Billed as "uptown comfort food," this hip, modern take on a cafeteria is a far cry from the dull, hot table version of the last century. Along with meatloaf and grilled steak, you will find maple chicken-fried quail, plus pastas, salads (dubbed leafs and oils), sandwiches, and burgers. The first Wed of the month features wine-tastings. Grown-up fare and a kid-friendly menu make it popular with young families. Open Mon through Sat for lunch and dinner; Sat and Sun for brunch.

*FONDA SAN MIGUEL $$$–$$$$
2330 West North Loop Blvd.
(512) 459-4121
www.fondasanmiguel.com
Some of Austin's finest restaurants are found in unexpected places. Fonda San Miguel is situated in an everyday neighborhood, but once you step over the threshold it is easy to assume you are in Old Mexico. This is an accurate rendition of both Mexican architectural style and food under the direction of Chef Miguel Ravago. Designed to evoke the atmosphere of an old hacienda, the entrance to the restaurant, the bar area, is a small courtyard complete with fountain and plants. Inside, the walls are decorated with antiques and ceramics representative of colonial Mexico. This is the place to come to understand the complexities and nuances of classic Mexican cuisine. The menu features regional specialties from throughout the country. The doyenne of Mexican cooking, Diana Kennedy, has held cooking classes here. A good way to sample a variety of fare is to make a reservation for Sunday brunch. This meal evokes the Sunday custom in Mexico, where families sit down for a long, leisurely meal comprising snacks, entrees, desserts, coffee, and long conversation. The restaurant is open daily for dinner and on Sun for brunch. Reservations are recommended.

KIM PHUNG $
7601 North Lamar Blvd.
(512) 451-2464
www.kplamar.com
Asian noodle aficionados tout this humble-looking cafe as one of the best places in town to sample a wide variety of the Vietnamese specialty. There are more than 40 varieties of noodle dishes on the menu. The restaurant is in a strip shopping center, and the surroundings are plain. Open from midmorning to evening daily.

MUSASHINO
SUSHI DOKORO $$–$$$
3407 Greystone Dr.
(512) 795-8593
The extensive menu at this Northwest Austin sushi bar features traditional Tokyo-style offerings and some hybrid American takes on Japanese classics. Sushi enthusiasts hail Musashino as among the best in town. The

atmosphere is quietly elegant. Open daily except Mon for dinner only.

SATAY $$

Shoal Creek Plaza,
3202 West Anderson Lane
(512) 467-6731
www.satayusa.com

The spice trade was a two-way affair, bringing spices from the countries in South Asia to Europe and importing Dutch, British, Spanish, and Portuguese customs to the region. Satay celebrates that trade with a menu that reflects Indonesian, Thai, Vietnamese, and Malaysian dishes. Dutch traders adopted the Indonesian custom of serving a variety of dishes at one course, dubbing it "rijsttafel," or rice table. At Satay it is a great way to share a meal with several friends. The menu also features curries, both Thai and Indian-inspired. Satay is well-known not only for its diverse menu but also its food products, including a peanut sauce served with satay, which are sold in local food stores. The restaurant is in the Shoal Creek Plaza shopping center, but inside the decor is exotic and features artwork from the South China Seas region. Satay's sauces and food products are sold in local grocery stores and online at their website. Open daily for lunch and dinner.

TAJ PALACE $$

6700 Middle Fiskville Rd.
(512) 452-9959
www.tajpalaceaustin.net

Both vegetarians and meat-eaters will find an abundant selection at this traditional Indian restaurant near Highland Mall. The vegetarian specialties include saag paneer, a homemade cheese and spinach sauté, and malai kofta, cheese and vegetable dumplings simmered in a cream and almond sauce. Carnivores can dig into tandoori dishes such as barra kebab, lamb marinated in spiced yogurt and then grilled. The menu also features a variety of curries with varying degrees of heat, and the tandoor oven-baked breads are not to be missed. There is an all-you-can-eat daily lunch buffet. Open for dinner daily.

THREADGILL'S RESTAURANT $$

6416 North Lamar Blvd.
(512) 451-5440
www.threadgills.com

Janis Joplin sang here at the legendary (a much overused word, but justified) restaurant and club founded by Kenneth Threadgill on a mundane section of North Lamar Boulevard. Of course, back when Threadgill got a liquor license for the former Gulf gas station, this was the far northern reaches of Austin, practically a rural outpost. "There's music on the menu" is the boast these days, and the mix of Southern hospitality, music, and homestyle cooking packs 'em in. A second Threadgill's has opened near downtown (see the South Central listings), and both locations offer similar food: old-fashioned favorites such as chicken-fried steak, fried chicken, meat loaf, hamburgers, and lots of veggies. Open daily for lunch and dinner and until midnight on Fri and Sat. (Read more about the Threadgill's legacy in The Music Scene chapter.)

UCHIKO

4200 North Lamar Blvd.
(512) 916-4808
www.uchikoaustin.com

The name means "child of Uchi" in Japanese reflecting its connection to Uchi, Tyson Cole's renowned restaurant in South Central Austin. The aesthetic embraces the Japanese farmhouse in its simplicity of line and tranquility, while the menu reflects Cole's wonderful translation of Japanese dishes with a passion for the best source local and imported product. For example, a cold dish might be maguro sashimi served with local goat cheese, Fuji apple and pumpkin seed oil, while a hot delight might be sake shio salmon with a tomatillo and ponzu sauce. Open daily from 5 p.m. to 10 p.m., 11 p.m. on Fri and Sat. reservations are advised, but walk-ins to the sushi bar are welcome.

NORTH

ANDIAMO $$
2521 Rutland Dr.
(512) 719-3377
www.andiamoitaliano.com
Unfortunately some patrons judge a restaurant by its surroundings or by the decor. While the setting is important to enjoying food, don't let a location in a strip shopping center turn you off. Despite its ritzier neighbors in this part of the city, for example the restaurants at the Domain shopping village, Andiamo's serves up great Italian seasonal food in a charming interior. The menu features locally grown products and the restaurant has received plaudits from local critics and customers. Open Mon through Fri for lunch and dinner. Dinner only on Sat. Closed Sun.

JASPER'S $$
11506 Century Oaks Terrace
(512) 834-4111
www.jaspers-restaurant.com
Jasper's is located in the upscale (there's that word again!) shopping center, the Domain (see the Shopping chapter), and is a sister restaurant to Kent Rathbun's acclaimed Dallas and Houston restaurants. The decor is modern, natural, minimalist cool, while the

menu features "gourmet backyard cuisine." Open daily for lunch and dinner.

NORTHEAST

LA PALAPA $–$$
6640 US 290 East
(512) 459-8729
www.lapalapaaustin.com
The thatched roof is a reminder of La Palapa's roots south of the border—a palapa is a thatched shelter in Mexico. The restaurant has ties to two La Palapas, one in Laredo, the other in Nuevo Laredo, Mexico. Under the thatch, patrons will find several variations on the fajita theme plus enchiladas and Tex-Mex fare. On Sat night the restaurant features an all-you-can-eat fajita bar, and Sun there is an all-you-can-eat lunch buffet. The restaurant's cantina has live music and karaoke on Wed, Fri, and Sat nights. La Palapa is open daily for lunch and dinner

i A favorite late-night dining spot among Austin chefs is T&S Seafood, a Chinese restaurant located in north Austin, 10014 North Lamar Blvd., (512) 339-8434. Open until 1 a.m., except on Tues.

EAST

ARKIE'S GRILL $
4827 East Cesar Chavez St.
(512) 385-2986
www.arkies.weebly.com
This old-fashioned diner in a working-class neighborhood on the edge of East Austin serves breakfast and lunch. The cooking is homestyle with generous servings, especially those luncheon side dishes of home-cooked vegetables. The cooking attracts a wide variety of faithful customers. No credit cards.

CISCO'S $

1511 East Sixth St.
(512) 478-2420

Rudy "Cisco" Cisneros is no longer with us, but his east-side cafe where the likes of President Lyndon B. Johnson took breakfast is still a fixture. The small bakery and restaurant continues to attract the powerful and famous for breakfast or lunch, and the walls are plastered with photos of both current and former politicos. The menu is not extensive; simple Tex-Mex fare is offered along with sweet rolls and cookies from the bakery. Cisco was something of a humorist, so the walls are covered with cartoons, jokes, and even a sign hung on an old gasoline pump that says: Out of Gasoline, We Sell Beans. Cisco's is open for breakfast and lunch only.

EASTSIDE CAFE $-$$

2113 Manor Rd.
(512) 476-5858
www.eastsidecafeaustin.com

Those looking for ways to revive older neighborhoods should visit this cafe east of the Interstate in an area of the city that is a mix of economically depressed businesses and urban pioneers. A small, homey cottage has been turned into a thriving enterprise that includes a large kitchen and herb garden plus a cooking and garden shop. Visitors can stroll through the kitchen garden before or after brunch, lunch, or dinner. The menu is a variety of pastas, enchiladas, grilled fish and chicken dinners, and sandwiches and salads. Brunch begins with mimosas (champagne and orange juice) or poinsettias (champagne and cranberry juice), and then patrons can choose from rich waffle dishes or classics such as eggs Florentine. After dining here, wander through the on-site store, where the house salad dressings are sold plus cookware and

garden tools. Eastside is open daily for lunch and dinner, brunch on the weekends.

EL AZTECA $-$$

2600 East Seventh St.
(512) 477-4701

Wander the Mexican-American neighborhoods of South Texas and you will find family-owned restaurants like El Azteca, where the menu goes beyond the familiar Tex-Mex as served up by many chain restaurants. The Guerra family has run El Azteca for 40 years. Cabrito, spit-roasted baby goat, is a house specialty at this East Austin restaurant, about a mile and a half east of the Interstate. Another popular dish is the barbacoa de cabeza (barbecued beef head), but don't wince until you have sampled the meat; the moist and tender cheek meat is touted as the best for folding inside a soft flour tortilla. El Azteca also serves carne guisada, a slow-simmered stew that is served with flour tortillas for a lick-your-fingers meal, and chicken mole enchiladas, dressed in the rich chocolate-chile mole sauce. The menu also features vegetarian dishes. The walls are hung with portraits honoring Mexican president Benito Juarez and American presidents Abraham Lincoln and John F. Kennedy plus Senator Robert F. Kennedy. The cafe is open for lunch and dinner every day except Sun.

EL CHILE CAFE $-$$

1809 Manor Rd.
(512) 457-9900
www.elchilecafe.com

Created by a couple of sous-chefs from Austin's top flight restaurant Jeffrey's (see Central listing), this cafe serves foods flavored and inspired by interior Mexican fare. The brunch on weekends features dishes like the Yucatecan Huevos Motulenos, a

Chihuahua-inspired steak and eggs, while dinner might offer a Oaxacan mole or an achiote roasted pork. Open daily for lunch and dinner, brunch on the weekends.

HOOVER'S COOKING $–$$
2002 Manor Rd.
(512) 479-5006
www.hooverscooking.com
When you can't get home to Mom and you need a comfort food fix, Hoover's is the place. Hoover's, created by founder Hoover Alexander, an icon on the Austin food scene, doesn't look like much inside or out—it occupies a storefront in a neighborhood where working folks live—but the food is down-home good. Chicken-fried steak is a specialty, as it should be since it occupies a special place in the pantheon of Texas homestyle cooking, plus pork roast, macaroni and cheese, catfish, and barbecued ribs. There is a new Northwest location, also. Open Mon through Fri for lunch and dinner, weekends for breakfast, lunch, and dinner.

J. KELLY'S BARBECUE $
900 East Eleventh St.
(512) 499-0910
www.jkellysbbq.com
"We ain't pizza" the owners of the old Ben's Long Branch Barbecue used to boast, and after 31 years in the neighborhood Ben's proved it. Carrying on that tradition in the same location is the new J. Kelly's, part of the restaurant renaissance in this old Austin neighborhood. Open daily from 11 a.m. to 9 p.m.

JUSTINE'S $$–$$$
4710 East Fifth St.
(512) 385-2900
www.justines1937.com
Hip Austin has jumped the Interstate into East Austin, once the heartland of the city's

Mexican-American barrio. Dubbed a "pitch-perfect French bistro" by the *New York Times*, Justine's focused menu features traditional fare like escargots and coquilles St. Jacques, onion soup and steak frites, all served in a cozy cottage or outdoors on the patio. The neighborhood is transitional with working class homes and old industrial buildings, but the vibe is very *moderne*. Open for dinner Wed through Mon.

NUEVO LEON $–$$
1209 East Seventh St.
(512) 479-0097
www.nuevoleoninaustin.com
Dishes inspired by the family's Northern Mexican roots are served at this colorfully decorated restaurant that has found success in a second Southwest location. Lunch and dinner are served weekdays; breakfast, lunch, and dinner on weekends.

SAM'S BAR-B-CUE $
2000 East Twelfth St.
(512) 478-0378
Sam's biggest fan was famed guitarist Stevie Ray Vaughan, and the walls of this authentic barbecue joint offer homage to the late musician with pictures and newspaper clippings. The menu is simple: brisket, chicken, sausage, and ribs plus spicy beans and potato salad. Take-out is available at this humble neighborhood cafe. Lunch and dinner are served daily. Open to 3 a.m. on Fri and Sat. No credit cards.

SOUTHEAST

CATFISH PARLOUR $$
4705 East Ben White Blvd.
(512) 443-1698
www.catfishparlour.us

For more than two decades Catfish Parlour has been pulling in the crowds for all-you-can-eat catfish and more. Both baked and fried catfish are served, plus fried shrimp and chicken. The menu has Cajun touches with hush puppies and gumbo, plus there is a large salad bar. There is a second location in north Austin. Open daily for lunch and dinner.

MARISCO'S SEAFOOD   **$**
1504 Town Creek Dr.
(512) 462-9119
In search of an authentic neighborhood restaurant? Marisco's is housed in an A-frame building east of I-35 on a busy street. The food here is very cheap and simple; seafood entrees are simply prepared, either boiled, fried, or broiled, but there are Mexican touches such as the vuelve la vida (back to the good life) seafood cocktail, ceviche, and seafood soup. Marisco's is open daily for lunch and dinner.

PATSY'S COWGIRL CAFE   **$–$$**
501 East Ben White Blvd.
(512) 444-2020
www.patsyscafe.com
Famed Austin comic performers Shannon Sedwick and Michael Shelton of Esther's Follies fame (see the Nightlife chapter) own this country cafe on the road to Austin's airport. It is a good place to learn local history since many of the dishes are named after local celebs, many connected to the liberal political scene, like Ann Richards, or of musical fame, like Kinky Friedman. Down-home food daily for lunch and dinner, and live music Tues through Sat.

NIGHTLIFE

Austin's nightlife is so vibrant we had to divide it into two chapters: The second, The Music Scene, is a comprehensive look at the musicians and clubs that have made it possible for Austin to claim the title Live Music Capital of the World. This chapter also lists a great many music and dance venues and takes a look at some of the other spots where residents and visitors gather after the sun goes down.

Austin after dark can be a quiet glass of wine in a subdued, sophisticated setting; or a cold brew among friends at a cheery pub; perhaps a shot of tequila and a salsa dance; a glass of sherry with tapas; a beach blanket bingo movie with Coke and pizza; or an evening of satire with Austin's favorite comedy troupe, Esther's Follies.

One thing that is constant about the Austin nightlife scene is it is evolving and growing by leaps and bounds. The historic center of the city's night scene is, of course, Sixth Street, sometimes called Austin's Bourbon Street. The scene there has evolved over the past three decades. The liveliest nightlife is to be found downtown around Sixth Street, both east and west of Congress; in the Warehouse District/Second Street District just west of Congress Avenue; and south of the river in SoCo, the South Congress Avenue neighborhood, which is a mix of restaurants, bars, cafes, shops, and street theater.

OVERVIEW

Two of the best places to keep track of the city's evolving nightlife are the *Austin Chronicle,* the city's popular alternative newspaper, and the *Austin American-Statesman*'s website, www.austin360.com. We have divided this chapter into Bars; Sports Bars; Brewpubs & Pubs; Wine Bars; Coffeehouses; Comedy Clubs; Dance Clubs & Nightclubs; Gay Nightlife Scene; and Movie Houses. In addition, the Close-up in this chapter is dubbed "Hangouts" and offers a look at the places that Austinites, well, hang out—be it a beer garden where Fido is welcome; a place to watch the sunset; or a party spot where the gang from the office can plot a management coup over nachos and 'ritas.

Austin swings every night, and most clubs and bars are open every day, except where we have noted in the listings. Where there is music, either live or electronic, there is likely to be a cover charge of a few dollars, but rarely do those covers top $10. Bars must stop serving alcohol at 2 a.m. by Texas law, and no one younger than 21 can be served, though some clubs do admit them. Some upscale clubs have a "no one under 25" rule in a bid to keep college students at bay. Driving-while-intoxicated laws are very strict, and bar owners are also held responsible under the state's liquor licensing laws for making sure customers do not overindulge. Taxis cruise the city's major nightlife areas, and patrons who overindulge are wise to take a ride home.

Close-up

Hangouts

The dilemma: It is a restaurant with a great view or vibe, but the food is not really that great. It is a bar, but kids are welcome. And where do you go to find the "real" Austin?

Solution: Check out these hangouts.

KIDS AND DOGS

Austin has a booming population of 24- to 35-year-olds, but some adult gathering spots are just not kid-friendly. How does dad enjoy a brewski while junior munches on chicken fingers?

South Austin, a popular settling spot for upwardly mobile young families, boasts a few solutions for the couple caught in the parent trap. **Freddie's Place,** 1703 South First St., (512) 445-9197, www.freddiesplaceaustin.com, is where we saw a table of rugrats munching on hot dogs while a decidedly hot dog, a pug, sat two tables away being fed off a fork by his "mom." The dads, meanwhile, were sipping one of the 20 or so brands of cold beers offered on the menu. Freddie's has a washer-pitching ring so it's almost a sports bar, but the playscape and sandpit make this a kid-friendly spot. On Sun there is a stupid pet tricks contest and all the dogs get a Freddie's treat, but most of them prefer the fries. There is free brisket during happy hour on Tues, Wed, and Thurs, and there is live music to drown out the squeals of the kids as they fall off the slide. Simply said—a hangout.

Another kid-friendly/Dad-and-Mom-can-be-a-grownup-again place is **Doc's Motorworks,** 1123 South Congress Ave., (512) 448-9181, www.docsaustin.com. This SoCo bar and restaurant is always packed and noisy. (A second location has opened in Southwest Austin.) The video games, shuffleboard and washer pit keep the youngsters and not so youngsters busy. The old metal porch chairs out front on the patio give the place that laid-back, South Austin vibe. Lots of beer varieties on the menu, plus fish tacos, burgers, and finger foods for the young 'uns.

POST-SORORITY BLUES

Remember that Cancun spring break and the wet T-shirt contest? There are a couple of spots in Austin where the ambience hits a memory nerve. **Carlos 'N Charlies** is "proud"

BARS

THE APPLE BAR
120 West Fifth St.
(512) 322-9291

There's a whiff of the cosmopolitan Big City about this place, but its size (small) and the ambience (sophisticated, subdued) make it friendly and relaxing. The apple martini is, of course, a favorite.

THE BELMONT CLUB
305 West Sixth St.
(512) 457-0300
www.thebelmontaustin.com

The inspiration here is Las Vegas/Palm Springs/Rat Pack—leather banquettes, dark wood, and dim lights. The restaurant serves a full menu, but the bar offers snacks late into to be the first north-of-the-border branch of the famous Mexican restaurants created by Carlos Anderson. Located on Lake Austin, 5973 Hiline Rd., (512) 266-1683, www .cncaustin.com, this lively party spot boasts a dock so patrons can drop in after a day on the water. There's music, margaritas, parrots, margaritas, bikini tops, margaritas. You get the picture. Closer to downtown Austin, but also on the water, **Chuy's Hula Hut,** 3825 Lake Austin Blvd., (512) 476-4852, www.hulahut.com, touts its "Mexonesian" menu and vibe, Polynesian meets Mexico. A typical fusion dish is the shrimp pipeline enchilada. Popular for group celebrations, the Hula Hut is a casual bar and restaurant where the menu apologizes for requiring shoes and shirts for "health, sanitation and safety" reasons.

THE REAL AUSTIN HANGOUT

What happened to the old Austin? Does it still exist? Can we go home again? The answer is, yes if you like dark, dingy bars with cheap beer and a great jukebox. The **Deep Eddy Cabaret** (cabaret—that's a joke worthy of the old Austin!) has one of the best jukeboxes in town, featuring Elvis, Otis Reading, even Edith Piaf. The beer is downright cheap and always very cold, brands like Lone Star, Shiner and yes, even Pearl. No liquor. No wine. No cigarettes (thanks to the new Austin), although the walls are a rich brown with years of tobacco smoke. A former grocery store, turned bait shop, then neighborhood bar, this hallowed hangout is near Deep Eddy Pool just west of downtown, 2315 Lake Austin Blvd., (512) 472-0961. Keeping Austin weird is no problem at **Ginny's Little Longhorn Saloon,** a legendary North Austin hangout that *Texas Monthly* put on its Bucket List. As one post on Yelp.com noted, Ginny's is filled with "50 dudes whose only income is playing Santa for one month a year," some of whom show up at 9 a.m. when the bar opens. The small cottage that looks a little like a neighborhood church also attracts lovers of rockabilly music who listen to Dale Watson and the Lonestar Trio performing out in the yard on weekends (bring chairs). Beer only, but Ginny, who presides over the bar, does provide setups and takes charge on Sun when the legendary Chicken S—t Bingo games are held. A live chicken determines the winning numbers by, shall we say, "deposits" on the call board. Ginny's is located at 5434 Burnet Rd., (512) 458-1813.

the night and the patio features live music midweek, plus movies on Mon.

THE BROWN BAR
201 West Eighth St.
(512) 480-8330
www.thebrownbar.com
The renovation of the historic Brown Building in downtown Austin has created not only an architectural gem where lucky loft owners can hang their hat but also has given birth to one of the city's best bars. The Brown Bar with its, yes, brown walls, brown ceilings, and dark furnishings has a comfy, yet sophisticated feel. The clientele is a mix of hip 20-somethings and downtown powerbrokers, lobbyists, and lawyers.

i One way to give new meaning to the term "pub crawl" is to take one of Austin's pedicabs from nightspot to nightspot. Austin Bicycle Cabs operate in the downtown area; (512) 930-8791, www.austinbicyclecabs.com. Others include Roadkill Pedicabs, (512) 300-3784, www.roadkillpedicab.com, and Capital Pedicabs, (512) 448-2227.

☀CEDAR DOOR
Second and Brazos Streets
(512) 473-3712
www.cedardooraustin.com

When they built the Cedar Door, they should have put wheels on the building. That would have saved this cherished neighborhood-style bar some money. The Door has moved, literally, several times—the first location is now occupied by a high-rise on Twelfth Street downtown. Originally a typical Austin cottage-turned-bar, it now lives west of the city's convention center. A popular watering hole for bureaucrats, courthouse lawyers, politicos, and journalists, it has all the hallmarks of an old favorite with mismatched chairs and tables, old prints and posters, a munchie menu, plus bartenders who know their regulars well. Its signature drink is the Mexican martini, a hybrid margarita-martini.

CEDAR STREET COURTYARD
208 West Fourth St.
(512) 495-9669
www.cedarstreetaustin.com

The patio of this hip bar, dubbed "the king of gin joints," is a few steps down from the elevated sidewalks that once served as loading docks in the Warehouse District, east of Congress Avenue. Live music fills the air most nights, often jazz music, and the patio is flanked by two dark, cool indoor bars that

make a nice retreat on steamy nights. The renovated buildings were designed by one of Austin's most noted architects, Sinclair Black.

☀CLUB DEVILLE
900 Red River St.
(512) 457-0900
www.clubdeville.com

The exterior of Club DeVille looks vaguely 1950s, definitely funky, and is certainly Austin, with its mix of patrons, some dressed up for a posh night on the town, others in jeans and sandals. The guys who founded this Sixth Street–district club did so because they needed a place to hold their regular weekend cocktail parties. One of the owners is Mark McKinnon, a former *Daily Texan* editor and former Democratic political consultant who amazed his friends and political cohorts when he signed on with then Governor George W. Bush as a media consultant. One newspaper critic has described the decor as "hanging out in Grandma's basement while she's in Florida." There is a large outdoor, dog-friendly deck equipped with funky furniture and blankets for chilly nights. The bar does get busy on the weekends, but the relaxed atmosphere is constant.

DRISKILL HOTEL LOBBY BAR
604 Brazos St.
(512) 474-5911
www.driskillhotel.com

The venerable Driskill Hotel (see the Hotels chapter) is like an island of style amid the cacophony of Sixth Street. The lobby's cool marble floors and pillars, ornate gilt mirrors, and chairs a person can sink into make for a plush surrounding for the hotel's piano bar. Happy hour draws people in, and they often stay to unwind to the sounds of classic lounge hits played on the grand piano. Later in the evening, folks gather around and even join in as the old romantic hits are played.

THE ELEPHANT ROOM
315 Congress Ave.
(512) 473-2279
www.elephantroom.com
This smoky, dark basement bar in the heart of downtown is a longtime gathering spot for jazz aficionados. For more information about the jazz scene at the Elephant Room, see The Music Scene chapter.

FINN & PORTER
500 East Fourth St.
(512) 493-4900
www.finnandporter.com
This clublike, comfy bar in the Hilton, upstairs from the restaurant of the same name, is a great place for a quiet drink and conversation. Sophisticated, and if you get the munchies there is a sushi bar downstairs.

FIREHOUSE LOUNGE
605 Brazos St.
(512) 478-3473
You might spot a celebrity in this comfortable, but classy lounge built in a restored firehouse; however, the management boasts that everyone is a VIP. Quiet in the early evening, a little more lively as the night progresses with a DJ.

✳FOUR SEASONS LOBBY BAR
98 San Jacinto Blvd.
(512) 478-4500
www.fourseasons.com
The lobby bar of this downtown luxury hotel (see the Hotels chapter) is a great place to people-watch. The patrons here might be top Texas businesspeople, foreign investors, high-tech wizards, top-name

musicians and movie stars, politicians, or media personalities. The bar offers an extensive list of single malt whiskey and cognac plus wine and snacks, none of them inexpensive. In the afternoons, tea and sandwiches are available.

✳HOTEL SAN JOSÉ
1316 South Congress Ave.
(512) 444-7322
www.sanjosehotel.com
The interior garden courtyard of the restored Hotel San José in SoCo is an oasis of calm and inspiration. A wonderful place for an end of the day glass of wine and bite of cheese, perhaps with someone you care about, or simply alone for a moment of reflection.

LUSTRE PEARL BAR
97 Rainey St.
(512) 494-4120
www.lustrepearlaustin.com
The Rainey Street neighborhood, tucked in a corner of downtown south of Cesar Chavez and west of the Interstate, is the latest old central neighborhood to be revived as a nightspot. Lustre Pearl occupies an old house with a large backyard where patrons can relax under the stars, enjoy a conversation of hoola hoop—yep hoola hoop—or play table tennis. There is also a gypsy food trailer out back serving tacos. Other neighborhood-style bars are opening in the area.

MALAGA'S WINE AND TAPAS BAR
440 West Second St.
(512) 236-8020
www.malagatapasbar.com
A fixture in the Warehouse District scene, this wine and tapas bar moved 2 blocks south into the Second Street District. The food is inspired by the wonderful Spanish tradition

of nibbling on savories while drinking sherry or wine. There is a full bar, and noshes can be ordered until 2 a.m. on weekends and midnight during the week and Sun.

MALVERDE
400 West Second St.
(512) 705-0666
www.malverdeaustin.com
With a nod to its downstairs neighbor, La Condesa restaurant where the menu reflects trendy Mexico City cuisine, Malverde offers drinks with a Latin flair—South American liqueurs, wines, beers, and spirits, all served with a view of Austin's dramatic City Hall.

MOLOTOV
719 West Sixth St.
(512) 499-0600
www.molotovlounge.com
The decor as this quasi-neighborhood bar in the loft-sprouting neighborhood near Whole Foods Landmark Store is retro-Communist with hammers and sickles, splashes of red, even a pointer on the website that turns into a flaming Molotov cocktail (the hand-made gasoline bombs were contemptuously named after a Russian official by the Finns after Stalin invaded their country in 1939). But the atmosphere is much more pleasant with the open-to-the-street walls and the upstairs deck decorated with some very non-Commie, large comic-style portraits of bikini-wearing girls. There is also a karaoke night where it is doubtful you will hear the *Internationale,* the Communist workers' anthem.

PECHE
208 West Fourth St.
(512) 495-9669
www.pecheaustin.com
With the legalization of absinthe, often called the Green Fairy, in 2007 this potent, herbal distillation is back on bar menus. Peche highlights the historic drink that often inspired the artists and writers of 19th-century Paris.

STAR BAR
600 West Sixth St.
(512) 477-8550
Just beyond the downtown Warehouse District, West Sixth Street has developed into one of the hottest spot in town for new restaurants and bars. Star Bar once was a paint shop, but the '50s-style building is now a very hip place to be seen and to watch Austin's 20-something set at play. The store's big plate-glass window looks out on a small street-side patio, while inside the low ceiling and retro furnishings give the place an intimate, jazzy sort of feel.

TOWNHOUSE
303 West Fifth St.
(512) 472-5288
www.infusedhouse.com
This warehouse district bar serves classic cocktails plus ingenious new concoctions made from spirits infused by exotic flavors, spices, herbs, and even rose petals.

SPORTS BARS

In addition to the sports bars listed here, check the Brewpub section, since many local pubs also turn on the TV when there is a hot sports event.

AUSSIE'S VOLLEYBAR AND GRILL
306 Barton Springs Rd.
(512) 480-0952
www.aussiesbar.com
Volleyball takes center stage at this South Central Austin bar and grill (see the

Restaurants chapter), but sports enthusiasts also gather at the bar to watch sporting events on several television sets. A favorite drink is, of course, Foster's—the national beer of Australia, mate.

BLACK SHEEP LODGE
2108 South Lamar Blvd.
(512) 707-2744
www.blacksheeplodge.com

A combo neighborhood bar, hamburger joint, and sports bar, the Black Sheep has 20 beers on tap, a streetfront deck, pub grub like fried pickles and jalapeños, burgers and hot dogs, plus plenty of screens tuned to the sports channels.

COMMON INTEREST
8440 Burnet Rd.
(512) 453-6796
www.ciaustin.com

This sports bar in North Central Austin boats 20 big screens, plus a paintball karaoke stage where patrons can vent their frustrations if their team loses.

DIRTY MARTIN'S PLACE
2808 Guadalupe St.
(512) 477-3173
www.dirtymartins.com

Faithful Longhorn fans have been flocking here since the 1920s, long before HDTV, when it was known as Martin's "Kumback." Classic burgers and fries are on the menu for fans watching the big game inside or out on the patio. Dirty's is open daily for lunch and dinner.

LEGEND'S
8901 Business Park Dr.
(512) 343-0888

Housed in the Holiday Inn in Northwest Austin, Legend's focus is simply sports, cold beer,

and all-American fare. This is the quintessential sports bar: The 22 televisions are always tuned to sports, and the menu features food like hamburgers and steaks. Occasionally there is a cover charge when special sports broadcasts are scheduled.

SHOAL CREEK SALOON AND SPORTS PARLOR
909 North Lamar Blvd.
(512) 477-0600

New Orleans Saints fans are drawn to this Central Austin sports bar, perhaps because the pub's menu features Cajun dishes like gumbo and fried catfish.

THE TAVERN
922 West Twelfth St.
(512) 320-8377
www.austintavern.com

Opened in 1916 as a grocery store on what was then the edge of the city, the building has had several incarnations including, legend has it, serving as home to a brothel. After Prohibition, the Tavern came into its current life and is now a popular place for friends to gather for a burger, a game of pool, or a beer or two during a football game on the big screen.

WAREHOUSE SALOON & BILLIARDS
509 East Ben White Blvd.
(512) 443-8799
www.warehousesaloon.com

This large pool hall is also home to a sports bar where patrons can watch regularly televised events or pay-for-view specials. In addition to 25 tables, the Warehouse also offers video games, pinball, and shuffleboard.

BREWPUBS & PUBS

In 1993 the Texas Legislature permitted homemade brew products to be sold in public bars, despite the opposition of the big breweries and beer distributors. Microbreweries are as fashionable as coffeehouses these days.

B. D. RILEY'S PUB
204 East Sixth St.
(512) 494-1335
www.bdrileys.com

This is a real Irish pub that was built in Dublin and shipped over to Austin by owner John Erwin, whose grandmother, Bessie D. Riley, gave her name to the joint. Beer here is served in Imperial pints for two-fisted drinkers, and the pub grub is some of the best in Texas. In addition to being home of the Austin branch of the Notre Dame club, Riley's offers music, football nights, and pub quiz nights, a popular tradition in the old country.

i The Southwest Brewing News (512-443-3607, 800-474-7291; www.brewingnews.com/southwest) publishes the latest brew news in the Southwest. Features on new pubs, awards, and taste tests are included in the paper, which can be found in several Austin pubs.

THE BLIND PIG PUB
317 East Sixth St.
(512) 472-0809
www.theblindpigpub.com

Thirty varieties of beer and ale are offered at this pub-cum-sports bar on Sixth Street. The pub has a small beer garden, Foosball, and pool tables, plus big-screen televisions for watching sports events.

COPPER TANK BREWING COMPANY
514 Trinity St.
(512) 478-8444
www.coppertankaustin.com

This Sixth Street brewpub attracts a diverse crowd, including a large college contingent and sports fans, drawn by the bank of big-screen televisions. Local brewery critics give Copper Tank high marks for its brews like Big Dog Brown Ale and Firehouse Stout. Happy hour on Wed draws a large crowd, and the bar is popular among downtown workers who want a cold one on hot days.

THE CROWN & ANCHOR
2911 San Jacinto Blvd.
(512) 322-9168
www.crownandanchorpub.com

This UT campus–area pub is popular among students and perennial campus habitués. The aim here is to re-create an English pub, hence the dartboards and the wide selection of beers. Patrons can play pinball, Foosball, and video games and order a burger if they get hungry after a lively game. In balmy weather, patrons can enjoy a beer on the patio.

✳THE DOG & DUCK PUB
406 West Seventeenth St.
(512) 479-0598
www.dogandduckpub.com

This Central Austin bar is as close as Austin gets to an authentic English pub. The food here reflects a mix of English pub grub and popular American dishes, and the bar offers, like any English pub, a wide variety of beers on tap and in bottles.

THE DRAUGHT HORSE PUB AND BREWERY
4112 Medical Pkwy.
(512) 452-MALT
www.draughthorse.com

From the outside it looks like a reproduction of an English country town pub. Inside, the cozy atmosphere attracts a loyal clientele. In addition to stocking 80 different beer brands, the pub has been experimenting with several homemade brews.

FADÓ IRISH PUB
214 West Fourth St.
(512) 457-0172
www.fadoirishpub.com
Stepping into this Irish pub in the downtown Warehouse District, you almost expect to see John Wayne and Maureen O'Hara at the next table. It's not because the place looks like an old Irish pub, but because it looks more like the Hollywood-set version of an Irish pub. In addition to a menu of Irish-inspired dishes, the bar offers a wide selection of beer and whiskey, and the televisions in the bar tune in to satellite transmissions of rugby games, Gaelic football, hurling, and other interesting sports.

LOVEJOY'S TAP ROOM AND BREWERY
604 Neches St.
(512) 477-1268
The tables here are created from manhole covers, a coffin serves as a coffee table, and the walls are covered with the work of local artists. The seating ranges from comfy couches to tables and chairs where patrons can enjoy bar food and sample an extensive menu of bottled beers plus several homemade brews. A house specialty is Insomnia Coffee Stout, a strong brew made with coffee.

MAGGIE MAE'S
512 Trinity St.
(512) 478-8541
www.maggiemaesaustin.com
This well-known Sixth Street bar has grown with the years from a narrow, single-room pub noted for its live-music offerings (see The Music Scene chapter) to a major presence in the downtown nightlife scene. The pub has taken over adjacent buildings and has a rooftop patio for Sixth Street viewing.

MOTHER EGAN'S IRISH PUB
715 West Sixth St.
(512) 478-7747
www.motheregansirishpub.com
Imperial pints and frozen margaritas—no place but Texas! Mother Egan's has the feel of an Irish pub, with its wooden floors, cozy nooks, and dark paneled walls, but it also has an outdoor deck and large back room where patrons gather for bluegrass Sunday brunches, Celtic music, pub trivia games, and fish-n-chips nights—buy one, get one free.

NORTH BY NORTHWEST RESTAURANT AND BREWERY
10010 North Capital of Texas Hwy.
(512) 467-6969
www.nxnwbrew.com
Located just behind the Gateway Shopping Center in northwest Austin, this sleek, sophisticated restaurant and bar features several seasonal brews made on the premises. The glass-and-stone surroundings reflect the quality of the food and the on-premises brews. (See the Restaurants chapter.) North by Northwest also offers beer to go.

i Texas beers and barbecue are legend; Texas wines have made their way onto top flight menus; and, not to be outdone, Texas vodka is a favorite. Look for Tito's Handmade Vodka on the bar menu. It is made in Austin in the state's "first legal distillery" and has won industry awards, www.titos-vodka .com.

OLD PECAN STREET ALE HOUSE
& SOCCER BAR
310 East Sixth St.
(512) 474-6722

The name says it all here at this cozy Sixth Street alley pub, where the emphasis is on soccer. It serves a variety of beers, mixed drinks, and snacks in an old 19th-century building with limestone walls and well-worn floors, cozy seating, and dimmed lighting. The pub's television sets feature national and international soccer games.

OPAL DIVINE'S FREEHOUSE
700 West Sixth St.
(512) 477-3308
www.opaldivines.com

The original Opal's is housed in an old stone building on Sixth Street, next door to Austin's 24-hour deli, Katz's. This pub is named in honor of the owner's ancestor, who apparently enjoyed the good life as represented by pub food, a wide selection of single malt whiskies, and a large variety of beers. Two additional Opal's have opened, one at 3601 South Congress Ave. (512-707-0237) and the other at 12709 North MoPac (512-733-5353). All 3 have both indoor and outdoor seating and offer live music several nights a week.

✳SCHOLZ GARTEN
1607 San Jacinto Blvd.
(512) 474-1958
www.scholzgarten.net

This old German beer garden is many things to many people. In addition to being a popular restaurant (see the Restaurants chapter), a historical landmark, a favorite postgame gathering spot for University of Texas sports fans, and a political watering hole, the old stage in the shaded garden is also a music venue. A variety of live music is offered here.

Check local listings in the *Austin Chronicle* and the *Austin American-Statesman*.

SCOOT INN
1308 East Fourth St.
(512) 478-6200
www.scoot-inn.com

This East Austin beer garden lays claim to being the oldest bar in Austin. Back in 1871, wagoneers drove their loads to the railroad yard and cooled off with a beer in the saloon aside the tracks. The bar remained a working man's hangout and now the joint has been revived as a cool hangout for central city dwellers and visitors. A sign of the times: Capital Metro light rail now runs along the tracks.

UNCLE BILLY'S BREW & QUE
1530 Barton Springs Rd.
(512) 476-0100
www.unclebillysaustin.com

Brian Peters is a home brewer turned brewmaster with experience gathered at several Austin micro-breweries. Now he is serving up a wide variety of handcrafted beers—his own and other popular local beers—at this South Central Austin barbecue joint-hangout. The outdoor deck is popular and the menu features beer-appropriate noshes like barbecue sliders and all-you-can-eat 'que on Mon. The take-out menu even offers Peters' handcrafted jugs of brew. A second location on Lake Travis has opened.

WINE BARS

CORK AND CO.
308 Congress Ave.
(512) 474-2675
www.corkandco.com

A welcome addition to the downtown nightlife scene, this wine bar has an affordable happy hour and offers wine tastings for groups, small and large, plus classes in wine selection. There is also a retail shop on the premises.

CRU
238 West Second St.
(512) 472-9463
www.cruwinebar.com
Several businesses in the Second Street District are Austin branches of Dallas and Houston ventures, as is Cru, a popular wine bar. In addition to flights of wine, the bar and cafe offers "sharing plates" that can be paired with specific flights for optimum taste pleasure.

HOUSE WINE
408 Josephine St.
(512) 322-5210
www.housewineaustin.com
Tucked in a cottage behind the P. Terry's hamburger stand at the corner of Barton Springs Road and South Lamar Boulevard, and just a couple of blocks south of Lady Bird Lake is a neighborhood abuzz with a downtown vibe, this cozy wine bar offers weekly tastings, light noshes, and a front porch where patrons can watch neighborhood happenings and listen to live music.

VINO AND VINO
4119 Guadalupe St.
(512) 465-9282
www.vinovinotx.com
This Hyde Park wine bar has an Austin vibe, thanks to its location and the neighborhood clientele. The cafe offers a fresh menu, salads and soups, plus sandwiches and light dishes that might include beef carpaccio, salmon gravlax, vegetable tian, and cheese plates. There are also several light and delicious desserts.

Sixth Street

Long before Jell-O shots and nachos became a staple of the college diet, Austin's Sixth Street was a social hub of the city. When Austinites refer to Sixth Street, they generally mean the stretch of downtown street that runs west from I-35 to Congress Avenue. On any given weekend there are likely to be 20,000 patrons cruising the 7-block area, where more than 30 bars try to entice them with games, shots, Imperial pints, frozen margaritas, music, and tons of nachos. Many of the bars reinvent themselves with fierce regularity, changing names and decor to fit the fad of the moment.

Some of the venerable Sixth Street institutions remain amid the proliferation of shot bars and sports pubs, notably Esther's Follies (see Comedy Clubs in this chapter) is home to the city's favorite comedy troupe. The street is also popular on holiday nights like Mardi Gras, Halloween, and New Year's Eve.

COFFEEHOUSES

Austin's coffeehouses reflect their surroundings and the city's artistic, kooky, innovative population. Some are funky neighborhood hangouts, others serve as showplaces for local artists, while still others are favored by political activists.

AUSTIN JAVA COMPANY
1206 Parkway at Twelfth and Lamar
(512) 476-1829
www.austinjava.com

Austin Java Company has a relaxed feel, with picnic tables on the deck outside for those who enjoy a little sunshine with their coffee. Among the house specialties here are Vietnamese coffee, mocha shakes, and mocha chinos, little mocha lattes. The cafe has expanded its menu from snacks and pastries and now serves sandwiches, salads, and pasta dishes. Open daily for breakfast, lunch, and dinner. The coffeehouse also offers a late-night menu until 4 a.m. on weekends. There are four other locations in the city, including one in City Hall.

BOULDIN CREEK COFFEE HOUSE
& CAFE
1501 South First St.
(512) 416-1601
www.bouldincreek.com

This south-of-the-river coffeehouse caters to the local neighborhoods that are a mix of old and new Austin. The bright green exterior is in step with this part of the city where old Austin funky meets new Austin gentry. Inside old Austin hippie artists lucky enough to have hung on to their once modest, now high-priced homes rub shoulders with techies and lawyers. The cafe also offers an all-day vegetarian menu and has a fun website.

CAFE MUNDI
1704 East Fifth St.
(512) 236-8034
www.cafemundi.com

The *Austin Chronicle*, which is almost mandatory reading in the city's coffeehouses, has described Cafe Mundi as Parisianlike and an oasis. There is a quirkiness about this quiet eastside coffeehouse that sits amidst a small arts district along the abandoned railroad tracks in the city's eastside barrio, near downtown. The menu features the usual wide variety of coffees, chais and teas, plus breakfast, sandwiches, and salads. Small music groups also perform in the garden; the schedule is posted on the cafe's website.

CRESCENT CITY BEIGNETS
1211 West Sixth St.
(512) 472-9622

Tucked back from the busy street, this small restaurant is open from early morning to late evening, serving Cajun specialties in addition to those air-filled beignets coated in powdery sugar that are a hallmark of life in New Orleans. The coffee menu also includes that chicory-coffee blend that is a natural accompaniment.

i Many of Austin's coffeehouses are pet-friendly, particularly those with outdoor decks. For a list of where Fido can curl up with a bowl of latte, check out www.dogfriendly.com. Increasingly, Austin restaurants and bars with outdoor spaces are welcoming well-behaved leashed dogs; call ahead first.

*DOLCE VITA GELATO AND
ESPRESSO BAR
4222 Duval St.
(512) 323-2686

The name means "the sweet life," and there are layers of meaning to that phrase for this Hyde Park–area coffeehouse. The menu is rich with sweets, many with an Italian flavor—gelato, sorbet, granitas, tiramisu, cannoli—and there is also a relaxed, easy-living

European atmosphere at this neighborhood cafe. The menu also features Italian sodas, coffees, a full bar, and a variety of grappas. Dolce Vita opens early for breakfast and stays open late for after-theater snacks.

FLIGHT PATH COFFEEHOUSE
5011 Duval St.
(512) 458-4472
www.flightpathcoffeehouse.com
Old Austin hands know that this small, neighborhood coffeehouse was once in the flight path for planes landing at what used to be the city's main airport, Robert Mueller Airport. Located in the heart of the Hyde Park neighborhood at Fifty-first Street and Duval, the Flight Path is a popular gathering spot for families, students, and artists, some of whom exhibit their work here.

FLIPNOTICS
1601 Barton Springs Rd.
(512) 480-8646
www.flipnotics.com
If the oversize cafe au lait doesn't make you flip for Flipnotics, nothing will. It is made from whole milk and condensed milk and served in a cup as big as a soup bowl. Not far from Zilker Park (see the Parks & Recreation and Attractions chapters). Flipnotics offers a light menu of sandwiches, muffins and bagels, wine, beer, and coffee, of course. In the evening, local musicians often perform. It is open until midnight every night except Sun, when it closes at 11 p.m.

GREEN MUSE
519 West Oltorf St.
(512) 912-7789
There is a relaxed, laid-back feel to this South Austin java joint not far from the St. Edward's University campus. The exterior is decorated with murals; inside, the couches, bookcases, and assorted tables give the place a true coffeehouse aura—dare we say groovy? There is a patio out back. Light snacks are on the menu. Given its location near St. Ed's, it is busy in the morning. The coffeehouse is open daily and closes at midnight Sun through Thurs, and 1 a.m. on weekends.

JO'S COFFEE
1300 South Congress Ave.
(512) 441-3627
www.joscoffee.com
Jo's is a true neighborhood hangout in SoCo where the locals gather to gossip, read, or hang out. The staff at Jo's is tuned into neighborhood happenings and art events. They even conjure up special happenings like the Average Jo's Fashion Show, held in the neighboring Hotel San José (see the Hotels chapter) parking lot, featuring retro chic clothes and aimed at raising money for animal rescue groups. Success has led to the opening of a second location in the Second Street District at 242 West Second St. (512-469-9003).

LITTLE CITY ESPRESSO BAR AND CAFE
916 Congress Ave.
(512) 476-CITY
www.littlecity.com
Just a few blocks from the capitol, Little City has helped give new meaning to the word *avenue*. Little City was among the first downtown cafes to promote the idea of putting tables and chairs on the wide sidewalks that line the city's main street. The cafe serves coffee, tea, juices, granitas, breakfast items like bagels and muffins, and lunch and snack food, including sandwiches and savory pastries. Little City is open until midnight during the week, until 1 a.m. on Fri and Sat, and until 9 p.m. on Sun.

MOJO'S DAILY GRIND
2714 Guadalupe St.
(512) 477-6656

A coffee shop with a bohemian bent, Mojo's is popular with UT students and campus habitués. The 19th-century-home-turned-cafe is open 24 hours daily except Sun. The purple neon lights and the giant coffee mug sign mark the spot. Mojo's prides itself on presenting the work of cutting-edge, and sometimes controversial, artists working in a variety of mediums including photography, painting, and collage. There are also poetry events held at the cafe; check the listings section of the *Austin Chronicle*. The popular house drink is the Iced Mojo, a cold, creamy brew. Munchie offerings include coffeehouse-style eggs steamed at the espresso machine, bagels, muffins, oatmeal, pastries, and empanadas. Beer is also served at Mojo's.

MOZART'S COFFEE ROASTERS
3825 Lake Austin Blvd.
(512) 477-2900
www.mozartscoffee.com

This West Austin cafe, which boasts a large deck overlooking Lake Austin, is a good spot for a late-afternoon cappuccino or a late-night espresso. On Wed and Sat local artists perform contemporary music under the stars on the deck, which seats 350 people. In addition to an extensive coffee bar menu, the cafe also serves iced, herbal, flavored, and chai (soy-based) teas, granitas, Italian soda, pastries, and snacks. There is a juice bar on the premises as well as a bookstore specializing in arts, travel, and literature. Mozart's also roasts and sells a variety of coffee beans. Mozart's is open until midnight during the week and on Sun, 1 a.m. on Fri and Sat.

QUACK'S 43RD STREET BAKERY
411 East Forty-third St.
(512) 453-3399
www.quacksbakery.com

Quack's, as the UT students call it, is lively and sometimes noisy at night. Quack's offers work areas, however, for aspiring poets and playwrights to plug in their laptops. The cafe hosts a weekly poetry workshop under the auspices of Austin Poets At Large (APAL). The work of local artists is featured on the walls, and classical music plays in the background. Serving breakfast, lunch, and late-night snacks. Quack's is open until 11 p.m. daily.

✳RUTA MAYA COFFEE COMPANY
3601 South Congress Ave.
(512) 707-9637
www.rutamaya.net

If there was a single coffeehouse that captured the mood and spirit of Austin, it was Ruta Maya, which occupied an old building in the heart of the warehouse district west of Congress Avenue in downtown Austin. The patrons here were a true Austin mix, and on any given night you could see young professionals, aging hippies, Jack Kerouac wannabes, even a spinning yogi chanting mantras on a rotating platform.

Why do we speak in the past tense? Because Ruta Maya closed down at its old location in early 2002, and Austinites held their breath to see if it would maintain its fabled ambience at a new location near St. Edwards University. Some of the funkiness has gone, but the new industrial-style building offers lots of wallspace for art and space for cultural and political gatherings. In fact, then-Vermont Governor Howard Dean held a fund-raiser here in October 2003.

Ruta Maya serves coffees produced in Latin America. In 1990 the company was formed to help Latin American farmers sell their products and make a fair return. Ruta Maya Negra Lager Beer, brewed in El Salvador at La Constancia Brewery, is sold at the coffeehouse. In addition to coffee, the cafe serves soups and snacks. There are regular music events and poetry readings, plus yoga and wellness programs. The walls of the coffeehouse are covered in local artwork and notices on all manner of cultural and political events. Ruta Maya is open until 2 a.m. on weekends and 1 a.m. during the week and on Sun.

> **i** Penalties for driving under the influence are high in Texas, so consider using Square Patrol, (512) R-U-DRUNK (783-7865), www.square patrol.com, to get you home or back to your hotel. The patrol arrives with a folding moped that is stored in your trunk, the driver takes you home, unfolds his moped, and buzzes back to headquarters. Donations are accepted by the nonprofit. On holidays like Halloween and New Year's Eve when Sixth Street is packed, www.austinsoberride .com, (512) 657-2999, offers free cab rides.

SARADORA'S COFFEEHOUSE
& EMPORIUM
101 East Main St., Round Rock
(512) 310-1200
Not all the coffeehouse action is in Austin. This Round Rock cafe is housed in an old building in the heart of the town's historic district. Local artists sell their jewelry and artwork here, and there is live music several nights a week. Saradora's is open until 10 p.m. during the week and midnight on Fri and Sat, and until 6 p.m. on Sun.

SPIDER HOUSE
2908 Fruth St.
(512) 480-9562
www.spiderhousecafe.com
This coffeehouse just north of the University of Texas campus is packed with old stuff—not really antiques and not really junk, just old stuff like Christmas lights and soft drink machines, old radios, and a miscellany of chairs and tables. The large outdoor deck is a stage for local musicians. Late-night noshes include tamales and pasta dishes.

COMEDY CLUBS

Austin is well known as a funny place—especially when the State Legislature is in session. There is not a session that goes by without some Texas legislator making national headlines for offering one wacky proposal or another.

Visitors will find political humor is high on the agenda at local comedy outposts, notably Esther's Follies, a longtime Austin troupe that takes aim at both local and national politicians. There are only a handful of nightclubs dedicated to comedy alone, but a few of the city's live music venues also take a comedy break now and then. That list expands greatly during the annual Big Stinkin' International Improv and Sketch Comedy festival held in Apr each year (see the Annual Events & Festivals chapter).

CAPITOL CITY COMEDY CLUB
8120 Research Blvd.
(512) 467-2333
www.capcitycomedy.com
This Northwest Austin club has pulled in some of the big names in comedy, including Ellen DeGeneres, Jeff Foxworthy, and Bobcat Goldthwait. While nationally known comics appear on Fri and Sat nights, up-and-coming

comedians, including local talent, are featured on other nights.

*ESTHER'S FOLLIES/ESTHER'S POOL
525 East Sixth St.
(512) 320-0553
www.esthersfollies.com
Like Barton Springs and the old Armadillo World Headquarters, Esther's Follies is part of the fabric of Austin. The comedy troupe performs every Thurs, Fri, and Sat at Esther's Pool on Sixth Street on a stage where the backdrop is three floor-to-ceiling windows looking out on the street. The audience can watch the antics of the troupe and their interactions with the passersby on Sixth Street.

Esther's is named for Esther Williams, the actress and water ballet artist who made all those swimming movies in the 1950s. The group took that name in the 1970s when they performed skits between music sets at another legendary spot, Liberty Lunch. Founders Michael Shelton and Shannon Sedwick (he is co-owner of Esther's and the announcer, she is a star of the troupe and co-owner) say they chose the name because the troupe would perform in the Texas heat wearing swimsuits and get cooled by the stage sprinklers.

Satire and outrageous, campy comedy are the troupe's mainstays. National and local politicians are spoofed, caricatured, and mimicked. The show changes routines regularly and puts on special holiday shows, so repeat visitors are never disappointed. On Fri and Sat it is wise to arrive early to ensure a seat. Performances are at 8 p.m. on Thurs and 8 p.m. and 10 p.m. Fri and Sat. Tickets are $18 for students, seniors, and military on weeknights, $20 open seating general admission, $27 online for reserved seats.

THE HIDEOUT
617 Congress Ave.
(512) HIDE-OUT
www.hideouttheatre.com
There are two theater stages where everything from comedy classes to ghost tours are offered. Improv and parody nights are popular also.

VELVEETA ROOM
521 East Sixth St.
(512) 469-9116
www.thevelveetaroom.com
If Esther's Follies is the jewel in the crown of the Austin comedy scene, then the Velveeta Room is the jester. Housed on Sixth Street, next door to Esther's Pool, local and visiting comic talent try out some of their more outrageous and irreverent routines here. Sketches and improvisations are performed Thurs, Fri, and Sat nights. There is a $6 admission charge.

DANCE CLUBS & NIGHTCLUBS

Whether it is the Texas two-step, salsa, merengue, swing, even the Lindy hop, there is a club in Austin where dancers can strut their stuff. Even disco, heaven forbid, is alive and well as the 20-something crowd explores retro fashions. Those looking for a Texas experience should consider visiting one of the city's country dance spots, notably the Broken Spoke, which has been described as the best example of a Texas honky-tonk in Austin. But don't miss out on another important cultural experience: dancing to the Latino beat, ranging from tango to Tejano.

THE 311 CLUB
311 East Sixth St.
(512) 477-1630
An old favorite on Sixth Street featuring blues music. The old-style bar attracts a

diverse crowd, and there are open-mic nights when the regulars can sing the blues.

> **i** Want to experience a real Texas country dance hall? Head for The Coupland Dance Hall (512-856-2226; www.couplanddancehall.com) on Highway 95 between Taylor and Elgin, east of Austin. On weekends this old dance hall is "just a two-step back in time," as its slogan says.

ATOMIC CAFE
705 Red River St.
(512) 457-0644
The outside of this downtown nightclub looks as grungy as the inside, but that is part of its charm for the metalhead fans who gather here. The club serves up hard rock nightly, and there are special fetish nights for those who want to show off their chains, piercings, and tattoos.

AZUCAR
Fourth and Colorado Streets
(512) 478-5650
Salsa and merengue continue to be hot trends on the Austin dance scene. This downtown club touts itself as "the only 100 percent salsa and merengue club" in Austin. Salsa is not only an exotic way to get a great physical workout, it can be a good opportunity to spot some of the city's "stars," since many of the Hollywood types enjoy a salsa workout when they are in town, notably film star Sandra Bullock.

✳BROKEN SPOKE
3201 South Lamar Blvd.
(512) 442-6189
www.brokenspokeaustintx.com

An original honky-tonk that merits the description "legendary" (hence its inclusion in The Music Scene chapter), the Spoke is also a great place to dance a little, drink a little, and eat a lot. There is live music here Tues through Sat, and the cover charges vary. The low ceiling, the tall men in big hats, and the wooden dance floor give this place the feel of an authentic Texas roadhouse. No visit to Austin should end without dropping by the Spoke in South Austin for a longneck.

CLUB CARNAVAL
2237 East Riverside Dr.
(512) 444-6396
Southeast of downtown, along East Riverside Drive, there are several authentic Hispanic nightclubs that celebrate Mexican-American and Latin dance traditions. Club Carnaval is noted for its *norteño* dances, which originated in Northern Mexico and flourish in South Texas. Male dancers don Western wear, including large belt buckles, tight pressed jeans, and white cowboy hats, while the women dance in full skirts or jeans and Western shirts. Some of the top names in *norteño* music play here in a setting that has an Aztec motif. In addition to *norteño* music, the club also features salsa, Tejano, merengue, and cumbia music. Cover charges vary.

COPA BAR AND GRILL
217 Congress Ave.
(512) 479-5002
www.copabarandgrill.com
During the daytime, Copa is a lunchtime spot with a Tex-Mex flavor, but at night it turns into a nightclub swinging to a Latin beat. The Copa also offers salsa lessons several times a week. Patrons tend be to "dressy" in their attire and there is a cover fee.

DESPERADO'S
9515 North Lamar Blvd.
(512) 834-2640

There are several different kinds of Latino music, but the homegrown kind here in Texas is called Tejano—the state was, after all, named "Tejas" when it was part of Mexico. The music has a fast-paced swing, a sort of cross between country and salsa. The outfit of choice celebrates the "vaquero," the northern Mexican cowboy whose dress influenced cowboys north of the border. Both men and women wear cowboy boots and the men wear cowboy hats, while the women wear either Western-style skirts or jeans. This 11,000-square-foot dance club has three full-service bars.

> **i** The Capital City Murder Mystery Theatre appears at various restaurants around Austin offering a dinner theater experience. The group also performs at private parties. Call (512) 404-9123 or visit www.capcitymystery.com for more information.

EL BORINQUEN
2728 South Congress Ave.
(512) 447-5087

This tiny restaurant and bar re-creates the atmosphere of Old San Juan. The food and drinks are Puerto Rican, as are many of the customers, but the dance floor also draws a diverse crowd that enjoys dancing to salsa and merengue sounds on Fri and Sat nights.

ELYSIUM
704 Red River St.
(512) 474-2285
www.elysiumonline.net

One of the city's liveliest dance clubs. Theme nights are popular here, including Regression Night on Sun when the '80s are celebrated. The club also hosts fashion shows.

FLAMINGO CANTINA
515 East Sixth St.
(512) 494-9336
www.flamingocantina.com

The Flamingo gets consistently good reviews for the bands that it books, and the club also offers rock and reggae that keep the place packed on weekends. The decor and the sounds are designed to evoke the Caribbean with a grass-thatched roof over the stage and pictures of Bob Marley on the walls. There is an upstairs open-air deck where you can dance under the stars.

MIGUEL'S LA BODEGA
415 Colorado St.
(512) 472-2369

Miguel's is the hot spot in the downtown Warehouse District for the Latino dance scene. Salsa and merengue rule here, and the uninitiated can take midweek lessons on the premises. Live bands on the weekends provide a constant salsa beat, and just to make sure you stay in a south-of-the-border mood, the club serves a Latino menu.

PARADOX
311 East Fifth St.
(512) 469-7615

The *Austin Chronicle* calls this Sixth Street–area club the "Wal-Mart of dance clubs," suggesting it is both popular and cheap. It is always packed on the weekends and is popular with the college crowd. Paradox also stays open after the bars close at 2 a.m. The Wal-Mart designation aside, there is a dress code here (primarily on Fri and Sat). Guys may get turned away at the door if their jeans are too ragged or their T-shirts have gaping holes.

SPEAKEASY
412 Congress Ave.
(512) 476-8017
www.speakeasy.com
Listed in The Music Scene chapter, Speakeasy is also a classy spot for a martini or glass of wine. Housed in one of Congress Avenue's older buildings, recently a used appliance store, the renovation has produced one of the fancier nightspots. A mezzanine theme, hence the emphasis on jazz and gin.

TEJANO RANCH
7601 North Lamar Blvd.
(512) 834-2640
www.tejanoranchaustin.com
Tejano music is designed for dancing, and some of the biggest acts in the genre appear at this North Austin nightclub, notably on the weekends. The crowd here is generally older than 30 and familiar with the Tejano scene. The club has a South Texas atmosphere with neon mustangs outside and a large Selena mural inside, plus the chairs are covered in cowhide.

GAY NIGHTLIFE SCENE

The gay nightlife scene in Austin seems to divide into two categories—sophisticated downtown clubs where beautiful people gather and country swing clubs. However, there are also a couple of neighborhood bars that offer relaxing atmosphere after work hours.

1920'S CLUB
918 Congress Ave.
(512) 479-7979

This Congress Avenue club, 3 blocks south of the capitol, has a '20s theme. Dubbed a "speakeasy," the club features jazz music and martinis, but there is also a food menu.

'BOUT TIME
9601 North I-35
(512) 832-5339
Gay patrons, both men and women, are attracted to this nightclub that aims for a neighborhood tavern theme, dubbed "Cheers for queers," by the *Chronicle*. Indoors there are pool tables and darts, while outdoors there are sand volleyball courts. The bar also features a big-screen television and video games.

BOYZ CELLAR
213 West Fourth St.
(512) 479-8482
This warehouse district club has two bars and a large dance floor. The club also features exotic dancers, movie nights, and special musical events.

CHAIN DRIVE
504 Willow St.
(512) 480-9017
www.chain-drive.com
This Central Austin bar is described as Austin's only "leather bar," but this is soft and cuddly leather. Chain Drive is headquarters for a group calling itself the Heart of Texas Bears, a self-described social group for masculine, bearded, and/or hairy gay men and their admirers. The bar has pool tables and a small dance floor and is open daily from early afternoon until 2 a.m.

CHARLIE'S
1301 Lavaca St.
(512) 474-6481
www.charliesaustin.com

A longtime fixture on the gay scene, Charlie's is noted for its clubby atmosphere and party mood on weekends plus drag contests that include an annual Cher look-alike contest. On Sun night, the downtown club hosts drag shows, while on Tues the steak and chicken dinners draw crowds. There is a dance floor, dartboards, pool tables, 2 bars, and television sets for special programming. The outdoor patio is a popular gathering spot when the weather cooperates.

i A good source for gossip about the gay nightlife scene in Austin is "The Gay Place" column in the *Austin Chronicle*. The column is a play on the title of the classic Texas novel by Billie Lee Brammer, which was all about old-style Austin politics, not sexuality.

DICK'S DEJA DISCO
113 San Jacinto Blvd.
(512) 457-8010
The gay and lesbian community comes to this downtown club to kick up its collective heels and dance to the top country sounds or the retro sounds of disco music.

OILCAN HARRY'S
211 West Fourth St.
(512) 320-8823
www.oilcanharrys.com
Some have dubbed this Warehouse District bar a neighborhood bar for Austin's gay, beautiful set. Named as one of the top 50 clubs in the world by *Out* magazine, the large bar is a major feature of the club, but the dance floor with its fog machine is the focal point. A patio in the back of the club offers a retreat from the frenzy of the dance floor. Although the majority of the customers are gay, straight patrons also enjoy the

atmosphere here—and the dancing. Open 2 a.m. to 2 p.m. daily.

RAIN ON 4TH
217B West Fourth St.
(512) 494-1150
www.rainon4th.com
This upscale downtown club offers sophisticated events like a black tie Christmas gala, plus amateur strip nights that have a much naughtier air. Other evenings are set aside to celebrate the music of the '80s and '90s.

MOVIE HOUSES

Check the daily *Austin American-Statesman* and the weekly *Austin Chronicle* for featured movies. The following movie houses feature classic, foreign, and independent films.

ALAMORITZ
320 East Sixth St.
(512) 476-1320

✳ALAMO DRAFT HOUSE LAKE CREEK
13729 Research Blvd.
(512) 219-5408

✳ALAMO DRAFT HOUSE VILLAGE
2700 Anderson Lane
(512) 476-1320

✳ALAMO DRAFT HOUSE SOUTH
1120 South Lamar Blvd.
(512) 476-1320
www.drafthouse.com
Tired of sitting in movie theaters where the average age of the audience is younger than your family dog? Try the Alamo Draft House, where there is no sticky Coke on the floor and munchie choices go beyond dill pickles and Butterfingers. The original Warehouse District movie theater is now a nightclub, but the old Alamo movie theater

was transformed into a concept that has spread throughout the city. Alamo theaters feature first run flicks and cult favorites and classics, everything from beach movies to horror flicks served in a nightclub setting where patrons can order beer, wine, and food to accompany the evening's celluloid offerings. The Alamo creators took that concept to three other locations around the city, salvaging old movie houses like the Ritz on Sixth Street. On the weekends there are midnight flicks and sometimes the movie house puts on special presentations, such as a presentation of the movie *Like Water for Chocolate* featuring dishes mentioned in the book. Some of the best independent movies can be found playing in Alamo theaters, also, and if you want a movie at your next party rent the "Alamo Rolling Road Show," a huge 20 x 40-foot inflatable screen.

GOLD CLASS CINEMA
3225 Amy Donovan Plaza
(512) 568-3400
www.goldclasscinemas.com

The Domain shopping center in North Austin is home to an upscale version of the Alamo, part of the national Gold Class Cinema chain. Patrons relax in reclining seats and can request pillows, blankets and wait service for gourmet treats and beverages, both alcoholic and family friendly. Ticket prices reflect the amenities offered and come in around $30 each.

PARAMOUNT THEATRE FOR THE
PERFORMING ARTS
713 Congress Ave.
(512) 472-5411
www.austintheatre.org
The beautifully restored theater on the city's main avenue hosts a summer film festival featuring the great classics of Hollywood. Also, given Austin's emergence as a movie-making venue, premieres are held at the downtown theater.

THE MUSIC SCENE

If this chapter were set to the tune of Austin music, the savory sounds of country, blues, folk, funk, punk, pop, jazz, bluegrass, Tejano, and rock 'n' roll would waft off the pages and fill the air like a Saturday night on Sixth Street. While we can't reproduce the sounds, we can tell you about some of the artists, the venues, the free concerts, and the record stores that constitute the Live Music Capital of the World. So whether you're a music lover eager to explore the sounds of Austin or you've arrived with a guitar on your back and a pocketful of songs, get ready to enter a truly remarkable realm.

No matter what you may have heard about Austin's live music scene, there really is nothing that prepares newcomers for the jolt of firsthand experience. Music is, indeed, here, there, and everywhere in Austin. On any given Friday night, music lovers can choose from among well over 90 venues offering just about any style of music you can imagine, including those exotic strains created by our true Texas hybrids. No weekend-warrior music mentality exists here, however, as our club scene rocks seven nights a week. From national touring shows and top local acts to the most exciting up-and-coming artists and youngsters (some barely past puberty) taking the stage for the very first time, Austin is tuned in to music.

OVERVIEW

You'll find live music in record stores and bookstores. There's live music to accompany your Sun brunch and live music to stir your evening coffee. Austin's premier gourmet grocery offers live music at its two locations on the patio (see the Feeding Frenzy Close-up in the Shopping chapter). You can listen to live music in our museums and art galleries, and there's live music in our parks and on our sidewalks. Austin's Sixth Street is an entire district dedicated to live music and dance halls, while our own nationally televised music TV show has celebrated Austin music for more than 35 years. **Austin City Limits,** which has been called the city's cultural calling card to the world, is Austin's top showcase for musical talent. Our city also hosts one of the most important live music

festivals in the country, South-by-Southwest (see the Close-up in the Annual Events & Festivals chapter), in the spring, as well as the ever-popular Austin City Limits Festival in the fall, and a variety of other festivals throughout the year.

Though Austin took the motto "The Live Music Capital of the World" in the early 1990s, it gained prominence long before that as a haven for artists seeking to follow their own music and create their own sounds without much interference from the commercial establishments in L.A., New York, and Nashville. *Billboard* magazine has called Austin a "mecca for musical mavericks," saying Austin is known as "a creative oasis, a place that puts music first and career far behind." While it's true that many artists are drawn to

Austin for its no-strings-attached spirit, so to speak, it is also true that some current and former Austin regulars have found the magic formula that cracks the charts, including Willie Nelson, the late Stevie Ray Vaughan, Robert Earl Keen, Pat Green, Shawn Colvin, Lyle Lovett, and Jerry Jeff Walker .

In fact, Austin is one of the few cities in the United States where young musicians can go from learning to play, to having a garage band, to performing in a club, to burning their own CDs, to getting an independent record contract, to earning a major-label deal without ever moving their base of operations.

Austin's music scene appears as dynamic today as ever, as more and more young musicians pour into town seeking the freedom to explore their music and the comfort of Austin's appreciative audiences. The constantly changing array of artists onstage—our classic legends and old main- stays combined with young newcomers and emerging talents—renews Austin's status as a musical mecca each and every night. So whether you prefer a lone singer onstage strumming a folk tune on an acoustic guitar or a 10-piece band rocking off the roof, you'll find that Austin has a sound all its own—the sound of originality.

CATCH 'EM IF YOU CAN

With an entire city of musical artists deter- mined to travel to the beat of their own drummers, it's no wonder Austin offers so many choices for the music lover. A city that re-establishes itself as the world's live music capital 7 nights a week makes it hard on those of us trying to assemble a list of must-see acts. There are just so many tal- ented musicians worthy of mention. The art- ists listed here are among Austin's favorites,

but don't think for a minute that this list is all-inclusive. A little experimentation and willingness to explore the live music scene will bring its own reward. We've called this section Catch 'em if You Can because Austin's favorite artists are often the most in demand for concerts around the country and around the world. So catch them while they're here. You can't go wrong.

Asleep at the Wheel: Led by founder/ singer/songwriter/guitarist Ray Benson, Asleep at the Wheel has perhaps done more to preserve and expand the Western Swing sound popularized by the legendary Bob Wills than any other band. From the group's 1973 debut record *Coming Right at Ya* to its recent release, *Asleep at the Wheel* with the Fort Worth Symphony Orchestra, this nine-time Grammy-winning band has con- tinued to impress fans with its fiddle- and steel guitar-driven sound. The group recently collaborated with Willie Nelson on a 2010 Grammy-nominated album *Willie and the Wheel.*

i *Austin City Limits* moved in 2011 from little Studio 6A on the UT campus to Moody Theater north of City Hall. The new space more than doubles the seating capacity for live music tap- ings, so the chance of scoring a spot has improved. Free tickets are still distrib- uted on a space-available basis at www .austincitylimits.org.

Marcia Ball: *CD Review* called Ball's 1994 release, *Blue House,* "another gusto-filled col- lection of tunes informed by the grit of Texas honky-tonk, the stomp of Louisiana Delta rhythms, and the soul of New Orleans– style blues." This piano-playing dynamo with a full-bodied, earthy voice continues to enchant audiences across the country. Known for her soulful "Gulf Coast Sound," she won the Pinetop Perkins Piano Player Award at the Blues Music Awards in Memphis in 2009 and was inducted into the genre's Hall of Fame in 2010.

The Band of Heathens: With a stage at the 2010 Austin City Limits Music Festival, an appearance on the *Austin City Limits* TV show and a couple of nominations for Americana Music Association Honors, this young quintet is way past getting its foot in the door.

BettySoo: Texas-born Korean American BettySoo (no, that's not a stage name), is a singer/songwriter with a folk-rock bent. Although she occasionally performs with a band, BettySoo is best known for her one-woman shows—just her and her guitar. The powerful voice that comes out of her 5-foot-tall body is impressive!

Black Joe Lewis: J. J. Lewis, known by his stage name Black Joe, is a multi-award-winning star on Austin's soul music scene. This young man was inspired by blues greats of the past, but has a sound all his own. He's been recording and performing lately with the Honeybears.

Boombox ATX: With the release of its first CD, *Feel the Boombox*, in 2007, this multi-faceted band finally came together. Although it often is categorized as a hip-hop group, there is something more to these guys. Playing a little bit of jazz and a lot of funk-infused hip-hop, the guys have been described as "Earth, Wind & Fire meets hip-hop."

Gary Clark Jr.: If blues is your thing, you can't go wrong seeing a show headlining Clark. *Texas Music* magazine has called him "probably the most talented Texas guitarist since a certain SRV." Born and raised in Austin, he's a movie actor, too.

W. C. Clark: Few living artists epitomize Austin blues better than W. C. Clark. Born on Austin's east side on November 16, 1939, Clark developed his musical style playing bass and then guitar with the likes of T. B. Bell and Blues Boy Hubbard at the landmark Victory Grill, Charlie's Playhouse, and other black blues clubs of the era. He still performs regularly in Austin.

Del Castillo: "Our music is kind of like the band, we all come with our own influences," Del Castillo percussionist Mark Holeman once told the *Austin Chronicle*. "We got a Gipsy Kings/flamenco groove, but then we've got this Steven Tyler–Mick Jagger lead singer out there. It was either going to work or be the biggest train wreck of our lives. Luckily for us, it works." Austin agrees. This six-member Spanish-language band has taken home a slew of Austin Music awards.

Shawn Colvin: With *A Few Small Repairs,* Austin's gem of the New Folk scene solidified her reputation as an important singer/songwriter. Colvin's first platinum album, *Repairs,* produced the single "Sunny Came Home," which won two 1997 Grammys for Record of the Year and Song of the Year and proved to the world what her fans have known all along: This songwriter can play the guitar and owns a set of provocative pipes to boot.

The Derailers: Combining the country sounds of Buck Owens, Merle Haggard, and others of the Bakersfield Sound era with influences of rock, R&B, and pop, the Derailers are making a major contribution to the music scene in Austin, and now around the country.

Kat Edmonson: It's jazz all the way for this Austin starlet, who "brings Billie Holiday's style into the 21st century," says the *Austin Chronicle*. For a nice taste of Kat's style, download her album *Take to the Sky*. There's still time to catch her shows around the city.

Roky Erickson: When we began this listing back in the 1990s, we never thought we would be including this giant of the 1960s Austin music scene. Erickson, whose band 13th Floor Elevators was one of the seminal groups of that era, suffered mental difficulties and dropped out of sight for decades. But in the late 2000s Erickson staged what the *Statesman* called "one of the most improbable comebacks in music history," winning the *Chronicle*'s 2008 Musician of the Year award. We're not sure how much he will be performing now, but catch him if you can—and find out for yourself what all the fuss is about. In 2010 Erickson released *True Love Cast Out all Evil* with Okkervil River (see this list).

Alejandro Escovedo: It's hard to believe that a guy who launched his musical career by playing in his own student film about a rock band that couldn't play could have come so far. His songs, according to his biography, "blend lyrical strings and woodwinds with the gritty sound of crunching, sawed-off guitars and pumping pianos." We couldn't have said it better.

The Flatlanders: The flatlands of West Texas have produced some of our state's most inspired musicians. Buddy Holly, Roy Orbison, and Waylon Jennings all hail from that sparse outpost of pure Texas. In 1972 **Jimmie Dale Gilmore** and fellow Lubbock singer/songwriters **Joe Ely** and **Butch Hancock** formed a little acoustic band called the Flatlanders and recorded *One Road More* in Nashville. When the album fizzled, so did the band. Little did they know the album was to become a collector's item. It was later rereleased under the more appropriate title *More a Legend Than a Band*. All three went on to form successful solo careers and got together once in a while for a show or two. Fans everywhere got a real treat when the Flatlanders reunited in 2001 for shows across the United States and over into Europe. The three have been performing gigs together ever since. They also make musical magic in records and performances as solo artists—so catch them if you can.

Ruthie Foster: This Texas-born and -raised singer/songwriter has a voice that embodies the Lone Star State in so many ways. A hybrid of blues, gospel, roots, and folk music flows like a backcountry stream whenever she opens her mouth in song. Foster received a 2010 Grammy nomination for Best Contemporary Blues Album for *The Truth According to Ruthie Foster*.

Kevin Fowler Band: This hot Austin band plays the real stuff: traditional country music that its leader says is for "pickup driving, Wrangler wearing, everyday working-class people like me."

Davíd Garza: "His future's so bright, he's gotta wear shades." That's what the *Austin American-Statesman* said, quoting Austin group Timbuk3 about this pop singer/songwriter following the release of his 1998 major-label debut *This Euphoria*. His music, rooted in quirky yet alluring rock/pop melodies and lyrics, is sort of early Beatles but freshened for the times.

Ghostland Observatory: This rockin', experimental duo of front man Aaron Behrens and producer/drummer Thomas Turner has released its fourth CD, *Codename: Rondo,* and is wowing audiences at home and around the country. Their live performances are inspired.

The Gourds: The music of Austin's rollickin', good-timin' country/rock band is just impossible to describe. No one can ever tell quite where it's going, but everyone knows they're having a grand time anyway. They've been making dang good music around these parts—and around the country—for some time now.

Pat Green: Green's second major-label album, 2003's *Wave on Wave,* which hit No. 1 on Country Music Television's Top 20 Countdown, and an appearance on *Austin City Limits* helped his well-deserved fame spread beyond the Texas border, and now he's packing auditoriums all over the place. His music is personal, and he's found success by doing things his own way.

Patty Griffin: *Billboard* magazine called Griffin's 2002 album, *1,000 Kisses,* "the most magnetic album yet by one of the most compelling recording artists in popular music." Of course, her legions of fans here in Austin and across the country were already well aware of this singer/songwriter's amazing talents. Griffin, a multiple Grammy nominee, was nominated again for a 2010 award for her country collaboration with Dierks Bentley, *Beautiful World*.

Sara Hickman: A superb live performer, Hickman is an acoustic rock 'n' roller who mixes folk sweetness with open-eyed humor—and not just a touch of mischievousness. This is another Austin artist who breaks the female singer/songwriter mold—due, perhaps, to the fact that she is inspired by all kinds of music.

Sarah Jarosz: Nominated for a 2010 Grammy for Best Country Instrumental Performance for her song *Mansinnedof,* young Sarah Jarosz is a rising star on the Austin music scene. She was chosen as a performer for the Country Music Association Awards and has appeared on Garrison Keillor's National Public Radio show, *A Prairie Home Companion*. A multiple nominee in the 2010 Austin Music Awards, Sarah took the honors for Best Female Vocalist, Best Country/Bluegrass Band, and Best Folk Band.

Eric Johnson: Guitar-player extraordinaire and Grammy Award winner Eric Johnson is one of those rare Austin musicians who actually was born here. This tall Texan won his Grammy in 1991 for Best Rock Instrumental Performance for his song "Cliffs of Dover" on the *Ah Via Musicom* album, which proved to the country that lyrics aren't an essential part of rock music. Johnson also sings and writes, but guitar is his forte.

Jimmy LaFave: LaFave's talents as a singer, songwriter, and guitarist have catapulted him to the top ranks of Austin musicians. This poetic lyricist with a wonderfully raspy voice alternates easily between rock numbers and romantic ballads. While he has many CDs, it's still much more fun to see him perform live.

Los Lonely Boys: "Texican rock 'n' roll." That's how this young rock/blues/country/Mexican band describes its unique sound. This hit trio, which composes original songs in both English and Spanish, is made up of the Garza brothers: Henry (guitar), JoJo (bass), and Ringo (drums, of course).

James McMurtry: If that last name sounds familiar to all you fans of the books *Lonesome Dove* and other modern classics by novelist Larry McMurtry, you're on the right track. James is the author's son. This McMurtry, however, has taken a different writing path. As a singer/songwriter known for his intelligent, narrative-oriented rock 'n' roll songs, McMurtry tells stories his own way.

Willie Nelson: Willie turned 77 in 2010, but he doesn't appear to be slowing down at all, performing at various venues in Austin throughout the year. Nelson released his 4-disc, career-spanning CD, *One Hell of a Ride*, in 2008. His musical style? Do you have to ask?

Okkervil River: *The Chronicle* called Okkervil River's 2007 album *The Stage Names* "a poignant pop masterpiece." This band tours constantly, but stopped home long enough to pick up a 2008 Austin Music Award for Best Indie Band—and perform in the show.

Omar & The Howlers: This dynamite rockin' blues band is one of those quintessential Austin groups that just shouldn't be missed.

Reckless Kelly: "Reckless Kelly . . . could do for alternative-country what Nirvana did for grunge," according to the *Houston Chronicle*. Austin remains impressed with this long-standing quintet, awarding it several Austin Music Awards.

Bruce Robison: If you're a country music fan from outside of Austin, Bruce Robison is one of those guys you probably didn't know you knew. His songs have been recorded by the Dixie Chicks, George Strait, and Faith Hill and Tim McGraw, among others. If you are from these parts, you know that Bruce is also an outstanding performer and recording artist who has graced the stages of some of the best country bars and honky tonks in the region and beyond. Originally hailing from out west in Bandera, Texas, Austin gets to claim him as our own these days. His brother, Charlie Robison, is also a dang fine singer/songwriter. Bruce often performs with his wife, Kelly Willis (see this list.)

Bob Schneider: The driving force behind several distinctly unique and very popular Austin party bands, Schneider launched a solo career with the self-released CD *Lonelyland* a few years ago, and he continues to be a hot live act around the city—and the country. Along with a bunch of other honors, Schneider was named Austin Musician of the Year in the *Austin Chronicle*'s 2010 Music Awards.

Charlie & Will Sexton: These two brothers, both of whom made major-label record deals when they were just teenagers and then spent more than a decade each developing separate musical identities, are great performers and worth waiting for. Charlie, a member of the Austin superband Arc Angels, has been touring again with Bob Dylan.

Speak: This up-and-coming Austin quintet, which delivers a lively, funky dance-pop sound, took home honors as Austin's Best New Band in the 2010 Music Awards. Now's the time to catch them here at home.

Spoon: Currently playing at sold-out shows around the country, Spoon has won multiple Austin Music Awards, including Band of the Year and Album of the Year (*Ga Ga Ga Ga Ga*). Led by songwriter Britt Daniel, this 4-man rock band might be hard to find in Austin, but the search is worth it.

Vallejo: Perennial hometown favorite Vallejo is a rock band with a Latin beat.

Kelly Willis: Country crooner and darling of the Austin club circuit, Willis is one of those performers who makes your jaw drop the minute she hits her first note. First, that powerful voice of hers comes charging at you like a bull on wings. Then you realize this young woman is mixing up some of the best traditional country sounds with a perfect dose of rock 'n' roll.

THE STAGES

Janis Joplin overcame her insecurities and launched her singing career in the early 1960s in an Austin beer joint. George Strait was a relative unknown when he first started singing around town. Stevie Ray Vaughan was just another teenager with a used guitar and a dream when he found a stage here. Austin's own Willie Nelson is a regular on our club and music hall scene. While not every artist who performs on an Austin stage goes on to fame and fortune, many of the hottest acts on the nation's club scene today got their start on an Austin stage.

From dark, intimate clubs to big concert halls to superb outdoor venues, Austin's club scene swings 7 nights a week, bringing a wide array of live music from around Austin and around the country. Few other cities in the nation come close to Austin in the number of live acts performed onstage every night.

If Austin is the Live Music Capital of the World, then downtown is the Live Music Capital of Austin. The lively strip known simply as Sixth Street, on East Sixth between Congress Avenue and I-35 (and now grown to includes side streets as well), touts nearly a score of live music venues, plus restaurants, comedy clubs, T-shirt shops, and tattoo parlors. Because of its national reputation, Sixth Street often gives tourists their first taste of Austin's music scene. But downtown also has the popular Warehouse District, another one coming into its own around Second Street, and some good clubs on Congress Avenue. Austin's East Side is also being discovered—or shall we say rediscovered—as a great area to hear live music. While some of the clubs and restaurants that line East Sixth present hot acts and fascinating up-and-comers, this street also offers plenty of cover bands, DJs, and unproven performers. So experience the awesome Sixth Street scene, but check out downtown's other great clubs and music halls as well as those scattered around Austin.

Of course, what would Austin be without music by the side of the lake? Several spots are known for presenting great live bands—some that cover popular songs and old favorites and others doing original stuff. While the places listed here under The Shores are mainly known as restaurants, we couldn't miss out on telling you about them in this section. Austin music and the lakes are meant to be together like a singer and a guitar.

While there are just too many clubs around Austin to list them all, we've provided you with information about some of Austin's favorites, as well as some of our own. For news about who's playing where, check the listings in the *Austin Chronicle* and the *Austin American-Statesman* (or see the Insiders' Tip earlier in this chapter).

We're not providing specific information on cover charges because these can vary greatly depending on the night of the week, the artist onstage, or, it seems, the alignment of the stars in the heavens. Hours vary, too, so check with the club. Some clubs admit minors; many don't. Again, check with the club. The drinking age in Texas is 21. Most clubs sell tickets at the door only. Some clubs offer tickets for advance purchase. Check out the specific club's website to see the policy and order tickets when available.

Around Town

*ANTONE'S
213 West Fifth St.
(512) 320-8424
www.antones.net
If there's one local club practically the whole world has heard of, it's Antone's—Austin's home of the blues. Since 1975 this club, now in its fourth Austin location, has featured some of Austin's best blues performers as well as top blues artists from around the country. In recent years Antone's lineup has expanded to include rock, pop, and country acts also. This Austin institution swings with live music almost every night of the week, offering a continuous parade of some of the best live music from Austin and around the country.

AUSTIN ACOUSTICAL CAFE
2874 Shoal Crest Ave.
(512) 474-5921
www.austinacousticalcafe.com
Want to sit back and enjoy some great acoustical music from local and national singer/songwriters, maybe even bring the kids? This alcohol- and smoke-free venue might be just the place. Located in the Lamar Activity Center, the Acoustical Cafe presents live musical acts on Sat evenings once a month. The shows begin early enough—7:30 p.m. for the headline act—to bring kiddies ages 8 and up. Of course you don't have to be a parent to enjoy this acoustically excellent space.

AUSTIN MUSIC HALL
208 Nueces St.
(512) 263-4146
www.austinmusichall.com
One of Austin's premier venues for national touring shows and local performers, the Austin Music Hall's contribution to the local music scene is enormous. And now, thanks to a major renovation and expansion, it is bigger and better than ever. Outstanding performing artists from around the country have performed at this venue, including Bruce Springsteen, the Neville Brothers, Sarah McLachlan, and John Fogerty. This hall, which is indeed a glorified big black box with removable metal chairs for seats, also hosts the annual Austin Music Awards and other South by Southwest events.

*THE BACKYARD
13742 Bee Cave Pkwy., Bee Cave
(512) 263-4146
www.thebackyard.net
Opened in 2010 at this new location just down the road from the original (which was nudged out by development in the area), The Backyard has been an Austin favorite since its 1993 debut. Bonnie Raitt, Gypsy Kings, Paul Simon, Willie Nelson, the Allman Brothers, and many, many more national touring shows favor this outdoor venue and

its beautiful Hill Country surroundings. The new, larger amphitheater, with room for as many as 7,000 music fans, rocks the night during its Mar-to-Nov season. Even though it's bigger, get your tickets early for really popular shows, as these events can sell out. Operated by Direct Events, the people who bring us La Zona Rosa and Austin Music Hall, The Backyard offers season tickets—a sure way to get one of the best seats in the house. There's great local food and drink on site, so come hungry, too!

i Save some gas money and help out our planet by carpooling to The Backyard outdoor amphitheater. Its located "just three songs west of downtown," operators say. You'll be rewarded with a prime parking spot at the new "green" Backyard.

✳BROKEN SPOKE
3201 South Lamar Blvd.
(512) 442-6189
www.brokenspokeaustintx.com
Willie Nelson has called the Broken Spoke his favorite watering hole. *Texas Highways* magazine has named it the Best Honky-Tonk in Texas, while *Entertainment Weekly* has said it's the best country dance hall in the country. The Broken Spoke has appeared in a host of movies, documentaries, and commercials (including one for Foster's beer that made the Spoke a household name in Australia). Since 1964 the Broken Spoke has been dishing up a steady stream of the best country music Austin has to offer—along with a full menu of down-home Texas cookin'.

✳CACTUS CAFE
Texas Union Building
Twenty-fourth and Guadalupe Streets
(512) 475-6515
www.utexas.edu/universityunions
This excellent club in the Student Union on the University of Texas campus has been serving up live music for nearly 80 years. Opened in 1933 as the Chuck Wagon, the club was among Austin's first hippie hangouts in the 1960s, catering to an emerging group of "folkie" musicians that included a young Janis Joplin. Later up-and-comers included Lyle Lovett, Robert Earl Keen, Nanci Griffith, and others. After going through a few names, the club was renamed the Cactus Cafe in 1977 but continues to be one of Austin's prime venues for singer/songwriters presenting acoustic performances. The Cactus suffered a close call in 2010 when UT's Union Board announced plans to close the venue, citing money woes, but a deal with local PBS radio station KUT saved the cultural icon. This club is a popular daytime hangout for UT students, faculty, and staff. Evening shows draw both students and members of the public.

i In the old days Austin's downtown east-west streets were named for trees. Sixth Street was called Pecan Street, which is why you still see references to Pecan Street in business names or in our annual Old Pecan Street Festival. The street names were changed to numbers around 1897.

CAROUSEL LOUNGE
1110 East Fifty-second St.
(512) 452-6790
www.carousellounge.net

Located just east of I-35, the Carousel Lounge has been serving up drinks and music since 1963. The Carousel features an eclectic range of live music—usually swing, jazz, Big Band, country, rock, or lounge acts—Tues through Sun nights. The lounge looks much as it did a quarter century ago, with those miniature jukeboxes (not in service) over the tables, an aqua-colored padded bar, and a big jukebox that's loaded with lots of old music. This treasured Austin landmark is now being discovered by a whole new generation of music fans.

CEDAR STREET COURTYARD
208 West Fourth St.
(512) 495-9669
www.cedarstreetaustin.com

Jazz under the trees. Since Cedar Street opened in 1994, this lovely outdoor venue loaded with live oak trees has gained a reputation for featuring excellent local jazz musicians as well as acts from around the country. This is also the place for some good ol' partying to the tune of some cover bands playing tunes from the 1970s and 1980s. Tucked between two buildings a few steps down from sidewalk level in the Warehouse District, this intimate setting is the perfect place for live music—7 nights a week.

✳CONTINENTAL CLUB
1315 South Congress Ave.
(512) 441-2444
www.continentalclub.com

Perhaps it's the perennial odor of day-old beer that lends this club its primo atmosphere. More likely, it's the long, long list of top Austin acts that have earned their musical wings at the Continental Club over the years—it celebrated its 53rd anniversary in 2010. Whatever the reason, the Continental

Club is one of Austin's premier live music venues, with an excellent reputation not only locally but around the country. There's generally always somebody worth seeing within these dark walls.

COOL RIVER CAFE
4001 Parmer Lane
(512) 835-0010
www.coolrivercafe.com

This venue in far north Austin is really three distinct places in one: An elegant, and quiet, restaurant on one side; a sophisticated, and quiet, cognac lounge in the middle; and then a jam-packed and deliciously loud party bar on the other side, featuring live music and lots of dancing Thurs through Sat. This is one hot spot for both the young and old(er)—anyone who is looking for a good time.

EGO'S
510 South Congress Ave.
(512) 474-7091

This dark, low-ceilinged room on South Congress Avenue is a popular spot with the underground music crowd. The L-shaped corner stage for eclectic musical acts is intimate and the sound system alert. Strange that one of the city's most likable venues is buried inside a parking garage. Did we mention the pool tables and video games?

ELEPHANT ROOM
315 Congress Ave.
(512) 473-2279
www.elephantroom.com

Voted Best Jazz Bar in Austin 7 years in a row by the Clarksville Jazz Festival—and in 2007 named by *USA Today* as one of the country's top 10 "places to get jazzed about"—the Elephant Room presents a wide variety of live jazz, including Latin jazz, fusion, traditional, and funk. This cozy basement club presents an excellent assortment of Austin bands as well as bands from around the country. Audiences are treated to the cool sounds of live jazz 7 nights a week. (Yes, some of the artists and members of the audience do don sunglasses—it's that cool.)

FRANK ERWIN CENTER
1701 Red River St.
(512) 471-7744,
(512) 477-6060 (Texas box office)
www.uterwincenter.com
Austin's largest venue for national touring musicians is also home to University of Texas basketball as well as Disney on Ice shows, circuses, and scores of other events throughout the year. When it comes to music, however, there just isn't any space in Austin as large or as comfortable for the crowds that have turned out to see world-class musical performers, including, of course, many Austin music legends. The Erwin Center also hosts plenty of classical musical performers. Depending on the stage setup, the Erwin Center can hold anywhere from 4,000 to 18,000 fans. Performances are announced well in advance.

THE GHOST ROOM
304 West Fourth St.
(512) 879-4472
www.theghostroom.com
Opened in late 2009 this club quickly earned a reputation for great atmosphere, superior sound, and an impressive and diverse lineup of acts. Just a few months later it picked up the 2010 Austin Music Award for Best New Club. Located in a century-old building in the popular Warehouse District downtown, the club is indeed living up to its early hype.

Shows usually run Thurs through Sat nights at the 350-person venue. Careful not to sit on the *real* ghost who actually inhabits the place!

HANOVERS DRAUGHT HOUSE
108 East Main St., Pflugerville
(512) 670-9617
www.hanoversaustin.com
The suburbs have grown and grown around historic downtown Pflugerville, once a small, quiet Central Texas town. Not only has new life come to the fields surrounding downtown, there also is new life for some of the town's old buildings. Once a saloon, then a hardware store, this 1899 stone building is alive again with the sounds of Texas. The bar features 76 types of beer. In addition to the music stage, there is a back room with pool tables and dart boards, plus a large outdoor beer garden that can seat up to 1,000. For nourishment, there is barbecue, of course. The live music shows are presented Wed, Fri, and Sat.

HILL'S CAFE
4700 South Congress Ave.
(512) 851-9300
www.hillscafe.com
The chicken-fried steak isn't the only thing on the menu at this South Austin landmark, owned by top country music radio personality, Bob Cole. How about a helping of the down-home country performers who are giving this place a reputation for presenting great live music? Tues is songwriter night, a fine time to hear some new sounds.

HOLE IN THE WALL
2538 Guadalupe St.
(512) 477-4747
www.holeinthewallaustin.com
This Austin institution almost didn't make it to its 30th anniversary in 2003. Closed for

nearly a year while the building was up for sale, the local Austin Pizza chain revived the space and returned the 200-capacity venue to its original configuration. Bands now play in the front; the back room has pool tables, pinball machines, and a jukebox. Located on The Drag near the University of Texas campus, this really is just a hole in the wall. But over its nearly four decades in business, this club and eatery has earned a reputation for presenting excellent up-and-coming as well as established bands.

LAMBERTS DOWNTOWN BARBEQUE
401 West Second St.
(512) 494-1500
www.lambertsaustin.com
This spot in downtown's historic Schneider Brothers Building (built in 1873 as one of Austin's first general stores) gained popularity first as a "fancy barbeque" restaurant for both lunch and dinner. Its upstairs stage, however, is now gaining a loyal audience of music lovers, thanks a great deal to the venue's excellent booking choices. Live music, including blues, jazz, Western swing, and other genres, is offered on the weekends.

LA ZONA ROSA
612 West Fourth St.
(512) 463-4146
www.lazonarosa.com
A longtime Austin tradition, formerly a quaint Mexican eatery and music hall, La Zona Rosa now concentrates on outstanding live music. It is high on the list of hot Austin clubs known for providing consistent quality entertainment. La Zona Rosa presents both national touring shows and some of Austin's favorite artists. Its two rooms can be made into one for shows that seat up to 1,200 people.

LUCKY LOUNGE
209 A West Fifth St.
(512) 479-7700
www.theluckylounge.com
Featuring live music 6 nights a week, this lounge with 60s-inspired decor and soft neon lighting is located in the heart of Austin's Warehouse District. The musical styles—rock, hip-hop, funk, and more—are as eclectic as the patrons who flock to this popular establishment.

MOMO'S
618 West Sixth St.
(512) 479-8848
www.momosclub.com
One of the best things about this downtown club, besides the live music of course, is the rooftop patio, which offers a view over the city and a look at the inside stage and dance floor. The club has had several incarnations and now features all sorts of music, including singer/songwriters.

✳SAXON PUB
1320 South Lamar Blvd.
(512) 448-2552
www.thesaxonpub.com
Saxon Pub started out as a folk music club when it opened in South Central Austin in 1990, but Saxon is now gaining a reputation as a great blues club. Country and rock bands also have found a home. To the delight of music fans, some of the country's most popular musicians also have been known to drop in for a jam session or two, including Bonnie Raitt and Kris Kristofferson.

SCOOT INN
1308 East Fourth St.
(512) 478-6200
www.scoot-inn.com

Although Scoot Inn's Eastside location dates back to the 1870s as a music venue, it has had quite a checkered past. Like some other historic East Austin music venues, Scoot Inn is making a comeback and is becoming known as a hip place to hang out and listen to an eclectic array of music acts. Part of the attraction here is the indoor and outdoor stages—and the beer garden—but really it all comes down to the live music.

SPEAKEASY
412 Congress Ave.
(512) 476-8017
www.speakeasyaustin.com
This upscale club in the Warehouse District downtown features live music on most nights. This is the place to play billiards and hear bands play some great standards from the '30s and '40s as well as some original music. The Speakeasy offers plenty of blues, jazz, salsa, lounge music, swing, and some country tunes. The rooftop terrace (for those willing to make the trek up the 59 stairs) offers a fantastic view of downtown. Hint: the entrance is down the alley.

TC'S LOUNGE
1413 Webberville Rd.
(512) 926-2200
Austinites who have been flocking to this lopsided barn of a blues haunt for years probably will be none too happy with us for "outing" their little secret. TC's Lounge, they will argue, is already crowded enough, especially on Mon nights when The Little Elmore Reed Band is on stage and the dance floor is packed. It's kinda dirty from years of good use, and the air conditioning is iffy, but if you like great blues and R&B, at reasonable prices, you'll make the trip over to East Austin.

THREADGILL'S
6416 North Lamar Blvd.
(512) 451-5440
www.threadgills.com
With two Austin locations, the original "Old No. 1" on North Lamar and the "World Headquarters" on Riverside, Threadgill's embodies Austin music history. Both of these excellent restaurants offer some of the best down-home cooking around these parts, but they also are an integral part of the music scene, serving up a juicy selection of musical acts. The evening music schedule varies at both the North Lamar indoor spot and the Riverside outdoor beer garden, although both have Sun brunch shows around 11 a.m. The North Lamar brunch features bluegrass music; at Riverside it's gospel. Another location is at 301 West Riverside Dr. (512-472-9304).

Sixth Street/Red River Districts

The Sixth Street Entertainment District has grown over the years to include parts of Fifth and Seventh Streets, while the Red River District is an offshoot of this district on the northeast side of Sixth. This listing includes our favorite clubs in both areas.

BEERLAND
711½ Red River St.
(512) 479-7625
www.beerlandtexas.com
The *Austin American-Statesman* calls this punkish club with a gay vibe "the heart and soul of Red River Street," although well-established Emo's down the block might dispute that. The decor is Old World cabaret.

THE CHUGGIN' MONKEY
219 East Sixth St.
(512) 476-5015
www.thechugginmonkey.com

With a name like Chuggin' Monkey, this club was destined for Sixth Street. The stage is tiny but it is right up front on Sixth. The Monkey packs in the crowds.

ELYSIUM
705 Red River St.
(512) 474-2285
www.elysiumonline.net
Specializing in synthpop, gothic, industrial, rock, EBM (electronic body music), as well as alternative rock and electronica genres, Elysium is one popular nightspot for those who eschew the ordinary. The club presents live music on Thurs and Fri; DJs the other nights.

EMO'S
603 Red River St.
(512) 505-8541
www.emosaustin.com
This Austin club just off Sixth Street is drawing oodles of fans for its eclectic mix of underground music. With two stages, one inside and one outside, there's always an act worth seeing. If it's punk/indie/electronica/garage/emo stuff you like, Emo's is your place.

FLAMINGO CANTINA
515 East Sixth St.
(512) 494-9336
www.flamingocantina.com
Calling itself "Austin's Good Vibes Club," this well-established place is where Austin goes to hear the city's best reggae music, as well as ska, Latin, and world beat. You might also catch some hip-hop, rock, or alternative acts. Carpeted bleachers line two walls, offering great views of the band onstage. Of course there's a dance floor, for when swaying in your seat just isn't enough, and an upstairs open-air deck for dancing under the stars.

MAGGIE MAE'S
323 East Sixth St.
(512) 478-8541
www.maggiemaesaustin.com
With three different stages offering simultaneous music on weekends, an airy rooftop bar upstairs, and private courtyard downstairs, Maggie Mae's has no trouble drawing a crowd. Named for a famous London lady of the evening, Maggie Mae's offers live music most nights. One band is featured during the week, but on Fri and Sat this 2-story club rocks with different types of music in three different rooms, including at least two live bands. The building, originally a general store built in 1874, predates Sixth Street's historic Driskill Hotel by a dozen years. Maggie Mae's is one of this strip's longest running and most successful clubs.

i Austin's venerable Paramount Theatre and Bass Concert Hall also book music performers—to great success. Check out their websites at www.austintheatre.org and www.texasperformingarts.org for a list of upcoming shows.

MOHAWK
912 Red River St.
www.mohawkaustin.com
This popular spot on the outer limits of the Sixth Street Entertainment District says it draws its inspiration "not from the hairdo," but from the Native American culture of the Northeast. An eclectic mix of music—hip-hop, jazz, indie, rock, and so on—is offered on both the indoor and outdoor stages Thurs through Sun. By the way, the club says if you happen to have a mohawk (the hairdo) "bring it on over."

*THE PARISH

214-C East Sixth St.
(512) 473-8381
www.theparishaustin.com

This has been a hot Sixth Street nightclub for quite some time, and deservedly so. *Austin American-Statesman* music critic Michael Corcoran has called it "one of the last places to hear live original music on Sixth Street" and "Austin's most handsome room." All sorts of top bands play in this acoustically excellent space.

RED EYED FLY

715 Red River St.
(512) 474-1084
www.redeyedfly.com

The emphasis seems to be on rock and funk here, but really it's an electrically eclectic mix of great sounds, with some heavy metal and a bit of country rock tossed in the mix. There's definitely some musical experimentation going on here.

RED 7

611 East Seventh St.
(512) 476-8100
www.red7austin.com

If you like punk and hardcore music—and who doesn't?—you'll love Red 7. Great bands perform outdoors on the covered stage.

*STUBB'S

801 Red River St.
(512) 480-8341
www.stubbsaustin.com

It's hard to say which is more enticing at this Austin hangout, the excellent barbecue or the live music acts that perform on both the indoor and outdoor stages. The building itself is a historical gem. Built in the 1850s, it has been remodeled into a 6,000-square-foot 2-level restaurant with mahogany and cherry bars that date from the 1870s. Outdoors, two decks and bars overlook the stage. Today Stubb's showcases both national touring acts and some of Austin's finest musicians. The Gospel Brunch every Sun is not to be missed—reservations highly recommended.

The Shores

Music snobs may reckon that venues known primarily as lakeside eateries are unworthy of mention in the same listing with such Austin classics as Antone's, the Broken Spoke, and others. You might not always hear original music at these restaurants, but sometimes you will. Besides, even the cover bands we've heard at several of these places beat the music many visitors will find at home. And you get to enjoy being out on the lakes at the same time. Water and music—now that's an unbeatable Austin combination. This is just one more dimension of the Live Music Capital of the World. To find more about most of these eateries, see the Restaurants chapter.

IGUANA GRILL

2900 RR 620
(512) 266-8439
www.iguanagrillaustin.com

The excellent view of Lake Travis and the great Mexican restaurant draw crowds of Austinites and out-of-towners, but the Iguana also offers live music mainly Fri through Sun starting around 6:30 p.m., and on random other nights. Check the website for the music calendar.

SKI SHORES WATERFRONT CAFE

2905 Pearce Rd.
(512) 394-7511
www.skishoresaustin.com

Getting raves from Austin crowds since 1954, and newly updated and expanded in 2010, this is a super-casual place where you can just boat right up to the dock and hop in for a burger, a beer, or an evening of live music. Located on Lake Austin, Ski Shores is one of our favorite outdoor eateries. The stage, presenting Austin singer/songwriters during the summer, is so close to the water that the wake from the boats going by could almost serve as the rhythm section.

STARLIGHT TERRACE AT THE OASIS
6550 Comanche Trail
(512) 266-2442
www.oasis-austin.com
Situated high above Lake Travis, the Oasis is famous for its fabulous view of the sunset. But the multilayered outdoor decks are also perfect for dining—and for listening to live music. The bands play all kinds of music, including Top 40, jazz, salsa, and much more. Austin bands, performing both original hits and popular contemporary music, make this place an inviting stop for those who want to experience the outdoor music scene in Austin.

Free Concerts

＊AUSTIN'S FOURTH OF JULY PICNIC
Auditorium Shores, Riverside Drive and South First Street
(512) 476-6064
www.austinsymphony.org
Austin's biggest free concert is the performance by the Austin Symphony Orchestra at the annual July Fourth Concert and Fireworks Show on the shores of Lady Bird Lake. See the Annual Events & Festivals chapter for more on this giant concert/picnic/party.

AUSTIN SYMPHONY'S SUMMER CONCERT SERIES
Hartman Concert Park, The Long Center
701 West Riverside Dr.
(512) 476-6064
www.austinsymphony.org
Presented on Sun evenings June through Aug, these outdoor concerts are performed by different ensembles of the Austin Symphony. Genres include jazz, light classical, pops, and even film scores, so each week brings a new surprise! This is a casual event, so grab some picnic food and a blanket and head on down to the show. The event is officially known as the Hartman Foundation Concerts in the Park, in tribute to the generous benefactor that makes these concerts possible.

BLUES ON THE GREEN
Zilker Park
2100 Barton Springs Rd.
www.kgsr.com/other/blues
This excellent series of six outdoor blues concerts has been a summer staple in Austin for more than two decades. Presented every other Wed evening beginning in June, these concerts are always packed with Austin music lovers. Bring a blanket or lawn chair—then sit back and enjoy the show! You don't even need to pack the picnic basket, as food and nonalcoholic drinks are sold at the concert. The venue is on the east side of the park near Barton Springs Pool.

CHRISTMAS SING-A-LONG CONCERT
Riverbend Centre
4214 North Capital of Texas Hwy.
(512) 476-6064
www.austinsymphony.org
Another family friendly event presented by the Austin Symphony and chorus, the

Christmas concert is held around mid-Dec at the beautiful Riverbend Centre. Santa Claus is in attendance, as are Frosty the Snowman, and other beloved characters of the Christmas season. The songs are all familiar—*Joy to the World, Silent Night, Rudolph the Red-Nosed Reindeer*, and many others—so the sing-a-long is a snap! Although the one-night-only event is free, seating is limited so tickets must be obtained in advance. They usually become available around Dec 1 at the Symphony box office. Check the website.

LIVE FROM THE PLAZA
City Hall Plaza
301 West Second St.
www.ci.austin.tx.us/music/live.htm
There are two seasons to this wonderful outdoor concert series, featuring an eclectic assortment of Austin music acts. Sponsored by the city of Austin, the concerts are held on Fri from Mar to June and from Oct to Nov. Most are hourlong concerts that begin at noon, although the first and last shows of both seasons begin after work, around 5:30 p.m. If you can't make it in person to the show, you can tune in via the city's government access TV channel.

i If you visit The Long Center make sure to stop in the area known as the City Terrace overlooking Lady Bird Lake. You'll find engraved discs bearing the names of the inductees to the Austin Music Memorial. The memorial honors several dozen of our city's music icons.

ZILKER HILLSIDE THEATER CONCERTS
2206 William Barton Dr.
(512) 477-5335
www.ci.austin.tx.us/zilker/hillside.htm

The fabulous natural amphitheater near Barton Springs Pool in Zilker Park presents an array of free concerts during its season, which runs from late Mar to mid-Oct. Performances are given by the Austin Symphonic Band, the Austin Civic Orchestra, the Austin Civic Wind Ensemble, and other groups. The Civic Orchestra's 2-night Pops Concert and the Symphonic Band's Father's Day Concert, both in June, are just a couple of the highlights.

MUSIC STORES

Record stores, yet another dimension to the city's music scene, feature a wide variety of music from jazz to Tejano, hip-hop to blues, classical to funk, and of course, Austin's own local artists. Furthermore, some of these stores go out of their way to promote Austin's music scene by sponsoring live in-store performances, setting aside special sections featuring CDs by local musicians, and offering advice and tips on the Live Music Capital of the World. Stop in any of the shops we've listed here for a taste of Austin. The large chain bookstores all over town, including Barnes & Noble, also sell records.

ANTONE'S RECORD SHOP
2928 Guadalupe St.
(512) 322-0660
www.antonesrecordshop.com
Reflecting the music played at the venerable Austin club of the same name (see the listing in this chapter), Antone's focuses on blues music. There is also a large selection of Texas and Cajun music, country sounds, soul, vintage rock 'n' roll, rockabilly, and jazz at this Central Austin store. Customers can buy, sell, and trade here. This is also the place to buy advance tickets to shows at Antone's club (see The Stages section of this chapter).

CHEAPO DISCS
914 North Lamar Blvd.
(512) 477-4499
www.cheapotexas.com
Housed in the old Whole Foods store, just north of the West Sixth shopping district, not far from downtown in Central Austin, Cheapo features used CDs, one of the largest selections in Austin. The shop buys used CDs. Technically, Cheapo is part of a small Minnesota-based chain, but it retains the atmosphere of an independent outfit. Check the website for an impressive schedule of live in-store performances.

END OF AN EAR
2209 South First St.
(512) 462-6008
www.endofanear.com
This Austin record store wasted no time in capturing a loyal clientele base when it first opened a few years ago. Offering an eclectic mix of sounds, not to mention a huge collection of used LPs, the store aims to please. Music lovers can find everything from indie and French pop, to jazz, techno, soul, funk, punk, reggae, and much more. It also hosts free in-store music events. This is a good-size shop as independent record stores go, making it an inviting place to browse.

MUSICMANIA
3909-D North I-35
(512) 451-3361
East of the Interstate in the Fiesta grocery store center, this East Austin record store has a reputation for one of the best R&B and rap music collections in the country. In addition to CDs, the store has a large collection of vinyl records, posters, magazines, and music-related merchandise.

TURNTABLE RECORDS
1903 South First St.
(512) 462-2568
For a small space, this South Austin shop has a nice collection of breakbeat, retro, disco, Top 40, and other sounds, including both domestic and imported albums and singles.

✳WATERLOO RECORDS
600–A North Lamar Blvd.
(512) 474-2500
www.waterloorecords.com
Consistently voted the Best Record Store in town in the annual *Austin Chronicle* Readers' Poll, Waterloo is at the heart of the West Sixth Street shopping district. The shop has a fabulous selection of records and CDs—both new and used—reflecting a wide variety of styles and sounds, and there are plenty of listening stations to sample the music. In-house performances and CD-release concerts are held regularly to highlight the work of popular artists, both up-and-coming and well known. Waterloo arranges its records alphabetically instead of by music type, which makes this store extremely user-friendly. Waterloo also stocks lots of other music-related items. Trying to decide what band to hear when you're in town—and you can't find any on our "Catch 'em if You Can" list? Stop in at Waterloo and ask the advice of owner John Kunz or any other member of the knowledgeable sales staff. Waterloo is also one place to purchase tickets for shows around town and for wristbands or individual tickets for SXSW events and the Austin City Limits Music Festival (see the Annual Events & Festivals chapter). It's no wonder this store has been going strong since 1982.

SHOPPING

You can never be too adventurous to enjoy shopping in Austin. Sure there are big malls with big parking lots to match, but while they provide Austin shoppers with the opportunity to buy appliances at national discount chain prices or shop at namebrand department stores, local merchants present a dazzling array of arts, crafts, collectibles, folk art, funk, vintage redux, and just plain fun items.

First is a look at the city's shopping districts, then a brief overview of the area's major malls and outlet stores. This is followed by listings, by category and area, of an assortment of unique shops in Austin. It is impossible to list every noteworthy and intriguing shop in the city, especially as the city grows and the shopping districts multiply, but this list aims to give the reader the flavor of the shopping scene in Austin, plus tips on finding shops that the city's zeitgeist.

Several categories of shops are not included here—bookstores appear in the chapter on The Literary Scene, art galleries are showcased in The Arts chapter, and music stores are featured in The Music Scene. In addition, sporting goods that cater to a specific sport are found in our Parks & Recreation chapter. In recent years there has been a blossoming of retail in Austin. On the one hand, national giants such as Whole Foods Market and Dell Computer have emerged from the Austin earth; on the other hand, the personal has flourished. Older boulevards and city streets in Austin have seen small, unique shops sprout like cabbages as young at heart Austin goes in search of expression and joy. Fashionistas will find the city's clothing stores a mix of small high end boutiques located in shopping districts like Jefferson Square on Thirty-eighth Street, the Second Street District downtown, or the Domain, an upscale outdoor shopping center in north Austin, or shops and studios in SoCo and other emerging neighborhoods where Austin's young fashion designers celebrate their art.

Given Austin's lively night scene, many bookstores and specialty food shops keep late hours. The burgeoning shopping scene along South Congress Avenue is one example of a late-night shopping district—some of the stores stay open until midnight, particularly on weekends. During the Christmas holiday season, many stores and malls also extend their hours.

SHOPPING DISTRICTS

One of the liveliest shopping districts is on South Congress Avenue, in the neighborhood called "SoCo," south of Lady Bird Lake in South Central Austin. Congress Avenue is wide and magnificent here, but for many years the shops and businesses along the street decayed and stagnated. Now there is new life on the avenue, and resale shops featuring vintage clothing, toy emporiums, retro furnishing stores, and folk art shops flourish (if they can afford the escalating rents, a controversial subject these days)— some staying open in the night hours to give the street an after-dark vitality.

West of the South Congress shopping district is South Lamar Boulevard, where some of the city's really funky stores can be found. Vintage clothing stores, "junque" shops, antiques stores, and several thrift stores are located on this road to downtown Austin. Running parallel and in between South Lamar and Congress is South First Street, which is also home to offbeat stores, gypsy food trailers, and old-fashioned Mexican bakeries.

The nexus of West Sixth and North Lamar Boulevard is one of the hippest shopping districts in Austin. At its heart is the Whole Foods Landmark Market, the natural foods grocery store that is a leitmotiv for the Austin economy. Founded more than 30 years ago as a natural foods store by a couple of hippies with a vision, it now serves as the anchor of the country's largest natural foods grocery store empire. Across the street, to the north, is Austin's quintessential bookstore, Book People, a place where incense fills the air and the titles outnumber any chain store in town. Next door is a branch of the national fashion/home decor chain Anthropologie.

The area east of the Sixth Street-Lamar nexus, leading to the so-called Warehouse District, is also seeing a boom in bars, restaurants, shops and galleries catering to the fast-rising number of downtown residents. Just south of the Warehouse District is downtown's most upscale shopping, the Second Street District (www.2ndstreetdistrict.com) anchored around City Hall and the neighboring lofts. The shops here are trendy, upscale (that word that is creeping into the Austin lexicon) and many of them aimed at dressing those downtown loft-dwellers and decorating their habitats.

Another shopping district in the making is the area along Burnet Road leading from North Austin down into Central Austin. This is a mix of antiques shops, ethnic bakeries and grocery stores, and crafts stores catering to potters and glassmakers.

One of the city's shopping corridors lies east of MoPac along Thirty-fifth Street, flowing into Thirty-eighth Street and then north on Lamar Boulevard to Central Park, home of the city's second-biggest tourist draw, Central Market (see the Close-up in this chapter), a grocery store that belies its pedestrian name. There are no big signs here, but Austin residents know this is where they can find some of the best shops in Austin in small shopping centers like 26 Doors and Jefferson Square along Thirty-fifth Street.

To the northwest along US 183 is the Arboretum, the Rodeo Drive of Austin. This is where some of the top merchandising names in the country have a foothold. Saks has a store in the Great Hills Trail area near the open air Arboretum shopping center.

To the north of the city, just east of MoPac Boulevard and north of US 183 is The Domain (www.thedomainaustin.com), a definitely upscale shopping experience built to resemble a European town center. Here you will find Tiffany's, Neiman Marcus, Burberry, Coach, and several top-notch restaurants, cafes, and even a tea room.

To the east, at 10901 North Lamar Blvd., is another exciting addition to the Austin shopping scene, Austin's new Chinatown (www.chinatownaustin.com). The Chinatown Center, anchored by the MT Supermarket (see the Food shopping listings) is home to several restaurants and cafes featuring Chinese, Indian,

Japanese, Korean and Vietnamese food, plus home decor and herb shops.

Back in the central city is The Drag, the section of Guadalupe Street that runs alongside the University of Texas campus. Here there is an odd mix of hip fashion stores and Vietnamese egg roll stands, old hippie vendors and souvenir shops selling all things Longhorn. Just north of The Drag is The Triangle, another town center concept that is home to small shops and cafes.

The Austin ethos dictates that nobody shops simply to shop; Austinites shop to find, to discover, to enjoy. If these listings are packed with stores selling folk art, food, and plants, it is an indication that Austin residents are sensual folk who love to dip into the unknown, find the new, and enjoy the past.

MALLS

We have it on good authority that when the Queen of England came to Austin, her staff and ladies-in-waiting ventured to a local shopping mall to sample the wares. There are some local merchants in the area's malls, but like much of America, the shopping mall is the home of chain stores, big-name department stores, and fashionable merchants of the moment.

The malls are open 7 days a week, usually from 9 a.m. to 9 or 10 p.m. Mon through Sat and from noon to 6 p.m. on Sun, although hours are extended greatly during the Christmas shopping season and for special promotional sales.

The major shopping malls include **The Arboretum** (10000 Research Blvd.) in northwest Austin, an open-air mall that is home to many upscale national stores. Barton Creek Square, a large indoor mall, sits atop a hill in West Austin at 2901 Loop 360 (Capital of Texas Highway) and is home to several

department stores, including Foley's, Nordstrom's, Sears, Dillard's, and JCPenney. **Lakeline Mall** (11200 Lakeline Mall) serves the fast-growing northwest greater Austin area. It also is home to such major department stores as Foley's, Sears, Dillard's, and JCPenney. **Highland Mall** (6001 Airport Blvd.) was Austin's first mall in what was then far North Austin and is now considered the edge of Central Austin, near the intersection of I-35 and US 290. It has several major department stores on the premises.

New malls include the aforementioned Domain at 11506 Century Oaks Blvd. and the Hill Country Galleria, home to many well-known national merchandising names, located in the Village of Bee Cave at the intersection of US 71 and RM 620 in what was once rolling, empty hill country pasture west of the city—proof that much of Austin's growth has been in the coveted land near the lakes.

Shoppers who love to hunt for bargains at outlet stores have a major source of pleasure in San Marcos, about 45 minutes south of Austin. Both sides of I-35 are lined with outlet stores located in 2 malls, Prime Outlet Mall and Tanger Outlet Center, both located at exit 200 on the Interstate. Another area favorite is the large IKEA store located on I-35 in Round Rock.

ANTIQUES/COLLECTIBLES/FOLK ART

Central

BOB LARSON'S OLD TIMER CLOCK SHOP
1803 West Thirty-fifth St.
(512) 451-5016
www.bobsclocks.com
The Old Timer Shop has been a treasured resource for years for Austin residents. The

shop not only sells beautiful old clocks and watches but also offers a fine repair service.

DREYFUS ANTIQUES BROCANTE
1901 North Lamar Blvd.
(512) 473-2443
www.dreyfusantiques.com
The large wrought-iron replica of the Eiffel Tower is a surefire tip to what shoppers will find inside—a selection of 18th- and 19th-century French antiques, including armoires, tapestries, tables, architectural pieces, and chairs.

*EL INTERIOR
1009 West Lynn St.
(512) 474-8680
www.elinterior.com
This Clarksville store is one of the best and oldest folk art stores in Austin. The owners really know where to find the best pottery, jewelry, and textiles south of the border. The selection of Oaxacan ceramics is notable, and the store also stocks Guatemalan fabric by the yard. The store features the work of notable Mexican and Southwestern folk artists and often brings them to the store for special appearances.

There are two large antiques marketplaces in the Austin area that house dozens of small dealers under one roof. Two are in north Austin, Austin Antique Mall, 8822 McCann Dr., (512) 459-5900, www.austinantiquemall.com, and Antique Marketplace, 5350 Burnet Rd., (512) 452-1000.

KERBEY LANE DOLL SHOPPE
3706 Kerbey Lane
(512) 452-7086
www.kerbeylanedollshop.com

This store sells both antique dolls aimed at the collectors' market and exquisite, new dolls for that special niece or granddaughter. The owners also offer on-site doll repair.

LOTUS ASIAN ART AND ANTIQUES GALLERY
1211 West Sixth St., Suite 100
(512) 474-1700
www.lotusasianart.com
Don't just think Chinese here, in addition to a large collection from Asia, the gallery also has African antiques, ancient pottery and even some Viking pieces.

*WHIT HANKS ANTIQUES AND DECORATIVE ARTS
1009 West Sixth St.
(512) 478-2101
www.whithanksantiques.com
Several top flight antiques and arts dealers can be found under one roof at Whit Hanks, an antiques showcase on West Sixth Street at the heart of one of Austin's best shopping districts. The website has a detailed list of the stores under one roof here and links to individual dealers, some of whom show extensive catalogs online. From the large, Tuscan-style pottery urns on its lawn to the myriad collectibles inside, this is one of the most pleasant and amenable antiques venues in Austin. The building, located next door to Treaty Oak (see the Attractions chapter), is a popular spot for a weekend outing. Several Austin artisans display their original iron, ceramic, and woodworking pieces here also.

South Central

MI CASA
1700A South Congress Ave.
(512) 707-9797
www.micasagallery.com

The entrance to this rabbit's warren of treasures is actually on West Milton, just half a block off Congress Avenue. Room after tiny room features rustic ranch and primitive furniture, while the walls hang with Southwestern and Mexican folk art. The store also sells textiles and cotton clothing from Mexico and Guatemala.

i Keeping up with the dizzying pace of Austin's design and fashion scene is made easier by reading "The Goods" blog on the *American Statesman*'s website, www.statesman.com, and the "Chronique" blog at the *Austin Chronicle,* www.austinchronicle.com.

TEN THOUSAND VILLAGES
1317 South Congress Ave.
(512) 440-0440
www.tenthousandvillages.com
This store is part of a growing number of "fair trade" stores across the country and Canada that sell crafts, jewelry, and home furnishings from countries around the world. The goal is to offer support for Third World countries and communities.

✳TESOROS TRADING CO.
1500 Congress Ave.
(512) 479-8377
www.tesoros.com
Nudged off Congress Avenue north of the river by a hotel development, Tesoros has relocated in SoCo. It features a wide selection of Mexican and Latin American folk art, jewelry, Day of the Dead tableaux, amulets, loteria art, old Mexican postcards, Moroccan mirrors, jewelry from all over the world, purses made in Vietnam from old Pepsi cans,

Mexican grocery store calendars, retablos, Peruvian good luck pigs, etc. The store's Christmas ornaments, particularly those from Latin America, are popular Austin collectibles. This SoCo store is one of those must-see stops for any visitor.

THE TURQUOISE DOOR
1208 South Congress Ave.
(512) 480-0618
Mexican folk art, notably works from famous ceramic artists like Josefina Aguilar, plus wonderful Southwestern jewelry make this store a popular spot for folk art collectors.

✳UNCOMMON OBJECTS
1512 South Congress Ave.
(512) 442-4000
www.uncommonobjects.com
There seems to be a competition in the South Congress shopping district to see which store can qualify for the Best Stuff award. Here, Mexican doors, architectural elements, lamps, and clothing all compete for attention, making the store a surefire contender for top spot.

Northwest

MARCO POLO'S ATTIC
9828 Great Hills Trail, Suite 330
(512) 342-0111
www.marcopolosattic.com
Walking around owner Renata Marsilli's "attic" is like going on a trek through the world's exotic places. There are many large pieces suitable for the garden or for grabbing attention in any room—antiques from Tibet and Thailand, Indian textiles and Italian marble. Some really unique stage setters here.

North

COURTYARD SHOPS/NEGREL ANTIQUES
5453 Burnet Rd.
(512) 477-1616
www.negrelantiques.com
Several antiques dealers and crafters are creating a small shopping and craft center on Burnet Road, all part of the spontaneous revival of this street as a place to roam for special items and bargains. The center of the shopping area is a small courtyard decorated by garden artist Bud Twilley. He uses old garden stoneware from Europe and Mexico to create fountains, topiaries, and garden art. Negrel Antiques, headquartered at Whit Hanks (see above) has a warehouse here and holds periodic sales.

DRAGON'S LAIR COMICS & FANTASY
4910 Burnet Rd.
(512) 454-2399
www.dlair.net
Comic books, games, fantasy fiction, and videos, particularly those featuring the work of John Wu and Jackie Chan, are sold here. Japanese comic books are particularly popular. The Austin Board Game Group meets here every month, as the store hosts games on-site.

GYPSIES ANTIQUES
5202 Burnet Rd.
(512) 451-6200
www.gypsiesantiques.com
The store owner gathers European and American antiques, often mixing them with whimsical finds and affordable gift items like British bread boards and old china. Gypsies also participates in the spring Round Top antiques show (see the Annual Events & Festivals chapter).

TURQUOISE TRADING POST
6103 Burnet Rd.
(512) 323-5011, (888) 887-7864
www.turquoisetradingpost.com
In addition to offering a wide selection of contemporary and traditional Native American jewelry, the store also has a collection of Zuni fetishes and Navajo kachinas, plus pottery and sculpture from the Southwest.

ARTS & CRAFTS

Central

CLARKSVILLE POTTERY & GALLERIES
Central Park, 4001 North Lamar Blvd., Suite 200
(512) 454-9079
www.clarksvillepottery.com
This pottery shop found life in the old Central Austin neighborhood of Clarksville (hence the name); however, this shop now has a gallery in Central Park featuring pottery by local artists, including decorative pieces and very practical, sturdy everyday ware; also stone fountains, lamps, beautiful wooden boxes, and hummingbird feeders. The store also showcases unusual and unique jewelry pieces, including a collection of wedding rings.

THE NEEDLEWORKS
4401 Medical Pkwy.
(512) 451-6931
www.theneedleworks.com
A mecca for needlework enthusiasts, this store features all manner of needlework supplies and kits, including traditional yarns, specialty fibers, accessories, books, instruction, and finishing. Classes also are offered, and there is an extensive online store.

RENAISSANCE MARKET
West Twenty-third and Guadalupe Streets
www.austinartistsmarket.com

Some folks joke that Austin is an elephant's graveyard for old hippies, and Renaissance Market may be evidence of that. This small plaza on The Drag is home to a variety of crafters and artists who specialize in Woodstock-era items—tie-dyed shirts and skirts, silver jewelry, sun catchers, leather pouches and purses, etc. The outdoor market also attracts jugglers and mimes. A mural, dubbed "Austintatious," shows the city's life in the hippie heyday. Despite its laissez-faire atmosphere, the market is tightly regulated, and the operation is under the auspices of a special city oversight committee that makes sure only authentic hippie stuff is sold here. No place but Austin! Open daily.

i Christmas shopping takes on special meaning in Austin because of two popular annual events: the Austin Junior League Christmas Affair in late November and the Armadillo Christmas Bazaar in Dec. Check our Annual Events & Festivals chapter for details.

South Central

FANNY'S OUTLET FABRIC STORE
1150 South Lamar Blvd.
(512) 442-8255

The antithesis of an outlet, this small, friendly south Central Austin neighborhood shop features an assortment of fabrics and samples, plus decorating staples such as wide linen and Egyptian cotton. It is also a good spot to pick up information on the Austin fashion scene and the various events and classes held in the area.

HILL COUNTRY WEAVERS
1701 South Congress Ave.
(512) 707-7396
www.hillcountryweavers.com

For over two decades this store has been a vital resource for the "fiber community" that includes weavers, knitters, and basket makers. Supplies, classes, and news about shows and events.

North

FEATS OF CLAY
4630 Burnet Rd.
(512) 453-2111
www.featsofclaypottery.com

Local potters buy supplies at this Central Austin store, plus the store offers kiln firing for homemade pieces. The store also features stoneware, earthenware, and porcelain by local potters. Pieces include dinnerware, batter bowls, large tureens, teapots, and bird feeders.

MITCHIE'S FINE BLACK ART GALLERY AND BOOKSTORE
7801 North Lamar Blvd., Building B
(512) 323-6901
www.mitchie.com

Mitchie's celebrates African-American, African, and Caribbean culture, selling arts, crafts, and books that illustrate these regions and the work of the people who live there. The store has a large print collection celebrating the lives of sports figures, cultural and religious heroes, historical figures from the American Civil Rights movement, and celebrations of African and African-American life and art.

RENAISSANCE GLASS COMPANY
5200 Burnet Rd.
(512) 451-3971
www.rencoglass.com

Specializing in stained glass, this arts and crafts store also sells supplies and tools for stained-glass artists.

East

✳SILK ROAD
2832 East Martin Luther King Jr. Blvd., Studio 111
(512) 302-0844
www.srfabrics.com
Formerly housed in a plain-looking, small building across from Central Market, Silk Road has relocated to the Flatbed Building in East Austin where it continues to draw fabric hounds from Austin and beyond. The store sells natural fabrics from around the world, including cottons, silks, linens, batiks, and velvets, plus it has an unusual collection of bone, glass, jet, pewter, and wood buttons.

CLOTHING/FASHION

Central

✳BY GEORGE
524 North Lamar Blvd., Suite 103
(512) 472-5951
www.bygeorgeaustin.com
The two By George shops are a favorite among young, hip, and well-heeled dressers. The look is simple and very modern; the price tag is not so simple. Designers featured include Stella McCartney, Vera Wang, Lanvin, Marc Jacobs, plus some lesser known names. The other location is at 1400 South Congress Ave. (512-441-8600).

CAPRA & CAVELLI
3500 Jefferson St., Suite 110
(512) 450-1919
www.capracavelli.com
This men's boutique features classic looks and designs, casual wear, or button-down

office outfits. The aim is to provide personal service to customers who want to look their best and be comfortable in the Austin climate. A second location has opened in the lobby of the downtown Hilton hotel at 509 East Fifth St. (512-477-2020).

CREATURES
1206 South Congress Ave.
(512) 707-2500
Sweatshop-free fashions by Misile and kooky shoes by the likes of French designer Colico give the wares here a decidedly young, hip feel. The boutique also has clothes for men and babies, really cute shoes for toddlers.

DRESS SHOP
315 Congress Ave.
www.dressshopaustin.com
This on-the-avenue shop is an ideal location for Austin's professional woman shopping for a stylish daytime and classy evening look. Owner Leslie Gandy, an experienced retailer, offers creations by New York City designers.

FETISH
1112 North Lamar Blvd.
(512) 457-1007
Sexy, smart, sleek shoes by designers like Isaac Mizrahi and Cynthia Rowley are sold here. The shop also stocks fashions to match, with designs by Diane von Furstenberg and Laundry, among others.

INSTEP
1010 West Thirty-eighth St.
(512) 476-5110
www.instepaustin.com
If your trusty Birkenstocks ever need fixing, this is the place; a repair shop is on site. The store also sells a line of leather-free "vegan" shoes and chef's clogs.

HATBOX
115 East Sixth St., Suite N
(512) 476-1203
www.hatbox.com
Classic hats for both casual wear and dapper toppers for men and women, even children's hats are featured at this downtown shop. Whether you are hunting for a trilby, a shady straw hat, a tweed cap to wear while touring in that rented convertible, or an Easter bonnet, check out the small store across the street from the Driskill Hotel.

JULIAN GOLD
1214 West Sixth St.
(512) 473-2493
www.juliangold.com
Catering to well-dressed, well-heeled (both in the bucks and the shoes departments) Texas women, Julian Gold has four stores in the state, where shoes, clothes, and accessories by designers like Escada, Bill Blass, and Valentino can be found, plus popular collections created by Ellen Tracy, Missoni, Ferragamo, Anne Klein, and Isaac Mizrahi are featured in the shoes department, and there are bridal, fur, evening wear, and cosmetic departments also.

T. KENNEDY
1011 West Lynn St.
(512) 478-0545
The emphasis is on natural women's clothing here at this small Clarksville area store—easy, natural design and natural fabrics including linen, cotton, and flax. Batik clothing is a specialty, and the store also features jewelry and accessories.

✳THE TEXAS CLOTHIER
2905 San Gabriel St.
(512) 478-4956
www.texasclothier.com

Owners Dain and LaDonna Higdon have survived the economic roller coaster during 30 years of business in Austin. After working for years in retail, Dain Higdon started his own store in 1976, and ever since Austin's busy, top businessmen and attorneys have turned to him for fashion advice. Higdon's clients insist on quality and are willing to pay for it.

South Central

BLACKMAIL
1202 South Congress Ave.
(512) 326-7670
www.blackmailboutique.com
One of several quirky fashion spots in SoCo, it's all about black here (although an occasional dash of red or spot of brown creeps in). Both the clothes and the home furnishings urge shoppers to "think noir!"

LUTHER'S
1200 South Congress Ave.
(512) 442-7000
www.thelutherstore.com
This SoCo shop was created by Cory Moore, Jimmie Vaughn's manager, to sell clothes for "normal guys," manly fashions that reflect Moore's tastes for sturdy clothes that are practical and comfortable to wear. Moore, a partner in the hot rod/auto restoration shop, the Austin Speedshop, sells Dickies workshirts decorated with the shop's logo at his clothing store, plus "rock star" jewelry.

MAYA STAR
1508 South Congress Ave.
(512) 912-1475
www.mayastar.com
The name evokes Latin colors and both the clothes and jewelry here have an exotic flair. Unique pieces like Israeli silk jewelry

are showcases, and wrapped semiprecious stone pieces are a top seller.

Southwest

LAST CALL
Brodie Oaks Shopping Center
4115 South Loop 360
(Capital of Texas Highway)
(512) 447-0701
www.lastcall.com

This is Neiman Marcus without the posh surroundings and posh prices. The famous department store has its outlet store at this location in a small mall in Southwest Austin. The store features men's, women's, and children's fashions, shoes, some small decorative furniture items, and a few household items including sheets, pillows, and knickknacks. Items are discounted up to 70 percent.

SUE PATRICK
5222 Burnet Rd., Suite 150
(512) 452-7701
www.suepatrick.com

Dressing comfortably and smartly in Austin's climate can be a challenge given the hot summer weather and sudden temperature changes in the winter. Sue Patrick offers a wide variety of casual and dressier fashions well suited to the Austin lifestyle. Some of the casual but comfortable fashions often have a hint of Texas in their cut or design. This is the place to go for fashionable burnt orange casual clothes celebrating allegiance to the University of Texas.

CLOTHING/KIDS

Central

BRIGHT BEGINNINGS
1006 West Thirty-eighth St.
(512) 454-KIDS
www.bestdressedkids.com

Owner Sally Whitehouse keeps the Austin lifestyle in mind when stocking her stores. Just like their elders, Austin kids like to play, and that means casual clothes, preferably in natural fabrics. Even the dress-up clothes here emphasize easy wearing and easy caring. The Medical Parkway store, dubbed Best Dressed for Less, features discounted fashions. Two other locations are 701 South Capital of Texas Hwy./Loop 360 (512-328-8989) and 3811 Medical Pkwy. (512-453-0433).

North

DRAGONSNAPS
2438 West Anderson Lane
(512) 445-4497

Owned by the same folks who own Terra Toys (see the Toys section in this chapter), Dragonsnaps seeks to bring the Terra Toys free spirit to kid's clothing. The clothes are easy to wear, fun, and eye-catching.

West

LAMBS-E-DIVEY
3663 Bee Caves Rd.
(512) 306-0566

This West Austin store features both casual wear for kids and outfits for those special occasions, such as Easter, Christmas, and family weddings.

CLOTHING/WESTERN

There is an old saying in Texas: "That boy is all hat," meaning, of course, there's too much image and not much substance. If you are going to don Western wear, you have to have the panache and some bucks. Good boots, a well-made hat, and a sturdy leather belt with a finely made belt buckle do not come cheap.

In Austin, Western attire is not seen as much as in other parts of the state, although at some Western and Mexican dance clubs (see the Nightlife chapter) you will see both men and women dressed in fine Western wear. While you won't see a lot of Stetsons in Austin (outside the dance halls), you will see boots, particularly well-worn, much loved old boots, usually worn with jeans or a long skirt. Boots with no hat is okay, but a hat and no boots is a social faux pas. Nothing says "Yankee" like a guy in a cowboy hat and a pair of loafers.

There are several boot outlet stores in Austin, but the well-heeled will turn to one of the city's master boot makers or specialty shops for a custom-made pair—well-heeled because a good pair of boots can run to several hundred dollars. If you can't afford a pair, settle for a kerchief or two. A faded cotton kerchief, dipped in cold water and tied around your neck on a hot day, is an authentic cowboy tradition.

One word about two stores not listed in this section. Cabela's, a national chain catering to all things outdoors in terms of hunting and fishing, plus Callahan's, a local Austin "feed store" and more, both sell Western wear. We chose to list them in our Food section since they are both wonderful resources for foodies, selling cookware, preserving tools, and all manner of gadgets, but they are also a great resource for Western wear, outdoor, and hunting equipment.

TEXAS HATTERS
911 Commerce St., Lockhart
(512) 398-4287, (800) 421-HATS
www.texashatters.com
What does Prince Charles have in common with Willie Nelson? They both own hats created by one of the most famous Western wear artists in the United States, the late Manny Gammage. For decades, country western music stars, politicians, presidents,

and future kings have worn what are generically called "cowboy hats." Gammage, like his father before him, blocked his hats by hand rather than by machine. Gammage passed away in 1995, but his family has carried on the tradition out of their Lockhart store.

i Singer Jerry Jeff Walker made Capitol Saddlery famous when he sang about the talents of late master boot maker Charlie Dunn. The store had an old-fashioned air, with boots, saddles, tack, and assorted leather wear stacked everywhere. Sadly, the store has closed, but the large sign still hangs outside the building at 1614 Lavaca St. which has been turned into a six-figure, converted downtown residence. Look for the large boot-shaped sign hanging outside the old building, just a few blocks west of the Capitol.

South Central

✳ALLEN'S BOOTS
1522 South Congress Ave.
(512) 447-1413
www.allensboots.com
This Western wear store has been on South Congress for years and now finds itself in the midst of a South Austin shopping revival. This is a great place to find Western wear and boots at reasonable prices. Enjoy the ambience. This is a Western wear shop without the glitz and urban cowboy atmosphere found in some other large Texas cities.

COMPUTERS

Austin has more computer stores than Los Angeles has car dealers. Perhaps not factually true, but metaphorically speaking it captures the tech mood in Austin. In addition to several major chain operations, there is an ever-growing subculture of small stores and resale outlets in Austin. Judging from online ads, it might appear that there's more money in motherboards than mother's old Buick. However, putting a system together from bits of this and that is easily done in Austin, provided you know your bytes from bits. Keep track of the ads, know who is a fixture on the landscape as opposed to a fly-by-night operation, and ask questions. Here is one unique Austin store for geeks:

GOODWILL COMPUTER WORKS
1015 Norwood Park Blvd.
(512) 637-7501
www.austincomputerworks.org
Whether you're looking for a cheap PC or an old classic Mac, this may be the place. Given Austin's intense high-tech industry growth and level of computer ownership, the town's closets are filled with old models. So Goodwill decided to provide a home for the abandoned. Old computers are donated to the shop, fixed up, and sold at bargain-basement prices. It's a great place to find a computer for a schoolchild or grandma without spending a fortune. There is an informal "museum" on-site, also.

FLEA MARKETS
Central
AUSTIN CITY-WIDE GARAGE SALES
Palmer Events Center
900 Barton Springs Rd.
(512) 441-2828
www.cwgs.com
The Palmer Events Center on Lady Bird Lake is host to a large sale, usually held once a month (except Dec), featuring more than 180 vendors selling a variety of flea market merchandise. Dates vary, so check the website for each monthly sale.

Northeast
AUSTIN COUNTRY FLEA MARKET
9500 US 290 East
(512) 928-2795
www.austincountry.citymax.com
This is the real thing: an old-fashioned, take-your-chances flea market. A jumble of clothing, rugs, pottery, tools, records, furniture, CDs and videos, and sporting goods. Beware, some of the "brand-name" items may not be the real thing. The market's Mexican herb stalls and Latino music stands give the market a south-of-the-border flavor. You also can have your palm or tarot cards read, or enjoy a snow cone and a barbecue sandwich. The market is approximately 5 miles east of I-35 and is open only on weekends.

Southwest
MARKET DAY
Lions Field, Wimberley
(512) 847-2201
www.visitwimberley.com/marketdays
On the first Sat of the month, Apr through Dec, flea market mavens flock to Wimberley, southwest of Austin, to comb the multitude of stalls at the famed Wimberley Market Day. Vendors number in the hundreds, and the wise get there early—to get first choice get there by 7:30 a.m. The Lions Club sells sausage wraps for breakfast and barbecue later in the day, plus a couple of local churches operate cake and cookie stands.

FARMERS' MARKETS

A good resource for keeping track of local farmers' market activities and the status of locally produced vegetables and fruits is the

Texas Department of Agriculture's website www.picktexas.com, especially if the family plans a peach-pickin' weekend. Austin's Sustainable Food Center offers a guide to local farmers' markets, farms, and special events on its website, www.sustainablefoodcenter.org.

Central

AUSTIN FARMERS' MARKET
422 Guadalupe St.
www.sfcfarmersmarketdowntown.org
The downtown market is the latest addition to the farmers' market scene in Austin, turning Republic Square, 2 blocks west of Congress Avenue, into a busy mix of food stalls and craftspeople every Sat morning. The market's website lists many of the vendors and links to their websites.

> **i** It is really a love story, a tale of how Sara Bolton with her family and friends created an award-winning goat cheese dairy and farm in the hills just west of Austin. Sara passed away at 52, surrounded by her loved ones, but her family continues to produce incredibly delicious cheese at Pure Luck Farm (available at local stores including Whole Foods and Central Market), and visitors can arrange for tours. There are also open house days and special classes. Check the farm website www.purelucktexas.com.

South

SOUTH AUSTIN FARMERS' MARKET
2910 South Congress Ave.
(512) 285-4758
www.austinfarm.org
Local farmers set up shop in the parking lot of the El Gallo restaurant on Sat morning from spring to fall.

Southwest

SUNSET VALLEY FARMERS' MARKET
3200 Jones Rd.
www.sfcfarmersmarketsunsetvalley.org
The large Toney Burger stadium parking lot in southwest Austin is home every Sat morning to a large farmers' market. Some of the best-known names in Austin foodie circles have a presence here.

West

BARTON CREEK FARMERS' MARKET
MoPac and Capital of Texas Highway
(512) 280-1976 (Sat number),
(512) 443-0143 (weekday number)
www.bartoncreekfarmersmarket.org
This westside farmers' market sets up in the Barton Creek shopping mall parking lot every Sat morning.

North Central

TRIANGLE FARMERS' MARKET
4600 North Lamar Blvd.
www.sfcfarmersmarket.com
The Triangle "village," a development of small shops, apartments, and restaurants just north of the UT campus, hosts the farmers' market from midafternoon to early evening every Sat.

East

*BOGGY CREEK FARM
3414 Lyons Rd.
(512) 926-4650
www.boggycreekfarm.com
It is almost unbelievable that just 2½ miles east of downtown Austin in an old East Austin neighborhood is a 5-acre organic farm that offers its products for sale every Wed and Sat morning throughout the year. Boggy

Creek Farm is noted for its fruit and vegetable crops, particularly its tomatoes. Owners Larry Butler and Carol Ann Sayle send out a weekly e-mail to customers, announcing what is in season. But there's more; the e-mail also includes a link to wonderfully written glimpses into farm life that offer busy urbanites a moment's pause for reflection.

HOPE FARMERS' MARKET
414 Waller St.
www.hopefarmersmarket.org
Crafts and food products are featured at this small eastside farmers' market held every Sun afternoon from 11 a.m. to 3 p.m.

FOOD/GOURMET/ KITCHENWARE

Austin is a city that considers food a significant part of life, not in a highfalutin way, although the city's restaurants boast a fair number of top-notch chefs, but in a way that celebrates the mix of food and friends, new tastes and familiar comforts. It is no surprise that when out-of-town visitors arrive, many Austinites take them on a discovery tour of the city's food stores. Foodies have an abundant choice of stores where they can shop for kitchen and pantry supplies (check the listings under General Stores for several of our favorite hometown hardware stores that also cater to the culinary shopper).

Central

ACE MART RESTAURANT SUPPLY CO.
2415 South Congress Ave.
(512) 482-8700
www.acemart.com
A little-known secret in cooking circles is that many restaurant supply companies are open to the public. Ace sells both to the

trade and to the individual customer. Thrifty cooks and hostesses will check out the price of plates, glasses, silverware, and party ware here. There are two locations, a new one in central Austin since its Fifth Street location was sold to a loft developer, and a second in north Austin at 411 North Lamar Blvd. (512-832-9933).

ANDERSON COFFEE COMPANY
Jefferson Square
(512) 453-1533
www.andersonscoffee.com
Jefferson Square, just off West Thirty-fifth Street near Kerbey Lane, is a collection of small, older homes turned into cozy shops, a fitting setting for Anderson Coffee Company, founded in 1972 and which sells coffees, teas, mugs, and teapots, plus culinary spices—comfort stuff. Singer-songwriter Lyle Lovett is said to be a fan of Anderson's coffee.

i Shopping for a special gift that captures the creative spirit in Austin? Check out the online crafty community that sells its wares on www .etsy.com. Many crafters and artists with online shops gather at www.etsy-austin.blogspot.com where the motto is "Keep Austin Crafty."

CENTRAL MARKET
Central Park, Fortieth Street, and Lamar Boulevard
(512) 216-1000
www.centralmarket.com
The two Central Market supermarkets are must-see stops for foodies (see the Close-up in this chapter). The other location is at Westgate, Ben White, and South Lamar Boulevards (512-899-4300).

CIPOLLINA
1213 West Lynn St.
(512) 477-1237
www.cipollina-austin.com

The name is Italian for a special, small sweet onion, often grilled or roasted in a sweet balsamic vinegar, and it is a fitting symbol for this popular take-out deli in the Clarksville neighborhood created by the owners of one of Austin's favorite restaurants, Jeffrey's (see the Restaurants chapter). A great place to stop for picnic fare or a take-home dinner feast.

✳DAI DUE
Republic Square Park, Fourth and
Guadalupe
(412) 524-0688
www.daidueaustin.net

One of our favorite local food producers, Dai Due (the name derives from an old Italian phrase advising wise choices in choosing food) is both a butcher's shop and the force behind the Dai Due Supper Club, which hosts special dinners at charming indoor and outdoor locations during the culinary year. At their butcher's facility, Jessie and Lily Griffiths use carefully and lovingly selected local ingredients to create a variety of sausages, pâtés, and relishes that can be ordered online and picked up at Austin farmers' markets, usually the downtown market on Sat morning. They also offer butchering and cooking classes during the year.

PASTA & CO.
3502 Kerbey Lane
(512) 453-0633
www.austinpasta.com

Pasta to go is the theme here. The company makes numerous kinds of pasta and sauces, including jalapeño fettuccine, wild-mushroom ravioli, and ancho-pecan pesto.

For those who can't bring themselves to boil a pot of water, the store also features ready-cooked pasta dishes that simply need reheating. For Valentine's Day, the store makes special heart-shaped varieties.

PORTABLA
1200 West Sixth St.
(512) 481-TOGO (8646)
www.portabla.com

Casual eating is a hallmark of the Austin scene, and this take-out deli (affiliated with nearby Sweetish Hill Bakery; see below) offers a variety of dishes, many with a Mediterranean flavor. Portabla also caters small and large parties. During football season, there is a tailgate menu offered to feed the fans in style. Closed Sun.

SAVORY SPICE SHOP
1201B West Sixth St.
(512) 524-1093
www.savoryspiceshop.com

The Austin branch of a popular Denver spice shop founded by Mike and Janet Johnston, hosts of a Food Network show, sells all manner of spices and extracts, plus special blends and sauces.

SWEETISH HILL BAKERY
1120 West Sixth St.
(512) 472-1347
www.sweetishhill.com

One of Austin's most noted bakeries, Sweetish Hill is famed for its breads, cookies (the lemon bars are addictive), and European-style pastries. This is a great place to order a special birthday cake, and many Austinites insist on a chocolate or mocha buche de noel (a French cake shaped and decorated like a log, complete with meringue mushrooms) at Christmas time. The bakery is also a popular breakfast and lunch spot (see the Restaurants chapter). A second location is at 98 San Jacinto Blvd. (512-472-1347).

WALTON'S FANCY AND STAPLE
609 West Sixth St.
(512) 542-3380
www.waltonsfancyandstaple.com
Walton's is yet another symbol of movie star Sandra Bullock's love affair with Austin (see her down the street bistro Bess in our restaurants chapter). Bullock opened the store on Sixth Street and emblazoned its motto—"Perishable, Cherishable, Fetishable" on the old-fashioned painted sign. The store sells coffee and deli-style food, plus baked goods that can be eaten in-house or as take-out. They also make Sweets2Go and Fancy2Go gift baskets, packed with chocolates, Bess signature candles (inspired by Bullock's favorite natural scents), and fresh flowers.

WHEATSVILLE FOOD CO-OP
3101 Guadalupe St.
(512) 478-2667
www.wheatsville.com
Wheatsville is an old-fashioned cooperative grocery store where the customers own the store. Members pay a nominal annual fee or purchase a share, but anyone can shop here. The co-op specializes in natural foods, and there is a vegetarian deli.

WIGGY'S
1130 West Sixth St.
(512) 474-WINE (9463)
If you are picking up a picnic at nearby Portabla, Cipollina, or Sweetish Hill, these two small central Austin stores are a good place to find a wine to complement your menu. The staff is knowledgeable and the shops offer a wide range of wines, some bargains,

others more expensive. The stores also have a large selection of cigars and spirits. The other location is at 1104 North Lamar Blvd. (512-479-6045).

WILLIAMS-SONOMA
Barton Creek Square
2901 Capital of Texas Hwy.
(512) 328-5220
www.williams-sonoma.com
Austin has two branches of the well-known kitchen shop, both located in major shopping malls, one west and the other northwest. The second location is at The Arboretum Market, 9722 Great Hills Trail (512-231-1813).

South Central

FARM TO MARKET GROCERY
1718 South Congress Ave.
(512) 462-7220
www.fm1718.com
A loaf of bread, a jug of wine, and a can of tomatoes. This SoCo neighborhood grocery store (look for the big radish sign) provides essentials and staples for home cooks in the nearby neighborhoods. The owners emphasize local and organic produce and products.

✳LA MEXICANA BAKERY
1924 South First St.
(512) 443-6369
www.la-mexicana-bakery.com
Mexican pastries are intended to be mood-lifters, a little sweet bite to accompany mid-morning coffee, or a late-night snack with a cup of hot Mexican chocolate. Many contain no salt or preservatives, so they are best eaten the day they are made. La Mexicana offers a variety of cookies and cakes, empanadas stuffed with pumpkin, gingerbread pigs, and sugarcoated conchas (shell-shaped cakes).

Close-up

Austin's Feeding Frenzy

One surefire way to judge how people regard their hometown is to ask them where they take out-of-town visitors for an Insider's view of their city. Three spots appear on most short lists—Barton Springs Pool, the State Capitol, and the grocery store. The grocery store? Yep, but not just any grocery store and not just one. Austin is the birthplace of two marvelous grocery stores, Central Market and Whole Foods. One is the creation of an old Texas family-owned grocery store chain, H-E-B; the other grew out of the imaginations of several hippies, for want of a better word, who took the old concept of a health food store to places they could only dream of 30 years ago. In fairness, we have listed them alphabetically, but any serious food enthusiast should visit both and take a large shopping bag.

Central Market now ranks among the city's most visited landmarks, and it has become a living symbol of the city's lifestyle. On any given weekend, when the store is at its busiest, it is possible to see Austinites from all parts of the city, of all ages and backgrounds, speaking a variety of languages. So popular was the original Central Market, a second has opened in Southwest Austin—Central Market Westgate.

The Central Market concept is the creation of the H-E-B grocery store chain, a family-owned South Texas chain now headquartered in restored buildings in the historic King William District in San Antonio. H-E-B has been an innovator, both in its concept developments and its growth both in Texas and Mexico. The original Central Market in Austin is the model for others around the state, all designed to evoke the spirit of an Old World marketplace. Visitors enter a vegetable and fruit market first, then proceed to a fish and meat market, a wine shop, a specialty food area, a bakery, a deli, and a cheese shop, finally reaching the front of the store, where a flower shop stands. The original Central Market building itself is a blend of local materials and design elements taken from 19th-century Texas buildings with a hint of Italian inspiration. A large tile mural by Austin artist Malou Flato at the front of the store depicts Barton Springs pool. The second location also borrows Austin icons, and there is a replica of the city's moonlight towers (see the Attractions chapter) out front, plus more tile murals of wildflowers by Flato.

Among Central Market's most crowded spots on the weekend are the butcher shop and fishmonger. The meat market features aged premium choice beef, lamb, veal, naturally raised pork, and poultry raised on organic grains, as well as custom-made sausage. Special cuts of meat can be ordered. The seafood counter offers numerous varieties of both saltwater and freshwater fish, shellfish, and sushi.

The market sells numerous domestic and imported wines, plus an extensive collection of beers. The specialty foods section features a large selection of olive oils and vinegars, numerous barbecue sauces, salsas, fresh pastas, an olive bar—and the list goes on. Then there is the bakery, where French baguettes are baked daily and fresh tortillas roll off the conveyer belt of the tortilla machine. The deli has prosciuttos from Italy, smoked salmon from Scotland, pâtés, and organic cold cuts. The cheese shop offers cheeses from the best producers in the United States and Europe. Both stores also have an extensive prepared food to go counter. The original store houses the Central Market Cooking School, where internationally known chefs as well as top Austin chefs have taught. Both stores also feature a Central Market Cafe (see the Restaurants and Kidstuff chapters), a popular family gathering spot where patrons can eat inside or listen to a variety of local musicians while eating on the deck. The original location at 4001 North Lamar Blvd. is open from 9 a.m. to 9 p.m. daily, and the cafe is open from 7 a.m. to 10 p.m. daily. Call (512) 206-1000 for general information, (512) 206-1013 for the meat market, (512) 206-1012 for the seafood market, and (512) 458-3068 for the cooking school. The Westgate location at 4477 South Lamar Blvd. is open from 9 a.m. to 9 p.m. daily, and the cafe from 7 a.m. to 10 p.m. daily. Call (512) 899-4300 for all departments. During the holidays, notably Thanksgiving and Christmas, both stores extend their hours in the evening. For more information check out www.centralmarket.com.

The first **Whole Foods Market** was in a tiny store not much bigger than a 7-11—the premises are now occupied by Cheapo Discs at 914 North Lamar Blvd. But just 2 blocks to the south is the world headquarters of Whole Foods, where the corporate offices make the old store look like a crowded VW bus. Whole Foods was founded in 1980—back then the store had 19 employees, now it has 32,000 and operates 180 stores in three countries, including Canada and the United Kingdom. Its stock is listed on NASDAQ, and like the Austinites who bought stock in Dell years ago, it has made some people very, very happy. But commercial success aside, the company strives to keep the old ethic going that it developed in its first days, according to CEO John Mackey, using a team member approach where employees share profits and have input into company policy. True to its roots, many of the store's offerings are organic, but it is also a veritable gold mine of foods from various cultures. The meat and seafood departments are large and offer not just various cuts but also smoked meats, aged beef, shucked oysters, and ready-to-go cooked foods of all varieties. There is a barbecued meat counter, smoked fish counter, and a large variety of fresh sausages.

From the moment the shopper enters the store and sees Lamar Street Greens, a fresh food cafe, he or she is surrounded by not just a multitude of grocery choices but also in-house mini restaurants. Pasta, salads, a cheese and wine bar, ethnic foods, a pizza oven, a smoked nut bar, noodles and sushi, satays and soups, coffee and raw foods, you name it, Whole Foods likely has it and you can eat it here, on the rooftop garden, or take it home.

Just in case you can't find what you want, there is a concierge desk at the front of the store where you pick up an iPod and take a tour. The Whole Foods Landmark Store is open from 8 a.m. to 10 p.m. daily and is located at 525 North Lamar Blvd.; (512) 476-1206, www.wholefoods.com. A second, smaller store is located in northwest Austin in the Gateway Plaza, 9607 Research Blvd., (512) 345-5003.

SHOPPING

Be sure to ask the names of the varieties—often they are a wonderful play on the
shape, ingredients, or taste of the item. The
bakery also sells Mexican sodas, barbacoa
(Mexican barbecue), tortillas, and carnitas
(slow-roasted pork) to go.

PHOENICIA BAKERY & DELI
2912 South Lamar Blvd.
(512) 447-4444
www.phoeniciabakery.com
Phoenicia is a Mediterranean deli specializing in imported foods. In addition to olives,
olive oils, peppers, spices, sauces, pasta, and
grains, the store also sells cold cuts, plus
cheeses from the region, pickles, stuffed
grape leaves, freshly made tahini, and hum-
mus. There is a frozen food section where
bakers can find phyllo dough. The deli also
makes sandwiches and has a small bakery
selling pita bread and baklava, plus other
regional delights. In addition to the original
location in South Central Austin, a second,
larger new store has opened in uptown
Austin on Burnet Road. Another location is
at 4701 Burnet Rd. (512-323-6770).

Northwest

FARADAYS
1501 RR 620 North, Lakeway
(512) 266-5660
www.faradayskitchenstore.com
Cooks in the western 'burbs don't have to
drive into Austin to shop for the best culinary
tools or even take cooking classes.

North Central

ASAHI IMPORTS
6105 Burnet Rd.
(512) 453-1850

It is easy to miss this store with its unassuming storefront in a strip shopping center, but
its selection of everyday Japanese ceramics,
sake sets, rice bowls, teapots, plus origami
kits and Japanese food items (tea, rice candy,
plum wine) is well worth seeking out, both
for price and quality.

LAMME'S CANDIES
5330 Airport Blvd.
(512) 310-2223, (800) 252-1885
www.lammes.com
The Lamme family has been making candies in Austin since 1885. Famed for Texas
Chewie Pecan Pralines, Lamme's also heralds
the early summer with its chocolate-dipped
strawberries. The company's headquarters
is on Airport Boulevard, but there are other
locations around the area: Lamar Village at
Thirty-eighth Street in Central Austin, downtown at Sixth and Congress, Northcross Mall
in North Austin, Barton Creek Mall in West
Austin, Highland Mall in North Austin, Lakeline Mall in Northwest Austin, RR 620 and
I-35 in Round Rock, and at San Marcos Factory Outlet stores.

MANDOLA'S ITALIAN MARKET
4700 West Guadalupe St.
(512) 419-9700
www.mandolasmarket.com
The creation of Texas chef Damian Mandola,
this namesake store and cafe features all the
essential Italian ingredients and goodies.
Fresh bread, meats and cheeses, pastas both
dried and homemade, olive oils, vinegars
and antipasto essentials. For desserts, there
is a gelati bar and bakery with biscotti and
ladyfingers for tiramisu. Another location is
at Beecave Galleria, Loop 620 and Highway
71 (512-600-8500).

MGM INDIAN FOODS
7429 Burnet Rd.
(512) 459-5353
www.mgmindianfoods.com
This is the city's oldest Indian grocery, stocking herbs, vegetables, dried fruits and nuts, and other vital ingredients for Indian cuisine. Recently the owner, who hails from the state of Kerala in India, has added foods from Ghana and Nigeria to meet customer demands.

MI VICTORIA BAKERY
5425 Burnet Rd.
(512) 458-1898
Owner Anita Becerra creates Mexican specialties at this small bakery on Burnet Rd. One seasonal item worth seeking out is her pan de muerto or Day of the Dead bread, which celebrates the annual Mexican holiday on All Souls Day. (See the Annual Events chapter for more on All Souls Day.)

SPEC'S LIQUORS
5775 Airport Blvd.
(512) 366-8300
www.specsonline.com
This Houston-based warehouse-sized liquor store, wine shop, and deli was a welcome addition to the Austin foodie scene for bargain hunters. There are three locations, one north central, one southwest, and a third northwest—the other two are at 4960 West US 290 (512-366-8260) and 10515 North MoPac Blvd., Arborwalk shopping center (512-342-6893). Pay with cash or a debit card and get an extra discount.

North

HONG KONG SUPERMARKET
8557 Research Blvd.
(512) 339-2068
A stroll around this North Austin supermarket, which was formerly a neighborhood grocery store, is like a culinary tour of Asia. The owners filled the facility with Asian foodstuffs, fresh, frozen, and canned, to meet the needs of Austin's growing Asian population. The meat and fresh fish section features cuts and types of fish and fowl popular among cooks. There is a cooked meat section with barbecued ducks and meats, plus several aisles featuring kitchen and household goods. It is a good place to buy noodles, tea, and rice in bulk.

MT SUPERMARKET
10901 North Lamar Blvd.
(512) 454-4804
www.mtsupermarket.com
This 55,000-square-foot supermarket serves Austin's growing Asian population and aficionados of Asian cuisine. The supermarket is the anchor to Austin's Chinatown market (www.chinatownaustin.com), and has vast aisles of fresh vegetables, fish tanks, and staples to stock Chinese, Thai, Japanese, Indian, Filipino, Korean, and Vietnamese kitchens. Chinatown is the location for traditional Asian festivals like Chinese New Year and the shopping center joined in the Chuy's Christmas children parade (see the Annual Events & Festivals chapter) with a popular Hello Kitty float.

SUR LA TABLE
11410 Century Oaks Terrace
(512) 833-6905
www.surlatable.com
This Austin branch of the foodie favorite national chain offers chef's tools; the best cooking pots, pans, and devices; plus wonderful linens and crockery. Spend a few dollars or go whole hog on tools to enhance your kitchen skills. Sur La Table is located on

the ritzy main street of The Domain shopping center.

East

CALLAHAN'S GENERAL STORE
501 US 183
(512) 385-3452
www.callahansgeneralstore.com
Callahan's sells sausage-stuffing machines, canning equipment, cast iron cookware, and all manner of supplies for cooks, both kitchen-bound and out in the wild. In addition, they have Western wear, boots, saddles, and supplies for the farm and ranch.

✳EL MILAGRO
910 East Sixth St.
(512) 477-6476
www.el-milagro.com
El Milagro—the Miracle—is an authentic tortilla factory that sells both wholesale to Austin grocery stores and restaurants and retail to the walk-in customers (look for their tortillas at Central Market and Wal-Mart). Buying from the source can be fun, and it gives you an opportunity to see the inner workings of an authentic culinary tradition both south of the border and in Texas. Ambitious cooks who plan to follow a Texas tradition and make Christmas tamales can buy freshly ground masa (cornmeal) from the factory. Some Austin foodies swear the "Blancas" white corn tortillas are the best in town. Check out the website for its great music and recipes.

FIESTA MART
3909 North I-35
(512) 406-3900
www.fiestamart.com
A branch of the Houston supermarket chain, Fiesta takes a multicultural approach to the grocery store business. Everything from banana leaves for tamales to British custard mixes can be found on the shelves here. If your Puerto Rican pen pal or your great-aunt from Australia is coming to town, check the shelves here for those grocery essentials. Another location is at 5510 South I-35 (512-373-7800).

South

CABELA'S
15570 I-35, Buda
(512) 925-1100
www.cabelas.com
Maybe the only store that some shopping-averse men will go to with enthusiasm. This national chain sells all things for the outdoor life, hunting, fishing, camping, etc., but we like it for its wide range of foodie supplies. Cast iron cookware, home preserving and sausage-making equipment. Big fryers for that southern fried turkey, chili pots big enough to feed the team, plus picnic and barbecue supplies.

West

TRIANON COFFEE ROASTERS
3201 Bee Caves Rd.
(512) 328-4033
www.trianon.com
This French-style coffee boutique sells freshly roasted beans, pastries, chocolate, and candies.

GARDENING
South Central

FLORIBUNDA
2401–B South Lamar Blvd.
(512) 441-6145
www.floribundaworks.com

Tucked behind a bead shop and a vintage clothing store, Floribunda is like a small magic garden. Austin-friendly plants, vibrant pots, seeds, tools, and garden ornaments are arranged artfully in this hidden garden. Ivan Spaller, a young Austin garden artist who once worked at the Bush Kennebunkport, Maine, home, has designed several garden follies, including a literal lawn chair—an oversize lawn-covered sofa that sits in one corner of the garden—and a 4-poster lawn "bed."

THE GREAT OUTDOORS
3730 South Congress Ave.
(512) 448-2992
www.gonursery.com
Huge live oaks cover this South Austin nursery across from the St. Edward's University campus, making it a pleasant place to meander while choosing plants and daydreaming about garden projects. The garden center offers advice on growing in the challenging Austin climate and has special tips on bamboo, fruit trees, banana palms, and other tropicals that can tolerate both hot summers and sudden cold snaps. Another attraction is the on-site outdoor cafe, the Mad Bird Juice Garden, where smoothies, coffee, muffins, cookies, and sandwiches are served amid the horticultural surroundings.

South

IT'S ABOUT THYME
11726 Manchaca Rd.
(512) 280-1192
www.itsaboutthyme.com
Newcomers to Austin who enjoy gardening may be frustrated if they try to grow plants that flourish in cooler, northern climes, but they won't be disappointed if they stick to native plants and those herbs that do well in

Mediterranean countries—rosemary, oregano, basil, and thyme. This South Austin herb nursery, 2 miles south of Slaughter Lane, has a wide selection of herbs and related items. The shop also sells antique roses, which do quite well in the Austin climate, and xeriscape and pond plants.

Southwest

✳THE NATURAL GARDENER
8648 Old Bee Caves Rd.
(512) 288-6113
www.naturalgardeneraustin.com
Owner John Dromgole is a well-known radio personality who preaches the benefits of organic gardening every Sat morning on KLBJ–AM. The extensive gardens and nursery, tucked away on a country road in Southwest Austin (technically lying just inside our West region, but for driving access it is listed here), are always busy on the weekends as Austin gardeners flock here for plants, flowers, vegetables, seeds, a wonderful variety of tools and garden ornaments, advice and inspiration. There is an antique rose collection, plus xeriscape plants for low water–maintenance gardens. The nursery also sells a line of soils and fertilizers, including Dillo Dirt, a soil enhancer made from recycled Austin sewage wastes. Shoppers can bag their soils or have large amounts delivered.

West

BARTON SPRINGS NURSERY
3601 Bee Caves Rd.
(512) 328-6655
www.bartonspringsnursery.net
This West Lake Hills nursery features an extensive collection of native plants. Newcomers soon learn that native is often the best way to go in the Austin climate, and

many varieties and species can be found here. The owners and staff have a warehouse of knowledge to help gardeners overcome the challenges of Hill Country gardening. The center also has a collection of wildflower seeds and garden ornaments.

i It is a dream shopping trip for anyone fascinated by architectural salvage, plus the drive is a pretty one on a spring day. Discovery Architectural Antiques, 409 Saint Francis St., in Gonzales, a small town 60 miles southeast of Austin, boasts a vast array of doors, old ceiling tiles, sinks, bathtubs, and hardware—all salvaged from old homes. (830) 672-2428; www .discoverys.net.

East

BIG RED SUN
1102 East Cesar Chavez St.
(512) 480-0688
www.bigredsun.com
This garden design and landscaping business also houses a wonderful garden shop with strikingly modern planters, imported ceramic pots, and "retro-botanicals" that match the Austin climate and hip personality. A small store on-site, Little Green Moon, sells unusual clothing for children, reflecting the fact that this is a family business, and there is a housewares section also.

PITCHFORKS AND TABLESPOONS
2113 Manor Rd.
(512) 476-5858
www.eastsidecafeaustin.com
They grow their own vegetables and herbs at the Eastside Cafe (see the Restaurants chapter), so it was only logical that a small food and garden shop open on-site at

this—the name says it all—eastside cafe. In addition to gourmet and homestyle pantry items, patrons can find balm to soothe those garden-stressed hands, birdhouses and butterfly kits, herbs, and natural fertilizers.

GENERAL STORES/HARDWARE
Central

✳BREED & COMPANY
718 West Twenty-ninth St.
(512) 474-6679
www.breedandco.com
This is the kind of store that actually can bring couples closer together, and even heal marriages. One partner can stroll the nuts and bolts section, while the other daydreams about the days when the entire collection of cooking equipment will find its way to his or her kitchen. The store stocks hard-to-find and everyday hardware and paint supplies, cleaning solutions, china and crystal, a perfumery, a specialty food section, garden supplies, picture frames, decorative accessories, throw rugs, coffee beans, bird feeders, knives, cutting boards, and all manner of cookware. Breed also offers bridal and gift registries and cooking classes and events. Another location is at 3663 Bee Caves Rd. (512-328-3960).

ECO-WISE
110 West Elizabeth
(512) 326-4496
www.ecowise.com
Located in SoCo, this hardware and more store is dedicated to selling earth-friendly materials to area home rehabbers and homeowners, making it a popular spot for the city's green builders, both professional and amateur. In addition to ecowise tiles flooring, paints, glues, etc., the store also sells green

living goods for the home, family, kitchen, garden, and even the office.

HARRELL'S SUPPLY AND SERVICE CENTER
1409 Oltorf St.
(512) 442-5966
www.harrellssupplyandservice.com
This third-generation south central hardware store is legendary at our house for always having the right bit to solve a household dilemma. The store stocks plumbing and pipe supplies, plus tools, especially retro fittings for older homes. Their motto is "Together we can do it yourself!"

ZINGER HARDWARE AND GENERAL MERCHANT
2436 West Anderson Lane
(512) 533-9001
www.zingerhardware.com
This north central store is a treasure trove, a veritable "A to Zinger" as the store's motto proclaims of finds for the home, the kitchen, the garden, even for Fido and Kitty. From architectural hardware for home rehabbers, to handmade furniture, even fountain pens wrapped in rattlesnake skin.

GIFTS
Central

ATOMIC CITY
1700 San Antonio St.
(512) 477-0293
Toys are us—for grown-ups that is. Atomic City is the place to find Godzillas that spit fire, fighting nuns, and other Japanese toys to keep on the desk for those moments when the brain bombs. The store also has a large collection of tin toys, lava lamps, Hawaiian shirts, even boots and shoes to add just the

right sartorial touch to a toy player's tropical outfit.

CAPITOL COMPLEX VISITORS CENTER
112 East Eleventh St., Capitol Annex
(512) 305-8400
www.texascapitolgiftshop.com
The capitol police report the occasional ardent tourist attempting to remove part of the capitol's wrought-iron fence, a doorknob, or door hinge as a memento. But law-abiding visitors head to the capitol's gift shop where gifts reflecting these architectural elements can be bought without risking arrest. Replicas of the capitol's door hinges serve as bookends; other architectural elements are reproduced in paperweights. The store has a first-class collection of posters, flags, and books about Texas flora, fauna, travel, and history. The small shop also sells Texas foods and T-shirts.

COWGIRLS AND FLOWERS
508 Walsh St.
(512) 478-4626
www.cowgirlsandflowers.com
One of the most popular flower shops in the central city, noted for its artistic, modern arrangements.

THE MENAGERIE
1601 West Thirty-eighth St., Suite 7
(512) 453-4644
www.themenagerie.com
Bucatelli, Christofle, Saint Louis, and Wedgwood are just some of the top names in crystal, china, and silver that can be found at this small, elegant Jefferson Square shop. The bridal registry is a favorite among some of Austin's old families. The shop also sells jewelry and collectibles.

MORNING STAR TRADING COMPANY
1919 South First St.
(512) 476-1726
www.morningstarcompany.com
The major trade here is in oils and essences aimed at making folks feel better. The store sells massage, relaxation, and bath oils, plus other body-care products.

OAT WILLIE'S
617 West Twenty-ninth St.
(512) 482-0630
www.oatwillies.com
Remember the term "head shop"? A visit to Oat Willie's is a jaunt down memory lane for anyone who grew up in the '60s. Whenever you see an "Onward through the Fog" bumper sticker, you are a looking at an Austin hallmark—this was Oat Willie's slogan. Oat Willie once ran for President, and his T-shirts are now collectors' items. T-shirts are still sold at Oat Willie's, along with comic books, videos, toys, and clothing. Two other locations are at 1931 East Oltorf St. (512-448-3313) and 9505 Burnet Rd. (512-836-6289).

PAPER PLACE
4001 North Lamar Blvd., Suite 540
(512) 451-6531
www.paperplaceaustin.com
The stock here goes beyond invitations, celebratory cards for all occasions, and stationery to include a large stock of handmade papers that can be used in a variety of crafts.

POSITIVE IMAGES
1118 West Sixth St.
(512) 472-1831
Part of the so-called West End shopping district, this store has a delightful mix of handcrafted jewelry, wooden boxes, and glass art. The store also sells fantastical furniture—carved,

painted, and decorated with inspirational and witty sayings—woodland animals, pastoral scenes, and fairy-tale fantasies.

THINGS CELTIC
1806 West Thirty-fifth St.
(512) 472-2358
www.thingsceltic.com
The name says it all here. The shop features arts, crafts, and food items from the Celtic world—Scotland, Ireland, Wales, Cornwall—and Celtic artists in the United States. Celtic lace, Belleck china, Waterford crystal, and Irish tea are sold in this small shop in the Thirty-fifth St. shopping area. The shop also sells kilts, socks, walking sticks, and Celtic jewelry. The shop's operators have information on the Austin Celtic Association, which holds an annual festival in Oct (see the Annual Events & Festivals chapter). The website offers online shopping and a link to the association.

UNIVERSITY CO-OP
2244 Guadalupe St.
(512) 476-7211
www.coop-bookstore.com
If God isn't a Longhorn, why did he paint the sunset burnt orange and then fill this store on The Drag with all that burnt-orange stuff? That philosophical question needs no answer in Austin. UT fans can find just about anything in their team colors here.

South Central

THE HERB BAR
200 West Mary St.
(512) 444-6251
www.theherbbar.com
Herbs, both culinary and medicinal, can be found here, plus tinctures and body oils designed to soothe what ails you. The small

SoCo shop also offers massage and alternative medicine information.

HOME FURNISHINGS
Central

FEATHER YOUR NEST
3500 Jefferson St.
(512) 206-3555
www.featheryournesthome.com
Luxurious European linens, table linens, lamps, and home furnishings are sold at the charming Jefferson Square shop in the Thirty-fifth St. shopping district.

✳FINCH
417 West Second St.
(512) 236-1414
www.shopfinch.com
Frankly, some of the newcomers to the shopping scene lack an "Austin feel," but not Finch in the hip Second Street District. Owner Kristi Pruett favors pieces that reveal the hand of the maker and have a modern, but charming look and feel, notably her collection of Heath ceramics.

JAYA
902 North Lamar Blvd.
(512) 457-1255
www.jayafurniture.com
David and Jacque Hooks travel to China, India, and Southeast Asia to bring back exotic furniture and home furnishings for their central Austin store. They also take special orders that craftsmen in faraway places construct to meet your needs. Many of them are built from old woods to modern specifications.

TIPLER'S LAMP SHOP
1204 West Fifth St.
(512) 472-5007
www.tiplerslampshop.com

Tipler's has a selection of hanging lamps from the 1900s to 1940s, plus a large variety of antique and custom-made lamps. The store also has an extensive selection of lampshades and provides repair and restoration services.

WILDFLOWER
908 North Lamar Blvd.
(512) 320-0449
www.wildflowerorganics.com
Natural is the keyword at this home furnishings boutique in the North Lamar–West Sixth shopping district. Natural bedding, shabby slipcovers, organic cotton mattresses, and furniture from reclaimed wood are among the items for sale in this boutique. The store also sells natural clothing for the whole family, including babies.

South Central

AVIARY
2110 South Lamar Blvd.
(512) 916-4445
www.aviarydecor.com/index
Proof that South Lamar Boulevard is a shopping destination that reflects Austin creativity, Aviary is a mix of travel finds from Canada, Sweden, Argentina—not your usual finds in Austin where Latin America, Italy, and France often dominate—plus local home furnishing creations by local designers.

OFF THE WALL
1704 South Congress Ave.
(512) 445-4701
www.offthewallaustin.com
A mix of antiques, retro furniture, vintage china and glassware, even old cowboy boots in the store's "Odd Stuff" corner that might include souvenir glasses, vintage cameras, old cigarette lighters, etc., are for sale in this SoCo store.

West

FURNITURE BROKERS OF WESTLAKE
4201 Westbank Dr.
(512) 329-8421
www.furniture-brokers.com

The showroom for this upscale furniture consignment store is in a small shopping center across from Westlake High School. Given its West Austin location, much of the furniture here comes from some of Austin's more affluent residents. The store also sells collectibles and artwork.

Southeast

FOUR HANDS HOME
2090 Woodward St.
(512) 371-7575
www.fourhands.com

Imported furniture from the Far East and India, much of it with an ethnic, but modern feel. Massive wooden tables, Oriental cabinets, leather chairs with a contemporary, boxy look, are among the many pieces sold out of the warehouse just southeast of the intersection of I-35 and Ben White Boulevard. Look for the yearly sales for bargains.

JEWELRY

Central

BELL AND BIRD
1206 West Thirty-eighth St.
(512) 407-8206
www.bellandbirdjewelry.com

For a glimpse of the exquisite offerings at this small Jefferson Square boutique, peruse the shop's website which features an ever-changing inventory of antique and custom-made pieces.

ELIZA PAGE
229 West Second St.
(512) 474-6500
www.elizapage.com

Owner Elizabeth Gibson Serrato describes her inventory as "new classics from small designers," many of them local. The day and evening wear are showcased in a gallery setting in the Second Street District.

GALLERIE ESTATE JEWELERS
3500 Jefferson St., Suite 105
(512) 451-3889
www.galleriejewelers.com

Antique and estate sale jewelry is sold at this Jefferson Square–area jeweler. The store also accepts consignments.

RUSSELL KORMAN
3806 North Lamar Blvd.
(512) 451-9292
www.russellkormanjewelry.com

This is another Austin success story. Back in the '70s, Korman worked on The Drag near the university selling beads; now he is selling custom-made pieces made from precious metals and jewels.

South Central

SCHATZELEIN
1713 South First St.
(512) 382-0969
www.schatzeleinaustin.com

The name means "sweetie" in German and owner Christine Fail chose it to reflect the personal fondness and affection jewelry often expresses. In addition to her own pieces, she selects handcrafted pieces from artists near and far. The works are affordable and unique.

North

NOMADIC NOTIONS
2438 West Anderson Lane
(512) 454-0001
www.nomadicnotions.com
Nomadic Notions sells beads from more than 35 countries, some 5,000 varieties ranging in price from pennies to around $50 apiece. The store also sells jewelers' supplies and offers instruction to those eager to make their own distinctive jewelry.

PHOTOGRAPHY

Central

*PRECISION CAMERA AND VIDEO
3810 North Lamar St.
(512) 467-7676
www.precision-camera.com
A favorite among Austin's professional and amateur photographers, Precision has grown from a small shop near the university to this large store just north of Thirty-fifth Street. Services include film and digital processing, classes, camera rental, and repair. Check out the store's used-camera department.

South Central

HOLLAND PHOTO
1700 South Lamar Blvd.
(512) 442-4274
www.hollandphoto.com
This is a full-service photographic lab used by many of Austin's professional photographers. It offers a variety of services to both professionals and amateurs alike, including fast film processing, computer imaging, custom enlargements and restoration, and film and photo supplies.

RESALE SHOPS/CHARITY

Recycling is a subject close to Austin's heart, so it is no wonder that resale shops abound. Many are dedicated to raising money for charity; others seek to extend the life of bell-bottoms well beyond their expected life span. Goodwill (www.austingoodwill.org), the Salvation Army (www.satruck.com), the MaryLee Foundation, the Junior League, St. Vincent de Paul (www.svdpusa.org), and other worthy institutions all operate thrift stores in Austin. Donations are encouraged, and listings for the stores can be found on the organizations' websites. Here we have listed those charity stores with a specific mission or those with a unique presence in Austin.

Central

BUFFALO EXCHANGE
2904 Guadalupe St.
(512) 480-9922
www.buffaloexchange.com
Founded in Phoenix, Buffalo Exchange shops are sprouting across the country. The innovative concept is to recycle and re-use clothes by encouraging customers to bring in their cast-offs and swap them or get cash in return. The shops sometimes join with the Humane Society to accept old fur coats to be recycled into beds for injured wildlife.

JUNIOR LEAGUE OF AUSTIN
   RESALE SHOP
6555 Burnet Rd.
(512) 459-4592
www.jlaustin.org
One of several fund-raising efforts by the Junior League (the popular Christmas Affair show is another; see the Annual Events chapter). The store is a good place to find children's clothing.

NEXT TO NEW

5308 Burnet Rd.

(512) 459-1288

www.next2new.org

The Next to New shop is a nonprofit organization sponsored by St. David's Episcopal Church. Staffed by community volunteers, the store's profits go to community outreach programs and to the restoration of historic church buildings.

TOP DRAWER THRIFT

4902 Burnet Rd.

(512) 454-5161

www.topdrawerthrift.com

This store supports people living with HIV/AIDS. Proceeds from the sale of donated merchandise benefit Project Transitions, which provides a homelike environment to meet the physical, emotional, and spiritual needs of persons experiencing the dying process.

Northwest

GOODWILL OUTLET

12317 Technology Blvd.

(512) 249-5231

www.austingoodwill.org

Known in Austin's sewing and fashion circles as the "Blue Hanger" stores—their original name—these two Goodwill stores generate millions for the group each year in Austin. All clothing is $1.25, no matter how fancy or plain. Rummaging through the piles are bargain hunters, moms with a tight budget and funky fashion mavens on the prowl for retro looks. The second store is in East Austin. The other location is at 916 Springdale Rd. (512-928-8832).

East

*HABITAT FOR HUMANITY RE-STORE

310 Comal St.

(512) 478-2165

www.re-store.com

The large Comal Street warehouse features donated household fittings such as faucets, miniblinds, bathroom cabinets, stove tops, even the kitchen sink, plus doors, windows, and construction lumber. Many of the items are used and have been donated by homeowners and builders upgrading or replacing older items, but some are new. All proceeds benefit Habitat for Humanity, the organization that builds homes in low-income neighborhoods.

RESALE/VINTAGE CLOTHING & STUFF

Vintage clothing stores abound in Austin, so much so that the Austin Convention and Visitors Bureau provides a "treasure map" of vintage stores around town and the *Austin Chronicle* website offers the definitive vintage and kitsch list. There are four general areas where the stores can be found: the South Congress Avenue shopping district (see the chapter introduction), on South Lamar Boulevard between Barton Springs Road and Oltorf Street, along The Drag, Guadalupe Street near the university campus, and around North Loop Street and Fifty-first Street in North Austin.

Central

BANANA BAY TRADING COMPANY

2908 San Gabriel St.

(512) 479-8608

www.camonow.com

Banana Bay is Austin's version of an Army-Navy store. Located on a triangle of land east of Lamar and just north of Twenty-ninth Street, Banana Bay features a variety of military clothing, ammo boxes, tents, and survival kits.

HOG WILD
100A East North Loop Blvd.
(512) 467-6515

Is this a toy store or a clothing emporium? It's both, thanks to joint owners with different interests. On the clothing side, customers find Hawaiian shirts, velvet bell-bottoms, miniskirts, and leisure suits, all divided by decade. On the toy/collectible side there are *Star Wars* toys, Barbies, even *Welcome Back, Kotter* games.

South Central

BIG BERTHA'S BARGAIN BASEMENT
1050 South Lamar Blvd.
(512) 444-5908
www.bigberthasbargainbasement.com
/frames.html

It is not in a basement, but it is in an old shopping center that seems to capture the essence of South Austin (see the Relocation chapter). The word *funky* is overused in Austin, but this is one case where it fits. The funky shopping center is home to several resale shops, a classic gym, a music store, and this clothing resale store that owner Henry Tarin calls "extreme vintage." The store has a wild assortment of clothes that attracts retro fans and the theatrical community in Austin.

✳BITCH'IN THREADS
1030–D South Lamar Blvd.
(512) 441-9955

Grace Faulkner is a diminutive woman with a small treasure trove of a shop, located near her good friend Henry Tarin's Big Bertha's (see above). A native of Australia, she relies on an old school chum to ship her pre-World War II kimono (she will politely tell you that the plural of kimono is kimono, not kimonos) from Japan. Collectors come from throughout the country to see what she is offering. In addition to kimono, Grace also sells "top-quality" vintage fashion, suits, cocktail dresses, evening gowns, shoes, and purses, classy enough to clad Audrey Hepburn on a world cruise.

BOHEMIA RETRO-RESALE
1606 South Congress Ave.
(512) 326-1238

Good junk from every era is the boast here. The ever-changing stock includes clothes, furniture, and housewares. Like other South Congress stores, Bohemia keeps late hours to encourage after-dinner browsing.

FLASHBACK
1805 South First St.
(512) 445-6906

The shops along South First and South Lamar Boulevard are tucked between businesses, bus stops, car washes, and apartment homes, and, if anything, they are even funkier than those found on the burgeoning South Congress Avenue shopping strip. This vintage clothing store is one of the longtime fixtures in this area and boasts a large selection of shoes.

FLIPNOTICS
1600 Barton Springs Rd.
(512) 480-8646
www.flipnotics.com

If the retro clothes here smell a little more like coffee than the usual thrift shop aroma, it is because there is a coffee shop with the same name on the premises. Among the finds here are surfer shirts, 50s-style rock 'n' roll wear, and fanciful little cocktail dresses.

LET'S DISH
1102 South Lamar Blvd.
(512) 444-9801

The vintage clothing at Let's Dish ranges from the turn of the 20th century through the ever-popular '70s disco style. The store also has an extensive vintage jewelry collection and sells pottery, dishware, and maps dating from the 1920s to the 1950s.

LUCY IN DISGUISE WITH DIAMONDS AND ELECTRIC LADYLAND
1506 South Congress Ave.
(512) 444-2002
www.lucyindisguise.com

That's the real name of the store, perhaps the most famous shop in SoCo, certainly one of the most photographed storefronts. The emphasis here is theatrical, with both gorilla suits and French maid's uniforms in stock. Disco wear also is big, and the store boasts that Bob Dylan shopped here.

North Central

BANANA BAY TRADING COMPANY
5102 Chisholm Ave.
(512) 479-8608
www.camonow.com

Banana Bay is Austin's version of an Army-Navy store. Located near the intersection of Fifty-first Street and Airport Boulevard, Banana Bay features a variety of military clothing, ammo boxes, tents, and survival kits.

North

IT'S NEW TO ME
7719 Burnet Rd.
(512) 451-0388
www.itsnewtomeaustin.com

A variety of furniture is displayed in the store's 8,000-square-foot showroom, including some good-quality pieces from furniture producers such as Henredon. This is a consignment shop where Austin residents sell their quality furniture.

TOYS

Central

HOG WILD
1001 East North Loop Blvd.
(512) 467-9453
www.hogwildtx.com

These toys are for grown-ups who long for their childhood years—retro toys at a retro clothing store (see above under Resale/Vintage Clothing).

KIDS-N-CATS
5732-A Burnet Rd.
(512) 458-6369

All things feline here—toys, jewelry, china cats, pens shaped like kitties, posters, cards, and kitty knickknacks. Despite its name, the store also has other sections devoted to dinosaurs, horses, and spacemen—in other words, all things kids hold dear. The shop is also a good resource for party favors.

MOMOKO
705 West Twenty-fourth St.
(512) 469-0232

This small store and bubble tea shop sells all things by Sanrio. If you don't know Sanrio, then likely you don't know any preteen girls who love the star of the Sanrio line, Hello Kitty. There is also a sushi restaurant and bubble tea bar in the store.

ROOTIN' RIDGE
26 Doors, 1206 West Thirty-eighth St.
(512) 453-2604
www.rootinridge.com

Georgean and Paul Kyle have been making toys since 1975, and their store in 26 Doors features their own creations, plus handcrafted quality wooden toys, puzzles, and musical instruments.

✳TOY JOY
2900 Guadalupe St.
(512) 320-0090
www.toyjoy.com

"You are never too old to play" might be the motto of this store, which boasts of selling toys for kids and grown-ups. Japanese toys are a specialty, plus there is a large selection of lava lamps, stickers, novelty items, and puppets.

North

TERRA TOYS
2438 West Anderson Lane
(512) 445-4489
www.terratoys.com

This is a favorite place for shopping for stocking stuffers and unusual children's toys for Christmas. Terra Toys left its longtime Congress Avenue locations as rental rates climbed when SoCo became a hip address, but fortunately, this wonderful toy shop has found a new home in north Austin.

WORLD WIND KITE SHOP
7208 McNeil Dr.
(512) 250-9454
www.worldwindkites.com

The store's slogan is "A Hobby to Some. A Way of Life to Us!" Listing it under "toys" may be misleading, since this shop sells not only indestructible kid kites but also high-grade kites for competition. The store also offers repair services and kite-flying lessons.

East

PIÑATA PARTY PALACE
1704 East Cesar Chavez Blvd.
(512) 236-0975

Custom-made piñatas for parties, particularly kid's birthday parties, can be ordered here. Piñatas are papier-mâché forms, covered with colorful tissue paper and stuffed with candies and little toys. The piñata is strung up over a tree limb and the birthday boy or girl is blindfolded and given a baseball bat to take whacks at the piñata until it breaks open—then there is a mad scramble for the candy and toys. The store also sells ready-to-go piñatas, flags, balloons, and party supplies.

South Central

ANNA'S TOY DEPOT
2620 South Lamar Blvd., Suite B
(512) 447-8697
www.annastoydepot.com

None of the frenzy of a modern toy shop here. Anna's sells traditional toys, some of them gently used. It also caters to special-needs children and youngsters who can benefit from play-therapy toys.

TRAVEL/ADVENTURE/ OUTDOORS

For sporting goods stores focused on a particular sport (e.g., soccer or cycling), see the Parks & Recreation chapter and also see listings for Cabela's and Callahans in our Food shopping section.

Central

ARMADILLO SPORT
1806 Barton Springs Rd.
(512) 478-4128

An Austin surf shop? Housed in a former diner-style restaurant along the Barton Springs restaurant row (see the Restaurants chapter), Armadillo also sells sports equipment that you can use in nearby Zilker Park, including in-line skates, wakeboards, swimsuits, and lacrosse equipment.

MCBRIDE'S GUNS
Thirtieth Street and North Lamar Boulevard
(512) 472-3532
www.mcbridesguns.com
Popular among hunters, anglers, and collectors, McBride's is noted for its extensive collection of antique guns. The store also sells archery equipment and provides gunsmithing services. The store also has a complete line of fishing tackle and lures.

WHOLE EARTH PROVISION CO.
2410 San Antonio St.
(512) 478-1577
www.wholeearthprovision.com
Before Austinites head for the hills, they head for Whole Earth. Not only does the store sell the top labels in camping, hiking, diving, biking, and kayaking gear, it also has wonderful rainwear and sweaters, plus imported clothes from Latin America. The shoe shop has everyday, sturdy wear and great hiking boots. Whole Earth also sells tents, backpacks, climbing gear, toys, guidebooks, knives, flashlights, freeze-dried foods,

desktop Zen gardens, and telescopes. If you are not sure you want to buy a tent, you can rent one here. There are three stores, one central, the second uptown, and the third in Southwest Austin. The other locations are at 1014 North Lamar Blvd. (512-476-1414) and Westgate Shopping Center, 4477 South Lamar Blvd. (512-899-0992).

West

SPORTSMAN'S FINEST
12434 Bee Cave Rd.
(512) 263-1888
www.sportsmansfinest.com
This West Austin store sells new and used firearms, hunting and fishing gear, travel equipment, and offers information on guide services and classes.

North

GOLFSMITH
11000 North I-35
(512) 821-4050
www.golfsmith.com
This North Austin outlet is a mecca for golf enthusiasts. The facility boasts that it has the largest golf inventory in the world, where shoppers can buy Golfsmith and Harvey Penick golf clubs. The store has a snack bar, computerized swing analyzer, and educational and practice facilities. In addition, visitors can take a factory tour. There is a second, smaller store at the Arboretum.

ATTRACTIONS

irst, a word of appreciation to our sponsor: Nature. It is, after all, our greatest attraction. The bluebonnets in springtime; the sparkle of sunlight on the lakes; the limestone cliffs and green rolling hills; the crisp, rushing creeks; the fresh air; the fauna; the fault and the foliage. Austin's natural beauty and bounty attracted our first visitors, drew our first settlers, and continue to entice our newest arrivals. Nature was Austin's greatest artist, perhaps an inspiration to the others who came to create some of the phenomena that give Austin its individuality. So while you're busy enjoying the production that is Austin, take a moment to acknowledge the set design.

While some of the sites below come to us courtesy of Nature, we've devoted much of this chapter to giving you a tour of the landscape of invention, the visual sensations contributed by the ingenuity of Austin's own people over the past 150 years or so. Here you'll find attractions to tickle your fancy, tease your brain, touch your heart, and, perhaps, stir your own imagination. Among these curiosities, historic treasures, and modern marvels you'll discover a provocative portion of Austin's story.

We've also pointed out some of our most interesting pieces of public art. Here, you'll receive an introduction to a few of the sculptures, statues, paintings, murals, and fountains that are on view for all to appreciate. These artistic creations enhance Austin's natural beauty and provide a window into the city itself. For some excellent guided tours of Austin and the surrounding area, don't miss the Touring Greater Austin section at the end of this chapter.

Of course, Austin wouldn't be Austin without the many spots dedicated to celebrating our unique natural habitat. So for more outdoor attractions, don't miss the chapter on Parks & Recreation, where we've introduced you to Lake Travis, Lady Bird Lake, and many, many other alfresco wonderlands. If you still yearn for more things to see and do, check out the chapters on The Arts, Kidstuff, The Music Scene, Nightlife, and Spectator Sports. Come to think of it, much of this book is dedicated to Austin attractions, in one form or another. Note: Because of the high concentration of Attractions in Central Austin, we've divided this section into three smaller parts to make it easier for you: Downtown, The University of Texas, and Central.

DOWNTOWN

THE AUSTIN HISTORY CENTER
810 Guadalupe St.
(512) 974-7480
www.ci.austin.tx.us/library/ahc

While Austin was among the last major Texas cities to build a public library, the city made up for its delay by constructing a facility that was both inspiring and advanced in its design. This Moderne-influenced, Classical Revival–style building opened in 1933 to replace the city's temporary public library, a wooden structure built in 1926. A showcase for some of Austin's finest crafters in its day, the building features loggia frescoes, a carved mantel, and ornamental ironwork balconies. The ironwork was done by a noted family of ironworkers, the Weigls. The History Center, which served as the city's library for nearly 50 years, now houses the leading local history collections in the state. Here, visitors will find more than one million items documenting the history of Austin from before it was founded to the present day. The center has received national recognition for its collection of more than 600,000 photographic images, which document the people, events, architecture, and social customs of this region. The center also has more than 1,000 maps of Austin and Travis County from the mid-1800s to the present as well as 25,500 drawings and documents from local architectural projects. The center also features regular temporary exhibits of interest to the Austin community. The History Center, part of the Austin Public Library system, is next door to Austin's main public library at the corner of Ninth and Guadalupe Streets. It is open from 10 a.m. to 6 p.m. Tues through Sat, and from noon to 6 p.m. Sun.

i To get a great feel for the unique people and places that make greater downtown Austin so special, tune in to the award-winning documentary series DOWNTOWN at www.downtownaustintv.org, or check the listings on PBS channel KLRU-TV. These short productions are awesome!

✳ THE BATS
Congress Avenue Bridge at Lady Bird Lake
Get your cooler and a comfy blanket and head out to Lady Bird Lake for a truly unique Austin experience. The largest urban bat colony in North America—as many as 1.5 million Mexican free-tails—resides in the crevices beneath the Congress Avenue Bridge for nearly 8 months of the year. When they take off from under the bridge for their evening flight for food, the spectacle is astounding. On their nightly forage the bats devour up to 30,000 pounds of insects. Aug is the best month for viewing the bats because they often come out before sunset. But they can be seen at other times from about mid-Mar to early Nov. You can see the bats from either side of Lady Bird Lake under the bridge or from the top of the bridge. There also are options to view the bats from boats or kayaks. See the Touring Greater Austin section in this chapter.

Austin was scandalized when the huge colony first took up residence here in the early 1980s, even going so far as to petition to have the colony eradicated. But when citizens learned that the bats consume so many insects—thus cutting down the need for chemical insecticides—and that the bats pose no danger to the community, Austin changed its mind in a big way. Today our bat colony is a welcome addition to Austin. Nearby is the enormous bat sculpture, *Night Wings,* by artist Dale Whistler.

✳ THE BOB BULLOCK TEXAS STATE HISTORY MUSEUM
1800 North Congress Ave.
(512) 936-8746
www.thestoryoftexas.com
This museum was Bob Bullock's dream. Who was he? Perhaps the quintessential Texas politician of the last half of the 20th century. Bullock rose to become the state's lieutenant governor and was known for his tough politics and his unmitigated love of all things

Texas. Former President George W. Bush, a Republican, credited Bullock, a Democrat, with being a major influence on his political life, and the two men grew to be very close. When "Governor Bullock"—all lieutenant governors in Texas are called "Governor"—set a goal, nothing could stop him. He decided the great state of Texas needed a museum, just as he decided the Texas State Cemetery where he now rests needed a much needed restoration (see later in this chapter). The building echoes the colors, textures, and style of the nearby Texas Capitol, and its huge star out front says "This is Texas!" The 3 floors inside celebrate Texas's ancient cultures and pre-Republic days; the volatile days of the Republic of Texas, the state's admission to the Union and the tragedy of the Civil War; and finally the energy that has made modern Texas.

In addition to permanent exhibits, the museum has rotating exhibits on each floor. There is a cafe, an IMAX theater, plus the Texas Spirit Theater that echoes the traditional Texas town opera house and where an electronic Sam Houston introduces the audience to a colorful history of Texas. The museum is open 9 a.m. to 6 p.m. Mon through Sat and noon to 6 p.m. Sun. Parking is available nearby or for a fee in the underground parking lot. Ticket prices are affordable. There are additional admission prices for the IMAX theatre and Texas Spirit Theater.

CAPITOL VISITORS CENTER
112 East Eleventh St.
(512) 305-8400
www.texascapitolvisitorscenter.com
The Capitol Visitors Center must be added to any list of places to visit while in Austin, for both what it was and what it is today. Completed in 1857, this is the oldest remaining

state office building in Texas and, both for its architectural and historic values, one of the most significant properties owned by the state. Designed by German-born architect Christopher Conrad Stremme for use as the Texas General Land Office, the building is an excellent example of Medieval-inspired architecture and is listed on the National Register of Historic Places. Today, the 2-story "castle" hosts a variety of exhibits relating to the State Capitol and to the history of the Old Land Office itself.

We recommend stopping here before taking a tour of the Capitol. For one thing, the 20-minute film *Lone Star Legacy: A History of the Capitol*, narrated by Walter Cronkite, will serve as a great initiation to the capitol tour itself. And don't miss the space next to the "small, dark spiral stairway" dedicated to the writer known as O. Henry. (See the O. Henry Museum listing in this chapter.) O. Henry worked as a draftsman in the Land Office from 1887 to 1891, and two of his stories are set there, "Georgia's Ruling" and "Bexar Scrip No. 2692," in which he refers to the spiral stairway.

Upstairs in the wing dedicated to the history of the Land Office, visitors will find two surveyor's transits. Peek through one to get a close-up view of the Goddess of Liberty who stands so regally on top of the Capitol Rotunda. (Her features are exaggerated to be seen from afar.) The gift shop here is great and so are the people who work as information assistants inside the front entrance. The center is open 9 a.m. to 5 p.m. Mon through Sat and noon to 5 p.m. on Sun.

DEWITT C. GREER BUILDING
125 East Eleventh St.
What with the splendor of the State Capitol, this building just across the street is easy to miss. But take a moment to enjoy its

wonderful Art Deco architecture. Built in 1933, the building features three bronze panels over the main entrance depicting changes in Austin's modes of transportation: a Native American on horseback, a covered wagon, and an automobile. There are also two stylized eagles over the entrance and a number of other details from the era that are worth a look. The building, home to the Texas Transportation Commission, was named for Greer, a state highway engineer and commissioner from 1969 to 1981.

DICKINSON MUSEUM
411 East Fifth St.
(512) 974-3830
www.ci.austin.tx.us/dickinson
This museum, opened in 2010, celebrates the life and times of Susanna Dickinson, the "Messenger of the Alamo" and one of Texas's most famous historical women. Dickinson, the young wife of US Army artillerist Almeron Dickinson, and her infant daughter were the only two Anglo survivors of the 1836 Battle of the Alamo. When the bloody siege ended, victorious Mexican General Antonio Lopez de Santa Anna chose Dickinson to deliver a message to Texas General Sam Houston that further opposition would end in defeat as well. (Houston ignored the warning.) Susanna lived, married again and again—and prospered—for almost half a century after the infamous battle, bearing witness to and participating in Texas's early Anglo history.

Susanna and her fourth husband, Joseph Hannig, built this home in downtown Austin in 1869. Saved from destruction and moved to this new location next door to the O. Henry Museum, the structure is officially called the Joseph and Susanna Dickinson Hannig Museum. The permanent exhibit focuses on Susanna and her first husband's participation in the Texas Revolution, her life in the aftermath of the Alamo defeat, and her later move to Austin with Hannig. A temporary exhibit, expected to remain into 2012, centers on the surviving wives and children of men who died at the Alamo. The museum is open Wed through Sun, noon to 5 p.m. Admission is free.

✳THE DRISKILL HOTEL
122 East Sixth St.
(512) 474-5911
www.driskillhotel.com
Built in 1886 for cattle baron Jesse Driskill, the Driskill Hotel was restored in 1998 to its original splendor. This Richardsonian Romanesque–style hotel is uniquely Austin and should not be missed. (See the chapter on Hotels and Motels for more details.)

> **i** You've most likely heard of the legendary Texas Rangers. But have you heard of the Downtown Rangers? These friendly folks roam the greater downtown area, offering help, advice, and making sure all is well. These rangers are not police and do not carry weapons, but they use two-way radios that allow them to contact authorities if anyone needs help.

GOVERNOR'S MANSION
1010 Colorado St.
(512) 463-5518
www.governor.state.tx.us/mansion
Fire caused by a suspected arsonist greatly damaged a good portion of the Governor's Mansion in the early morning hours of June 8, 2008. The mansion, which was in the midst of a major renovation project, was unoccupied at the time of the blaze and

no one was injured. Repair and restoration work finally began in late 2010, although the historic structure remains closed to the public for the foreseeable future. Check the website for information about when it might reopen for tours.

MILLET OPERA HOUSE
110 East Ninth St.

Now the private Austin Club, tourists can enjoy this edifice from the outside only. But it's definitely worth a walk by when you're visiting downtown. Built in 1878, the opera house became a cultural center for the city. Its auditorium boasted 800 movable seats. The building, made of Texas limestone, was listed on the National Register of Historic Places in 1978.

MOONLIGHT TOWERS
Corner of Ninth and Guadalupe Streets

At this location, which features a historical marker, visitors will find just one of the 17 Moonlight Towers that remain in Austin from 1895, when the towers provided the city's first public electric lights. Austin is the only city in the world to preserve its earliest electric street lamps. And they still work. At 165 feet, they're the city's tallest street lights and a truly unique attraction. The City of Austin contracted the Fort Wayne Electric Company to install 31 towers with carbon arc lamps, believing they would be easier to maintain than many small street lamps throughout the city. Some residents of Hyde Park, however, weren't so sure. They feared that the lights, sometimes called Austin moonlight, would trick the vegetables in their gardens into growing day and night. The 17 towers that remain, now with mercury vapor lights, can be found around downtown, in Hyde Park, and in Clarksville. The Moonlight

Tower in Zilker Park, moved to the park from Congress Avenue in the 1960s, is used every Christmas to support the 3,500 multicolored lights on the Zilker Park Christmas Tree (see the chapters on Kidstuff and Annual Events).

O. HENRY MUSEUM
409 East Fifth St.
(512) 472-1903
www.ci.austin.tx.us/ohenry

William Sydney Porter, who earned international fame as a short-story writer under his pen name, O. Henry, lived in this simple Queen Anne–style cottage for 3 of his nearly 11 years in Austin. Simply named Will Porter when he arrived as a bachelor in 1884, Porter would see some of his greatest personal triumphs and his most devastating public humiliation during his era in Austin. It was here where Porter sold his first short story to a national publication, launched his weekly newspaper, *The Rolling Stone*—and was convicted of embezzlement and sentenced to prison. (A mock court trial conducted at the UT School of Law in 1998, the 100th anniversary of the original trial, exonerated him.)

The cottage is much as it was during Porter's 3 years in it, from 1893 to 1895. Once slated for demolition, the home was moved twice in the 1930s from its original location at 308 East Fourth St. Here visitors will find many furnishings and personal possessions belonging to Porter, his wife, and daughter. Here also are first editions of O. Henry books, magazines featuring his stories, copies of *The Rolling Stone*, and family photographs. The museum hosts the O. Henry Pun-Off World Championship, a lively and popular event held every May since 1977. The museum is open noon to 5 p.m. Wed through Sun. Admission is free. Guests are asked to wear flat, soft-soled shoes to prevent damage to the original Bastrop pine floors.

THE OLD BAKERY AND EMPORIUM
1006 Congress Ave.
(512) 477-5961
www.ci.austin.tx.us/parks/bakery1.htm
When Swedish immigrant Charles Lundberg opened his bakery in 1876, Austinites gathered to buy such delicacies as ladyfingers, sponge cake, and glazed kisses. Used as a bakery until 1936, the building then housed a number of different businesses, including a nightclub. By 1963 the Old Bakery, vacant and deteriorating, was scheduled for demolition. That's when the Austin Heritage Society and the Junior League stepped in to save it, through hard work and donations. Today the Old Bakery is registered as a national landmark. Owned and operated by the Austin Parks and Recreation Department, the bakery is home to Austin's Senior Citizens' Craft Project, and visitors will find scores of handicrafts made by Austin's most experienced artists, those age 50 and older. The Old Bakery also has a hospitality desk that provides information and brochures about Austin attractions. Just a half block down Congress from the State Capitol, the Old Bakery is a great place to stop on your tour of Austin. It's open Mon through Fri 9 a.m. to 4 p.m., though it opens on Sat in Dec before Christmas. It generally is closed on weekends and holidays.

PARAMOUNT THEATRE
713 Congress Ave.
(512) 472-2901
www.austintheatre.org
An Austin jewel, the Paramount Theatre opened in 1915 under the name Majestic Theatre. Now, beautifully restored to the last detail, the neoclassic structure is one of the nation's classic theaters. Katharine Hepburn performed here, as did Sarah Bernhardt, Helen Hayes, and Cab Calloway. Today it hosts film festival screenings; music, dance, and theater performances; and classic movies. (See the chapter on The Arts.) The Paramount series for kids is a summer extravaganza. And finally, the Paramount is offering tours. Fifty-minute tours are conducted Wed through Sun at 10:30 a.m. Reservations and tickets, $10 for adults, are available through the website.

SCHOLZ GARTEN
1607 San Jacinto Blvd.
(512) 474-1958
www.scholzgarten.net
Built in 1866 by German immigrant August Scholz, the Scholz Garten has been serving up beer and German food ever since. This building is listed as a National Historic Site and as a Texas Landmark. General Armstrong Custer, who was stationed 2 blocks away during Reconstruction, reportedly ate here, and the University of Texas football team celebrated its first undefeated season here in 1893. Photographs from days of old adorn the walls.

SIXTH STREET ENTERTAINMENT DISTRICT
Downtown between Congress Avenue and I-35
If you haven't spent an evening in the Sixth Street area, you haven't really experienced Austin. These few blocks, filled with live music venues, DJ clubs, shops, and restaurants, continue to make up the entertainment district for Austin in many people's minds, even though downtown now offers several other hip areas. Within walking

distance of many hotels, Sixth Street is one of Austin's top tourist draws. Nowadays, the Sixth Street District also encompasses parts of Fifth and Seventh Streets on either side of Sixth, as well as Red River Street on the eastern side. This district really comes alive after 5. (See the Music Scene chapter for a listing of some of the clubs.)

SYMPHONY SQUARE
1101 Red River St.
(512) 476-6064
www.austinsymphony.com/about/square

Four historic limestone buildings and a wonderful 350-seat outdoor amphitheater still used for live performances make up this complex, which serves as the offices of the Austin Symphony Orchestra and the Women's Symphony League and houses Serranos Tex-Mex restaurant (see the Restaurants chapter). Located on the banks of historic Waller Creek since the 1970s, Symphony Square represents the efforts of a group of leading citizens, the City of Austin, the Urban Renewal League, and the Symphony itself to save and restore these 19th-century buildings. The provocative triangular shaped building at the corner of 11th and Red River Streets is believed to be one of just three stone triangular buildings remaining in Texas today. Built in 1871 by Jeremiah Hamilton, one of nine African-American legislators who served in the Texas Legislature, the building today bears his name and is used as the symphony's main office. Symphony Square also contains the Michael Doyle House, considered one of the few remaining examples of a simple, one-story stone cottage in Austin. The Hardeman House, also native limestone, was moved from its original location to the square and is home

to Serranos Cafe, which features a lovely outdoor patio overlooking the amphitheater. On Wed mornings in June and July, the Austin Symphony Orchestra hosts Children's Day activities in the square. For information on that and for other children's activities sponsored by the symphony, see the chapter on Kidstuff. Also see the chapter on The Arts for more about the Symphony and its seasonal performances at the Long Center.

i Its picture seems to be everywhere these days (even on the Visitor Center website) and yet if you're just visiting you might never happen upon it. We're talking about the gorgeous arched, rust-steel bridge that spans Lake Austin on Capital of Texas Highway (Loop 360). Locals just call it the 360 Bridge, but it's officially the Pennybacker Bridge.

✳ TEXAS STATE CAPITOL
1100 Congress Ave.
(512) 463-0063
www.tspb.state.tx.us

"Here glitters a structure that shall stand as a sentinel of eternity to gaze upon the ages." Now, more than a century since those words were spoken, visitors from all over the world come to gaze upon this magnificent monument to Texas. Temple Houston, the youngest son of Texas hero Sam Houston, dedicated Texas's new State Capitol, our "sentinel of eternity," on May 16, 1888. This Renaissance Revival–style structure made of Texas pink granite and native limestone, now stands as gracious and grand as Texas itself on the hilltop overlooking Austin's historic Congress Avenue. Perched atop the soaring Rotunda—which at 311 feet is taller than our nation's Capitol—is the 15½-foot statue called the

Goddess of Liberty, a 1986 aluminum replica of the original zinc goddess. Marble statues of Stephen F. Austin and Sam Houston carved by German-born sculptor Elisabet Ney grace the south foyer as does a portrait of Davy Crockett, martyr of the Alamo, holding his famous coonskin cap. The painting of the *Surrender of Santa Anna,* which depicts a watershed event in Texas history, is among the meaningful works of art that can be found throughout the building.

More than a monument, more than a museum, the State Capitol is the seat of Texas government. In this building, among the pioneers of Texas's past, work the leaders of Texas's future. Among many other state government headquarters, the offices of the governor and secretary of state are here, along with the magnificent Senate and House chambers, occupied during the legislative sessions held every 2 years.

No trip to the capitol is complete unless you've stood on the Rotunda floor and looked up at the Texas star and the 2-foot letters spelling out T-E-X-A-S on the ceiling. From below, they look about 3 inches tall. After you've gazed up, be sure to look down. Here are the seals of the six nations whose flags have flown over Texas: France, Spain, Mexico, the United States, the Confederate States of America, and, of course, the Republic of Texas. On the Rotunda's circular walls you will find the portraits of every president and governor of Texas beginning with the current chief executive. That means that each time a new governor is elected, every portrait in the Rotunda must be moved back one space.

Visitors can choose to walk through the capitol themselves or take a free regularly scheduled guided tour. We suggest the tour. Not only are the guides interesting and informative, they also will point out details you might miss and can also take you into areas otherwise locked, such as the Senate and House chambers. And these are definitely worth a look. When the Legislature is in session—every other year on odd years—visitors can watch our lawmakers in action from the third-floor public gallery, open on a first-come, first-served basis. Guided tours are also available of the capitol grounds. The massive grounds, with their many statues, sculptures, and beautiful old trees, are a sight unto themselves. And don't forget to visit the Capitol Complex Visitor Center nearby. (See the previous listing in this chapter.)

The capitol is open 7 a.m. to 10 p.m. weekdays, 9 a.m. to 8 p.m. on weekends and holidays. Tours are offered on weekdays from 8:30 a.m. to 4:30 p.m., Sat 9:30 a.m. to 3:30 p.m., and Sun noon to 3:30 p.m.

TRAIL OF TEJANO LEGENDS—ART
600 River St. and other locations
www.austinlatinomusic.com/trail.html
www.ci.austin.tx.us/aipp
Honoring the contributions to the Austin music scene of important Latino musicians from the 1940s and 1950s, the City of Austin renamed five Austin sites for specific artists and installed impressive outdoor sculptures by nationally recognized Austin artist Connie Arismendi at three of the sites.

The trail begins at 600 River St., site of the Mexican American Cultural Center (see listing in The Arts chapter), whose Perez and Ramos Plaza features Arismendi's sculpture, *Una Cancion de Fe y Familia* (A Song of Faith and Family). The metal sculpture, which honors brothers Ruben and Ernest Perez, and Alfonso and Ruben Ramos, depicts the Perez brothers playing the saxophone and the Ramos brothers singing. Another cut metal sculpture, *Tenderly*, is of Nash Hernandez Sr., a legendary trumpeter and orchestra leader. The sculpture portrays Hernanez atop a base that bears lyrics from his famous song, *Tenderly*. The sculpture is on Nash Hernandez Sr. Road in East Austin's Festival Beach Park. Finally, there's the 18-foot-diameter shade canopy *Estamos en Tejas!* (We're in Texas), which honors recording artist Roy Montelongo and his long-running radio show *Estamos en Tejas!* This sculpture is at the Roy Montelongo Scenic Overlook near East Austin's Metz Park on Lady Bird Lake. Two other East Austin stops on the 5-mile Trail of Tejano Legends are a pavilion named for conjunto accordionist and orchestra leader Johnny Degollado and a park named for Tejano music pioneer Manuel "Cowboy" Donley and his musician brother, Robert.

THE UNIVERSITY OF TEXAS

The University of Texas at Austin (www .utexas.edu), founded in 1883 on 40 acres, has grown to 357 acres, and that's just the main campus. Its historical significance, size, and allure as one of Texas's most beloved universities make UT a major tourist attraction. The university is roughly bounded by Twenty-sixth Street on the north, Martin Luther King Jr. Boulevard on the south, I-35 on the east, and Guadalupe Street on the west.

Getting information about UT and its many small and large treasures is much easier these days, thanks largely to user-friendly improvements to the university's website. For a campus overview, go to the main website. For more specific information about tours, go to www.utexas.edu/tours. We highly recommend spending some time navigating the tours section of this site before you arrive on campus, as it will provide you with some good basic information about what to see. Plus, it offers some interesting virtual tours, including "The University of Texas Virtual Campus," which provides photographs and details about the 40 Acres. Here's where you go to find out about student-led campus walking tours, the after-dark tour called the Moonlight Prowl, and tours of the UT Tower Observation Deck. You'll also find an excellent self-guided tour.

Those interested in visiting the UT campus should be aware that streets inside the campus are closed to normal traffic (cars must bear an authorized sticker to enter) during school hours. It's okay to enter after 4 p.m. daily. The university recommends that visitors use one of the seven public parking garages scattered around campus, although these, too, can fill up. For information and maps about UT parking, go to www.utexas .edu/parking/parking/visitor. If you happen to find a parking space near UT on The Drag, don't buy a lottery ticket for a while, as you've just used up your luck for the foreseeable future.

Information on the university's most noteworthy attractions follows.

BATTLE OAKS/BARBARA JORDAN STATUE
Near Twenty-fourth Street and Whitis Avenue

In an interesting twist of words, the historic Battle Oaks, three live oak trees at the northwest corner of the campus, are named in honor of the man who saved them, not the battle he waged to do so or the other trees in the grove that were destroyed earlier to build a fortress to protect the capital. The trees are named for Dr. W. J. Battle. His efforts to save the trees, slated for the ax to make room for a new biology building, have now taken on mythic grandeur. Some stories have him perching with a shotgun on one of the largest branches; others say he was on the ground with the shotgun to keep the tree choppers away. Neither version is probably true, but the story is fun anyway.

Of course, way before Battle, and perhaps one of the reasons he saved the trees was a UT legend about this grouping of trees, which existed when Austin was home to Native Americans. According to the story, the largest of the three trees learned to speak the native tongue. When the new settlers came, the trees learned the ways of these people and provided shelter for them beneath their branches. When the only son of an old man was killed in battle, the oaks brought comfort. And when Northern troops were descending on Austin during the Civil War, all the trees in this grove, but the three remaining, gave their lives for the fortress.

On the northeast corner of the Battle Oaks stands a statue of Barbara Jordan, hands on hips and smiling down at her audience. The first African-American woman from the South to serve in the US Congress and a champion of civil rights, Jordan was a professor at UT's LBJ School of Public Affairs. The statue was dedicated in 2009.

THE DRAG
Guadalupe Street from Martin Luther King Jr. Boulevard to Twenty-sixth Street
The University of Texas meets Austin on this section of Guadalupe Street on UT's western side. Fondly known as The Drag, it once comprised mostly locally owned shops and eateries. Now, with the closing in 2010 of the venerable Dobie Theater and the considerable presence of national chains, including a Wells Fargo Bank in a prime location, The

Drag has lost some of its former Austin "weirdness." Still, the outdoor Renaissance Market (see the Shopping chapter) remains, where you can buy tie-dyed clothes and jewelry made by Austin artisans. This is also a great place to select UT souvenirs, T-shirts, and other memorabilia or just take a break from campus sightseeing.

HARRY RANSOM CENTER
Near Guadalupe and Twenty-first Streets
(512) 471-8944
www.hrc.utexas.edu
Among the Ransom Center's exceptional properties are a rare Gutenberg Bible and the world's first photograph. The center is much more inviting to the general public since a major renovation was completed in 2003. See The Arts chapter for more about the center's world-class collections.

JACK S. BLANTON MUSEUM OF ART
200 East Martin Luther King Jr. Blvd.
(512) 471-7324
www.blantonmuseum.org
The Blanton Museum opened in early 2006, featuring 18,000 feet of exhibition space to show off the University of Texas's enormous art collection. For more about the museum, see the chapter on The Arts.

i Ahhhhh, Austin in springtime. The weather is perfect, and the fields and roadsides are filled with miles of bluebonnets. It's an annual tradition to find a field of bluebonnets and take your loved ones' pictures against this stunning backdrop. The Lady Bird Johnson Wildflower Center has tons of bluebonnets, but there are plenty all around the city.

LITTLEFIELD BUILDING
At the northwest corner of
Twenty-fourth Street and Whitis Avenue

Built in 1894, this ornate red stone-and-brick Victorian mansion belonged to Major George W. Littlefield, an important UT benefactor and member of the Board of Regents. Standing on the edge of the original 40 acres, the mansion was bequeathed to the university in 1939. It was first used as practice rooms for UT music students and in World War II as headquarters for Naval Reserve Officers Training Corps, who set up a firing range in the attic. Sadly, the mansion is no longer open to public tours.

LITTLEFIELD MEMORIAL FOUNTAIN
Twenty-first Street and Whitis Avenue

Visit this fabulous fountain to enjoy its beauty and to mingle with the college students who come here to sit, have lunch, and socialize. Dedicated on March 26, 1933, the fountain has become a prominent landmark on the UT campus. Designed by Italian-born sculptor Pompeo Coppini, the fountain is meant to symbolize the revival of American patriotism during World War I, a spirit that Coppini felt had been lost during the Civil War. The large fountain consists of 3-tiered pools with water jets spraying the larger-than-life bronze goddess standing on the prow of the battleship *Columbia* as it rushes to aid democracy abroad. The goddess Columbia holds in one hand the torch of freedom and in the other the palm of peace. The bronze figures of three horses rearing out of the water represent the surging ocean. On the left side of the grouping stands a young lad representing the army. Over the years this fountain has attracted all kinds of mischief. Soap bubbles and detergent have turned the normally still waters into a foaming spectacle, while an interesting array of reptiles, including alligators, have turned up in the fountain. The memorial, which includes the nearby statues of Texas and national notables, is dedicated both to "the men and women of the Confederacy who fought with valor and suffered with fortitude that states' rights be maintained." and to the "sons and daughters of the University of Texas" who died in World War I. The fountain is about half a block east of Guadalupe Street at Twenty-first Street.

✳THE LYNDON BAINES JOHNSON LIBRARY AND MUSEUM
2313 Red River St.
(512) 721-0200
www.lbjlibrary.org

While Americans have not gone in for a lot of fanfare about our former presidents, other than the Washington memorials, we do make an exception when it comes to our presidential libraries. And one of the greatest expressions of this American political tradition is the library and museum dedicated to President Lyndon Baines Johnson. Nowhere on earth can visitors see, hear, and learn as much about this compelling figure in American history and about the official politics of the turbulent 1960s as in the LBJ Library. The Vietnam War, the Civil Rights Movement, the War on Poverty, and the Great Society all are represented, as well as some aspects of the '60s cultural scene. Here visitors will learn about Johnson's long and colorful political career, view mementos of the lives of President and Lady Bird Johnson, and visit the replica of the Oval Office as it was during Johnson's time. (Note especially the number of television sets and the news wires here. Johnson was a real newshound.)

There also are two short video presentations of LBJ himself. A 5-minute tape shows how he worked, and a 7-minute presentation gives great insight into the humor and personality of this charismatic Texan who was the nation's 36th president. For even better perspective, start your tour by watching the 20-minute movie that traces Johnson's life from his childhood on the banks of the Pedernales River west of Austin (see the Day Trips chapter) to the nation's highest office. The library houses 40 million pages of historical documents. The museum and gift shop are open from 9 a.m. to 5 p.m. every day of the year except Christmas. And, because Johnson did not want people to have to pay to see his museum, it's the only presidential library that does not charge an entrance fee. Parking is free, too, in the lot on Red River Street.

THE MUSTANGS SCULPTURE
San Jacinto Street at the base of the Texas Memorial Museum

Dedicated to the "spirited horses that carried the men who made Texas," this gorgeous statue of seven plunging mustangs is a landmark at the University of Texas. Unveiled in 1948, the statue is the work of Phimister Proctor, a famous sculptor of Western subjects. Proctor reportedly spent almost a year observing and measuring the anatomical details of a herd of painstakingly chosen puros españoles, Spanish mustangs. (FYI: It was the Spanish who introduced these powerful and wonderful horses to Texas.) The results are marvelous. Proctor created a band of horses that, since 1948, appears as if it could come to life at any moment.

SANTA RITA OIL RIG
At the corner of Trinity Street and Martin Luther King Jr. Boulevard

History buffs will want to search out this rig while touring the University of Texas campus. This little piece of machinery stands as a powerful symbol of the riches UT gained from the legendary Santa Rita oil well in West Texas. On the morning of May 28, 1923, oil gushed forth from the well in Big Lake Oil Field on UT lands. For 19 years this oil rig worked to draw the black gold to the surface and help catapult the struggling university to fame as a first-class institution. (UT became one of Austin's economic pillars along the way.) For just short of 67 years, the Santa Rita oil well pumped money into the UT system.

TEXAS MEMORIAL MUSEUM
2400 Trinity St.
(512) 471-1604
www.utexas.edu/tmm

Opened in 1939 as a permanent memorial of the Texas Centennial celebrations, the Texas Memorial Museum is a showcase for the natural and social sciences. Here, among the bones, rocks, fossils, and dinosaur tracks, visitors will discover the distant—and not so distant—past. Life-size dioramas of Texas wildlife, habitat groups of native Texas birds, and displays of Texas's poisonous and harmless reptiles are just some of the treasures awaiting visitors in this museum.

Among the museum's many special attractions is the original 16-foot statue of the Goddess of Liberty that stood atop the State Capitol for nearly 100 years until she was replaced with a replica in 1986. The star she holds in her hand, however, is not the original. That can be viewed in the Capitol Complex Visitor Center. There's also the Onion Creek mosasaur, which serves as the centerpiece of the Hall of Geological History. Here ancient amphibians and reptiles mingle with some of the giant Ice Age mammals, including saber-toothed cats and mastodons..

Although the museum focuses on Texas, there's also much to be seen about the Southwest and Latin America. The building itself is a work of art and a true attraction. The museum is open 9 a.m. to 5 p.m. Mon through Fri, 10 a.m. to 4:45 p.m. Sat, and 1 to 4:45 p.m. on Sun. There's no entrance fee, but contributions are encouraged.

✳THE UT TOWER
(512) 475-6633, (877) 475-6633
www.utexas.edu/tower

Just look up when you're on the UT campus and you'll find this 307-foot landmark, the most recognizable symbol of the university, which stands at the very heart of the original 40-acre campus. The Tower of the Main Building was completed in 1937 on the site of the university's first academic building, Old Main. The 27-story tower features a clock whose 4 faces are 14 feet, 8 inches, in diameter and the Knicker Carillon with its 56 bells that chime on the quarter hour and hour and are played at other times by the university's carillonneur.

The tower once shared the Austin skies with only one other soaring rival, the State Capitol. Its construction drew the ire of some Austin citizens back then, most notably Austin's master storyteller and UT professor J. Frank Dobie, who suggested the tower be laid on its side. Why, he complained aloud, with all the space in Texas, did a building here have to look like one in New York.

The soaring observation deck, however, afforded an excellent view of the city and quickly became a popular tourist attraction. But a tragic mass murder committed from the tower (see the History chapter) as well as a rash of suicides caused university officials to close the tower to the public in 1975. After being closed for nearly 25 years, the tower underwent a renovation and is once again open to the public for guided tours. Tickets for the nearly hourlong tour, including about 35 minutes on the observation deck, cost $6. Advance reservations are strongly recommended, as the tours fill up early. Call one of the numbers listed above to reserve. Tickets cannot be reserved on the website, but the site contains other important information about the ticketing process.

The Spanish Renaissance–style structure, designed by Paul Cret of Philadelphia and built of Bedford Indiana limestone, is lighted to commemorate achievements in athletics and academics. There are so many different lighting schemes, each with its own significance, that the university once issued a guide to Tower lighting.

CENTRAL

ELISABET NEY MUSEUM
304 East Forty-fourth St.
(512) 458-2255
www.ci.austin.tx.us/elisabetney

This museum, once the Hyde Park home and studio of celebrated 19th-century artist Elisabet Ney, features an array of about 50 portrait busts and full-figure statues of European notables, Texas heroes, and other figures. An entire section of the museum is dedicated to the life of this amazing sculptor who helped to establish Austin's artistic traditions. This is one museum that should not be missed on any tour of the Austin arts. For more information about the museum and the Ney home, called Formosa, see the chapter on The Arts.

Lady Bird Johnson: A National Treasure

One of the first display cases that visitors encounter at the Lyndon Baines Johnson Library and Museum contains mementos of the whirlwind courtship between the future president of the United States and the woman who would be his bride, Lady Bird Taylor. Among the documents is a handwritten letter from the 21-year-old recent University of Texas graduate to her suitor.

"Lyndon, please tell me as soon as you can what the deal is," the letter reads. "I am afraid it's politics—Oh, I know I haven't any business—not any 'proprietary interest'—but I would hate for you to go into politics."

The year was 1934. Mrs. Johnson spent more than six decades in the public eye. During those years she evolved from the shy, nervous girl who deliberately dropped her grade point average in high school to avoid making the speech required of the class valedictorian to become one of the great First Ladies in American history. Although Mrs. Johnson died in 2007, she will forever remain an American treasure, a Texas icon, and Austin's most beloved citizen. Each spring, Central Texas residents need only look to the roadside to see Lady Bird Johnson's reflection: There wildflowers abound, planted by both Mother Nature and the state highway department as a tribute to her advocacy.

On November 22, 1963, an assassin's bullet thrust Mrs. Johnson into the role of First Lady of the United States. Asked later what image she hoped to project to the nation, Mrs. Johnson replied, "My image will emerge in actions, not words."

Indeed. A genteel Southern woman whom fate would place at the very center of the turbulent 1960s, Mrs. Johnson's vigorous campaign in the Bible Belt helped the JFK-LBJ ticket take Texas and win the 1960 national election. In 1964, when it was her husband's turn to seek the presidency in his own right, Mrs. Johnson embarked on a massive whistle-stop tour through eight Southern states, often facing hostile crowds because of Johnson's support for civil rights. As First Lady she traveled to some of America's poorest regions to address the crisis of poverty in the country.

She also became the first First Lady to actively campaign to get a bill made into law. In 1965, despite strong opposition, her noble vision for America paid off with the passage of the Highway Beautification Act, which sought to eliminate billboards and other eyesores from America's highways.

In 1977 President Gerald Ford gave her the nation's highest civilian honor, the Presidential Medal of Freedom. President Ronald Reagan added the Congressional Gold Medal in 1988. "She claimed her own place in the hearts and history of the American people. In councils of power or in homes of the poor, she made government human with her unique compassion and her grace, warmth, and wisdom. Her leadership transformed the American landscape and preserved its natural beauty as a national treasure," reads her Medal of Freedom certificate, on display along with the medal at the LBJ Library.

As a child growing up in the small East Texas town of Karnack, the girl born Claudia Alta Taylor on December 22, 1912, came to cherish the native flowers that flourished around her home. The daughter of Thomas Jefferson "T. J." Taylor, the wealthy owner of the town's general store, and Minnie Pattillo Taylor, Claudia was just 5 years old when her mother died after falling down a flight of stairs. The role of mothering was left to her maiden Aunt Effie Pattillo, a well-educated, cultured woman who came from Alabama to help raise Claudia and her two older brothers. It was a nursemaid who gave Claudia the name that would remain with her for life, saying she was just "as purty as a lady bird."

Lady Bird was 17 years old when she entered the University of Texas at Austin in 1930. Four years later she graduated with honors with degrees in journalism and history as well as with a teaching certificate. In Austin she met Lyndon Baines Johnson, the up-and-coming assistant to a Washington congressman. Within one day of their meeting, Johnson proposed and within two months they were married in San Antonio. He had literally swept her off her feet.

After World War II broke out and LBJ joined the service, Lady Bird ran his congressional office for the half a year Johnson was away. In 1943 the Johnsons, with Lady Bird at the helm, bought a small Austin radio station, KTBC. Mrs. Johnson, who did everything from paint the station walls to sign the checks, proved she was an astute businesswoman. On Thanksgiving Day 1952, KTBC became Central Texas's first television station and the cornerstone of the family's multimillion-dollar fortune.

Following President Johnson's death, Mrs. Johnson divided her time between Austin and the family ranch in Stonewall, which the Johnsons donated to the American people as a national historic site. Through all these years she remained at the forefront of the American environmental movement, not as a figurehead but actively involved in the effort to preserve and protect the nation's natural beauty. In Austin she chaired the Town Lake Beautification Project, a community effort that resulted in the creation of the city's magnificent Lady Bird Lake Hike and Bike Trail (see the Parks & Recreation chapter). The city wanted to name Town Lake for Lady Bird, but she demurred. Following her death on July 11, 2007, however, Town Lake was officially renamed Lady Bird Lake in her honor. In 1982, on her 70th birthday, Mrs. Johnson founded Austin's National Wildflower Research Center. On a glorious spring day in 1998, the acclaimed center (see the listing in this chapter) was officially renamed the Lady Bird Johnson Wildflower Center in honor of this remarkable woman, whom First Lady Laura Bush called "the conductor of the symphony of wildflowers that bloom across Texas."

Mrs. Johnson, wearing a sunflower-bright yellow suit and her trademark radiant smile, received a warm standing ovation as she stood to unveil the new name on the center's logo. "I had great fun campaigning with Lyndon and falling in love with the natural beauty and diversity of this country," she told the audience, speaking in the soft East Texas drawl that charmed even her staunchest opponents throughout her lifetime.

The museum is open Wed through Sun noon to 5 p.m. Admission is free.

THE NEILL-COCHRAN HOUSE MUSEUM
2310 San Gabriel St.
(512) 478-2335
www.neill-cochranmuseum.org

Austin's master builder Abner Cook designed and built this stately home in 1855 following a design plan that is similar to the Cook-built Governor's Mansion. Now a museum run by the Colonial Dames of America in the State of Texas, the home is a glorious example of Greek Revival architecture. Classic furnishings from the late 18th and early 19th centuries can be viewed throughout this beautifully kept home. The National Trust for Historic Preservation has called this house a "jewel and perfect example of the Texas version of the Greek Revival in the South." The home, originally built for Washington L. Hill, was purchased in 1876 by Colonel Andrew Neill. Judge T. B. Cochran bought the house in 1895 and made additions. The museum is open from 2 to 5 p.m. Tues through Sat. General admission is $5.

TREATY OAK
Baylor Street, between West Fifth and West Sixth Streets

The poignant tale of Austin's beautiful and historic Treaty Oak will tug at your heart strings. Estimated to be between 500 and 600 years old, the Treaty Oak once stood more than 3 stories high and its branches covered more than half an acre. In the Hall of Fame of Forestry, the tree was described as "the most perfect specimen of a tree in North America." Legend has it that the Father of Texas, Stephen F. Austin, and leaders of local Indian tribes signed a treaty under the mighty oak, supposedly dividing the city between them. Although there is no historic evidence that this meeting ever took place, the legend persevered and people came from all over the country just to look at this incredible specimen.

Poisoned in 1989 by a man who was later caught and sentenced to 9 years in prison, the majestic Treaty Oak is now about a third its original size but still definitely worth a visit. Austin's heroic effort to save the Treaty Oak is another chapter in the tree's rich history. Specialists were brought in, sunscreens were erected, and people from all over the country prayed and sent letters along with more than $100,000 in donations to help save the tree. Since then, acorns and cuttings from the tree have been planted in Austin and the Treaty Oak was cloned so that identical copies of it are growing in Texas and other parts of the country. It's a story of survival. It's a story of Austin.

i Who is that crazed-looking woman lighting a cannon on the corner of Sixth Street and Congress Avenue? She's Angelina Eberly portrayed in bronze by Pulitzer Prize–winning cartoonist Pat Oliphant. Eberly was the 19th century innkeeper who helped ignite Austin's "Archive War," which kept Austin as Texas's capital.

AROUND AUSTIN
South Central

AUSTIN NATURE AND SCIENCE CENTER
301 Nature Center Dr.
(512) 327-8181
www.ci.austin.tx.us/ansc

A perfect place to enjoy Austin's great outdoors, the Austin Nature and Science Center in the Zilker Park Nature Preserve features 2 miles of trails with cliffs and a scenic outlook (see the Parks & Recreation chapter). But the facilities here go far beyond trails. In the Visitor Pavilion, guests will learn about the two ecosystems—Hill Country and Caves, and Grasslands—that meet right smack in the middle of Austin. Displays also provide information on two minor ecosystems found throughout Central Texas: Ponds and Creeks, and Woodlands. Wildlife exhibits and a birds of prey exhibit are just a couple of the attractions found at this wonderful spot. (See the Kidstuff chapter for more information on the center.) It is open 9 a.m. to 5 p.m. Mon through Sat, and noon to 5 p.m. on Sun throughout the year. Admission is free.

PHILOSOPHERS' ROCK SCULPTURE
Entrance to Barton Springs Pool

This exquisite bronze sculpture by artist Glenna Goodacre depicts three of Austin's illustrious figures engaged in animated conversation—just as they were accustomed to doing in life. Life-size images of historian Walter Prescott Webb, naturalist Roy Bedichek, and J. Frank Dobie, humorist and folklorist, are presented in this large work, installed November 21, 1994. Webb stands fully clothed next to the rock (he never swam), while Dobie and Bedichek are seated, wearing swimming trunks. As you view this lively sculpture, it's difficult not to wonder what these three great "philosophers" are discussing.

STEVIE RAY VAUGHAN MEMORIAL
Auditorium Shores, South side of Lady Bird Lake near Riverside Drive and First Street

This larger-than-life bronze statue of the late blues/rock legend stands near the site where Vaughan played his last Austin concert on Auditorium Shores. The sculpture by artist Ralph Helmick depicts Vaughan in a relaxed pose wearing his trademark black hat and holding his guitar like a walking stick in his left hand. A long bronze shadow trails behind. When it was dedicated on November 21, 1993, Vaughan fans gathered in tribute to the Austin-based music man who died in a helicopter crash in 1990. The piece continues to draw admirers of both the artist it depicts and the artist who created it. (For more on Stevie Ray Vaughan, see the Close-up in The Music Scene chapter.)

UMLAUF SCULPTURE GARDEN & MUSEUM
605 Robert E. Lee Rd.
(512) 445-5582
www.umlaufsculpture.org

The outdoor setting of this wonderful sculpture garden combines Austin's love for the outdoors and for the arts. Acclaimed artist Charles Umlauf, whose works are on display in museums and public collections across the country, lived in Austin from 1941 until his death and was a University of Texas professor until 1981. The garden is the perfect outdoor setting for dozens of Umlauf's bronze and cast-stone pieces. (For more on this inspiring Austin museum, see the chapter on The Arts.) The museum is open Wed through Fri 10 a.m. to 4:30 p.m. and on Sat and Sun 1 to 4:30 p.m. There is a nominal admission charge.

ZILKER BOTANICAL GARDEN
2220 Barton Springs Rd.
(512) 477-8672
www.zilkergarden.org

The theme gardens in this beautiful spot are just some of the attractions at this lovely botanical garden, managed jointly by the

Austin Area Garden Council and the City of Austin Parks and Recreation Department. Here visitors stroll among the 31 acres of displays and gardens to learn about different species of plants, get ideas for their own gardens, or just appreciate the beauty of nature. The Butterfly Garden and trail has been filled with flowers and plants that attract many species of Texas butterflies. The Green Garden is a showcase of water-tolerant plants and the principles of xeriscaping. The Prehistoric Garden re-creates a dinosaur habitat, in tribute to the dinosaur tracks and bones discovered here in 1992. In the Japanese Garden visitors will discover a series of waterfalls, lotus ponds, and an authentic teahouse. There also are gardens dedicated to roses, herbs, and cacti. The Garden Council also sponsors a number of educational and cultural programs on-site as well as several popular annual events, including the Zilker Garden Festival in the spring.

Here, too, visitors will find Pioneer Village, which includes two original log structures from the 1800s, a blacksmith shop, and an organic garden. The Swedish Log Cabin, built about 1838 on the "Govalle" Ranch—meaning "good grazing land" in Swedish—and moved to the botanical garden in 1966, is fully furnished with such 19th-century necessities as a spinning wheel, loom, and baby cradle. Next to the cabin is the Esperanza School Building. Built in 1866, the log building was one of the earliest one-room rural school houses in Travis County. The interior of this school also is furnished as schoolchildren would have occupied it in the 19th century. The Botanical Garden opens daily at 7 a.m. Admission is free. No food or picnicking is allowed.

North

THE REPUBLIC OF TEXAS MUSEUM
510 East Anderson Lane
(512) 339-1997
www.drt-inc.org/museum.htm
This fascinating space, which is meticulously run and cared for by the Daughters of the Republic of Texas, is packed with Texas history. Here visitors will learn about the men and women who fought for Texas independence and led the Republic of Texas from 1836 to 1846. The museum features award-winning permanent exhibits and a variety of touring shows. One outstanding section is called Great Grandma's Backyard, where visitors get to see and touch the household implements used by families in the mid-19th century. The museum also features an excellent collection of guns from that period, portraits and statues of Texas leaders, and much, much more. (See also the chapter on Kidstuff.)

South

ST. EDWARD'S UNIVERSITY
3001 South Congress Ave.
(512) 448-8400
www.stedwards.edu
Don't miss the beautiful Gothic Revival–style Main Building and the other great attributes of this 180-acre campus. The Main Building is one of Austin's most stunning landmarks—a grand structure in the Southwest when it was built in 1889 and just as grand today. (For more information on this historic university, see the Higher Education chapter.)

SOUTH AUSTIN MUSEUM OF POPULAR CULTURE
1516 South Lamar Blvd.
(512) 440-8318
www.samopc.org

A true Austin original, this funky little space it worth a stop by any visitor who wants to view some of the music posters and other graphic art that were created during the 1960s psychedelic era, the 1970s cosmic cowboy era, and into the 1980s. For more information, see the listing in The Arts chapter.

Southwest

AUSTIN ZOO
10807 Rawhide Trail
(512) 288-1490
www.austinzoo.org
Located on the edge of Hill Country about 20 minutes from downtown Austin, the Austin Zoo is a great escape from the hustle and bustle of the city. Here visitors get a close-up view of domestic and exotic animals as well as a relaxing, enjoyable experience in a natural setting. (For more on Austin's zoo, see the Kidstuff chapter.)

BARSANA DHAM
400 Barsana Rd.
(512) 288-7180
www.barsanadham.org
About 20 minutes from downtown Austin, this Hindu temple and ashram is a stunning sight to behold in the Texas Hill Country. Located on 200 acres, the 35,000-square-foot architecturally magnificent compound is one of the largest Hindu temples in the United States. The most impressive feature is the dome, which towers high above the temple, but that is only one of the attractions here. The main hall and prayer hall, as well as the compound's fountains, pools, and shrines also are impressive. The temple, which represents the holy district of Braj, India, is surrounded by fields of wildflowers, a stream and ponds in a parklike setting

that includes picnic benches and other outdoor seating. Best of all, this temple is extremely visitor friendly. General visiting hours vary, but visitors also are invited to attend prayer services. The temple also hosts festivals throughout the year, as well as an open house and fair in the spring, which features carnival games, booths, entertainment, Indian food and sometimes even elephant and camel rides! Check the website for a virtual tour and calendar of events.

✴LADY BIRD JOHNSON WILDFLOWER CENTER
4801 La Crosse Ave.
(512) 232-0100
www.wildflower.org
Established in 1982 as the National Wildlife Research Center, this delightful center was renamed in March of 1998 in honor of its founder, Austin's own Lady Bird Johnson. (See the profile of the former First Lady of the United States in this chapter.) This 42-acre Hill Country gem overflows with a brilliant variety of native plants and flowers and has become one of Austin's most visited spots. Here visitors will see and learn about our own state flower, the bluebonnet, as well as the glorious Indian paintbrush, which is as splendid as its name, and more than 500 other species of native plants. The center's many perennial and seasonal gardens display in living color the bounty of Texas's botanical beauties. Much more than a showcase for the magnificent plant life of Texas, however, the center is an ecological sanctuary dedicated to the preservation and reestablishment of native plants—wildflowers, grasses, shrubs, and trees. It's the only national nonprofit organization fulfilling that mission and has become the leading

national authority on native American plant life.

The place to begin a tour is at the Visitor Gallery, where visitors are introduced to the Wildflower Center and can view interesting displays on the region's plant life. Young children especially will delight in hearing Ralph, the talking lawn mower, just one of the many features designed to appeal to children. The grounds are open Tues through Sat 9 a.m. to 5:30 p.m., and Sun noon to 5:30 p.m., though check the website for extended hours in the spring. The Visitors Gallery closes earlier. General admission is $8.

Northwest

CYPRESS VALLEY CANOPY TOURS
1223 Paleface Ranch Rd., Spicewood
(512) 264-8880
www.cypressvalleycanopytours.com
When we visited Costa Rica a few years ago, one of our most thrilling adventures was taking the zip-line canopy tour, soaring hundreds of feet above the forest floor over the treetops suspended only by wires and harnesses. You can imagine our pleasant surprise, then, when we learned that the patriarch of a former Austin family had done the same—and decided to open up a canopy tour in the cypress-covered area near his family's new home about 35 miles northwest of downtown Austin. The adventurous can choose between the Canopy Tour or the more advanced Canopy Challenge. Check the website for details, as there are minimum and maximum weight requirements as well as other restrictions. There is also an option of staying overnight among the trees—and zipping to your room!

East

FRENCH LEGATION MUSEUM
802 San Marcos St.
(512) 472-8180
www.frenchlegationmuseum.org
After King Louis Philippe of France officially recognized the fledgling Republic of Texas in 1839, he named Alphonse Dubois de Saligny as charge d'affaires and sent him to Austin. De Saligny, a flamboyant character, bought 22 acres of land on a beautiful Austin hilltop and began construction on his luxurious residence and carriage house, which are considered modest by today's standards. De Saligny, who insisted he be called Count, was anything but noble and more like a no-account scoundrel, leaving a trail of debts and angry citizens during his short stay here. While he awaited completion of his residence, de Saligny lived in downtown Austin, where he launched the infamous Pig War. Complaining that his neighbor's pigs were destroying his garden, de Saligny ordered his servant to shoot any pig that even looked as though it was going after the garden. The neighbor, Richard Bullock, retaliated by whacking the servant and threatening to come after de Saligny himself. That was about all de Saligny could take of Texas, and vice versa. He headed back to Louisiana and never occupied the home. The home was purchased by Dr. Joseph Robertson in 1848, and it remained in the family's hands for a century. In 1948 the state of Texas bought the property and placed it in custody of the Daughters of the Republic of Texas. They restored the home and opened it to the public in 1956. Today visitors will find many of the Robertson family furnishings as well as other period pieces. Guided tours include a visit to the original house and the reconstructed French Creole kitchen, which is fully equipped and contains many unique items. The replica

of the carriage house contains an 1828 carriage, other exhibits, and a gift shop. Tours are conducted Tues through Sun 1 to 4 p.m. The French Legation is also a popular spot for weddings. There is a small admission fee.

The French equivalent of our Independence Day, Bastille Day, July 14, is celebrated here with French song, food, and dance, and the legation also hosts a popular Christmas event when Pere Noel arrives to celebrate the season with a Gallic flair (see the listing in our Annual Events chapter).

GEORGE WASHINGTON CARVER MUSEUM AND CULTURAL CENTER
1165 Angelina St.
(512) 974-4926
www.ci.austin.tx.us/carver

Distinguished for being the first African-American neighborhood museum in the state of Texas, this 36,000-square-foot facility includes 4 galleries, a 134-seat theater, a dance studio, conference room, classroom, darkroom, and archival space. The museum's core exhibit is on Juneteenth, the oldest nationally celebrated commemoration of the ending of slavery in the United States. There also is a permanent exhibit on Austin African-American families, an Artists Gallery, and a children's exhibit on African-American scientists and inventors, including George Washington Carver, of course. It's open 10 a.m. to 9 p.m. Mon through Thurs, 10 a.m. to 5:30 p.m. Fri, and 10 a.m. to 4 p.m. Sat.

HUSTON-TILLOTSON UNIVERSITY
900 Chicon St.
(512) 505-3025
www.htu.edu

While the campus has modernized over the past 135 years, two of Huston-Tillotson's historic buildings remain as splendid examples of turn-of-the-20th-century architecture. The Evans Industrial Building, built in 1911–12, was completely renovated in 1984 and designated as a Texas Historical Site. The Old Administration Building, constructed in 1913–14, is one of the few remaining examples of the Modified Prairie Style popularized by Frank Lloyd Wright. This now-restored building was entered in the National Register of Historic Places in 1993. (For more on this historic African-American university, see the chapter on Higher Education.)

OAKWOOD CEMETERY
Sixteenth and Navasota Streets

Austin's oldest cemetery is a scene of tranquility and beauty. Created in 1839, the cemetery is the final resting place for many Austin pioneers, prominent Austin families, and community leaders from the past and present. Athol Estes Porter, wife of short-story writer O. Henry, is interred here, as are former Texas Governor James Hogg and his daughter Ima. Mary Baylor, a driving force in the preservation of the Clarksville neighborhood, was buried here in 1997. Susanna Dickinson Hannig, the "Messenger of the Alamo," also rests here. The cemetery, which is chock-full of towering trees that provide wonderful shade in summer, was added to the National Register of Historic Places in 1988.

✳TEXAS STATE CEMETERY
901 Navasota St.
(512) 463-6600
www.cemetery.state.tx.us

A must-see for anyone who wants to comprehend the scope of Texas history, the 18-acre Texas State Cemetery manages to be both tranquil and exhilarating at the same time. Visitors who walk among the tombs of many of Texas's most noted heroes and legends can't help envisioning the drama of the lives and times of these leaders. Stephen F. Austin, the Father of Texas, is buried here under a bronze statue that shows him standing with his right hand raised and holding a manuscript in his left hand inscribed with the words TEXAS 1836. Confederate General Albert Sidney Johnson lies under the recumbent statue of him carved by Elisabet Ney, the German-born sculptor who made Austin her home. Among the other Texas leaders interred here is Barbara Jordan. A beloved scholar, teacher, and politician, Jordan was the first African American from Texas elected to the US House of Representatives. Three-term Texas Governor John B. Connally is buried here along with the bullet fragments left in his body from when he was wounded during the Kennedy assassination. Lt. Governor Bob Bullock, the force behind the Texas State History Museum (see earlier in this chapter), is also interred here. And there are many more, including 10 other Texas governors, many famous writers and historians, and about 2,200 white marble headstones for veterans of the Confederate Army. Among the graves is that of General Edward Burleson, a vice president of the Republic of Texas and the first person to be buried in the cemetery after its creation in 1851.

The cemetery is open daily 8 a.m. to 5 p.m., although the visitor center is closed weekends. Guests can call ahead to arrange for guided tours, or they can do a self-guided tour with the help of information packets available at the visitor center. There's also a new audio tour available for download.

> **i** When planning outdoor activities, remember that Austin does have four seasons: November, December, January, and Summer. Or, as some like to say, Almost Summer, Summer, Like Summer, and Christmas.

West

✳AUSTIN MUSEUM OF ART AT LAGUNA GLORIA
3809 West Thirty-fifth St.
(512) 458-8191
www.amoa.org

One of two facilities of the Austin Museum of Art, Laguna Gloria is important as much for its facilities as for the artworks it exhibits. Constructed in 1915–16 as a private residence, the Mediterranean-style villa covers more than 6,000 square feet. The outdoor amphitheater hosts a variety of performance artists throughout the year. It's also a great place just to sit by the lake and have a picnic. The sculpture garden is wonderful. (For more information on Laguna Gloria, see the chapter on The Arts.)

MOUNT BONNELL
At the top of Mount Bonnell Road off West Thirty-fifth Street

This scenic spot overlooking Lake Austin has been attracting nature lovers—and romantic ones—for more than 160 years. At 785 feet above sea level, Mount Bonnell is one of the highest points in the Austin area and offers a view to end all views. Choose your partner wisely to make that first climb up the steps. According to local lore, two people who make their first climb together will fall in love. Some say Mount Bonnell was named after George W. Bonnell, a newspaperman and mercenary. Others claim it was named for Golden Nell and her "beau"—beau-nell—who leapt off the summit to their deaths in order to avoid capture by Native Americans. Visitors can also reach Mount Bonnell off FM 2222 (Bull Creek). (For more information on Mount Bonnell, see the chapter on Parks & Recreation.)

TEXAS MILITARY FORCES MUSEUM
Camp Mabry, 2200 West Thirty-fifth St.
(512) 782-5659
www.texasmilitaryforcesmuseum.org

Tanks, transport vehicles, vintage aircraft, cannons, and other big guns are just a few of the items on display at this sprawling museum, which traces the history of Texas's military forces from 1823 to the present. The museum's five galleries and outdoor exhibit areas are absolutely loaded with items that bring to life the story of Texas's fighting men and women. Visitors will find a seemingly infinite number of weapons dating from before the Texas Revolution all the way to the War on Terror. There are dioramas of the battles of the Alamo and San Jacinto, a model of the Bridge Over the River Kwai built by members of the "Lost Battalion" during World War II, an exhibit on the Choctaw code-talkers of World War I, a Soviet M1946 130mm Field Gun captured in Iraq during Operation Desert Storm, and so much more. This museum really must be visited to be fully appreciated. It's open Wed through Sun 10 a.m. to 4 p.m., and admission is free.

A word about getting there and getting in: This museum is only one part of Camp Mabry, a military installation of the Texas National Guard, so all adults must show a photo ID to gain admittance. Also, the museum does not have its own address so the address listed above is for the Camp itself. Check the website for detailed instructions on how to find the entrance, which is on Maintenance Drive.

Northeast

✳JOURDAN-BACHMAN PIONEER FARMS
10621 Pioneer Farms Dr.
(512) 837-1215
www.pioneerfarms.org

This living history museum, originally part of a 2,000-acre cotton farm, treats visitors to a journey back in time to witness the lifestyle of Central Texas's early settlers. From the dwellings to the farm implements and household items to the guides' dress, everything out here is historically correct. There are plenty of hands-on activities for the whole family. See the chapter on Kidstuff for more about this enlightening slice of early Texas life.

Lake Travis

✳THE OASIS
6550 Comanche Trail
(512) 266-2442
www.oasis-austin.com

Consistently named one of the Top 10 Austin Area Attractions by the Austin Convention and Visitors Bureau, the Oasis offers one of the most stunning views in this entire area. From a vantage point of 450 feet above Lake Travis, the multitudes of outdoor decks and the indoor dining rooms look out across the lake and the Texas Hill Country. Struck by lightning on June 1, 2005, much of the Oasis was destroyed by the resulting fire. Within weeks the Starlight Terrace was reopened and other decks were being reconstructed. This is one of the best places to drink a margarita or two while watching a fabulous Austin sunset. The Oasis hosts live bands Thurs through Sun nights. This establishment is also a full-service restaurant leaning heavily on Tex-Mex cuisine.

NATIONAL REGISTER DISTRICTS

While Austin has numerous residences and commercial buildings listed on the National Register of Historic Places, many of which we've mentioned in this chapter, the city also boasts a number of entire districts listed on this important National Register for historic preservation. Those who don't want to miss one stop on their tour of historic Austin should consider taking a walking tour of some of these uniquely Austin locations. See the listing under Austin Tours in this chapter if you're interested in a guided walking tour of some of the following neighborhoods. You can also pick up copies of the free "Historic Walking Tours" series from the Austin Visitor Center at 209 East Sixth St. (www .austintexas.org). They have brochures for Hyde Park, the Bremond District, and Congress Avenue and East Sixth Street. These brochures describe each building in detail and give some interesting tidbits about the buildings' former owners. There's also a brochure available on Camp Mabry.

Barton Springs Archaeological & Historic District

This district within Zilker Park in South Central Austin includes our favorite swimming spot and a most endangered treasure, Barton Springs Swimming Pool. Named to the National Register in 1985, this place is Austin through and through and should not be missed on any tour of Austin, prehistoric, historic, or otherwise. Barton Springs, comprising four principal springs, is the fifth-largest group of springs in the state of Texas. One of the many reasons this site is listed on the National Register of Historic Places is that human habitation has been traced back to approximately 6000 BC. Archaeologists have found chipped-stone arrowheads, bone fragments, and prehistoric ceramics while digging in this area.

The springs are named for one of Austin's earliest modern settlers, William Barton, who moved to the springs in 1837 and built a home. While nothing remains of his homestead, there is evidence (a cistern) of the home built on the property in 1867 by the Rabb family, who came to Texas as part of Stephen F. Austin's first colony of Anglo settlers (see the History chapter). More modern structures that contributed to the springs' selection for the National Register include the concrete Zilker Amphitheater, built around one of the springs by Austin civic leader and philanthropist Andrew Jackson Zilker in the first decade of the 20th century. And then there's the famous Bath House. Built in 1946, this cool structure has been a source of pride for Austin for more than half a century. During a period when Texas architecture was largely ignored by the national press, the Bath House was the subject of a long article in *Architectural Digest* magazine. The article praised architect Dan Driscoll's ingenuity in designing an imaginative structure that was entirely appropriate for its site. The Bath House, still in use today next to the pool, is practically unchanged from the day it was built. (For more information on this 1,000-foot-long spring-fed pool, see the chapter on Parks & Recreation.) The pool itself is located at 2201 Barton Springs Rd., but the register district is bounded on the north by Barton Springs Road, on the east by Robert E. Lee Road, and on the west by Barton Creek and is situated on both banks of the creek.

Bremond National Register District

For a glimpse into the lifestyles of the rich and prominent from a century ago, include this district, simply called the Bremond Block, on your tour of downtown Austin. Here are some of the most elegant and elaborate 19th-century homes still found in the city. Italianate, Greek revival, colonial revival, Queen Anne, and Second Empire are just some of the architectural styles borrowed for this collection of 14 homes built between 1854 and 1910. Many of these fabulous homes are historic landmarks.

Three of the homes—the Walter Bremond House, the Pierre Bremond House, and the stunning John Bremond Jr. House—were built by Austin builder George Fiegel, who is notable for having planned, constructed, or remodeled many of the buildings on historic Congress Avenue.

The histories of those who built and occupied these dwellings are as interesting as the structures themselves. Eugene Bremond and his siblings grew up just a couple of blocks away as the children of wealthy merchant John Bremond Sr. As it happened, the Bremond homestead was catty-cornered from the homestead of another Austin merchant, John Robinson Sr. The warm friendship between the patriarchs of these two families must have cast a spell over both houses, because Eugene and two of his sisters married Robinsons. Eugene, who parlayed his father's wealth into a fortune first as a lender—it's said he charged 18 percent interest on loans made to early settlers—and then as a banker, bought the north half of the block in 1866 that was to bear his family's name. Over the years, as the families' children grew and married, the block became the Bremond family compound, just as Eugene had envisioned. Not all the homes in this district were owned by the Bremond line, however. Other wealthy Austinites also lived in this compound, including the Harvey North family, the Henry Hirshfelds, and William Phillips, one of Austin's first doctors. The district is between Seventh and Eighth Streets and Guadalupe and San Antonio Streets.

i *The Unforeseen* is a documentary film about the forces of real estate developers on Austin's beloved Barton Springs. The award-winning film is moving, magical—and not just a little sad—but it is a wonderful way to discover the strong feelings many Austinites have about Barton Springs. Rent it if you can.

Clarksville National Register District

Clarksville is one of four Austin communities founded by African Americans in the years following the end of slavery, on June 19, 1865. Named for Charles Clark, the name taken by freed slave Charles Griffin, the neighborhood started when Clark purchased two acres of wilderness land on what was then just west of the Austin city limits. In 1977 Clarksville became the first African-American neighborhood in Texas to be listed on the National Register of Historic Places. Many of the homes in this neighborhood were built between the 1870s and the 1930s (see the Relocation chapter). Today visitors can find the 1930s basilica-style building that houses the Sweet Home Missionary Baptist Church at 1725 West Eleventh St. The church was founded in the 1880s by the freed men and women who built new lives in this district. The neighborhood is in Central Austin and is bounded by MoPac on the west, Tenth Street on the south, Waterston Avenue on the north, and West Lynn Street on the east. And don't miss Mary Baylor Clarksville Park at 1811 West Eleventh St. This park was named in 1997 in honor of Mary Baylor, who passed away earlier that year. This dynamic community leader, the great-granddaughter of original Clarksville residents, spent a lifetime fighting to preserve Clarksville's unique character.

Congress Avenue National Register District

With our grand Texas State Capitol as its crowning glory, Congress Avenue is a showcase for some of the city's finest late-19th-century commercial architecture. As you walk this 10-block district from the Capitol south to Cesar Chavez Street, keep in mind that this street was once Austin's main thoroughfare and the nerve center for the capital of a fledgling frontier state. Of note on this street is the Johns-Hamilton Building at 716 Congress Ave. Built in 1870 with an elegant Gothic Revival storefront, the facade has been reconstructed. Just a few doors down are the Walter Tips and Edward Tips Buildings at 708–712 Congress Ave. These two German-born brothers immigrated to the United States about 1850. Older brother Edward opened his hardware business at 708 Congress Ave. in 1865 and gave his brother a job as clerk. Not to be outdone, Walter built a much more elaborate structure for his business next door, which dealt in heavy machinery. The Walter Tips Building is a 3-story structure that features Corinthian architecture on the first floor and Venetian Gothic architecture on the top 2 floors. Interior columns and girders in this building are made of recast exploded Confederate shells.

At the corner of Sixth Street and Congress Avenue is the Littlefield Building, which we mentioned in our chronicle of the Sixth Street Historic District. Down the block, at 512–520 Congress, is the Littlefield's rival, the Scarborough Building, which housed the preeminent department store in Texas until the early 1980s. Built in 1909 in the Chicago style, the building's exterior was changed to an Art Deco style in 1931. Next to Scarborough's, at number 504, is the Robinson-Rosner Building. Built in the mid-1850s, this is the oldest known building on Congress Avenue. We must also point out one of Abner Cook's buildings on this avenue. Cook was Austin's master builder during this era and is responsible for some of the city's most historic landmarks, including the old Governor's Mansion (which suffered extensive damage in a June 2008 fire) and the Neill-Cochran House (see the listings in this chapter). He also built the Sampson-Henricks Building at 620 Congress Ave. in 1859. This, too, is one of Congress's oldest buildings and is distinguished for its Italianate style and excellent craftsmanship.

Hyde Park National Register District

Hyde Park represents the vision of Monroe Martin Shipe, an entrepreneur who came to Austin from Abilene, Kansas, in 1889. As president of the Missouri, Kansas, and Texas Land and Town Company, Shipe had resources as big as his dream. He bought the tract of land that was then in far North Austin, named it Hyde Park, for the distinguished London address, and spent the rest of his life living in and promoting his beloved neighborhood. Elisabet Ney, the sculptor famous for carving the marble statues of heroic Texans found in Austin, was among the first to build her home and studio in this 207-acre suburb, now listed as a National Register District. (See more about Elisabet Ney in this chapter.)

The site of the State Fair of Texas from 1875 to 1884, the area back in Shipe's day still had a prominent horse racing track, and those who raced horses there would walk their horses up and down one of the main streets, which became known as the Speedway because of it. Speedway is still one of the major avenues in this Central Austin area.

One of Shipe's first actions to promote development of this suburb was to connect it to the city via his own electric streetcar system. Then he turned the southwest section into a resort that included a dance pavilion and tree-lined walking paths. The middle-class homes, built mostly of wood between 1892 and 1925, reflect a variety of architectural styles and tastes (see the Relocation chapter). The first of Austin's historic Moonlight Towers was built in this neighborhood, and it still works. You'll find it at Forty-first Street and Speedway (see the previous listing in this chapter). A lovely park and playground, now called Shipe Park, was added in 1928 and remains a popular spot for neighborhood families today. The homes are privately owned and not available for tours. Do take a moment to stop in at the Avenue B. Grocery at 4403 Avenue B. This small neighborhood store will take you back in time. This district is in Central Austin between Thirty-ninth and Forty-fourth Streets and Avenue B to Avenue H.

Sixth Street National Register District

By night, this strip defends its reputation as Austin's most-visited strip when tourists and residents out for a good time pack its lively, music-filled clubs and restaurants. By day, Sixth Street takes a breather. That's the time to stroll along the uncluttered sidewalks and take in the sites of one of Austin's most historic streets. This section is about East Sixth Street by day, when the sun illuminates the past. Known as Pecan Street in Austin's early days, this district is filled with more than two dozen fascinating examples of Victorian commercial architecture. Many of the buildings here were constructed during the building boom of the 1870s. Others followed in the 1880s and 1890s. Of course, these structures don't disappear at night. They're just a little harder to appreciate. The district

encompasses a 9-block street from Lavaca Street on the west to I-35 on the east.

Start your tour at the corner of Sixth and Brazos Streets at the famous Driskill Hotel, built in 1886. (See the chapter on Hotels & Motels for more on this landmark.) As you walk east on the north side of Sixth Street, you'll discover many more examples of Victorian architecture. Among the noteworthy structures on Old Pecan Street is the Hannig Building, once the property of cabinet-maker and undertaker Joseph Hannig (the fourth husband of Alamo "Messenger" Susanna Dickinson). Built in 1875 at 206 East Sixth Street, this Renaissance Revival–style structure is considered one of Austin's finest late-19th-century, Victorian commercial buildings. The Padgitt-Warmoth Building, built in 1885, is next at number 208. Once a saddlery and leather business, this is one of Old Pecan Street's most interesting buildings, with its fleur-de-lis cutouts and a Star of David cap.

In the next block is the Platt-Simpson Building at 310 East Sixth St. This structure, built in 1871, was a livery stable and later a hardware store. St. Charles House, at number 316, was built in 1871 and once was a hotel and restaurant. Among the historic structures in the 400 block is the beautifully restored Dos Banderas at 410 East Sixth St. Once a saloon and bawdy house, the building was closed in 1961 for housing "nefarious activities." Next door is the Quast Building, built in 1881 as a residence and later operated as a grocery store. This is one of the oldest stone buildings on the strip. The Risher-Nicholas Building at 422–424 East Sixth St. is another of the building-boom structures. Built in 1873, it became a drugstore in the early 1900s. Owner J. J. Jennings, a black physician, was once lauded for his work at building up "a trade that would do justice to any drugstore owned by any other race." The *Austin Watchman,* an early African-American newspaper, was published here in the early 1900s.

On the south side of Sixth Street, at 421 East Sixth St., is the 2-story stone and masonry Paggi Carriage Shop, constructed around 1875. Owner Michael Paggi is said to have been the first to bring an ice-making machine from France to Texas. Also on this block, visitors will find two 1875 structures, the J. L. Buass Building at number 407 and the Driskill-Day-Ford Building at number 403. The Cotton Exchange Building next door at 401 East Sixth also was built about this time. Across the street, at 325 East Sixth St., is the Smith-Hage Building. Built in 1873, this building is a good example of commercial Victorian architecture during this time period, with its 3 arched windows on the second floor and topped by an elaborate metal cornice. One of Austin's few remaining cast-iron–front buildings can be found at 209 East Sixth St. This is the Morely-Grove Drug Store, originally built as a 2-story structure in 1874. The third floor and a Queen Anne bay window were added about 20 years later. At the corner of Sixth and Congress is the Littlefield Building. Completed in 1912 and built for Major George Washington Littlefield (whose opulent home and the fountain named for him are on the UT campus), this elegant structure once was the tallest building between New Orleans and San Francisco. The building originally had 8 floors, but Littlefield added another floor when the rival Scarborough Building matched the Littlefield's height.

Swedish Hill National Register District

This district is close to the Oakwood Cemetery just east of I-35 in East Austin. Visitors who walk along East Fourteenth Street, East Fifteenth Street, Olander Street, and Waller Street will discover 10 architecturally significant residences built from about 1880 to 1938, none open to the public. The neighborhood, now only partially intact, got its name from the area's Swedish immigrants.

i When you're looking for downtown attractions or lodging, remember that an address that includes the word "south" means south of Lady Bird Lake. Also know that Lady Bird Lake is that river-looking body of water. It's a lake only because the river is dammed.

Zilker Park National Register District

This great Austin Park, which includes many historic structures and buildings, including a limestone Boy Scout hut built in 1934 and a Girl Scout lodge built the same year, was added to the National Register of Historic Places in 1997. (For more on Austin's favorite community park, see the chapter on Parks & Recreation.)

TOURING GREATER AUSTIN...
...On Foot & Wheel
AUSTIN ASTRONOMICAL SOCIETY TOURS
Wild Basin Wilderness Preserve
805 North Loop 360 (Capital of Texas Highway)
(512) 327-7622
www.austinastro.org
A bit off the beaten path but well worth the time are the popular Stargazing (during a crescent moon) and Moonlighting (at or near a full moon) tours offered at Wild Basin Wilderness Preserve by members of the Austin Astronomical Society and Wild

Basin volunteers. Although the tours can be canceled if the sky is overcast, these events are extremely popular and do fill up, so reservations are highly recommended. Call the number above to reserve. Tour guides suggest that visitors bring a flashlight, binoculars, drinking water, and a cushion or small folding chair. The preserve entrance is about 1 mile north of Bee Caves Road on the east side of Loop 360.

AUSTIN GHOST TOURS
(512) 853-9826
www.austinghosttours.com
Boo! For those looking for the decidedly unusual, the well-established Austin Ghost Tours offer a variety of adventures unlike any other tour company. Jeanine Plumer serves as both historian and storyteller as she takes visitors through Austin's haunted haunts. The Ghosts of the Capitol District Tour conjures up the spirit world in a 90-minute walking tour that includes stops at the capitol and the Driskill Hotel. The Servant Girl Annihilator Tour traces the steps of the girl who terrorized our city in the 1880s. There is also a popular Halloween Tour, which runs many nights in Oct—even on the night itself. All tours are conducted in the evening and depart from the Moonshine Patio Bar and Grill at 303 Red River St. Look, too, for Jeanine's book, *Haunted Austin*, at area bookstores and on Amazon.

AUSTIN OVERTURES
(512) 659-9478
www.austinovertures.com
From the vantage point of a comfortable bright-fuchsia van, Austin Overtures offers 90-minute narrated tours of Austin that include 30 of Austin's major historical and cultural attractions on a 30-mile tour route. Experienced tour operators Dow and Mary

Davidson launched this company in 2003, offering interesting, fun-and-fact-filled introductions to many of the places and people that make Austin what it is, such as *Austin City Limits*, the LBJ Library, Barton Springs, and the Congress Avenue bat colony. The tours are narrated by Dow, a Texas history buff whose great-great-grandfather founded the Texas town of Leakey. There are three daily scheduled departures from the Austin Visitor Center, and reservations can be made through the phone number or website above. Special group tours can also be arranged.

AUSTIN VISITOR CENTER
209 East Sixth St.
(512) 478-0098, (866) GO-AUSTIN
www.austintexas.org
The Visitor Center offers free guided walking tours from Mar through Nov of historic Congress Avenue and Sixth Street, and the Bremond District. The Congress Avenue/Sixth Street tour begins at 9 a.m. sharp Thurs through Sat and at 2 p.m. on Sun. The Bremond Block Historic District tour, a glimpse into Austin's Victorian era, begins on Sat and Sun at 11 a.m. These tours leave from the south steps of the State Capitol. Reservations must be made 48 hours in advance by phone or through the website. The Visitor Center also has brochures for self-guided walking tours.

SEGCITY SEGWAY TOURS
621 East Sixth St.
(512) 402-9299
www.segcity.com
If you travel with tweens and teens, you've probably witnessed the eye-rolling and suffered the protests at the mere suggestion of sightseeing. But promise a Segway tour of Austin as part of the day and you'll very likely get a much different reaction. SegCity

offers a variety of 1½- to 2½-hour narrated tours of the downtown Austin area, including the Ultimate City Tour, a 6.5-mile trip that starts at Lady Bird Lake and goes up to, and inside, the Capitol. Other tours include stops to see the Congress Avenue Bats (in season) and a Haunted History Tour in the evening. The tour guides are young, lively, and knowledgeable. Segways balance themselves, but you can count on the guides to provide some basic training before you head off on your tour. Of course, you don't have to be traveling with the kids to enjoy these rides and these guides. Reservations can be made through the website.

i Join the Austin Visitor Center's Insiders Club (we like the name!) to get discounts off goods and services at local businesses. Registration is free on the center's website at www.austin texas.org. The much-improved site is also worth a visit if you're looking for a vacation package or current happenings—or even if you want to listen to or buy some music by Austin artists.

TEXPERT TOURS
(512) 383-8989
www.texperttours.com
Known locally as "the Texas Back Roads Scholar," Howie Richey offers entertaining, insightful tours of Austin and the Texas Hill Country based on his excellent knowledge of and love for this region. His enlightening tours of downtown Austin provide much more than a look at buildings and scenery. He's got the scoop on the history, geography, and quirky qualities of our fair city and exudes a hearty respect for the region's natural wonders. You'll think you've got your very own university professor in the vehicle with

you. Howie is a longtime Austinite and University of Texas grad (twice!) who also hosts shows on Austin public radio. He offers four tours—Witty (top Austin sights), Wild (wineries and nature in the Hill County), Wacky (artsy/offbeat Austin), and Wondrous (music, music, music). Howie also can tailor an outing to satisfy any group's interests. He offers several departure times daily. It's important to reserve in advance, as he customizes the trip for each group. Reservations can be made on his website. (Hint: Be prepared to tell him your favorite food, music, and drink!)

. . . On Hoof

AUSTIN CARRIAGE
Tours starting and ending at several downtown locations
(512) 243-0044
www.austincarriage.com
With Austin's weather so beautiful most of the year, one great way to see the sites of historic downtown and enjoy the outdoors in style is to hop on a Vis-A-Vis. That's French for face to face. Indeed. These white horse-drawn carriages operated by Austin Carriage have seating for up to 6 people, facing one another, and each features a top that can be raised in case of light rain or harsh sunlight. The carriages, reproductions of a servant-driven carriage from the 18th century, are drawn by draft horses that stand about 6 feet tall and weigh 1,800 to 2,200 pounds. Austin Carriage offers a variety of regular tours during the day and at night that take in the sights on Congress Avenue, Sixth Street, Lady Bird Lake, and more. In most cases there's no need to make a reservation. Just walk up and enjoy the ride. A carriage can also be dispatched to a specific location by making arrangements in advance. Drivers are friendly and also serve as guides on your historic tour. Fees vary according to the

length of the tour, which ranges from about 20 minutes to 80 minutes.

DIE GELBE ROSE CARRIAGE
(512) 477-8824
www.austinsdiegelberosecarriage.com
This carriage company (whose name is "The Yellow Rose" in German) offers 25- to 75-minute horse-drawn carriage tours around downtown's most comely sights. There are tours of the State Capitol area, Sixth Street, Lady Bird Lake, or you can design your own tour. The service, will pick you up at any one of more than dozen hotels and restaurants downtown. Call ahead if you prefer to have a carriage waiting at a certain time to whisk you away. Magnificent Clydesdales are the horses used for this task.

. . . On Rail

AUSTIN STEAM TRAIN
(512) 477-8468
www.austinsteamtrain.org
Like the carriage rides above and the boat rides that follow, the mode of transportation for these tours is a big part of the fun. Take one—or all—of a number of rides on this popular tour. Choices, depending on the season, include a daylong trip through the Texas Hill Country, a half-day Hill Country tour, and specialty excursions, including the North Pole Flyer (with Santa Claus on board), and a number of Murder Mystery Specials. The Hill Country trains, which depart from Cedar Park in north Austin, run on the same tracks built in 1881 for the Austin & Northwestern Railroad. The pink granite used to build our State Capitol was hauled over these tracks in the 1880s.

Although the main locomotive for these trips is Southern Pacific #786, a steam engine built in 1916, the vintage locomotive was still undergoing a massive overhaul in 2011, and diesel-powered engines have been called into action. Check out the website for a schedule, rate information, and news on when the steam train will be back in service. The trains are operated by the Austin Steam Train Association, a community-based non-profit organization whose volunteers go out of their way to make these trips fun for all.

. . . On Water

CAPITAL CRUISES
Hyatt Regency Hotel Boat Dock,
208 Barton Springs Rd.
(512) 480-9264
www.capitalcruises.com
For private or public cruises of Lady Bird Lake, Capital Cruises offers a variety of tour options. Public tours, held Mar through Oct, include weekend dinner cruises and sightseeing tours as well as the popular bat-watching excursions. Capital Cruises also offers private cruises by reservation year-round, and can accommodate groups big and small. These include private and group dinner cruises, party boat cruises, and company outings. They even have a margarita machine for rent during your tour! (You supply the booze.) Check the website to see options and make reservations.

LAKE AUSTIN RIVERBOATS
On Lake Austin
(512) 345-5220
www.austinriverboats.com
These two stern-wheel riverboats are for chartered cruises on gorgeous Lake Austin, complete with food and beverage service if you like. *Commodore's Pup* is for groups of 130 people or fewer, while the riverboat *Commodore* can hold up to 220 people. They can do weddings, casino nights, corporate meetings, or just about anything else.

Entertainment can also be arranged for that special party. Call for rates.

LIVE LOVE PADDLE
(512) 804-2122
www.livelovepaddle.com

Kayaks are the mode of transportation offered by this newcomer to the Austin tour scene. Led by professional kayakers and whitewater rafters Casey Vick and Beverley Chrystal, Live Love Paddle is all about the water. There's a 1½-hour Bat Tour in which kayakers paddle up Lady Bird Lake to the Congress Avenue Bridge to see and learn about Austin's famous bat colony. They also offer 3- to 5-hour trips on one of the area's rivers, as well as overnight kayaking and camping on the San Marcos River. Kayaks, paddles, flotation devices, and water are provided. You can reserve through the website.

LONE STAR RIVERBOAT
On the south shore of Lady Bird Lake, between the Congress Avenue Bridge and South First Street Bridge
(512) 327-1388
www.lonestarriverboat.com

Electric pontoon cruisers seating 34 or 60 people take visitors on a one-hour cruise of scenic Lady Bird Lake (with the ever-changing Austin skyline as a backdrop) from Mar through Oct. *Lone Star* offers a variety of cruise times, including a sunset tour with a close-up view of the evening flight of the bats from the Congress Avenue Bridge. There's also a 1-hour weekend tour offered about mid-afternoon on Sat and Sun, as well as holiday cruises. Group and private charters aboard an all-electric, double-decked, paddle-wheel riverboat are also available. The schedule changes according to the time of year. Reservations are taken by phone at the number above.

. . . On Water & Land

AUSTIN'S COSMIC COWBOY TOUR
(512) 589-5564
www.austincosmiccowboy.com

All aboard the Cosmic Duck—a bright yellow amphibious vehicle—for a 2-hour evening tour of Austin on the streets and on Lake Austin. What makes this fun tour unique is it includes a real live (and real good) musician on board as well as food, drinks, and a stop at one of Austin's clubs, pubs, or saloons. Owner and tour guide Greg Strake knows Austin! Public tours depart across the street from the Hilton Hotel at 500 East Fourth St. Private and group tours also are offered. Check the website for details.

AUSTIN DUCK ADVENTURES
(512) 477-5274
www.austinducks.com

What's that amphibious truck emitting a loud quacking sound rolling down Congress Avenue? It is one of the Austin Duck Adventure vehicles, which goes from the road straight into Lady Bird Lake for a cruise along the river. As you ride/float you get to see and hear about Austin from lively, knowledgeable tour guides. Tickets can be purchased online or at the Austin Visitor Center, 209 East Sixth St. There are several departures daily, and all trips leave from the visitor center. This is not Splash Mountain so no need to wear swimsuits. But do be prepared to quack!

KIDSTUFF

One of the first things you'll notice when you visit Austin is our abundance of trees and flowering plants. From our magnificent urban forest to the scores of species that adorn our private gardens and lawns, it's clear that Austin both values and nurtures its greenery. We love our trees so much that in 2007 the city created Austin's Tree of the Year Award, so far recognizing an outstanding Bald Cypress as well as Texas Persimmons, and Escarpment Live Oaks. While we don't have an Austin Child of the Year Award (hmmm?), we do tend to lavish our kids with care and attention so they, like our trees, will grow upright, strong, and resilient. Creative Austin entrepreneurs and community leaders have put a great deal of energy into providing recreational, educational, cultural, and downright fun activities for youth of all ages. The greater Central Texas area provides even more diversion, including that guaranteed kid-pleaser, the giant amusement park. So whether yours is a little sprout, a precocious sapling, or a young tree whose branches are reaching for the sky, Austin offers plenty of sunshine, water, and fertilizer for all.

OVERVIEW

If you want your sprouts to enjoy their trip to Austin, be sure to visit some of the places listed here. We've provided six categories designed to direct you to Central Texas's most appealing attractions for "growing" children.

Fertilize Well: While this list includes those attractions designed to stimulate the mind, there's plenty of fun to be found, too.

Just Add Water: What would Central Texas be without diversions designed to get you nice and wet?

Supply Sunshine: These are a few of Austin's outdoor delights that appeal to children.

Let 'em Grow Crazy: For when the kids just need to let loose and have fun.

A Garden of Delights: Check this out for relaxing and entertaining spots that are sure to please.

Don't Eat the Daisies: Sure, Austin has all the fast-food chains that appeal to children, but here are a few local favorites, both homegrown and outside imports. See the Restaurants chapter for even more places to feed yourself and the kids.

Please see the Parks & Recreation chapter for information on many more activities that are practically guaranteed to delight kids of all ages. The chapters on Attractions, Spectator Sports, and The Arts offer locales and events for the young and young at heart. The Attractions chapter also lists some guided tours, several via fun modes of transportation that might help get the kids out the door. The Literary Scene chapter provides information about our libraries and bookstores, which all have story times or other activities designed especially for kids. You'll also find some comic bookstores listed!

FERTILIZE WELL

AQUARENA CENTER
921 Aquarena Springs Dr., San Marcos
(512) 245-7570
www.aquarena.txstate.edu
Take a ride on a glass-bottom boat or kayak on Spring Lake to view the pristine waters and aquatic life of Aquarena Springs, one of Central Texas's natural wonders. The freshwater springs that created the San Marcos River were formed millions of years ago by a fracture in the earth's crust, known today as the Balcones Fault. The river is home to more than 100 varieties of aquatic life, including several endangered species found nowhere else on earth. Well-informed tour guides take you on a relaxing adventure as you witness, through the bottom of the boat, the springs bubbling up from the Edwards Aquifer. There are also the underwater remains of an archaeology dig that unearthed 12,000 years of history, including mastodon bones, Spanish gold coins, and arrowheads.

This former theme park was acquired in 1994 by Texas State University, which changed the focus here from amusement to preservation and education. Aquarena Center features a lovely park next to the lake, a historic village, a gift shop, and snack bar, as well as a fascinating 5,400-gallon aquarium where visitors learn about the Texas blind salamander, the San Marcos salamander, and other aquatic life. Admission to the park and exhibits is free, but a fee is charged for a variety of boat tours. To get to the springs, take I-35 south from Austin, exit 206 to Aquarena Springs Drive, and go about 1.5 miles west.

✳AUSTIN CHILDREN'S MUSEUM
Dell Discovery Center,
201 Colorado St.
(512) 472-2499
www.austinkids.org
Fun *and* educational. What better combination is there to please children and parents alike? The Austin Children's Museum at Dell Discovery Center is a 12,500-square-foot playscape filled with galleries and hands-on activities designed to entertain and educate even the youngest visitors. This facility is just packed with permanent and temporary exhibits—all aimed at encouraging youngsters to explore and use their imaginations.

The museum is open Mon 9 a.m. to noon for children under 3 years old only, Tues through Sat 10 a.m. to 5 p.m. and Sun noon to 5 p.m. Admission is by donation on Wed from 5 to 8 p.m. and free Sun from 4 to 5 p.m. The museum also offers a wide range of summer camps, school tours, and special activities for children throughout the year.

i *Austin Family* magazine, www .austinfamily.com, sponsors a Camp Fair each Jan. This is a great place for long-time residents and newcomers alike to check out the many kids' camps available in Austin.

✳AUSTIN MUSEUM OF ART AT LAGUNA GLORIA
3809 West Thirty-fifth St.
(512) 458-8191
www.amoa.org
Housed in a historic villa, this great West Austin museum also hosts the city's art school for children and adults alike. While small children may feel too restricted in the exhibition space, the museum sits on a 12-acre site, complete with sculpture garden that gives

kids plenty of room to move around while still enjoying works of art. The school is in a separate building on-site. The museum also hosts several family friendly outdoor festivals each year. Operating hours for the villa and the grounds vary, so check the website before heading out. Public tours are held at 1 p.m. on weekends. (See The Arts chapter for more details.)

AUSTIN NATURE AND SCIENCE CENTER
301 Nature Center Dr.
(512) 974-3888
www.ci.austin.tx.us/ansc
Children will get a kick out of looking through microscopes and magnifying glasses for close-up views of specimens, viewing more than 90 animals native to Texas, and working in a paleontological dig in the Dino Pit at this great center in the Zilker Park Nature Preserve. Owls, hawks, and vultures are featured in the Birds of Prey exhibit, while the Small Wonders exhibit displays 20 of Austin's small animals. Kids can also earn points for correctly identifying the Monthly Mystery Object. The Nature and Science Center is a perfect introduction to Austin's unique ecosystems and to the wonders of Austin nature. The center is open 9 a.m. to 5 p.m. Mon through Sat and Sun noon to 5 p.m. Admission is free.

THE BOB BULLOCK TEXAS STATE HISTORY MUSEUM
1800 North Congress Ave.
(512) 936-8746, (866) 369-7108
www.thestoryoftexas.com
This downtown museum just north of the State Capitol is a must visit for visitors of all ages, but kids will love the colorful exhibits, many of them interactive, which present the story of Texas from before we were even called Texas. Because this is a noncollecting museum, some exhibits come and go—so visit often! The museum also houses Austin's only IMAX theater and the Spirit Theater. (For a complete description of the museum, see the Attractions chapter.)

GEORGE WASHINGTON CARVER MUSEUM AND CULTURAL CENTER
1165 Angelina St.
(512) 974-4926
www.ci.austin.tx.us/carver
Distinguished for being the first African-American neighborhood museum in the state of Texas, the George Washington Carver Museum and Cultural Center is a 36,000-square-foot facility that includes 4 galleries, a 134-seat theater, a dance studio, conference room, classroom, darkroom, and archival space. The museum's core exhibit is on Juneteenth, the oldest nationally celebrated commemoration of the ending of slavery in the United States. There also is a permanent exhibit on Austin African-American families, an Artists Gallery, and a children's hands-on exhibit on African-American scientists and inventors, including George Washington Carver, of course.

INNER SPACE CAVERN
4200 South I-35, Georgetown
(512) 931-2283, (877) 931-2283
www.myinnerspacecavern.com
People tend to think that attractions located right beside the Interstate are just tourist traps designed to get your money. This one, however, is one of the best and most accessible attractions around for both children and their families. Estimated to be 100 million years old, Inner Space Cavern was discovered in 1963 by workers testing core samples for construction of the Interstate. It

seems everywhere they drilled they found air pockets. Now opened for all to appreciate, this living cavern—meaning it continues to grow and develop—features an excellent array of formations beyond the typical stalactites and stalagmites. Guides on the Adventure Tour will lead you on a 75-minute walk and point out such fascinating shapes as the Flowing Stone of Time, the Lake of the Moon, and more, including the bones of prehistoric animals who died in here. Other tours also are offered. At a temperature of 72 to 74 degrees, this is the perfect spot to escape both the sizzling summer heat and the winter chill. Outside, the family can pan for gems and minerals. Admission for the standard tour is about $18 for adults and $10 for children, though children ages 3 and under are admitted free. Tours depart regularly throughout the day.

*JOURDAN-BACHMAN PIONEER FARMS
10621 Pioneer Farms Dr.
(512) 837-1215
www.pioneerfarms.org
Children will enjoy stepping back in time to witness the lives of Central Texas settlers at this living history museum, which is open to the public Fri through Sun from 10 a.m. to 5 p.m. The farm, originally part of a 2,000-acre cotton farm, presents the story of rural life in the late 19th century. Visitors can stroll around the three historic farmsteads and view demonstrations of blacksmithing, woodworking, spinning, and weaving. They also can see firsthand the historically correct crops, food, clothing, farm implements, and dwellings on this large property. On other days, farm personnel offer guided tours for schoolchildren and other groups. Admission is $8 for adults and $6 for children.

MEXICAN AMERICAN CULTURAL CENTER
600 River St.
(512) 974-3772
www.ci.austin.tx.us/macc
The Mexican American Cultural Center (MACC) is a wonderful addition to the Austin kids' scene. This Hispanic-focused facility (see The Arts chapter) offers countless activities for children, from classes in dance, sewing, filmmaking, writing, and art to children's theater and music productions. The ongoing exhibits and movies will inspire adults and children alike.

NATURAL BRIDGE CAVERNS
26495 Natural Bridge Cavern Rd.
(210) 651-6101
www.naturalbridgecaverns.com
Located just north of San Antonio and southwest of New Braunfels off I-35 exit 175, Natural Bridge Caverns boasts more than 10,000 formations, including such wonders as Sherwood Forest, the Castle of the White Giant, and the King's Throne. These living caverns, discovered in 1960, present many spectacular sights, including one underground room that's as big as a football field. The cool caverns (average temperature is 72 degrees) are nestled amid Texas Hill Country terrain and provide plenty of shaded space outside for picnicking or relaxing. Various tours are offered, beginning at about $18 for adults and $10 for children. Operating hours vary depending on the season.

THE REPUBLIC OF TEXAS MUSEUM
510 East Anderson Lane
(512) 339-1997
www.drt-inc.org/DRTmuseum.htm
Do you know where and when the Texas Declaration of Independence was signed?

How about the year Santa Anna was elected president of Mexico or the reason washing clothes was dangerous for women in the 1800s? The answer to these questions, and many more, can be found in the Republic of Texas Museum, a compact but fun and educational space for the whole family. Children and adults are given a separate list of scavenger hunt questions, the answers to which can be found by touring the exhibits. The littlest ones get to answer questions such as where is the chair with the two ears located or find the three chickens in the museum and what are their names? This museum, run by the Daughters of the Republic of Texas, is dedicated to the era of the Texas Republic (1836–46). Young children especially like Great Grandma's Backyard, a collection of hands-on household items and implements used by families in the mid-19th century. There's something of interest for people of all ages here. The museum is open 10 a.m. to 4 p.m. Mon through Fri. General admission is $5, $2 for students.

SPLASH! INTO THE EDWARDS AQUIFER
2201 Barton Springs Rd.
(512) 478-3170
www.ci.austin.tx.us/splash
This hands-on educational exhibit at Barton Springs Pool is a 1,400-square-foot interactive space on the Edwards Aquifer. Splash! features a continuously running 4-minute video, *Carved in Stone*, which shows how the springs were formed. An interactive 3-dimensional relief map that uses animated lights to show the movement of the water lets children push the buttons to make the water flow. There's also a fascinating aquascape model of the aquifer. Aquariums here house specimens of the aquifer's aquatic life. This is a great place to learn about the Barton Springs salamander,

an endangered species found only in Austin. Splash! is part of the Beverly Sheffield Education Center run by the city's Nature and Science Center. The various exhibits are designed for use by children in 4th grade and up. Splash! is free to the public, although there may be a charge for guided tours. Call for hours of operation. (For more about Barton Springs, see the Close-up in the Parks & Recreation chapter.)

STARGAZING
T. S. Painter Hall Observatory, near
Twenty-fourth Street and Inner Campus
Drive
(512) 232-4265
http://outreach.as.utexas.edu/public
/painter.html
No. We're not talking about the kind of stargazing that involves Austin's film industry. This is the old-fashioned, out-of-this-world kind. The University of Texas Astronomy Department offers free stargazing experiences on the UT campus almost every Fri and Sat night while UT is in session. (No viewings on Sat during UT home football games.) Families with children seem especially attracted to this kind of educational fun. Astronomy students lead visitors on a tour of the stars, using a cool 9-inch telescope built in 1932. Viewing times vary, and the event can be canceled due to weather, so UT asks that participants call the number above.

TEXAS STATE CAPITOL
1100 Congress Ave.
(512) 463-0063
www.tspb.state.tx.us
There's just no better way to introduce your youngsters to the legends and lore of Texas history than taking them on a tour of the

Texas State Capitol. We've found the guides to be especially kind and patient with children, making sure to answer all their questions. (For more on this monument to Texas, see the Attractions chapter.)

UMLAUF SCULPTURE GARDEN
& MUSEUM
605 Robert E. Lee Rd.
(512) 445-5582
www.umlaufsculpture.org
Ask for the treasure hunt map when you visit the Umlauf Sculpture Garden, and your child will be delighted to chase around looking for some of Charles Umlauf's magnificent sculptures. (The diversion will allow you more time to enjoy the sculptures, too.) Because most of the statues are outdoors, this is a great place to introduce children to a museum. They don't have to keep quiet, and they don't have to keep their hands to themselves. (Yes, they can touch the outdoor sculptures!) They'll love you for it. (To find out more about this outdoor garden and indoor museum, see the Attractions chapter.)

WONDER WORLD PARK
1000 Prospect St., San Marcos
(512) 392-3760
www.wonderworldpark.com
Unlike other caves in Texas that were formed by rushing water, this fascinating underground fissure was formed by a massive earthquake millions of years ago. You can actually see where the earth split, leaving jigsaw puzzle–like sections of rock that would fit right into each other if pushed back together. And because it's not growing, kids get to put their hands anywhere they like. Wonder World, said to be the only earthquake-formed cave in the country open for tours, drops more than 160 feet beneath the

earth's surface but is accessible for children of all ages. Kid-friendly guides take visitors on a 45-minute tour of this Texas marvel, pointing out all the prehistoric treasures and naturally glowing rocks. Wonder World also has a 190-foot aboveground observation tower, a train ride to the petting park, and an antigravity house. Theme park prices and coupons are available on the website. Wonder World is open 8 a.m. to 8 p.m. Memorial Day to Labor Day; shorter hours the rest of the year.

JUST ADD WATER

✳BARTON SPRINGS
Zilker Park, 2201 Barton Springs Rd.
(512) 476-9044
www.ci.austin.tx.us/parks/barton
springs.htm
There's nothing like a cool—and we mean cool—dip in Austin's treasured spring-fed swimming pool to chill out the kids on a hot summer day and make them feel like real Austin Insiders. The water in the pool remains a constant 68 degrees throughout the year. (For more on this historic spot and for Austin's other great swimming spots, see the Parks & Recreation chapter.)

DEEP EDDY POOL'S SUMMER MOVIES
401 Deep Eddy Ave.
(512) 974-6700
www.ci.austin.tx.us/parks
Leave it to Austinites to figure out a way to combine water fun and flicks. West Austin's Deep Eddy Pool, one of our favorite swimming spots, presents family movies right next to the pool on Sat night throughout the summer, starting in late June. The schedule has included such winners as *Antz, 101 Dalmatians, George of the Jungle, Dr. Doolittle,* and *Creature from the Black Lagoon,*

presented in 3-D. Come around 8 p.m., and bring a picnic basket or buy pizza at the pool. The films begin at about 9 p.m. or so, just around sunset. A nominal admission fee is charged.

> **i** Take a float along with you when you go to Deep Eddy's Summer Movies—and watch the flick from the pool. That will keep you cool.

✳SCHLITTERBAHN WATERPARK RESORT
305 West Austin St., New Braunfels
(830) 625-2351
www.schlitterbahn.com
Never mind that this waterpark is about 50 miles south of Austin in New Braunfels. Schlitterbahn is one place many Austin families visit at least once, if not several times, during summer. Located on the banks of the spring-fed Comal River, Schlitterbahn is 65 acres of high-tech water rides, slides, pools, inner tube floats, and kiddie parks. The park has plenty of hair-raising rides sure to please the stoutest thrill-seeker in your group. Schlitterbahn also claims the world's first uphill water coaster. Although food and beverages are sold here, picnic baskets (no glass or alcohol, please) are welcome, and there are plenty of shaded areas and tables. The park is open late Apr to late Sept, but on weekends only during the school year. The fun starts at 10 a.m. daily and goes until closing time, which varies from 6 to 8 p.m. Note: Schlitterbahn has obtained approval from Cedar Park, Austin's northern suburb, to build a new park there, possibly as early as 2012. Check the website if you're in the area after that time.

✳SEA WORLD ADVENTURE PARK
10500 Sea World Dr., San Antonio
(800) 700-7786
www.seaworld.com
Promise your youngsters a trip to Sea World and you're sure to get at least a day or two of good behavior in exchange. While there are plenty of thrilling water rides, waterscapes, cool amusement park adventures, and shows, your kids can actually learn something here, too. But keep that part under your hat. This giant park features the only major display of hammerhead sharks in North America, dozens of penguins, sea lions, whales, and, of course, the great Shamu. Sea World says it's the world's largest sea life adventure park. While not all the rides are designed to get you wet, there are plenty to keep you cool on a hot summer day. Be sure to pack the swimsuits. Sea World is open Mar through Oct, mostly on weekends until school gets out. But all summer long this exciting place is open 10 a.m. to 10 p.m. Admission is in the $50 to $60 range, but print your tickets online and save. Two-day passes and season tickets also are available. This is definitely worth a trip to San Antonio.

TUBING
City Park, near University and Bobcat Drives, San Marcos
(512) 396-5466
www.tubesanmarcos.com
To many Texans, the Hill Country is synonymous with river tubing, in which you ride down the river on big inner tubes. This inexpensive, low-tech pastime is loads of fun, especially on hot summer days. While some tubing areas can be dominated by older kids and young adults, the Lions Club operates a family-oriented tubing, swimming, and snorkeling spot on the San Marcos River in

nearby San Marcos. They provide rides back to the park once you've gone downriver. You can even rent an extra tube, tie it to your own, and cart a cooler downstream if you like. This is refreshing and exhilarating fun, and all proceeds go to charity. All-day rental prices are very reasonable. It's open daily late May to early Sept from 10 a.m. to 7 p.m. The Lions Club also rents life vests for the little ones and lockers. Take I-35 south to exit 206 and follow Aquarena Springs Drive. Turn left onto Charles Austin Drive, then turn right behind Strahan Basketball Stadium and follow the signs.

i **If you go to Schlitterbahn, most locals know to stake a claim on a picnic table early in the day. Put your coolers and towels there and make it your base of operations. Don't leave valuables, of course.**

VOLENTE BEACH WATER PARK
16107 FM 2769, Volente
(512) 258-5109
www.volentebeach.com
For those hot, hot, hot summer days in Austin, this compact water park on Lake Travis offers some cool options. It features four great water slides of varying thrill levels, as well as a pool for swimming or volleyball and other fun water activities. Sprouts can play in the shallow pool and climb on the pirate ship in the middle. The sandy beach on the lake is large, even if the swimming area is not. There are WaveRunners and other boats for rent. Volente Beach is Austin's only water park and is small in comparison to a sprawling Fiesta Texas or Splash Town water park, but that doesn't prevent it from being a popular spot for kids of all ages. The Blu Parrot Lakeside Bar and Grill serves entrees,

desserts, and beverages, and visitors may also bring ice chests with food and soft drinks. (No glass, or uncooked foods.) The water park is open weekends in Apr, May, and Sept and daily June through Aug.

SUPPLY SUNSHINE

AUSTIN'S PARK 'N PIZZA EXPERIENCE
16231 North I-35
(512) 670-9600
www.austinspark.com
Open 365 days a year, this 22-acre park offers fun activities for all the kids—and for the kid in all of us. The hardest part of the day is trying to choose from among the park's many attractions, which include miniature golf, bumper boats, laser tag, go-karts, batting cages, a driving range, an indoor climbing wall, a huge arcade, and a thrill ride: the Ejection Seat, which shoots passengers 150 feet into the air. Of course all this exercise is going to work up some huge appetites. For that, there's the reasonably priced all-you-can-eat pizza, pasta, salad, and dessert buffet. The park, 15 miles north of downtown Austin at exit 248, is open Sun through Thurs from 9 a.m. to 10 p.m., Fri and Sat from 9 a.m. to 11 p.m., but call or check the website as hours can vary by season.

AUSTIN ZOO AND ANIMAL SANCTUARY
10807 Rawhide Trail
(512) 288-1490, (800) 291-1490
www.austinzoo.org
This Hill Country escape about 20 minutes southwest of downtown Austin is a perfect place to bring young children for a close-up look at the animals, a picnic, a pony ride, or a train ride. Compared to the sprawling superzoos many cities boast, Austin's zoo is small, rustic, and very laid-back. That makes it

easy on young ones and their parents—you don't need to rush madly around the park to see everything. Here visitors will find Bengal tigers, wolves, capybaras, African lions, monkeys, potbellied pigs, and many more animals. There's a petting corral where you can purchase food to feed the animals. The zoo features a wonderful tortoise barn in which children can get a close-up view of several species. The Austin Zoo is open 10 a.m. to 6 p.m. most of the year. Admission is $8 for adults, $5 for children ages 2 to 12, and free for children younger than 2.

BUTLER PARK PITCH & PUTT GOLF COURSE
201 Lee Barton Dr.
(512) 477-4430

Tiger Woods would have loved this place when he was just a toddler trying to master the game of golf. This specially designed, 9-hole Par 3 course in South Central Austin features holes about a third as long as standard ones—61 to 118 yards long—and also rents short clubs for the kids. Of course, adults who want a quick game of golf enjoy this wonderful course, too, which includes all the fun and frustrations of a regular course, including water hazards and the rough. Run by the Austin Parks and Recreation Department, this golf course is sure to please. It's open year-round. Greens fees are family-friendly. Club rental is extra.

CHILDREN'S DAY ART PARK
Symphony Square, 1101 Red River St.
(512) 476-6064
www.austinsymphony.org

Children are encouraged to bang the drums, blow the horns, and fiddle the strings at the instrument "petting zoo," just one exciting feature of the Austin Symphony Orchestra's summer art park for children. These delightful outdoor events, held every Wed morning in June and July at historic Symphony Square, feature performances by symphony ensembles and by a variety of children's performers, including salsa bands, folk singers, and ballet folklorico. Symphony musicians are on hand each week to demonstrate the use of various instruments and to provide guidance. When the musical performance ends, children follow the Pied Piper down Waller Creek for more hands-on activities and face painting under a big tent. The Austin Symphony, Austin's oldest performing group, has sponsored these art parks for kids for more than 35 years. They're designed for kids ages 3 to 8, but everyone is invited. Very small admission fee. Check out the art park from 9 to 11:30 a.m. (See the chapter on The Arts for more symphony events for the whole family.)

i Kids can test their gaming skills at the giant chess set (knee-high to adults) in Woolridge Park downtown almost every Sat year-round from about 12:30 to 3:30 p.m.

PETER PAN MINIGOLF
1207 Barton Springs Rd.
(512) 472-1033
www.peterpanminigolf.com

If you've got a hankering to play miniature golf until midnight—at least on Fri or Sat—this is the place for you. Peter Pan offers two 18-hole miniature golf courses and a whole lot of fun for the little ones. What is it about this game that attracts so many kids and adults? It must be the challenge of trying to get that little ball up the hill around the obstacle and into the hole without screaming! Peter Pan is open year-round. You can arrive 20 minutes before opening to get signed up.

SLAUGHTER CREEK METROPOLITAN PARK
4103 Slaughter Lane

Do you have an in-line skating fanatic in the family? This is the outdoor place for those who just couldn't leave home without the skates. The park features a 3-mile veloway (it's nice and smooth) and is popular with skaters and bikers. The park also offers a playground, nature trail, sports courts, and picnic facilities, too. This Southwest Austin park is next to the Lady Bird Johnson Wildflower Center. (See the Parks & Recreation Chapter for more about indoor roller rinks.)

WILD BASIN WILDERNESS PRESERVE
805 North Capital of Texas Hwy.
(512) 327-7622
www.wildbasin.org

Open from sunup to sundown, this is a perfect place to educate the kids, and yourself, about Austin's beautiful Hill Country terrain. This 227-acre preserve in West Austin is also great for nature walks as it features a trail system that runs throughout the area. The preserve gives school tours during the week, so tour guides know just how to talk to youngsters and are prepared for the guided tours for visitors on weekends. Or you can take a self-guided tour and explore this park yourself. For the budding astronomer in the family, the Austin Astronomical Society holds a family-oriented stargazing party here each month as well as many other kid-friendly events. (See the Parks & Recreation chapter for information about other parks and preserves in the area.)

ZILKER PARK
2100 Barton Springs Rd.
(512) 472-4914

If, as they say, Barton Springs is the crown jewel of Austin, then Zilker Park is the crown.

This 400-acre site is the city's largest park and definitely one of its most popular. There's a great playscape for kids, rides on miniature trains, jogging trails, and plenty of space to just run, play soccer, throw a Frisbee, or toss a ball. Tuck your swimsuits in the trunk when you head for the park, as Barton Springs Pool is right here and you might be tempted. (See the Parks & Recreation chapter for more details.)

LET 'EM GROW CRAZY

BLAZER TAG ADVENTURE CENTER
1701 West Ben White Blvd.
(512) 462-0202
www.blazertag.com

Billing itself as the "largest laser tag arena in Texas," this giant complex is blaster Nirvana. Whether your kids need to release some pent-up energy after a week of school or a weekend of sightseeing, Blazer Tag is the place to go. The 3-story, 10,000-square-foot arena offers players of all ages plenty of space to track down and then blast away at their opponents. Games are 20 minutes long and start every 20 minutes. The center, which also features a video arcade and snack bar, sponsors a competitive laser tag league for kids ages 13 and up. It's also a popular spot for parties of all kinds. Blazer Tag is closed Tues and Wed for private functions.

CHAPARRAL ICE CENTER
14200 North I-35
(512) 252-8500
www.chaparralice.com

Kids can come daily for skating on their own or sign up for Learn-to-Skate classes at either of these two family-run facilities. The well-maintained skating rinks offer a wonderful variety of year-round activities for children and adults, so be bold and lace up some skates for yourself. There also are classes in ice dance and hockey as well as hockey leagues for children and adults. Chaparral does birthday parties and has a full summer of camps for children. Call for the current schedule. Admission and skate rental fees are family friendly. The other location is at 2525 Anderson Lane, Northcross Mall (512-451-5102).

CHUCK E CHEESE
8038 Burnet Rd.
(512) 451-0296
www.chuckecheese.com

Ahhhh, the coveted token! There just never seem to be enough of those discs of gold to satisfy even the youngest of competitors. To match wits with a machine and win those esteemed tickets is, at that very moment, the most awesome adventure on the planet. All of Austin's Chuck E Cheese locations are filled with interactive arcade games, playscapes, and air hockey tables that are sure to please. The good news for parents is that the food is pretty darn good too. There is pizza and hot dogs, snacks and soft drinks, and even a salad bar. At the end of the day, your youngsters get to go home with the prizes they've won in exchange for the tickets. Chuck E Cheese does birthday parties, too. Hours vary by location. The other locations are at 502 West Ben White Blvd. (512-441-9681) and 10515 North Mopac Expressway (512-372-4700).

CYPRESS VALLEY CANOPY TOURS
1223 Paleface Ranch Rd., Spicewood
(512) 264-8880
www.cypressvalleycanopytours.com

There is a minimum weight requirement of 70 pounds for the thrilling zip-line rides at Cypress Valley Canopy Tours, but your older kids—especially your teenagers—will have a blast soaring through the cypress trees and over the creek at this spot not far from Austin. (See the Attractions chapter.) Make your reservations in advance if you will have only limited time in Austin. And check out the "one child flies for free" offer on the website.

MAIN EVENT
13301 North US 183
(512) 401-0000
www.maineventusa.net

With 75,000 square feet of entertainment space, there is something here for kids of all ages. With bowling (including exciting Laser Jam events), laser tag, rock climbing, cool arcade and interactive games, and even an 18-hole glow-in-the-dark miniature golf course, the kids will want to spend hours here. But that's not a bad thing because Main Event caters to adults, too. The Shots Bar offers an assortment of alcoholic and nonalcoholic drinks, as well as billiards and darts. When it's time for a food break, the whole family can enjoy burgers, pizzas, nachos, wings, subs and more at the Main Street Cafe. Main Event is open daily from 11 a.m. (10 a.m. on Sat) and closes as late as 2 a.m. on some nights. The games are priced individually.

✳SIX FLAGS FIESTA TEXAS
17000 I-10 West, San Antonio
(210) 697-5050, (800) 473-4378
www.sixflags.com

You'll need to drive down to San Antonio for this one, but our resident kid advisor insists you'll gain major points with your children by letting them know that, yes, Central Texas offers a fantastic amusement park. Fiesta Texas is a blast—and not just for the kiddies. Thrilling rides like Poltergeist, Goliath, and

Superman: Krypton Coaster (the largest steel coaster in the Southwest) will have your heart in your throat in no time. There also are plenty of exciting rides sure to get you wet—and cool! This giant park offers rides for people of all ages, a special children's area, plenty of shops and restaurants, great shows, and, to top it off, the wonderful White Water Bay waterpark—don't forget to bring your swimsuits. This immaculate facility is so fun and so huge that many people purchase 2-day or season passes. Fiesta Texas is open 10 a.m. to 10 p.m. daily throughout the summer and on weekends, with shorter hours in spring and fall. The park is closed Nov to Mar. Daily admission is around $40 for everyone if you buy tickets online.

YMCA
1100 West Cesar Chavez St.
(512) 322-9622 (main office)
Locations throughout the area
www.ymca.com

With many locations in Austin and our surrounding communities, there's sure to be a YMCA somewhere near you. They all offer plenty of sporting facilities and equipment, classes, and just plain fun. The good news for Austin members is that your membership card at one "Y" allows you access to all Austin locations. There is an initiation fee, and membership is offered by the month.

i The upscale Arboretum Shopping Center at 10000 Research Blvd. in Northwest Austin has a lovely park that features five life-size granite cows that kids like to climb on. An Amy's Ice Cream shop and picnic tables are right there.

A GARDEN OF DELIGHTS

*THE BATS
Congress Avenue Bridge at Lady Bird Lake

Children ogle in wonder when North America's largest urban bat colony sets off en masse on the evening flight for food during spring and summer. This is a spectacle the whole family can enjoy. (For more on these Mexican free-tails, see the Attractions chapter.)

CAFE MONET
4477 South Lamar Blvd., Suite 560
(512) 892-3200
www.cafemonet.org

This popular paint-your-own pottery studio attracts budding artists young and old(er) at two Austin locations. Patrons simply pick out the ceramic piece they want to decorate, choose their colors, paint, and leave the pottery to be fired, picking it up a few days later. Of special interest to parents is Kids Night Out, held on the first Fri of the month at the Guadalupe Street store in the commercial/condo development known as the Triangle. Children ages 6 and up can spend an evening painting ceramics and enjoying a pizza party, while mom and dad slip out for dinner or a movie. The cafe also offers children's parties for 8 to 18 kids, as well as fun summer camps. The other location is at 4700 West Guadalupe St., Suite 11 (512-906-2200).

CERAMICS BAYOU
3620 Bee Cave Rd.
(512) 328-1168
www.ceramicsbayou.com

This paint-it-yourself ceramics studio offers a wide range of items—everything from simple tiles and coffee mugs to plates, platters, and animals. Children will delight in using their creative powers to design and paint their own piece. Cost is based on the piece selected, as Ceramics Bayou no longer charges for studio time. Finished pieces are fired in the kiln and ready for pickup in a few days. Hint: These make excellent gifts for parents, friends, or Grandma or Grandpa on their birthday. Speaking of birthdays, Ceramics Bayou hosts those too, as well as private parties.

i It's mid-summer and the kids are too hot to take even one more step with you on your tour of Austin. Why not let them cool off at a splash pad, where they can get wet (clothes and all) from the sprays of water? Don't worry, they'll dry off soon enough. There's a great splash pad downtown just south of Lake Austin in Butler Park (next to Palmer Events Center).

✳ZILKER TREE HOLIDAY FESTIVAL
Zilker Park, 2100 Barton Springs Rd.
(512) 472-4914

It only lasts a few weeks once a year, but this is one of THE places to take your kids if you're here around the Christmas holiday. The "tree" is formed using Zilker Park's 165-foot-tall Moonlight Tower as the trunk and strings of multicolored lights—3,500 of them—to form the tree's cone shape. Children love to stand inside the tree and twirl around until the lights blur. The recession forced the Austin City Council to scale down the second part of the Yule Tide light show, the famous Trail of Lights (with its gazillion lights—and enormous electric bill), beginning in 2009. Time will tell whether the full Trail of Lights makes a return. Admission to the park is free.

DON'T EAT THE DAISIES

BIG TOP CANDY SHOP
1706 South Congress Ave.
(512) 462-2220

If you prefer to visit the museums or the malls, but can't convince the kids, try bribing them with the promise of a trip to the Austin-original Big Top Candy Shop in the trendy SoCo neighborhood south of Lady Bird Lake. This big store with a circus theme is chock full of sugar in all its best forms, both pre-wrapped and in bulk. Of course, one giant bin is dedicated to circus peanuts. On First Thursday, the monthly street party on South Congress, the store sometimes features entertainers such as clowns and musicians. There's an old fashioned soda fountain here, too. (A few doors down, and operated by the same owner, is the toy store Monkey See, Monkey Do.)

CENTRAL MARKET CAFE
4001 North Lamar Blvd.
(512) 206-1020
www.centralmarket.com

The great outdoor patio filled with picnic tables and a playscape that's close enough to keep your eye on the kids are among the attractions for families at North Lamar Central Market Cafe. This casual restaurant, an extension of Austin's gourmet grocery store, has an extensive menu for people of all ages: burgers, pasta, salads, pizzas, gourmet fare, and much more, including great desserts. The second location at 4477 South Lamar Blvd. (512-899-4300) has a patio, but not the wide green space of the original. You place your order at the counter and retrieve your meal when your beeper lights up. Both Central Market locations also have indoor dining for when it's just too hot outside to breathe. There's live music on the patio at both locations several evenings a week. It's a great way to introduce children to the Austin music scene and get them fed, too.

DAVE & BUSTER'S
9333 Research Blvd.
(512) 346-8015
www.daveandbusters.com

Guests ages 18 and under must be accompanied by an adult at this establishment, even in the gaming area, but that doesn't prevent it from being one extremely popular spot with Austin kids. Why? Eat well, play games, win prizes! One side of the huge facility is filled with all sorts of arcade and interactive games, including table shuffleboard and pocket billiards. Yes, adults must come along here, too. The dining room, which is separated from the gaming room, is much more upscale than the typical fun center, one of the reasons this Dallas-based chain is growing. It offers plenty of kid-pleasing menu items, including burgers, pizza, and pasta. For heartier appetites there are steaks, chicken, and ribs. D&B's is open daily from 11:30 a.m. Closing time varies.

GÜERO'S TACO BAR
1412 South Congress Ave.
(512) 447-7688
www.guerostacobar.com

This Austin institution on funky South Congress Avenue is a popular family eatery. While Chelsea wasn't with former President Clinton when he ate here years ago, we're sure she would have been satisfied with the Mexican fare. The kid's menu includes quesadillas, breakfast tacos, chicken breast tacos, and enchiladas. All entrees come with rice and beans. The salsa bar is serve-it-yourself, so the food isn't too spicy for the kids. You

won't have to chide the kids for squirming here. It's just comfy Austin.

HUT'S HAMBURGERS
807 West Sixth St.
(512) 472-0693
www.hutsfrankandangies.com

Are the kids screaming for burgers? Why take them to one of those ubiquitous fast-food chains? You won't know whether you're in Austin, Boston, or Kalamazoo. Hut's, a '50s-style diner decorated with college sports memorabilia, is an Austin legend. Better yet, your kids will love the food. The menu includes 20 types of burgers—or mix and match to build your own—plus chicken-fried steak, fried chicken, meat loaf, and, of course, french fries and thickly sliced onion rings. True to diner law (it must be written somewhere), Hut's also offers a daily blue plate special. If you want to experience a real Austin burger joint, visit Hut's on West Sixth Street. And if the kids are leaning more toward pizza and pasta instead of burgers, we can suggest the Hut's-affiliated Frank and Angie's Pizzeria, which is just behind Hut's at 508 West Ave.

KERBEY LANE CAFE
3704 Kerbey Lane
(512) 451-1436
www.kerbeylanecafe.com

Children just seem to love the huge plate-dwarfing pancakes served round the clock at this popular Austin eatery. But there are many more delicacies sure to please. The children's menu includes enchiladas, tacos, hamburgers, peanut butter and jelly sandwiches, ham and cheese, and other guaranteed kid pleasers. Prices are very reasonable, and with four Austin locations—the other three are at 2606 Guadalupe (512-477-5717);

12602 Research Blvd. (512-258-7757); and 2700 South Lamar Blvd. (512-445-4451)— Kerbey Lane is easy to find. All four stores are open 24 hours a day.

MAGNOLIA CAFE
2304 Lake Austin Blvd.
(512) 478-8645
www.themagnoliacafe.com

Homegrown and down home, Magnolia Cafe serves an excellent assortment of meals for children, including some nutritious items, like steamed broccoli with cheese or a grilled chicken dinner. There are plenty of other kid pleasers as well, including a chicken black bean taco, kid burger with home fries, fish taco, kid French toast, and a kid breakfast that includes an egg, pancake, and sausage or bacon and is served all day. There's nothing fancy about Magnolia Cafe but the food. Adults will be happy, too, and there's a good selection of vegetarian dishes. Both Magnolia Cafes are open 24 hours a day. The second store is at 1920 South Congress Ave. (512-445-0000).

PHIL'S ICEHOUSE
5620 Burnet Rd.
(512) 524-1212
www.philsicehouse.com

An outdoor playscape complete with bridges and slides, a shuffleboard game, and plenty of outdoor seating create the perfect kid-friendly atmosphere at this Austin burger joint, brought to you by the folks at Amy's Ice Creams. Burgers—big beefy ones, mini ones, chicken ones, veggie ones—and fries (a mix of regular and sweet potato) are the stars at Phil's, but there are also footlongs, corn dogs, frito pies, fish sandwiches and more. And if this recommendation isn't enough, Austinites have voted Phil's the best place to bring the kids in a *Chronicle*'s Readers' Poll. To finish off the meal, take the family next door for some Amy's Ice Cream. Phil's even hosts occasional live music and outdoor movies, so check the website for upcoming events.

SHADY GROVE
1624 Barton Springs Rd.
(512) 474-9991
www.theshadygrove.com

This super-casual eatery with both indoor and outdoor dining spaces is sure to please the kids. The menu offers everything kids love, including hot dogs, burgers, tacos, and nachos, as well as plenty of nourishment for adults. (See the Restaurants chapter). The "Unplugged at the Grove" music series features Austin musicians performing live every Thurs evening in the spring and fall.

ANNUAL EVENTS & FESTIVALS

Weekends are the raison d'être for life in Austin. Weekday workdays are the equivalent of bench time, as far as many Austinites are concerned. The generally benign climate affords residents and visitors the opportunity to live life outdoors, and perhaps that is why so many weekend activities are linked to appreciation of sun, sky, and landscape. It is significant to note that springtime is the most active of all seasons when it comes to outdoor fiestas and festivals. This, after all, is when the Hill Country blossoms, the sun shines, and the sky is generally blue. (It is also the time when hotels are full and few rental cars are available.)

It is impossible to list all the annual events and festivals that take place in Austin and the surrounding Central Texas area. We have chosen some favorites and those that are both widely popular and long-standing. One characteristic of this list is the number of annual events that celebrate local culture, ethnic traditions, and historic events. Texans, nonnatives and newcomers will note, are eager to explore their past and have a strong sense of their state's history and culture. Other events are just sheer expressions of what could be called Texas joy, an embracing of local life and folkways. Whether it is a Woodstock-style romp or an old-fashioned church picnic, the operative word is celebration. So go forth and celebrate!

One note before you do: Admission prices, times, and even dates may vary from those listed. Many events are sponsored by nonprofit groups that face the vagaries of economic needs and demands, so it is a good idea to check the local media and make a call for additional information before you go.

JANUARY

FRONTERAFEST
Hyde Park Theatre, 511 West Forty-third St.
(512) 479-PLAY
www.hydeparktheatre.com
The annual performance festival runs for 5 weeks beginning in late Jan and includes more than 50 productions put on under the auspices of Frontera @ Hyde Park Theatre, the theater company in one of the most popular neighborhoods in Central Austin (see Hyde Park in the Relocation and The Arts chapters). Ticket prices vary and usually begin at around $3. Discount passes are available.

FEBRUARY

BLACK HISTORY MONTH
Austin Visitor Center,
301 Congress Ave.
(512) 478-0098, (866) GO-AUSTIN
www.austintexas.org
Throughout Feb there are numerous celebrations and events relating to African-American history. In the very early days of

the city, almost a quarter of the city's residents were African Americans, some 155 out of 856 people living in the city. The Austin Convention & Visitors Bureau (telephone and website listed above) produces the *Austin African-American Visitors Guide,* listing historic sites, cultural facilities, clubs, churches, and a guide to Austin's historic African-American neighborhoods. The guide can be picked up at the visitor center, and visitors also can request more information online indicating specific areas of interest, including African-American history and culture in Austin. Another great resource for events and celebrations in the African-American community is the Carver Branch Library, 1161 Angelina St., (512) 974-1010, www .austinlibrary.com.

i Need a breath of fresh air on New Year's Day? Take a blanket to the hills or shores around Lake Travis (see the Parks & Recreation chapter) and watch the Austin Yacht Club's Annual Redeye Regatta, www.austin yachtclub.org.

CARNAVAL BRASILEIRO
Palmer Events Center, 900 Barton Springs Rd.
(512) 452-6832
www.sambaparty.com
For more than 20 years, Austin has danced to the Brazilian beat of samba in a pre-Lenten festival of conga lines, costumes, and cacophony. A couple of thousand or more revelers gather, usually the Sat before Lent, which can fall in Feb or Mar, to emulate Rio's famous Carnival. The costumes are hilarious and sometimes minimalist, which makes this a decidedly grown-up affair. The live music features top names in samba. Tickets

are on sale at various popular record and bookstores in Austin.

MARCH

SPRING FESTIVAL AND TEXAS CRAFT EXHIBITION
Winedale, near Round Top
(979) 249-2085
www.roundtop.org
This tiny village near Round Top, some 90 miles east of Austin, has served as the center for study of Texas culture under the auspices of the University of Texas. The collection of historic buildings is now a center for cultural events and antiques shops and home to artists and crafters. (See the Day Trips chapter for more information on this historic area.) The third weekend in Mar, Winedale holds its annual Spring Festival and Texas Crafts Exhibition. This area is an easy drive from Austin but worth an overnight stay at one of the country bed-and-breakfasts in the area.

STAR OF TEXAS FAIR & RODEO
Travis County Exposition and Heritage Center
7311 Decker Lane
(512) 919-3000
www.staroftexas.org
For 2 weeks in mid-Mar, country music fans flock to the livestock and rodeo show at the Expo Center in far East Austin, where top-name stars perform. The live music begins after the rodeo performances each night. In addition to the music, there are livestock shows, a carnival, barbecue and food booths, and children's activities. Rodeo tickets are in addition to grounds admission fees. There is extensive coverage of the event in the local media. Note: The show usually overlaps with the SXSW Festival (see the Close-up in this chapter), and hotel rooms and rental cars

are at a premium in Mar. (See the Spectator Sports chapter for more information.)

ℹ️ It seems not a month goes by that the historic Hill Country town of Fredericksburg does not have a spring festival. In July there is the Night in Old Fredericksburg festival that celebrates the town's German roots and Hispanic culture, the Food and Wine Festival and the Mesquite Art Festival in Oct, and the Candlelight Homes Tour at Christmas. Check the calendar at the Chamber of Commerce website, www.fredericksburg texas.com (and see the Day Trips & Weekend Getaways chapter).

✳️ZILKER GARDEN FESTIVAL
Austin Garden Center
Zilker Botanical Gardens
(512) 477-8672
www.zilkergarden.org
To paraphrase the pitch for the popular local public television show *Central Texas Gardener*, what flourishes in gardens elsewhere can end up in the compost heap in Austin given the local climate—sometimes too much rain, too much drought, sudden frost, summer heat, year-round shade, year-round sun, and occasional high wind. That is not to say gardening cannot be rewarding in Austin; it simply means newcomers have to learn the rules. Garden enthusiasts can find many of the answers at this annual event, plus plants for sale, advice, brochures, books, gardening tools, and equipment. There is a small admission fee.

ZILKER KITE FESTIVAL
Zilker Park, 2100 Barton Springs Rd.
(512) 448-KITE (5483)
www.zilkerkitefestival.com

Mar winds help more than 200 handmade kites take flight in one of the city's most popular free outdoor events. Usually held on the second Sun of the month in the city's large downtown park. Anyone can come fly a kite, but there is also an organized competition. Categories include the smallest kite, the strongest-pulling kite, the highest kite, and the most creative kite, but everyone's favorite is the largest kite. The event begins at 11 a.m. and is free. Parking at Zilker Park events can be a headache. In addition to parking in the park, additional space is available under the MoPac overpass to the west.

APRIL

THE ANNUAL AUSTIN RUGBY TOURNAMENT
Zilker Park, 2100 Barton Springs Rd.
www.austinrugby.com
Since 1968 this rugby tournament has attracted enthusiasts from across the region. Organizers tout it as the oldest and largest rugby tournament in the Southwest. There are several divisions of play in the 2-day tournament and, true to rugby tradition, a post-tournament party on Sixth Street. The tournament's website lists telephone numbers for team contacts. (See the Rugby section in the Parks & Recreation chapter for more information on the local rugby scene.)

ANNUAL BLUEBONNET FESTIVAL
Historic Square, Burnet
(512) 756-4297
www.burnetchamber.org
This is one of several Hill Country events celebrating the wildflower season. Burnet is northwest of Austin on US 281. In addition to an arts and crafts show, children's activities, a parade, and 5K and 10K runs, the festival also features a golf tournament, a classic

car show, and special appearances by an association of vintage airplane owners. The festival is held in conjunction with the Highland Lakes Bluebonnet Trail, a scenic route through the Hill Country where many of the best stands of wildflowers can be viewed. Maps and stories about the best bluebonnet spots are frequently printed in the Austin newspaper.

ANNUAL SHAKESPEARE FESTIVAL
Zilker Park, 2201 Barton Springs Rd.
(512) 454-BARD (2273)
www.austinshakespeare.org
The Sheffield Zilker Hillside Theater is the outdoor site of this late Apr/early May dramatic festival. Usually, one of the Bard of Avon's comedies is presented along with a Shakespearean drama on alternate nights. Bring along a blanket, a picnic, and perhaps a sweater if cooler weather is lingering.

ART CITY AUSTIN
Downtown Austin
(512) 609-8591
www.artallianceaustin.org
This juried art show, originally known as the Laguna Gloria Art Fiesta, features the works of more than 200 nationally recognized artists. To make the event festive there is music and children's activities, plus related events at local galleries and public spaces. The festival is sponsored by the Austin Arts Alliance, and both the exhibitions and the creations of craftsmen that are offered for sale are top quality. Admission fee.

AUSTIN INTERNATIONAL POETRY FESTIVAL
Various venues
P.O. Box 41224, Austin, TX 78704
www.aipf.org

Usually held in mid-Apr, this citywide festival celebrates poetry in a variety of forms. Readings are held in bookstores, coffee shops, and pubs as well as public places and feature published poets and inspired amateurs. The festival also includes several workshops and films.

i The Austin Convention and Visitors Bureau maintains an extensive website calendar for all kinds of events in the city: www.austintexas.org.

THE BOB MARLEY FESTIVAL
Auditorium Shores, Riverside Drive and South First Street
www.austinmarleyfest.com
This laid-back music concert celebrates the life of reggae singer Bob Marley. Attendees are asked to bring a donation for the food bank, and there is an admission charge. The event has collected more than 100,000 pounds of food for the needy. The all-day festival features both local and national reggae favorites.

THE CAPITOL 10,000
Downtown, shores of Lady Bird Lake
(512) 445-3598
www.austin360.com
This 10K race is listed among the top 100 road races in the country by *Runner's World* magazine. First held in 1978, it has become a very popular event and attracts approximately 15,000 competitors and hundreds of spectators. The course changes every year but always ends on the shores of Lady Bird Lake. Entry fees vary.

EEYORE'S BIRTHDAY PARTY
Pease Park, Parkway Street off West Twelfth Street
(512) 448-5160
www.eeyores.com

Close-up

South by Southwest

Since 1986 when the first **SXSW Music and Media Conference** (South-by-Southwest, for the uninitiated) was held, it has grown to significant proportions. There is so much energy, growth, and creativity associated with this annual festival that it literally takes over the city, as nightclubs, theaters, conference halls, restaurants, and hotels get in on the action. The economic impact on Austin is estimated in the millions, and the number of musicians and entertainment professionals is counted in the thousands. In addition to the SXSW Music festival, there is now a SXSW Film Festival and Conference and a SXSW Interactive Festival. The essence of the festival is to produce a creative critical mass that spills out and energizes all who come into contact with it. Hence, the city of Austin is awash in musicians, filmmakers, and high-tech multimedia types for the last two weeks of Mar. (A word of warning to anyone planning to come to Austin during the festival—make your hotel, air, and car rental reservations well in advance.)

In the beginning, the conference was seen as a vehicle to focus attention on the Texas music scene, the so-called Third Coast. The festival is still kicked off at the Austin Music Hall with the Austin Music Awards, a decidedly funky version of the Grammys in which winners are chosen by the public at large—and top names in Austin music perform. The local alternative newspaper, the *Austin Chronicle,* organized the first festival (and remains a primary host), but the conference quickly grew and has expanded at record rates every year. The number of bands participating is approaching the 1,000 mark, performing at more than 50 venues in Austin. The acts include national and international headliners. So extensive is the performance list that SXSW press releases tend to look like the contract you sign to buy a refrigerator at Sears: pages and pages of tiny print.

You don't have to be a full-time flower child to enjoy Eeyore's Birthday; however, it helps if you have a touch of Woodstock in your heart. (That makes it easier to understand the Summer of Love drumbeat.) Both old and young free spirits meet on the final Sat of the month at Pease Park in Central Austin to listen to music, dress up (costumes with a pun are favored), paint their faces, dance, watch the jugglers—all for free from mid-morning to sunset. Despite the Winnie the Pooh connection, some aspects of Eeyore's Birthday Party might not be suitable for children, but there are areas set aside for face painting and other kid-friendly activities.

THE MIGHTY TEXAS DOG WALK
(512) 891-9090
www.servicedogs.org
The route changes each year as Central Texas dog lovers and their pooches gather to try to set a new Guinness World Record for a dog walk over their rivals in England. In 2010, some 8,000 furry participants made the march, not quite enough to beat the Brit record of 10,000, but plenty to help raise money for the Texas Hearing and Service Dogs organization.

OLD SETTLER'S MUSIC FESTIVAL
Salt Lick Pavilion, Camp Ben McCullough Road, Driftwood
(512) 346-0999
www.oldsettlersmusicfest.org

Everyone is on alert during the festival to seek out the next wave. The panelists at the conference count among their numbers major record producers and influential music and film professionals who have come to view SXSW, according to festival sponsors, as "one of the most influential musical events in the world." While conference participants sign up for the whole shebang of seminars and panel discussions ("Parenting in the Music Business" and "So IS Paul Dead?"), music enthusiasts opt to pay for a wristband that allows them to roam the nightclub scene and hear as many of the bands as possible. Conference fees cost several hundred dollars, but wristbands have been described as affordable. However, grumbling has been heard in recent years as wristband prices approached $100. Availability and cost of wristbands have caused rumors of rebellion in the Austin ranks, but that has not detracted from the success of SXSW.

The creators of SXSW also launched a SXSW Film Festival, which has been described as "early Sundance," since entrants must be chosen by a panel in order to show their films. The 4-day festival includes panels, workshops, meetings, mentor sessions, demo reel sessions, and the presentation of more than 150 films at various locations in Austin. Major agents, directors, and up-and-coming film producers attend. Another spin-off festival held in conjunction with the film and music conferences is the SXSW Interactive Festival, dedicated to discussions and explorations of new media technology. Again, there are panel discussions, star speakers, and a trade show featuring local and national high-tech companies. The entertainment events include such things as cyberoperas and intercontinental Internet concerts. The best way to absorb all the SXSW possibilities is to visit www.sxsw.com or get on the mailing list. Write to SXSW, P.O. Box 4999, Austin, TX 78765; call (512) 467-7979, or fax (512) 451-0754.

This folk music festival originated in Old Settler's Park in Round Rock, north of Austin, hence its name. But as it grew, the celebrants sought a larger site and moved south to Driftwood, a tiny community about 12 miles south of US 290 on FM 1826, southwest of Austin. The 2-day celebration of acoustic, bluegrass, jazz, and folk music is usually held on the first weekend of the month, drawing crowds that make a weekend of the event by camping out on-site. A 2-day ticket costs about $50, but book early since tickets, especially camping sites, sell out early. One-day tickets are also available.

TAYLOR JAYCEES NATIONAL RATTLESNAKE SACKING CHAMPIONSHIP

Murphy Park, Lake Drive, Taylor
www.taylorjaycees.org

Not for the faint of heart, this annual event takes place in the small community of Taylor, northeast of Austin. Amateur teams compete for the prize; even young snake handlers test their skills. Visitors can also answer that age-old question—does fried rattlesnake meat taste like chicken? Admission fee.

THE TEXAS HILL COUNTRY WINE & FOOD FESTIVAL
Various locations
(512) 249-6300
www.texaswineandfood.org

Texas chefs, vintners, cheesemakers, herb growers, and gourmets gather in Austin on the first weekend in Apr to celebrate Texas wine and foods. The first festival was held in 1985 and was the brainchild of several nationally and internationally recognized chefs, including Dean Fearing, executive chef of Dallas's Mansion on Turtle Creek, and Robert Del Grande, executive chef of Houston's Cafe Annie. Events take place at restaurants, posh and funky, throughout the city and locations outside the city. Experts in cuisine, wine, cigars, and famous chefs and culinary authors from across the country conduct seminars and tastings, create special menus, and host field trips. Admission to events varies from triple digits for a ticket for a celebration dinner to an affordable amount for a Taste of Texas sampler, featuring Texas foods, wine, and beer at a country barbecue. Chocolate cigars might be the dessert at a dinner, while bock beer-battered quail is likely to be on the menu at the outdoor tasting. For a brochure and information, write to the festival at 12731 Research Blvd., Suite 112A, Austin, TX 78759.

THE TEXAS RELAYS
The University of Texas Memorial Stadium, San Jacinto Street at Manor Road
(512) 471-3333, (800) 982-BEVO
www.texassports.com

The relays have been run at UT for more than 70 years and feature top high school and collegiate track and field competitors from across the nation. Usually scheduled for the first weekend in Apr, sessions begin on Fri morning and end Sat afternoon. The preliminaries are held on Wed and Thurs and are free. Tickets available for one day or the entire event. An all-session ticket costs $10. Call the toll-free number for additional information and advanced ticket purchase.

✳WILDFLOWERS DAYS FESTIVAL
Lady Bird Johnson National Wildflower Research Center
4801 La Crosse Ave.
(512) 292-4100
www.wildflower.org

The research center celebrates the Hill Country spring wildflower season with a daylong festival featuring native plant experts and authors, an arts and crafts exhibit, and live music. Admission is $3.50 for adults, $2 for students and seniors, and $1 for children 5 and younger.

YESTERFEST AND THE SALINAS ART FESTIVAL
Bastrop City Park and Main Street, Bastrop
(512) 321-2419
www.bastropdba.com

Bastrop, the historic small community just east of Austin on Highway 71, is a town that has worked hard at maintaining its ties to the past. Several historic buildings line Main Street, where the art festival takes place on the third Sat of the month. Out at the city park, the locals celebrate their pioneer past with historical exhibits, reenactments, craft demonstrations, music, and food. It all winds up in a Main Street dance at night and a campfire stew dinner. Admission charge to the park. Parking is available at the Bastrop High School, and shuttles run to the park. Yesterfest begins at 10 a.m. and closes at 5 p.m.

MAY

CATHOLIC CHURCH SPRING PICNIC
American Legion Park, Shiner
(512) 594-4180
www.shinertx.com

Shiner is a small Central Texas town southeast of Austin well known as the home of Shiner beer. The town retains much of its German-American flavor, and one of the best ways to experience that is to visit the annual Catholic church picnic. The event, which dates back to 1897 and is one of the biggest church picnics in the area, is free and features a country store, food, games like horseshoes, and dancing all day to polka bands. The fun continues into the evening with more dancing and a church dinner, featuring Shiner Picnic Stew, sausage, fried chicken, and all the fixin's. The event is held the Sun before Memorial Day.

CINCO DE MAYO
Fiesta Gardens
2101 Bergman St.
www.cincodemayoaustin.com

On May 5, 1862, Mexican General Ignacio Zaragoza (who was born in Texas) defeated the army of French Emperor Louis Napoleon at Puebla, east of Mexico City. That blow against European imperialism is now a special holiday celebrated in song and dance both in Mexico and Texas. In addition to celebrations at Fiesta Gardens in East Austin, folkloric dancers and mariachi bands often perform at the State Capitol in the rotunda. Most Cinco de Mayo events are free, but some of the evening celebrations at Fiesta Gardens may charge an entrance fee. Another place where celebrations of Mexican-American life are held is the new Mexican American Cultural Center, 600 River St., (512) 478-6222, www.ci.austin.tx.us/macc.

FUSEBOX FESTIVAL
Downtown Austin
www.fuseboxfestival.com

A 10 day contemporary arts festival celebrating theater, film, dance, music, and art on Austin's downtown streets and in buildings, even bridges—the emphasis here is on modern.

HISTORIC HOMES TOUR
Various locations in Austin
(512) 474-5198
www.heritagesocietyaustin.org

On Mother's Day weekend, the Heritage Society of Austin offers history buffs an opportunity to tour some of the city's most historic homes. Each year, the tour has a different theme. The society has played an important role in saving Austin buildings. One of its first projects was to rescue the Driskill Hotel on Sixth Street back in the 1970s. Tickets are available in advance or at the homes on the tour.

THE O. HENRY WORLD CHAMPIONSHIP PUN-OFF
O. Henry Museum
409 East Fifth St. in Brush Park
(512) 472-1903
www.ci.austin.tx.us/library/ahc/ohpun off.htm

If you are a pun-lover, and apparently there are hundreds of them in Austin, this is the event for you. Each year, on the first Sun in May, up to 2,000 people gather at the O. Henry Museum (see the Attractions chapter) to watch and participate in the pun-off. The famous short-story writer William Sydney Porter, who wrote under the nom de plume of O. Henry, was a master punster. The event is free. To join the pun-off, simply show up.

THE SUMMER CONCERT SERIES
Waterloo Park, Red River and Fifteenth Streets,
downtown Austin
(512) 440-1414

Organized by the Austin Federation of Musicians, this series of free outdoor summer concerts is held every Wed in May at 7 p.m. on Auditorium Shores, the south shore of Lady Bird Lake, just west of South Congress Avenue. Concerts also are held on Sun afternoon at the Zilker Hillside Theater at 3 p.m. The concert series features a variety of bands and music, including rhythm and blues, Tejano, samba, and jazz. Bring a blanket or a lawn chair. Some refreshments are sold at concession stands, but many music lovers bring along a picnic.

JUNE

AUSTIN SYMPHONY ORCHESTRA
   CHILDREN'S DAYS
1101 Red River St.
(512) 476-6052
www.austinsymphony.org

Each Wed in June and July the symphony entertains and educates children in the little stone amphitheater at Symphony Square. There's music, dance, stories, and a little education thrown in for good measure.

BLANCO LAVENDER FESTIVAL
Courthouse Square, Blanco
(830) 833-5101
www.blancolavenderfestival.com

The Hill Country is now home to a burgeoning new crop—lavender and this festival celebrates its role in the culinary and home-keeping arts. Tours of local lavender farms are offered and stalls on the courthouse square demonstrate lavender arts and sells crafts and food. There's music, also.

CHISHOLM TRAIL ROUNDUP
City Park, Lockhart
(512) 398-2818
www.chisholmtrailroundup.com

Back in 1840, Lockhart residents fought their way into the history books by defeating the Comanches at the Battle of Plum Creek. Later this small town southeast of Austin became a staging center for cattle being driven north on the Chisholm Trail to Abilene, Kansas. Lockhart had a reputation as a wild town, famous for its shoot-outs and feuds. The town history is celebrated with a reenactment of the battle, city tours, and a chili cook-off. The weekend-long festival in late May also includes dances, arts and crafts shows, and live music. Admission for events varies.

FESTIVAL INSTITUTE AT FESTIVAL HILL
Round Top
(409) 249-3129
www.festivalhill.org

In the early 1970s, classical pianist James Dick founded the festival at Round Top, the small German settlement east of Austin in Fayette County. Round Top has come to represent the best of the Texas cultural scene, combining great music, historical settings, and a bucolic atmosphere. There are concerts once a month throughout the year at the institute site, but a special midyear series dubbed Summerfest takes place on each weekend in June and the first two weekends of July. Concerts range from the strictly classical to the popular. For a concert schedule write to Festival Institute, P.O. Box 89, Round Top, TX 78954.

JUNETEENTH
Various locations

Juneteenth is an original Texas celebration and marks the day that Texas slaves learned of the Emancipation Proclamation. On June

19, 1865, Union commander Major General Gordon Granger took Galveston and announced to Texas slaves that they had been freed 2 years earlier. The day is now marked by festivals of music, barbecues, parades, celebrations of African-American culture, and gospel sings. Check the *Austin American-Statesman* and community newspapers for details of this yearly event. Juneteenth is now a state holiday.

ORIGINAL ROUND TOP ANTIQUES FAIR
Round Top
(512) 237-4747
www.roundtopexasantiques.com
Round Top is a wonderful, culture-rich community located in Fayette County, about 65 miles east of Austin. Two of the most renowned antiques fairs in the United States, one in the spring, the other in Oct, are held here. *Country Home* magazine has named this fair "one of the 10 best antique fairs in the country," and dealers come from all over the United States and even the world to sell, shop, and mingle. Founded by the legendary dealer Emma Lee Turney, the show at the Big Red Barn on TX 237 is now held by Susan Franks and features furniture and home furnishings from all regions of the country, plus British and European works. (For more information on Round Top, see the Day Trips chapter.) In addition to the two big fairs, there are other antiques sales events and crafts shows, as well as theater presentations and music concerts throughout the year, so check out the small town's website: www.roundtop.org.

JULY

AUSTIN CHAMBER MUSIC FESTIVAL
Various locations
(512) 454-0026
http://austinchambermusic.org

Imagine a chamber ensemble performing in the Victorian ballroom of the Driskill Hotel, or a music workshop for kids at the Austin Children's Museum. This 3-week festival celebrating chamber music utilizes a variety of locations around the city, including churches, public spaces indoors and out, and evocative settings like the Driskill's ballroom.

AUSTIN SYMPHONY ORCHESTRA JULY FOURTH CONCERT AND FIREWORKS
Auditorium Shores, Riverside Drive and South First Street
(512) 476-6064
www.austinsymphony.org
As Austin grows, the size of the crowd gathering on the shores of Lady Bird Lake to watch the July Fourth concert gets larger and larger. The orchestra sets up on the southern shore of Lady Bird Lake on Auditorium Shores. The grand finale is, of course, Tchaikovsky's "1812 Overture," complete with cannon and fireworks. The music begins at 8:30 p.m., but many families come down earlier and enjoy a family picnic. Parking is a major headache, and after the concert the city's major thoroughfares out of the downtown area are jammed, making the trip home a slow one. The concert is free.

BARTON SPRINGS DIVING CHAMPIONSHIPS
Barton Springs Pool,
2201 Barton Springs Rd.
(512) 476-9044
www.ci.austin.tx.us/parks/barton springs.htm
Elvis is alive and diving at Barton Springs. At least he was in 1997, when he won the "Most Original" prize in this annual contest. The contest includes best splash, best dive,

and most-original dive categories. Participants range in age, and their entry fees help fund environmental exhibits. Local musical groups also perform before and after the diving competition, which takes place on the third Sun of the month. Flyers advertising the event and containing registration forms are widely distributed at Austin's pools, local grocery stores, and other outlets. Spectators pay an admission charge. Participants pay a registration fee. You can save a few dollars by preregistering.

BASTILLE DAY
The French Legation,
802 San Marcos St.
(512) 472-8180
www.frenchlegationmuseum.org
The legation was the home and office of Comte Alphonse Dubois de Saligny, charge d'affaires to the Republic of Texas. Francophiles and homesick French citizens gather on the Sun closest to July 14 to celebrate the French equivalent of Fourth of July in the US. The food is French, of course, and very good since it is concocted by local chefs. The music also is French, and the dancers, jugglers, and mimes celebrate traditional French culture. Admission fee.

SHAKESPEARE AT WINEDALE
Winedale Historic Center, near
Round Top
(979) 278-3530
www.shakespeare-winedale.org
Each summer, University of Texas English literature students gather at historic Winedale (see the Day Trips chapter) to study and perform Shakespeare's plays. The students perform three plays in the theater barn in the historic settlement, beginning the last week of July and continuing through

mid-Aug. Performances are Thurs and Fri at 7:30 p.m. and Sat at 2 and 7:30 p.m. Admission fee. Winedale is about a 90-minute drive east of Austin.

WILLIE NELSON'S JULY FOURTH PICNIC
www.willienelson.com
Willie Nelson is renowned for his concerts, and no one gets shortchanged when he takes to the stage. Over the years, the picnic has changed locations, so it is wise to keep an eye on local music coverage in the media for prices, admission, and ticket numbers. It is an event that is popular, and concertgoers from all over Texas come to hear Willie sing, so book tickets well sin advance.

ZILKER SUMMER MUSICAL
Zilker Hillside Theater, Zilker Park
(512) 479-9491
www.zilker.org
Each summer, for more than 40 years, talented Austin musicians and actors have put on a popular Broadway musical in the open-air hillside "arena" adjacent to Barton Springs in the city's major downtown park. The musical is free and performances are at 8:30 p.m. Thurs through Sun from mid-July through Aug.

AUGUST

✳AUSTIN CHRONICLE HOT SAUCE FESTIVAL
Waterloo Park, 403 East Fifteenth St.
(512) 454-5766
www.auschron.com
This combination cook-off and foodie fest brings together amateurs, chefs, and commercial salsa makers who try to woo the taste buds of Austin's hot sauce aficionados. There is a competition, lots of samples, plus

music—so what better way to cool off on a hot summer than with some hot sauce. Proceeds benefit the local food bank.

AUSTIN LATINO COMEDY FIESTA
713 Congress Ave.
(512) 472-5470
www.teatrohumanidad.com

The historic Paramount Theatre is home to this annual comedy festival that celebrates Austin's Latino culture. Stand-up comics and sketch artists perform at the weekend festival.

BAT FEST
Ann Richards Congress Avenue Bridge
(512) 441-9015
www.roadwayevents.com

Underneath the bridge lives the 1.5-million-strong colony of Mexican free-tail bats (see the Attractions chapter) and mid-summer is a great time to watch the swarm fly out at dusk to feast on bugs all around Central Texas. This family friendly festival features all things "batty," including a "bat wing" eating contest (think chicken) and all manner of bat costumes and bat hats. Admission fee.

i On any given weekend throughout the year, the air is filled with the smoky aroma of slow-cooked brisket. The Central Texas Barbecue Association keeps a calendar of barbecue cookoffs and contests on its website, www.ctbahome.com.

FALL CREEK GRAPE STOMP
Fall Creek Vineyards, Llano County
(915) 379-5361
www.fcv.com

This Hill Country vineyard has established a national reputation for the quality of its wines. Located on the shores of Lake Buchanan, about 70 miles northwest of Austin, Fall Creek is a popular place to visit while touring the Hill Country. The peace and quiet of the winery is broken by the cheers and hollers of barefooted kids and grown-ups stomping the grapes. The winery opens its doors from 11 a.m. to 5 p.m. so that visitors can roll up their jeans, strip off their socks, and jump into vats of red grapes. The experience is free.

GILLESPIE COUNTY FAIR
Fairgrounds, Highway 16, Fredericksburg
(830) 997-6523
www.gillespiefair.com

This is the oldest county fair in the state and is well worth a visit for a glimpse of a time when the county fair was an important date on the local calendar. The fair includes a traditional livestock show, handicrafts and home-baked goods, horse races, a carnival, and dances in the evening. The fair usually takes place at the end of Aug over 4 days and nights. Fairground admission is $5, free for children. Additional admission charges may be in place for other events.

ZILKER PARK JAZZ FESTIVAL
Zilker Park Amphitheatre, Zilker Park
(512) 440-1414
www.ci.austin.tx.us/zilker

There is no better way to spend a warm summer night than listening to the cool sounds of jazz float across Zilker Park, the city's favorite gathering spot throughout the seasons. (See the Parks & Recreation chapter.) Bring a blanket and something cold to drink, and enjoy the free summer festival.

SEPTEMBER

AUSTIN CITY LIMITS FESTIVAL
Zilker Park,
2100 Barton Springs Rd.
www.aclfestival.com

The same folks who brought America the legendary *Austin City Limits* television show on PBS sponsor this 3-day festival of music, food, arts, and crafts in the city's most famous park (see the Parks & Recreation chapter). There are multiple stages across 15 acres of parkland, plus an "Austin Food Court" and an art show. Capital Metro provides transportation to the site. The festival runs a very detailed website, where lists of bands, schedules, and information can be found and tickets may be purchased. Daily or 3-day tickets are offered.

AUSTIN GAY AND LESBIAN INTERNATIONAL FILM FESTIVAL
Various venues
(512) 302-9889
www.agliff.org

In keeping with Austin's building reputation as a film center, this 2-week festival brings a variety of films to Austin theaters around the city.

DIEZ Y SEIS DE SEPTIEMBRE
Various locations

This is a major fiesta both north and south of the border, celebrating Mexico's demand for independence from Spain. Like the US July Fourth celebration, serious history and fun are combined on Diez y Seis. Mariachi bands perform, folkloric dancers celebrate their heritage, and everyone eats really well. Austin's celebrations center on Fiesta Gardens, on the shores of Lady Bird Lake in East Austin. Nearby Elgin also holds its Chili Pepper Fest, with celebrations of the Mexican fiesta.

There are ceremonies in Austin on the actual day of the holiday, but the fiesta is usually carried over to the weekend closest to the 16th, with events on several consecutive days. Check the local newspaper for details.

OATMEAL FESTIVAL
Bertram
(512) 335-2197
www.bertramtx.com

This tongue-in-cheek Labor Day weekend festival has helped to revive a small community northwest of Round Rock on FM 243. The festivities include an oatmeal cook-off and eat-off, an oatmeal sculpture contest, and the Miss Bag of Oats (you have to be 55-plus) pageant. For the kids, there is a grasshopper parade where children can parade their pet insects. Most events are free.

OCTOBER

AUSTIN FILM SCREENWRITERS CONFERENCE AND AUSTIN FILM FESTIVAL
Various locations in the city
(512) 478-4795
www.austinfilmfestival.com

This fall festival, usually held at the beginning of the month, is fast becoming recognized as a significant film and cultural event. The conference offers screenwriters the opportunity to listen to panel discussions by top screenwriters, directors, and studio executives. Participants have included director Oliver Stone, actor Dennis Hopper, Mike Judge (creator of *King of the Hill* television show), screenwriters Eric Roth (*Forrest Gump*), Randall Wallace (*Braveheart*), Al Reinart (*Apollo 13*), and Buck Henry (*The Graduate*), and many more. The accompanying film festival features either movies scheduled for release or movies that are making the festival circuit. The two festivals vary in admission prices. Tickets to individual films are available on show day. Passes to panel discussions and films also can be purchased for around $200, and full registration is approximately double that. The festival also includes a juried competition for screenwriters, and some of the winners have seen their work make it to the big silver screen as a result of the exposure here.

i October is Texas Archaeology Month, celebrated statewide with hands-on exhibits, demonstrations, workshops, and opportunities to explore the rich Texas past. The Texas Historical Commission posts an events calendar on its website, www.thc.state.tx.us, or archaeology buffs can call (512) 463-6096 for more information.

EMMA LEE TURNEY'S ROUND TOP FOLK ART FAIR
Round Top
(281) 493-5501
www.roundtopfolkartfair.com
Twice a year the cognoscenti of the antiques world flock to this small Texas town (see the fair listing in Apr for details). The fall event celebrates American folk art and is under the direction of the legendary antiques dealer Emma Lee Turney.

FRONTIER DAYS
Old Settlers Park, Round Rock
(512) 255-5805
www.roundrocktexas.gov
The only shoot-outs these days in Round Rock involve high school basketball tournaments. The only masks being worn are those donned by high-tech workers. But Round Rock, now a booming suburban community, was a typical frontier town back in 1878

when the streets were the setting for one of the most famous of Texas shoot-outs between the law and outlaw Sam Bass. "Texas's Beloved Bandit," as Bass was dubbed, rode into town intent on robbing the bank, but he ended the day buried in the local cemetery. Bass likely was dubbed "Beloved" because, in the grand Texas tradition of Bonnie and Clyde, bank robbers are somehow elevated to folk hero status. On the second weekend of the month the community celebrates Frontier Days, complete with a reenactment of the shoot-out, which is the headline event of the 2-day festival. There is also a frog-jumping contest and hands-on demonstrations of butter-churning, whittling, soap making, and other pioneer skills. Admission fee.

✳HALLOWEEN ON SIXTH STREET
Sixth Street, between Congress Avenue and I-35
Wholesale Halloween madness is one way to describe this event. As many as 60,000 costumed revelers have gathered on the street for the celebration. Several blocks are roped off to vehicular traffic. The noise level is high, and some partygoers do become a little rowdy. This is strictly a grown-up celebration and not recommended for children.

HOGEYE FESTIVAL
Elgin
(512) 281-5724
www.elgintx.com/hogeye.asp
Famed for its sausage, Elgin is a small town 19 miles east of Austin on US 290 East. This typical Texas small-town festival features cow patty bingo, a sausage cook-off (of course), a hog-calling contest, music, arts and crafts, and a street dance.

LIVE STRONG CHALLENGE
Various sites in the city
(888) 4-CHALLENGE
www.livestrongchallenge.org
One of Austin's most beloved residents is legendary bicyclist Lance Armstrong. According to the Lance Armstrong Foundation, Lance's cycling buddies first organized a Ride for the Roses race to show support for Lance's battle with cancer in 1997. The original race paralleled the training ride Lance and the group made through the hills west of Austin. Today the event has become the Live Strong Challenge and takes place in four cities. It has multiple features and spans a weekend. Some 7,000 participants enter bicycling events, plus there is a gala, silent auction, a 5K fun run, a health and sports expo, a Kids CARE ride at Auditorium Shores, and music venues featuring local and national bands.

OKTOBERFEST
Market Square, Fredericksburg
(830) 997-4810
www.oktoberfestinfbg.com
Fredericksburg has a strong German heritage; in fact, some of the older residents still speak in a form of German heard in 19th-century Europe. The traditional community festival features beer-hall singing, waltz contests, and lots of sausage. Admission fee; free for those 6 and younger.

NOVEMBER

AUSTIN CELTIC FESTIVAL
Fiesta Shores on Lady Bird Lake
www.austincelts.org/festival
Touted as the largest gathering of the clans in Central Austin this 3-day festival features Celtic music and dance, plus food. Admission fee.

AUSTIN JUNIOR LEAGUE CHRISTMAS AFFAIR
Palmer Events Center,
900 Barton Springs Rd.
(512) 467-8982
www.jlaustin.org
A sure sign that Christmas is just around the corner is the transformation of Palmer Events Center into a shopping wonderland. More than 200 specialty merchants offer a variety of Christmas gift ideas, some easily affordable, others high-priced. Not everyone shops at the affair, although the league raises hundreds of thousands of dollars for its community projects at the event; some just stroll, sip some Christmas spiced wine, and window-shop or gather decorating ideas for their own holiday celebrations. The affair is held the third weekend in Nov. Daily admission fee.

CHUY'S CHILDREN GIVING TO CHILDREN PARADE
Congress Avenue
(888) 439-2489
www.chuysparade.com
This is a great way to teach children to give thanks on Thanksgiving weekend. Balloons, some up to 80 feet high, depicting popular children's characters lead the parade, followed by marching bands, floats, dancers, clowns, and trucks filled with toys donated by children along the route. The donations go to the Austin Police Department's Operation Blue Santa, which gives toys to needy kids at Christmas. The parade is sponsored by Chuy's, the popular local restaurant (see the Restaurants chapter).

DIA DE LOS MUERTOS
Mexic-Arte Museum
419 Congress Ave.
(512) 480-9373
www.mexic-artemuseum.org

It means "Day of the Dead," and this quintes-sentially Mexican fiesta is celebrated on All Souls Day, Nov 1. In Mexico, families take food to the local cemetery on that day for a 2-day celebration in honor of their ancestors. Families set up altars at the gravesite, offer-ing food and drink. Day of the Dead folk art is highly collectible, and much of it is humor-ous, mocking human foibles. Mexic-Arte Museum (see The Arts chapter) sponsors several Day of the Dead events, including the construction of a variety of *ofrendas* by local artists at its downtown museum site. Admission fee. There is also a parade down East Sixth Street onto Congress Avenue in celebration of Mexican and Chicano culture. Spectators are urged to wear typical Day of the Dead costumes, angels or skeletons, and watch low riders, dancers, and musicians parade on the avenue. Check the local paper for additional Dia de los Muertos events.

TEXAS BOOK FESTIVAL
Texas Capitol and various locations
(512) 477-4055
www.texasbookfestival.org
This very successful celebration of Texas literature (thanks in great part to First Lady Laura Bush) includes book signings, semi-nars, discussions, and celebrations of literary history. (See The Literary Scene chapter for more on this event.)

WURSTFEST
Wurstfest Grounds, Land Park, New Braunfels
(830) 625-9167, (800) 221-4369
www.wurstfest.com
Wurstfest is the city's version of Oktoberfest and attracts tens of thousands of visitors, who eat sausage, drink beer, sing songs, and spend money. Admission fee. Children 12 and younger are free.

DECEMBER

✳ARMADILLO CHRISTMAS BAZAAR
Palmer Events Center
900 Barton Springs Rd.
(512) 447-1605
www.armadillobazaar.com
This annual arts and crafts fair was originally held at the legendary Armadillo World Head-quarters (see The Music Scene chapter) but now is housed in the Palmer Events Center. The 'Dillo is long gone, but the spirit of the bazaar lives on as a showplace for local art-ists and craftspeople, some of them creating fanciful jewelry and whimsical toys. Local musicians also perform nightly at the 2-week event, which begins in mid-Dec and ends Christmas Eve. It is open from 11 a.m. to 11 p.m. daily. Admission fee. Children younger than 12 are admitted free.

CHRISTMAS AT THE FRENCH LEGATION
French Legation, 802 San Marcos St.
(512) 472-8180
www.frenchlegationmuseum.org
The Daughters of the Texas Republic offer a glimpse of Christmas past as it might have been celebrated in the mid-19th century. The legation (see the Attractions chapter) was built for Comte Alphonse Dubois de Saligny, France's charge d'affaires to the Republic of Texas. In addition to Christmas displays, choirs perform Christmas carols and holiday refreshments are offered. Pére Noel, the French Santa Claus, is on hand. The celebration takes place on the first Sun of the month from 1 to 5 p.m. Admission fee.

CHRISTMAS MUSIC AND THEATER
Various locations

With its rich and talented arts community, Austin offers a large variety of Christmas musical events. There are the long-standing traditions of the holiday, like the annual performances by the Austin Civic Ballet of *The Nutcracker* at Bass Concert Hall, (512) 469-SHOW. Handel's "Messiah" is performed by several musical entities, plus there is the annual "Sing It Yourself Messiah" at St. Matthews Episcopal Church, where the audience can join in with the Austin Civic Chorus. Call (512) 454-TIXS for information and tickets. Local theater and comedy troupes offer a variety of performances. Check the listings in the *Austin American-Statesman*.

CHRISTMAS OPEN HOUSE
Winedale Historic Center, near Round Top
(409) 278-3530
www.roundtop.org

Christmas at Winedale is celebrated each year in a different historic home in this wonderful old settlement in Fayette County, east of Austin (see the Day Trips chapter). Usually held the Sun before Christmas, the celebration features seasonal music and food. The many antiques shops offer one-of-a-kind Christmas gifts. Call for hours. There is a small admission charge.

FAMILY CHRISTMAS NIGHT
Downtown Round Rock
(512) 255-5805

On the first Sat of the month, the City of Round Rock closes the downtown streets for a family celebration. At the heart of the event is the town's historic town square where Santa appears to assure Round Rock kids that he knows who has been naughty and who has been nice. The festivities begin at 7 p.m., and admission is free.

FELIZ NAVIDAD!
Various locations

There are a variety of Christmas events with a Mexican flavor held in Austin during the holidays. Plays depicting the Nativity, folk music concerts, and folk art are popular at this time of year. *La Pastorela*, the traditional Latino Nativity play, is performed by several groups. But one of the most interesting and authentic traditions takes place in mid-Dec as members of our Lady of Guadalupe Church, 1209 East Ninth St., enact La Posada. This is a tradition both in Mexico and Texas as the faithful reenact Joseph and Mary's search for a place to stay in Bethlehem. The faithful follow members, who are dressed as the Holy Family, as they go from door to door, asking for shelter. When the parade reaches the church there is a mass followed by Christmas treats, tamales, and Mexican hot chocolate. Check the arts and events listings in the *Austin American-Statesman* and local community newspapers.

FIRST NIGHT
Downtown Austin
(512)739-9900
www.firstnightaustin.org

This family friendly celebration is a farewell to the old year and a great way for the whole family to ring in the new. A "celebration of the arts," it is centered around City Hall on the northern banks of Lady Bird Lake (formerly Town Lake) and is a gift by various major corporate donors to the city. There is poetry, dance, mummers and musicians, artwork and clowns, some exhibitions have a Cirque de Soleil feel and even the buildings become canvases for artists. There is an early evening welcoming for the New Year, plus the traditional midnight fireworks and its free!

ICE SKATING AT WHOLE FOODS
525 North Lamar Blvd.
(512) 476-1206
www.wholefoodsmarket.com
The rooftop of the Whole Foods Landmark store and corporate headquarters becomes a winter wonderland during the Christmas holiday, no matter if the temperatures remain balmy. The skating rink offers a wonderful view of the downtown holiday lights.

KWANZAA
Various locations
The Swahili word means "fruits of the harvest," and Kwanzaa, created in 1966, has proved fruitful as millions of African Americans embrace the celebration's principles. From Dec 26 to Jan 1, the 7 days of Kwanzaa are dedicated to 7 principles. In recent years African-American leaders in Austin have taken Kwanzaa from a family event to a community celebration. During the festival there are a variety of public events. Check the *Austin American-Statesman* and local community newspapers for details.

✳THE LIGHTING OF THE ZILKER PARK CHRISTMAS TREE
Zilker Park, 2100 Barton Springs Rd.
This annual event and Austin ritual on the first Sun of the month is a true sign that Christmas is nigh. One the city's moonlight towers (see the Attractions chapter) was moved to the park and serves as the main "trunk" of the tree. Thousands of colored Christmas lights are strung from the top of the 165-foot tower to resemble a Christmas tree shape. Tradition calls for children to stand inside the pyramid and whirl around, making the lights blur.

Young children are whisked around in their parents' arms. It is one of those simple holiday traditions that children never forget. Admission to the park is free.

LIGHTS OF THE BLACKLANDS
Small towns east of Austin
(512) 285-5721
www.elgintx.com
The holidays can be stressful, but one of the most relaxing ways to enjoy the season is to take a leisurely evening drive through some of the area's small towns and view the Christmas decorations. The towns east of Austin in what are called the Blacklands, a reference to the rich blackland prairie soil, suggest a tour beginning in Elgin on US 290 and then on through Coupland, Thrall, Bartlett, and LaGrange. The route is featured on the Elgin City website.

NEW YEAR'S CELEBRATION ON SIXTH STREET
Sixth Street, between Congress Avenue and I-35
www.6street.com
New Year's Eve in Austin's club scene is wild. Many clubs and downtown restaurants have special performances or menus in celebration. Check the local entertainment press for the particulars. Local television and radio stations camp out on Sixth Street rooftops to watch Austin's version of the "big ball" fall. The big ball falls at midnight, but that doesn't end the craziness as the party goes on in clubs and on the street itself until the wee hours.

PIONEER FARM CHRISTMAS CANDLELIGHT TOUR
Jourdan-Bachman Pioneer Farm
11418 Sprinkle Cut-Off Rd.
(512) 837-1215
www.pioneerfarms.org

Traditional Christmas activities reflecting the pioneer lifestyle are celebrated each weekend leading up to Christmas, many of them conducted by candlelight just as they would have been done in frontier days. Admission is $6. (See the Kidstuff chapter for information on the farm.)

i There is one Austin neighborhood that takes Christmas decorating very seriously. On Thirty-seventh Street east of Guadalupe Street in Central Austin's Hyde Park neighborhood, neighbors try to outmatch each other in Christmas light exhibitions. Walk or drive the street, but be sure to make a donation to the electricity fund.

TEXAS HILL COUNTRY REGIONAL CHRISTMAS LIGHTING TRAIL
Various locations
(860) 997-8515
www.fredericksburgtexas.com
Some of the most picturesque Christmas light shows can be seen in the small towns around the Austin area. Most of the lights are put up in early Dec and taken down after New Year's Day. Below are a few locations well worth visiting. The phone numbers are for the local chambers of commerce and visitor bureaus. Check the chambers' websites, also.

Bastrop, to the east, decorates its historic downtown and Old Iron Bridge, (512) 321-2419. **Blanco,** southwest of Austin, decorates the old courthouse with thousands of lights, (210) 438-2914. **Johnson City,** west of Austin, is ablaze as the local residents cover homes, businesses, and the Blanco County Courthouse with lights, (830) 868-7684. **Llano,** northwest of Austin, decorates the historic town square and the old courthouse with 10 miles of lights, (915) 556-5172. **Marble Falls,** northwest of Austin, boasts it uses one million lights to decorate its Walkway of Lights, (800) 759-8178. In **Austin** the local television meteorologists often highlight spectacular Austin neighborhood decorations. One of the best is Thirty-seventh Street, east of Guadalupe Street in Central Austin. Walking through this neighborhood is recommended, rather than driving. In **Round Rock** the downtown historic district is decorated for the holidays, and in **Cedar Park** the Hill Country Flyer (see the Attractions chapter) departs from the train station in midafternoon for Burnet, then returns in the evening so that passengers can view the Hill Country homes decorated with lights. Call (512) 477-8468 for information.

THE ARTS

What do 20-something slackers, a zany town named Tuna, a statewide high school competition, a giant university, and a celebrated European sculptor have in common? They all have added a few broad brush strokes to the colorful canvas of Austin arts. Austin attracts artists. While that phenomenon dates back to the 1800s, Austin's status as a hub for artists has developed largely since the 1970s, when enough musicians, actors, writers, and painters had gathered to form an arts scene. Over the past few decades, more and more talented artists have found inspiration in Austin's artistic communities, and many of those have helped Austin earn a reputation for both appreciating and producing high-quality art. Read about the dynamic people and places in this chapter as well as in The Music Scene, Nightlife, and Attractions to discover many of the reasons Austin always gets such high praise in the national media. In this chapter we'll tell you about the visual artists and theater troupes, the dancers and filmmakers, the classical performers, and the choirs that make Austin sing.

OVERVIEW

Elisabet Ney, who had sculpted some of the great figures of Europe, was nearly 60 when she moved to Austin in the late 1800s. Back then, Austin had more gambling dens and brothels than galleries and theaters. Ney's celebrity status attracted influential men and women, many who believed, as did she, that art, music, and dance rank up there near water and air to sustain life. As Ney's hands transformed crude blocks of marble into glorious statues of Texas heroes, her spirit and her passion shaped a culture that prized the arts. Along the way, she became a pioneer of artistic development in the state of Texas. Her ability to inspire others during a time when the arts weren't exactly on the top of the Texas agenda led to the creation of the Texas Fine Arts Association (now called Arthouse) and later the Texas Commission on the Arts and the University of Texas art department.

The University of Texas gets major billing among the stars of Austin's cultural scene. The university's highly respected film and fine arts schools have turned out some of the best-prepared graduates in the country. It's impossible to estimate the number of UT alumni, and professors, who are making significant contributions in Austin and around the country in the fields of dance, film, visual art, theater, literature, and music. UT's Texas Performing Arts is a world-class arts complex for student and professional performers alike. The University Interscholastic League (UIL), a program started in 1910 to encourage educational development in Texas high schools through competition, began as a sports program. Since the 1920s the UIL has included an annual theater competition in which high school students from across the state vie for top honors. This Texas theater tradition, which produced Broadway's Tommy Tune and others, gets students hooked on theater at an early age.

Speaking of addictions, Austin—and most of the country, it seems—has developed a taste for Tuna. The crazy-quilt of characters that inhabit the fictional Tuna (Texas's third-smallest town) come to comic life onstage through actors Joe Sears and Jaston Williams, the Austinites who cowrote (with Ed Howard) *Greater Tuna* and its spin-offs. *Greater Tuna,* an Off-Broadway hit in the early 1980s, was followed by *A Tuna Christmas* and *Red, White and Tuna.* Quick-change artists Sears and Williams perform the parts of more than two dozen characters—male and female—in their fictional town of Smut Snatchers and hanging judges. *Greater Tuna,* presented in touring versions around the country, in an HBO production, in command performances at the White House, and in theaters all over the United States, has placed Austin on the national theatrical map.

What Tuna is to theater, *Slacker* is to film. This 1991 low-budget film by Austinite Richard Linklater made a bundle when it was released nationally and proved to the country that Austin has what it takes to make movies. A year later, Austin's Robert Rodriguez hit it big with *El Mariachi.* Since those films debuted, Austin filmmaking has jelled into an industry. The various film festivals now held throughout the year, including the venerable SXSW festival, are one testament to Austin's dynamic movie-making scene.

Meanwhile, Austin's large and small theater companies, visual artists, cutting-edge dancers, and performance artists are doing their parts to shake up the arts world, not just locally. Austin's rapid artistic development has not come without speed bumps. While small warehouse-type theaters/ galleries were popping up all over, Austin still cried out for large state-of-the art venues to host both local and national productions. In response, a dedicated team of arts patrons mounted a $77 million private fund-raising campaign to convert the old Palmer Auditorium on the south shore of Lady Bird Lake into a world-class facility. Renamed the Joe R. Long and Teresa Lozano Long Center for the Performing Arts—the Long Center for short—it now complements the city's other large venues, including the lavishly renovated Bass Concert Hall on the UT campus. Austin will always need more performance space, but with the opening of The Long Center and other facilities around town, things are looking up. This chapter presents the Austin art scene on center stage—and the curtain is rising.

PERFORMING ARTS

Theater

When William Shakespeare wrote that "all the world's a stage," he might have been looking into the future at Austin. With more than 250 different shows a year produced by both national touring companies and the dozens of local troupes that perform at varying intervals, it often seems as though the whole city has been bitten by the bug. Check the local theater listings if you're in doubt. Many times, theater patrons have the luxury of choosing from as many as two dozen productions—at once.

Austin does theater in a variety of ways: blockbuster Broadway and Off-Broadway shows like 2010's *Shrek the Musical* at UT's Bass Concert Hall and *Celebrity Autobiography* at the Long Center; popular performances by the wacky Tuna guys at the Paramount; and the ambitiousness of a locally produced *Rent* at Zach Theatre. There also are lots of experimental shows staged in small converted warehouses, delightful productions geared toward kids, bilingual comedies and dramas, and performances celebrating the Bard himself on an outdoor stage.

Austin also is becoming increasingly known as an incubator of playwrights, many of them qualifying as finalists for the Actors Theatre of Louisville's Heideman Award, a prize given for the best play submitted to ATL's National Ten-Minute Play Contest. In fact, an Austinite has won the prize in the past. Each of these writers came out of the dynamic, locally founded organization Script-Works (www.scriptworks.org), which offers services to playwrights across the country at every stage of project development.

While theater can pop up in just about any nook and cranny around the city, we've identified Austin's main performance stages and theater troupes here. The stages are divided into three categories: The Main Stages are the city's larger, cushier, most formal theaters; The Outdoor Stage presents Austin's natural amphitheater; and The Small Stages highlight vintage buildings and warehouses that have been converted into performance spaces. Additionally, we have a category called The Gypsies, which includes our favorite theater troupes that perform anywhere they can find a space. Keep in mind that theater is fluid here in Austin, so those troupes we've associated with a particular stage may perform in other locations as well.

This list will direct you to some of the best and most interesting theater Austin offers. For even more theater, check out the lineup at Austin's colleges and universities. The Austin Circle of Theaters (see Arts Organizations in this chapter) calculates there are about 80 theater companies in the city. Some present works occasionally, while others, as you'll see here, are busy all the time.

We may all be actors on the stage of life, as Shakespeare suggested, but those who choose the theater as their life make it so much more interesting for the rest of us—as we like it.

The Main Stages
CEDAR PARK CENTER
2100 Avenue of the Stars, Cedar Park
(512) 600-5000
www.cedarparkcenter.com
They play professional hockey and basketball here (see the Sports chapter), so this ultra-modern space seats thousands! However, since its opening in the fall of 2009 the Cedar Park Center has also hosted a nice variety of musical and theatrical shows, including the children's production *Yo Gabba Gabba Live!*, comedian George Lopez, and 2011's *Cirque du Soleil: Dralion*. On the northern outskirts of Austin, Cedar Park is a hop, skip away, and this gorgeous facility is another reason to visit.

✳THE LONG CENTER
701 West Riverside Dr.
(512) 457-5100
www.thelongcenter.org
A 15-year-effort to bring another world-class performing arts center to Austin paid off in 2008 with the grand opening of The Joe R. Long and Teresa Lozano Long Center for the Performing Arts, known as the Long Center. Located on beautiful Auditorium Shores on Lady Bird Lake, the center is the performance venue for Ballet Austin, the Austin Lyric Opera, and the Austin Symphony. Additionally, it presents an eclectic mix of both local and nationally known

artistic performers—everything from Broadway-style shows to musical acts to children's theater and much more.

The center features the 2,400-seat state-of-the-art Dell Hall, whose acoustics can be arranged to maximize the effect of each performance. It also has the smaller black-box-style Rollins Studio Theatre, also acoustically excellent, which can be arranged to seat anywhere from 80 people in a cabaret-style configuration, to 232 people in a theater-in-the-round design.

While Dell Hall is a sight to behold, one of the main attractions at The Long Center is the spectacular view of the shores, the lake, and the downtown Austin skyline. Lobbies on either side of Dell Hall, one glass-enclosed and one open-air, were designed to maximize the view. The center not only sits on the site of a long-time Austin icon, the former Palmer Auditorium, its construction actually incorporates about 65 percent of the old Palmer, including its columns, its distinctive ring shapes and, most notably, the green, brown and beige metal tiles that adorned Palmer's roof. (Some of the hail-dented tiles are used as decorative accents inside the new building).

The center is operated by a nonprofit arts organization, which raised $77 million from more than 4,000 Austin donors to get this newest Austin icon up and running.

ONE WORLD THEATRE
7701 Bee Cave Rd.
(512) 330-9500
www.oneworldtheatre.org
It was originally intended to be a mansion in West Austin, but it took a musician who was dubbed "a California dreamer" by the *Austin American-Statesman* to turn it into a wonderful performing arts center, which specializes in world-class musical performances by artists from around the globe Founder and Executive Director Hartt Stearns runs the nonprofit theater, which also has a hugely popular program for schoolchildren.

One World Theatre is a modern, Italianate structure that is an eye-grabber along Bee Cave Road. From its verandas visitors can look out over the Hill Country and the burgeoning upscale neighborhood. Inside, the 300-seat auditorium wraps around the stage, offering the audience close-up, intimate views of the performers. The eclectic offerings in past seasons have included Russian ballet stars, Tibetan monks, world-famous classical guitarists, the top names in chamber music, popular contemporary music stars, rock groups, and jazz legends. Stearns, a percussionist who toured for 14 years with the acclaimed Argentine band Arco Iris, often performs at the venue, as does his wife, Nada, a singer and pianist.

✳PARAMOUNT THEATRE
713 Congress Ave.
(512) 472-5470
www.austintheatre.org
On a stage once graced by the Ziegfeld Follies, Helen Hayes, George M. Cohan, John Philip Sousa, the Marx Brothers, and more of history's great performers, the Paramount Theatre presents top artists from Austin and around the country. Built in 1915 as the Majestic Theatre, a vaudeville house that presented variety acts, this elegantly restored venue was designed by one of the most respected theater architects in the United States, John Eberson of Chicago. This is one of the few theaters left in the country that showed the movie *Casablanca* when it was originally released more than half a century ago.

Now listed on the National Register of Historic Places, the Paramount itself is one of the city's main attractions. In 2010 votes from loyal patrons placed the Paramount first in a nationwide competition sponsored by the National Trust for Historic Preservation. The $25,000 prize in the "This Place Matters Community Challenge" will go toward preserving this Austin jewel.

And the attractions onstage are just as inspiring as the venue. The Paramount, which seats nearly 1,300, is active most nights, bringing live theater, dance, music, comedy, and film to audiences of all ages. This is where Austin's own blockbuster live comedy *Greater Tuna* got its start and where the two Tuna sequels packed the house. *A Tuna Christmas*, one of the sequels, continues to draw crowds during the holidays. Other recent hits include the 2010 premiere of Austin director Robert Rodriguez's film *Machete*, and performances by recording artists Chris Isaak and Lyle Lovett and his Large Band.

i Stargazing, and we don't mean through telescopes, is alive and well in Austin—for good reason. Several A-List personalities, including Academy Award-winner Sandra Bullock and director Robert Rodriguez, call Austin home. Many others stop by for film festivals or other events. The lobbies of the Four Seasons or new W Austin hotels are good places to "gaze."

RIVERBEND CENTRE
4214 North Capital of Texas Hwy.
(512) 327-9416
www.riverbendcentre.com
Musical and theatrical stars performing in a house of prayer? Well, yes. This elegant

2,300-seat venue in one of Austin's most picturesque settings has drawn acts like bluegrass singer Alison Krauss, pop star Kenny Loggins, and the Austin Symphony Orchestra. Built in 1998 as the Riverbend (Baptist) Church's "Home for Hope," the hall is one of Austin's largest performing arts venues, although it has a limited performance schedule. Check the website for listings.

TEXAS PERFORMING ARTS
Bass Concert Hall, Twenty-third Street and East Campus Drive
(512) 471-2787
www.texasperformingarts.org
We've said it before, and we'll say it again. Being home to one of the country's largest universities has many advantages. Texas Performing Arts (formerly the Performing Arts Center), is one of the biggies. This huge network of theaters, studios, rehearsal halls, and classrooms spreads to several campus locations. At the heart of the system is Bass Concert Hall at 23rd and East Campus Drive.

This immense structure, which houses two theaters as well as rehearsal halls, offices, and massive support facilities, is one of the finest performing arts centers in the United States. Bass, UT's flagship theater, is a 3,000-seat auditorium with an orchestra pit that can accommodate even the largest musical group. Some of the finest touring artists and companies in the country have performed at Bass. Big Broadway touring shows in the recent past have included *Mamma Mia* and *Shrek the Musical*. Bass, which reopened in 2009 after an 18-month $14.7 million renovation, has state-of-the-art acoustics, an expanded atrium area, improved lighting, and restaurant space for patron dining. Also in this complex is the McCollough Theatre, which seats 400 people and is used by both professional and student performers.

Many people tend to think of the Texas Performing Arts as the Bass complex alone. In fact, there's much more. The complex also includes Bates Recital Hall in the Music Building adjacent to Bass. The recital hall is a 700-seat theater designed for acoustic excellence and equipped with a 3-story pipe organ. This theater hosts musical performances by some of the best virtuoso performers of the day, as well as leading names in jazz, chamber and organ music, and more.

Other theaters around campus are the B. Iden Payne Theatre, a 500-seat facility used for both professional events and student theatrical productions, and Hogg Auditorium, a recently reintroduced theater that's almost as large as the Paramount and is also used for both professional and student events. A few smaller theaters and a dance studio complete the system.

While Texas Performing Arts is perhaps most known to the public at large for the world-class events it presents, we can't fail to mention the quality and range of many student productions offered at some of these theaters throughout the school year. UT students of theater, dance, film, and music present shows that are definitely worthwhile for any fan of the performing arts.

✳ZACH THEATRE
1510 Toomey Rd.
(512) 476-0541
www.zachtheatre.org
Home of one of Austin's most exciting and innovative professional theater companies, Zach Theatre has been wowing Austin audiences for years with its broad spectrum of plays and musicals, including many performed for the first time by a regional theater in the United States. Additionally, Zach has given Austin audiences wildly popular revues such as *Beehive,* as well as *Shear Madness,* the longest-running play in Austin history. Zach, Central Texas's oldest resident theater, began in 1933 when it was incorporated as the Austin Civic Theatre. The theater was renamed in 1972 in honor of Zachary Scott, an Austin-raised actor who went on to a successful Hollywood film career.

Zach presents 8 to 10 productions during its yearlong season that runs from Sept through Aug on both stages—the 230-seat main Kleberg Stage and the 130-seat Whisenhunt Arena Stage. Several of Zach's shows have been so popular that the company has needed to rent Austin's larger Paramount Theatre to accommodate the huge audiences. But, in 2011, Zach launched a $22 million fundraising campaign to complete construction on its new 420-seat Topfer Theatre by 2012. Theater buffs should include a visit to Zach on any tour of Austin.

The Outdoor Stage
✳ZILKER HILLSIDE THEATER
2206 William Barton Dr.
(512) 477-5335
www.ci.austin.tx.us/zilker/hillside.htm
Casual outdoor free arts! What better tribute to Austin than this great venue on a natural grassy amphitheater that hosts some of the city's most anticipated free shows. Start with the annual Zilker Summer Musical, an Austin tradition for half a century. This big, splashy show draws more than 2,000 people a night to Zilker Park for some of the best outdoor performances Austin offers. Another outstanding event, Austin Shakespeare's 4-week engagement of an excitingly staged and costumed Shakespeare play, also attracts huge audiences. You don't have to wait for

an annual event to experience this great Austin theater, however. Bring a blanket and a picnic basket and enjoy the outdoors while watching any number of dance, musical, or theatrical events held in this comfy spot near Barton Springs Pool. All events are free, but there is a small charge for parking. No reservations are required although rules about drinking, smoking, and seating are enforced, so check the website before heading out to the theater.

The Small Stages
AUSTIN PLAYHOUSE
3601 South Congress Ave., Building C
(512) 476-0084
www.austinplayhouse.com
Home to the award-winning Austin Playhouse Acting Company, this facility is located in the sensitively redeveloped Penn Field complex off South Congress Avenue. Built in 1914 at a flight training center for the Army Air Corps, the building reopened as a 150-seat theater in 2002. Two years later a second stage was added, the 70-seat Larry L. King Theatre. The year-round lineup has included original plays, including *Travesties* by Austin playwright Tom Stoppard and Dug Up by Austinite Cyndi Williams, as well as such perennial favorites as *Kiss Me Kate* and 2011's *The Importance of Being Earnest*.

BLUE THEATER
916 Springdale Rd.
(512) 684-3220
www.bluetheatre.org
A former truck shop built in the 1950s, this 99-seat facility is located in a warehouse complex in East Austin. It opened as an arts venue in 2000 to offer theatrical productions, visual art, dance, music, and film. Recent productions include Civil War Blues—"a blue's

song for today's hard times"—by local alternative group No Direction Productions.

CITY THEATRE
3823 Airport Blvd., Suite D
(512) 524-2870
www.citytheatreaustin.org
City Theatre Company wasted no time catching the public's—and the critics'—eye when it first appeared on the scene a few years ago. It has won rave reviews and several local theater awards with productions such as *Parallel Lives*, *The Boys Next Door*, and, more recently, *A Raisin in the Sun* and *How the Other Half Lives*. Operating out of this venue in East Austin, City Theatre is also one of the most ambitious companies around, opening a new production within days of closing another. It presents classics such as *Death of a Salesman* and *The Taming of the Shrew*, as well as dramas from the likes of Neil Labute and Tom Stoppard. Its season also includes summer productions aimed at kids.

COLD TOWNE THEATER
4803 Airport Blvd., Suite B
(512) 524-2807
www.coldtownetheater.com
Tragedy in the form of 2005's Hurricane Katrina brought members of this exciting comedy improv troupe from New Orleans to Austin. Since the group's founding, Cold Towne has won a bundle of impressive awards, including the B. Iden Payne Award for Outstanding Improv Ensemble, *Chronicle* Readers' Poll awards for Best Comedy Troupe, Frontera Fest—Best of Week, and the O. Henry Pun-Off World Championship. All forms of comedy are performed at the theater, including improv, sketch, and stand-up. Check the website for the current schedule of events. The Cold Towne Conservatory also

offers sketch-writing classes. In its short existence here, the troupe has grown so much it's hoping to raise enough cash to move into a new, larger space. Check the website for updates.

DOUGHERTY ARTS CENTER THEATER
1110 Barton Springs Rd.
(512) 974-4000
www.ci.austin.tx.us/dougherty
Built in the 1940s as a Naval and Marine Reserve Center, this wonderful facility was taken over by the Austin Parks and Recreation Department in 1978 and turned into one of the busiest arts venues in town. (The center includes a 1,800-square-foot art gallery, classrooms, and plenty of studio-lab spaces.) Not nearly as large as the Main Stages listed above, the theater at Dougherty Arts Center nonetheless seats 150 people quite comfortably, and is always hosting one show or another. Austin's Ballet East Dance Theatre performs here, as do a host of other local theater, dance, and musical groups. Because this is a city-run facility, admission prices to the shows are often very reasonable.

ESTHER'S FOLLIES
525 East Sixth St.
(512) 320-0553
www.esthersfollies.com
They call themselves "Texas's premier magic and comedy troupe," and we can't argue with that. We've taken more than one out-of-town guest to see Esther's Follies' great performances, which combines some classic routines with constantly updated political satire. The follies can be found in a converted 1800s-era building on Austin's historic East Sixth Street. Read more about this laugh-

a-minute riot of a comedy show in the Nightlife chapter.

HYDE PARK THEATRE
511 West Forty-third St.
(512) 479-7529,
www.hydeparktheatre.org
Since its founding in 1992, Hyde Park Theatre has grown into one of Austin's most well-respected and popular small troupes, presenting bold alternative works by both Austin artists and others from around the country, including several world premiere events each season. Hyde Park also runs the largest and most intriguing fringe performance festival in the Southwest: FronteraFest. This annual 5-week festival, held in Jan and Feb, provides a venue for hundreds of high-caliber local, regional, and national artists who present nearly 100 separate acts (see the Annual Events & Festivals chapter). In addition to producing its own shows, Hyde Park Theatre also serves as a performance venue for some Austin gypsy troupes and fringe artists.

THE OFF CENTER
2211–A Hidalgo St.
(512) 476-7833
www.rudemechs.com
This 93-seat theater in a converted feed store presents shows by one of the city's most "Austin-tacious" theater troupes: Rude Mechanicals. Founded in 1995, Rude Mechs has become one of Austin's most renowned and original companies and is known for its enormously creative—and brave—theatrical vision. The company received national attention and acclaim for its stage adaptation of *Lipstick Traces,* which played in New York and other American cities. A longtime favorite among Austin theater buffs, Rude

Mechanicals was featured in the *New York Times* as one of three companies in the country "making theatre that matters." The group also manages The Off Center.

SALVAGE VANGUARD THEATER
2803 Manor Rd.
(512) 474-7886
www.salvagevanguard.org
This theater's resident company, Salvage Vanguard, is an exciting experimental group that has earned a reputation for presenting hot new writers to Austin in shows that, in recent seasons, were paired with a local band—so music fans no longer have to miss out on an interesting theater experience. Catering to Austin's hip crowd, Salvage Vanguard is known for performances that rock the ceiling. The theater also presents works by other Austin gypsy troupes, including the acclaimed Trouble Puppet Theater Co. and Gnap Theater Projects. The 100-seat facility is in East Austin.

SANTA CRUZ CENTER FOR CULTURE
1805 East Seventh St.
(512) 524-4278
This established cultural center is home to Austin's well-respected Aztlan Dance Company (see the Dance listing in this chapter) as well as the ProArts Collective and Proyecto Teatro. The theater, which opened in 1988 in a converted WWI-era warehouse, seats 120 people and has become a center for both well-established and up-and-coming Latino arts projects on the East Side.

TEXARTS THEATER
Morris Theater, 2300 Lohman's Spur
(512) 852-9079
www.tex-arts.org

Founded in 2005 TexARTS has had its ups and downs, but it has remained true to its mission of producing classic, Broadway-quality musicals and other high-caliber shows for Austin-area audiences. The group got its feet wet with well-received productions of *The Music Man, Big River, Carousel,* and others at the Paramount Theatre. TexARTS has since moved out to a Lakeway strip mall near Lake Travis, opening Keller Williams Studios and its main performance venue, the 99-seat Morris Theater. TexARTS also offers an Off-Broadway Series, which has presented *Always . . . Patsy Cline,* and a Cabaret Series, which included a performance by Shirley Jones at the Riverbend Centre.

THE VORTEX
2307 Manor Rd.
(512) 478-5282,
www.vortexrep.org
Home to Austin's Vortex Repertory Company since 1994, the Vortex has become the place to go to see original cutting-edge performances that have included *Wisdom of the Crone,* conceived and directed by producing artistic director and Vortex founder Bonnie Cullum. Among the leaders of Austin's alternative theater scene, Vortex has produced scores of successful works since it was founded in 1988. World premieres, new plays, Texas premieres, and vibrant works by Shakespeare have all been presented on the Vortex stage. This East Austin theater, a once-abandoned warehouse that has been converted to an intimate 90-seat venue with comfortable theater seats, is used by other individual performers and theatrical companies for shows of all kinds. Vortex presents several major productions a year as well as a number of smaller performances that showcase this company's talents. Vortex also has

earned a reputation in Austin for presenting shows by nationally known performance artists.

The Gypsies
AUSTIN SHAKESPEARE
701 Tillery St., #9
www.austinshakespeare.org
Mention Austin Shakespeare around these parts and folks will immediately think of the wonderful free outdoor Shakespeare plays produced annually for the past two decades at the Zilker Hillside Theatre. Austin Shakespeare also presents shows indoors, including *The Tempest* at The Long Center's Rollins Studio Theatre. Shakespeare aficionados might want to attend the company's weekly "Shakespeare Aloud," a reading of the Bard's works.

DIFFERENT STAGES
(512) 454-TIXS
www.main.org/diffstages
Launched in 1980, Different Stages is a community theater company that produces works by playwrights who are defining forces in theater: Moliére, Shakespeare, Shaw, and O'Neill, to name a few. The company also has been the first to introduce Austin to new playwrights and has produced original works by Austin playwrights Ann Ciccolella and Tom White. Under the artistic directorship of Norman Blumensaadt, the company has presented dozens of plays, including romantic, neoclassic, realistic, and surrealistic. The company's actors and productions have won a variety of Austin's prestigious B. Iden Payne awards. Different Stages presents a full season of performances, most often at the Austin Playhouse or the Vortex. Last we heard, the company was raising funds for a permanent home.

DANCE & MUSIC

More and more Austin audiences are getting the "pointe" about Austin's rich dance scene, which includes a number of established companies and even more individual dancers and choreographers who bring their unique styles to stages all over the city. In addition to the dance companies we've listed here, be sure to look for special performances by troupes formed for a specific production. Austin dancers offer a wonderful cross section of styles, including classical ballet, tap, modern, postmodern, and folklorico. Austin's main dance organization, Dance Umbrella, also sponsors dance and performance-art shows throughout the year by Austin talent as well as nationally and internationally known performers (see the Arts Organizations listing in this chapter).

Whether you like a toe-tapping good time, the skirt-swirling grandeur of a Mexican folk dance, the awesome power and grace of a dancer on pointe, or the stylized foot- and bodywork of modern dance, you'll be inspired by Austin's dance performances.

While Texas's mecca for classical music artists is about 70 miles east of Austin in Round Top (see the Day Trips chapter), you'll be pleased to know that you don't have to travel to hear exciting ensembles. In fact, in 2003 Austin's classical music scene took a giant leap forward when the University of Texas snagged highly coveted string ensemble the Miró Quartet (www.miroquartet.com) as its resident quartet. This internationally renowned foursome performs for the public at large. Additionally, Austin claims about two dozen classical music groups, about half choral, half instrumental. The two mentioned here are among Austin's leaders, but look, too, for outstanding performances by the Austin Choral Union, the Austin Vocal

Arts Ensemble, River City Pops, the Austin Lyric Opera Chorus, and the Texas Chamber Consort. Those interested in performing will discover that these and many other musical groups, including barbershop and gospel choruses, accept new members by audition. Austin also claims several groups for children.

The classical guitar scene is also alive and well in Austin and has attracted enough outstanding guitarists to maintain the Austin Classical Guitar Society. The only nationally syndicated classical guitar program is produced right here in Austin and airs out of radio station KMFA. The crème de la crème of Austin's classical guitarists is world-class player and recording artist Adam Holzman (www.adamholzman.com). This virtuoso, who plays recital halls throughout the world, including Carnegie Hall, has won many prestigious international guitar competitions and has created UT's classical guitar program. In a music city dominated by singer/songwriters and rock 'n' rollers blasting chords through amplifiers, Holzman is the artist the *Austin American-Statesman* has called "the best guitar player in Austin you've never heard of."

Dance

AZTLAN DANCE COMPANY
Santa Cruz Center,
1805 East Seventh St.
(512) 524-4278
www.aztlandance.com
Both the critics and the public are raving about this dance company, which combines original contemporary choreography with traditional Latino folk steps, often set to the music of popular Latino recording artists. Founded in 1974, this company for many years performed mainly the classic regional folk dances of Mexico. In the past few years,

however, choreographer and general director Roen Salinas has introduced a modern format that reflects the danza folklorico heritage but addresses the Hispanic culture of today's Texas. Instead of the flamboyant costumes typical of some regional dances of Mexico, for example, Aztlan dancers have worn blue jeans and T-shirts while dancing to the music of Los Lobos.

Aztlan still does Mexican folk dances, and does them extremely well, but this new choreography adds an exciting artistic dimension to the troupe. The company is based at East Austin's Santa Cruz Center but also performs at the Paramount and the Bass Concert Hall. Aztlan also has performed at venues all over the country and in Hong Kong and Great Britain. Academia Aztlan, which aims to promote a greater understanding of the Hispanic cultural arts, offers dance classes, workshops, lectures, art exhibits, and more at the Santa Cruz Center and elsewhere in Austin.

✳BALLET AUSTIN
501 West Third St.
(512) 476-9151
www.balletaustin.com
Austin's premier classical ballet troupe has soared to new heights since 2000, when Stephen Mills stepped up as artistic director. Mills, who has been with the organization since 1987 as dancer, choreographer, and associate artistic director, received rave reviews and attention from across the country for his world-premiere production of *Hamlet* during his first year as director. In 2002 the company performed sold-out shows of *A Midsummer Night's Dream* at the Kennedy Center in Washington, D.C. Mills's national and international accomplishments as both a dancer and a choreographer are

Close-up

First Thursday: SoCo's Monthly Celebration

Live music, beer gardens, casual dining, shopping—and free hugs! Those are just a few of the attractions at the increasingly popular First Thurs event in the trendy SoCo district of South Congress Avenue from about the 1200 block to the 1800 block. On the evenings of the first Thurs of each month, district merchants keep their doors open until 10 p.m. (or later), many of them hosting special events or activities, while outdoor marketeers offer their wide assortment of handicrafts and other goods in several spots along the strip.

The focus here is on dining, shopping and services—and why not? Few other strips offer the eclectic assortment of choices available on South Congress. Visitors can find new, designer clothes as well as vintage apparel, costume rentals, hair salons, toys and candies, antiques, art galleries, fine jewelry, home furnishings, international imports and much more. There is even Allens Boots, a whole store dedicated to cowboy boots and Western wear, as well as an Amy's Ice Creams shop, and Austin's famous Continental Club live music venue (which really gets going after the festivities).

This is not a rollicking street party like that which occurs regularly on Sixth Street because alcoholic drinks are served only in the restaurants and beer gardens, but it is a lively event nonetheless, with plenty of live music under the stars. It's no wonder the event is popular with the old and young alike: singles, families, groups of friends, and couples. There even are more than a dozen college-age kids offering free hugs—and each one is most warmly received. While you are here, take a moment to check out the roof at Lucy in Disguise with Diamonds (in the 1500 block) to enjoy a piece of Austin's landmark art, a giant zebra dressed as Carmen Miranda—complete with Carmen's iconic fruit-filled headpiece!

This also is a perfect place to find Austin originals, from the "Keep Austin Weird" T-shirts and mugs, (as well as the alternative "Keep Austin Batty," a tribute to the local bat population) to handcrafted jewelry, candles and soaps, as well as photographs of Austin scenes. SoCo also offers an assortment of restaurants, including the extremely popular Güero's Taco Bar and El Sol y La Luna restaurant (see the Restaurants chapter). Beyond those two, there is Doc's MotorWorks Bar & Grill, which features a large outdoor patio, as well as hamburger and pizza joints, an outdoor coffee shop, Japanese fast food, and more.

Parking is available right on South Congress, but those spots fill up quickly. The best bet is to park in the free lot at One Texas Center (505 Barton Springs Rd.) and then grab the free orange 'Dillo trolley car that runs all evening. For information on the event, and the SoCo merchants, see the website at www.firstthursday.info.

astounding. Under his leadership Ballet Austin is becoming one of the nation's finest developing ballet organizations.

Ballet Austin presents five seasonal ballets, including the much anticipated annual performances of *The Nutcracker* in December. Other Austin favorites have included performances of *Firebird*, *Ulysses*, and *Cinderella*. This accomplished company traces its roots to 1956, when it was chartered as the

Austin Ballet Society. Over the years, the ballet evolved from a civic, all-volunteer group to become a professional organization.

One major aspect of this company is the Ballet Austin Academy, also established in 1956, which offers classical ballet training as well as jazz, modern dance, and fitness classes to dancers from age 3 to adult. Ballet Austin II, an apprentice program, provides professional development for the 10-member second company. Ballet Austin's performances are held at The Long Center on West Riverside Drive. The company also offers full-length and mixed-repertoire performances throughout Texas. This community-based company goes all out to educate school students and adults alike. The season runs from Oct to May.

BALLET EAST DANCE COMPANY
3111 Garwood St.
(512) 385-2838
www.balleteast.org

Founded by Rodolfo Mendez in 1982, Ballet East is a well-known community dance troupe made up of professional and emerging dancers and choreographers from many ethnic backgrounds. The company in residence in East Austin has a solid reputation for developing young dancers and for showcasing the talents of some of Austin's finest dancers and choreographers, including Toni Bravo, Andrea Ariel, and Melissa Villarreal. The company also works with guest choreographers from nationally known companies, including the Alvin Ailey American Dance School in New York and the Joyce Trisler Danscompany. Ballet East, which most often offers mixed repertoire programs, performs several times a year at various locations in Austin, most often at the Dougherty Arts Center.

BLUE LAPIS LIGHT
P.O. Box 1821, Austin 78767
(512) 288-1929
www.bluelapislight.org

Choreographer and performer Sally Jacques is the creative mastermind behind some of the most spellbinding and offbeat dance/performance art productions around these parts. She creates site-specific aerial dance performances, meaning that one production is developed for, say, a temporary construction scaffolding while another is developed for an airport hangar, and another for Barton Creek, and so on. A native of England, Jacques has received many Austin awards as well as important grants in recognition of her work, including those from the National Endowment for the Arts, Art Matters of New York City, and the Texas Commission on the Arts.

DEBORAH HAY DANCE COMPANY
1703 Alta Vista Ave.
www.deborahhay.com

World-renowned and multi-award-winning dancer, choreographer, writer, and teacher, Deborah Hay is Austin's dance elite. Unfortunately for local audiences, that means she spends *a great deal of time* performing around the globe. An experimental dancer whose work is not easily pegged (one reviewer called it a "moment-to-moment process of creating movement"), Hay did stop home for a sold-out performance at The Long Center. UT's Center for Gender and Women's Studies hosted a symposium attended by an international audience of performers, choreographers, dance critics, and producers to discuss and highlight Hays's contributions to the world of dance. This is one act to catch—if you can.

KATHY DUNN HAMRICK DANCE COMPANY

P.O. Box 160432, Austin 78716
(512) 934-1082
www.kdhdance.com

This modern dance company has dazzled Austin audiences and critics since its first performance more than a decade ago. *So Close*, performed with dancers moving behind, in front of, and through the audience, was named one of the Top Ten Dance Events of the year by the *Austin Chronicle*. It's no surprise, then, that the company and its founder/artistic director/dancer/choreographer Kathy Dunn Hamrick have won plenty more awards and accolades. Dunn Hamrick, a UT graduate, creates imaginative dances often accompanied by live musical ensembles.

TAPESTRY DANCE COMPANY

2302 Western Trails Blvd.
(512) 474-9846
www.tapestry.org

Founded in 1989 by rhythm tap dancer Acia Gray and ballet/jazz artist Deirdre Strand, Tapestry is an acclaimed multiform dance company that has delighted audiences all over Austin and in other parts of the country during the company's national performance tours. This professional company presents seasonal multiform concerts at various venues around town, including The Long Center and Salvage Vanguard Theatre. and has thrilled Austin audiences by hosting a number of international dance and musical artists. Tapestry's annual Soul to Sole Tap Festival brings the world's finest rhythm tap artists to Austin for tap jams, concerts, film screenings, and more. The company also operates a pre-professional program and a downtown dance academy that offers classes for children and adults in rhythm tap, jazz, and ballet. Tapestry is also known for hosting numerous ethnic and cultural events, including Irish step dancing, clogging, and tango.

Music

✳AUSTIN LYRIC OPERA

901 Barton Springs Rd.
(512) 472-5927
www.austinlyricopera.org

Since its founding in 1986, Austin Lyric Opera has grown dramatically to a seasonal attendance in the tens of thousands, an outstanding record for a city the size of Austin. The company, led by internationally renowned conductor Richard Buckley, is known for presenting both the most popular of the operatic repertoire as well as works that explore the boundaries of opera, including *The Ballad of Baby Doe,* the company's first American work. Central Texas's only professional opera company brings major international and American artists to Austin each season, and the results have included many world-class performances. *La Traviata* and *La Bohème* are just two of the performances that have highlighted past seasons. The company also has teamed up with the gang at Esther's Follies for a comedic, all-Austin version of Johann Strauss's *Die Fledermaus.* All main-stage performances are held at The Long Center.

Opera attendance is on the rise nationwide, and one of the reasons is the use of supertitles, the simultaneous translation into English of the opera on a small screen above the stage. Patrons of Austin Lyric Opera and of operas throughout the country no longer have to speak a foreign language to understand the story. Austin Lyric Opera has its own 65-member orchestra and a 60-member semiprofessional chorus.

The Opera has opened a modern facility, the Armstrong Community Music School at Barton Springs Road, which houses a recital hall, a multimedia lab, classrooms, and teaching studios.

✳AUSTIN SYMPHONY ORCHESTRA
1101 Red River St.
(512) 476-6064
www.austinsymphony.org

Austin's oldest performing arts group, the Austin Symphony Orchestra was founded in 1911. In 1998 American Peter Bay arrived in Austin as the symphony's conductor and music director, following a 2-year search for the perfect conductor to lead the orchestra to new artistic challenges and to expand its audience even further in Austin. Bay, especially known for his skill at conducting large contemporary scores and complex pieces, has introduced more works of American composers and thematic programs, including music from film scores, to the orchestra's extensive repertoire of classical music. In 2003 the symphony performed with famous singing group the 5th Dimension. The orchestra also presented concerts commemorating President John F. Kennedy on the 40th anniversary of his assassination. The performance of *JFK: The Voice of Peace* (a work by local composer Dan Welcher) was narrated by ABC News's Hugh Downs and accompanied by the symphony.

The Austin Symphony Orchestra, which performs its classical series Sept through May at The Long Center, also presents festive pops concerts, as well as the annual Halloween Children's Concert, for which the entire family is invited to come dressed in costume. Another annual tradition is the presentation in Dec of Handel's *Messiah*.

CHORUS AUSTIN
(512) 719-3300
www.chorusaustin.org

Chorus Austin is the umbrella organization for two of the city's most popular choral groups: Austin Civic Chorus and Austin Vocal Arts Ensemble. Founded in 1965 with just 32 singers, Austin Civic Chorus today has up to 140 voices ranging from high school students to senior citizens. This excellent chorus performs several major choral/orchestral masterpieces a year for huge audiences from all over Central Texas and is often a featured chorus with the Austin Symphony Orchestra. Past performances have included *Songs of the American People* and Beethoven's *Mass in C*. The Civic Chorus also has performed *The Passion According to St. John* by Bach and works from many other masters. One major highlight of the year is the annual Sing-It-Yourself Messiah in December, a holiday tradition for hundreds of Austin families.

The Austin Vocal Arts Ensemble is a chamber chorus of 40 singers that performs to music or a capella. The ensemble's repertoire ranges in style from Renaissance to contemporary. The groups most often perform in churches around the area.

✳CONSPIRARE
1033 La Posada Dr., Suite 130
(512) 476-5775
www.conspirare.org

Since its founding in 1991, Conspirare has developed into a world-class, Grammy-nominated ensemble known for its entertaining, innovative, and varied vocal music concerts. This professional chorus and orchestra specializes in music for the human voice. Conspirare has never been known to limit itself to just one genre. Choral, classical, jazz, ethnic, experimental, Broadway, old masterworks, and contemporary compositions are all presented by this company, which the *Austin American-Statesman* recently called "Austin's most original classical music group." Founded as New Texas Festival by renowned conductor Craig Hella Johnson, Conspirare started out as an annual weeklong series of vocal music performances. Now the choir performs concerts throughout the year, including the annual "Christmas at the Carillon" show performed in a historic chapel in West Austin.

THE VISUAL ARTS

We can think of few better ways to spend an afternoon or a whole day than by visiting some of Austin's exceptional art museums and galleries. Access to the master artists of the past and present, including celebrated Austin and Texas artists, couldn't be easier. Austin offers two significant museums dedicated to the works of eminent sculptors Elisabet Ney and Charles Umlauf, who both lived and worked in Austin until their deaths. The gallery scene offers an excellent opportunity to view works by both established and emerging artists. There's always a chance you'll come face to face with the artists themselves, either working or simply enjoying the company of people like yourself who've come for the experience. You may return home with an art treasure that will delight you for years to come, or perhaps turn out to be a shrewd investment. At the very least, we guarantee you'll be enlightened. Austin seems dominated by so many "alternative" galleries that the term has lost its meaning to a certain extent. Alternative to what? we might ask. Prepare yourself for the unusual.

Austin still has not achieved the status of Dallas and Houston as a major hub for art buyers, but what it lacks in patrons is more than made up by a dynamic artistic community. Austin has several artists whose work is recognized, and coveted, far beyond the state's borders. What better way to become acquainted with these talented visionaries, as well as the city's many emerging artists, than by seeing exhibits of their work on their home turf. You'll be astounded by the range of styles and the diverse media on display by the painters, sculptors, photographers, and fine crafters working in Austin today.

Austin also is distinguished for producing fine arts prints. Master printmaker Sam Coronado, Flatbed Press, and Slugfest are leading the way in that arena. Austin's galleries are not limited to Austin-based artists, however. Among the galleries we've listed below you'll find work by some of the most interesting and well-known artists in the country today.

> **i** In recent years a huge community of artists has sprung up just east of I-35 from the Cesar Chavez Street area up to around $38\frac{1}{2}$ Street. The best way to see the more than 100 artist studios in this area is to take part in the annual East Austin Studio Tour (E.A.S.T.) event, held over two weekends in the fall. For details click www.eastaustinstudiotour.com.

Don't let the idea of visiting a museum or gallery intimidate you, even if you're not an art expert. Austin's showrooms are staffed by knowledgeable, accessible experts, sometimes artists themselves, who are more than willing to offer on-the-spot advice, tips, and information about the artists and their works. Those of you who want to extend your study of the visual arts even further may want to check out some of the true art colonies that circle Austin in small towns like Salado, Wimberly, and Fredericksburg. For more information on local museums and galleries, visit the Austin Museum Partnership's website at www.austinmuseums.org.

Art Museums

ARTHOUSE AT THE JONES CENTER
700 Congress Ave.
(512) 453-5312
www.arthousetexas.org

Arthouse operates this prime downtown space as part of its efforts to nurture artists, promote contemporary Austin and Texas artists, and improve public awareness and appreciation of the state's visual artists. Formerly called the Texas Fine Arts Association, Arthouse was established in 1911. It is the oldest statewide visual arts organization in Texas and the only one devoted solely to contemporary art. Arthouse hosts a variety of exhibitions throughout the year, as well as special programs devoted to contemporary art. In 2010 Arthouse reopened after an architecturally stunning renovation that tripled its floor space to nearly 21,000 square feet. The update added new galleries, studios, a screening room, and a rooftop space with a giant movie screen!

AUSTIN MUSEUM OF ART—DOWNTOWN
823 Congress Ave.
(512) 495-9224
www.amoa.org

After the Austin Museum of Art (AMOA) outgrew its location at Laguna Gloria, the institution opened this additional 12,000-square-foot space in November 1996. The downtown space focuses on presenting temporary exhibits of significant

20th-century American visual art. Works by artists from the United States, Mexico, and the Caribbean are presented, including a strong showing of artists from Austin and around Texas.

The museum hosts 10 to 12 exhibitions annually, including those organized in-house and by other museums around the country. The museum is closed on Mon and hours vary daily, so check the website before heading out. There is a nominal admission fee. Reduced parking rates are available at the 823 Parking Garage on Ninth Street, or you can try to find a spot at the meters on the street.

AUSTIN MUSEUM OF ART—LAGUNA GLORIA
3809 West 35th St.
(512) 458-8191
www.amoa.org

One of Austin's most cherished treasures, Laguna Gloria is a restored Italian-style villa, which is registered as a National Historic site. Built in 1916 and designed with meticulous care by its original owner, Clara Driscoll, the 5-story, 15-room villa sits on 12 acres beside Lake Austin. The gardens surrounding the estate, including a sculpture garden, also have been restored to reflect Driscoll's vision. The grand lady herself ensured that her home would one day become a museum, deeding it in 1943 to the Texas Fine Arts Association (known today as Arthouse). The museum presents small-scale, long-term exhibitions and special events and is home to the museum's educational programs. This West Austin site was the only city art museum until the larger downtown facility opened in 1996. Members receive free admission to the museum, invitations to special events, subscriptions to museum publications, and more. The Art School at Laguna Gloria, in a separate facility on the grounds, offers both children's classes and instruction for adults in painting, sculpture, graphic arts, and more. The school can be reached at (512) 323-6380.

JACK S. BLANTON MUSEUM OF ART
200 East Martin Luther King Jr. Blvd.
(512) 471-7324
www.blantonmuseum.org

The University of Texas's Jack S. Blanton Museum of Art, now the largest university museum in the United States, features two art buildings as well as a 145,000-square-foot public plaza and garden. It's no surprise, then, that the Blanton is a key component of Austin's cultural scene. The complex includes The Mari and James A. Michener Gallery Building that houses the permanent collection and temporary exhibitions. The Blanton Museum's outstanding permanent collections are the most expansive in Central Texas, especially in the areas of American and contemporary art, Latin American art, and prints and drawings from all periods. Especially noteworthy is the museum's celebrated Suida-Manning Collection of Renaissance and Baroque paintings, drawings, and sculptures, as well as the Michener Collection of 20th-century American paintings. In all, the collection includes more than 17,000 works of art spanning the history of Western civilization from antiquity to the present. The newer Edgar A. Smith Building features The Blanton Cafe restaurant, an expanded museum store, a state-of-the-art auditorium, and classrooms.

The Blanton, named for former chairman of the UT Board of Regents and arts advocate Jack Blanton, offers a constantly changing array of temporary exhibits of works by internationally known artists, major Texas artists, and University of Texas fine arts graduate students. The museum, a strong research-oriented teaching institution, also hosts an ongoing series of public lectures by museum curators, artists, and art historians from UT and around the country. Admission is free for UT students, about $9 for adults. The museum is closed on Mon.

> **i** Want to take in the stunning view from the Long Center, but can't afford the price of admission to the major events in Dell Hall? Buy a ticket instead to the usually less expensive events in the center's Rollins Theatre and then wander on over to the Dell Hall's scenic-view lobbies.

MEXICAN AMERICAN CULTURAL CENTER
600 River St.
(512) 974-3770
www.ci.austin.tx.us/macc

One of the newest additions to the Austin arts scene, the city of Austin's Emma S. Barrientos Mexican American Cultural Center, opened in September 2007—though in many ways it was hundreds of years in the making. Known as the MACC, the center celebrates Hispanic art, history, and culture through exhibitions, film, dance, music, educational programs and more. It features a large, airy art gallery that presents the works of well-known and up-and-coming Latino artists. It also has an auditorium for performances, film presentations, and lectures. The MACC sits literally a stone's throw from Lady Bird Lake on a sprawling lawn (some of it earmarked for future MACC expansions) that makes a perfect spot for outdoor performances and activities—as well as picnicking on a warm Austin afternoon. The center is family friendly and offers classes of all kinds for kids and adults. Admission to the center is free, though there could be a charge for special programs. The MACC is one site on Austin's Trail of Tejano Legends (see the Attractions chapter for details).

MEXIC-ARTE MUSEUM
419 Congress Ave.
(512) 480-9373
www.mexic-artemuseum.org

Since its founding in 1984, Mexic-Arte Museum has been dedicated to presenting and promoting art created by both local and internationally known Mexican and Latino artists. The museum presents works from Mexic-Arte's permanent collection as well as from touring shows and exhibits organized by the museum staff.

Among the more memorable shows in recent years, and there have been many, is *From Revolution to Renaissance: Mexican Art from the Aaron Collection*, which included works by Rufino Tamayo, David Siqueiros, Dr. Atl, and others. The annual Young Latino Artists Exhibition showcases the work of artists under age 35. Mexic-Arte works with the Mexican Consulate in Austin to bring exhibitions and programs from throughout Mexico.

This museum was founded by Sylvia Orozco, Pio Pulido, and Sam Coronado, three Austin artists who painted a mural at the former Arts Warehouse in Austin in exchange for exhibit space back in 1983. In its current location since 1988, the museum also presents musical, theatrical, and performing arts events. The museum also houses an impressive gift shop that offers works by local artists. It's open 10 a.m. to 6 p.m. Mon through Thurs, 10 a.m. to 5 p.m. Fri and Sat, and noon to 5 p.m. Sun. Admission is about $5.

ELISABET NEY MUSEUM
304 East Forty-fourth St.
(512) 458-2255
www.ci.austin.tx.us/elisabetney

Celebrated sculptor Elisabet Ney put her artistic career back on track when she moved to Austin's Hyde Park in the late 1800s and built Formosa, now an extraordinary museum dedicated to the life and works of this sophisticated woman. Here visitors will discover a provocative array of about 50 portrait busts and full-figure statues of Texas heroes and of the European notables Ney sculpted as a young artist in Europe. Also here are the glorious sculptures of Lady Macbeth, Prometheus Bound, and Sursum (a Latin word meaning "to uplift your heart"), a delightful sculpture of two young nude boys.

The building itself, which Ney designed as her home and studio, also glorifies Ney's artistic sensibilities. Built in two phases and named Formosa, meaning "beautiful" in Portuguese, the studio lives up to its name. The first studio section, reminiscent of a Greek temple, was built in 1892, when Ney was 59 years old. Living quarters, which included a Gothic tower study for her husband, philosopher/scientist Edmund Montgomery, were added 10 years later. Today Formosa is listed on the National Register of Historic Places as well as both the Austin and Texas Registers. The museum includes a wonderful section on the life of Ney herself. Here visitors will find many of the artist's tools as well as a hat, watch, teacup, glasses, and many other items used by the artist. Excellent written accounts of her life are on display here also. Visitors will learn that this great talent came to Texas from Europe with the idea of forsaking her career for, as she put it, the "more important art of molding flesh and blood"—in other words, to raise her two boys. Tragically, one son died at age 2. Twenty years later Ney accepted a commission to sculpt the figures of Sam Houston and Stephen F. Austin that stand in the Texas State Capitol today. Her career had resumed.

The museum stands as a monument to Ney's influence on the arts in Texas. Her ability to inspire others during a time when Texas slighted the arts led to the creation of the Texas Fine Arts Association (known today as Arthouse) and later the Texas Commission on the Arts and the University of Texas art department. The Elisabet Ney Museum, one of the oldest museums in Texas, was founded after her death in 1907 by those Ney inspired during her lifetime. Ney's work can also be seen at the Texas State Cemetery, at UT, at the Smithsonian Institution in Washington, D.C., and in other museums in the United States and Europe. The museum is open Wed through Sun from noon to 5 p.m. Admission is free, as is parking on the residential streets around the building.

HARRY RANSOM CENTER
Near Guadalupe and Twenty-first Streets
(512) 471-8944
www.hrc.utexas.edu
Officially named the Harry Ransom Humanities Research Center, the emphasis here has always been on providing researchers with access to the world-class collections of art, literary manuscripts, photography, music, and more. A $14.5 million renovation completed in 2003 lets the light shine in on this Austin gem. The glass walls and open spaces invite visitors to come in and stay awhile, while the arrangement of the collections makes it easy for the general public to enjoy. There certainly are plenty of reasons to spend some time here. Among the center's

exceptional properties is a 1455 Gutenberg Bible, one of just five existing complete copies of the first book printed with movable type, as well as the world's first photograph, taken by Frenchman Joseph Nicephore Niepce in 1826. There are important paintings by Mexican artists Diego Rivera, Frida Kahlo, and Rufino Tamayo, as well as artworks done by some literary greats, including D. H. Lawrence and Tennessee Williams. Literary manuscripts include works by Ernest Hemingway, William Faulkner, and Samuel Beckett.

In all, the Ransom Center houses 30 million literary manuscripts, 1 million rare books, 5 million photographs, and more than 100,000 works of art. Obviously it's impossible to display all these treasures at once, so the Center presents numerous exhibitions and events showcasing its collections. The galleries are open from 10 a.m. to 5 p.m. Tues, Wed, and Fri; from 10 a.m. to 7 p.m. Thurs; and from noon to 5 p.m. on weekends. Admission is free.

SOUTH AUSTIN MUSEUM OF POPULAR CULTURE
1516 South Lamar Blvd.
(512) 440-8319
www.samopc.org
The more Austin gentrifies and sprawls—not only literally, but figuratively as well—away from its core, the higher the need for a museum like this. A visit to this funky South Austin hole in the wall is a trip down musical and artistic memory lane for some and a portal into the past for those who missed the 1960s, '70s, and even into the '80s when Austin was making its biggest impact on US popular culture. On these walls, visitors will find posters advertising music shows around town, underground cartoons, as well

as other music-related graphics and ephemera of the era. And they will also learn about the personalities that put Austin graphic art on the map during those years, including Jack "Jaxon" Jackson, Jim Franklin, Ken Featherston, Frank Kozik, and others. One of the feature attractions here is a giant mural, *Peyote Dreams*, done by Featherston in 1974. This museum is just getting going in establishing its collection, which is to include more paintings, album covers, T-shirts of the era, musical recordings, photographs, and other important music memorabilia from the psychedelic period, through the cosmic cowboy years and beyond. The museum is open Thurs through Sun 1 p.m. to 6 p.m. There is a nominal admission fee.

✳UMLAUF SCULPTURE GARDEN & MUSEUM
605 Robert E. Lee Rd.
(512) 445-5582
www.umlaufsculpture.org

Directors of the Umlauf Sculpture Garden & Museum like to say this garden epitomizes Austin: It's outdoors, casual, and lovely. And they have a great point. Here, in a totally Austin xeriscape garden and pond next to Zilker Park, visitors are treated to the fabulous sculptures of acclaimed artist Charles Umlauf, who came to Austin in 1941 and remained for the rest of his life.

The garden, terrace, and surrounding land provide a perfect outdoor setting for 62 of Umlauf's bronze and cast-stone sculptures. The pieces, which range from the realistic to the abstract, represent a wide range of subject matter, including children, family groupings, mythological and religious figures, and sensuous nudes. Many other smaller sculptures made of exotic woods, marbles, and terra-cotta are inside the glass-enclosed museum.

Umlauf, who taught in the University of Texas art department for 40 years, won nearly every professional award offered, including a Guggenheim Fellowship and a Ford Foundation Grant. His works can be seen in museums and public collections across the country. In 1985 Umlauf and his wife, Angeline, donated their longtime home and studio and more than 200 pieces of his work to the city of Austin.

The museum is open Wed through Fri from 10 a.m. to 4:30 p.m., and 1 to 4:30 p.m. on Sat and Sun. General admission is $3.50. Umlauf's pieces can also be found on the UT campus and around town, including the Austin Museum of Art at Laguna Gloria and the Texas State Cemetery.

VISUAL ARTS CENTER
University of Texas Art Building,
Twenty-third and Trinity Streets
(512) 471-1108
www.utvac.org

One of Austin's newest contemporary art spaces, opened in fall 2010, comes courtesy of the University of Texas's Department of Art and Art History. Exhibiting works by emerging artists from around the world and renowned UT faculty, as well as notable students and alumni, the VAC, as it is known, is a 25,000-square-foot center with 5 galleries and 3 public spaces. Each of the galleries—the Vaulted Gallery, the Arcade, the Mezzanine Gallery, the East Gallery, and Center Space—is unique. The Vaulted Gallery, for instance, is so named because its ceiling rises 2 stories. This is one place to come to discover artists before they become household names. UT has pledged that the space will have a strong student presence, and the Center Space Project, the VAC's student organization and curator of the exhibitions in that gallery, is honoring that commitment. The VAC also presents films, music and artistic performances.

> **i** If you happen to be walking by the busy UT intersection at Twenty-third and Trinity Streets and see huge picture windows with art videos showing through, even at night, you've found the hot new contemporary art space, Visual Arts Center. Go on in. You'll thank us later.

Galleries

ART ON 5TH
1501 West Fifth St.
(512) 481-1111
www.arton5th.com
One of Austin's largest and most diverse art galleries, Art on 5th features work by famous artists such as Miró, Picasso, and Dr. Seuss as well as exceptional undiscovered artists from around the world working in many genres. This well-designed, visitor-friendly gallery is owned by Joe Sigel, who owned galleries in Santa Fe and California for many years.

AUSTIN GALLERIES
1219 West Sixth St.
(512) 495-9363
www.austingalleries.com
After a tour of Austin and the surrounding Hill Country, you might be tempted to search out paintings that capture the stunning beauty of the hills. Among the more than 2,000 original works of art offered at Austin Galleries is a huge selection of Texas landscape paintings, as well as Impressionist, abstract, and classical paintings and original prints signed by Andy Warhol, Picasso,

Jasper Johns, and others. And that's just the beginning.

CLARKSVILLE POTTERY & GALLERIES
4001 North Lamar Blvd.
(512) 454-9079
www.clarksvillepottery.com
Clarksville Pottery & Galleries has grown from a small, one-man pottery shop and studio back in the '70s into a major retailer of fine arts and crafts with 2 prominent Austin locations (the other is at 9828 Great Hills Trail, Suite 110, 512-794-8580). The stores offer handmade pottery by local and nationally known potters as well as an impressive selection of jewelry, glass, wall art, fine woodcrafts, fountains, and more. The stores do a brisk business because they offer some of the finest crafts available in Austin today. In fact, the business has been chosen by *Niche* magazine as a "Top 100 Retailer of American Crafts."

> **i** Many people have asked us whether Austin has a museum dedicated to the musicians who put Texas on the map. The answer is yes— kind of. For now the museum is a small space in the Marvin C. Griffin Building at 1009 East Eleventh St., although a 100,000-square-foot, multi-galleried permanent home is envisioned. To follow the progress, or get involved, visit www.texasmusicmuseum.org or call (512) 472-8891. The current space is worth a look, too.

FLATBED PRESS AND GALLERY
2830 East Martin Luther King Jr. Blvd.
(512) 477-9328
www.flatbedpress.com
Flatbed Press's master printmakers work with some of the finest artists of the day to

create limited editions of original etchings, lithographs, and woodcuts. This press has a national reputation for producing state-of-the-art work. Additionally, the gallery exhibits and sells original paintings as well as works on paper by leading contemporary artists, including Austin's Michael Ray Charles and Melissa Miller. Flatbed also offers about a dozen classes in printmaking and other techniques for novice to experienced artists.

IMAGES OF AUSTIN AND THE SOUTHWEST
4612 Burnet Rd.
(512) 451-1229
www.imagesofaustin.com
Austin artist Mary Doerr runs this gallery in a small house in Central Austin that showcases Doerr's attractive illustrations and watercolors, often depicting Austin, as well as the work of a number of other selected artists. The gallery features Southwestern sculptures and wall hangings as well as pottery, gourds, jewelry, limited-edition prints, and paintings.

L. NOWLIN GALLERY
1202-A West Sixth St.
(512) 626-9301
www.lnowlingallery.com
Well-known Austin photographer Lesley Nowlin runs this young photography gallery, which exhibits work by artists from Austin and around the world, including some of Nowlin's own photographs. Just up some stairs off West Sixth in the West End District, the gallery features a steady stream of provocative group exhibitions and one-person shows in an array of genres, including black and white, fine art, and documentary. The space is adjacent to the Wally Workman Gallery (see below).

OKAY MOUNTAIN GALLERY
1312 East Cesar Chavez St., Suite B
(512) 451-1229
www.okaymountain.com
Okay Mountain Collective, a group of 10 artists in their late 20s and 30s, is generating a buzz in the national art world these days, and their East Austin gallery is one fine place to find out what the hoopla is all about. Art school graduates all, they each produce their own work. However, they also are getting raves for their collective projects, for which some or all 10 contribute to the final drawing, video installation, or other piece. "Maximal," is how the *Austin-American Statesman* describes the collective's style. "All are unapologetic progeny of Austin's pop culture-saturated, consumer-driven American culture—as celebratory of its absurdities as they are careful observers of those absurdities," *Statesman* art critic Jeanne Claire van Ryzin noted. The gallery presents the members' work, as well as that of other young artists from around the world. In 2010 Okay Mountain's video installation *Water, Water Everywhere, So Let's All Have a Drink,* was exhibited at the Austin Museum of Art before heading to New Orleans and Illinois. The artists are Sterling Allen, Tim Brown, Peat Duggins, Justin Goldwater, Nathan Green, Ruan Hennessee, Josh Rios, Carlos Rosales-Silva, Michael Sieben, and Corkey Sinks.

SLUGFEST PRINTMAKING WORKSHOP & GALLERY
1906 Miriam Ave.
(512) 477-7204
www.slugfestprints.com
Slugfest is a stellar printmaking operation that produces limited-edition original prints for both novice and established artists. Opened in 1996 by Margaret Simpson and

Tom Druecker, both MFAs in printmaking and teachers at Austin universities, this press has an excellent reputation for producing museum-quality prints. The gallery hosts an excellent variety of shows. Slugfest also offers introductory workshops in lithography, relief printing, monotype, collograph, book arts, and letterpress.

WALLY WORKMAN GALLERY
1202 West Sixth St.
(512) 472-7428
www.wallyworkmangallery.com
This well-established art gallery in a 2-story historic house in Austin's artistic West End District represents nearly 50 artists, mostly from Austin. Owned and operated by Wally Workman, a female University of Texas graduate in art history, the gallery has been a strong supporter and promoter of Austin artists for 30 years. Local connoisseurs will recognize the names of the artists she represents, including Will Klemm, Ian Shults, Jennifer Balkan, Helmut Barnett, Gordon Fowler, Margie Crisp, Jan Heaton, and many others.

WILD ABOUT MUSIC
115 East Sixth St.
(512) 708-1700, (877) 370-1700
www.wildaboutmusic.com
What better combination for Austin than an art gallery and gift shop that celebrates music? Everything in the locally owned shop has a music or performing arts motif, including accessories, clothing, jewelry, glass, and stationery. Wild About Music features exceptional work by more than 100 artists, including some nationally known Central Texas artists as well as others from around the country. This shop also hosts a variety of special events, including art demonstra-tions, touring art shows, and live music performances.

WOMEN & THEIR WORK
1710 Lavaca St.
(512) 477-1064
www.womenandtheirwork.org
This statewide nonprofit organization dedicated to promoting women in the arts celebrated its 32nd anniversary in 2010. Make no mistake—this is much more than just an art gallery. Women & Their Work is the only organization of its kind in Texas that embraces all the arts. The organization promotes women artists in visual art, dance, music, theater, literature, and film, and it is one of Austin's premier resources for the arts. There's also a nice gift shop here that, like the gallery, is open Mon through Sat. Gallery exhibitions featuring painting, sculpture, photography, fine crafts, and works on paper change regularly. Women & Their Work presents more than 50 diverse events each year, including juried and invitational exhibitions of Texas artists as well as solo and group exhibitions. The organization also produces dance, musical, and theatrical performances featuring local, regional, and national performing artists, often collaborative ventures with other groups. We especially like this organization's motto: "Women & Their Work is dedicated to the belief that women artists should be seen and heard. And paid."

i Wondering how to dress for a classical performance in Austin? The answer is almost any way you want. Although some people like to take the opportunity to dress up, you'll also find patrons in casual, even laid-back, clothing. Shoes and shirts are necessary, of course.

YARD DOG FOLK ART
1510 South Congress Ave.
(512) 912-1613
www.yarddog.com

Fascinating is the word that comes to mind to describe the work of the artists, many of them nationally known, represented here. Art dealer Randy Franklin opened this gallery on now-trendy South Congress Avenue in 1995, focusing on folk and outsider art from the American South. The space has evolved since then and now features paintings and other works by many contemporary artists who the shop says "work in a folky, funky vernacular." This area is a fun place to visit even if you're not an art buff. The strip is lined with other funky shops and restaurants that will satisfy any craving for the unusual.

ARTS ORGANIZATIONS

ART IN PUBLIC PLACES
1110 Barton Springs Rd., Suite 201
(512) 397-1455
www.ci.austin.tx.us/aipp

Established in 1985, the City of Austin's Art in Public Places (AIPP) program was Texas's first municipal effort to purchase and place works of art in public areas. Since then, AIPP has installed artworks at the Austin-Bergstrom International Airport, the Austin Convention Center, libraries, parks, recreation centers, and many more spots for everyone to enjoy. The program has involved talented artists of local and national renown, while the collection represents the broad range of media, styles, and cultural sensibilities. The organization also has sponsored a Public Art Academy for Artists and other events designed to educate and support local artists. The organization's website features an excellent map to the art installations around the city. Check out also the art from more than 100 artists at the People's Gallery in City Hall downtown.

AUSTIN VISUAL ARTS ASSOCIATION
3707 Home Lane
(512) 457-0075
www.avaaonline.org

For more than 30 years the Austin Visual Arts Association has worked to promote knowledge and appreciation of the visual arts in the city. Its members include working artists as well as arts' patrons, museum professionals, and gallery owners. AAVA not only provides its members with a networking structure and opportunities to exhibit, it also hosts seminars and other events for the city's visual artists. In 2009 the association presented its first Austin art awards.

DANCE UMBRELLA
3710 Cedar St., Suite 286
(512) 450-0456
www.danceumbrella.com

Whether it's bringing local and internationally renowned dance companies to the Austin stage or helping a young dance company find its legs, Dance Umbrella has been supporting the movement arts in the city since it was founded in 1977. This nonprofit organization with about 100 artistic members also aims to promote dance and dance companies throughout the region with its many programs and services. After all, the organization is based on the philosophy "that the arts help describe, define, and deepen our experience of living." Membership is open to one and all and provides discounts on performances.

GREATER AUSTIN CREATIVE ALLIANCE
701 Tillery St., Suite 9
(512) 247-2531
www.austincreativealliance.org
www.nowplayingaustin.com

This outstanding nonprofit organization works to nurture, support, and promote the city's performing and visual artists and arts communities, as well as attract new audiences to artists of all disciplines. For the public at large, the alliance sponsors the excellent AUSTIX box office, which offers easy access to full- and half-price tickets for many of the city's art events. Its Now Playing Austin website listed above is a treasure trove of current happenings in music, theater, dance, visual arts, comedy, and much more. The site also has a link to half-price tickets available through AUSTIX. The alliance is a strong voice of arts' advocacy in the Austin community.

TEXAS FOLKLIFE
1317 South Congress Ave.
(512) 441-9255
www.texasfolklife.org

Modern-day Texas culture is a rich blend of ethnic and regional traditions dating back hundreds of years. There's no better way to discover how well those traditions have survived than by attending events sponsored by Texas Folklife. This dynamic nonprofit organization brings the best of those living, breathing cultures to the forefront of public awareness today through a comprehensive calendar of events in Austin and around the state.

Texas Folklife works with folk artists all over the state to document living traditions and present them to the public in many forms, including exhibitions, concerts, radio programs, and demonstrations. Among its many successful projects is Texas Folk Masters, whose performances pay tribute to legendary singers and songwriters in the state. The organization also offers photography exhibitions that showcase traditional Texas blues clubs and its honky-tonk culture. And there's more: gospel music, powwow craft traditions, works in wood by folk artists, and songs and ballads of the Texas-Mexico border.

Texas Folklife also operates the Apprenticeships in the Folk Arts program, which encourages master folk artists to pass their traditions on to qualified apprentices in their community. Check the website often to keep fully informed of the organization's extensive list of events. Better yet, join the community and help present, preserve, and promote the folk arts and folklife of the Lone Star State.

THE LITERARY SCENE

"The tempo of the earth-dwellers to whom I have been listening for many years is the tempo of growing grass, of a solitary buzzard sailing over a valley, of the wind from the south in April, of the lengthening of a tree's shadow on a summer afternoon, of the rise and fall of flames in a fireplace on a winter night." With those words, J. Frank Dobie, Texas's first nationally known writer, introduced his book *Tales of Old-Time Texas,* published in 1928 and still available, along with many of his other two dozen collections, at bookstores today. In this chapter we'll delve into Austin's rich literary history and describe its current status as a writers' mecca. But for those of you in a rush to explore the Austin of letters, we'll get right to the point: If you like books, you'll love Austin.

OVERVIEW

J. Frank Dobie is one of the reasons. Dobie, a University of Texas professor from 1914 to 1947, with occasional absences, was born in the Texas brush country and lived in and around Austin for most of his adult life—that is, when he was not off wandering around Mexico and the American Southwest in search of someone with a tale to tell.

"Frank Dobie became a hunter of legends and a gatherer of folk tales and the result was one of the most important bodies of literature produced by a Southwesterner," wrote Neil B. Carmony, who edited a collection of Dobie's stories for the book, *Afield with J. Frank Dobie,* published in 1992, 28 years after the writer's death.

Names of other luminaries grace Austin's past, including historian Walter Prescott Webb and naturalist Roy Bedichek, who together with Dobie formed a triumvirate of intellectuals that electrified the city's literary ambience. William Sydney Porter, who later was to gain international notoriety as the short-story writer O. Henry, published his first short fiction here in his literary magazine the *Rolling Stone.* A Porter story that appeared in the October 27, 1894, issue of the *Rolling Stone* gave Austin one of its most endearing nicknames: City of the Violet Crown. (See the chapter on Attractions for more about O. Henry.) Austinite and LBJ aide Billy Brammer is still known around these parts for his 1962 political novel, *The Gay Place.*

John Henry Faulk, for whom Austin's central library is named, was a multitalented writer, actor, New York radio show host, and defender of the First Amendment. As vice president of the American Federation of Television and Radio Artists, Faulk insisted the union take a stand against McCarthy-era blacklistings of entertainers—and was himself blacklisted. Faulk fought back and as a result won the largest libel judgment awarded up to that time. He was one of Dobie's students.

Internationally celebrated short-story writer Katherine Anne Porter (1890–1980) grew up 20 miles down the road from Austin in the small town of Kyle. Her relationship with Texas, however, was a stormy one. It infuriated her, for example, that the Texas Institute of Letters chose to honor Dobie instead of her when it gave its 1939 award for the best book by a Texas writer. (Folklorist Sylvia Ann Grider has written that "Porter's emotional attachment to her home state fell victim to the cowboy mentality that has traditionally proclaimed Texas a fine place for men and horses, but hell on women and oxen.") Of course her fame eclipsed Dobie's, which probably brought her no small amount of satisfaction. While Porter lived most of her adult life outside Texas, she nevertheless wrote some of her finest fiction about her home state and chose to be buried in Texas.

Pioneering Texas journalist Bess White-head Scott, who broke gender barriers in 1915 as the first woman news reporter in Houston, was a beloved member of the Austin writers' community until her death in 1997 at age 107. Noted folklorist and poet J. Mason Brewer, the first African American to become a member of the Texas Institute of Letters and the first African-American vice president of the American Folklore Society, found inspiration among members of his own family in their East Austin home. Dobie called Brewer's work "genuine and delightful." Pulitzer Prize–winning author James Michener is another illustrious writer who found inspiration in Austin—and inspired others. (Find out more about Michener's contributions to Austin's literary scene in the Close-up in this chapter.)

Austin also was home to the late liberal syndicated columnist and best-selling author Molly Ivins, who forever will be known for her sharp tongue, her ability to skewer politicians, and her colorful commentary on what she called the "reactionary, cantankerous, and hilarious" state of Texas. She also was the person who gave President George W. Bush the nicknames "Dubya" and "Shrub."

Some of these trailblazers not only established Austin's literary traditions but also helped this city earn a reputation as a haven for writers and free thinkers, a distinction that has endured. Austin's literary scene, in fact, is more vibrant today than ever before. Perhaps even Dobie would be amazed at the sheer number of Austin writers and at the contributions many of them have made to the nation's literary wealth. To read Austin writers is to take a joyride on the roller coaster of literary expression: novels, mysteries, science fiction, cyberpunk, suspense, history, poetry, travel, books for children and young adults, essays, memoirs, how-to books, cookbooks, political satires, biographies, screenplays, short stories. The list goes on. Austin claims best-selling and award-winning writers in a number of genres—including 2007 Pulitzer Prize–winner Lawrence Wright (*The Looming Tower: Al-Qaeda and the Road to 9/11*)—as well as a host of successful poets, playwrights, and screenwriters.

i While Austin Public Library cards are free to Texans, out-of-state visitors may purchase a three-month card for $20. Youth 16 and under can get a card for free regardless of where they live. If you're visiting Austin and just have to read a book, this could be your answer.

It's impossible to pinpoint just one catalyst for Austin's literary explosion. We'd have to include Austin's own magnetism. Once experienced, Austin is hard to abandon. The superlative efforts of the Writers' League of Texas to promote and encourage the city's writers have had impressive results. The league, with more than 1,500 members, is one of the largest writers' organizations in the country.

Two Austin publications, *Texas Monthly* magazine and the *Texas Observer,* have long and rich traditions of attracting excellent writers to Austin, many of whom have gone on to achieve literary fame. The vibrant music scene and flourishing film industry, illuminated by excellent local songwriters and screenwriters, add further dimension to Austin's literary landscape. (See the chapter on The Music Scene and the Close-up on the film industry in The Arts chapter.) Of course, the presence of outstanding intellectuals at the University of Texas, St. Edward's University, and the other colleges and universities has added untold riches to Austin's writing legacy. Adding further dimension to the scene are the university presses and many small- and medium-size publishing houses that are willing to gamble that an author's work will be of interest to others.

Austin's esteemed independent superstore, BookPeople, and several stores operated by Barnes & Noble and Half-Price Books are some of the many shops in our area to offer great reads and welcoming surroundings for book lovers. BookPeople and Barnes & Noble host a great assortment of readings by national and local authors, as well as book signings and other literary events that bring the written word to life. Several of Austin's small- and medium-size bookstores also have long traditions of providing venues for local and national writers of poetry and prose, as do a number of other venues

around town, including the University of Texas and St. Edward's University. The James Michener Center for Writers co-sponsors readings by national and international writers and poets, both on and off the University of Texas campus.

Texas Writers Month, first organized in 1994, has become an outstanding statewide celebration of Texas's literary artists. The annual May festival, held in Austin and other major cities around the state, includes book panels, readings, children's events, literacy benefits, signings, musical events, and film. Texas Writers Month, originally conceived to convince booksellers to give local authors more prominence in their stores, has become a premier celebration of Texas writers.

The Texas Book Festival, started in 1996, is another major Austin event for writers and readers alike. Laura Bush was a driving force behind the festival when she was first lady of Texas. The Nov festival, which raises money for Texas public libraries, features readings and panel discussions by more than 100 authors who have been published the previous year. A giant book fair, musical events, children's activities, and more highlight this celebration of the state's literary heritage. The Austin International Poetry Festival (www.aipf.org), held in Apr since 1993, draws poets and poetry fans to Austin from around the globe.

BUY THE BOOK

As if in a scene by Kafka, you innocently walk through a door and suddenly you're transformed—into a worm, no less. As you look around you realize the room is crawling with all kinds of worms: big ones, baby ones, curly-haired ones, bearded ones, coffee-drinking worms, worms wearing ties, worms

Close-up

James Michener: A Memorable Character

Pulitzer Prize–winning author James Michener, whose 1991 memoir is titled *The World Is My Home,* chose Austin as his home for many of the last, always prolific, years of his life. Over the course of the Michener Age here, Austin was to become a richer city, not merely because of the millions in art and monetary endowments he gave to the University of Texas but also because of Michener's generosity of spirit.

Here was a man whose own life was one of America's great rags-to-riches tales; a man whose appetite for adventure and unquenchable thirst for knowledge were matched only by a gift—he called it a passion—for telling a story; a man who spent his life, and most of his fortune, giving back to the people and communities that had embraced him.

Michener was no stranger to the Capital City when he arrived in 1982 to begin work on his sweeping saga of the Lone Star State. He had known the Austin of the 1940s, when he came as an editor following publication of his first book, and he'd known the Austin of the 1960s, when he returned to donate his huge 20th-century American Art collection to the University of Texas. By the time the 1980s rolled around, Michener had been decorated with America's highest civilian honor, the Presidential Medal of Freedom. His reputation as America's Storyteller was as solid as his hefty novels—and so was his fame as one of the country's most generous writers. At the time of his death, it was estimated that Michener had given $117 million to museums, libraries, individuals, and universities around the country. The largest beneficiary of Michener's generosity was the University of Texas at Austin, which received $44.2 million from the late-in-life Austinite.

Michener's first novel, *Tales of the South Pacific,* published in 1947 when the author was 40 years old, had earned him a Pulitzer Prize. The bestsellers that followed, including *The Fires of Spring, The Bridges at Toko-ri, Sayonara, Caravans, The Source, Iberia, Centennial, The Drifters,* and *The Covenant,* earned him millions of loyal readers who found his fictionalized version of history more exciting, more moving, and even more educational than anything they'd read in nonfiction. It warranted not even a pause when critics called his work too preachy, his characters too one-dimensional, or his dialogue too contrived. Readers made Michener famous as they stampeded to the bookstores to

taking notes. It's a community, a coterie, a coven of worms. Ahhhh.

You're right at home. Whether it's 10 in the morning or 10 at night, Austin's bookstores are teeming with those literate critters known as bookworms. Austin consistently ranks among the top 10 cities in per capita sales of books, according to nationwide studies done by the book industry. Readings and book signings by nationally known and local authors, comfy couches, and cafes are just a few of the features some bookstores offer to lure readers—and to add life to Austin's literary scene.

Throughout Greater Austin

BARNES & NOBLE BOOKSELLERS
Six stores in Austin and Round Rock
(512) 328-3155
www.bn.com

get their hands on his latest epic. Perhaps it was his ability to create characters with whom readers could identify that won him such a loyal following.

"I have endeavored to center my writing upon ordinary but memorable characters whose lives shed a kind of radiance, whose behavior, good or bad, illuminated what I was striving to impart, and whose noble, craven, godlike or hellish deportment stood surrogate for the behavior of human beings the reader has known," he wrote in his memoir.

Bill Clements, then governor of Texas, invited Michener to Austin in 1981 to work on a book about Texas for the sesquicentennial. Published in 1985, when Michener was 78, the 1,096-page epic turned out to be his longest work. Like *Hawaii, Space,* and *Chesapeake* before it, and *Poland, Alaska, and Mexico* that followed, *Texas* required no dramatic title. The image the title conjured in people's imaginations, and the bold name of the author below it, was enough to turn *Texas* into a million-copy block-buster.

Michener and his wife, Mari, found a home in Austin during the years the author spent researching and writing his Texas saga. According to the *Austin American-Statesman,* Michener once told a friend as they walked down the West Austin street where he lived, "You know, I think I'm happier living on this street than any street I've lived on in my life." That statement said a great deal about the man who considered the world his home. His memoir features a cover photograph of the author sitting atop Austin's breathtaking Mount Bonnell (see the Attractions chapter).

In his half century of work, Michener wrote nearly 50 books of nonfiction and fiction, many of them as thick as bricks. Along the way, Michener found time to establish the Texas Center for Writers—renamed the James Michener Center for Writers following his death in 1997—to enlighten writers for generations to come.

In a 1988 interview on *Good Morning America,* Michener talked about his craft. "I think I have a passion for telling a story and then working on it until I think it's coherent," he said. "I'm proud of my profession. I'm a writer. I never say I'm an author, that's somebody else. I'm a real good writer." He was also a real good human being.

This large New York–based chain arrived in Austin in 1994 and has grown to include 6 superstores around the greater metropolitan area. Barnes & Noble wasted no time in becoming part of, and promoting, Austin's literary, musical, and artistic communities. Each store hosts a number of monthly book discussion groups on a variety of areas of interest, including fiction, nonfiction, science fiction, and Texana. The stores are a popular place to attend regular book readings and book signings by local, national, and international writers and screenwriters. The stores also are extremely active in promoting and hosting events for the annual Texas Writer's Month celebration. Barnes & Noble also works in conjunction with local and national organizations that promote literacy and is involved with the Austin Independent School District's Adopt-a-School program. The website gives the addresses of all B&N stores in the area.

HALF PRICE BOOKS
(512) 454-3664
www.halfpricebooks.com
With four Austin locations, one in Round Rock and one in Cedar Park, Half Price Books offers Central Texans easy access to its wide selection of used and new books, including rare and out-of-print titles and Texana titles not easily found elsewhere. We especially like the well-stocked used magazine section, where patrons often can find recent issues of their favorite magazines without having to pay full price for them. For the environmentally minded—and this is Austin, so there are many of us—this is a great place to recycle used magazines and books. The Dallas-based chain opened its first Austin store in 1975 and gradually built up to its current number. Half Price Books has a good selection of children's books as well as music in all formats, magazines, and DVDs. New books sell for half the current retail price or less. The store buys used books, magazines, DVDs, and music.

Central

AUSTIN BOOKS
5002 North Lamar Blvd.
(512) 454-4197
www.austinbooks.com
This locally owned store, serving Austin since 1977, has gone through several incarnations over the years and now specializes in comic books, Japanese manga, anime action figures, Japanese graphic novels, and trade paperbacks. The store stocks about 500 new titles of comic books as well as thousands more classics and collectibles. For collectors and diehard comic book fans, the store offers an e-mail service listing new titles for the week, as well as a simple response asking employees to set aside certain titles for pickup later.

i To mark the 35th anniversary of *Austin City Limits,* the longest-running popular music series in American television history, the University of Texas Press in 2010 published a fabulous coffee-table book, *Austin City Limits: 35 Years in Photographs.*

BOOKPEOPLE
603 North Lamar Blvd.
(512) 472-5050
www.bookpeople.com
This Austin institution was the city's first book superstore and continues to be one of Austin's major literary venues. With more than 200,000 titles, BookPeople is one of the largest bookstores in Texas. It definitely is one of Austin's favorite spots to shop for books and to hear authors read from their works. Founded in 1970 by two University of Texas students, the store later became Grok, an alternative bookstore. BookPeople, still locally owned and operated, has grown to encompass a huge selection of books in all genres and is especially known for an excellent selection of books on alternative healing, computers, and cooking. The store features a wonderful children's section and great newsstand as well as books on tape, gift items, and computer software for children and adults. BookPeople's contributions to the Austin literary scene through the years have been enormous. This store goes out of its way to sell books written by local authors, even going so far as to buy books that are self-published. The store features a section of books about Texas and another dedicated to Texas authors. BookPeople sponsors regular book

discussion groups and hosts three weekly story times for children, including one for preschoolers. Check out the store's monthly calendar for upcoming events.

BOOK WOMAN
5501 North Lamar Blvd., Suite A–105
(512) 472-2785
www.ebookwoman.com

This Austin original celebrated its 35th anniversary in 2010. Book Woman specializes in new books by and about girls and women, but that tells only part of the story. Since 1975 this shop has been a showcase for women writers and musicians. Book Woman, owned by Austinite Susan Post, sponsors a monthly book club for women and hosts readings and book signings by local and national writers. In addition to its great fiction section, the shop stocks an impressive collection of books on such subjects as self-help, women's health and psychology, girls and teens, memoirs, biographies, spirituality, and feminism. It has a wonderful section dedicated to Latina and Chicana books and another section of lesbian fiction and nonfiction. The community bulletin board, which displays information on events and services of interest to women, is a popular feature of this store. Book Woman is part of the feminist bookstores network and can do special orders from that catalog.

FUNNY PAPERS
2021 Guadalupe St.
(512) 478-9718
www.myspace.com/funnypapersaustin

This is one of Austin's one-stop shops for fans of comic books, role-playing games, collectible card games, collectible figurines, and more. Funny Papers sells comic book–related collectibles and many types of players' handbooks that go along with role-playing games. This unique store, which opened in Dobie Mall near the UT campus in 1990, receives about 100 new comic book titles each week and also stocks a wide selection of back issues and trade paperbacks. Funny Papers has an assortment of collectible card games as well as Magic cards and all the supplies needed for card collectors. Regular comic book subscribers receive a discount.

i The Literacy Coalition of Central Texas sponsors the annual Great Grown-Up Spelling Bee, a fun—but challenging—event in which costume-clad teams of professionals attempt to spell such words as *rhizoidal* and *poikilotherm*. In 2010 the event raised $75,000 to fight illiteracy in the region. Visit www.willread.org for information.

HART OF AUSTIN ANTIQUARIAN BOOKS
1009 West Sixth St.
(512) 477-7755

Locally owned and operated since 1992, this large antiquarian bookstore is tucked away inside the delightful Whit Hanks Antiques complex. Owner Pat Hart offers several thousand used and rare books in all genres. The store also buys books and offers appraisals.

UNIVERSITY CO-OP BOOKSTORE
2246 Guadalupe St.
(512) 476-7211, (800) 255-1896
www.universitycoop.com

Founded in 1896, the University Co-op is owned by the students, faculty, and staff of the University of Texas at Austin. The bookstore offers UT and Austin Community College textbooks as well as books for UT Extension classes, correspondence courses, and informal classes. This is also a great place to shop for UT apparel, gifts, and souvenirs as well as greeting cards, art, and school supplies. The store has been on The Drag right across the street from the UT campus since 1919. The Co-op East Bookstore at 2902 Medical Arts St. also has some souvenirs but mainly carries textbooks for the LBJ School of Public Affairs, the UT Law School, and other schools in the area.

South Central

RESISTENCIA BOOK STORE
1801–A South First St.
(512) 416-8885
www.resistenciabooks.com
Founded by the late Austin poet Raul Salinas, Resistencia adds an important dimension to the Austin literary scene. This specialty store, established in Austin in the early 1980s and located in South Central Austin since 1992, is well known for promoting the literary arts through its sponsorship of regular poetry readings, book signings, and book readings by local and national authors. The store specializes in Native American, Chicano, Latino, African-American, and feminist literature, poetry, and history. Resistencia also features CDs and tapes by local and international musicians in its specialty areas. The store offers literary magazines, T-shirts, and posters and features a community bulletin board announcing literary events.

WHOLE LIFE BOOKS
1006 South Lamar Blvd.
(512) 443-6794
This nonprofit bookstore, music store, and gift shop specializes in books on alternative health, metaphysics, spirituality, meditation, health, and New Age topics. Whole Life Books, which opened in 1983, is the only store of its kind in Austin that does not exist for commercial purposes. Austinite Ted Lanier, former UT graduate student in psychology and the former owner of a "hippie bicycle shop," started the operation as a reading room so that people could investigate for themselves the possible approaches to discovering nonmaterial spiritual reality. His patrons, however, wanted to buy the books they discovered in the reading room—and a business was born. The store now stocks about 50,000 titles as well as a wide assortment of CDs. Candles, wind chimes, incense, and jewelry can also be found at Whole Life Books. One nice thing about this store is it hours. It's open Mon through Sat from 11 a.m. to 10 p.m., and Sun noon to 7 p.m.

North Central

RECYCLED READS
5335 Burnet Rd.
(512) 323-5123
www.austinlibrary.com/branches
Opened by the Austin Public Library in 2009 and staffed by volunteers, this bookstore offers thousands of used books, CDs, DVDs, and other and media items at prices as low as 50 cents and a dollar. Best sellers and coffee table-style books go for a whopping $2. The collection, which also includes signed and out-of-print books, is made up of materials withdrawn from the library system and from donations. All proceeds go to the library system. The shop is open from noon to 6 p.m. Thurs through Sun.

BORROW THE BOOK

As centers of learning and for community outreach, Austin's public libraries are among its greatest public assets. Despite the bookstore boom of the 1990s, which brought hundreds of thousands of books to the community, more and more citizens are turning to the public libraries for their reading material. Of course there's no place like the library for doing research, getting on the Internet free of charge, or checking out that vintage recording. Those attractions, and the surge in Austin's population in recent years, have put a strain on already limited library resources.

Authorities say the materials collection at the current Central Library is about a third the size it should be to meet Austin's needs. Despite limited resources, however, the library system has won a number of awards for its efforts to make reading and research materials available to everyone, to increase literacy in the city of Austin, and to provide after-school tutoring. Although Austin has outgrown its existing Central Library, the projected opening date for a brand new downtown facility is 2015.

ℹ️ "Connected Youth" (www.connectedyouth.com) is a partnership between the Austin Public Library and the Michael and Susan Dell Foundation. The program hosts special events as well as book clubs for young readers, including one focusing on comic books! Teens can also check out laptops through the program.

The Austin public library system is made up of 23 facilities that include the John Henry Faulk Central Library, the Austin History Center, 20 branch libraries located all over the city, and a used bookstore. The hub of the interconnected system continues to be the Central Library, which is more than 10 times the size of some of the branches. While branch libraries do not always have the book you want, the library system allows

for books to be sent from the Central Library or another branch, usually within a couple of days. The Central Library is open 7 days a week, while the branches are open 5 to 6 days a week. Call the numbers listed for hours.

Central

AUSTIN HISTORY CENTER
810 Guadalupe St.
(512) 974-7480
This building, which served as Austin's city library for nearly half a century, is now home to one of the leading local history collections in the state. The History Center houses more than one million items documenting the history of Austin to the present day. It's closed Mon. (See the Attractions chapter for more about this wonderful facility.)

JOHN HENRY FAULK CENTRAL LIBRARY
800 Guadalupe St.
(512) 974-7400
www.cityofaustin.org/library
Named for revered Austinite John Henry Faulk, Austin's Central Library has more than 360,000 books, manuscripts, periodicals, artistic prints, and recordings. It also features 26 computers that connect to the Internet as well as wireless Internet connections for those who wish to connect to the web using their own computers. The library is open Mon through Thurs from 10 a.m. to 9 p.m., Fri and Sat from 10 a.m. to 6 p.m., and Sun noon to 6 p.m.

YARBOROUGH BRANCH
2200 Hancock Dr.
(512) 454-7208

South Central

TWIN OAKS BRANCH
1800 South Fifth St.
(512) 974-9980

North

LITTLE WALNUT CREEK BRANCH
835 West Rundberg Lane
(512) 974-9860

NORTH VILLAGE BRANCH
2505 Steck Ave.
(512) 974-9960

South

MANCHACA ROAD BRANCH
5500 Manchaca Rd.
(512) 974-8700

East

CARVER BRANCH
1161 Angelina St.
(512) 974-1010

CEPEDA BRANCH
651 North Pleasant Valley Rd.
(512) 974-7372

OAK SPRINGS BRANCH
3101 Oak Springs Dr.
(512) 974-9920

TERRAZAS BRANCH
1105 East Cesar Chavez St.
(512) 974-3625

West

HOWSON BRANCH
2500 Exposition Blvd.
(512) 974-8800

Northwest

MILWOOD BRANCH
12500 Amherst Dr.
(512) 974-9880

OLD QUARRY BRANCH
7051 Village Center Dr.
(512) 345-4435

SPICEWOOD SPRINGS BRANCH
8637 Spicewood Springs Rd.
(512) 974-3800

Northeast

SAINT JOHN BRANCH
7500 Blessing Ave.
(512) 974-7570

UNIVERSITY HILLS BRANCH
4721 Loyola Lane
(512) 974-9940

WINDSOR PARK BRANCH
5833 Westminster Dr.
(512) 974-9840

Southeast

PLEASANT HILL BRANCH
211 East William Cannon Dr.
(512) 974-3940

RUIZ BRANCH
1600 Grove Blvd.
(512) 974-7500

SOUTHEAST AUSTIN COMMUNITY BRANCH
5803 Nuckols Crossing Rd.
(512) 462-1452

Southwest

HAMPTON BRANCH AT OAK HILL
5125 Convict Hill Rd.
(512) 974-9900

University of Texas Libraries

It pays to have one of the largest universities in the country right in your own backyard, especially when that university has a great library system—the fifth-largest academic library in North America to be exact. The UT library system comprises 17 facilities, including 14 general libraries—all but the Marine Science Library located in Austin and most open to the public. Texas residents who wish to use these UT libraries may acquire a Courtesy Borrower Card, available for a $100 annual fee, or apply for a free TexShare card from the Austin Public Library. Information is available at the Courtesy Borrower Services Desk at the main UT library, the Perry-Castañeda Library (512-495-4305). Brochures describing the libraries, their locations, and hours of operation, which vary, can also be obtained at the Borrower Services Desk. For general information call (512) 495-4350.

We've provided information about the main libraries here. For information about all UT libraries and their locations, visit the library system's website at www.lib.utexas .edu. Vehicular access to the main campus is restricted during normal school hours, so if you'd like to visit one of the UT libraries, it's best to park in one of the lots or parking garages located off campus nearby.

FINE ARTS LIBRARY
Doty Fine Arts Building, Third Floor, Near Twenty-third and Trinity Streets
(512) 495-4481
www.lib.utexas.edu/fal
The library includes materials on art, the performing arts, and music, including plenty about Austin's modern music scene. The art collection emphasizes 19th- and 20th-century art of the Americas but includes materials on all art movements and schools,

the philosophy of art, art education, and aesthetics. The music collection provides support for teaching and research in applied music, music education, musicology, and more. The performing arts collection is designed to support studies in drama history, performance, play production, playwriting, drama education, and dance. The library also houses the Historic Music Recordings Collection, with facilities to play selections.

i If you have a TexShare card from the public library in Austin, you can borrow materials from the University of Texas, Austin Community College, and public libraries outside the city without having to pay a membership fee. Ask at your local library for details.

NETTIE LEE BENSON LATIN AMERICAN COLLECTION
Sid Richardson Hall, Manor Road, Between Red River Street and East Campus Drive
(512) 495-4520
www.lib.utexas.edu/benson
Adjacent to the LBJ Library on campus, the Nettie Lee Benson Latin American Collection is an internationally renowned collection of books and many more materials on subjects relating to Latin America and writings by Latin Americans. The collection includes the Mexican American Library Program, which collects materials relating to all aspects of Spanish-speaking people in the United States, especially Mexican Americans.

PERRY-CASTAÑEDA LIBRARY
Twenty-first and Speedway Streets
(512) 495-4250
www.lib.utexas.edu/pcl

The main library of the UT system contains about 3 million volumes in all subject fields. The PCL, as it is known, emphasizes the humanities, the social sciences, business, and education. Subject strengths are American and British history, the South, 20th-century American literature, and modern German literature. The PCL also houses the Map Collection, the East Asian Program, South Asian Program, and the Middle Eastern Program. US government and United Nations documents can also be found here, along with other collections. Most of the books available for loan are found on levels 3 to 6.

Community Libraries

CEDAR PARK PUBLIC LIBRARY
550 Discovery Blvd., Cedar Park
(512) 401-5600
www.cedarparktx.us/cp/li.aspx
Opened in 1981, the Cedar Park Public Library now holds more than 70,000 book titles as well as videos, books on tape, music CDs, and more than 100 magazine and newspaper titles. The library also has Internet-connected computers for public use. The library is free for Cedar Park residents. Others may obtain a card for $20 for 6 months or $35 per year. The library is open Mon through Thurs from 9 a.m. to 9 p.m., Fri and Sat from 9 a.m. to 5 p.m., and Sun 1 to 6 p.m.

LAKE TRAVIS COMMUNITY LIBRARY
2300 Loman's Spur, Suite 100
(512) 263-2885
www.laketravislibrary.org
This library serves Lake Travis community residents as well as all those summer visitors who flock to the lake. In addition to the fiction and nonfiction sections, the library features a good-size children's section, large print books, newspapers and magazines,

audio and video cassettes, as well as Internet computers for public use. This library also features an ongoing bag-of-books sale to raise funds. Volunteers who staff this library in summer say this program is especially popular with out-of-town visitors. The library is open Mon and Tues from 10 a.m. to 7 p.m., Wed through Fri from 10 a.m. to 6 p.m., Sat from 10 a.m. to 4 p.m., and Sun from 1 p.m. to 4 p.m.

PFLUGERVILLE COMMUNITY LIBRARY
102 Tenth St., Pflugerville
(512) 251-9185
www.cityofpflugerville.com/library
Once housed in an old home in what was euphemistically called "downtown" Pflugerville, the library, like other city services, has found itself overwhelmed by the growth of the once-quiet little town northwest of Austin. The 12,500-square-foot facility, opened in 1999, has already been deemed too small, and plans are to open a new expansion by 2012. The current collection includes 56,000 items, including books, CDs, and DVDs. The library is open Mon through Thurs 10 a.m. to 9 p.m., Fri 10 a.m. to 6 p.m., Sat from 10 a.m. to 4 p.m., and Sun from 1 p.m. to 6 p.m.

ROUND ROCK PUBLIC LIBRARY
Robert G. and Helen Griffith Building,
216 East Main St., Round Rock
(512) 218-7000
www.roundrocktexas.gov/library
The city's library, located in the heart of Round Rock's historic district, encompasses 43,000 square feet and is named in honor of library patrons Robert G. and Helen Griffith. The library now boasts more than 160,000 items, including books, videos, CDs, and books on CD. There are 31 computer stations, including 15 filtered computers for

young patrons to use to access the Internet. Round Rock residents use the facility for free, while patrons from outside the city limits pay a small fee for a card. The library is open Mon through Thurs 9 a.m. to 9 p.m., Fri and Sat 9 a.m. to 6 p.m., and Sun 1 to 6 p.m.

WRITERS' ORGANIZATIONS

Writers, like other addicts, need support and there's no better comfort to be found than at the meetings of the groups listed here. We have yet to hear of one that has cured writing fever, however.

TEXAS INSTITUTE OF LETTERS
www.texasinstituteofletters.org
This honorary organization, established in 1936, recognizes practicing writers who have demonstrated substantial literary achievement, as well as others who have had a positive influence on the literary arts. Members, who are invited to join, must have a substantial connection to Texas. Most important for nonmembers, the TIL, as it is known, determines the winners of more than $22,000 in annual writing prizes that are backed by foundations or individuals. The prizes include the prestigious $6,000 Jesse Jones Award for Fiction and the $5,000 Carr P. Collins Award for Nonfiction. Other awards are given for poetry, journalism, short stories, children's books, and book design. Additionally, the TIL and the University of Texas determine the winners of two annual fellowships, which give writers a residency at J. Frank Dobie's Paisano Ranch and a large stipend. The goals of the TIL are to stimulate interest in Texas letters, recognize distinctive achievement

in the field, and promote fellowship among those interested in the literary and cultural development of the state.

✳WRITERS' LEAGUE OF TEXAS
611 South Congress Ave., Suite 130
(512) 499-8914
www.writersleague.org
Established in 1981, the Writers' League of Texas has grown from a group of writers gathered in an Austin backyard to include more than 1,500 members, more than half living outside Central Texas. Formerly called the Austin Writers' League, the name was changed to reflect the membership base as well as the many programs the league offers to writers throughout the state. This fine organization, the largest in Texas, is highly involved in developing the Austin literary scene and providing support for its members. League members host many informal classes, workshops, and retreats for writers of many genres. The league also sponsors annual writing contests and scholarship programs..

The nonprofit organization maintains a library and resource center that contains more than 1,500 volumes and includes books written by members that can be checked out. The league's monthly newsletter, *Scribe*, provides a wealth of information for writers and book lovers. General meetings, open to the public, are held the third Thurs of each month and feature a speaker or panel of experts on topics of interest to writers. The league also has information about local writers' groups for specific genres. Individual membership is $50 a year.

PARKS & RECREATION

No one who has stood on the edge of a Hill Country pasture in springtime could deny the beauty of Central Texas, but even long after the riot of colorful wildflowers is gone there is much to admire in the landscape of the Hill Country. Familiarity breeds admiration and learning about the particulars makes both residents and visitors appreciate the whole. Central Texas is not only home to some of the world's intriguing and delicate fauna and flora but is also a land where residents enjoy a generally benign climate. This is a place where Christmas Day may be celebrated with a walk in the sun along Lady Bird Lake or a swim in Barton Springs Pool. Life, for much of the year, is lived outdoors in Austin. Though Austin's nightlife and music scenes are touted, it is also the city's fondness for outdoor activities and an abundance of parks, greenbelts, and preserves that give Austin a reputation as a livable city. Pockets of greenery are fiercely defended against the pressures of urban sprawl. The Highland Lakes, which bring nature into the heart of the city via Lady Bird Lake, serve as a natural lifeline between the Hill Country and the city dweller. The city also rises to the modern challenge to provide its citizens with something to do on the weekends other than mow the lawn. There are 5K runs, 10K runs, marathons, bicycle races, kite-flying contests, and rugby games. There are rocks to be climbed and Frisbees to be thrown. This chapter offers a look at area parks and gives an overview of the many recreational activities popular in Central Texas. It is divided into four general sections: Parks, Nature Preserves, Recreation, and Water Sports.

PARKS

State Parks

There are at least two dozen state parks within an easy 2-hour drive of Austin under the management of the Texas Parks & Wildlife Department (800-792-1112, www.tpwd.state.tx.us). This is a first-class website with downloadable maps and PDF files that detail the state's parks, wildlife management areas (WMAs), and areas of interest, including biking, camping, driving tours, equestrian activities, fishing, hunting, and wildlife viewing. Visitors can make reservations online or by e-mail, plus fax and telephone numbers for campsites and cabins are listed.

Among the 41 historical sites are several national landmarks, including the Admiral Nimitz Museum and Historical Center in Fredericksburg and Lyndon Johnson State Park in Stonewall, both to the west of Austin and easily accessible (see the Day Trips chapter).

Other state parks in Central Texas offer visitors an opportunity to experience Texas natural history. Most offer camping, water sports, nature trails for hiking, walking, or mountain biking, plus picnic facilities and perhaps equestrian trails.

Admission to most state parks is between $1 and $5 per person. There is a 12-month pass, the Texas State Parks Pass, which sells for $60 for each family vehicle and allows unlimited visits to state parks and historic sites. Pass holders also qualify for a 50 percent camper's discount (some restrictions apply on popular holidays), a 10 percent discount at state park stores and a reduced subscription rate to *Texas Parks and Wildlife* magazine. The state also offers the Texas Parklands Passport, also called the Bluebonnet Pass, which offers discounted admission to parks and historic sites for seniors, veterans, and disabled visitors.

Most state parks have camping facilities. Advance reservations are advised. Most parks are open for day visitors from 8 a.m. to 10 p.m., but call ahead for hours of operation, particularly on holidays. Parks that have certain natural attractions, greenbelts, nature trails, or swimming holes may have special hours and blackout dates.

BASTROP STATE PARK
Highway 21, 1.5 miles east of Bastrop
(512) 321-2101

This 3,503-acre park 32 miles east of Austin is popular, perhaps because its landscape is so different from the surrounding countryside. The park is home to the "Lost Pines," a forest of pine trees (Texans call them "piney woods") that would seem to be more at home in East Texas. During the Depression, the Civilian Conservation Corps built several log cabins at the park, which are now popular for family getaways. There are 12 cabins accommodating from 2 to 8 persons. Reservations and a deposit are required. All cabins have bathrooms, kitchen facilities, air-conditioning, and wood-burning fireplaces.

Prices range from $65 to $110. For reservations call (512) 389-8900. No pets are allowed except for those aiding the physically challenged. The park also has camping facilities, a swimming pool open in the summertime, fishing on a 10-acre lake, hiking, golfing on a 9-hole course, and hiking trails. Park rangers offer guided nature tours, popular from Jan to Mar during the breeding season of the endangered Houston toad. Scenic Park Road 1 connects with Buescher State Park, 15 miles east.

i The best time to call the state parks reservation number (512-389-8900) is midweek (Wed and Thurs), when call volumes are lighter. Mon and Tues and the week before major holidays are the busiest times. Before you go, visit the park you have chosen online at www.tpwd.state.tx.us to download a detailed map in PDF format.

BUESCHER STATE PARK
FM 153 off Highway 71, Smithville
(512) 237-2241

This 1,016-acre park, pronounced "Bisher" State Park, is a favorite spot for area fishermen. A 30-acre lake is stocked with trout, bass, and other fish. There are campsites, screened shelters, and picnic areas. Unlike nearby Bastrop State Park, oak trees and Blackland prairie dominate the landscape here. Popular activities at the park include biking, hiking, swimming, and boating.

COLORADO BEND STATE PARK
FM 580, west of Lampasas near Bend
(915) 628-3240

This 5,328-acre park offers primitive camping, hiking, fishing, swimming, mountain biking, birding, cave tours, and nature walks to the beautiful 60-foot-high Gorman Falls, particularly popular with birders.

✳ENCHANTED ROCK STATE NATURAL AREA
RR 965, north of Fredericksburg
(830) 685-3636

The major feature of this 1,643-acre park is Enchanted Rock, a 640-acre granite outcropping, a vast stone dome that rises above the Hill Country landscape, similar to its geological cousins Uluru (Ayers Rock) in Australia and Stone Mountain in Georgia. Hikers who are in good form can hike to the top (it's easier than Uluru) to enjoy an unparalleled view of Texas. See the Fredericksburg section of the Day Trips chapter to learn more about the Native American origins of the "enchanted" part of the name. It is the "rock" part of the name that beckons the more down-to-earth types who are interested in rock climbing. In addition, there is camping, both tent and primitive; hiking; nature trails; and picnicking. Given its spectacular views and easy access from major population centers, the park reaches its visitor and parking limits early on weekends. Get an early start.

INKS LAKE STATE PARK
Highway 29 on Park Road 4, near Burnet
(512) 793-2223

This 1,201-acre Highland Lakes park 9 miles west of Burnet offers camping, minicabin facilities, recreational vehicle hookups, backpacking, hiking, golfing, boating, canoeing (canoes and paddleboats for rent), water-skiing, scuba diving, and fishing. It is a favorite for boaters and anglers. The park offers nature trail walks and canoe tours in spring and fall. There is a sunset bat watch, and a grocery store is on-site. A 9-hole golf course is operated by

Highland Lakes Golf Club (512-793-2859), and the daily fee is $10 or less, depending on the day and time.

MCKINNEY FALLS STATE PARK
5808 McKinney Falls Pkwy.
(512) 243-1643

Located just 13 miles southeast of downtown Austin off US 183, this 744-acre park encompasses the lands around the confluence of Williamson and Onion Creeks. The park is named for Texas pioneer Thomas McKinney, whose ruined home still stands near the confluence of the creeks. He was one of Stephen F. Austin's original 300 colonists. The pool under the falls is a popular swimming spot, but it is limited to those days when park rangers deem it safe. On some days the bacteria count may be high due to pollution from upstream, nonpoint sources, so call ahead if you want to swim. The park also has hiking, biking, fishing, picnicking, several screened shelters with bunk beds (no mattresses), and camping facilities. There are nature study areas, a dirt-bike trail, and group picnic facilities.

PEDERNALES FALLS STATE PARK
FM 3232, near Johnson City
(830) 868-7304

The spectacular falls are the highlight of this 5,211-acre park, formerly part of the Circle Bar Ranch. The falls are even more spectacular after a sudden spring rain, when the Pedernales River exhibits all the dangerous beauty of a Hill Country river in flash flood. With its vast tumble of boulders and Hill Country plants and trees, the falls are beautiful, even on dry summer days. The park has fishing and nature study facilities, picnic sites, a hike and bike trail, swimming in the lower 3 miles of the river, and an equestrian trail.

i The Texas state parks system celebrated 75 years of stewardship in 1998. One handy guide to the state system is a map of Texas showing all the state park sites. Call (800) 786-8644. The cost is $3.11 to cover postage and handling.

The Lake Parks

The image of Texas as a land of deserts and vast, treeless wilderness owes a lot more to Hollywood than reality, but in Central Texas, where lakes abound, most of them are not nature's work but owe their existence to people with gigantic imaginations who roamed the Texas political landscape in the first half of the 20th century.

Between 1843 and 1938 several devastating floods washed through the Hill Country along the path of the Colorado River. The horror of flooding was contrasted with the blight of drought. Texas leaders looked to the hills and dreamed of damming the river to stem the floods, defeat droughts, and harness the river's power to electrify the wilderness. With the help of engineers and laborers, they succeeded, and now the Highland Lakes climb 646 feet, stretch more than 150 miles long, and encompass 56,000 acres of water and 700 miles of shoreline, making up the greatest concentration of fresh water in Texas.

In 1934 the Texas Legislature created the Lower Colorado River Authority (LCRA), a state agency that administers the chain of artificial lakes and dams created to harness the Colorado River. Today it is one of the most influential state agencies in terms of environmental policy.

Hydroelectricity may be a very small part of the function of the Highland Lakes these days, but the lakes are still a vital force in the battle against floods and are a critical water supply for some communities in the area. They also provide water for rice farms downstream, a major Texas agricultural crop, and are a huge draw to tourists.

There are three major links in the lake chain in the area around and in Austin. The most urban link in the chain is Lady Bird Lake, 5 miles long from Tom Miller Dam in West Austin, near Redbud Trail, to Longhorn Dam in East Austin near Pleasant Valley Rd.

Lake Austin is 20 miles long, stretching from Mansfield Dam on Lake Travis to Tom Miller Dam. Lake Austin is the oldest of the Highland Lakes.

Lake Travis is 64 miles long and was formed by the construction of the 266-foot-high, 7,089-footlong Mansfield Dam, which was built in 1941 and named for Texas Congressman J. J. Mansfield. Not only is the lake an increasingly popular recreational spot but its shores also are prized real estate.

With the booming growth, the Highland Lakes are just one focus of the debate among environmentalists and the development community. On the recreation front, there are increasing concerns about crowding on the lakes as personal watercraft, yachts, swimmers, scuba divers, waterskiers, Windsurfers, and cigarette boats vie for space. Personal watercraft have been banned from the lakes during the three major summer holiday weekends: Memorial Day, Fourth of July, and Labor Day. Following verbal clashes and some accidents between motorized crafts and sailing vessels, there has been some discussion by the LCRA of "zoning" the lakes for various activities.

To the west of Lake Travis is Lake Buchanan, pronounced Buck-ANN-un by the locals (see the Texas Pronunciation guide in the Overview chapter). Created by the Buchanan Dam, the 31-milelong lake is the highest in the chain and covers the largest surface area, although Lake Travis contains more water. The LCRA has set aside 16,000 acres for parks and reserves along the Colorado River—developed parks, environmental learning centers, recreational areas, and river access sites. The LCRA's website is a valuable resource and offers detailed guides and downloadable maps, which can be very handy when trying to locate remote areas and boating docks. These parks typically feature little artificial landscaping—hills have not been leveled, and large green spaces are usually Hill Country meadows rather than planted lawns. Picnic and campsites are shaded by oak trees and trails are lined with juniper trees.

For more information about all the Highland Lakes, see the Day Trips chapter.

THE LOWER COLORADO RIVER AUTHORITY (LCRA)
(512) 473-3200, (800) 776-5272, ext. 3366
www.lcra.org

In addition to a wealth of information on water safety and quality, weather forecasts, and utility, energy, and conservation issues, the agency also offers newcomers and visitors a park visitor's package.

LCRA Primitive Areas

The river authority operates a primitive recreation system along the lake system. These campsites are in natural areas where the typical rugged Hill Country landscape has been minimally disrupted. Most of the sites are in out-of-the-way places, and visitors will

need detailed directions or a good area map to find them. Call (512) 473-3200, ext. 4083 for directions and information. Some charge a nominal use fee, around $5.

GLOSTER BEND PRIMITIVE AREA
Lake Travis, off FM 1431

Approximately 6 miles west of Lago Vista, this lakeside site has camping and picnic facilities. Day use only is recommended, but the boat ramp is available 24 hours a day.

GRELLE PRIMITIVE AREA
Lake Travis, off Highway 71 near Spicewood

Grelle is a 400-acre park with woods, trails, camping, and access to the lake. The hiking trails are challenging. Next door is the popular Krause Springs swimming hole (see the Swimming section of this chapter). Overnight camping is allowed.

MULESHOE BEND PRIMITIVE AREA
Lake Travis, off Highway 71 past Bee Cave

A 900-acre facility with trails, lake access, camping, and picnicking near the Ridge Harbor subdivision on Burnet County Road 414. This wilderness area is very popular with mountain bikers.

THE NARROWS PRIMITIVE AREA
Lake Travis, off Highway 71 near Spicewood

This rugged site has a boat ramp, picnic areas, and primitive campsites. This is one of the smallest parks in the system, encompassing only 250 acres. It is used primarily as a boat ramp facility (the only public ramp on the upper south side of the lake), since there are neither potable water nor restrooms on-site.

SHAFFER BEND PRIMITIVE AREA
Lake Travis, off FM 1431

A 535-acre park with camping, picnicking, and lake access about 17 miles west of Lago Vista. The terrain is rough and suitable to trucks and 4-wheel-drive vehicles.

TURKEY BEND (EAST) PRIMITIVE AREA
Lake Travis, off FM 1431

A 400-acre park with great views of the lake and surrounding countryside. The park has camping and picnic facilities and lake access. The park is about 10 miles west of Lago Vista.

Travis County Parks

Travis County, home to the capital city, operates 26 parks under its Travis Natural Resources department (TNR), many of them on the banks of Lake Travis and Lake Austin, and other small, urban parks in suburban areas beyond municipal limits. A wide variety is listed here and, keep in mind, as the population grows more parks are being added. Generally the Lake Austin parks charge no fees, but those on Lake Travis may have vehicle charges and individual entrance fees. You can reach Travis County Parks Visitor Information and Reservations at (512) 854-7275, www.co.travis.tx.us/tnr/parks.

ARKANSAS BEND
16900 Cherry Lane, Lago Vista

This 195-acre LCRA park on the shores of Lake Travis is not as primitive as some other LCRA parks and is operated by the county. The Hill Country landscape is a backdrop to picnic areas equipped with barbecue pits. The park has hiking trails, swimming facilities, a boat ramp, and campsites.

BEN FISHER
600 Carrie Manor St., Manor

This park is in eastern Travis County and has picnic and barbecue facilities, hiking trails, and sports courts. The landscape east of Austin is called Blackland Prairie, and much of it is fertile farmland. Parks in this area have undulating hills, meadows covered with wildflowers both spring and fall, and large pecan trees. Pecan harvesting is a favorite fall pastime.

BOB WENTZ PARK AT WINDY POINT
7144 Comanche Trail, Lake Travis

This 21-acre LCRA lakeside park has barbecue pits, picnic sites, hiking trails, playgrounds, a swimming area, showers, and a boat ramp for sailboats. It is popular among Windsurfers and scuba divers.

CYPRESS CREEK
13800 Bullick Hollow Rd., Lake Travis

The landscape in this LCRA park on Lake Travis retains its wild character, but there have been some additions, including barbecue pits and picnic areas. The park offers access to the lake for swimming and primitive camping.

DINK PEARSON PARK
3011 Lohman Ford Rd., Lago Vista

Dink Pearson is a lakeside park with picnic and barbecue facilities, access to the lake for swimmers, and a boat ramp.

FRITZ HUGHES
3100 Fritz Hughes Park Rd., Lake Austin, near Mansfield Dam

This is a good spot for family picnics but is not suitable for swimming. The park has picnic and barbecue facilities plus a playscape.

HIPPIE HOLLOW
7000 Comanche Trail, Lake Travis

This is an Austin landmark. (Its formal name is MacGregor Park, but nobody calls it that.) This clothing-optional LCRA park is open to individuals age 18 and older and is particularly popular among gay sun seekers. You can swim in the lake, sunbathe on the park's beach and rocks, or hike on the trails (shoes recommended). Admission fees. Day use only.

LITTLE WEBBERVILLE
100 Water St., Webberville

This Colorado River park 20 miles east of Austin, near the community of Webberville, has both picnic and barbecue areas. The park also has playscapes and a boat ramp. It is a popular entry point on the river for kayakers and canoeists.

MANSFIELD DAM
4370 Mansfield Dam Park Rd., Lake Travis

On Lake Travis, just west of Mansfield Dam, this county park offers picnic and barbecue facilities, swimming, a boat ramp, and overnight camping facilities. It is a short walk to the dam, which offers a close-up view of engineering feats in Central Texas. The dam is also a favorite place for hawks and other birds of prey to ride the thermal wind currents.

PACE BEND
2501 Pace Bend Park Rd., Spicewood
(512) 264-1482

This 1,000-acre-plus park (sometimes called Paleface Park) has equestrian facilities, trails, campsites, picnic and barbecue facilities, plus swimming in the lake.

RICHARD MOYA
10001 Burleson Rd.

This park is a favorite spot for family picnics, particularly on Mexican-American holidays and birthdays, when the smell of fajitas cooking and the sound of piñatas being whacked fill the air. Portions of the original downtown Congress Avenue Bridge, ca. 1884, now span Onion Creek in the park. This day-use park is only 20 minutes from downtown and is a popular location for baseball and softball tournaments.

SANDY CREEK
9500 Lime Creek Rd., Leander

Another rugged hillside park on Lake Travis, this park has hiking trails, offers access to the lake for swimmers and boaters, and has primitive camping facilities.

SELMA HUGHES PARK
11921 Selena Hughes Park Rd., Lake Austin

This is the site of a popular boat ramp on busy Lake Austin. There are picnic facilities with barbecue pits.

TOM HUGHES PARK
12714 Hughes Park Rd., Lake Travis

Swimming is the popular attraction in this small county park, which is open in daylight hours only.

WEBBERVILLE
2305 Park Lane, Elgin

This large and popular county park is 3 miles east of Webberville in eastern Travis County on the banks of the Colorado River at the Travis/Bastrop County line. There are picnic and barbecue facilities, hiking trails, playscapes, a boat ramp, ballfields, sports courts, and equestrian facilities. The large picnic pavilions can be reserved for gatherings by calling the Travis County parks reservations number at (512) 473-9437.

WINDMILL RUN
7306 Kirkhaven Lane

Windmill Run is a neighborhood park near the Windmill Run subdivision in Oak Hill, with picnic and barbecue facilities, hiking trails, and ballfields.

Austin City Parks

The city boasts nearly 208 city parks, 25 hike and bike trails, and numerous greenbelts (www.ci.austin.tx.us/parks/greenbelts.htm), plus 11 nature preserves (see the Nature Preserves section in this chapter), all encompassing more than 16,076 acres of urban retreats.

Given the large number of city parks, we have picked out several of particularly interesting character and detailed them below. The city offers detailed information about all city parks in several brochures, available on request from the Parks and Recreation Department (PARD) and on the city's website, both listed below. The parks are listed alphabetically, ending with Zilker Park, the city's major park in the heart of the city and home to Barton Springs Pool, an icon that is perhaps the ultimate natural symbol of Austin life (see the Close-up in this chapter).

Austin has more than 20 miles of surfaced scenic paths in the city's natural greenbelts, plus untold miles of wooded tracks. Bicycles are permitted, but motorized vehicles are not. Pets on leashes are allowed. The city's parks department has been building separate trails for hikers, joggers, walkers, and bikers, but there are several popular trails, notably around Lady Bird Lake, where the groups must coexist. Rock climbers on the Barton Creek greenbelt also have been at odds with mountain bikers. Peaceful coexistence is encouraged.

The curfew on all trails is 10 p.m. They reopen at 5 a.m. To access a greenbelt, head for the address listed with each park. Parking is limited at some greenbelt locations, and space is at a premium on weekends, particularly when the weather sends much of Austin outdoors.

AUSTIN PARKS AND RECREATION DEPARTMENT (PARD)
200 South Lamar Blvd.
(512) 974-6700
www.ci.austin.tx.us/parks

Residents and visitors alike should stop by the main office of PARD and pick up a wealth of material on Austin recreational activities and facilities. The city's website also has extensive information and downloadable maps.

✳BARTON CREEK GREENBELT
3755-B Loop 360 (Capital of Texas Highway)

This is one of the city's most popular, and most crowded, greenbelts. The trail follows Barton Creek through the canyon that cuts across Southwest Austin. Barton Creek has 6 official access points, called trailheads, and one very popular unofficial entry. The designated trailheads are at Zilker Park, west of Barton Springs Pool; the intersection of Spyglass Drive and Barton Skyway; 2010 Homedale Dr., behind Barton Hills Elementary School; the Gus Fruh Access at 2642 Barton Hills Dr.; the Brodie Oaks office complex, off Loop 360 west of Lamar Boulevard; and the intersection of Camp Craft Road and Scottish Woods Trail. The Gus Fruh and Brodie Oaks access points are wheelchair accessible. The unofficial access point is easily spotted on a balmy weekend afternoon. The shoulder of the access road leading from Loop 360 (Capital of Texas Highway) onto MoPac south is lined with cars. Just a few yards away, a wide stretch of the creek creates a swimming hole that attracts large crowds on warm days.

BOGGY CREEK GREENBELT
1114 Nile St.

This East Austin trail runs 3 miles from Rosewood Park to Zaragosa Park. Trails in the eastern half of the city, roughly defined as east of I-35, have different flora from those in the western half. The eastern half of the city is built over Blackland Prairie—rich, black soil, compared with the rocky, limestone landscape in the west. The creeks and greenbelts in the east are often shaded by pecan trees and have woodland plants along their banks.

BULL CREEK PARK AND GREENBELT
7806 North Capital of Texas Hwy.

This is a popular spot, particularly in spring when the rains fill the creek, attracting swimmers and waders. In summer the creek is usually very low or dry. There are picnic facilities and hike and bike trails. The 120-acre greenbelt attracts hikers and mountain bikers. The park is off Loop 360 (Capital of Texas Highway) and south of Spicewood Springs Rd.

EMMA LONG METROPOLITAN PARK
(CITY PARK)
1600 City Park Rd.
(512) 346-1831

This large 1,147-acre park with 3 miles of Lake Austin shoreline has boat ramps and picnic sites. It is the oldest city park and is more traditional, showing the human hand in its landscaping and facilities.

JOHNSON CREEK GREENBELT
2100 Enfield Rd.

A milelong urban trail runs from Lady Bird Lake to Enfield Road, paralleling MoPac. Trail users can access the greenbelt from the Austin High School parking lot.

LADY BIRD LAKE METROPOLITAN PARK

Along the Colorado River from Tom Miller Dam in West Austin to the US 183 bridge in East Austin, this park graces the Colorado River as it winds through the heart of downtown Austin. No other Austin city park, with the exception of nearby Zilker Park, so captures the Austin spirit. From dawn to beyond dusk, the Hike and Bike Trail is filled with joggers, walkers, bicyclists, nature lovers, and dog walkers enjoying the riverside pathways. Spring is an especially beautiful time for a stroll along Lady Bird Lake (formerly Town Lake) as flowering cherry trees, some of them gifts from Japan, bloom alongside native redbud trees. The parks department also periodically offers the public the opportunity to plant a tree in the park and dedicate it to a loved one.

The southern shore of Lady Bird Lake, just west of South First Street, is known as Auditorium Shores and is the site for outdoor concerts, including the annual July Fourth Pops Concert (see the Annual Events & Festivals chapter) and various festivals.

In quieter moments, wildlife, particularly turtles, ducks, and swans, can be seen swimming and feeding along the banks of Lady Bird Lake. Only nonmotorized craft are allowed on this stretch of the lake, such as canoes, kayaks, and paddleboats, which can be rented in nearby Zilker Park (see the Boating section in this chapter). The Austin Rowing Club has its clubhouse on the north shore near the Four Seasons Hotel, and lone rowers can be seen sculling in the early morning through the light fog rising from the lake. No swimming is allowed in the lake.

On the northern bank of Lady Bird Lake and east of I-35 is Fiesta Gardens, a popular community concert and celebration spot. Two notable Mexican-American holidays are celebrated here, Cinco de Mayo and Diez y Seis de Septiembre (see the Annual Events & Festivals chapter).

LAKE WALTER E. LONG METROPOLITAN PARK
6614 Blue Bluff Rd.
(512) 926-5230
In Northeast Travis County, this 1,300-acre lake is well known for its fishing and water activities. There are campsites, hike and bike trails, plus park roads that are popular with bicyclists and runners.

MARY MOORE SEARIGHT METROPOLITAN PARK
907 Slaughter Lane
The 344 acres contain an 18-hole disc (Frisbee) golf course, a 2-mile hike and bike trail, a 2½-mile equestrian trail, and a fishing pier over Slaughter Creek. There are basketball, tennis, and volleyball courts, plus baseball and soccer facilities, barbecue pits, and a picnic gazebo for large parties.

MOUNT BONNELL PARK
3800 Mount Bonnell Rd., off Scenic Road
For 140 years tourists have been coming to Mount Bonnell and climbing the 99 steps (785 feet) to the peak for a great view of the city. No mountain, but a sturdy climb. Several local legends purport to account for the mount's name. One claims it is named in honor of George W. Bonnell, a New Yorker

who came to Texas to fight in the War of Independence against Mexico. He fought the Native Americans and was a sometime newspaper editor. He met his death on December 26, 1842, when he was captured and shot by Mexican troops. Others say the name is a corruption of the names Beau and Nell, two lovers who were married on the peak minutes before a Native American attack. After their first kiss, they leapt to their death. Other legends are variations on this theme, involving Native American princesses and beautiful Spanish senoritas, all forced to take a dive. On a serious note, visitors should be careful at the peak, since an unfortunate few have slipped and fallen down the hillside. Mount Bonnell is the stuff of romance and a popular spot for young couples who want to watch the stars come out over Austin—a particularly romantic spot for University of Texas students, who can get a clear view of the UT Tower, aglow in orange light when the university's athletic teams win. It is also a great spot for a picnic with a view. The park opens at 5 a.m. for sunrise viewing and closes at 10 p.m.

PEASE PARK
1100 Kingsbury St.
Along Shoal Creek between Twelfth and Twenty-fourth Streets, this Central Austin park is popular among lunchtime picnickers and joggers. The land was donated by former Governor Elisha M. Pease, hence the name. During the Civil War General George Armstrong Custer camped on this site and buried 35 of his men here. There are legends of buried treasure here involving a lost cache of money supposedly stolen by a paymaster in the Mexican Army. Digging, of course, is forbidden. These days it is known for happier occasions, including Eeyore's Birthday, an

annual free-spirit celebration—sort of a mini Woodstock-meets-Mardi Gras event—that includes both the whimsical and the outrageous (see the Annual Events & Festivals chapter).

i Woolridge Square is a little gem of a park in downtown Austin—squeezed between the Travis County Courthouse and the Austin History Center, Ninth and Tenth Streets on Guadalupe. The park's Victorian bandstand sits in the center of a natural amphitheater and has been the site of weddings, political rallies, small concerts, and one murder (according to legend).

SHOAL CREEK HIKE AND BIKE TRAIL
Lamar Boulevard, from Thirty-eighth Street to Lady Bird Lake
This wide, 3-mile-long greenbelt along the urban pathway of Shoal Creek, roughly paralleling Lamar Boulevard, winds through the heart of Central Austin and can be accessed at many points along the way. Like other urban Austin creekbeds, Shoal Creek has an early-warning system in place to alert residents and emergency workers of flash floods. These high-tech devices can be seen near bridges and low crossings on city creeks. They look like large traffic signal boxes and are equipped with solar panels and antennas.

SLAUGHTER CREEK METROPOLITAN PARK
507 West Slaughter Lane
Adjacent to the Lady Bird Johnson Wildflower Center in Southwest Austin, this park is at its best in spring, when the Hill Country wildflowers bloom. The prime attraction is the 3-mile veloway, which attracts bicyclists

and in-line skaters. The park also has a nature trail, picnic facilities, playground, soccer fields, volleyball, and basketball courts.

WALLER CREEK GREENBELT
703 East Fifteenth St.
Stretching from Fifteenth Street to Lady Bird Lake, the Waller Street greenbelt is a mixture of urban greenbelt and urban blight. The northern stretch is quite pleasant. City voters recently approved a bond election to improve the southern end of the trail.

WATERLOO PARK
403 East Fifteenth St.
This central city park lies just east of the capitol and is a quiet retreat in the heart of the city. It is also a popular spot for several gatherings during the year (see the Annual Events chapter).

ZILKER BOTANICAL GARDENS
2200 Barton Springs Rd.
(512) 477-8672
Just north of Zilker Park (see the subsequent listing) and part of the Zilker experience, the gardens are also home to the Austin Garden Center. There are several gardens within the grounds, including a rose garden (a popular site for weddings), a cactus and succulent garden, fragrance and butterfly gardens, and woodland trails. There is also a xeriscape garden, where native plants are shown off to great advantage. Admission to the garden center is free except for certain weekends (see the Annual Events & Festivals chapter) when garden shows are held on the grounds.

The most beautiful part of the garden center is the Taniguchi Oriental Garden, created by the late Isamu Taniguchi, a native of Osaka, Japan. Taniguchi moved to the United States as a young man, worked as a farmer in California and the Rio Grande Valley, and then retired to Austin in the 1960s. Taniguchi, whose son was a noted Austin architect, spent 18 months creating the garden along the hillside site. He worked for free with his own plans and no oversight or interference from city planners. His creation is a symbol of peace, just as Taniguchi wished. He died in 1992 at age 94. The best time to visit the garden is on a quiet weekday, since it is a popular attraction on weekends.

✳ZILKER PARK
2100 Barton Springs Rd.
(512) 472-4914
This 400-acre downtown park became a city park in 1917 when Colonel A. J. Zilker donated the land to the city. The most famous and revered attraction in the park is Barton Springs Pool (see the Close-up in this chapter), but it is also a place of pilgrimage for other reasons. At Christmas one of the city's so-called moonlight towers (see the Attractions chapter) serves as the trunk of the Zilker Park Christmas Tree (see the Annual Events & Festivals chapter), visible from miles around. The "tree" is created by Christmas lights strung in maypole fashion from the tower to the ground. Tradition calls for children to stand inside the tree and spin around until the lights are blurred and the kids are dizzy. Small children are spun around in a grown-up's arms, making both kid and grown-up enjoy the dizzy spell.

Zilker is home to a miniature train, playscape, picnic grounds, a "folf" (Frisbee or disc golf) course, rugby and soccer fields, and a canoe and kayak concession (see the Boating section in this chapter). A grass-covered hillside serves as a natural amphitheater for summer musicals (see the Annual Events & Festivals and The Arts chapters for more

information). The park is open daily from 6 a.m. to 10 p.m. and is free. There is a small parking fee on weekends when the park is very busy.

Area Parks Departments

CEDAR PARK PARKS AND RECREATION (PARD)
715 Discovery Blvd., Suite 111
(512) 401-5500
www.ci.cedar-park.tx.us
As Cedar Park grows, the number of city parks increases as the city attempts to keep up with the area's booming population. There are 11 neighborhood parks, most of them with picnic facilities and playscapes. Many also have tennis and basketball courts, and some have sand volleyball facilities. The city's parks and recreation department offers information on all city parks and recreation programs.

PFLUGERVILLE PARKS AND RECREATION DEPARTMENT (PARD)
400 Immanuel Rd.
(512) 251-5082
www.cityofpflugerville.com
The city of Pflugerville boasts that the city's parks are a "hometown kind of place, where you and your friends and coworkers can celebrate without a lot of big-city fuss and bother." The city's PARD has developed a master plan aimed at helping the city make the transition from a tiny, rural town to a growing suburban community. The city's parks are connected by an integrated trail system, connecting many of the neighborhoods in the city. PARD also provides swimming, gymnastics, aerobics, soccer, volleyball, and basketball programs. There is the Summer Pfun Camp and PARD-organized events such as 5K Pfun Run and Walk, Pfall Pfest, and the Pumpkin Pflyer bicycle tour.

Close-up

Austin's Beloved Waterin' Hole

Barton Springs Pool has been called the soul of Austin, and that is really not an exaggeration. This treasured, spring-fed pool stands both as a symbol of Austin's lifestyle, a measure of its commitment to the environment, a political rallying point, and even a place of spiritual and psychological renewal. This 1,000 x 125-foot unchlorinated swimming pool, fed by natural spring waters, stands at the heart of Zilker Park and serves as a touchstone for all that was and is Austin.

The pool is fed by spring waters that bubble up at the rate of 35 million gallons a day through the 354-square-mile Edwards Aquifer, an underground limestone formation that stretches from downtown Austin west through the Hill Country. Rains that fall on the hills west of the city filter down through the limestone and emerge at temperatures between 67 and 70 degrees Fahrenheit.

Native Americans gathered around the springs, according to archaeologists. Later, Spanish explorers paused to rest here. In the 19th century among the settlers who came to Austin was William "Uncle Billy" Barton. He set up a homestead near the springs in 1837 and eventually gave his name to both the springs and the creek. For the next 70 years, the land passed through several owners, eventually being sold to Colonel A. J. Zilker in 1907. Ten years later, Zilker left his land to the city and his bequest became Zilker Park.

At first just male residents swam there, but in 1880 a ladies swimming club was formed. While some ethnic minorities swam there in the latter years of the 19th century, by the 1950s the overwhelming majority of African Americans and Mexican Americans did not swim at the pool until the Civil Rights Movement in the 1960s. Now the city pool is a gathering place for all Austinites and visitors.

Since the late '60s, Austin environmentalists, let's dub them the "Greens," have faced off against the "Developers." Barton Springs became a symbol of that fight when the Save our Springs Alliance (SOS) was formed in the 1980s to do battle against development over the Edwards Aquifer, the watershed that feeds the springs—a fight that had limited success as any aerial view of the land west of Austin will show. In the early 1990s the tiny salamander that had been swimming underfoot for years was declared to be a rare species found only in the waters of the spring and pool under the federal Endangered Species Act (ESA). The inch-long salamander has a pale yellow-cream body, flat snout, long limbs, four toes on its front legs, five on the back, and a short, finned tail marked with a narrow orange-yellow stripe and is unique to the springs. It also was the star of a series of lawsuits and political wranglings that kept the development battle blazing throughout the 1990s.

ROUND ROCK PARKS AND
RECREATION DEPARTMENT (PARD)
301 Bagdad St., Suite 250
(512) 218-5540
www.roundrocktexas.gov

The city's parks department operates about 30 parks in the city limits, most of them small neighborhood parks that serve as play areas for neighborhood children and places to relax, perhaps jog, play tennis, or shoot a few baskets for teens and adults. The city's PARD publishes a program brochure and guides to the city's parks that are available on request. In addition to athletic programs, PARD offers

In January 1998 an attorney who had, in the past, represented landowners and developers, filed suit on behalf of two scientists against the city, charging that the City of Austin was violating the ESA by killing salamanders during routine pool cleanings, when the water level was lowered and the pool bottom scrubbed. The Greens said the lawsuit was aimed at shutting down the pool and claimed that mean-spirited developers were behind the action, but the attorney and his clients insisted they only wanted the city to follow the federal laws and protect the salamander. Some observers said the Greens had been hoisted on their own petard.

After a great deal of legal maneuvering, US District Judge Sam Sparks of Austin refused to stop the pool cleanings, issuing his ruling in a poem:

> Barton Springs is a true Austin shrine,
> A hundred years of swimming sublime.
> Now the plaintiffs say swimmers must go
> 'Cause of "stress" to critters,
> 50 or so.
> They want no cleaning 'cause of these bottom feeders,
> Saying it's the law from our
> Congressional leaders.
> But really nothing has changed in all these years
> Despite federal laws and these plaintiff's fears
> Both salamander and swimmer enjoy the springs that are cool.
> And cleaning is necessary for both species in the pool.
> The City is doing its best with full federal support,
> So no temporary injunction shall issue from this Court.
> Therefore, today, Austin's citizens get away with a rhyme;
> But, the truth is they might not be so lucky the next time.
> The Endangered Species Act in its extreme makes no sense.
> Only Congress can change it to make this problem past tense.

The salamanders are a popular feature on T-shirts and in paintings that decorate the pool bathhouse. Few swimmers claim to have actually seen a Barton Springs salamander, but for those who regard Barton Springs Pool as more than a place to swim, the knowledge that the little creatures also enjoy the waters just adds to the beauty and wonder of the place.

For information about pool hours and admission, see the listing under Swimming in this chapter.

country and ballroom dance classes, Jazzercise, programs for toddlers and seniors, preschool and youth programs, plus Cool Kids Camp, an afternoon recreation program for elementary kids.

NATURE PRESERVES

Within the Austin city limits are several nature preserves that offer visitors a glimpse of the wild beauty of both the Hill Country and the prairie to the east of Austin. In addition to city preserves, Travis County and the

LCRA are also guardians to several nature areas.

> ℹ️ **Wildlife, notably birds and deer, are abundant around Austin, but so are insects and snakes, so pack insect bite treatment and wear sturdy boots when hiking on nature trails. Snakes play a vital role in the ecosystem and are usually shy creatures that avoid human contact. Most snakebites can be treated successfully if aid is sought quickly. If you plan to be outdoors frequently in Austin, familiarize yourself with the snakes found in the Texas countryside.**

Austin Nature Preserves

The city operates 11 nature preserves and a nature center. There are strict rules of behavior within the preserves, designed to protect the ecosystems. Access to some of the preserves is by prearrangement only, and group tours are available. For information call (512) 327-7723 or visit www.ci.austin.tx.us /parks/preserves.htm. The preserves' pages on the city's PARD website offer downloadable maps and brochures.

Motorized vehicles, bicycles, pets, firearms, and hunting are prohibited in the nature preserves. Visitors are required to keep noise levels low and stay on trails and may not remove plants or animals from the area.

AUSTIN NATURE AND SCIENCE CENTER
303 Nature Center Dr.
(512) 327-8181
The center's central exhibit is "The Nature of Austin," illustrating four habitats found in the area—ponds, grasslands, woodlands, and a Hill Country cave. The live exhibits feature Texas wildlife—animals that have been rescued and because of permanent injury or extensive human contact cannot be returned to their habitat. The center also has a discovery lab and is surrounded by 80 acres of nature preserve with 2 miles of trails. The "dino pit" exhibit features fossils and bones found at a Congress Avenue building site.

BARROW PRESERVE
7715 Long Point Dr.
This 10-acre preserve is on the upper reaches of Bull Creek in Northwest Austin. It has spring-fed canyons and hiking trails.

BLUNN CREEK PRESERVE
1200 St. Edwards Dr.
This preserve near the St. Edward's University campus in South Austin boasts two lookout points that offer great views of the city, one of which is atop a 100-million-year-old coral reef. This area of Central Texas once was an inland sea. Within its confines can be seen the remains of volcanic ash deposits spewed out by a dozen active volcanoes that rumbled in this area some 80 million years ago.

COLORADO RIVER PRESERVE
US 183 at the Montopolis Bridge,
5827 Levander Loop
On the banks of the Colorado River, west of the Montopolis Bridge in East Austin, this 43-acre preserve offers views of river life, including turtles, herons, and cranes along the sandy banks of the river.

INDIANGRASS WILDLIFE SANCTUARY
Walter E. Long Metropolitan Park,
6614 Blue Bluff Rd., off US 290 East
The sanctuary is in a 200-acre section of Walter E. Long Park in Northeast Austin and is designed to protect Blackland Prairie

habitat, notably a variety of prairie grasses. The wetlands along Lake Long are home to an abundance of wildlife. Access is limited to guided tours only.

GOAT CAVE KARST PRESERVE
3900 Deer Lane

This interesting preserve is off Brodie Lane in Southwest Austin and adjacent to the Maple Run subdivision. Karst is the name scientists have given to the type of honeycombed limestone formations found in several areas of the world, including the Texas Hill Country. This 8-acre site, and this part of Austin, is riddled with sinkholes, caves, and honeycombed limestone.

MAYFIELD PRESERVE
3505 West Fifteenth St.

This is a small city enclave that reflects 19th-century Austin. The 22-acre preserve in Central Austin embraces 5 lily ponds, palm trees, woodlands, and several old cottages, including one from the late 19th century. A cross between a preserve and a park, this quiet spot is very popular with children, who can approach the peacocks (watch out, they have tempers!) and tame deer for close-up viewing. The preserve is next door to Austin Museum of Art Laguna Gloria (see The Arts chapter) in West Austin.

i Austin Metropolitan Trails Council is a coalition of public, private, and nonprofit organizations, neighborhood associations, and individuals working to "promote a comprehensive system of greenways and trails in the greater Austin area." You can contact the council through the Austin Parks and Recreation Department at (512) 974-2000.

ONION CREEK PRESERVE
7001 Onion Creek Rd.

This secluded preserve is north of Highway 71 along Onion Creek and is open to guided tours by reservation only.

ZILKER WEST NATURE PRESERVE

This is a 60-acre preserve at the western end of the park (see the listing under Austin Parks in this chapter), which includes 2 miles of trails along cliff edges on the banks of Barton Creek.

Balcones Canyonlands

The Austin growth boom has led to a great loss of natural habitat, particularly west of Austin in the rugged Hill Country, a land whose outward appearance belies its sensitivity. Following a grand political tug-of-war between pro-development forces and environmentalists, city leaders, environmentalists, developers, and concerned landowners sat down and forged an agreement for a unique preservation effort, dubbed the Balcones Canyonlands Conservation Plan (BCCP).

What has emerged is one of the most significant preservation efforts in Texas. The BCCP embraces more than 30,000 acres west of Austin, and more acreage is being sought to add to this vast area just west of the city. Part of the BCCP is the Balcones Canyonlands National Wildlife Refuge, an area run by the US Fish and Wildlife Service. The City of Austin, Travis County, the LCRA, and several private landowners also are part of the BCCP effort. The Austin BCCP office is located in Marble Falls, northwest of Austin, but this Austin area telephone number provides information on hours and programs, (512) 339-9432. All the agencies involved have information about the BCCP and maps to access points on their respective websites, but one way to get a wealth of information and find links to all the agencies and environmental groups involved in the effort is to visit www.friendsofbalcones.org.

i Inside the City of Austin, dogs must be leashed, but even Fido can enjoy the city's famous free-spirit lifestyle in certain designated parks. One of the most popular spots is in Zilker Park in an area bounded by Stratford Drive, Barton Springs Road, and Lou Neff Drive. For a complete list of places to let Fido feel the wind in his hair, free and unfettered, call the parks department at (512) 974-6700, or check the city's dog parks website www.ci.austin.tx.us/parks/offleash areas.htm. Another resource for dog-friendly parks and facilities is www.dog places.com.

BALCONES CANYONLANDS NATIONAL WILDLIFE REFUGE

The public areas of the refuge are located near the community of Lago Vista, northwest of Austin. The refuge gets its name from the Spanish explorers who, when they saw the terraced hills west of what is now Austin, dubbed the land "Balcones." From afar, the land looks dry and scrubby, but numerous creeks run through, over, and under the terrain, and wildflowers, grasses, trees, and plants abound. This is home to the endangered golden-cheeked warbler and black-capped vireo, two little birds whose songs can still be heard thanks to efforts like the BCCP.

The refuge has two public areas: Warbler Vista Trail, just outside Lago Vista on FM 1431, and Doeskin Ranch, located on FM 1174. Warbler Vista has two trails through the limestone terraces—Cactus Rocks Trail is a 0.6-mile one-way trail and is an easy to moderate hike. This trail winds through golden-cheeked warbler habitat of juniper and hardwood trees. The warblers arrive from Mexico and Latin America in mid-Mar and leave in July. Pick up a guide pamphlet at the parking lot kiosk. Keep in mind this is a delicate ecosystem dedicated to the birds, so no pets or rowdy activity. The Vista Knoll Trail is 1⅓ miles round-trip and is a moderate hike. This trail offers great views of Lake Travis and Lago Vista. The Shin Oak Observation Deck is set in the middle of black-capped vireo habitat. The deck is closed for a short period in spring just as the vireos arrive to minimize the disturbance to the birds. Check the refuge website for the specific dates the deck is closed each year. Once the birds settle into nesting activities, the observation deck is reopened to visitors. The refuge is open from sunrise to sunset, but some areas may be closed for public hunts or bird nesting activities.

The Texas Ornithological Society and the Travis Audubon Society conduct field trips to the refuge, and several annual events throughout the year offer information and tours. One of the most popular events is the Annual Texas Songbird Festival hosted by the Lago Vista community in late Apr or early May. Master naturalists lead area birding expeditions, some to the refuge and others to backyard habitats. There are workshops and seminars on bird photography, butterfly gardening, landscaping fort wildlife, etc. Local craftspeople also show their wares. Contact the Lago Vista Chamber of Commerce at (512) 267-7952, (888) 328-5246, or visit http://songbirdfestival.homestead.com.

LCRA Preserves

The Lower Colorado River Authority (LCRA) operates two preserves near

Austin—McKinney Roughs and Westcave Preserve, listed below—and Canyon of the Eagles, detailed in the Day Trips & Weekend Getaways chapter.

MCKINNEY ROUGHS NATURE PARK AND PRESERVE
**North Bastrop, Highway 71
(512) 303-5073, (800) 776-5272,
ext. 8014
www.lcra.org**

Located a little more than 13 miles east of the Austin-Bergstrom International Airport on Highway 71, this 1,100-acre preserve includes rolling canyons, wildflower meadows, and meandering river bends illustrating four unique ecosystems. The preserve is open to canoeists, hikers, horseback riders, birders, and picnickers who simply want to enjoy the pastoral scenes. The Mark Rose Environmental Learning Center hosts educational programs and activities for students, teachers, and the general public. The center has a 128-room dormitory and is home to the Academy in the Roughs, an overnight environmental learning program for children. There is small entrance fee, reduced for seniors and children; horseback riders pay a larger fee and provide their own horses.

WESTCAVE PRESERVE
**Hamilton Pool Road, RM 3238
(830) 825-3442
www.westcave.org**

Not far from Hamilton Pool Preserve (see below) is an almost mystical place, a natural collapsed grotto that was formed 150,000 years ago, effectively creating a giant terrarium covered by towering cypress trees. The sheltered environment creates a unique ecosystem where orchids and other semitropical plants flourish. Temperature differences between the grotto floor and the surrounding countryside above can be as much as 25 degrees—a wonderful place for a summer escape. Westcave's 30 acres also are home to several endangered species, including the golden-cheeked warbler. The preserve is operated by the LCRA and the private Westcave Preservation Corporation and is open only on weekends or for special visits. Access is limited to guided tours at 10 a.m., noon, and 2 and 4 p.m. Tours also are limited to 30 persons at a time. In March 2003 a study center designed by well-known Texas architect Robert Jackson opened on the site, and this sensitively designed building now operates as a study and education center. There is a nominal entrance fee.

Travis County Preserves

HAMILTON POOL PRESERVE
**24300 Hamilton Pool Rd., Dripping Springs
(512) 264-2740
www.co.travis.tx.us/tnr/parks**

Hamilton Pool Preserve is part of the Balcones Canyonlands (see the listing above). At the heart of the preserve is the pool, a natural pool fed by a waterfall along Hamilton Creek, a branch of the Pedernales River. The waters spill out over limestone outcroppings and create a 50-foot waterfall into the box canyon. The flora of the canyon and the surrounding grasslands vary in color and texture with the seasons. In addition to endangered and rare birds, there are several rare plant species in the preserve. Because of the sensitive, fragile nature of the land, visitors are limited to 75 a day; and because of the beautiful swimming, the parking lot fills up fast. Call ahead, or perhaps plan a weekday visit. Visitors may picnic, hike, or engage in group nature walks and study groups. There is no over-night camping, and pets are not allowed. Guided tours are available every Sun at 10 a.m. or by appointment. Sturdy shoes and lots of drinking water are recommended. During dry weather the waterfall may slow to a trickle, but the pool remains filled; how-ever, the pool is closed to swimming when the bacteria count climbs. In heavy rains the park may be closed because of typical Hill Country flooding. The preserve has no concessions. Admission fee.

✳WILD BASIN WILDERNESS PRESERVE
805 North Capital of Texas Hwy.
(512) 854-7275
www.wildbasin.org
The traffic whizzes by on Loop 360, but just a few steps off the roadway is a 227-acre wilderness literally within minutes of down-town Austin. Travis County operates this preserve, but it exists because of the efforts in the 1970s of seven extraordinary women who were dubbed the "Now or Never" group. Their goal was to establish the natural area as an outdoor lab for children's science edu-cation and teacher training, and the seven women took the task on as a Bicentennial Project. For more on how they won the day, visit www.wildbasin.org, the home page of the volunteers who still help maintain and fund the project. There are 2½ miles of hiking trails that pass through woodland, grassland, and streamside habitats that are home to threatened and endangered species and hundreds of native plants, animals, and birds. Wild Basin's nature education programs are funded by special events, memberships, cor-porate donations, and grants. The entrance to Wild Basin is on the east side of Loop 360 at 805 North Capital of Texas Highway, 1½ miles north of Bee Caves Road, or 3¼ miles

south of the Loop 360 bridge over Lake Austin. The preserve is open from sunrise to sunset, and while there are no entrance fees, donations are accepted. There is a small gift shop at the site.

RECREATION OPPORTUNITIES

Looking to play rugby? Climb a rock wall? Join a soccer club? Find the best place to go in-line skating, or view the sunrise from a hot-air balloon? This Recreation section offers a play-by-play breakdown on sports activities in Austin. Area municipal parks departments are a good starting point for finding information on a particular sport in the area. Austin Parks is listed below, for other cities' departments see the Parks list-ings above.

AUSTIN PARKS AND RECREATION
DEPARTMENT (PARD)
200 South Lamar Blvd.
(512) 974-6700
www.ci.austin.tx.us/parks
The City of Austin Parks and Recreation Department (PARD) operates 17 recreation centers throughout the city, which offer a wide variety of activities, day camps, youth programs, lessons in sports activities, and league supervision. PARD is a good place to begin when researching availability of facili-ties, lessons, and league activity.

UNIVERSITY OF TEXAS RECREATIONAL
SPORTS OUTDOOR PROGRAM
(512) 471-3116
www.utrecsports.org
The university offers noncredit courses in outdoor sports, including canoeing, rock climbing, windsurfing, cycling, hiking, fit-ness and personal training, massage, and health education. Classes are open to UT

staff, students, faculty, and members of the community. They are very popular, so sign up early.

YMCA

There are six YMCA branches in the greater Austin area. A branch in Round Rock area and another in Cedar Park are both under the auspices of the Williamson County YMCA. As the area grows, additional facilities are planned.

METRO YMCA OFFICE
(512) 322-9622
www.austinymca.org
This office offers information on programs and facilities at all Y branches in the area. The website has detailed descriptions of each branch, plus downloadable maps and information on child care, summer camps, and special events.

EAST COMMUNITIES BRANCH
5315 Ed Bluestein Blvd.
(512) 933-9622

NORTH PARK FAMILY BRANCH
9616 North Lamar Blvd., Suite 130
(512) 973-9622

NORTHWEST FAMILY BRANCH
5807 McNeil Dr.
(512) 335-9622

SOUTHWEST FAMILY BRANCH
6219 Oakclaire Dr.
(512) 891-9622

TOWNLAKE BRANCH (DOWNTOWN)
100 West Cesar Chavez Blvd.
(512) 542-9622

Bicycling

Bicycling has taken off in the Hill Country, where both road-racing and mountain-biking enthusiasts face some rugged challenges. One of Austin's most famous residents is international racing champion Lance Armstrong. (See the Close-up profile of Armstrong in the Spectator Sports chapter.)

The 3-mile Veloway in Slaughter Creek Metropolitan Park (see the Austin Parks section of this chapter) is a popular spot for cyclists. Other popular trails include Loop 360 west of the city and the Lady Bird Lake Hike and Bike Trail. Local mountain bikers also enjoy riding the trail in the Barton Creek Greenbelt. Check the Parks section of this chapter for other area venues for road and off-road cycling.

The Bull Creek Greenbelt in Northwest Austin (see the Parks listings above for more details on all these sites) has a hilly bike path in unspoiled, natural surroundings. The Shoal Creek Hike and Bike Trail wends through the center of the city in a more urban parklike setting, while the 2-mile trail in Southwest Austin at the Mary Moore Seabright Metropolitan Park flows through the rolling, wooded hills, typical of the natural landscape in this area.

Local cycle shops sell maps of the area showing popular trails. Among the most popular are Colorado Bend State Park (again, see the Parks listings above) and McKinney Falls State Park. The latter has a 3½-mile trail characterized by woodlands and gently rolling hills. Since McKinney is just 13 miles southeast of Austin, this is easily accessible to local riders.

One popular road route among cyclists is Park Road 1C between Buescher and Bastrop State Parks, about a 40-minute drive east of Austin. This is a very challenging ride, as the 13 miles of paved road climbs through steep hills.

The emergence of cycling as a popular sport has brought road-racing events to Austin. Bicyclists are respected in Austin—the city even has a bicycle coordinator on its planning staff (see the Getting Here, Getting Around chapter).

i The LCRA's excellent website (www.lcra.org) offers several "adventures" pages, which give tips to mountain bikers and equestrians, among others. The site also has links to parks and preserves that are wheelchair friendly.

AUSTIN CYCLING ASSOCIATION
www.austincycling.org

The group publishes a monthly newsletter that previews upcoming events, describes the best places to test your skills, and keeps track of the bicycle scene, including recreational and transportation issues.

AUSTIN RIDGE RIDERS
www.austinridgeriders.com

Dedicated to the Austin mountain-biking community, the Ridge Riders organize fun rides and races and offer information on popular trails in Central Texas.

BICYCLE SPORT SHOP
5175 South Lamar Blvd.
(512) 477-3472
www.bicyclesportshop.com

Just west of Lamar Boulevard and Riverside Drive, this local shop offers sales, rentals, and information on the local scene. Other locations are at 10947 Research Blvd., (512-345-7460) US 183 in Northwest Austin, and 9900 West Parmer Lane (512-637-6890).

✳MELLOW JOHNNY'S
400 Nueces St.
(512) 473-0222
www.mellowjohnnys.com

When famed cyclist and Austin resident Lance Armstrong announced his plans for Mellow Johnny's he told the *Austin American-Statesman* he was planning "the coolest bike shop in the world" and this downtown paean to all-things cycle-ly is just that. It is an homage, albeit a very practical one, to cycling. The shop sells the best bikes in the world and not just the famed Trek brand Lance rode to glory, but all manner of machines suited to play and transportation. The shop also has a coffee bar where customers can view bike mechanics at work. There are showers and lockers for commuting cyclists—Lance is a big advocate of biking to work—and there are training facilities in the large store, which occupies an old warehouse space in downtown Austin. Biking memorabilia, including some of Lance's Tour de France mementos, decorate the walls—in a word, a mellow place indeed.

i The 3-mile veloway in the Slaughter Creek Metropolitan Park was designed for cyclists, but in-line skaters also find this winding paved trail through the park a wonderful place to roll. No joggers are allowed on the veloway. The park is located at 4103 Slaughter Lane in Southwest Austin and is open seven days a week from sunrise to sunset.

UNIVERSITY CYCLERY
2901 North Lamar Blvd.
(512) 474-6696

This University of Texas area store offers rentals, sales, repairs, and information on the Austin cycling scene.

Bird Watching

Texas is the center lane of the migratory pathway of many North American birds, making the state a popular spot for bird watching. Local environmentalists are working hard to raise the consciousness of newcomers about endangered species in the area, and several nature preserves are dedicated to protecting these species. For more information see the Preserves section of this chapter.

TRAVIS COUNTY AUDUBON SOCIETY
3710 Cedar St.
(512) 300-BIRD (2473)
www.travisaudubon.org
There are more than 2,500 members of this local chapter of the society, which meets every month and usually holds at least one field trip a month. From backyard birding to treks into the Hill Country in search of elusive and endangered species such as the golden-cheeked warbler, the society offers practical advice to both members and nonmembers who are eager to protect and conserve the ecosystems so vital to bird life in Central Texas. Every Dec the group holds a Christmas bird count, its contribution to the national count.

VANISHING TEXAS RIVER CRUISE
Lake Buchanan
(512) 756-6986, (800) 474-8374
www.vtrc.com
In addition to offering wildflower cruises in spring, this company also offers winter river cruises up the Colorado River Canyon to view the largest colony of American bald eagles in the state.

Bowling

Austin has hosted professional bowling tournaments, and most lanes offer facilities for disabled bowlers plus party planning for large groups. The latest craze to hit local lanes is Electric Bowling, known in other parts of the country as Extreme Bowling or Glow-in-the-Dark Bowling. By pumping up the music and bringing down the lights, the bowling facility owners hope to attract a younger crowd and boost interest in the sport.

Two area associations are a good place to obtain information about local bowling activity and league play: the Austin Bowling Association located at 8820 Business Park Dr. (512-670-9315, www.austin.bowling .org), and the Austin Women's Bowling Association, located at 5700 Grover Ave. (512-453-8714).

HIGHLAND LANES
8909 Burnet Rd.
(512) 458-1215
www.highlandlanes.com
This North Austin bowling facility is home to Electric Bowling 3 times a week, on Fri and Sat from 11 p.m. to 1 a.m. and Tues evening from 8 to 10 p.m. Highland Lanes also offers bumper bowling for kids, eliminating gutter balls and ensuring that kids hit at least some of the pins. There are leagues on-site for teens, women, men, and seniors. The lanes are open from 9:30 a.m. to midnight Sun through Thurs and 9:30 a.m. to 1 a.m. Fri and Sat.

SHOWPLACE LANES
9504 North I-35
(512) 834-7733
A large 52-lane facility in North Austin, Showplace is open 24 hours a day. There is a sports bar on-site, plus 2 video game rooms and a nursery. A dart league also holds its events here.

WESTGATE LANES
2701 William Cannon Dr.
(512) 441-2695
www.westgatelanes.net
Home to several popular summer youth leagues, Westgate has 40 lanes and is located in South Austin. The bowling alley is open daily from 10 a.m. to midnight Sun through Thurs and 10 a.m. to 2 a.m. on Fri and Sat.

Camping

Camping is not just a recreational activity in Central Texas, it is a way of life for some residents who have chosen to make their homes in the area's private facilities. Perhaps the most famous "campsite" for motor homes is the Shady Grove RV Park smack in the middle of town in an old pecan grove and a few blocks from Zilker Park. Campsites catering to short-term visitors can be found along the I-35 corridor and on the shores of the Highland Lakes.

The Parks section lists area parks with camping facilities, and we have included some of the most popular here in this section, along with privately operated facilities. The Lower Colorado River Authority operates several parks with primitive camping areas (see the LCRA Primitive Areas section). Two guides that are very useful for campers visiting Central Texas are *The Texas State Travel Guide*, published by the Texas Department of Transportation (800-452-9292), and the *Lower Colorado River Authority (LCRA) Visitors Package* (800-776-5272, ext. 4083, or 512-473-4083).

In addition to the websites for the state, county, city, and LCRA (see above), other good resources include:

AUSTIN VISITOR CENTER
209 East Sixth St.
(512) 478-0098, (866) GO-AUSTIN
www.austintexas.org

TEXAS ASSOCIATION OF CAMPGROUND OWNERS
6900 Oak Leaf Dr., Orange
(512) 459-8226, (409) 886-4082
www.tacomembers.com

TEXAS PARKS & WILDLIFE DEPARTMENT
4200 Smith School Rd.
(512) 389-8900, (800) 792-1112
www.tpwd.state.tx.us

TEXAS TRAVEL INFORMATION CENTER
Old General Land Office Building,
Capitol Grounds
112 East Eleventh St.
(800) 452-9292
www.traveltex.com

i Many Texas landowners, farmers, and ranchers have turned to ecotourism to help them survive difficult financial times in rural America. Others simply want to share the wonders of Texas with visitors. The state agency charged with boosting Texas tourism, the Texas Department of Economic Development (TDED), has developed a website where visitors can find ecotourist opportunities, including birding, trail riding, wilderness camping, and fishing—check out traveltex.com.

RV Resorts

AUSTIN LONE STAR RV RESORT
7009 South I-35
(512) 444-6322
www.austinlonestar.com
There are 159 RV sites, 8 cabins, and camping facilities at this South Austin campground. Campsites rent and cabins are available for under $50 a night. Access to the site is controlled, and there are facilities for wheelchair

visitors. The main lodge has a fireplace, a full kitchen, color television, jukebox, and swimming pool. There is a small grocery store and laundry facilities on-site. Telephone hookups, compatible with modems, and television hookups also are available.

AUSTIN RV PARK NORTH
4001 Prairie Lane
(512) 244-0610
The 25 spaces at this North Austin park, near the intersection of I-35 and FM 1325, may be rented on a daily basis for around $20 a night, a little more than $100 a week, and around $400 a month. The sites all have electricity, water, and sewage hookups.

ARMADILLO RV
4913 Hudson Bend Rd.
(512) 266-9012
This Lake Travis–area RV park has 38 large shaded lots, all with a view of Lake Travis, that rent for around $20 a day, or approximately $250 to $275 a month. Cable television and telephone hookups are extra. There is an on-site laundry facility, a grocery store nearby, and 3 marinas within a half mile of the facility. Children and pets are welcome.

BUESCHER STATE PARK
FM 153, off Highway 71, Smithville
(512) 237-2241
A popular spot for angler, Buescher (pronounced "Bisher") State Park has 34 campsites (20 for tents or pop-ups and 14 for RVs) and 4 screened shelters. Showers and restrooms are available for campers. Admission to the park is $3 and free for those 13 and younger. Tent campsites are $12 a night; RV sites with water and electricity are $15 a night.

EMMA LONG METROPOLITAN PARK
(CITY PARK)
1600 City Park Rd.
(512) 346-1831
This large 1,147-acre Austin park with 3 miles of Lake Austin shoreline is a popular weekend camping spot (see the Austin City Parks section of this chapter). There are 20 sites with water and electricity, plus 50 tent sites. Campers may stay for up to 2 weeks. The entry fee to the park is $3 during the week and $5 on weekends. Tent sites are $6 per night and $10 for sites with utilities. The campsites are on an alluvial plain, adjacent to Lake Austin with the hilly park in the background. This is a very popular site, so reservations should be made early.

ENCHANTED ROCK STATE NATURAL
   AREA
RR 965, north of Fredericksburg
(830) 685-3636
This popular and legendary state park, detailed above under State Parks, is 18 miles north of Fredericksburg (see the Day Trips chapter). Only walk-in campers and backpackers may pitch their tents in this carefully protected natural area. There are no facilities for RVs or pop-up campers. Campers must call the state's camping reservations number at (512) 389-8900. Walk-in campers pay the park admission fee of $6 for those 13 and older, plus $15 a day camping fee with a maximum of 8 people at a walk-in site. Backpackers pay the entrance fee, plus $10 daily camping rate with a maximum of 4 people at each campsite.

HUDSON BEND RV PARK
5104 Beason Dr.
(512) 266-8300
www.hbrv.com

Sites are available at this Lake Travis–area facility by the day ($25), week ($85), or month ($280), and all are served with water, electricity, and free cable television. There are 29 pads at this shady site and also 6 storage sheds available for rent to extended-stay campers.

MCKINNEY FALLS STATE PARK
5808 McKinney Falls Pkwy.
(512) 243-1643

Its location, just 13 miles southeast of downtown Austin off US 183, ensures that this 640-acre state park is usually filled with campers on holidays and weekends. (See the State Parks section for a full description of the park.) There are 81 sites in the park for tents, pop-ups, or RVs, and these cost $12 a night, including water and electricity. There are 8 walk-in primitive sites for hikers, costing $12 a night. The park entrance fee is $4 per person, free for those 13 and younger. McKinney also rents 3 screened shelters for $30 a night. The 2-room shelters are furnished with 8 bunk beds, a cold-water sink, picnic table, and barbecue grill.

PACE BEND PARK
2011 North Oace Bend Rd., Spicewood
(512) 264-1482

This 1,000-plus-acre Travis County park (sometimes called Paleface Park) is likely to be packed with campers on weekends and during summer holidays. The park, described in the Travis County Parks section above, has more than 400 sites for tents, pop-ups, and RVs. There are also primitive tent sites. Admission to the park is $8 per vehicle, $15 for overnight stays. Sites with water and electricity cost $20 a night. The park has a strict quiet time in effect from 10 p.m. to 7 a.m., and dogs can be allowed to run free if their

owners are in control of them. Reservations are critical at this park, since it fills up very quickly on major holiday weekends.

RECREATION PLANTATION
3550 Pursley Rd., Dripping Springs
(512) 894-0567
www.rpcampground.com

If you're looking to camp with a crowd, then consider renting this self-described "event facility." For $750 a weekend, the minimum rate, you can rent this 40-acre campsite with its own creek frontage and swimming hole. The facility also has a 2-bedroom cabin on the property and a stage. There are tent sites and RV hookups, also, making this a great place for family reunions and corporate getaways.

City Leagues

One of the best resources for information on local team sports is the city's parks and recreation department or PARD offices. See the full listing of PARD offices in the previous Recreation introduction.

Another good resource for information on team sports is the YMCA. The Y has 6 locations in Austin, offering basketball, volleyball, soccer, basketball, and T-ball. Listings for the facilities are also listed in the previous section.

The area has an abundance of baseball leagues for all ages. Check with the area PARD for Little League, Optimist, and Kiwanis league teams. The Austin PARD supervises several basketball leagues, and the Y offers league and pickup games.

Central Texas is home to soccer moms and dads by the thousands, but the sport also attracts Gen-Xers and even older "footballers" from the expatriate crowd in Austin. There are numerous soccer leagues; the vast majority fall under the auspices of two organizations.

The Capital Area Youth Soccer Association at 1029 Reinli St., Suite 6 (512-302-4580, www.caysa.org), has more than 15,000 members. It is an umbrella group that oversees youth league and tournament play in the Central Texas area. The association also offers coaching and referee training sessions and hosts two annual invitational tournaments.

One of the best ways to keep track of league play at all levels is to visit one of the Austin area soccer stores. Soccer World has four locations: 5446 US 290 West (Southwest area), (512) 899-1135; 221 South Lamar Blvd. (Central), (512) 320-8447; 13376 Research Blvd. (Northwest), (512) 257-8560; and Soccer World Indoor Center, 1404 Royston Lane, (512) 990-3100.

Another center of soccer activity in the Round Rock–Pflugerville area is the Longhorn Soccer Club, run by Laszlo Marton, a former Hungarian and Austrian professional soccer player. The club offers top-quality coaching and training for soccer players of all ages and summer camps. Contact the camp at 1235 Blackthorn Dr., Round Rock (512-990-1234, www.longhornsoccerclub .org).

Softball is an extremely popular sport year-round in Austin. The Austin PARD serves as the major clearinghouse for schedules, league, and fee information. Call the PARD Athletics Office at (512) 480-3015. Many of the teams play at the Pleasant Valley Sports Complex, 1225 South Pleasant Valley Rd., (512) 445-7595. For softball league information in Round Rock, call (512) 218-5540.

Disc Golf (Folf)

Pitching a Frisbee at a target is a popular sport in Austin, and many of the area's neighborhood parks feature either 9- or 18-hole golf courses. The discs can be found at local sporting goods stores.

i League officers change with the seasons, and with the advent of the Internet many city sports leagues are relying on their website to reach out to fellow sport fans—abandoning the answering machine in favor of e-mail. Consequently, some listings in this chapter show only a website. If you have no access to the Internet, call the city PARD office at (512) 974-6700; they will put you in contact with the appropriate league official.

AUSTIN RECREATION CENTER
1301 Shoal Creek Blvd.
(512) 476-5662
www.ci.austin.tx.us
The Austin Recreation Center offers classes to would-be folf masters.

BARTHOLOMEW PARK
5201 Berkman Dr.
(512) 974-6700
This 18-hole course is in Northeast Austin.

MARY MOORE SEARIGHT PARK
907 Slaughter Lane
This 18-hole course is part of a fairly new park in Austin's growing southern suburbs.

OLD SETTLERS PARK
3300 Palm Valley Rd., Round Rock
This course is in Round Rock's major city park and claims to be the longest folf course in America (see the Parks section above).

PEASE PARK
1100 Kingsbury St.

This course is very popular among University of Texas students who live in the neighborhood.

SLAUGHTER CREEK METROPOLITAN PARK

5507 Slaughter Lane

This pleasant, relatively new Southwest Austin park boasts a new 9-hole golf course and gets 4 stars from www.discrevolution.com.

WELLS BRANCH GREENBELT

Wells Branch Parkway at Wells Port Drive
(512) 251-9814

A new 9-hole course in the Wells Branch subdivision of North Austin, this facility is open to Wells Branch residents only.

ZILKER PARK

2100 Barton Springs Rd.

You'll find this 9-hole course at the western edge of the city's premier park. It's a popular weekend course, also ranked at 4 stars.

Fishing

Texans have a reputation for telling tall tales, but when it comes to fishing they have lots to boast about. The state has more than 5,175 square miles of inland fresh water, including lakes, rivers, and creeks, plus 624 miles of shoreline. There is a wide variety of fish available for the taking, provided the fish are biting. Native fish include black bass, crappie, bluegill, and catfish. Freshwater fishing areas also have been stocked with nonnative species, including Florida bass, walleye, and rainbow trout, and saltwater species, including redfish and striped bass. The Texas Parks & Wildlife Department reports that several Texas lakes are producing striped bass weighing over 30 pounds—some Texas tale!

Texas residents can buy an annual combination fishing-hunting license for $25. Fishing licenses vary in cost and can be purchased on an annual or 2-week basis by residents. Nonresident anglers over the age of 17 must purchase a license, and these can cost $30 for an annual license or $20 for a 5-day license. There are additional charges for stamps for certain fish.

Licenses are sold at sporting goods and tackle stores, some county courthouses, Parks & Wildlife offices, and by some local game wardens. The Texas Parks & Wildlife Department also produces several excellent guides to Texas fishing. The department's magazine (see the Media chapter) is also an excellent resource.

TEXAS PARKS & WILDLIFE DEPARTMENT

4200 Smith School Rd.
(512) 389-4800, (800) 792-1112
www.tpwd.state.tx.us

The Highland Lakes are popular among anglers (see the Parks listings in this chapter for access and location). Lake Austin record catches include a 43-pound striped bass. Bass fishing is popular in the quieter areas of Lake Austin and Lake Buchanan. Fishing is permitted on Lady Bird Lake in Central Austin, and after years of concern about urban runoff, the city has lifted its warning about consuming your catch. In fact, the river has been stocked with trout.

BASTROP STATE PARK, BASTROP

Highway 21, 1.5 miles east of Bastrop
(512) 321-2101

Lake Bastrop boasts a lighted pier. The record catch here is a 43.5-pound catfish. See the State Parks section of this chapter for a description of facilities here.

BUESCHER STATE PARK, SMITHVILLE
FM 153, off Highway 71
(512) 237-2241
This state park is considered an angler's paradise by some. The park's 30-acre lake is stocked with catfish, bass, crappie, perch, and rainbow trout.

Fishing Gear

GIT BIT
(512) 713-7401
www.gitbitfishing.com
This fishing guide service, run by Mike Hastings, a national tournament fisherman and commentator, offers half-day and full-day bass fishing trips on Lake Travis, a noted hot spot for summertime bass fishing.

SPORTSMAN'S FINEST
12434 Bee Cave Rd.
(512) 263-1888
www.sportsmansfinest.com
This West Lake Hills angling and outdoor sports supply and travel company provides guides and other services to hunters and fishermen.

Fitness Centers

Fitness centers, gyms, aerobics classes, tai chi sessions, health clubs—Austin has them all. Some offer activities priced per session, while others offer membership. There is a wide range of services and amenities, from the basic nuts-and-bolts weight rooms to highly personalized training programs. Several national chains are present in Austin, and the number of fitness centers has grown with the city. Here, we list some of the non-chain centers that have an Austin "vibe." A great source of information on local gyms and other fitness resources is *Austin Fit* magazine (www.austinfitmagazine.com).

CRENSHAW ATHLETIC CLUB
5000 Fairview Dr.
(512) 453-5551
www.crenshaws.com
This is an old Austin favorite, home for more than 50 years to generations of Austin's families. Located in Central Austin, Crenshaw is noted for its family facilities and popular children's gym. The club has an indoor pool and track, plus weight rooms and cardio training equipment.

GREGORY GYMNASIUM
2101 Speedway on the UT campus
(512) 471-6370
www.utrecsports.org
Under the auspices of its RecSports program (see the Recreation Opportunities listing earlier in this chapter), students, ex-students, faculty, staff, and community members can enjoy the extensive facilities at the UT gym. The facilities are vast and include basketball and volleyball courts, indoor jogging, squash courts, weight rooms, climbing walls, even a big-screen TV and a coffee shop.

THE HILLS FITNESS CENTER
4615 Bee Caves Rd.
(512) 327-4881
www.thehillsfitness.com
Located on a beautiful 12-acre wooded campus, the center features both indoor and outdoor pools; racquetball, squash, and basketball courts; and a child-care center and cafe, among other amenities.

✳HYDE PARK GYM
4125 Guadalupe St.
(512) 459-9174
www.hydeparkgym.com
"No chrome. No contracts." is the advertising motto of this university-area gym in

one of Austin's favorite and most colorful neighborhoods, Hyde Park. The owners describe the place as down-to-earth, and it is, with cement floors, free weights, and no fancy contracts to sign. Personal trainers are available.

PREMIERE LADY AND SPA
7028 Wood Hollow Dr.
(512) 418-9399
www.premiereladyfitness.com
A very popular fitness center in Northwest Austin, this facility caters to women only. In addition to fitness equipment, the center also has a pool, whirlpools, and steam and sauna rooms. There are aerobics and fitness classes, plus clients can avail themselves of personal care services, such as a hair and nail treatment, facials, massage therapy, and tanning. The club has in-house child care available. Another location is at 6800 Westgate Blvd. (512-707-7700).

YMCA
See a list of YMCA branches under Recreation Opportunities, earlier in this chapter.

Flying

See the Getting Here, Getting Around chapter for information on flying lessons and sightseeing tours.

Hiking

Austin's greenbelts, hike and bike trails in Cedar Park, Pflugerville, and Round Rock (see the Parks section above), and hundreds of miles of trails in nearby state parks offer a great variety of terrain, levels of difficulty, and scenic views for hiking enthusiasts.

Some of the easiest trails to access are within the Austin Greenbelt network. For more information and brochures showing trails and access points, call Austin PARD at (512) 499-6700. One good way to get started is to join the Sierra Club for its city hikes (www.sierraclub.org/austin). The Lone Star Chapter is headquartered at 1202 San Antonio St., (512) 477-1729.

Popular scenic hikes include the trails at McKinney Falls State Park in Southeast Austin and Wolf Mountain Trail in Pedernales Park and Hamilton Pool Park, both west of Austin (see the Parks section in this chapter). A good resource for hikers is the Hill Country Information Service (512-478-1337, www.txinfo.com), which offers US Geological Survey maps and other illustrated guides to Hill Country. Other good resources are outfitters listed in the Shopping chapter.

Horseback Riding

True to its Texas character, there are several major rodeo and equestrian events in Austin each year. (See the Annual Events & Festivals chapter for details.) Several area ranches offer horseback riding—be sure the owner/operator has a Texas Department of Health certificate posted.

BEAR CREEK STABLES
13017 Bob Johnson Rd.
(512) 282-0250
www.bearcreekstables.com
This 25-acre private trail riding facility is located in the area Austin residents call Manchaca, a small South Austin community that has been swallowed up by the growing metropolis. The horses are well behaved and the scenery bucolic, making it a great place for a family outing. Children under 7 years of age may not ride.

i Looking for the ultimate city slicker experience? How about a few days at a Central Texas dude ranch? The Hill Country town of Bandera, about 120 miles southwest of Austin, is home to several well-known dude ranches that offer horseback adventures, evenings on the front porch, and chuck wagon food; some find it quite high class. Check out www.duderanches .com/texas.

CAMERON EQUESTRIAN CENTER
13404 Cameron Rd., Manor
(512) 272-4301
www.cameronequestrian.com
This Northeast Austin stable and training center offers English- and Western-style lessons and riding opportunities.

WHITE FENCES EQUESTRIAN CENTER
10908 Jones Rd., Manor
(512) 282-6248
www.whitefencesaustin.com
The trail rides here meander through the rolling hills east of the city, where riders are likely to see a variety of Texas fauna and flora in quiet, serene surroundings. Family rides are available, and the little guys can rent ponies for the trek. The large facility also has a sale barn, picnic sites, and White Fences offers several types and levels of lessons

Hot-Air Ballooning

The skies over Austin are filled with balloons each Sept during the annual Lone Star Weekend Aloft. Before floating away, check the pilot's FAA certification. Most flights begin in the early morning, and prices per person can range from $150 to $350.

CENTRAL TEXAS BALLOONING ASSOCIATION
(512) 479-9421
www.centraltexasballooning.org
This group maintains a list of members who hold commercial hot-air balloon certificates.

Hunting

Deer hunting is a popular pastime in the Texas Hill Country, where more white-tailed deer live than in any other part of the country. So dense is the population that suburban Austin residents often find their gardens have become a favorite noshing place for small herds of deer. Driving in the Hill Country at night also can be a challenge, since the abundant deer love to graze on the roadside grasses—usually the grass on the other side of the road.

The Hill Country also is home to several exotic game ranches where, for a hefty fee, hunters can track and hunt wild Corsican rams, African aoudad sheep, Indian blackbuck antelope, and axis and sika deer. (Axis deer is a popular item on some area restaurant menus, notably Hudson's-on-the-Bend, one of Austin's leading restaurants. See the Restaurants chapter.)

Much of the hunting in Texas takes place on private lands where landowners rent out leases or allow hunters to come onto their land for a fee during peak season. The Texas Parks & Wildlife Department 4200 Smith School Rd., Austin, (512) 389-4800 or (800) 792-1112, offers several free comprehensive guides to Texas hunting, including *The Guide to Texas Hunting*. The website (www.tpwd .state.tx.us/huntwild) is a vast source of information on where hunters may apply online for permits.

Ice Sports

Ice sports are becoming more and more popular in Austin, perhaps because of the influx of new residents from colder climates. Youth ice hockey leagues are growing fast.

CHAPARRAL ICE CENTER
14200 North I-35
(512) 252-8500
www.iskateaustin.com
Public skating, classes, hockey leagues, birthday parties, and broom ball are all offered at these facilities in North Austin (second location at Northcross Mall, 2525 West Anderson Lane). They also offer a pro shop and locker facilities. Round Rock PARD offers ice-skating classes at the I-35 location. Skating admission is $5 for kids under 5 years old, $6 above, and skates rent for $4 a pair. The Lone Star Curling Club meets at the new Northcross rink every Sun morning. Call for hours and admission charges.

Rock Climbing

This is a fast-growing recreational activity in Austin. Central Texas Mountaineers Association (www.texasmountaineers.org) keeps track of area activities. A favorite outing for local rock climbers is to Enchanted Rock Park near Fredericksburg, about 90 miles west of Austin (see above under State Parks).

ASPIRE ADVENTURES
11008 Jollyville Rd., Suite 219
(512) 343-1071
www.aspireadventures.com
Hutto, just a stone's throw from Austin, is now regarded as part of the greater Austin metro area. Aspire is a guide service for rock climbers and also offers classes at facilities around Austin. The company's website lists numerous links to rock-climbing clubs and facilities around the state and beyond.

AUSTIN ROCK GYM
4401 Friedrich Lane, Suite 300
(512) 416-9299
www.austinrockgym.com
This Austin gym with two locations (the other is at 8300 North Lamar Blvd., Suite B102), has a 30-foot rock wall and offers classes for both kids and adults. There is a pro shop, plus patrons can rent equipment. Austin Rock also offers guide services for climbs around Central Texas.

UNIVERSITY OF TEXAS RECREATIONAL SPORTS
(512) 471-3116
www.utrecsports.org
Information about the classes is detailed in the Recreation section of this chapter. Rock climbing classes are included in the curriculum.

YMCA SOUTHWEST
6219 Oakclaire Dr., off US 290 West
(512) 891-9622
www.ymca.org
The Southwest branch of the Y has a rock-climbing wall and offers classes. Membership is required to enjoy the Y's facilities; however, guests may pay for one annual visit if they are accompanied by a member.

Roller-skating

These roller-skating facilities are generally open in the evenings until 11 p.m. Some offer afternoon sessions, particularly on weekends; however, be forewarned the rinks do close for private parties, so it is wise to call ahead. Admission prices are generally $4 and under; in-line skates cost a couple of dollars more. They also offer a variety of party packages ranging in price from around $5 to $9 per person, depending on whether party favors and snacks are included.

PLAYLAND SKATING CENTER
8822 McCann Dr.
(512) 452-1901
www.playlandskatecenter.com
The Northeast Austin center offers rollerskating, in-line skating, and special adults nights.

ROUND ROCK ROLLER RINK
15501 North FM 620
(512) 218-0103
This center touts its family activities, including skating for families and Christian music on Mon.

SKATEWORLD
9514 Anderson Mill Rd.
(512) 258-8886
Skating lessons and hockey leagues are featured at this Northwest Austin skating rink.

Rugby

Rugby can be an exciting game to watch, even if you don't understand the rules—or apparent lack of them. Spectators should remember rugby is a tough sport that often encompasses certain off-pitch lifestyle habits; i.e., revelry. There are three rugby clubs in Austin; several of their players hail from foreign countries where rugby is popular. Both teams have won titles, gone on tour, and hosted visits from foreign teams.

AUSTIN HUNS
www.hunsrugby.org
The Austin Huns RFC Pitch is in Zilker Park, and games are usually played on Sat afternoon. After the game the Huns head for Nasty's, "Homeland of the Huns," a neighborhood bar at 606 Maiden Lane in Central Austin. The Austin Huns Rugby Football Club was founded in 1972 when the second side of the Austin Rugby Football Club broke away to form their own team.

AUSTIN RUGBY FOOTBALL CLUB
P.O. Box 12932, Austin 78711
(512) 419-4784 hot line,
(512) 926-9017 clubhouse
www.austinrugby.com
The Austin Rugby Football Club was founded in the spring of 1967 and was the first club in the Southwestern United States. In 1978 the club became the first rugby club in the United States to purchase its own grounds, and in 1985 the team built a clubhouse—it is one of only two rugby clubs in the United States with its own clubhouse and grounds. Call the clubhouse for directions to the club in East Austin, which can be difficult to find without detailed directions.

AUSTIN VALKYRIES
www.austinvalkyries.com
The Austin Valkyries Women's Rugby Football organization is eager for new members. Ranked No. 2 in the Western United States, the Valkyries train Tues and Thurs at Burr Field, a facility the club owns in Northeast Austin. The site is hard to find, and the dirt road into the pitch is muddy in rainy weather. The Valkyries suggest using a 4-wheel-drive vehicle on wet days. Check the website for directions.

Running/Walking

There are 5K, 10K, and marathon events throughout the year in Austin. RunTex, which sells running equipment is a good source of calendar events (www.runtex.com). There are several RunTex stores in Austin, including one in Central Austin, 2201 Lake Austin Blvd., (512) 477-9464. The Austin Runner's Club serves as a clearinghouse of information; visit www.austinrunners.org. See the Austin Parks listings in this chapter for hike and bike trails in the city.

Tennis

In addition to private facilities at some of the area's top resorts (see the Resorts Close-up in the Hotels and Motels chapter) and country clubs, there are 28 first-come, first-served municipal tennis court facilities, some with 2 courts, others 4, located in all sectors of Austin. Tennis players also have access to several school courts during the summer months. For a complete list contact PARD at (512) 974-9350 (www.ci.austin.tx.us). Courts are concrete, asphalt, or laykold and are available free of charge. A wonderful resource for tennis players of all ages is www.austin-tennis-resource.com. This website has maps of tennis court locations, retail support for tennis players in the city, special events and tournaments, league stats, even some national and international tennis news.

Reservations are necessary and fees are charged to play on the courts at the city's 4 municipal tennis center facilities, which are larger and have lighting. All courts are laykold and lighted. Fees are $3 for adults and $2.50 for children in prime time, which is Mon through Thurs after 6 p.m. and Sat and Sun before 6 p.m. Fees are lower at other times.

The Capital Area Tennis Association at 3625 Manchaca Rd., (512) 443-1342, www .austintennis.org, is an excellent resource for tennis players. Organized in 1974 and dedicated to promoting amateur tennis competition, the association keeps its members informed of tennis activities in the greater Austin area; conducts educational tennis clinics and seminars; organizes competitive events to fund youth programs and new court construction; and offers consulting services to public officials about the development of tennis facilities. Membership fees are less than $15 a year for adults.

i There is a popular new sport on the Austin scene—cricket! Given the influx of immigrants from countries formerly colonized by the Brits, many of whom work in the high-tech industry, the sport has taken hold in Texas. There are four clubs in the area—the Round Rock Cricket Club, the Hill Country Cricket Association, the Austin Cricket Club, and the University Cricket Club. The cricket enthusiasts also are teaching area kids the sport. Schedules, contacts, league results, and special events are listed at www.centraltxcricket.org.

AUSTIN HIGH
1715 Cesar Chavez St.
(512) 414-2505
This tennis facility is in Central Austin, just east of MoPac at Austin High School. There are 8 courts available after school is out during the school year and daily during the summer months.

CASWELL
2312 Shoal Creek Blvd.
(512) 478-6268
www.lovetennis4caswell.com
This Central Austin tennis center has 9 courts and is open from 8 a.m. to 10 p.m. Mon through Thurs, Fri 8 a.m. to 9 p.m., and Sat and Sun from 8 a.m. to 6 p.m. A summer

tennis league is headquartered here, and lessons are offered.

PHARR
4201 Brookview Rd.
(512) 477-7773
This tennis center in North Austin has 8 full courts and is open daily from 8:30 a.m. to 10:30 p.m. Mon through Thurs and until 7 p.m. Fri, Sat, and Sun.

SOUTH AUSTIN
1000 Cumberland Rd.
(512) 442-1466
www.southaustintenniscenter.com
The city's South Austin facility has 10 courts and is open Mon through Fri from 9 a.m. to 10 p.m. and Sat and Sun from 9 a.m. to 6 p.m. In the summer, beginning in June, the center opens 30 minutes earlier.

Volleyball

Sand Volleyball
There are several sand volleyball courts in the city's parks, plus a few commercial locations where volleyball enthusiasts gather. Check out www.austinvolleyball.com.

AUSSIE'S BAR AND GRILL
306 Barton Springs Rd.
(512) 480-0952,
(512) 474-2255 (volleyball hot line)
www.aussiesbar.com
This is a haven for local sand court players. The restaurant operates league play throughout the summer.

AUSTIN PARK FACILITIES
Austin PARD
(512) 974-6700
There are 4 public sand volleyball courts with nets in Zilker Park in a green space area

north of Barton Springs Rd. The 3 courts at Pease Park lack nets, but you can rent them from PARD.

CARLOS 'N CHARLIE'S
5981 Hiline Rd.
(512) 266-1683
www.cncaustin.com
Cousin to those wacky Mexican restaurants south of the border, made popular by spring breakers in Cancun, this Emerald Point restaurant has a well-regarded sand volleyball complex. The restaurant rents out the volleyball court and party room for $200 a day for private parties.

VOLENTE BEACH
16107 FM 2769
(512) 258-5110
www.volentebeach.com
Volente Beach is a private lakeside park that offers volleyball, windsurfing, swimming, and other beach/lake activities. It opens at 11 a.m. daily, closing at 10 p.m. during the week and 11 p.m. on weekends. There are 3 lighted sand volleyball courts on site. Admission is $4.

Indoor Volleyball
The Austin PARD operates two indoor volleyball leagues: one located at the Austin Recreation Center, 1301 Shoal Creek Blvd., (512) 476-5662, and one located at the Northwest Recreation Center, 2913 Northland Dr., (512) 458-4107. League play is year-round and includes men's, women's, and coed teams. Another good resource is the Capitol City Volleyball Association, which operates out of the city recreation at 1301 Shoal Creek Blvd., (512) 476-5662, www.leaguelineup.com/directors.

WATER SPORTS

Newcomers to the Texas Hill Country often are taken aback by the abundance of lakes, rivers, and creeks in the area. There are several invaluable resources for the water sports enthusiast:

AUSTIN PARKS AND RECREATION
DEPARTMENT (PARD)
(512) 974-6700
www.ci.austin.tx.us/parks
PARD offers classes in canoeing, kayaking, and sailing. The department also operates Emma Long Metropolitan Park (see the Austin City Parks section above), the closest boat ramp to downtown Austin and the only city-run ramp on Lake Austin—Walsh Landing, 1 block north of the western end of Enfield Drive.

LOWER COLORADO RIVER AUTHORITY
(LCRA)
(512) 473-3200
www.lcra.org
Much of the Highland Lakes area falls under the auspices of the LCRA. In addition to operating parks along the lakes, the LCRA also offers boating safety classes. There are several public boat ramps in the LCRA parks and primitive areas (see the Lake Parks section in this chapter).

TEXAS PARKS & WILDLIFE
DEPARTMENT
4200 Smith School Rd.
(512) 389-8900
www.tpwd.state.tx.us
This state agency is not only charged with maintaining the state's parks but also enforcing water safety laws (see the Boating Safety information in this chapter). Copies of the

rules and guidelines on water safety can be obtained from the agency, in addition to information about state facilities, including boat ramps, on Texas lakes and rivers.

TRAVIS COUNTY PARKS
(512) 473-9437
www.co.travis.tx.us/tnr/parks
In addition to state parks and wildlife and LCRA wardens, the Travis County Sheriff's Office also has deputies aboard patrol boats on some areas of the lakes. Many of the county parks (see the Travis County Parks section above) include boat ramps.

Boating

Safety
Alarmed by the rising numbers of accidents on Texas waterways, the state legislature passed tougher boating laws in 1997. The highlights include:

- Teenagers 13 to 15 must take a boating education course before they can legally operate a boat of 15 HP or more without adult supervision. Since 2001 all 13- to 17-year-olds must complete water safety courses before they can operate a boat or watercraft without adult supervision.
- Children younger than 13 must be accompanied by an adult when operating boats of 10 HP or more or a sailboat longer than 14 feet.
- Jet Skis and other personal watercraft cannot be operated except at slow speed within 50 feet of other personal watercraft, stationary objects, the shoreline, or other boats.
- Driving a boat or personal watercraft while intoxicated is against the law.

Boat Rentals & Marinas

Literally dozens of companies rent boats, sailboats, canoes, pontoon boats, and even large party boats in the Austin area. Most also rent personal watercraft. Several of the larger marinas and rental companies are listed below. It is wise to check the Yellow Pages, then call around to check prices and availability. For busy holiday weekends, rentals should be made far in advance. Most require a deposit in the form of a credit card, and renters will be held liable for any damage to the craft.

Marinas offer both storage slips for sail and power boats, plus full service for gasoline and marine supplies. Many also rent boats, houseboats, and personal watercraft.

AUSTIN AQUA FUN
2507 Westlake Dr.
(512) 459-4FUN
This company rents boats on both Lake Austin and Lake Travis. Their stable includes pontoons, personal watercraft, and ski boats. The company also offers ski instruction. Pickups are arranged at various locations on the lakes.

BEACH FRONT BOAT RENTALS
Volente Beach, 16120 Wharf Cove
(512) 258-8400
www.beachfrontboats.com
The marina at this private lakeside park at the northern end of Lake Travis off RM 2769 rents personal watercraft and ski boats.

EMERALD POINT MARINA
5973 Hiline Rd.
(888) 870-3228
www.emeraldpointmarina.com
The marina is next door to the popular Carlos 'N Charlie's Bar & Grill on Lake Travis. In addition to being a full-service marina with store

and gas station, the facility rents houseboats, ski boats, and personal watercraft.

JUST FOR FUN WATERCRAFT RENTAL
5973 Hiline Rd.
(512) 266-9710
www.jff.net
This boat rental on Lake Travis Emerald Point Marina (and one at Hurst Harbor Marina, 16405 Clara Van St.; 512-266-1800; www.hh marina.biz), offer a variety of craft, including pontoon boats and party craft for groups up to 150 people.

LAKEWAY MARINA
103A Lakeway Dr.
(512) 261-7511
www.lakewaymarina.com
One of the larger marinas on the lake, this business offers boat rentals, lessons, fishing guides, and sunset cruises.

Canoeing & Kayaking

AUSTIN CANOE & KAYAK
9705 Burnet Rd.
(512) 719-4386
www.austinkayak.com
This North Austin store boasts the largest selection of kayaks and canoes for sale in Central Texas. In addition to sales of several major brands, the shop also offers rentals.

CAPITAL CRUISES
Hyatt Regency, 208 Barton Springs Rd.
(512) 480-9264
www.capitalcruises.com
Looking for a unique way to view the evening bat flight at the Congress Avenue Bridge? Consider renting a canoe, kayak, or electric pedal boat from this boat company based on Lady Bird Lake (formerly Town Lake).

ROWING DOCK AND PADDLE SPORTS
2418 Stratford Dr.
(512) 459-0999
www.rowingdock.com
This outfitter rents kayaks, paddle boards, and rowboats on the south bank of Lady Bird Lake on the western edge of Zilker Park.

✳ZILKER PARK CANOE RENTALS
2100 Barton Springs Rd.
(512) 478-3852
www.fastair.com/zilker
Since no motorized craft is allowed on Lady Bird Lake, one of the best ways to enjoy it is in a canoe or kayak, which can be rented at this concession in Zilker Park from 11 a.m. to dusk daily, Mar through Labor Day.

Cruises

AUSTIN PARTY CRUISES
2215 Westlake Dr.
(512) 328-9887 (Lake Austin)
www.austinpartycruises.com
Party boats can be rented for sunset cruises, birthday parties, scenic cruises of both lakes, and corporate events. The company also offers catering services.

CAPITAL CRUISES
Hyatt Regency
(512) 480-9264
www.capitalcruises.com
In addition to renting electric boats and canoes (see previous listing), Capital also offers dinner cruises on Lady Bird Lake, bat-watching parties, and sightseeing trips up and down the downtown lake.

RIVERBOATS
(512) 345-5220
www.austinriverboats.com

The company's two riverboats, *Commodore Riverboat* and *Commodore's Pup,* can accommodate 50 to 500 people as they cruise Lake Austin. The boats can be rented for parties, receptions, and corporate outings. Full food and beverage service is available on both boats.

✳VANISHING TEXAS RIVER CRUISE
Lake Buchanan
(512) 756-6986
www.vtrc.com
In addition to eagle-watching cruises (see Bird Watching in this chapter), Vanishing River offers fall foliage cruises, summer sunset dinner cruises, trips to admire the wildflowers in spring, and even tours of Fall Creek Vineyards (see the Close-up on Texas foods in the Restaurants chapter).

> **i** There are several sports programs for disabled children in Austin. The Austin Parks and Recreation Department offers therapeutic recreation programs, and the YMCA has several programs for special-needs children and adults.

Rowing

AUSTIN ROWING CLUB
(512) 472-0726
www.austinrowing.org
The advent of rowing on Lady Bird Lake has given Austinites the opportunity to view one of the most picturesque of early-morning city sights: a lone rower skimming the waters of Lady Bird Lake in the morning mist. The rowing club is on the northern bank of Lady Bird Lake, near the Four Seasons Hotel. The club serves as headquarters for collegiate team events on Lady Bird Lake and serves

noncollegiate members of the rowing club. Classes are offered for beginners.

Sailing

AUSTIN YACHT CLUB
5906 Beacon Dr.
(512) 266-1336
www.austinyachtclub.org
The club sponsors races every Sun out on Lake Travis and hosts several regattas and races throughout the year. The club is a good source of information on local sailing opportunities and practices, resources, and classes (see the chapters on Spectator Sports and Kidstuff).

COMMANDER'S POINT YACHT BASIN
4600 Commander's Point Dr.
(512) 266-2333
One of the few marinas on the lake that rents sailboats and offers training for beginners, Commander's Point is home to a large sailing fleet. The marina also rents captained boats for visitors who want to enjoy a sail on Lake Travis but do not know the ropes.

TEXAS SAILING
101 Lakeway Dr., Lake Travis
(512) 261-6193
www.texassailing.com
The academy has been offering sailing lessons on the lake since 1965. Day and weekly charters, captained cruises, and sailboat rentals are also available.

Scuba Diving

OAK HILL SCUBA INC.
6156 US 290 West
(512) 892-4900
www.oakhillscuba.com
This longtime scuba store offers several levels of instruction, also information on safety

practices, and coordinates scuba trips both affordable and exotic.

TOM'S DIVE & SWIM
5909 Burnet Rd.
(512) 451-3425
www.tomsscuba.com
Offering classes at all levels from beginners to advanced, plus specialties such as underwater archaeology, this North Austin diving facility has a 3,000-square-foot, 10-foot-deep pool. The school organizes local fun dives, outings to the Gulf of Mexico, and international dive trips to such places as Cozumel in the Yucatan.

Swimming

The Central Texas climate can make swimming a joy or, on a hot day, a necessity. Even on the coldest days of the year, enthusiasts will head for the constant 68 degrees of Barton Springs Pool (see the Close-up in this chapter), which, unlike many municipal and neighborhood pools, is open year-round. Of course, the area's lakes and creeks are open throughout the year, but there are dangers there. Diving into creek or riverbeds can be dangerous, as water depths can vary with the seasons, and rocky bottoms pose hidden dangers. The lakes are really water-filled valleys; rocks, buried tree limbs, and duckweed can pose dangers. No swimming is allowed in Lady Bird Lake, and it is unlikely you would want to swim there anyway given urban runoff problems. Instead, head for one of the many neighborhood pools, natural-fed pools, or favorite water holes in the area.

Swimming Lessons
AMERICAN RED CROSS
(512) 928-4271
www.centex.redcross.org

The Red Cross serves as a referral service to swimming lessons offered by various entities in the Austin area.

CRENSHAW ATHLETIC CLUB
5000 Fairview Dr.
(512) 453-5551
www.crenshaws.com

Fitness and water aerobic classes for swimmers with chronic disabilities, or those embarking on a health regimen, are offered at this Central Austin fitness center.

YMCA

All Y facilities listed in our Fitness section earlier in this chapter have indoor pools and a full schedule of swimming classes for all ages and ability levels.

Austin City Pools

There are two categories of city-run outdoor pools in Austin: municipal pools and neighborhood pools. Municipal pools are large, deep pools and charge small fees for daily use. Multivisit passes are available from the PARD. All municipal pools have wading areas, lap lanes, diving boards, concessions, and sunbathing areas. There are picnic sites adjacent to the pools. Generally neighborhood pools are free, open during summer months, and no deeper than 5 feet. All pools have lifeguards, and all may be rented before and after regular operating hours.

There are 27 neighborhood pools throughout the city. Call the Aquatics office below for a list and a map. The neighborhood pools usually open in May and operate on a weekend-only schedule until Memorial Day, when they go into daily operation. In mid-Aug they resume weekend-only operation and then close before Labor Day. Admission and hours of operation vary at each location.

AUSTIN AQUATICS OFFICE
400 Deep Eddy Ave.
(512) 974-9333
www.ci.austin.tx.us/parks/aquatics.htm

This city PARD hot line lists class schedules, fee information, and status of city pools.

BARTHOLOMEW POOL
1800 East Fifty-first St.
(512) 928-0014

This municipal pool serves Northeast Austin. Specific times are set aside for recreational swims, lap swimming, and lessons.

✳BARTON SPRINGS
Zilker Park, 2201 Barton Springs Rd.
(512) 476-9044

Revered as an icon, the "soul of Austin," this hallowed swimming pool is featured in the Close-up in this chapter. The pool is open daily, and even during the coldest days of winter you'll see swimmers enjoying the 68-degree water. It is open in spring and fall, from mid-Mar to Memorial Day, Labor Day to Oct 31, from 5 a.m. to 10 p.m. There are no lifeguards on duty from 5 to 9 a.m. and from 8 to 10 p.m. The pool closes on Mon and Thurs at 7:30 p.m. From Memorial Day to Labor Day, the pool is open from 5 a.m. to 10 p.m. There are no lifeguards from 5 to 9 a.m. and from 9 to 10 p.m. The pool closes at 7:30 p.m. Mon and Thurs. From Oct 31 to mid-Mar, hours are 5 a.m. to 10 p.m., and there are no lifeguards on duty from 5 to 9 a.m. and dusk to 10 p.m.

There are no entrance fees during the winter season. Admission during the rest of the year is $3 for adults; $2 for juniors (12 to 17); and $1 for seniors and children 11 and younger. Call to make sure the pool is open—cleanings and occasional heavy rains do close the pool. There is a gift shop and information booth at the bathhouse, plus a snack bar.

DEEP EDDY
401 Deep Eddy Ave.
(512) 472-8546

This West Austin pool is fed by an artesian well, and its fresh water is a major attraction, especially for families who let the little ones wade in the large, shallow end of the pool. Eilers Park at the intersection of MoPac and Lake Austin Boulevard is home to the pool. The early morning hours are set aside for lap swimmers.

GARRISON
6001 Manchaca Rd.
(512) 442-4048

Serving South Austin, Garrison opens in early May and closes in mid-Aug. Lap swimmers have the pool to themselves during early morning and late evening on weekdays. Recreational swimming and swim lessons also have designated hours on weekdays and weekends.

MABEL DAVIS
3427 Parker Lane
(512) 441-5247

This Southeast Austin pool opens in mid-May and closes in Aug. Lap swimmers have the pool to themselves on weekdays from 9 to 10 a.m. Swim lessons are also offered here during the week.

NORTHWEST AUSTIN POOL
7000 Ardath St.
(512) 453-0194

This Northwest Austin municipal pool opens a little earlier (late Apr) and closes a little later (mid-Sept) than some of the other city

pools. Lap swimmers enjoy early-morning and late-evening weekday hours here.

Swimming Holes

There are three natural swimming holes within a 90-minute drive of Austin. Not all are open year-round, and some may be closed when high water proves dangerous or park operators limit human traffic to protect delicate ecosystems. It cannot be overemphasized that swimmers must exercise caution when swimming in natural locations. Underwater hazards can prove deadly, and not a summer goes by without area residents mourning the loss of someone killed from diving into a natural hole.

BLUE HOLE REGIONAL PARK
333 Blue Hole Lane, CR 173, Wimberley
(512) 847-0025
www.blueholeregionalpark.com

Blue Hole has passed from private ownership to the City of Wimberley. *Texas Monthly* magazine named this swimming hole (featured in several movies) as one of the top 10 in Texas. It is along Cypress Creek, near Wimberley. There is a small admission fee and season passes are available for $10.

✳HAMILTON POOL
24300 Hamilton Pool Rd.
(512) 264-2740
www.co.travis.tx.us/tnr/parks/hamilton

The pool and the grotto that serve as the crown jewel of this 232-acre park (see the Travis County Parks section above) were formed when the dome of an underground river collapsed thousands of years ago. The grotto is now a unique ecosystem. The emphasis is on the environment here, so access to the pool for swimmers is limited. Calling ahead is vital. Once the 100-car parking lot is full, the park closes. Admission is $8 per car, $3 for pedestrians and bicycles.

KRAUSE SPRINGS
404 Krause Springs Rd., Spicewood
(830) 693-4181

Devotees of swimming holes tout this natural pool as a great place to take the family, since the waters are clear and shallow. The pool, which is listed on the National Register of Historic Places, is about 7 miles west of the point where the Pedernales River meets Highway 71. Turn north on Spur 191 and follow the signs. The pool is on privately owned land that is shaded by large cypress trees. There are picnic and camping facilities at the pool. Daily admission is $4 for adults and $3 for children ages 4 to 11. There are additional fees for overnight stays. No pets allowed.

Windsurfing

Windsurfing is a popular pastime on the Highland Lakes. There are two areas of Lake Travis where Windsurfers tend to gather—Mansfield Dam and Windy Point, both near Travis County Parks. Mansfield Dam Park is on RM 620 and Windy Point is off Bob Wentz Park (see the Travis County Park section).

AUSTIN WINDSURFER CLUB
www.austinwindsurf.org

The club has adopted Bob Wentz Park as its club project, working to keep the park clean and litter free. In addition to serving as a clearinghouse for Windsurfers, the club also meets socially every month, usually at a Lake Travis–area restaurant.

VOLENTE BEACH
16107 Wharf Cove
(512) 258-5109
www.volentebeach.com

This private lakeside park at the northern end of Lake Travis off RM 2769 rents Windsurfers. Admission is free for children 2 years of age and under; $14.99 for individuals under 42 inches in height; and $19.99 for anyone measuring over 42 inches.

Waterskiing

There are two area ski clubs that offer information on classes, tournaments, and tips about good ski locations.

CAPITAL AREA WATER SKI CLUB
P.O. Box 180875, Austin 78718
www.waterskiaustin.com

The club offers several tournaments throughout the year and touts itself as a "competitive ski club" where members can test their skills against members with similar skill levels. Coaching and clinics are also part of the club's activities.

GOLF

Austin is the home of the famous *Little Red Book*. "Aha!" some might say—at last, proof that Austin politics is decidedly more left-footed than the rest of Texas. No, we are not talking about Chairman Mao's little book here, but Harvey's. Harvey Penick was the revered golfing pro and teacher who is credited by some of the best players, both amateur and pro, with helping them better their game and reach inner golfing peace. Penick, who lived from 1904 to 1995, is more than an Austin legend. Long known in US golfing circles, Penick became a worldwide legend in the final three years of his life when his small, succinct, plain-talking books of golf wisdom became international best sellers. In 1992 Austin writer and screenwriter Bud Shrake teamed up with Penick to write the *Little Red Book*. When it became a runaway hit, they followed with a second little book, *And If You Play, You're My Friend,* followed by a third, *For All Who Love the Game.* They were working on a fourth when the much-loved Penick died.

Two weeks before he died in an Austin hospital, Penick was visited by one of his longtime students, pro golfer Ben Crenshaw, who was having trouble with his putting game. Penick gave him the advice he needed. Also, just days before he died, Penick saw another of his star pupils score a major breakthrough. Davis Love Jr. won the Freeport McMoran Classic in New Orleans and made the cut for the Masters. Penick died before the Masters ended, but Crenshaw and Love battled it out that year—Crenshaw winning, Love coming in second. Crenshaw said he felt Penick was the 15th club in his bag. Penick's "simple philosophies about golf and life" had helped him win.

Harvey Penick's life spanned almost a century of golf in Austin. He began as a caddy in 1913 and after high school took a job as the pro at the Austin Country Club (ACC). He taught Crenshaw and Tom Kite at the old ACC, now the Riverside Golf Club (see our listing in this chapter), and passed on his quiet knowledge of the game to several generations of golfers. A bronze statue of Penick, shown passing on tips to Tom Kite, stands near the ninth green of the ACC course in the hills of West Austin.

Penick, a religious man, mixed his love of golf with a wonder and praise of nature—easy to do on some of Austin's attractive golf courses. In addition to having some of the most beautiful and challenging golf courses in the country, Austin is also an egalitarian place. The city maintains several excellent municipal courses that can be played at very reasonable rates.

OVERVIEW

This chapter is divided into four parts—Austin Municipal Courses, Daily-Fee Courses, Private Courses, and Driving Ranges. For greens fees and cart rental prices, use the price code chart.

And for the ultimate pampered golf experience, we've listed several golf resorts.

Price Code

(for greens fees or cart rental)

$.....................under $25
$$ .... $25 to $50
$$$ .... $50 to $100
$$$$ .... More than $100

AUSTIN MUNICIPAL COURSES

There are 5 excellent municipal golf courses in the Austin area. Each course offers public league and tournament play, and lessons are available at each course. The city also hosts the Austin Junior Golf Academy for children ages 8 to 18. Call either the Austin Parks and Recreation Department's golf office at (512) 974-9350, www.austinpubliclinks.com, or the office at each course listed below.

Annual cards allow you to play at any municipal course. You also pay a small surcharge of around $2 per round for seniors and juniors and a little more per round for adults. (Fees, of course, may change as government budgets are scrutinized every year.) Seniors and juniors also get a considerable discount on daily greens fees.

> **i** Approximate prices for the annual cards are $1,000 for an individual and considerably less for seniors, college team players and junior golfers.

JIMMY CLAY GOLF CLUB $
5400 Jimmy Clay Dr.
(512) 444-0999

There are two courses at this municipal golf club located in Southeast Austin. The 6,749-yard Roy Kizer Course is 18 holes, par 71, and has a driving range. The course is described as a "thinking man's golf course" because of its carefully laid out design. It is named after a legendary figure in Austin golf who was the course superintendent at the Lions course (below) from 1937 until 1973. The 57 acres of lakes and marshes surrounding the course add to its natural beauty. Tee times for weekdays are taken 3 days in advance; Fri, Sat, and Sun tee times are taken on Tues beginning at 7 a.m. Greens fees depend on the day of the week and time of day. The 6,857-yard Jimmy Clay course has 18 holes, par 72. Tee times for weekdays are taken one day in advance; weekend tee times are taken Fri beginning at 7 a.m. A third, 4-hole course designed to encourage new players has been built on the site of an old water treatment plant and has 22 acres of wetlands and a 35-acre lake to attract wildlife. The small course is named The Joe Balandar Learning Center in honor of another notable Austin golfer.

> **i** The Austin Golf Association has members of all ages, genders, and backgrounds and encourages tournament play in the city, (512-961-8558, http://aga.ghinclub.com). The city's parks department also lists other associations on its website, www.austinpubliclinks.com.

HANCOCK GOLF COURSE $
811 East Forty-first St.
(512) 453-0276

Built in 1899, this is the oldest golf course in the state of Texas. Located in Central Austin, not far from the popular old Hyde Park neighborhood (see our Relocation chapter), this is a pretty course with rolling hills and a small creek that meanders through its heart. The 9-hole course is 2,633 yards, par 35. Reservations are not required, but groups of 4 or more can make a reservation one day in advance. Sun group reservations must be made Fri. Seniors and juniors pay reduced fees, and there are lower fees for evening and sunset play.

LIONS MUNICIPAL GOLF COURSE $
2910 Enfield Rd.
(512) 477-6963

In West Austin, south of Enfield and west of MoPac, this is the oldest municipal course in Austin, but nevertheless very popular. Ben Hogan, Byron Nelson, Tom Kite, and Ben Crenshaw have played here. This is a 6,001-yard course, par 71. There is an irons-only driving range, also. Tee times for weekdays are taken one day in advance; weekend tee times are taken Fri beginning at 7 a.m.

MORRIS-WILLIAMS GOLF COURSE $
4300 Manor Rd.
(512) 926-1298

This 18-hole municipal course is in East Austin, southeast of the old Robert Mueller Municipal Airport. When the airport site is developed, this golf course is likely to be a prime selling point for the residences that will be part of the new neighborhood. The 6,636-yard, par 72, course is built on an undulating landscape and has a driving range. Tee times for weekdays are taken one day in advance, weekend tee times are taken Fri beginning at 7 a.m. Greens fees depend on the age of the golfer, the time of day, and day of the week.

Round Rock

FOREST CREEK GOLF CLUB $$–$$$
99 Twin Ridge Pkwy.
(512) 388-2874
www.forestcreek.com

This municipal golf course has gained a great reputation not only for its challenging design but also for the quality of the pros who have worked at the club. J. L. Lewis, who went on to the PGA, was the club's first pro. The club is open daily. The par 72 course has 18 holes in 7,154 yards. The club has a golf shop, driving range, putting green, dining facilities, and even a stocked fishing lake.

DAILY-FEE COURSES

BLUEBONNET HILL
GOLF COURSE $–$$
9100 Decker Lane
(512) 272-4228
www.bluebonnethillgolf.com

Located in northeast Travis County near Manor, this public course was built to attract beginning golfers and has become very popular. It is popularly known as "the home of the 4-hour round." It takes its name from the rolling Hill Country landscape, particularly beautiful in spring when the bluebonnets bloom. Bluebonnet is rated one of the top 25 public courses in Texas according to the *Dallas Morning News*. The 6,503-yard course is 18 holes, par 72. Facilities include a driving range, snack bar, putting green, and chipping green.

BUTLER PARK PITCH AND PUTT
GOLF COURSE $
201 West Riverside Dr.
(512) 477-4430

For almost 50 years Winston Kinser operated this tiny private, very inexpensive course on city-owned land just south of Lady Bird Lake in the heart of Austin. Kinser died in 2000, but his dream lives on. The par 27, 805-yard course is tucked away just east of Lamar Boulevard and south of Riverside Drive. Each of the 9 holes is par 3, and the longest hole is No. 8, 118 yards. This is a great place to find out if golf is for you. You can rent clubs (you won't need a cart). The course opens at 8:30 a.m. and closes at dusk.

GREY ROCK GOLF CLUB $$$
7401 Highway 45
(512) 288-4297
www.thegolfclubatcirclec.com

This club was designed to give patrons of a daily-fee course a country-club feel. Near the southern end of MoPac in Southwest Austin in the Circle C subdivision, the course apparently succeeded. It was named one of the best new clubs in Texas in 1992 and has remained popular. The course was designed by Jay Morrish to attract new golfers and is regarded as a fun place to play. Circle C is next door to the Lady Bird Johnson National Wildflower Research Center, and the same rugged beauty preserved at the center is apparent around the golf course.

The 18-hole course is 6,859 yards, par 72. Players can avail themselves of the driving range, putting green, dining room, meeting rooms, and the 24-hour/10-day advance tee hot line. There is also shuttle service from area hotels.

RIVERSIDE GOLF COURSE $$
1020 Grove Blvd.
(512) 386-7077

This course is a part of golf history. Now a public course in Southeast Austin, this was the home of the Austin Country Club and the place where Harvey Penick taught golf luminaries like Ben Crenshaw and Tom Kite. Penick was the club pro when Austin Community College moved here in 1950. The course is lined with old oak and pecan trees that once stood witness as some of Austin's wealthiest citizens and future national golf champions played. Now it is owned by Austin Community College and open at very low fees to all comers. The 6,500-yard course is 18 holes, par 71. There is a snack bar and picnic area on site, plus a putting green, golf shop, and chipping green.

Pflugerville

BLACKHAWK GOLF CLUB $$
2714 Kelly Lane
(512) 251-9000
www.blackhawkgolf.com

Build it, and they will come! This is true of the Blackhawk Golf Club, which was built in the early '90s by John and Martha Leach in what was then the small country town of Pflugerville, northeast of Austin. These days the club is surrounded by the suburban boomtown of Pflugerville. John Leach turned to his sister-in-law for the design of the course—she is Hollis Stacy, 3-time US Women's Open Champion, who decided to enter the male-dominated profession of golf course architecture. Working with local architect Charles Howard, they turned a dairy farm into a highly praised public golf course with abundant water and trees. The 6,636-yard course is 18 holes, par 72. Facilities include a driving range, golf shop, and snack bar. Greens fees include a cart. There are reduced fees for twilight play and for seniors during the week.

PRIVATE COURSES

AUSTIN COUNTRY CLUB $$$
4408 Long Champ Dr.
(512) 328-0090
www.austincountryclub.com
This is the spiritual home of Harvey Penick, who was the club's first pro. A bronze statue of the revered teacher stands near the ninth green. He is shown giving tips to former student Tom Kite, the international golf champion who holds the course record, 64. This is the third home for the club, which was chartered in 1898, one of the two oldest in the state. The current course in West Austin was designed by Pete Dye, one of the world's top golf course designers. Experts rate this course as one of the toughest in the Central Texas area. The 6,822-yard course is on the shores of Lake Austin—18 holes, par 72.

BALCONES COUNTRY CLUB $$
Balcones Course
8600 Balcones Club Dr.
(512) 258-1621
www.balconescountryclub.com
There are two courses at this Northwest Austin club south of US 183, near Spicewood. Each course has its own club and pros, plus members enjoy an additional central clubhouse. The club is one of the largest in the Austin area and has given special emphasis to its junior program. The rolling hills of the Balcones course are favored by walkers. The 6,649-yard course is 18 holes, par 70. The 6,706-yard Spicewood course (11210 Spicewood Club Dr.; 512-258-6672) is 18 holes, par 72. Spicewood has greater elevation changes, plus more water elements. Twilight rates, after 4 p.m., are half price.

GREAT HILLS GOLF CLUB $$
5914 Lost Horizon Dr.
(512) 345-6940
www.greathillscc.com
This club is known for its wonderful, authentic Hill Country landscape with rolling hills, cliffs, and canyons. It is in West Austin but priced in a much more affordable range than its nearby neighbors—Barton Creek Resort and Austin Country Club. Great Hills is regarded as a great bargain and a challenging course. The 6,599-yard course is 18 holes, par 72. The clubhouse has both casual and formal dining rooms, a swimming pool, and tennis courts.

HILLS OF LAKEWAY GOLF COURSE $$$
26 Club Estates Pkwy.
(512) 261-7200
www.thehillscc.com
This Hill Country course west of RM 620 near Lake Travis has been ranked among the top 5 in Texas. It was designed by Jack Nicklaus, one of his first courses in Texas. The course follows a creek and offers wonderful vistas of the surrounding rugged hills. This 6,954-yard, 18-hole, par 72 course has a marina, tennis courts, swimming pool, driving range, and putting green on-site. The club also has three additional courses, plus club facilities.

LOST CREEK COUNTRY CLUB $$$
2612 Lost Creek Blvd.
(512) 892-1205
www.lostcreekclub.com
Located just west of Loop 360 (Capital of Texas Highway) in an area of rugged canyonland, this club is not far from Austin's most noted golf resort, Barton Creek. The land around the Lost Creek fairways and greens is rugged, and the precipitous drops along

the edges of the course make control even more important than usual. The natural rise and fall of the land, plus the hazards, make the course challenging. This 18-hole course is 6,522 yards, par 72. The clubhouse offers both golf and tennis pro shops, a swimming pool, and formal and casual dining areas. There is a driving range, practice bunker, and putting green on site. Closed on Mon.

ONION CREEK COUNTRY CLUB $$$
2510 Onion Creek Pkwy.
(512) 282-2150
www.onioncreekclub.com
This course was designed by Masters Champion Jimmy Demaret in collaboration with George Fazio. It has been described as a classic golf course, and for many years it was the home of the original Legends of Golf tournament on the Senior PGA Tour. The Legends was played here for 12 years, and it proved to be a major building block for the seniors' tour. Located in far South Austin, the course is the anchor for a country club–style residential development. The clubhouse has all the amenities. The 18-hole course is 6,367 yards, par 70.

RIVER PLACE GOLF CLUB $$
4207 River Place Blvd.
(512) 346-1114
www.riverplaceclub.com
On the shores of Lake Austin, west of the city, this course has been a symbol of the economic roller-coaster ride of the past 20 years. Originally planned to be part of an upscale Hill Country development on the shores of Lake Austin, it was caught up in the development versus antigrowth wars, then the real estate downturn of the 1980s. Finally, in 1991 it was placed on the auction block by the Resolution Trust Corporation.

Now, after a redesign by professional golfer Tom Kite, the course is described as attractive and sometimes challenging. The 18-hole course is 6,611 yards, par 71. Facilities include a driving range, snack bar, and putting green. Greens fees include carts. Twilight fees go into effect after 2 p.m.

i Avid golfers sometimes build a vacation trip around a visit to Austin's Golfsmith megastore, located in North Austin at 11000 North I-35, (512) 837-1245, toll-free (800) 813-6897 (www.golfsmith.com). The complex is home to the Harvey Penick Golfing Academy, created with the blessing of the legendary Austin teacher whose legacy is noted in the introduction to this chapter.

GOLF RESORTS

The three resorts listed here are detailed in the Close-up in our Hotels and Motels chapter.

BARTON CREEK CONFERENCE RESORT   AND COUNTRY CLUB $$$$
8212 Barton Club Dr.
(512) 329-4000, (866) 572-7369
www.bartoncreek.com
This resort with its four highly praised golf courses and beautiful 4,000-acre site is built on one of the most sought after and fought over pieces of land in Austin. Located just a dozen miles from downtown, the resort was created along the banks of Barton Creek, which winds through the hills before feeding the underground spring that, in turn, feeds Barton Springs. Some of Austin's most vocal environmentalists protested its construction, but others have praised the development for its ecological sensitivity—the golf courses are maintained without many

of the traditional fertilizers typically used on golf courses, and efforts have been made to embrace the local flora in the resort design. The greens and fairways are planted with drought-resistant grasses to cut down on water usage.

The club has four courses, described below, all designed by leading names in golf course architecture. Given the resort's popularity as both a country club and conference center, not all four courses are available every day to resort play, with the exception of the Lakeside course. Golf packages are available.While golf is a great reason to visit the Barton Creek club, the resort also offers other recreational facilities, including skeet shooting, tennis, and "supersports" for groups—volleyball, tug-of-war, and obstacle courses. Jogging, swimming, boating, fishing, horseback riding, sightseeing, even factory outlet mall tours are available. The resort has several dining facilities, including one of the few restaurants in Austin where a jacket is required. On-site there is a fitness center and a spa where you can have everything from facials to salt rubs, marine fango massages to aromatic loofah scrubs. There are 147 guest rooms at the resort with views of the golf course and the surrounding Hill Country. An additional 158 rooms were added to the resort in 2000.

The Crenshaw & Coore Course: This was designed by Austinite Ben Crenshaw and his partner, Bill Coore. True to Crenshaw's philosophy, the course is traditional and follows the terrain with broad, rolling fairways. This 18-hole course is 6,678 yards, par 71.

The Fazio Foothills Course: This is dubbed the resort's signature course, and its dramatic design shows the distinctive signature of Tom Fazio. There are cliff-lined fairways, waterfalls, and even caves. *Golf Digest* has rated this Fazio course one of the Best Resort Courses in America, second in Texas and 60th in the ranking of the 100 greatest golf courses in America. The course also has won the USGA's National Environmental Steward Award.

The Fazio Canyons Course: A second Fazio course has been added to the resort, and this one features more of the stunning Hill Country features Fazio incorporated into the first course, including hilltop views, meandering creeks, and small canyons where the native flora has been maintained.

The Arnold Palmer–Lakeside Course: Arnold Palmer designed this course, which opened in 1986 as the Hidden Hills Country Club. Barton Creek now owns and operates the course about 25 miles from the resort on the shores of Lake Travis. The course has been named among the most beautiful in Texas by the *Dallas Morning News*. Golfers enjoy great views from the clubhouse overlooking the lake. The 6,956-yard course is 18 holes, par 72.

LAKEWAY RESORT AND SPA $$$$
101 Lakeway Dr.
(512) 261-6600,
(800) LAKEWAY (525-3929)
www.lakewayresortandspa.com

This resort hotel on Lake Travis, west of the city, offers golfers and tennis players opportunities to pursue their sports while enjoying the other recreational activities available at the Highland Lakes. The hotel underwent a major restoration in 2000 and reopened with refurbished rooms, facilities, and restaurants. There are four golf courses made available to Lakeway guests, including the nearby Nicklaus-designed Flintrock Falls course at The Hills of Lakeway, and tennis players can enjoy the World of Tennis with its 26 indoor and outdoor courts. There is also a fitness center, outdoor jogging trails, 2 swimming pools, spa, and a marina.

Live Oak Golf Course was created in 1964 by designer Leon Howard. Development restrictions were not in place back then, and Howard was given permission to dredge soil from the lake bottom to spread on the course. Twelve years later, Howard built the Yaupon Course at the resort. Both offer dramatic views of the lake—two holes on Live Oak are adjacent to the marina.

Live Oak is 18 holes, 6,643 yards, par 72. Yaupon is 18 holes, 6,565 yards, par 72. The resort offers a variety of packages, and greens fees are included in the price of packages.

WOLFDANCER GOLF CLUB $$$–$$$$
The Hyatt Regency at Lost Pines,
575 Hyatt Lost Pines Rd., Bastrop
(512) 308-WOLF
www.visitlostpines.com
The club at this plush new resort just west of Austin in historic Bastrop is named in honor of the Tonkawa Indians who once roamed the woods here, named the "Lost Pines" since they are far from the typical piney woods of East Texas. The course is set down amid wild grasses, and the natural fauna and flora of the area have been preserved. The 18-hole, 72 par course designed by Arthur Hill has

been ranked as one the top fifty courses in Texas by the *Dallas Morning News*. The club also includes a short game area, 2 putting greens, a 13-acre driving range, and a clubhouse.

DRIVING RANGES

GOLFSMITH PRACTICE FACILITY
11000 North I-35
(512) 837-1810
www.golfsmith.com
Located next door to the Golfsmith Factory Outlet, the driving range has 70 lighted tees. Golfsmith offers custom golf clubs, clinics, practice greens, computerized swing analysis, factory tours, snack bar, and Harvey Penick irons and woods.

MISTER TEE
13910 North RM 620
(512) 335-4444
www.mrteegolf.com
There are 25 lighted tees at this Northwest Austin driving range.

OAK HILL GOLF RANGE
5243 US 290 West
(512) 892-5634
www.oakhillgolfrange.com
This Southwest Austin driving range has 65 lighted tees.

SPECTATOR SPORTS

et's face it. When it comes to professional sports, Austin isn't exactly in the big leagues. While the thousands of Austinites who enjoy major league sports find themselves sitting in left field, so to speak, there is still much to celebrate when it comes to sports in Austin and its environs. What our city lacks in major league teams is more than made up by Austin's passion for University of Texas athletics and the growing number of minor league sports in the area. While UT didn't coin the phrase "Winning isn't everything, it's the only thing," it has lived by that sentiment for more than a century of athletic achievement and has produced national championship teams in a wide range of sports time and time again. UT's nationally recognized Hook 'em Horns hand signal wasn't voted the best in the country by *Sports Illustrated* magazine in 1997 for nothing.

Greater Austin is home to the Texas Stars, a minor league professional ice hockey team that draws die-hard fans from all over the region; an NBA development team, the Austin Toros; and a very popular minor league baseball team, the Round Rock Express.

Sports spectators will discover that Austin boasts an important annual rodeo, a hugely popular marathon, and several spectacular boat races each year. Cyclists and runners will be pleased to note that not only is Austin home to seven-time Tour de France winner Lance Armstrong, our city also hosts his LIVESTRONG foundation's annual Ride for the Roses Weekend (bicycle rides from 10 to 90 miles) as well as the LIVESTRONG Austin Marathon and other events supported by the foundation. (See the Close-up of our hometown hero in this chapter.)

Another plus for sports fans is Austin's unique location between San Antonio, Dallas, and Houston, all within a three-hour drive of our city—and an even shorter flight. San Antonio is 80 miles south on I-35. This quirk of logistical fate affords Austinites incredible choices among major league sports teams in both men's and women's basketball, baseball, soccer, ice hockey, and, of course, football—the national pastime of Texas. For information on professional sports outside of Central Texas, check the website of the Dallas Cowboys, Houston Texans, San Antonio Spurs, WNBA Houston Comets and the other Texas teams.

Of course, one of the most popular spectator sports in this part of the world is the weekly high school football game, usually held on Thurs or Fri during the season. The TV show about high school football, *Friday Night Lights,* isn't filmed around these parts for nothing! Check the sports pages/website of the *Austin American-Statesman* for schedules, and take in a game on a cool fall evening.

Whether your competitive spirit is most roused by a whistle, a buzzer, a starter's pistol, or those simple words, "batter up," you're sure to find a Texas sport to call your own.

MINOR LEAGUE SPORTS

Baseball

※**ROUND ROCK EXPRESS**
Dell Diamond,
3400 East Palm Valley Blvd., Round Rock
(512) 255-2255
www.roundrockexpress.com

It took several major league players to bring minor league baseball to Round Rock, but when former Texas Ranger Hall of Famer Nolan Ryan and heavyweight techie Michael Dell are on the front line, success is assured. Naming the team was easy, given Ryan's nickname as "The Ryan Express" for his awesome fastball during his playing days. The Round Rock Express rolled into the Dell Diamond in 1999. The team was so successful, both in performance and in fan attendance, that owners felt confident enough to move on up from Double-A ball, announcing the purchase of the Triple-A Edmonton Trappers of Canada, who began play as the Express in 2005. Long the minor league affiliate of MLB's Houston Astros, the team switched in 2010 and is now the Texas Rangers' development team. Tickets to the games are available through the website or at the Dell Diamond Ticket Office. The season runs from Apr to Sept. General admission prices are family friendly, but make your reservations well ahead of time.

Home games are played at Dell Diamond, named to honor the Round Rock computer giant's efforts to bring minor league ball to Central Texas. The stadium, which includes luxury suites, is also designed with families and comfort in mind, and even the cheapest seats have chairbacks and cupholders. There's also a swimming pool complex and a children's fun center, which includes a climbing wall. Dell Diamond also hosts a variety of special events and benefits throughout the year, including Fri night fireworks shows and "Live in the Ballpark," a 2-day charity event of baseball, gourmet food, and live music.

i Sign up with Texas Box Office to receive notice—and advance purchase opportunities—of sporting events, concerts, family shows, and other events at the Frank Erwin Center and elsewhere around town. The website is www.texasboxoffice.com/register.

Basketball

AUSTIN TOROS
Cedar Park Center,
2100 Avenue of the Stars, Cedar Park
(512) 236-8333
www.austintoros.com

Minor-league basketball jumped into Austin in the fall of 2005 with the Austin Toros, one of four Southwest teams added to the young NBA development league, which has since grown to 17 teams. Now owned by the NBA's San Antonio Spurs, the Toros play about 23 home games during their Nov-through-Apr season. The team played 5 years at the Austin Convention Center but moved to the stunning Cedar Park Center for the 2010–11 season. The state-of-the-art venue holds more than 4,600 basketball fans. Cedar Park is only about a 3-point shot north of Austin.

Ice Hockey

TEXAS STARS
Cedar Park Center,
2100 Avenue of the Stars, Cedar Park
(512) 467-8277
www.texasstarshockey.com

A member of the 30-team American Hockey League, the main developmental league for the NHL, the Texas Stars first took the ice for the 2009–10 season at the new $55 million Cedar Park Center. The team, affiliated with the Dallas Stars, made it to the league finals its first season, playing to a more-than-capacity crowd of over 7,000 fans. The Stars play about 40 home games in their Oct-to-Apr regular season.

i For a rock-n-rolling good time, check out the Texas Rollergirls, www.txrollergirls.com, a high-spirited, heart-pumping roller derby born in Austin. Catch games played by the league's four teams—Hell Marys, Hotrod Honeys, Honky Tonk Heartbreakers, and Hustlers—at Playland Skate Center, 8822 McCann Dr.

UNIVERSITY OF TEXAS SPORTS

LONGHORNS BASEBALL
Disch-Falk Field, I-35 and Martin Luther King Jr. Boulevard
(512) 471-4602
www.texassports.com
UT baseball fans from across Austin share the blissful moment of striding past the turnstile, ticket in hand, through the stadium tunnel, and into the arena that is widely recognized as the best collegiate baseball facility in the country. This team, founded in 1895, has won an impressive 6 national championships, the latest in 2005. Disch-Falk Field, named for two former Longhorn coaches, holds 5,000 baseball fans in the main chairback area and can be expanded to hold more. As many as 8,000 fans have packed this facility for important, hotly contested collegiate games. However, this is one UT sporting event for which tickets can most often be purchased at the gate.

LONGHORNS BASKETBALL
Frank Erwin Center,
1701 Red River St.
(512) 471-4602
www.texassports.com
Few teams on the UT campus have captured the attention and admiration of Austin sports fans like our women's basketball team. Over the past 20 years, the team has attracted the most fans in women's basketball history with a total attendance of well over 1.5 million. Success on the court is the reason. During the 14-year history of the Southwest Conference, the Longhorns took 10 regular-season titles and won 9 tournaments. In 1986 the Longhorns became the first women's basketball team in the history of the National Collegiate Athletic Association to record a perfect season with a 34–0 record. The Longhorns, who moved to the Big 12 conference at the start of the 1996–97 season, draw an average of more than 5,000 fans to the Frank Erwin Center for the approximately 16 home games played during the regular season, which runs Nov through Feb.

i Efforts are afoot to bring Formula One car racing to Austin by 2012. As a host city for the world's top sporting event, Austin would become a major international sporting center. Organizers, who aim to build a $200 million Grand Prix racetrack in Southeast Austin, face many hurdles yet, so time will tell.

✳LONGHORNS FOOTBALL
Darrell K Royal–Memorial Stadium,
Twenty-third Street and Campus Drive
(512) 471-4602
www.texassports.com

No sporting event in Austin comes close to Texas football for the sheer number of burnt orange–clad fans that turn out to support this team. Longhorns fans—students, Texas Exes (alumni), and just plain football buffs—unite as one big family in Darrell K Royal–Memorial Stadium when the Longhorns play at home. In fact, Texas football is so popular here that many times over the years fans have stood to watch hotly contested games, jamming the stadium to way over capacity.

To attend a UT football game is to become part of a Texas tradition that dates back more than a century. Established in 1893, the Longhorns have left an impressive mark on national collegiate football. Over the years, Longhorn loyalists have been rewarded with a number of national and conference titles and more than three dozen NCAA postseason bowl games. In 2005, the Longhorns won their fourth National Championship, defeating USC 41–38 in a thrilling Rose Bowl game. In addition to witnessing these victories, fans have been treated to performances by Heisman Trophy–winner and future NFL Hall-of-Famer Earl Campbell, as well as by dozens of All Americans, future NFL players, and other trophy winners. In 1998 senior halfback Ricky Williams broke conference and national collegiate records, culminating his UT career with a Heisman Trophy. The list of accolades for this team goes on and on. Mack Brown, former head coach of the North Carolina Tar Heels, became Texas's 28th head football coach in 1998.

Known simply as Memorial Stadium since it was inaugurated in 1924, UT added legendary head football coach Darrell K Royal's name to the stadium in 1996. The five or six seasonal home games are usually played on Sat during the fall football season, which runs from Sept through Nov. It's best to get your tickets early, as these games can sell out.

LONGHORNS SOFTBALL
McCombs Field, Martin Luther King Jr. Boulevard and Comal Street
(512) 471-4602
www.texassports.com
McCombs Field is a $4.5 million softball complex that's arguably one of the best in the country. Of course the team that plays on it is also top notch. A varsity team since the late 1990s, the Longhorns have won several Big 12 Conference titles, most recently in 2010, and have appeared repeatedly in the College World Series. The team has included noted pitchers Christa Williams, a 1996 and 2000 Olympic gold medalist on the US Women's Softball Team, and Cat Osterman, who won an Olympic gold medal in 2004 as a member of the US team.

The Longhorns play about 15 home games, mostly double-headers, during the regular season, which runs Feb through Apr. These games can and do sell out, so get your tickets early. The team also has an exhibition-game schedule in the fall.

RUNNIN' HORNS
Frank Erwin Center,
1701 Red River St.
(512) 471-4602
www.texassports.com
With crowds averaging 13,000 fans for each home game, UT's Runnin' Horns men's basketball team is one of the biggest draws in town—and in college basketball anywhere. Founded in 1906, the Horns were members of the Southwest Conference (SWC) from 1915 to 1996. During that time the Horns

racked up an impressive 22 SWC titles (12 outright) and a 648–449 total record. In 1997 the Horns along with Southwest Conference members Baylor, Texas A&M, and Texas Tech merged with Big Eight teams to form the Big 12. The Runnin' Horns hold court for regular season games at the Erwin Center Nov through Feb.

i One good place to find out about running events in the Austin area and around the country is from the knowledgeable staff at one of our homegrown RunTex stores or on the local chain's website at www.runtex.com.

THE BEST OF THE REST

Car Racing

THUNDER HILL RACEWAY
24801 I-35, Kyle
(512) 507-1486
www.thunderhillraceway.com
Located just off I-35 exit 210, about 25 miles south of Austin, Thunder Hill Raceway presents exciting stock car racing on the second and fourth Sat of the month from Mar through Sept. This is not a sport to watch, it's a sport to experience as the cars speed around a ⅜-mile oval asphalt track, sometimes faster than 120 miles per hour. Thunder Hill opened in 1998 and features a 3,600-seat open-air stadium. Events include super stocks, grand stocks, and mini stocks, as well as special features, such as Texas pro sedans, late models, and pro trucks. Thunder Hill also host several special events, including the annual "Crash Fest," with a demolition derby and chain race among the featured events. Gates open at 4 p.m. and racing starts at 6 p.m. Tickets are on sale at the door.

i The University of Texas Longhorn Band, "The Showband of the Southwest," performs at UT football games and also makes appearances at important events around the country. The band owns the largest bass drum in the world, nicknamed "Big Bertha."

Running

✳LIVESTRONG AUSTIN MARATHON
Statesman Capitol 10,000
www.cap10k.com
www.youraustinmarathon.com
Austin is all about the great outdoors—and fitness. For tens of thousands of Austinites that means running, and our city offers something for everyone: Our Hike and Bike Trail along Lady Bird Lake is one popular place for joggers, as are our dozens of parks and recreational areas. For those with the competitive, charitable spirit, Austin hosts a variety of annual 5K and 10K races, relays, half marathons and a major full marathon. Two of the biggies are the LIVESTRONG Austin Marathon and Half Marathon, and the Statesman Capitol 10K.

The Austin Marathon (now partnered with Lance Armstrong's LIVESTRONG global cancer campaign) is usually held the second Sun of Feb, drawing thousands of participants and spectators. The 5,000 runners from around the world who participate in the long run, a Boston Marathon qualifier, get a nice tour of Austin—the old fashioned way!

In the spring Austin hosts the Capitol 10,000, the largest 10K run in the state and the fifth largest in the nation. This event is all inclusive, offering a Fun Run and Walk for casual participants (many of whom dress in silly costumes), a race for Wheelchair Athletes, and a Timed Race for competitive

Close-up

Lance Armstrong—Austin's Hometown Hero

"He's from Austin, you know."

Who among Lance Armstrong's hometown fans—and there are so many of us—has never heard those words drop impulsively from our lips? It's not just that Lance is a champion cyclist who won the Tour de France a stunning seven consecutive times. And it's not only because he first had to triumph over an advanced case of cancer, or because he formed a cancer foundation to help others even before he knew whether he'd survive the disease himself, although those are part of it, too. We're mostly proud of our hometown hero because he's lived his life—on and off the bike—with such dignity, such humanity, such heart. So when we casually mention that Lance Armstrong is one of us, or when we call the world's most famous bicycle race the Tour de Lance, we pay tribute to the neighbor we've come to admire these past years. He has reminded us just how high the human spirit can soar.

Each Oct, cyclists, runners, cancer survivors, and supporters from around the world converge on our city to participate in the LIVESTRONG Challenge (which includes a 5K run) and Ride for the Roses Weekend (see our Annual Events chapter), run by Armstrong's LIVESTRONG organization. LIVESTRONG is also a partner in the annual Austin Marathon (see Running in this chapter). Founded in 1997, LIVESTRONG (formerly the Lance Armstrong Foundation) has raised tens of millions of dollars to fund cancer survivorship programs and research. Not bad for an organization that Lance has said "started on a paper napkin in a Mexican restaurant in Austin, Texas." The foundation (www.livestrong.org), which opened new headquarters in East Austin in 2009, is just one of the many ways Lance has reached out to help others. In 1995, before he became a household name, he created the Junior Olympic Race Series to promote cycling among America's youth. He has co-written several best-selling memoirs that address in candid detail his struggle to survive cancer and get back to the business of living. And when he's not out there training for or winning races, Lance travels the globe on behalf of his foundation and others to raise cancer awareness and help strengthen the resolve of those stricken with the disease.

Born September 18, 1971, in the Dallas suburb of Plano, Lance gained fame in 1991 by winning the US Amateur Cycling Championship. In 1993, after picking himself up from a humbling last-place finish in his professional debut, Lance secured his spot in US cycling history with his victory in the million-dollar Triple Crown. By 1996 he was the number one–ranked cyclist in the world. Later that year he was diagnosed with testicular cancer, which had spread to his lungs and brain. Given less than a 50/50 chance of survival, Lance underwent two operations and a debilitating treatment program. While still battling the disease, he created the foundation. By 1998 he was cancer free—and ready to ride into history.

His stunning comeback victory in the 1999 Tour de France is now legendary, and the six Tour wins that followed are nothing short of miraculous. In 2002 *Sports Illustrated* named Lance its Sportsman of the Year, calling him "more than a bicyclist now, more than an athlete. He's become a kind of hope machine." In 2008 he was named one of Time magazine's 100 Most Influential People.

Wherever he goes from here, one thing is certain: Coasting is not in Lance Armstrong's nature.

athletes. This race has been going strong for more than three decades

Rodeo

✳STAR OF TEXAS FAIR & RODEO
9100 Decker Lake Rd.
(512) 919-3000
www.rodeoaustin.com
Yee haw!! There's nothing like a great rodeo to let you know you've arrived in Texas. Austin's big event is the annual Star of Texas Fair & Rodeo, a 2-week affair that begins around early Mar. This huge competition, on the official Professional Rodeo Cowboys Association (PRCA) circuit, draws thousands and thousands of people from all over the state for fun-filled days and nights of bull riding, calf roping, team roping, steer wrestling, barrel racing, saddle bronc riding, bareback riding, and much, much more. Rodeo events aren't the only highlight of this celebration. This is also the Travis County Fair and offers fun for people of all ages, including carnival rides and booths galore. To top it all off, the event features about 100 live musical acts, including a major concert performance each evening. Brooks & Dunn, Merle Haggard, Gretchen Wilson, Willie Nelson, and many more outstanding musical performers have appeared at this wildly popular event.

Sailboat Racing

AUSTIN YACHT CLUB
5906 Beacon Dr.
(512) 266-1336
www.austinyachtclub.org

Austin wouldn't be Austin if it didn't have a spectator sport that took advantage of our great waterways. The Austin Yacht Club sponsors a number of major annual sailboat regattas as well as a number of other races on Lake Travis throughout the year. Sailors may call the Yacht Club for information on how to participate in these events, while those with sailing experience may post information about themselves on the club's bulletin board if they would like to crew these boats. The Austin Yacht Club, founded in 1952, aims to promote the sport of sailboat racing. The club sponsors a summer sailing class for adults and camps for children.

Horse Racing

RETAMA PARK
1 Retama Pkwy., Selma
(210) 651-7000
www.retamapark.com
This modern 226-acre horse-racing park features a full calendar of thoroughbred and quarter horse racing. Retama also offers simulcast racing year-round from top horse and dog tracks across the country, including the Kentucky Derby, Preakness, Belmont, and the Breeders Cup. Retama has a spectacular indoor grandstand and clubhouse as well as a sports bar and terrace dining. Selma is about 65 miles south of Austin on I-35. Take the 174-A exit and follow the signs. Retama is just west of the Interstate.

DAY TRIPS &
WEEKEND GETAWAYS

Covering 267,339 square miles and boasting hundreds of miles of seashore, soaring mountains, plunging valleys, vast plains and prairies, pine forests, deserts, islands, lakes of all sizes and shapes, giant metropolises, small towns, and wide-open spaces galore, Texas is much more than a state—"It's a Whole Other Country," as Austin's boosters like to say. At the very heart of it all, in spirit if not precise geographic center, is Austin. It's no wonder, then, that when Central Texans plan a vacation we often look no farther than their own great big bountiful backyard. In fact, for trips covered in this chapter, we can't even include all the fascinating sights Texas has to offer. Some are just too far away to make even a weekend trip feasible. You'll soon find, however, that there are plenty of places to escape to right here in Central Texas.

OVERVIEW

One journey takes you to Johnson City, boyhood home of America's 36th president. We'll also introduce you to LBJ's beloved ranch, the "Texas White House" during the Johnson Administration, and the place where the elder statesman came home to retire following a lifetime of public service. Both of these areas make up the LBJ National Historic Park.

Not to overlook Texas's other US presidents, we'll present Bryan/College Station, home of the George H. W. Bush Presidential Library and Museum, site of sprawling Texas A&M University, and domicile of UT's archrival, the A&M Aggies. Of course #41, as the Bush family calls the first former President Bush, has a completed library, while #43 (our former governor), President George W. Bush, is building his library on the campus of Southern Methodist University in Dallas.

We'll tell you about Gruene, a former ghost town that emerged from ruin to become a thriving community, especially on weekends when the chicken-fried steak disappears faster than the time it takes to pronounce the city's name correctly. This is one place Austinites visit regularly to shop for antiques or to crowd into the historic Gruene Hall for an evening of first-class live music.

We had to include Round Top and Winedale, two communities east of Austin renowned as meccas of classical music and theater. One of the state's oldest communities, Round Top is home to the International Festival Institute, founded by a concert pianist. Winedale hosts the annual Shakespeare at Winedale festival. Austinites flock to these cities throughout the year to partake of their great annual events and to step back in time.

The little town of Salado, just a stone's throw from Austin, could have been a contender. An up-and-coming town in the 1880s, Salado was bypassed when the railroad finally came to Central Texas. While railroad towns thrived, Salado slipped into obscurity. Discovered by artists in the second half of the 20th century, Salado is now back on track, so to speak, and a popular day trip or weekend getaway from Austin.

Of course, we couldn't forget Fredericksburg, one of Austin's favorite weekend getaways and a prime example of Hill Country living. This quaint town, founded by German immigrants in 1846, boasts a Main Street that has earned a spot on the National Register of Historic Places. Main Street shops offering antiques, apparel, and arts and crafts do a bustling business on weekends as visitors pour in from all over the region. This is one great place to spot a movie star or two, or perhaps just enjoy an authentic German meal.

Considering the important German influences on the culture and development of Central Texas over the past 150 years, it wouldn't do to mention just one German-infused town. New Braunfels, too, retains much of its German flavor, literally. From the great German restaurants to the annual Wurstfest sausage festival, New Braunfels is a delight for the taste buds. We'll give you two other reasons this town attracts Central Texans year-round.

Appropriately, the Highland Lakes come last. After you've spent even a little time trying to see all the sights Central Texas has to offer, you may need to just get away from it all and relax for a while on a boat or on a beach. Any one of the four lakes we describe in this section will do the trick.

Before you head out, check the Annual Events & Festivals chapter for events in these day trip destinations. Also have a look at our Texas Pronunciation Guide in the Area Overview chapter so that you'll sound like an Insider when you get there.

Whether you decide to head north, south, east, or west to major cities, small towns, or a place of quiet solitude, you're sure to find a spot that is Texas through and through.

UP NORTH
Salado

The Village of Salado, 55 miles north of Austin on I-35, is just that—a village, and a charming one, that owes its existence now to the fact that history passed it by. Founded in 1859 at a low-water crossing of Salado Creek, it looked like Salado was destined to become a growing community, especially with the founding of Salado College in 1859. By 1884 the community was on its way to being a town with 7 churches, 14 stores, 2 hotels, 2 blacksmiths, and 3 cotton gins. But when the railroads were built to the north and east, Salado slipped back to being a village.

i If you're planning to explore several state parks, be sure to purchase a one-year Texas State Parks Pass for $60, which provides unlimited entry more than 90 state parks and historic sites, as well as a host of other benefits. The pass can be purchased at all Texas state parks and historic sites, (512) 389-8900.

Salado's population dwindled from 900 in 1882 to 400 by 1914 and only slightly more than 200 in 1950, according to the community's publications. But then artists and artisans began to settle in the area, buying up the old buildings and opening art galleries and antiques shops. Now the village has more than 130 businesses and attracts weekend visitors who come here to relax, browse the stores, and soak up the area's history. A great resource is the Salado website (www.salado.com), which offers information on lodging, shops, dining, events, and recreation in this historical community.

One of the best ways to learn about the area is to request a copy of the Driving Tour Tape prepared by the Bell County Historical Commission. Visitors can write to the Bell County Historical Commission, Bell County Courthouse, Belton, TX 76513, or ask at one of Salado's landmarks, like the Stagecoach Inn, 1 Main St., on the east side of I-35, (254) 947-5111, www.inn-at-salado.com.

The modern 82-room Stagecoach Inn stands adjacent to what remains of the Shady Villa Hotel, where Sam Houston was said to have slept in 1850. Other famous guests include General George Armstrong Custer and cattlemen Charles Goodnight and Shanghai Pierce, who stopped at this historic spot along the Chisholm Trail.

What remains of the old hotel is part of the inn's restaurant, which also includes an open-air atrium built around a 500-year-old burr oak. Newer dining rooms adjoining the original 2-story clapboard building serve guests at lunch and dinner, but in keeping with tradition the waitresses always recite the menu by heart—prime rib, plate-size steaks, fried chicken, baked ham and lamb, plus desserts such as homemade pie and cobbler.

Salado abounds with historical connections. In the 1830s Sterling C. Robertson, himself of Scottish heritage, established a colony here; many of the settlers were Scots. In November Salado's Central Texas Area Museum hosts the Annual Gathering of the Clans on the Village Green near the Stagecoach Inn. Hundreds of Texans and Americans of Scottish descent descend on Salado

for the weekend festival. Call (254) 947-5292 for information.

Visitors also flock to Salado for the annual Christmas Stroll & Holiday Home Tour, held on weekends in Dec. Salado is a favorite choice of Central Texans for Christmas shopping and celebrating the season, so the village's hotels and guest houses are booked in advance. There is also a large July Fourth picnic, a summer art fair in Aug, and a Dec village artists' sale. Call the Salado Chamber of Commerce, (254) 947-5040, for information on these events or check the calendar at www.salado.com. At the Table Rock Amphitheater, (254) 947-9205, an outdoor dinner theater in the community, the Tablerock Theatre group puts on annual performances of a historical pageant, Salado Legends, during the summer and dramatizations of Dickens's *A Christmas Carol* in December.

More than 130 buildings in Salado are listed on the National Register of Historic Places, and several of them serve as guest houses and bed-and-breakfast inns. Some are small cottages with cozy fireplaces, while others are large Victorian homes. Some are located in rural settings, others are just a few steps from the shopping district and most are listed on the chamber's website, www.salado .com. Duffers may want to ask about the Mill Creek Country Club & Guest Houses, (800) 732-8994, www.millcreek-golf.com, which has a Robert Trent Jones II 18-hole golf course as well as swimming and tennis facilities. The old homes also offer romantic and charming backdrops for dining in Salado. Several serve lunch and afternoon tea, including Browning's Courtyard Cafe on Salado Square, (254) 947-8666; Cathy's Boardwalk Cafe, (254) 947-8162; and the Pink Rose Tea Room on Main Street, (254) 947-9110. Gourmet dinners are served on weekends at the Inn on the Creek, (254)

947-5554, www.inncreek.com, a Victorian bed-and-breakfast on Center Circle. Reservations are required. Pietro's Italian Restaurant & Pizzeria, 302 North Main St., (254) 947-0559, offers a change of pace for lunch and dinner. The Range at the Barton House, Main Street (254) 947-3828, offers American cuisine with French and Mediterranean touches for lunch and dinner Wed through Sun. No Texas village would be complete without Mexican food, which can be enjoyed at the Salado Mansion, Main Street, (254) 947-5157. Mexican food served in an 1857 mansion—no place but Salado.

Sustenance is necessary in Salado since the village has so many shops it is impossible to list them all here. There are herbalists, antiques dealers, custom furniture stores—Barnhill-Britt sells handcrafted furniture constructed of antique longleaf pine taken from 19th-century Texas buildings; Benton's has custom-order iron beds—Amish quilts, children's fashions, Oriental rugs, Christmas ornaments, folk art, bride's gifts, rare books, top women's fashion, native plants, tribal art, gourmet foods, jewelry, and rabbits everywhere (Wigglesworth Place, Rock Creek at Main, a Salado Christmas favorite), paintings and sculpture, and on and on.

Salado is an unincorporated village, but the chamber of commerce estimates the population of permanent residents is about 1,500—which means there is a shop for about every 10 residents in the area. Most of the shops are open daily, although some do close on Sun. Most are in the immediate area of Main Street.

DOWN SOUTH

New Braunfels

Only an hour's drive from Austin, New Braunfels attracts visitors for two primary reasons—antiques shopping and water sports. The latter draws thousands of visitors, especially in summer, to a variety of artificial and natural waterways to tube, raft, swim, paddle, and plop in the cool, wet stuff.

The two sides of New Braunfels have led to a growth boom, and Comal County has been cited as the fastest growing county in Texas in recent years. Many of the visitors come to enjoy swimming in Landa Park, (830) 608-2165, the downtown home of the state's largest spring-fed pool and also home to a stretch of the Comal River. Another popular destination is Schlitterbahn, the state's biggest water park, which is detailed in the Kidstuff chapter. Given all the activities available in the area, crowds flock to New Braunfels on weekends in the peak summer season, but thanks to its old German roots the town has maintained its charm. The town is named after Prince Carl of Solms-Braunfels, a member of the Mainzer Adelsverein, or League of Nobles, who encouraged German emigration in the 1840s as an escape from economic hard times in Germany.

The young Republic of Texas offered land grants to the nobles as an inducement for European settlers. Prince Carl brought over a large contingent in 1844, many of whom died on the coast of Texas due to an epidemic. The survivors settled in New Braunfels in 1844, and by 1855 the town was the fourth largest in Texas. Meanwhile, Prince Carl had gone home since his fiancée refused to come to Texas.

There are several invocations of the Prince's name in and around the town, including Prince Solms Park, where tubers pay a small admission fee to tube in the Comal River, and the Prince Solms Inn, 295 East San Antonio St., (830) 625-9169, www.princesolmsinn.com, an upscale bed-and-breakfast in a restored Victorian home. Advance reservations are a must at this popular guest house. Another hotel with great character is the Faust Hotel, 240 South Seguin St., (830) 625-7791, www.fausthotel .com, just 1 block south of the town plaza. The Faust, now a National Landmark Hotel, was built in 1928 and has been restored to reflect that period. The rooms here all have character and are decorated individually.

New Braunfels is of great interest to architecture buffs, particularly for the tiny Sunday houses built by German farmers in the 19th century as weekend town cottages. Many have been restored, but others stand waiting for the deep pockets and eager hands of would-be restorers. Many of the town's antiques shops are housed in old German homes. The New Braunfels Chamber of Commerce, 390 South Seguin St., (830) 625-2385, www.nbcham.org, offers an "antique crawl" map.

The chamber also provides a historic walking tour map to guide visitors through the vibrant downtown area, where there are more than 30 historic buildings. The heart of the community is the plaza, where the traffic is slowed by a roundabout, and the restored buildings reflect the prosperity enjoyed by the town's forefathers.

Early life in New Braunfels is depicted at the Sophienburg Museum, 401 West Coll St., (830) 629-1572. Named for Prince Carl's fiancée, who declined to head for the frontier, the museum is built on a small hill where the prince had planned to build his honeymoon castle. The building housed his administrative offices and now has several exhibits showing life on the Texas frontier. The museum is open daily from 10 a.m. to 5 p.m. except Sun, when it is open from 1 to 5 p.m. There is a small admission fee.

Another New Braunfels museum is one of those little gems often tucked away in small towns that receive little attention in these days of theme parks. The Museum of Texas Handmade Furniture, 1370 Church Hill Dr., (830) 629-6504, features more than 75 examples of handcrafted furniture made by German cabinetmakers working in the mid-19th century on the Texas frontier. Housed in the Breustadt House, ca. 1858, and listed in the National Register of Historic Places, the museum is open to the public daily during the summer and on weekends the rest of the year.

Nearby, at 1300 Church Hill Dr., the city's Conservation Society has relocated a number of historic buildings in Conservation Plaza. They include several homes, a one-room schoolhouse, a music studio, a barn, and a general store. Some have been completely restored; others are awaiting restoration. The society holds a folklife festival here in early May, (830) 625-8766, and the buildings are open at irregular hours during the rest of the year (www.nbconservation.org).

Another good way to capture the spirit of 19th-century New Braunfels is to eat at one of the town's German-style restaurants. Krause's Cafe, 148 Castell St., (830) 625-7581, has been serving German dishes, barbecue, and just plain, old-fashioned American cooking since 1938. This is where the courthouse crowd and the business leaders come for breakfast and lunch. The cafe also serves dinner, including chili (William Gebhardt perfected his chili powder formula in downtown New Braunfels a century ago), steaks, and burgers. Leave room for pie—Krause's has a wide selection. The cafe is open for breakfast, lunch, and dinner daily; closed Sun and for three weeks in Sept. No credit cards are taken here.

True to its German roots, New Braunfels is noted for its sausage. The New Braunfels Smokehouse, (830) 625-2416, www.nbsmokehouse.com (they ship!), at the intersection of I-35 and Highway 46, began life as a smokehouse for local farmers and ranchers more than 50 years ago. Now it is a restaurant featuring several varieties of sausage and barbecue, plus smoked hams and turkeys. The restaurant is open for breakfast, lunch, and dinner daily, and there is a gift shop and mail-order business on the premises.

Sausage is celebrated with relish (and onions) at Wurstfest, the annual 10-day festival that attracts tens of thousands of visitors to New Braunfels every Nov. The festival centers on sausage eating, beer drinking, and polka dancing (see the Annual Events & Festivals chapter).

Gruene

It is pronounced "Green," and for the savvy developers who revived this ghost town north of New Braunfels, the name proved propitious. These days, old Gruene (www.gruenetexas.com) is anything but a ghost town, particularly on weekends when visitors stroll the narrow streets looking for antiques bargains, visiting craft shops and studios, kicking up a storm at the local dance hall, or digging into a chicken-fried steak. Ernest Gruene originally settled in New Braunfels and then moved his family to this area, about 5 miles north of New Braunfels, in 1872. His son, Henry D. Gruene, became very influential, and so the town was named after him.

After Henry died in 1920, Gruene suffered two fatal blows—the boll weevil killed the cotton crop and the Depression hit. The city turned into a ghost town, and the old buildings lay empty for years. When investors discovered the community, it looked as if time had stopped back in the '30s. Now this community on FM 306 just north of New Braunfels and about an hour's drive south of Austin on I-35 is listed on the National Register of Historic Places. There is only one intersection in Gruene, and most businesses lie either on Gruene Road or Hunter Road, making a tour of the town easy on the legs.

You will want to save some energy if you plan to spend the evening at Texas's oldest dance hall, Gruene Hall (830-629-5077, www.gruenehall.com), where some of the top names in country music have played, including Garth Brooks. The first dance was in 1878, and now the bar-cum-dance hall opens daily around midday so visitors can enjoy a longneck or two. The old hall has remained stuck in the years between the two world wars. The posters on the walls are advertisements from the era; there is no air-conditioning—the windows and doors are opened wide to catch the breeze—and there are burlap bags hanging from the ceiling. Cover charges for evening performances vary.

During the week, Gruene is quiet unless a popular band is playing, but on the weekends the little town fills up. Tubers are attracted to the Guadalupe River in summertime (Gruene is on the north bank of the river), while antiques hunters and shoppers come to the village to stroll the stores and galleries.

There is an abundance of bed-and-breakfast accommodations in town and the upscale Gruene Mansion Inn, located at 1275 Gruene Rd., (830) 629-2641 (www.gruenemansioninn.com), where guests stay in restored 1870 cottages with views of the Guadalupe River. The hotel also operates the Restaurant at Gruene Mansion Inn, (830) 620-0760, which serves lunch and dinner daily inside or out on the deck overlooking the river. The menu features a variety of cuisines, including Cajun, German, and continental. The Gruene Homestead Inn sits on 8 acres of farmland, and several of the old farm buildings have been renovated and converted to unique bedrooms. Cottages and old homes from the area also have been relocated on the farm and restored. The rooms at the inn are all individually decorated and have sitting areas or porches for relaxing after a day of activities on the river or among the shops nearby. The inn is located at 832 Gruene Rd., (800) 238-5534 or (830) 606-0216, www.gruene homesteadinn.com.

Also overlooking the river is the Grist Mill Restaurant at 1287 Gruene Rd., (830) 625-0684, www.gristmill.com, housed not in a gristmill but in a converted 100-year-old cotton gin. Lunch and dinner are served daily, and the menu features typical all-American fare—burgers, sandwiches, salads, steaks—plus some Tex-Mex and barbecue dishes.

Most of the businesses in Gruene offer free brochures illustrating walking tours of the community. One popular stop on the tour is the Guadalupe Valley Winery, also housed in an old cotton gin, at 1720 Hunter Rd., (830) 629-2351.

Hunter Road has several antiques stores and the old Gruene General Store, built in 1878, that now sells Texana, including cookbooks, cookies, and kitchen equipment, and offers sodas from the old-style soda fountain. Several artisans, including potters and ironworkers, have studios along Hunter Road, and the Gruene Antique Mall is home to several dealers. Gruene is popular year-round, but visitors mark their calendars for the monthly Market Days (www.gruene marketdays.com), held the third weekend of the month from Feb through Nov, when more than 100 arts and crafts vendors gather in Gruene. For more information on Gruene, call the Gruene Information Center at (830) 629-5077.

OUT EAST
Round Top & Winedale

These two tiny communities in Fayette County, about 90 miles east of Austin, have become world-renowned for their cultural events, their celebrations of music and theater that take place in several beautifully restored 19th-century Texas buildings set in landscaped grounds, and two nationally renowned antiques fairs. But even when there are no events scheduled at Round Top or Winedale, a day trip to the area can be an opportunity for city dwellers to catch a glimpse of small-town Texas.

> **i** Traveling around Texas by car will eventually lead you to a two-lane state highway. When these highways have wide shoulders, it's customary for slower vehicles to drive on the shoulder briefly to allow faster cars to pass. Frankly, we don't know if that's legal, but it's the Texas way.

Round Top is one of the state's oldest communities—the first Fourth of July in Texas was celebrated here in 1828, long before Texas was a republic or a state in the Union. In the mid-19th century, several German and Swedish families settled here, but the community never grew beyond a mere handful of homes. Then in the 1960s, artists and wealthy Texans began to be attracted to the area's natural beauty, buying up the old homes and restoring them.

In 1971 concert pianist James Dick chose Round Top as the home for his music institute, designed to offer students an opportunity to study with leading musicians. Dick established the International Festival Institute in historic Round Top. During its first 5 years, the Festival Institute leased facilities, but a master plan for development of a 200-acre campus was adopted. The first major facility, the Mary Moody Northern Pavilion, was acquired in 1973. It was the largest transportable stage in the world and was used for open-air concerts until 1983. Later it was housed in the 1,200-seat Festival Concert Hall, on which construction began in 1980, until the permanent stage was completed in the Concert Hall in 1993. An abandoned school building and 6 acres of land east of Round Top were acquired in 1973 for the campus, now named Festival Hill. The grounds are open to the public, and they make a great setting for a spring picnic.

Several historic buildings were moved to the festival site. The first historic structure moved to Festival Hill came from nearby LaGrange and was named the William Lockhart Clayton House in honor of the man who created the Marshall Plan. Built in 1885, it was renovated in 1976 for faculty offices, teaching facilities, and indoor concerts. The Menke House, built in 1902, was moved to Festival Hill from Hempstead and renovated as a faculty residence and conference center in 1979. Its Gothic Revival ceilings, woodwork, and staircases make it a showcase of Texas carpentry.

The historic sanctuary of the former Travis Street United Methodist Church of LaGrange, built in 1883, was moved to Festival Hill in 1994 for restoration as a center for chamber music, organ recitals, lectures, and seminars. It was renamed the Edythe Bates Old Chapel to honor one of the great Texan patronesses of the fine arts and houses an 1835 Henry Erben pipe organ. The Festival Institute Museum and Library exhibits art collections in the Festival Concert Hall and the historic house restorations.

There are now 17 musical programs during June and July each year. The Aug-to-Apr Concerts Series, the Early Music Festival, and other programs bring the total number of year-round concerts to more than 50. These include orchestral, chamber music, choral, vocal, brass, woodwinds, and solo performances. The repertoire extends from ancient to contemporary music.

The campus is also used for conferences, meetings, and retreats by businesses and professional organizations. A series of distinguished museum lectures is presented at Festival Hill each year. The campus, famed for its gardens, rare trees, herb collections, cascades, fountains, and unusual landscaping is a destination for visitors from all over the world; the grounds are open daily.

Tickets may be purchased at the Concert Hall beginning one hour prior to each concert, and season tickets are available. For information on the musical season or individual concerts, call (979) 249-3129, www .festivalhill.org.

Nearby Winedale has been a center for ethnic studies since Ima Hogg, daughter of a former Texas governor, donated the grounds and several historic buildings to the University of Texas in 1967. Winedale is also home to the Shakespeare at Winedale festival where UT students perform several of Shakespeare's plays in an 1894 barn-turned-theater at various times during the year (www.shakespeare-winedale.org).

Like Round Top, the grounds are open to the public, and there is a small admission charge. Winedale is open May through Oct on Sat from 10 a.m. to 6 p.m., Sun from noon to 6 p.m., and Nov through Apr from 9 a.m. to 5 p.m. on Sat and noon to 5 p.m. on Sun. Tours of the on-site historic buildings can be arranged, (979) 278-3530, and there is a marked nature trail. There are several annual events that bring visitors to Winedale, including a Christmas Open House featuring seasonal music and food, a spring festival and Texas Craft Exhibition, and a German Oktoberfest.

There are numerous bed-and-breakfast and guest house accommodations in the Round Top/Winedale area, and many are listed on the www.roundtop.org website. Some Austin residents prefer to stay overnight in the area after a concert or play, turning a night outing into a weekend getaway. Accommodations range in price. If you plan an overnight stay, book well in advance during those times when concerts and theater presentations are scheduled.

Several restaurants in the area feature country cooking, including Klump's restaurant, (979) 249-5696, in Round Top. It's open Wed through Sat for breakfast, lunch, and dinner and Sun and Tues for breakfast and lunch. Closed Mon.

The area also has become popular among antiques collectors. In addition to shops in the communities of Round Top, Winedale, Shelby, Warrenton, and Carmine, antiques dealers come from across the country for the first weekend in Apr and Oct to the Antiques Fair (see the Annual Events & Festivals chapter).

To reach Round Top or Winedale, take US 290 east toward Houston from Austin. Just beyond Giddings look for Highway 237; head south and follow the signs to Round Top. Winedale is just east of Round Top on

F.M. 2714. Many of the merchants in the area have tourist maps showing the locations of the various small communities and lists of accommodations and area attractions, and there is a visitor center on the square in Round Top. Another good place to gather information about local happenings is the Round Top Mercantile Company, on Highway 237, (979) 249-3117, www.round topmercantile.com, which is open 7 days a week. Look for the store's Texaco pumps on the west side of the highway as you drive into Round Top.

Bryan/College Station

Given the intense sports rivalry between the University of Texas and Texas A&M University, it's practically treason for an Austinite to tout the merits of College Station—home of the Aggies of A&M. This college town and neighboring Bryan (you can't tell where one begins and the other leaves off) offer all kinds of treats for the day-tripper or weekend visitor. College Station, 101 miles northeast of Austin, is an easy, stress-free drive along a route now designated as the "Presidential Corridor."

The corridor—US 290 East and Highway 21—connects Texas's 2 presidential libraries, the Lyndon Baines Johnson Library in Austin and College Station's George H. W. Bush Presidential Library and Museum, (979) 691-4000, http://bushlibrary.tamu.edu, at A&M University. It's worth the trip alone to visit this massive facility dedicated to the life and times of the 41st president of the United States. With more than 25,000 square feet of exhibition space, the museum chronicles Bush's life from his youth in Greenwich, Connecticut, to his service as a pilot in the US Navy and through his bold move to the Texas oil fields in the mid-1940s.

In vivid detail, visitors learn about Bush's career as a congressman, ambassador to the United Nations, director of the CIA, then vice president and president of the United States. Here visitors will find the largest and most complete exhibit in the country dedicated to the 1991 Gulf War. There's also a huge slab of the Berlin Wall, graffiti and all. One section of the museum is dedicated to former First Lady Barbara Bush's efforts on behalf of literacy, volunteerism, and AIDS prevention. Of course the library is also a research institution and includes 38 million pages of President Bush's official and personal papers. The library, located on the A&M West Campus, is open Mon through Sat 9:30 a.m. to 5 p.m. and Sun noon to 5 p.m. There is a $7 admission charge for adults.

Just a short distance from the Bush library is the main campus of Texas A&M University, Texas's oldest public college. A&M, the state's land grant college, was founded in 1876 as an all-male military college. On August 23, 1963, the name of the Agricultural and Mechanical College was changed to Texas A&M University. Today A&M is among the 10 largest universities in the United States, with more than 46,000 students, and ranks among the top three institutions nationally in undergraduate enrollment in agriculture, business administration, and architecture.

A&M's nationally known Corps of Cadets program—now open to men and women—has produced more military officers than any other institution in the country except for the service academies. Start your tour of this sprawling campus with a visit to the Appelt Aggieland Visitor Center in Rudder Tower on the main campus, (979) 845-5851, www .tamu.edu. Some points of interest include the Academic Building, built in 1912 on the site of Old Main, the first building on campus; the Albritton Bell Tower, a 138-foot tower that contains a 49-bell carillon; the Bonfire Memorial, erected in remembrance of the 12 students who were killed during A&M's 1999 bonfire tragedy; the Student Recreation Center, one of the largest student rec center's in the country; the Cadet Quad, home to those world-famous cadets; and Kyle Field, the impressive 70,210-seat football stadium—home to UT's archrival.

Check, too, for a listing of events at A&M's Reed Arena, (979) 862-7334, reed. tamu.edu. The arena features sporting events, concerts, ice shows, circuses, and much more. Also in College Station is Wolf Pen Creek Amphitheater, (979) 764-3408. This lovely outdoor arena hosts a wide range of music and entertainment, including some of Austin's finest musical performers.

Bryan is home to the Brazos Valley Museum of Natural History, (979) 776-2195, www.brazosvalleymuseum.org. The museum features a collection of fossils found in the Brazos Valley as well as a constantly changing array of temporary exhibits. Youngsters will find plenty to do in the nature lab and discovery room. The museum is open Tues through Sat 10 a.m. to 5 p.m. And be sure to take your children to the new Children's Museum of the Brazos Valley, (979) 779-5437, www.mymuseum.com. The museum features a wonderfully whimsical upside down entrance, and all kinds of hands-on learning activities and displays, including the inspiration gallery in which children can perform a puppet show, disassemble a VCR, or paint a Volkswagen Beetle. The museum is open Mon through Sat 10 a.m. to 5 p.m. and Sun noon to 4 p.m.

One of top spots in Bryan is the Messina Hof Winery at 4545 Old Reliance Rd., (979)

Close-up

Hitting the Trails to Hill Country Wines

It likely comes as no surprise to wine aficionados that Texas makes some excellent wines, many of them medal winners in national and international competitions. Those who are new to, or visiting, Central Texas, however, might be surprised to learn that the wine-making tradition in this region is alive and well—and growing. Today, the Texas Hill Country alone boasts almost two dozen wineries that vary in size, ambience, wine-making style, and, of course, "flavor." Austin, which sits at the eastern edge of Hill Country, is the gateway to all, as well as to other award-winning wineries within driving distance to the east and south of us.

As the popularity of Texas' homegrown wines has increased, so have the number of wine-related events.

Foremost on the list of Austin-area happenings is the Hill Country Wine & Food Festival, a 4-day event held annually in Apr, www.texaswineandfood.org. It is hard to pinpoint the highlight of this classy festival, which takes place at venues in Austin and the Hill Country, as every aspect of it is a true experience. The Village at the Shores, an outdoor food, wine, and live music extravaganza, and the Stars Across Texas Grand Tasting, a gala affair, are two of the most popular features, as are the cooking classes and the luncheons at Hill Country wineries.

Sixteen wineries have joined forces to create the Hill Country Wine Trail, www .texaswinetrail.com, to introduce newcomers to the wineries and to present the newest vintage. The calendar begins in February, with the Wine Lover's Trail held around Valentine's Day. The focus of this event is on the new vintage, but guests can enjoy "sweetheart" dinners, chocolates, and, of course, wine—in case the "bouquet" you want to present to your sweetheart is not the kind presented in a vase. The Wine & Wildflower Trail in Apr is timed to coincide with the annual spring blossoming of the Hill Country's bluebonnets. August brings the Harvest Wine Trail, Oct features the Texas Wine Month Passport Trail, while the Holiday Wine Trail is held in Dec. Another set of trails is outlined on the Texas Wine Trails website, www.texas winetrail.com, which includes two trails in the region. Some wineries are found on more than one trail, but if you want to get a fuller spectrum, check out all three.

It is not possible to visit all the wineries in the region in a day. Then again, why would anyone want to rush while visiting the quaint towns in the Hill Country? We suggest you select one area of the wine map on each trip and visit the wineries in that vicinity. First-timers might want to start in Fredericksburg, as it is the hub for several excellent wineries. And don't forget to take along a picnic basket. The Hill Country offers some excellent picnic spots, some at the wineries themselves.

To celebrate Texas Wine Month in Oct, don't miss the Fredericksburg Food & Wine Fest and the Gruene Music and Wine Fest, both within an easy drive of Austin. There's no need to wait for a special event to visit the wineries, however, as wine tastings and tours are held throughout the year. You might even come across a good old-fashioned grape stomp!

778-9463, www.messinahof.com. Established with the release of its first vintage in 1983, Messina Hof boasts a 200-year heritage with the family traditions of winemaker Paul Bonarrigo going back 6 generations to Messina, Sicily. Winery tours and tastings attract tourists from all over the region. Messina Hof produces a variety of red, white, and blush wines as well as ports and champagne. At the inviting guest center, visitors can purchase wines as well as a number of other gourmet foods made with the local product, including Riesling raspberry hazelnut fudge. Yum! The Vintage House restaurant serves international cuisine and is open Wed through Sat for lunch and dinner and Sun from 11 a.m. to 6 p.m.. For those planning a weekend trip to the area, the winery offers the Villa bed-and-breakfast.

As you make your way back to Austin, you might consider making a stop in Brenham to tour the cool business that put this town on the map. The Blue Bell Creamery, (800) 327-8135, www.bluebell.com, offers tours, topped off by servings of its great ice cream, for a $5 charge. Reservations are recommended.

For more information about Bryan/College Station, call the Convention and Visitor Bureau at (800) 777-8292 or visit the website at www.visitaggieland.com.

OUT WEST

✳ Johnson City/LBJ Ranch

No, Johnson City was not named after the 36th president of the United States, Lyndon Baines, but one of his ancestors. The young LBJ was raised in the town bearing his family name. Johnson City, 50 miles southwest of Austin, and the LBJ Ranch in Stonewall, about 13 miles farther west, combine to make a perfect day trip from Austin. As

you might expect, attractions in these two locations center on the life of the late President Johnson. The LBJ National Historic Park, www.nps.gov/lyjo, in fact, includes both the ranch and LBJ's boyhood home as well as the nearby Johnson Settlement.

Start your visit in Johnson City with a tour of the park's visitor center, at the intersection of Lady Bird Lane and Avenue G. Here you can pick up a map of the complex and a brochure on the park and also see the excellent exhibits, including scores of photographs, dedicated to the lives of LBJ and the former first lady. You can also listen to tape recordings of LBJ, Mrs. Johnson, and other state and national leaders speaking on major issues of the 1960s, including poverty, health, civil rights, and the environment. This modern stone facility also includes a gift shop and bookstore. It's open daily.

Nearby is LBJ's Boyhood Home. This simple but comfortable Folk Victorian–style house was LBJ's home from the age of 5 in 1913 until he married Lady Bird in 1934. It was here, on the front porch, that Johnson made his first public speech in 1937, announcing his candidacy for the US House of Representatives. National Park Service guides provide a brief introduction about the restored home and the career of LBJ every half hour throughout the day beginning at 9 a.m. A few items inside the home are original, but many are period pieces. An interesting collection of Johnson family photographs adorn the walls. Admission is free.

From here walk about 4 blocks along a cinder path through bucolic Hill Country terrain (you cannot drive it) to the Johnson Settlement. This exhibit hall is filled with displays detailing the selection of Johnson City as the site for the town in 1879 and features all kinds of fascinating stories about frontier life, including the cowboys, the cattle drives, the trails, and farming. The pleasant covered porch of this stone building is adorned with rocking chairs and has drinking fountains and restrooms. Another block down the path is the dogtrot cabin that once belonged to President Johnson's grandfather. The cabin, which has a shaded breezeway—through which a dog could easily trot—is typical of structures built during the 1800s.

This area also includes an authentic chuck wagon, used during cattle drives to haul food and supplies for the cowboys. There's also the James Polk Johnson Barn, built by the nephew of LBJ's grandfather in 1875, as well as a windmill, water tank, and cooler house. Across the field, in a penned enclosure, you might spy a herd of longhorn cattle grazing in the field.

While you're in Johnson City, you might also want to check out two attractions not related to LBJ. Take FM 2766 about 8 miles to Pedernales Falls State Park. The 4,800-acre park features waterfalls, fishing, swimming, hiking, camping, and great places to picnic. Children will enjoy visiting the Exotic Resort Zoo, (830) 868-4357, www.zooexotics.com, on Highway 281, 4 miles north of Johnson City. The zoo's trams take visitors on one-hour guided tours of the 137-acre park that is filled with more than 500 exotic animals from around the world, many that will come right up and eat out of your hand. It's open daily 9 a.m. to 6 p.m. This is also a great place to bring a picnic lunch.

Now, it's time to head for Stonewall and the LBJ Ranch, also known as the Texas White House. On your way to Stonewall, however, you might want to make a quick stop at the Hye Post Office, (830) 644-2465, which is right on US 290 about halfway between Johnson City and Stonewall. The

future president mailed his first letter here at the age of 4 and returned as president in 1965 to swear in Lawrence F. O'Brien as Postmaster General. This old post office and general store, built in 1904, is a Texas Historic Landmark.

i The Texas State Travel Guide is an invaluable resource when planning a trip around the state. It is available free at www.traveltex.com. See the Media chapter for more about this publication.

Follow US 290 west a few more miles until you arrive at a second visitor center, where you can pick up a map, CD, and free driving permit for a self-guided tour of the ranch from the comfort of your own vehicle. The tour includes all the areas of interest in this historic spread, including LBJ's reconstructed birthplace, the site where Johnson was born August 27, 1908 (the house was rebuilt by President Johnson in 1964); the show barn, which is the center of present-day ranching operations; and the Johnson Family Cemetery where generations of Johnsons are buried, including the president and first lady. The tour also takes you past the Junction School, where the future president learned to read at age 4, and the Grandparent's Farmhouse, where Johnson's paternal grandparents lived out their lives. The Ranch House, also known as the Texas White House, was added to the tour in 2008, following the death of Mrs. Johnson. Park Rangers are on hand to provide tours of the rooms of the home, including LBJ's office, that are open to the public.

You can now retrace your path to Austin or head farther west to Fredericksburg.

Fredericksburg

This Hill Country town is so packed with things to do that it is easy to make a half dozen day trips or weekend getaways out of this destination. There is something here for almost everyone!

Fredericksburg, named for Prince Frederick of Prussia, is kin to New Braunfels (see the day trip under Down South), as both were founded by the Society for the Protection of German Immigrants—New Braunfels in 1845 and Fredericksburg in 1846. The settlers moved into the Comanche territory, and in 1847 their leader, Baron Ottfried Hans von Meusebach, negotiated a peace treaty with the Comanche. That event is commemorated each year on the Sat before Easter with the Easter Fires celebration, a lighting of bonfires on the hills around the town and a pageant that involves townsfolk dressed as Easter bunnies, comanches, and pioneers. Fredericksburg has retained its German character in its architecture and cultural traditions. Indeed, many old-timers still speak what is called Old High German and can be heard talking among themselves on the streets and in stores. Local churches also offer German services and songs.

The heart of the town is listed on the National Register of Historic Places. One very wide street cuts through the town, wide enough, it is said, for a team of oxen and a wagon to be turned around. Most of the sights are on Main Street or just a block or two off the thoroughfare. During the Gold Rush of 1849, Fredericksburg merchants made their fortunes as prospectors stocked up at the last Western outpost before embarking into the heart of Indian Territory. These days there is a similar feel to the town as tourists browse the shops along Main Street and the locals talk about the latest movie star who has bought a little piece of the picturesque Hill Country. Some Austinites own weekend homes in the town.

Military history buffs won't want to miss the National Museum of the Pacific War at 340 East Main St., (830) 997-8600, www.pacificwarmuseum.org. This sprawling complex includes the nearby Admiral Nimitz Museum. Chester Nimitz, who commanded the Pacific Fleet in World War II, was born in landlocked Fredericksburg, and his grandfather once owned the hotel that now serves as the museum. One highlight of this museum is the 15-foot model of the aircraft carrier USS *Nimitz*.

The George H. W. Bush Gallery details the wartime experience of the 41st president, who was shot down in the Pacific. A highlight of the museum is an exhibit featuring one of the two-man submarines used in the attack on Pearl Harbor. Other interactive and audiovisual exhibits illustrate the fierce battles in the Pacific. The Plaza of the Presidents consists of 10 monoliths detailing the wartime service of 10 presidents, beginning with President Franklin Roosevelt. In stark contrast to the exhibits, the museum is also home to a Japanese Garden of Peace, given by the people of Japan to the facility. There is a replica of the study and teahouse used by Admiral Togo, Nimitz's counterpart in the Imperial Japanese Navy.

Adding to the military flavor of the Fredericksburg area is the Hangar Hotel, a 2003 addition to the abundant lodging scene in town. This unique hotel evokes a World War II Pacific Theater officer's club. The rooms are furnished with leather chairs and mahogany sleigh beds, and there is a '40s-era diner on-site. The hotel is located at 155 Airport Rd., (830) 997-9990, www.hangarhotel.com. Another military-related attraction is the reconstructed Fort Martin Scott, located just east of town at 1606 East Main St., (830) 997-9895. The ca. 1848 fort, one of the first frontier outposts in Texas, includes the original guardhouse as well as a reconstructed officers' quarters, a visitor center, and other buildings. Historical reenactments are periodically held here, and there is ongoing archaeological work at the site.

Many visitors are drawn to Fredericksburg by the architecture and rich pioneer history. The Pioneer Museum at 325 West Main St., www.pioneermuseum.net, is made up of several buildings, including a home and general store built in 1849, a barn and smokehouse, a firefighting museum, a pioneer log cabin, an 1855 church, and the Weber Sunday House. These tiny houses, sometimes just a single room, can be seen in both Fredericksburg and New Braunfels. They are called Sunday houses because they were built by farmers and ranchers as a place to bring the family on the weekend for Sunday church services. Many of them have been restored and are used as weekend homes by city dwellers. One of the best times of the year to see them is in spring when many of the tiny gardens are filled with wildflowers. An extension of the museum is the Vereins Kirche Museum (the People's Church Museum), a famous landmark in Market Square at the heart of the city. The octagonal building is a museum of local history.

The Fredericksburg Chamber of Commerce, (830) 997-6523, www.fredericksburg-texas.com, provides walking tour maps and other pamphlets that give detailed information about the Sun homes and other sights in the city. The maps and brochures also are available at many local businesses, including the German-style restaurants that dot Main Street. The Altdorf Restaurant, 301 West Main St., (830) 997-7865, www.altdorfbiergarten-fbg.com, has a beer garden and serves lunch and dinner daily, except Tues. The Old German Bakery and Restaurant, 225 West Main St., (830) 997-9084, serves breakfast, lunch, and dinner and sells typical German baked goods, including rye bread, which often runs out early in the day.

For great entertainment make plans to attend a live musical/comedy show at the Rockbox Theater just off Main Street at 109 North Llano St., (866) 349-6688, www.rockboxtheater.com. The professional entertainers at this nearly 400-seat theater present superb family-friendly shows from the golden era of rock 'n' roll. The shows change regularly, so we guarantee you'll want to go back! There are both evening performances and matinees so you can catch the show during a day trip.

Fredericksburg is also a popular destination for shoppers seeking hand-made, unique or one-of-a-kind items. Many of the scores of shops on Main Street offer the work of the area's, many artisans and artists as well as dealers in antiques and Texana. Candle-making and glassblowing are just two of the crafts demonstrated in town. One of the specialty shops is an outlet for Fredericksburg Herb Farms, www.fredericksburgherbfarm.com, where shoppers can buy oils and vinegars flavored with herbs grown in the Hill Country. In addition to the Easter Fires and the herb festival, there are several other annual events that draw visitors throughout the year. In Apr there is a large antiques show; "A Night in Old Fredericksburg" is celebrated in July with food, dance, and song; the oldest county fair in Texas takes place in Sept with a traditional livestock show, horse races, a crafts and home-baked goods competition, plus evening dances; Oktoberfest celebrates the town's German heritage; and at Christmas there is the Candlelight Homes Tour, which offers wonderful views of some of the city's historical homes. Some are detailed in the Annual Events & Festivals chapter.

Fredericksburg is 85 miles west of Austin on US 290, so it is an easy day trip from the city and can be combined with a trip to the LBJ Ranch or Johnson City. (If you're traveling in June or July, be sure to stop along the way at one of the peach stands lining the highway.) But it is also a great weekend getaway location since the town has a wealth of bed-and-breakfast facilities and guest cottages. The latter are perfect for a romantic weekend since they are very private. Listings appear on the town's website, above. Lovers of the outdoors also head for Fredericksburg to visit Enchanted Rock State Park, just 18 miles north of the city, where a granite dome rises some 325 feet from the earth and offers wide views of the area (see the Parks & Recreation chapter). There are also several vineyards in the countryside around Fredericksburg, so if you're interested in tasting the Central Texas fruit of the vine be sure to download a copy of the Texas Wine Tour map before heading out. (See the Close-up in this chapter.)

THE HIGHLAND LAKES

Perhaps you've already had the pleasure of making a trip out to Austin's beautiful Lake Travis, maybe even taken a swim in the refreshing waters or toured the lake from cove to inviting cove by boat. Possibly you've seen or boated up and down Lake Austin, that lovely stretch of Colorado River between West Austin's Tom Miller Dam and the Mansfield Dam. If so, you've seen two of Central Texas's six Highland Lakes. (Find out more about these two lakes in the Parks & Recreation chapter.)

Viewing Austin's two Highland Lakes does not mean you've seen them all, however. Lake Buchanan, Inks Lake, Lake LBJ, and Lake Marble Falls all have their own distinct personality, and the only way to discover their wonders is to spend some time visiting them—one by one. Each lake is 75 miles or less northwest of Austin, making visits to them either a perfect day trip or a wonderful weekend getaway.

The lakes, created by a series of six dams built on the Colorado River during the Depression of the 1930s and 1940s, vary immensely in size, shape, and degree of development. The dams were built and are managed by the Lower Colorado River Authority (LCRA), www.lcra.org, which aimed to control the flood-prone river while providing a dependable source of water and electricity for the Texas Hill Country. For information about the lakes, the dams, or any number of the parks and campsites operated by the LCRA, call (800) PRO-LCRA or phone the Park Information Hot Line at (512) 473-4083. The common denominator that unites all these lakes is the focus on water activities: swimming, boating, and fishing. Camping, either in tents or RVs, is extremely popular around these lakes, although in most cases the campsites are either primitive or just a step above, meaning you'll find restrooms in some but hardly ever showers. In most cases you'll enjoy the offerings much more by either taking along a boat, renting a pontoon or personal watercraft (PWC), or taking a guided cruise. While there are a few trails, the Highland Lakes are not renowned for attracting large numbers of hikers or bikers. If you're determined to hike, we'll point out a couple of good spots.

Lake Buchanan

Let's start with the granddaddy of them all: Lake Buchanan, known as "Big Buc" to the locals and fishermen in these parts. While it's the oldest, largest, and northernmost (farthest from Austin) of all the Highland Lakes, Lake Buchanan is also one of the most undeveloped, retaining the feel of a laid-back fishing haven. (Although more boating enthusiasts from the "big cities" are beginning to discover the lake.) The eastern shoreline stands out for its rugged, hilly terrain and towering cliffs. (Drivers should take special precaution here.) The western shore is closer to lake level and offers plenty of spots to just stop off and get your feet wet or take a swim.

i The bridge that spanned Inks Lake for decades has been replaced by a modern structure, but the old one remains as a pedestrian bridge—and it offers great views of the lake and Buchanan Dam.

This immense water basin, which covers 23,060 acres (36 square miles), was created with the completion of the 2.08-milelong Buchanan Dam in 1937. This lake is especially noted for its three scenic waterfalls—Fall Creek Falls, Deer Creek Falls, and Post Oak Falls—as well as for the gorgeous cliffs and rock formations that line the shores. Birds, deer, and other wildlife are common sights all the way up from the dam to Colorado Bend State Park, (915) 628-3240, on the northernmost end of the lake. The park, filled with towering shade trees, is one of the nicest campsites on the lake. It has portable restrooms but no shower facilities or electrical hookups. This campsite, on the western shore, is accessible from the

towns of Lampasas or Cherokee by car or by boat. Hikers and mountain bikers will be pleased to know this park also offers excellent choices for both.

Very important to know about boating on Lake Buchanan: This is not a deep lake even in times of abundant rainfall, so be sure to use your map, or better yet talk to the locals, and steer clear of sandbars and other hazards. Local experts warn that it is unsafe to try to boat upstream from Colorado Bend State Park, as you'll run into small but very rocky rapids. You'll find public boat ramps on both sides of the lake at the various parks, including Burnet County Park (Buchanan Dam), (512) 756-4297; Burnet County Park (White Bluff), same phone number, both on the eastern side of the lake; Llano County Park, (915) 247-4352, on the southwestern shore; and the Cedar Point Resource Area (LCRA Hotline) in the northwest. The various rental bungalows and cottages around the lake also feature boat ramps. You don't have to go way upstream to enjoy boating on the lake, however. The huge reservoir is perfect for sailing, speed boating, and bopping around on those ever-popular personal watercraft.

This lake also offers excellent scenic drives year-round but especially in springtime when the wildflowers are in bloom. Designated the "Bluebonnet Capital of Texas" by the state legislature, this area and neighboring Inks Lake attract scores of visitors to the Bluebonnet Trail each year during the spectacular wildflower season, which runs Mar through May depending on rainfall. The Lake Buchanan/Inks Lake Chamber of Commerce, (512) 793-2803, www.buchanan-inks .org, located at Buchanan Dam, offers an annual brochure and operates a hot line of the best viewing locations.

We suggest a stop off at the Buchanan Dam Museum and Visitor Center right off Highway 29 on the southeastern tip of the lake. It is open daily 10 a.m. to 4 p.m., except Tues. Here you'll find a fascinating pictorial history of the construction of the dam, comments from a few of the hundreds of workers who found highly coveted Depression-era jobs building the immense barrier, as well as information about the Kingsland Archaeological Center on Lake LBJ. The visitor center also features an 18-minute documentary about the dam itself. Also, this is where you'd come to take a free guided tour of the huge generating facility. Tours generally run from May to Sept. And don't miss out on the opportunity to take a stroll along the impressive pedestrian walkway that leads from the visitor center all the way out to the spillway. This is the best way to see for yourself what a huge undertaking this project was—and get a great view of Lake Buchanan at the same time. For those not interested in making the trek, there's an outdoor observation deck right off the parking lot.

i Early summer is peach season in the Texas Hill Country. If you're heading to Johnson City, Stonewall, or Fredericksburg, be sure to stop at any one of a number of businesses along US 290 that sell fresh, ripe peaches, homegrown tomatoes, and other fruits. Some even have homemade peach ice cream!

From here you can choose to either head up the eastern side of the lake or follow the western shore. Both have their own attributes and attractions, and you will find rental cabins and bungalows as well as places to eat on both sides of the lake. Going up north on the eastern shoreline is

the recreational development Canyon of the Eagles, (512) 756-8787 or (800) 977-0081, www.canyonoftheeagles.com. This 940-acre site includes a 64-room lodge, an RV park, camping facilities, a beach, general store, and, best of all, a nature preserve for wildlife such as the bald eagle and the golden-cheeked warbler. The Eagle Eye Observatory also is here, offering visitors a chance to peer through a 16-inch Ealing Cassegrain telescope and to chart the skies from a unique observing field. Stargazing parties are scheduled regularly. This is the place to catch the Vanishing Texas River Cruise on the Texas Eagle II, a 70-foot, 200-passenger boat with 2 observation decks.

Several tours are offered year-round, including the popular 2½ hour guided scenic wilderness cruise up the Colorado River Canyon. Bring your own picnic. Tours held Nov through Mar are especially fascinating because they take visitors upriver to see the winter habitat of the largest colony of American bald eagles in the state. Wildflower tours, vineyard tours, and sunset dinner cruises also are offered. You don't have to be a guest of the park to take a cruise. Call or check the website for a schedule and prices.

Inks Lake

Just a few miles west of the Buchanan Dam off Highway 29 is Inks Lake in what is known as the Central Texas Mineral Region. (Enter at Park Road 4 and travel south.) Only 4.2 miles long and just 0.6 mile at its widest points, Inks Lake is dwarfed by its gargantuan neighbor. Yet the lake is surrounded by such rugged natural beauty—highlighted by towering oak trees, wildflowers, scenic bluffs, and huge boulders of granite and pink gneiss—that it attracts nature lovers, campers, boaters, and fishing enthusiasts year-round. This lake was the second created on the Colorado River after the 1,548-foot Roy Inks Dam was completed in 1938.

Inks Lake features one of the most popular state parks in Texas. Inks Lake State Park, (512) 793-2223, is one of the most fully equipped parks in the region, offering both tent and RV sites, a few enclosed shelters, showers and restrooms, picnicking, swimming, trails, a boat ramp, and even a public golf course. The 1,200-acre park extends along the entire eastern shoreline of the lake. Be sure to stop at the scenic overlook along Park Road 4 and check out the Devil's Waterhole, which has a beautiful waterfall. Teenagers just love to climb on the huge granite boulders that adorn this area.

From Inks Lake you might want to follow Park Road 4 south about 10 minutes to Longhorn Cavern State Park, (512) 756-4680. While not on a lake, this wonderful 637-acre state park is nevertheless a great place for picnicking and hiking. No overnight camping is permitted. Of course the major attraction here is the cavern itself. Located in Backbone Ridge, a huge piece of Ellenburge limestone formed by a shallow sea more than 450 million years ago, the cavern is open for daily tours year-round. The 1¼-mile round-trip walking tour takes about 85 minutes.

Lake LBJ

If Buchanan and Inks Lakes are the rugged members of the family, Lake LBJ is the refined cousin. The Colorado River meanders down from Inks Lake and branches out to skirt the town of Kingsland before it widens near the towns of Sunrise Beach on the western shore and Granite Shoals on the east. Once called Granite Shoals Lake, it was renamed in 1965 to recognize President Lyndon Johnson's efforts on behalf of the LCRA. At 6,200 acres, this gorgeous lake is the second largest of these four. Created by the Wirtz Dam, Lake LBJ offers plenty of wide-open waters for speedboats, sailboats, and personal watercraft. Unlike Inks and Buchanan, however, Lake LBJ stands out for the upscale homes and large manicured lawns that surround the basin. This lake is becoming increasingly developed and includes the resort community of Horseshoe Bay and others.

i Sadly, there is not one great map of the Highland Lakes area available for purchase. The closest we have found is the Texas Hill Country Tourist Guide map, although it covers an area much larger than the Lakes. Try www.texasoutside.com/texaslakes.

Because of its emphasis on residential development, this lake is not stocked with rental units, although there are a few. For real pampering, stay at the beautiful Horseshoe Bay Resort by Marriott, (800) 452-5330, at 200 Hi Circle North, www.horseshoebaymarriott.com. This luxury property not only offers divine guest rooms, it also has golf, tennis, a spa—and its own airport. For other lodging options here and at the other lakes, we especially like the website www.lakesandhills.com.

If you're heading south on Highway 1431 from Kingsland, be sure to take a few moments to stop at Lookout Mountain, just a few miles south of TX 2342. This scenic overlook provides an excellent overall view of the Colorado River valley. A few minutes farther south off this highway is the Kingsland Archaeological Site, (830) 598-5261, which is open by reservation only.

The 10-acre site on the shores of Lake LBJ is a 5,000-year-old prehistoric campsite for hunter-gatherers along the Colorado River. Since it was discovered in 1988, archaeologists have uncovered more than 100,000 artifacts, including projectile points, grinding stones, and animal bone fragments. Photos of this site are on display at the Buchanan Dam Visitor Center.

Lake Marble Falls

Like Lake Austin, Lake Marble Falls is an inner-city lake that appears more like the river it is than a wide-open lake. Nevertheless, this 6-mile lake has grown so popular over the years that the community of Marble Falls and the huge Meadow Lake Country Club have grown up around it. The well-shaded 18-acre Johnson Park, (210) 693-3615, on the lake features a public boat ramp, a playscape for children, picnic area, overnight camping, and restrooms. Nearby is Lakeside Park (same phone), which also has a boat ramp but is designated for day use only. Entrance to both parks is free. RV campers will want to check out the Riverview RV Park, (830) 693-3910, on the shores of Lake Marble Falls at 200 River Rd., www.touringtexas.com/riverview. This site offers full hookups as well as restrooms, showers, and laundry facilities. If you're ready for a good, inexpensive home-style meal while in Marble Falls, try the famous Blue Bonnet Cafe in town at 211 Highway 281 South, (830) 693-2344, www.bluebonnetcafe.net. You'll find everything from burgers to chicken-fried steak, pot roast, fried chicken livers, and fried catfish. The homemade biscuits melt in your mouth, as do the pies. The Blue Bonnet is open for breakfast, lunch, and dinner Mon through Sat, and breakfast and lunch on Sun. For lakeside dining, we like the River City Grille at 700 First St., (830) 798-9909, www.rivercitygrilletx.com.

Once you've toured all the Highland Lakes, you'll know for yourself why they are the pride of the Texas Hill Country.

Appendix

LIVING HERE

In this section we feature specific information for residents or those planning to
relocate here. Topics include real estate,
education, health care, and much more.

RELOCATION

Growth is many things to Austin-area residents. For some it means opportunity, broader horizons, and wider dreams, but for others it has come to mean the struggle to maintain the city's identity and quality of life that have been Austin hallmarks. The spirit of Austin is treasured by both longtime residents and newcomers. One key to the preservation of the city's unique character is the vitality of its neighborhoods.

Even the word *neighborhood* is loaded with meaning in Austin. Some neighborhood organizations have wielded considerable political clout at City Hall, while others have created unique identities that act as a draw to both visitors and residents. In Austin, as in some of the smaller rural communities that have been absorbed by the city's growth, maintaining the neighborhood character, the particular sense of place, has been both a challenge and a goal. Many of the area's neighborhoods have succeeded; others have not. But with growth has come a dynamism that has revitalized some neighborhoods, created new ones, and, at a minimum, kept the quality-of-life issue on the front burner for every Central Texas resident.

OVERVIEW

The city has been leaping up the population list in record time in recent years. Beyond the city limits, the greater Austin metropolitan area is fast approaching the 2 million resident mark and demographers are predicting the area growth will continue into the second decade of this century.

While downtown maintains some of the flavor of a midsize city, there has been a boom in downtown development that promises to give the heart of the city more of the feel of a busy, urban area. Highrise condo towers and loft developments are changing the downtown vibe and skyline. There is a symbiotic growth between the numerous condo/loft projects and new restaurants, shops, and cafes. Businesses, particularly high-tech companies, are eager to locate downtown, many of the older high-rises and warehouses are being converted to offices and living spaces, and the nightlife and restaurant scenes are even more vibrant. (See the Restaurants and Nightlife chapters.)

Growth is leaving its mark on Central Texas in many ways. On the plus side, growth has given the city a more cosmopolitan air. There is a greater diversity of restaurants, and more shops and theaters, and the city's increasingly multicultural population celebrates ethnic traditions and cultural differences. The largest Hindu temple in North America is not far from one of the area's most popular country barbecue joints, the Salt Lick (see the Restaurants chapter).

Growth brings choice and there are numerous choices for homeowners in terms of location and price. But growth also means traffic jams. Rush-hour commutes are now a factor for homebuyers, in addition to access to city services—police, fire, EMS, libraries, even parks.

A word about prices in the Austin-area real estate market: The median price of a home in Austin was $151,000 in June 2005, according to *Money* magazine, a 29 percent increase in 5 years. By the end of 2010 that had risen to $195,000 and, despite the economic slowdown, family homes continue to hold their value and increase in the coveted areas of the city. That median price is about what a consumer will pay for a small "starter" home in the area, and it likely will be located on the fringes of Austin, perhaps even beyond. A good rule of thumb is the closer to downtown, the higher the price. Older neighborhoods, close to downtown, are now hot, and even a small cottage can cost upward of $350,000. For that same amount of money, a buyer can find a large, 3-bedroom family home in one of the newer neighborhoods on the city's outskirts. A great way to get a visual picture of Austin real estate prices is to visit the real estate website, www.trulia.com, where urban "heat maps" displaying price in coded colors can be viewed. Because Austin has a significant young population—the highest number of 25 to 34 year olds in similar "creative class" cities—many of the older neighborhoods that once were the Austin suburbs are being revived by young homeowners with a flare for reinventing 50s-style.

Several significant trends in Austin's growth offer insight into what makes Austin neighborhoods tick. We begin with a look at some of these trends, followed by a geographic tour of some of the city's neighborhoods.

NEW URBANISM

It's a phrase that is much discussed in planning circles and in architecture schools across the country. For the uninitiated, "new urbanism" might be simply summed up as a return to the old neighborhoods of fond memory.

Hal Box, former dean of the University of Texas architecture school, has adopted a litmus test for examples of the new urbanism—it is the "5-minute Popsicle rule." Every child should be able to walk or ride a bike to the neighborhood store for a Popsicle and be home safely within 5 minutes. There are several "Popsicle rule" neighborhoods in Austin. Some of them are in upper-income neighborhoods, others in some of the city's older, working-class neighborhoods.

Austin has hosted several important conferences on New Urbanism and in 1997 launched an effort to draft a building and planning code that would embrace the spirit of the movement.

DOWNTOWN DISCOVERY

Another important trend in the growth of Austin has been the rediscovery of downtown as a place to live and work. Thanks to the presence of the Texas Capitol and the city's vibrant music scene, downtown Austin is alive both day and night and has not suffered the sort of blight some of America's cities have experienced. Within blocks of the city's main street, Congress Avenue, apartments and lofts offer residents a downtown lifestyle, although not at bargain-basement prices.

Ten blocks to the west of Congress Avenue is the hub of another downtown center that has become a magnet and a model for inner-city growth. Once the corner of Lamar Boulevard and West Sixth Street was an area dominated by car lots and automobile showrooms. Now, at the heart of this hub are the headquarters of two quintessential Austin companies. These local legends—Whole Foods Market, headquarters of a NASDAQ-traded gourmet/health food grocery store chain, and GSD&M, an award-winning national advertising agency—were founded by Texas baby boomers. Whole Foods Landmark Store and GSD&M's "Idea City" headquarters are at the heart of an urban neighborhood of bookstores, ice-cream parlors, coffee shops, and bakeries, all within a stone's throw of several new loft and apartment developments. This is one of those Austin neighborhoods that locals love to visit.

The Second Street District just north of City Hall on Lady Bird Lake is another downtown neighborhood where high rises and lofts shade sidewalk cafes and shops. The urban boom along Fifth and Sixth Streets is fast bringing the Whole Foods hub and downtown into one vibrant neighborhood.

GENTRIFICATION

The downtown development trend is linked to two other Austin market characteristics: the gentrification of older, inner-city neighborhoods and what planners call "infilling." Eager to live closer to downtown, or in one of the city's colorful, older neighborhoods, buyers are looking for empty lots or run-down properties and then either building or moving older homes onto the property. Austin has grappled with the so-called McMansion trend where older homes have been razed and bigger, sometimes intimidating homes have been built next door to small cottages. Critics say they spoil the flavor of the neighborhood and Austin

has passed some building codes to address the problem.

Homes west of downtown have enjoyed prestige and market value for several decades. Now, that trend is beginning to occur south of Lady Bird Lake in older neighborhoods along South Congress Avenue, popularly called SoCo, and lately has spread east of the Capitol into what was once a depressed, primarily African-American neighborhood. Fortunately, the urban restoration has encouraged longtime businesses and homeowners to stay in the area. The East section of the Restaurants chapter is proof of the neighborhood's renewed vitality.

Many of the new residents are young, urban pioneers who are taking on the challenges of moving into older, run-down neighborhoods in areas north of the University of Texas campus and just west of I-35 around the Hancock Center shopping plaza. Generally, neighborhoods close to downtown and west of the capitol have been the first to ride the gentrification boom and are now firmly established as prestigious neighborhoods, where a relatively small home can cost $350,000—if you are lucky.

Of course, the other side of the gentrification trend is a growing lack of affordable housing. The picture is getting tougher for average families, and there has been a growing concern that working people, particularly those providing vital services—police, firefighters, teachers, and city workers—are being priced out of the market.

The key to finding a bargain, particularly in an older neighborhood, is knowing which neighborhoods are being revived and which are suffering from the usual urban ills, including problems with crime and vandalism. That can be difficult for a newcomer, but Austin's active neighborhood association infrastructure can provide assistance. The City of Austin maintains a community registry, a reference guide to the approximately 300 active neighborhood associations in the city. It can be requested by contacting the planning department's neighborhood section at (512) 499-2648, www.ci.austin.tx.us/housing.

SUBURBAN EXPANSION

While some Austin residents are looking to the heart of the city for a home, others are looking to the hills. The major growth trend in the past two decades has been the expansion of the greater Austin area to the west. Back in the 1970s, the Austin City Council adopted a growth plan that called for expansion along the city's north-south corridor defined by I-35. The council was reflecting the concerns of environmentalists, who wanted to protect the vast underground Edwards Aquifer, the underground watershed that feeds Austin's icon and symbol of community environmental sensibilities, Barton Springs Pool in downtown Zilker Park (see the Close-up in the Parks & Recreation chapter).

But the lure of the Hill Country with its distinctive flora and scenic views proved more overwhelming. Much of the growth has occurred in the northwest, west, and southwest. In fact, the word west has something of a cachet in Austin real estate circles. The area's most prestigious neighborhoods are in West Austin; West Lake Hills, the incorporated community west of MoPac (Loop 1); and in western Travis County toward the Highland Lakes.

Austin is built on the border of two distinct geographic areas. I-35 roughly tracks the break between the Hill Country and the Blackland Prairie. To the west are rolling hills, live oak trees, and scrub dominated by so-called cedar trees (actually junipers) growing in the thin soil that barely dusts the limestone ridges. East of the Interstate the land is flatter, covered with rich, black soil in which pecan trees flourish.

Both areas are picturesque, but the desire to live west may have more to do with age-old social patterns that have little to do with a modern, integrated Austin. Like so many other cities, the Interstate highway also serves as a barrier between downtown and Austin's predominantly ethnic neighborhoods. Austin's neighborhoods are well integrated, particularly newer subdivisions, but like most American cities, Austin still has two distinct neighborhoods east of I-35 that historically have been primarily African American and Hispanic. These neighborhoods have strong identities. Neighborhood groups there have fought both to preserve community identity and to improve city services in their communities. Those lines are being blurred, particularly as young urban "pioneers" seek a home close to the city center. The lure of living west has pushed development out beyond the Austin city limits, absorbing once small communities like Cedar Park, northwest of Austin in the next county. Just as the greater Austin area has pushed over the Travis County line into Williamson County in the northwest, in the southwest suburban developments have spilled over into Hays County. The small community of Dripping Springs, on US 290 West about 15 miles from the Austin city limits, is feeling the growth boom as homeowners eager for a spacious home on perhaps an acre or two of land are locating there. The search for the Hill Country life is now spreading out even farther west. Communities 60 miles or more from Austin are seeing home developments spring up in their communities. The growth also has spread east to some of the wonderful small, rural towns in the rolling farmland around communities like Smithville and Bastrop.

THE HIGH-PRICE BOOM

One of the hottest commodities in the Austin real estate market has been high-priced homes, those costing $1 million and up. Realtors attribute this trend to the impact of the city's growing high-tech sector. In 2000 the area had virtually full employment, as the experts define it, with the unemployment rate at 2 percent. In 2005 the jobless rate hovered just under 5 percent. The high-tech industry had produced a group of entrepreneurs and a large number of employees with valuable stock options.

Leading the pack, of course, was Michael Dell, founder of Dell Computer, who built a new home in West Lake Hills that has been compared to Bill Gates's mansion in Seattle. Dell's home was appraised by tax authorities at $22.5 million—an appraisal he challenged—which was only half of what Gates's home allegedly cost. However, it did symbolize the high-price boom in Austin. Even with the end-of-the-decade economic slowdown, high-priced homes held their value in the much-coveted inner city neighborhoods and west of downtown. An old ivy-clad mansion in the Enfield neighborhood close to downtown might sell for $2–3 million, while a sprawling lakeside home in the hills above Lake Austin might sell for $3 million. Some of the large homes in the hills reflect traditional Hill Country architecture with limestone walls, Mexican tile floors, and rustic timbers, while others are mock Tudor or French chateau–style.

We'll take a look at the city by geographic area.

NEIGHBORHOODS
Central

The geographic center of the City of Austin lies somewhere around Highland Mall at the intersection of I-35 and US 290 East, several miles north of the capitol. But most Austin area residents consider the center of the city to be the downtown area, along the shores of Lady Bird Lake and around the Texas Capitol. For the purposes of this book, we have separated the city into regions (see the Getting Around chapter) and as the city's far suburbs grow, the city's center has expanded also, hence the North Central and South Central listings in this book. The central area embraces some of the city's most prestigious addresses and some of its more run-down, older neighborhoods. It also contains one of the most quintessential neighborhoods, Hyde Park, defined by advocates of new urbanism as a perfect "Popsicle rule" community.

Hyde Park was the city's first planned suburb. In 1889 Colonel Monroe Martin Shipe, a businessman from Abilene, Kansas, came to Austin and purchased a 206-acre plot of land in what was then far north Austin. The new suburb had its own electric streetcar system, dance pavilion, and walking paths. Shipe first built large Victorian homes for some of Austin's leading citizens. Later, smaller Craftsman-style bungalows were added to the neighborhood.

Today, Hyde Park is not only a much-sought-after address but also a popular spot for lunch or coffee with friends from across the city. It's located north of the University of Texas campus and bounded by Guadalupe Street on the west and Thirty-eighth Street on the south.

Several miles southwest of Hyde Park is the Enfield neighborhood, east of MoPac (Loop 1) and west of Shoal Creek, which wends its way south through Central Austin to Lady Bird Lake, running alongside Lamar Boulevard for much of its course. As it crosses Shoal Creek, Fifteenth Street becomes Enfield Road, running west through this affluent old neighborhood.

You can still find a few small apartments tucked away over old garages and in some of the smaller houses of the area, and even a small ca. 1960s apartment complex or two along the major thoroughfare, Enfield Rd. But the area is best known for its large homes with hefty price tags, set back on wooded lots lining the area's curving streets.

Another central neighborhood with a unique character is Clarksville, just south of Enfield Park. Sometimes described as part of West Austin (a reflection of the days when the city was much smaller), Clarksville is bordered on the west by MoPac, on the south by Tenth Street, and north by Waterston Avenue. The property was originally owned by Texas Governor E. M. Pease, who gave the land to his former slaves in 1863 as an effort to keep them as workers on his plantation.

The neighborhood is named for Charles Griffin, who changed his last name to Clark after he was freed. Clark bought a 2-acre plot on Tenth Street in 1871. Some of the current residents are descendants of the founders, but the neighborhood has changed over the years. Originally, according to local historians, Clarksville was home to about 250 African Americans. That number has diminished as the demographics of the neighborhood have changed.

Clarksville remains a mix of comfortable, modest homes and some gentrified houses with high price tags. Within the neighborhood are several shops (see the Shopping chapter), bakeries, a pottery store, and restaurants, including one of Austin's top dining spots, Jeffrey's (see the Restaurants chapter).

Central and South Austinites have an affection for changing the names of streets and rivers as their paths cross the city. In fact, rivers even become lakes—Lady Bird Lake (formerly Town Lake), the portion of the Colorado River that runs through the heart of Austin, once represented a dividing line for some in the city. *Austin American-Statesman* humor columnist John Kelso helped engender the myth of North-South differences in the mid-'80s. North Austin, the mythology went, was the land of the yuppies while south of the river was occupied by "bubbas," laid-back old hippies, and assorted free spirits.

Those distinctions have faded somewhat, but South Austin is still viewed by some as a haven for free spirits. The distinctions have faded, perhaps, because the older neighborhoods south of the river are being eyed as fertile territory for downtown living. Prices in neighborhoods south of the river have escalated. One of the most popular neighborhoods is Travis Heights, an area east of South Congress Avenue, south of Riverside Drive, and west of I-35 where homes often sell for $500,000 and up.

> ℹ️ The Austin Neighborhood Council serves as a clearinghouse for Austin's diverse neighborhoods (www.ancweb.org).

The South Congress Avenue corridor is undergoing rapid change. Once known for its X-rated movie theaters, streetwalkers, and even an old feed store (now Güero's restaurant), the wide avenue is now alive with restaurants, antiques shops, bakeries, boutiques, and a software store. The changes have affected the Bouldin Creek neighborhood, located west of South Congress Avenue, north of Oltorf Street. Older homes in this area are being snapped up by buyers eager to live near downtown. The neighborhood remains a mix of run-down houses, fixer-uppers, and newly renovated homes. The southern portion of this area has a distinct Hispanic flavor, with popular Mexican bakeries and restaurants occupying the corner lots. (For more information on dining in this neighborhood, see the Restaurants chapter.) As we mention above, the boundaries of central Austin expand as residents and newcomers pursue the Austin lifestyle, hence the revival of neighborhoods along South First Street and South Lamar Boulevard. A similar trend is taking place in North Central Austin in old neighborhoods like Allandale and Rosedale near Burnet Rd.

The area south of Lady Bird Lake, west of Lamar Boulevard, and east of MoPac is one of Austin's most popular, older neighborhoods. Zilker Park wraps around the northern end of the area, while the Barton Creek Greenbelt winds around its western perimeter. Older homes in the Zilker neighborhood are much sought after. Farther south is the Barton Hills neighborhood where homes built 30 years ago are getting top dollar. The area has two critically acclaimed elementary schools, Zilker and Barton Hills, and enjoys quick access to downtown.

South Austin has continued to march southward, and neighborhoods age much like tree rings as the visitor drives south along the area's three major north-south streets— South Congress Avenue, South First Street, and Manchaca Rd.

Much of the area between Oltorf and US 290 West, locally known as Ben White Boulevard, is a mixture of older homes in working-class neighborhoods, some of them with a strong Hispanic flavor; others are home to free-spirit Austinites who frequent the area's ethnic restaurants. Loft-style apartments are being built along South Congress south of Oltorf. South of US 290 West, low- and middle-income homes, many of them built in the 1970s, give way to newer subdivisions. South of William Cannon Drive, neighborhoods like Cherry Creek, Southwest Oaks, Buckingham Estates, and Texas Oaks offer low- to midpriced homes, many of them dubbed "starter homes." These are traditional subdivisions with duplexes or apartments on the outer flanks of the neighborhood, single-family homes on the inner streets, and shopping facilities at nearby major intersections. Like most new homes in Austin, yards are enclosed with 6-foot privacy fencing, and most homes are constructed with at least the front wall faced in the local limestone or brick.

i One of the attractions of living in the hills west of Austin is the beauty of the natural surroundings. In addition to the flora—the wildflowers, the live oaks, redbud trees, and cactus flowers—there is the fauna. There are many species of birds, and in late summer the monarch butterflies pass through on their way to Mexico. And then there are the deer. Some Austinites feed the neighborhood deer; others complain about them. Nurseries sell deer-resistant plants, and neighbors swap stories of how to keep the deer out of their roses (human hair clippings).

It is clear to anyone driving on I-35 south of the city that growth is pushing the Austin suburbs farther and farther south. Small communities like Buda are now the focus of new home developments, some aimed at offering a country lifestyle, others targeted at middle-income families who are having a difficult time finding comfortable, larger homes at affordable prices.

Southwest

In 1980 the intersection of South Lamar Boulevard and US 290 West was bordered by a sheep farm. Now it is home on all four sides to shopping centers, and a major highway construction project has created a whirligig of flyovers and underpasses to speed traffic in all directions. A Neiman-Marcus outlet store now stands where the sheep once grazed.

Southwest Austin, roughly defined as the area south of US 290 West and west of Manchaca Road, is one of the fastest-growing areas of the city, despite efforts to slow growth through restrictive city planning ordinances. Much of the area sits above the recharge zone for the southern portion of the Edwards Aquifer, in the Barton Creek watershed. But the area's pleasant topography and easy access to downtown via MoPac have proved too much of a lure.

The Austin city limits do encompass much of this area, but a tiny island of real estate called the City of Sunset Valley marks the entrance to Southwest Austin, just west of the appropriately named Westgate shopping center, home to the southwest branch of Central Market. Westgate is lovingly dubbed the Bubbaretum, a reflection of the area's laid back South Austin style which stands in contrast to the upscale tone of the Arboretum shopping center in northwest

Austin This area has few homes but has fast become a shopping mecca for residents in this part of Austin. Two large farm homesteads occupied much of the small community for years but now have been sold to retail developers. Since Sunset Valley has a lower sales tax than the City of Austin, the shops here enjoy an advantage over other area merchants.

West of Sunset Valley, US 290 West passes through a community called Oak Hill. This area was settled in the 1840s and has long been a part of Austin, but it has clung to its name and some of its identity as a small community in the escarpment above the city. It was known by a variety of names until the locals settled on Oak Hill around the turn of the last century. The name is appropriate since the land here rises above the city and is shaded by hundreds, if not thousands of live oaks.

The massive US 290 West construction project has stripped the Oak Hill area of some its personality. One wag erected a sign when construction began asking WILL IT STILL BE OAK HILL WHEN THERE ARE NO OAKS AND NO HILL ANYMORE? The old highway was lined with a few small strip centers erected in pseudo Old West–style that gave Oak Hill its country character. One symbol of the old Oak Hill remains, the Rock Store, now a pizza restaurant, built by pioneer James Patton. It took Patton 19 years to build the store; he finished in 1898. The local elementary school is named in his honor.

Oak Hill is also the site of Convict Hill—a neighborhood is named in its honor. Here, from 1882 to 1886, convict labor was used to quarry limestone for the construction of the Texas Capitol. The stone was used in the capitol's basement. During the operation, 8 convicts died and are buried somewhere in the neighborhood on the hill in unmarked graves. The hill stands above the highway just as it splits with US 290 West heading toward Johnson City and Highway 71 heading northwest to the Highland Lakes. The split is called the "Y" by Austin residents.

Oak Hill is now surrounded by several new neighborhoods and a large Motorola plant close to the Y. The neighborhoods here are popular because of the proliferation of oak trees and the relatively easy commute into town. A nonrush-hour ride from the Y to downtown is about 15 minutes, and even a rush-hour commute is faster than a ride into the city from northwest suburbs.

Neighborhoods in this area include Westcreek, Maple Run, Legend Oaks, and The Village at Western Oaks. Homes are priced for middle-income residents. Southwest of the Y and south of Slaughter Lane is the Circle C Ranch development, named for the ranch that once operated in this area. This development was built under the auspices of a Municipal Utility District, a MUD, a device created by the legislature and much used in the Houston area by developers who sold bonds to support the infrastructure in non-incorporated areas. In early 1998 Circle C was annexed into Austin but not without protest from some of the homeowners.

Environmentalists had opposed the Circle C construction, but developers and residents boast of its attractive assets, including a large greenbelt, golf course, swim center, and community building. There are plans to add more amenities, including recreational and business centers. The developer, Gary Bradley, also donated Circle C land to house the nearby Lady Bird Johnson National Wildflower Research Center (see the Attractions chapter). Land also was donated for a veloway and nature trail for bicycle riders and walkers. Homes are in the mid- to upper mid-range pricewise. Development does not stop at the Austin southwest city limits. There are a growing number of housing developments along FM 1826, known as Camp Ben McCullough Road, which runs southwest off US 290 West, just west of the Y. Other developments can be found farther along US 290 West toward the Hays County line and Dripping Springs. Most of these homes are on larger lots, over an acre or two, and attract homebuyers who want a little rural atmosphere but a short commute into the city. Short is, of course, a relative term, and until improvements are made to the "Y" intersection, 290 through Oak Hill will continue to resemble a parking lot late on a Fri afternoon.

West

As noted earlier, the area known as Clarksville, just east of MoPac (Loop 1), once was a half mile outside the city limits. Today the Austin city limits do not extend much beyond that, but the hills above the city are home to people who consider themselves Austinites. For our purposes, West Austin is the area west of MoPac and north of US 290 West and south of Lake Austin and RM 2222.

Within the city limits, West Austin means two of the city's most prestigious neighborhoods. West of MoPac, between Enfield Road in the south and West Thirty-fifth Street in the north, are Tarrytown and Brykerwoods.

In the last century this part of Austin was home to several large estates. After World War II, the landowners began to subdivide the land. The neighborhoods have been built out over a period of 50 years by a variety of builders, and homes vary in size and personality. Price is consistent—it's high. The tiniest cottage in this area can cost as much as a large 4-bedroom home in the hills west of Austin, while large homes can sell for several million dollars. But the sheer variety of homes, the old trees, and beautifully landscaped gardens make this a favorite location.

The same amount of money can buy a whole lot more house in other parts of the city, but the Tarrytown or Brykerwoods address is still sought after. Many of the city's business and political leaders live in this area. Its proximity to downtown, the two highly rated elementary schools in the area, Casis and Brykerwood, plus the neighborhood's "village" atmosphere attracts homebuyers.

In addition to several small European-style shopping centers with cafes and shops, there are neighborhood churches, several parks, and the nearby Lions Municipal Golf Course. One of the city's popular swimming pools, Deep Eddy, is in this area.

Another of Austin's prestigious addresses is not in Austin at all. West Lake Hills is an incorporated city that overlooks downtown from the western hills, west of MoPac and east of Loop 360 (Capital of Texas Highway). A major attraction for homeowners in this area is the highly rated Eanes Independent School District, which encompasses West Lake Hills and much of the surrounding area. (See the Schools & Child Care chapter for more information.)

West Lake has its own city government, newspaper, the *West Lake Picayune* (www .westlakepicayune.com), and personality. Many of the homes are on steep, curved roads that have wonderful views of the downtown skyline. Homes in West Lake are varied in price, size, and style but generally are more expensive than most areas in Austin.

Tucked in between the southeast corner of West Lake Hills and MoPac is the small incorporated community of Rollingwood. Home prices here are generally upscale and expensive. Several large mansions line the cliffs above Lady Bird Lake in the Rollingwood area.

The major thoroughfare in West Lake Hills is RM 2244, popularly known as Bee Caves Rd. This winding, hilly road is lined with several shopping centers that serve the West Lake community. Growth has been a hot issue for West Lake residents, also, particularly the proliferation of large retail centers at the intersection of Bee Caves Road and Loop 360 (Capital of Texas Highway).

The development along Loop 360 is an indication of the boom in the hills west of Austin. The highway was originally planned as a scenic loop with few traffic lights. It has maintained its scenic quality, but there are now several major intersections along the roadway, many leading to new upscale subdivisions. Just west of Loop 360 and south of Bee Caves Road is Lost Creek, a neighborhood of large family homes on generously sized lots carved out of the hillsides on the eastern edge of Barton Creek. The creek, which feeds Barton Springs Pool, runs through the Lost Creek Country Club. On the western banks of the creek is the Lost Creek Estates development, and a little farther north is The Estates of Barton Creek, home of the Barton Creek Country Club. The development of the Barton Creek club was hard fought by environmentalists, but the developers have won recognition for their environmentally sensitive golf course design and landscaping methods.

The hills south of Lake Austin and north and west of West Lake Hills are home to an ever-increasing number of developments of large, comfortable homes. Among them are Rob Roy, Davenport Ranch, West Rim, and The Preserve. They remain outside the Austin city limits, but some are likely to be targeted for annexation by the City of Austin. West of Austin, out toward Lake Travis, are several new developments and one well-known, longtime incorporated resort area called Lakeway. The latter offers a variety of homes and condominiums that are popular as retirement and weekend homes since Lakeway offers a golf course, boating and tennis facilities, even a small airfield. Newer developments "out at the lake," as Austinites call it, like the Steiner Ranch, offer large family homes in the upper mid-range of Austin prices.

Northwest

On the north bank of Lake Austin, prices are not quite as steep as those developments west and south of the river. These new, comfortable family neighborhoods feature large family homes.

Northwest Austin is particularly attractive to employees working for the major high-tech companies, many located along US 183 North, dubbed Research Boulevard as it flows through Northwest Austin. South of Research are several neighborhoods built around the private Balcones Country Club.

The northwest corridor has seen the area's most explosive growth, and Austin has spilled over the Travis County line and into Williamson County. Children living in this area attend schools in the Round Rock Independent School District. While Austin has annexed a corridor of land along Research Boulevard, into Williamson County and to the Cedar Park city limits, beyond that strip fire, police, and EMS services are the responsibility of Williamson County authorities.

The residential area to the east and west of Research beyond Anderson Mill Road has seen home prices become static as market diversity increased. The growth along the Research Boulevard corridor also has led to long commute times for residents who have jobs in other areas of the city, a factor that may have contributed to static home prices.

North

The area north of RM 2222, known as Koenig Lane between MoPac and I-35, is a mixture of older, middle-class neighborhoods and some run-down areas. There has been periodic talk of turning Koenig Lane into a major east-west boulevard—the debate over east-west traffic flow is a perennial political topic—but it remains a 4-lane urban road.

i Most taxpayers in Central Texas pay property taxes to three jurisdictions—the local school district, the city, and the county. An Austin city resident pays taxes to Austin Independent School District, the City of Austin, Travis County, and Austin Community College tax district. School taxes are about 60 percent of a property tax bill in Central Texas.

Generally to the west of Burnet Road, particularly in the Allandale neighborhood along Shoal Creek, there are many spacious 1960s-era, ranch-style homes that are now attracting young would-be homeowners who want a fixer-upper within the city. The advice of a knowledgeable Realtor is well advised in shopping North Austin. There are pockets of wonderful older homes that have survived the urban onslaught of strip shopping centers and suburban flight, but there are also run-down neighborhoods. Just as in South Austin, the farther a visitor drives toward the city limits the newer the homes become. Many of the northern subdivisions are touted as ripe territory for "starter homes."

Adjacent to the northern city limits is a planned community, Wells Branch, developed as a Municipal Utility District (MUD). Wells Branch has a variety of homes, apartments, and condominiums that attract singles and young families. The MUD is well designed and landscaped. Shops and gas stations have inconspicuous signs that give the area a well-groomed look.

Northeast

Throughout the 1990s boom, the area east of I-35 and north of US 290 East escaped much of the growth frenzy found in other parts of the city. But the location of a large Samsung facility in the area just outside the city, plus the relocation of several government office buildings to light industrial parks in the northeast, has prompted suburban development. The new developments are, for the most part, targeted at middle-income families. A few developments farther out toward the small town of Manor list at lower prices.

Meanwhile, the older neighborhoods within the northeast sector of the city are being eyed as gentrification targets, particularly since the old airport has closed.

East

Roughly defined as east of I-35, south of US 290 East, and north of Lady Bird Lake, this large area of Austin is rapidly changing. Just east of the Interstate in the northwest quadrant of this section, the old Robert Mueller Municipal Airport has been developed as an urban village including housing, shops, and recreational facilities. Mueller includes

research facilities, film studios, homes, townhomes, parks, restaurants, cafes, and the Dell Children's Medical Center (see the Health Care & Wellness chapter). For a view of the new urban village visit www.muelleraustin.com. The airport closing also had an impact on prices of homes formerly in the flight path of the old facility.

Immediately to the north of the airport and to the southwest are two older neighborhoods that are beginning to attract the attention of homebuyers who want to live closer to the city center. Again, this is an area where the advice of a real estate agent is invaluable. It is also a good idea to talk to neighbors and check with city planners about the future of the area.

The Interstate has served as a dividing line in the city, particularly separating the predominantly older African-American and Hispanic neighborhoods that lie south of the airport. Efforts have been under way, with some success, to bring affordable housing and home ownership to this area of the city to ensure many residents with longtime family roots in the area remain, but the old neighborhoods also are attracting young families from all ethnic backgrounds and the residential racial divisions disappearing.

Austin neighborhoods are integrated, but like most other large cities, there are neighborhoods where there is an ethnic concentration. Generally, the area south of Rosewood Avenue and north of Lady Bird Lake has a distinctive Hispanic cultural flavor. Many popular Mexican restaurants are located here, as well as ethnic groceries and tortilla factories. Neighborhood associations in East Austin have fought to maintain their communities' identity and have resisted powerful forces, including the expanding University of Texas, which forged

a compromise with area residents over con-
demnation rights. But the neighborhoods
are attracting young Austinites of all ethnic
backgrounds.

Southeast

Just as the northeast has not matched
Northwest Austin in growth, so Southeast
Austin has not seen the boom experienced
by Southwest and Northwest Austin, but
that is slowly changing. There are many
apartment complexes east of I-35 along
the East Oltorf Street corridor, and there
have been several entry-level subdivisions
built in far Southeast Austin. At the south-
ernmost point of the Austin city limits, on
the east side of I-35, is one of Austin's well-
known golf communities. Onion Creek was,
for many years, home to the Legends of Golf
tournament. The secluded country club has
a variety of homes and condominiums that
attract retirees.

Round Rock

For many of their Austin neighbors, Round
Rock is viewed as a booming bedroom community on their northern border, a place to
avoid during rush hour if you are headed
north on I-35 to Dallas. But for Round Rock
residents, their fast-growing town is home,
and they are turning to historic preservation and neighborhood planning to keep it
that way.

Round Rock gets its name from a round
rock. The large rock is located in the middle
of Brushy Creek, which flows through what is
now a city. Brushy Creek was the name of the
village that sprang up here in 1852. Many of
the Victorian-era homes in the town center
now enjoy protective historic status.

Sam Bass, the infamous Texas outlaw,
is buried in the Old Round Rock Cemetery.
Until 20 years ago, the shoot-out between
Sam Bass and Texas Rangers, sheriff's deputies, and local citizens was the liveliest thing
that had ever happened in Round Rock.
But with the growth boom in Central Texas,
things have been humming in Round Rock
for the past two decades. (Demographers
predict the population of Williamson County
could reach almost a million by 2030.)

Round Rock offers a variety of new homes,
ranging from small homes suitable for a young
family or empty-nest couple at starter-home
prices to large homes with 5 bedrooms and
3 living areas priced less than the same home
would cost in West Austin. Some of the area
neighborhoods are west of the city limits—
several are in the tree-shaded countryside
near Brushy Creek. The city's historic homes
also are prized. Major employers, including Dell
Computer, have located in Round Rock, but
many residents do commute to nearby Austin,
making rush-hour traffic on I-35 a headache. A
second north-south toll road along the right-
of-way owned by the Missouri Kansas Railroad,
east of the Interstate has been opened, and
Texas 45 sweeps from south of the city around
the eastern edge and then west to link up with
RR 620 in the west near the lake communities.

Round Rock does have a reputation as
a good place to raise a family. The community's conservative values are touted by city
boosters, and comparisons are made with
the much more liberal politics and lifestyles
favored in Austin. These are clichéd images,
of course, but voting patterns and jury decisions tend to reinforce the two communities'
respective images.

Williamson County also touts its lower
crime rates compared with the more urban
Austin in Travis County.

Pflugerville

Ten years ago, about 4,000 people lived in Pflugerville, the small community southeast of Round Rock and northeast of Austin. In the last 3 months of 1997, the same number moved into the community. This small farming community is the latest home hot spot in Central Texas, particularly for homeowners who feel priced out of the Austin market. Like Round Rock, a dollar goes a little further in the home-buying marketplace here. Plus Pflugerville has maintained its small-town aura, locally run schools, and low crime rate.

i The Austin Convention and Visitors Bureau, in cooperation with the Historic Landmark Commission, produces an excellent walking tour guide to the Hyde Park neighborhood, one of several historic walking-tour brochures available at the bureau. The Visitor Information Center is at 209 East Sixth St., (512) 478-0098 or (800) GO-AUSTIN.

The area is experiencing some growing pains, and the city council has been forced to raise taxes and annex new areas to support city services. But the city is also putting taxes into city facilities like a recreation center and town library, hoping to add to the city's attractiveness as a good place to find an affordable home in which to raise a family. The new north-south Texas 45 toll road passes east of the community.

Cedar Park

The old-timers in Cedar Park remember how this community got its name. Cedar posts were the town's main business until a few years ago. The small community on US 183, northwest of Austin, was home to several cedar yards where fence posts were stacked before being shipped to ranches all over the West.

Every June, the town's history is celebrated at the Annual Cedar Chopper Festival. Before 1990 most of the festivalgoers came from out of town to enjoy the parade, sample the down-home cooking, and take a carnival ride. Back then the tiny community was just beginning to feel the boom wave heading from Austin, and the population in 1990 had grown to some 5,000. In 2010 it had topped 62,000. Cedar Park is trying to hold on to its history, but it is also attempting to attract high-tech companies and other businesses to help boost the local tax rolls and make Cedar Park something more than a bedroom community by developing a pedestrian-friendly downtown center. Homes in the area, which includes the neighboring community of Leander, offer homebuyers a variety of homes at more affordable prices than they will find closer downtown Austin. Developers are intent on creating neighborhoods, not just suburbs.

The area also features rural homes popularly known as "ranchettes," large country homes on 3- or 4-acre lots with enough room for a small horse stable or a kennel run.

APARTMENTS

Finding affordable housing in the rental category also is a challenge in Austin. The area's low unemployment rate is one factor in the expensive market, according to analysts. Another factor is the city's attraction to young college graduates, many of whom are attracted to Austin by the lifestyle and high salaries paid by high-tech industries. But the high prices have put some working Austinites in crisis. The Austin Tenant's Council,

(512) 474-1961, a nonprofit social service agency, tries to help apartment renters who cannot afford high rent.

Those who can afford the rents and are able to find a vacancy enjoy a lot of amenities. Most new apartment complexes are gated and provide residents with increased security. Many have security cameras in each unit that offer residents a view of the main gate and allow them to buzz visitors through after verifying their identities. Garages are an added feature, plus whole-home music systems. Most have recreational facilities, including workout rooms, swimming pools, and tennis courts. Others offer business centers. The extras offered by the newest apartment homes include gizmos like T1 lines for Internet access, cybercafes, and built-in computer desks. Want to get away from the high-tech world? Take a book to the "reading grotto" or stroll through the rose garden. Many of the new developments are located along the MoPac corridor, Loop 360 (Capital of Texas Highway), and in Southwest and Northwest Austin, but there also has been development along south Congress Avenue and north of the University in Central Austin.

Apartments for Rent is a monthly magazine that offers an overview of the area rental market, focusing on some of the newest developments and older apartment facilities. The magazine is available at many grocery

> **i** Central Texas enjoys a balmy climate for the most part, but heavy rainstorms can turn those picturesque Hill Country creeks into deadly torrents within minutes. Creeks, many of them dry creekbeds for much of the year, are part of the landscape tapestry in the region. When buying a home near a creek, check its location in relation to the floodplain. And if you are driving in a sudden rainstorm, never try to cross a water-filled creekbed.

stores and can be ordered at (512) 326-1133. The guide is published in 24 states and the District of Columbia. Out-of-town residents can order a complimentary copy of the *Austin* magazine by calling (900) 420-0040. There is a $4 charge for the call. There are numerous apartment search sites online.

REAL ESTATE RESOURCES

There are more than 9,500 real estate agents and Realtors in the greater Austin area, some operating as individuals, others as members of large, long-established firms. Most offer relocation and custom-building services. For a complete list of agencies, contact the Austin Board of Realtors at (512) 454-7636, www .abor.com, and check the website's listings, approximately 10,000 properties in 2010.

THE SENIOR SCENE

W hat can you say about a city where one of the leading senior citizens is Willie Nelson? The graying ponytail he once had may be one symbol of Austin's senior scene; another may be a subtle shift in attention to senior issues as more and more boomers slip into their 60s. Not all are famous, of course, but like so many other aging Americans they have a wealth of lifetime experience and energy to offer. Austin's active lifestyle and activist attitudes offer many outlets for that energy and experience.

POPULATION TRENDS

Austin's population is aging, but the percentage of people over the age of 65 in the Austin area is below the national average—7 percent in Travis and Williamson Counties, compared with 12 percent in the United States. When it comes to the number of residents 65 or older, among the 77 US cities with populations of more than 200,000, Austin ranks 71st.

The 1990 and 2000 US censuses revealed some interesting information about demographic trends in Texas. The fastest-growing segment of the state population is persons ages 25 to 44, representing around 40 percent of the Texas population, compared with about 30 percent nationally. The average age of an Austin city resident is 28.9 years.

However, as a Sunbelt state, retirees do come to Texas. They go particularly to the Rio Grande Valley near the Mexican border, where many retired Midwesterners spend their winters; San Antonio, whose extensive military infrastructure makes it attractive to retired military personnel; and the Hill Country to which many affluent retirees are attracted by the climate and lifestyle. In Central Texas the small communities of

Wimberly, southwest of Austin; Fredericksburg, west of Austin; and San Marcos, particularly along the Guadalupe River south of Austin, are attracting retirees.

In the Austin area the older-than-65 population is spread out across many neighborhoods. Austin's older neighborhoods, such as Hyde Park, Allandale, and Travis Heights, have their longtime residents. Many newcomers are attracted to the Highland Lakes area, where the many recreational facilities (see the Parks & Recreation and Golf chapters) offer amenities many seek. Two areas noted for their concentration of senior citizens are Lakeway and Lago Vista, both on Lake Travis, but these communities are by no means restricted to senior citizens.

In Round Rock and the Williamson County area, the percentage of persons older than 65 matches Travis County, 7 percent, but the number of residents younger than 18 is higher—24 percent in Travis, 31 percent in Williamson County.

Developers of retirement homes are finding Williamson County attractive because of its low crime rate, its small-town feel combined with nearby big-city health services, and, perhaps for some, its more conservative lifestyle. One major development is Del Webb's Sun City Georgetown in northern Williamson County.

Sun City is the latest manifestation of a fairly recent trend in Central Texas that has seen the development of housing alternatives for retirees. Compared with some other regions of the state and other Sunbelt communities, there is not an abundance of retirement communities in the area, but the numbers are growing. However, there already have been some tensions between retired residents and the local tax districts over increasing property taxes to support the booming public school systems in Williamson County. Another trend has been the relocation of empty-nesters from the suburbs to bustling downtown Austin.

SENIOR RESOURCES

In response to the aging of America, local businesses are beginning to recognize a market and, in true American fashion, responding to a need. One local Austin real estate company with longtime experience in the marketplace has created a new service to help people find a new, smaller house or a home in a retirement community.

Several agencies and organizations offer information, advice, and research on community housing and nursing homes. These are a good starting point before embarking on tours or visits to facilities aimed at attracting and serving seniors. All the experts emphasize that research and careful consideration are vital before making a move to a new home, a residential facility, or a nursing home.

The attorney general offers two publications for consumers: the *Rights of the Elderly* and *Selecting a Nursing Home*. For copies write to the Texas Attorney General, Attn:

Brochure Division, P.O. Box 12548, Austin, TX 78711, or call (512) 936-1737, or check the agency's website www.oag.state.tx.us.

AMELIA BULLOCK RELOCATION SERVICES
950 Westbank Dr., Suite 100
(512) 327-4800
www.ameliabullock.com
The company has been an Austin presence since 1969. In addition to its services for employees relocating to Austin, the company now offers Timely Solutions, a program to help seniors move to new homes, perhaps smaller homes or homes in communities geared to the senior lifestyle. A second location is at 8008 Spicewood Lane (512-345-2100).

AMERICAN ASSOCIATION OF RETIRED PERSONS (AARP)
98 San Jacinto Blvd.
(866) 227-7443
www.aarp.org
This downtown office serves as the state headquarters of the influential national group for 50-plus Americans. Well-known for its advocacy, the AARP also offers information on a variety of topics of interest to seniors. Members receive travel discounts, access to a mail-order pharmacy service, and insurance coverage. Many local chapters hold their meetings at the city's senior activity centers, listed later in this chapter.

AREA AGENCY ON AGING OF THE CAPITAL AREA
6800 Buelson Rd., Suite 165
(512) 916-6062, (TTY) (512) 916-6016,
(888) 622-9111
www.aaacap.org
This is a clearinghouse and ombudsman service agency for the 10 counties of Central

Texas. It is a good resource for information on nutrition, transportation, home help, health screening, and legal services. The agency's website also lists a variety of links to other agencies and programs including the following:

ADULT PROTECTIVE SERVICES, ADULT ABUSE AND FINANCIAL EXPLOITATION HOT LINE
(800) 252-5400
www.dfps.state.tx.us
To report elder abuse call or e-mail contact information on the website.

ALZHEIMER'S ASSOCIATION
(800) 272-3900
www.alz.org/texascapital

LEGAL HOT LINE, TEXAS LEGAL SERVICES CENTER
(800) 622-2520
www.tlsc.org

LOCAL SENIOR SERVICES
Dial 211

MEDICAID HOT LINE
(800) 252-8263

MEDICARE HOT LINE
(800) MEDICARE (633-4227)

NURSING FACILITY INFORMATION HELPLINE
(800) 252-8016

TEXAS ATTORNEY GENERAL CONSUMER HELPLINE
(800) 621-0508
www.oag.state.tx.us

TEXAS HEALTH AND HUMAN SERVICES COMMISSION
Agency Ombudsman
(877) 787-8999

VETERANS ADMINISTRATION BENEFITS INFORMATION AND ASSISTANCE
(800) 827-1000
www.va.gov

AUSTIN GROUPS FOR THE ELDERLY (AGE)
3710 Cedar St.
(512) 451-4611
www.ageofaustin.org
Housed in a wonderful Central Austin historic building, ca. 1902, AGE is an umbrella agency for more than a dozen nonprofit agencies. It is worth visiting the center both to enjoy the architecture and pick up information on a variety of services—adult day care, respite care, emergency residence for abused and neglected elders, family counseling, information, referral, mental health care, adult education, and computer learning center aimed at helping seniors become computer savvy, (512) 451-1932, www.seniornet.com.

i Austin Senior's Guide is published annually and gives tips on senior living in the Austin area, plus information on discounts and products of interest to seniors, (512) 257-7607, www.seniorsguide.net.

FAMILY ELDERCARE
2210 Hancock Dr.
(512) 450-0844
www.familyeldercare.org
Located in Central Austin, this nonprofit organization offers a wide variety of services for seniors. Eldercare receives some funds from the United Way. Programs include The Gatekeeper, a training program for social service workers and volunteers, plus business owners and members of community groups who interact with the elderly. The program

trains them to identify and assist seniors who are suffering from abuse or neglect or who are being exploited. Another Eldercare program is In Home Care and Respite Services, which provides care for home-bound adults. There is also an Alzheimer's program as part of this service. Volunteers are trained in the guardianship and money management program, and then they are matched with seniors who need legal guardians, representative payees, or money managers.

THE SENIOR ADVOCATE
3710 Cedar St.
(512) 451-7433
www.senioradvocatenews.com

The *Senior Advocate* has grown from a newsletter to a newspaper in the past 20 years and now has an online presence in addition to its paper format. The goal is to provide "interesting, accurate, and vital information on issues and resources important to seniors," according to its publishers, Dave and Dana Smith. The paper has won several awards for editorial excellence and community service. In 1999 the paper won the National Mature Media Awards, ahead of such publications as *Parade* and *Essence* magazines. The paper was also honored with an Outstanding Media Coverage award from the City of Austin in 1999 for publishing employment opportunities for seniors each month at no cost to the city. The job listings are a partnership effort between Austin's Senior Programs division and Experience Unlimited, a placement agency for individuals who are 50 years of age or older.

SENIOR HEALTH CARE CENTERS: PRIVATE SECTOR

Austin's two major health care providers run medical centers aimed specifically at the needs of seniors. St. David's Healthcare Partnership (www.stdavids.com) has two clinics, both in north Austin, one at 3300 West Anderson Lane, Suite 308, (512) 901-8250; the other at 5222 Burnet Rd., Suite 200 (512) 420-9775. The Seton Healthcare Network (www.seton.net) operates a senior clinic in the Lakeway area in far West Austin at 1602 Lohman's Crossing Rd., (512) 261-1758.

TEXAS DEPARTMENT ON AGING AND DISABILITY SERVICES (DADS)
701 West Fifty-first St.
(512) 438-3011, (800) 458-9858
www.dads.state.tx.us

This is a state agency designed to assist seniors. The hot line, at the 800 number listed above, offers information and referrals on senior services. In Texas, consumers can simply dial 211 and ask for DADS information.

TEXAS ATTORNEY GENERAL
(512) 463-2100, (800) 252-8011
www.oag.state.tx.us

Consumers may request two detailed brochures from the Texas Attorney General, the state's chief law enforcement officer who is empowered to bring suit against offending facilities, including nursing homes and residential homes for the disabled and the mentally handicapped. Both the current and previous attorneys general have filed suit to close down offending facilities. However, some consumer and advocacy groups have criticized the state legislature for allowing the nursing home industry to influence regulation. In 1997 legislation was passed aimed at responding to those criticisms. Write to: Research and Legal Support Division, Office of the Attorney General, Attn: Brochure Division, P.O. Box 12548, Austin, TX 78711.

TEXAS DEPARTMENT OF HUMAN SERVICES (TDHS)
(512) 438-3011, (800) 458-9858

This state agency can provide consumers with the last 2 years of compliance history of any facility. The agency says consumers should expect to see some compliance failures on any report, since even the most minor are listed by state inspectors. TDHS can answer four questions: How many complaints have there been in the last year? How many quality-of-care violations have there been in the past 2 years? When was the last visit by TDHS and why? Has the owner had other facilities recommended for closure?

TEXAS DEPARTMENT OF INSURANCE (TDI)
(512) 463-6169, (800) 578-4677
www.tdi.state.tx.us

The state agency charged with oversight of the insurance industry in Texas provides consumers free of charge and on request with *A Shopper's Guide to Long-term Care*. This brochure is published by the National Association of Insurance Commissioners. The agency also offers a great variety of insurance publications on all kinds of policies and state regulations, many of which are helpful to newcomers.

RESIDENTIAL OPTIONS

Making a move is a major step at any age, and certainly a step that is not be taken lightly. Experts recommend carefully weighing needs, both current and future; lifestyle habits and patterns; location; and, of course, cost. Another important part of the process is to visit the community and spend time there. Apply some of the same rules experts recommend in choosing a day care center for children—visit at different times; talk to the residents and the staff; compare notes with others (important for children helping their parents find a place to live); and read the fine print.

The number of retirement communities and facilities is increasing in Central Texas, and there also are attempts to build affordable housing in Austin, a growing need as housing prices soar. We've offered a sampling. The Area Agency on Aging of the Capital Area (above) offers an extensive list, www.aaacap.org. Another good resource is www.assistedlivingsource.com which lists a variety of facilities grouped by needs and location.

BUCKNER VILLAS
11110 Tom Adams Dr.
(512) 836-1515
www.bucknerretirement.org

This is a North Austin nonprofit rental community offering a variety of residential options in a Christian environment. The facility offers the flexibility for residents to change their environment as needs change, from independent and assisted living to nursing home care. Apartments have 2 bedrooms and full kitchens. The facility also has an Alzheimer's program.

BROOKDALE LIVING
The Heritage at Gaines Ranch,
4409 Gaines Ranch Loop
(512) 899-8400
www.brookdaleliving.com

Brookdale is a national company with several independent and assisted living facilities in Austin. The highrise Heritage is in Southwest Austin and is set amid landscaped gardens.

The community has both independent living apartments and an assisted-living program. There is an on-site health clinic, fitness and exercise programs, dining services, and 24-hour concierge, housekeeping, and transportation services. Brookdale operates these "Summit" facilities for both independent and assisted living in the area:

THE SUMMIT AT WESTLAKE HILLS
1034 Liberty Park Dr.
(512) 328-3775

THE SUMMIT AT LAKEWAY
1915 Lohmans Crossing Rd.
(512) 261-7146

THE SUMMIT AT NORTHWEST HILLS
5715 Mesa Dr.
(512) 454-5900

The three retirement communities at West Lake Hills west of Austin have been dubbed "retirement living for those who aren't the retiring type." The luxury rental communities have a variety of apartments, 24-hour security, transportation, catering, an on-site health care center, and recreational activities.

HOLIDAY CORPORATION:
THE CLAIRMONT
12463 Los Indios Trail
(512) 331-7195

THE CONTINENTAL
4604 South Lamar Blvd.
(512) 892-5995

ENGLEWOOD ESTATES
2603 Jones Rd.
(512) 892-7226

RENAISSANCE-AUSTIN
11279 Taylor Draper Lane
(512) 338-0995
www.holidaytouch.com

This national company operates four facilities in Austin. Each offers month-to-month rentals, catering of 3 meals a day, weekly housekeeping, paid utilities, planned activities, and on-site resident managers. Some have beauty shop and barber facilities and transportation services.

THE ISLAND ON LAKE TRAVIS
3404 American Dr.
(512) 267-7107, (800) 422-4753
www.islandonlaketravis.com

Literally on an island connected by causeway to the mainland, this independent living community is designed for active seniors. Rental apartments in this Lago Vista–area facility, northwest of Austin, have 24-hour security, indoor parking, an on-site restaurant, weekly housekeeping, and recreational facilities.

THE PARK AT BECKETT MEADOWS
7709 Beckett Rd.
(512) 891-9544
www.emeritus.com

The suburban assisted living facility in Southwest Austin is in a neighborhood favored by families, making it a good choice for elder family members who may need special care for Alzheimer's or dementia.

WESTMINSTER MANOR RETIREMENT
   COMMUNITY
4100 Jackson Ave.
(512) 454-4711
www.wmanor.com

This facility in Central Austin, near Seton Medical Center, has what it calls a Life Care Program, which allows residents to buy their apartments and a care program. Up to 90 percent of the entrance fee is returned to the buyer's estate, and a portion of the fee is deductible as a prepaid medical expense.

ADVOCACY

GRAY PANTHERS OF AUSTIN
3710 Cedar St.
(512) 458-3738
www.graypanthers.org
Located in Central Austin in the same facility as Eldercare, this senior citizen advocacy group has a national reputation for its organizational skills and education workshops. The group produces several handy publications, among them *A Caregivers Manual.*

TRANSPORTATION

Austin Capital Metro, (512) 389-7400, www.capmetro.org, the area public transportation service, has several programs designed for seniors. In a city some call an elephant's graveyard for hippies, the free bus pass for seniors is called an EasyRider; however, seniors must buy a $5 Capital Metro ID. These passes are free to citizens 65 who show proof of age with a Medicare card or driver's license. Passes are available at the downtown Metro office, 2910 East Fifth St., which is open from 7:30 a.m. to 5:30 p.m. weekdays. It just takes a few minutes to process the ID.

i In a booming area as property values grow, taxes can become burdensome for seniors on a fixed income. Check with the local tax assessor's office to learn of all the tax breaks and freezes afforded to seniors, for an overview check the Texas State Comptroller's Office, www.cpa.state.tx.us.

Groups of 20 seniors or more can request free transportation from 10 a.m. to 2 p.m. weekdays, 6 a.m. to 10 p.m. on weekends. Advanced reservations are required; call (512) 389-7583.

Capital Metro also offers curb-to-curb service and connections to medical services in some areas of the city. There is also a special transit service for the disabled. (See the Getting Here, Getting Around chapter.)

For general schedule information, call (512) 474-1200. Many grocery stores also stock bus schedules at their customer service counters.

MEDI WHEELS
3227 East Fifth St.
(512) 476-6325
www.mealsonwheelsandmore.org
This service offers rides to medical appointments to people 55 or older. Please call a week in advance of your appointment.

CITY OF AUSTIN SENIOR SUPPORT SERVICES
(512) 4768-7695
www.ci.austin.tx.us/parks//sractivity.htm
This PARD program offers nonemergency medical transportation for seniors 60 and older. Reservations are required, with 24-hour notice. Reservations can be made for medical, personal, and group travel.

LIFETIME LEARNING

AUSTIN COMMUNITY COLLEGE
5930 Middle Fiskville Rd.
(512) 223-7000
www.austincc.edu
The city's community college has several campuses around the area (see the Higher Education chapter). In addition to a full curriculum of credit courses, ACC offers a

variety of enrichment programs, some of them aimed at topics of particular concern to the elderly, including family care-giving, retirement and recreation, and aging classes.

ELDERHOSTEL
The University of Texas
(512) 471-3500
The University of Texas offers 5-day non-credit programs in the liberal arts at 7 Elderhostel sites. They are at University of Texas in Austin, Big Bend National Park in far Southwest Texas, San Antonio, Galveston, El Paso, and Fort Worth. Art, music, and literature are the themes of the various programs. Lodging, meals, and field trips are included in the tuition fee. The program also is a clearinghouse for Elderhostel programs around the state at other schools and cultural institutions.

LIFETIME LEARNING INSTITUTE
Concordia Lutheran College,
11400 Concordia University Dr.
(512) 313-3000
www.concordia.edu
In fall and spring, Concordia offers several 8-week courses for people 50 and older on a variety of topics such as art appreciation, foreign languages, Texas history, financial planning, and social and political history. Tuition is $15 per course, and classes are held at a variety of locations around the city.

SENIORNET
www.seniornet.com
This web-based site provides a wide variety of information for seniors, with links to local services. In conjunction with the site there is a computer training program in Austin located at Austin Groups for the Elderly (see earlier in this chapter).

UNIVERSITY OF TEXAS CONTINUING EDUCATION
The Thompson Conference Center,
Twenty-sixth and Red River Streets
(512) 471-4652
www.utexas.edu/cee
This facility is near the LBJ Presidential Library on the eastern edge of the campus. Two community outreach programs offer classes for seniors. There is an annual membership program, Learning Activities for Mature People, featuring a series lecture and classes in fall, winter, and spring for $125. Three 6-week programs, titled Seminars for Adult Growth and Enrichment, are offered annually in fall, winter, and spring. The cost is $195.

COMMUNITY ACTIVITIES

A wide variety of recreational activities are aimed at area seniors, and many of them can be found at a network of senior activity centers. These community facilities offer a place to meet for recreation, networking, and nutrition. Most city-run centers offer a hot lunch for a nominal fee, around $1.

The centers are operated by the Senior Program, which has numerous brochures and newsletters detailing programs and locations. Activities at the centers range from arts and crafts to health and fitness classes, line dancing, mah-jongg, poetry clubs and investment clubs, pool tournaments, stamp collectors' gatherings, and outings.

Austin

SENIOR PROGRAMS AND SERVICE CENTERS MAIN OFFICE
4201 Ed Bluestein Blvd.
(512) 478-7695
www.ci.austin.tx.us/parks/sractivity.htm
There are senior activities at all the city's recreation centers and several smaller senior

centers at various locations throughout the city. There are also three designated Senior Activity Centers in the city, listed below. All have extensive senior programs and support services, and all serve a hot lunch for a small charge. Transportation is provided on request.

CONLEY-GUERRERO SENIOR ACTIVITY CENTER
808 Nile St.
(512) 478-7695
The daily programs here are designed to enhance the quality of life for seniors in East Austin. Seniors gather at the senior center daily to exercise. Domino sessions are a popular pastime, as are the ceramics classes. The center also arranges out-of-town trips for shopping and recreation, and there are popular regular events like Blue Jean Day and Over the Rainbow Social Evenings.

LAMAR SENIOR ACTIVITY CENTER
2874 Shoal Crest Ave.
(512) 474-5921
The seniors at this Central Austin center are avid tripsters, heading off on theater and museum outings to Houston and Dallas, and visiting historic Texas sites, including the Bush Presidential Library in College Station. Ballroom dancing is a popular activity and dances are held usually three times a week. There is also an array of classes offered in games and arts and crafts. In addition, a driving safety class is offered that grants graduates a cut in their insurance premiums.

SOUTH AUSTIN SENIOR ACTIVITY CENTER
3911 Manchaca Rd.
(512) 448-0787
Bridge, dominos, and mah-jongg are popular pastimes at this South Austin center. Students in the ceramics classes can fire their creations in the on-site kiln. Oil painting classes are also offered. The center also organizes day trips to country music concerts, shopping trips to the outlet malls, and visits to major art exhibits in Dallas and Houston.

NUTRITION

Maintaining a healthy diet can be difficult for some seniors, particularly those on a tight budget or those who find themselves suddenly alone or unable to cook and shop for groceries. The programs listed below can lend a helping hand.

MEALS ON WHEELS AND MORE
3227 East Fifth St.
(512) 476-6325
www.mealsonwheelsandmore.org
This network of volunteers delivers hot, nutritious meals to the homes of more than 2,000 people who can no longer prepare food for themselves or leave their homes. The program also offers other services including:

- **Groceries to Go**—volunteers shop for participants who are unable to make a trip to the grocery store, and deliver vital groceries to their homes.
- **Medi Wheels**—volunteers provide transportation to and from medical appointments for more than 400 older people.
- **Care Calls**—volunteers brighten someone's day with a friendly telephone call, giving lonely seniors a chance to hear a friendly voice and talk to someone who will listen.
- **Handy Wheels**—volunteers perform minor home safety repairs such as installing smoke alarms, bathroom safety bars, house numbers, and replacing light bulbs, to the residences of the homebound.

All of these programs welcome volunteers. If you want to make a donation, check out the website, where you can buy Stubb's Gospel CD, music from the city's legendary barbecue joint.

SENIOR SUPPORT SERVICES
(512) 480-3005

This program provides lunches every weekday to senior citizens at 18 locations in Travis County, including the city's PARD Senior Activity Centers (see previous listing). To be eligible you must be 60 or the spouse of someone enrolled in the meals program. The cost of the hot lunch is minimal, as low as 50 cents, a little more in some locations. Additional activities include shopping, field trips, educational programs, and holiday events. Free transportation also is provided with 24 hours notice. Call (512) 974-1464.

CAREGIVERS
(512) 472-6339
www.faithinactioncaregivers.org

This national program relies on local churches, synagogues, and mosques to set up their own grassroots organization to reach out to needy members of the community in a variety of ways. Caregivers is a network of volunteers who help those seniors who want to remain in their homes maintain their independence. Volunteers do small but meaningful tasks for the seniors, including driving them to appointments or grocery shopping for them.

TELEPHONE REASSURANCE PROGRAM
United Austin for the Elderly
(512) 476-6325

This service, part of the Meals on Wheels program, offers a daily contact program for seniors who live alone. Volunteers also have Phone-A-Friend, a program aimed at contacting lonely seniors.

JOB OPPORTUNITIES

The high-tech field gets a lot of attention for its youthful workforce, but there are opportunities for talented, skilled workers of all ages in Austin. One good place to find information on job availability for seniors is at the Austin PARD website, www.ci.austin.tx.us/parks/seniors.htm.

AUSTIN SENIOR AIDES
(512) 480-3006

This PARD program matches seniors with nonprofit agencies for part-time work. On-the-job training is offered. To participate, a person must be 55 or older and have a low income.

EXPERIENCE UNLIMITED
(512) 480-3013

This PARD program encourages individuals 50 or older to register with the program's job referral bank. One of the program's innovative programs offered lifeguard jobs to seniors at the city's swimming pools.

OLD BAKERY AND EMPORIUM
1006 Congress Ave.
(512) 477-5961

A PARD program provides a showcase at the Old Bakery and Emporium for talented seniors to display and sell their crafts at this downtown attraction. (See the Attractions chapter.)

TEXAS WORKFORCE COMMISSION
South Austin Office,
4175 Friedrich Lane, Suite 200
(512) 381-1695
www.twc.state.tx.us

Formerly known as the Texas Employment Commission, this state agency offers employment counseling and referrals to Texas residents. The department also has a Mature Worker Services program that conducts seminars to help workers hone their interview and resume-writing skills. Other locations are the North Austin Office, 825 East Rundberg Lane (512-719-4145); the East Austin Office, 3401 Webberville Rd. (512-223-5400); and the Round Rock Office, 1609 Chisholm Trail (512-244-2207).

VOLUNTEER OPPORTUNITIES

Opportunities abound for those with a lifetime of skills to help others in the community. From local museums to the police department, rape-crisis centers to literacy programs, the possibilities for meaningful activity are enormous. We have listed several volunteer clearinghouse organizations and groups who seek out seniors. Each year, around Christmas, the *Austin American-Statesman* publishes a comprehensive wish list from various community groups seeking either volunteers or donations. Search for volunteer opportunities in the Central Texas area on www.volunteermatch.org.

i The Texas Silver-Haired Legislature is a nonprofit, nonpartisan group that works with the state legislature on senior issues. Delegates serve two-year terms. For participation information contact the Area Agency on Aging of the Capital Area at (512) 916-6062.

VOLUNTEER SOLUTIONS
www.volunteersolutions.com
In 1997 a group of MIT students was searching for a way to make the web work for America's needy. They came up with this website that tries to match volunteers with nonprofit agencies. The website has grown and now includes several cities across the United States, including an Austin site where more than 200 local nonprofits are listed. A great resource for anyone searching for a way to serve the community.

Following is a list of groups that use volunteers:

AMERICAN RED CROSS
Central Texas Office, 2218 Pershing Dr.
(512) 928-4271
www.centex.redcross.org

CARE CALLS
(512) 476-6325

COURT APPOINTED SPECIAL
   ADVOCATES (CASA)
(512) 443-2272
www.casatravis.org

FOSTER GRANDPARENTS
(512) 424-6130

RETIRED AND SENIOR VOLUNTEER
   PROGRAM (RSVP)
(512) 854-RSVP (7787)
www.rsvpaustin.org

UNITED WAY
(512) 472-6267
www.unitedwaycapitalarea.org

HEALTH CARE & WELLNESS

The first hint that Austin is a city that values wellness is the constant reminder over the airport public address system: Austin is a Clean Air City. Smoking is strictly verboten in most public places, although the battle over smoking in nightclubs suggested there was a backlash to political correctness among some Austinites. Perhaps that was an indication of another much-valued community trait—tolerance. That tolerance combined with a willingness to try new approaches also means Austin is a place where alternative therapies and health care options are widely available.

Health food stores, including the flagship store of the now international and publicly traded Whole Foods Market chain (see the Shopping chapter), are not only evidence of Austin's concerns about wellness but also serve as conduits for alternative therapy information. More and more mainstream stores stock organic foods, offer herbal supplements, and sometimes have on-site massage.

FINDING A PHYSICIAN

This can be a difficult task for newcomers to any city. Both Seton and St. David's operate physician referral services on their websites. Seton's Physician Referral number is (512) 324-4444. For information about the St. David's system, call (512) 482-4100; for physician referral call (512) 478-DOCS (3627). There are also several professional organizations that offer referrals to their members. They include the Austin Travis County Chiropractic Society Referral Service, (512) 263-3434; Capital Area Psychological Association, (512) 454-3706, www.austinpsychologists.net; Texas Chiropractic Association, (512) 477-9292, www.chirotexas.org; Texas Psychological Association, (512) 280-4099, www.texaspsyc.org; and the Travis County Medical Society, (512) 206-1249, www.tcms.org.

HOSPITALS
Central

BRACKENRIDGE UNIVERSITY MEDICAL CENTER
601 East Fifteenth St.
(512) 324-7000
www.seton.net
The city-owned hospital serves as the regional trauma center for the Central Texas area and is served by STARflight medical helicopter services. The hospital also has a children's emergency room facility that offers state-of-the-art crisis care. After grappling with deficits, the city turned operation of the downtown hospital over to the capable hands of the Daughters of Charity, who also run the Seton Healthcare Network, which includes other hospitals and clinics in the Austin area. The 360-year-old Catholic order has gained a reputation for providing quality health care for both insured and needy

Austin Cares

In the past couple of years, consolidations, expansions, and new developments have changed the medical scene. These changes are particularly apparent when reviewing the hospitals and clinics in Austin and surrounding areas. There are two major players in Austin—the Seton Good Health Network (www.seton.net) and the St. David's Healthcare Partnership (www.stdavids.com). Seton has expanded with clinic facilities in the suburbs as the city has grown. There are several health research facilities in Austin focused on drug and therapy trials. These research facilities frequently advertise in the local media for volunteers (sometimes with pay) to participate in drug trials.

adults," the hospital is focused on children's needs and family-centered solutions. The award-winning building is located on the site of the old Austin airport and is at the heart of a proposed health-care campus amid a town center development (www.muelleraustin.com). The green building uses art and nature to make children feel comfortable and the grounds are landscaped to remind them of the various flora in their hometown, be it a farm in the Blackland Prairie to the east or a town in the Hill Country. Inside, the surroundings are designed to be kid-friendly and not intimidating to youngsters who may be experiencing difficulties. Of course, the hospital also offers state-of-the-art pediatric medical care.

HEART HOSPITAL OF AUSTIN
3801 North Lamar Blvd.
(512) 407-7000
www.hearthospitalofaustin.com
This non-Seton, non-St David's entry on the Austin medical scene is situated at the southern end of a large swath of land sold by the state to private developers. The original Central Market sits on a portion of the land (see the Shopping chapter), and the hospital occupies a site to the south, just a few blocks east of the flagship Seton Medical Center Focused on heart health care, the facility also has a full-service emergency room.

patients while managing to retain profitability in a volatile marketplace.

Brackenridge is an acute-care hospital that, in addition to the trauma center, provides maternity, critical care, surgery, orthopedics, and nephrology services.

DELL CHILDREN'S MEDICAL CENTER OF CENTRAL TEXAS
4900 Mueller Blvd.
(512) 324-0000
www.dellchildrens.net
Thanks to generous donations by Austin entrepreneur Michael Dell and others, this Seton Network children's hospital is a showcase that serves a 46-county central Texas area. Rather than treat children like "little

HOSPITAL AT WESTLAKE MEDICAL CENTER
5656 Bee Caves Rd.
(512) 327-0000,
(512) 697-3628 (emergency room)
www.westlakemedical.com
The emergency room at this medical complex in West Austin offers emergency services and cardiac care. The campus-style

center houses a variety of clinics and medical specialists, including a sleep disorder clinic, wellness, and rehabilitation programs.

ST. DAVID'S MEDICAL CENTER
919 East Thirty-second St.
(512) 476-7111
www.sdhcp.com
Part of the St. David's Healthcare Partnership, this downtown hospital is an acute-care facility. Medical services include a rehabilitation center, a psychiatric center for children, maternity and reproductive technology services, and cardiac and urodynamics programs.

SETON MEDICAL CENTER
1201 West Thirty-eighth St.
(512) 323-1000
www.seton.net
The home base for the Daughters of Charity network of medical facilities in Austin, Seton Medical Center offers a wide range of medical and surgical services. It is in a "medical arts" area of Austin, where many of the city's physicians and medical support services are located. Offerings include a 24-hour emergency room, a neonatal center, a maternity facility, and cancer care services. It is also the headquarters for Seton's Good Health program, which focuses on wellness issues. For the families of patients, the hospital operates a nearby accommodations facility, Seton League House at 3207 Wabash Ave., (512) 323-1999. The Seton system also includes home care programs, senior health centers, and several clinics throughout the greater Austin area.

SETON SHOAL CREEK HOSPITAL
3501 Mills Ave.
(512) 452-0361
www.seton.net

This private psychiatric hospital also managed by the Seton network serves patients of all ages and is situated along a pleasant stretch of Shoal Creek in the central medical arts area of the city around Thirty-fifth Street.

South

SOUTH AUSTIN HOSPITAL
901 West Ben White Blvd.
(512) 447-2211
www.southaustinhospital.com
St. David's operates this acute-care facility in south Austin. The hospital has a 24-hour emergency room, a cardiovascular center, maternity services, and a neurological center. It also offers lithotripsy for noninvasive kidney stone removal.

Southwest

SETON SOUTHWEST MEDICAL CENTER
7900 FM 1826
(512) 324-9000
www.seton.net
In response to the fast-growing Southwest section of the city, the Seton network opened a new medical center and emergency room in 2000 on FM 1826, known to the locals as Camp Ben McCullough Rd. The facility is at the corner of FM 1826 and US 290 West.

Northwest

SETON NORTHWEST HOSPITAL
11113 Research Blvd.
(512) 324-6000
www.seton.net
This northwest branch of the Seton network has a minor emergency center, plus 24-hour emergency room, birthing units, and maternity services. Seton also offers Good Health School wellness programs on-site, and the facility houses the Seton Northwest Sports

Medicine practice. A similar facility is planned for Southwest Austin.

North

NORTH AUSTIN MEDICAL CENTER
12221 MoPac Blvd. North
(512) 901-1000
www.stdavids.com
Part of the St. David's Healthcare Partnership, this north Austin hospital has acute-care medical and surgical units, a 24-hour emergency room, an outpatient surgery center, maternity facilities, a women's center, rehabilitation services, and oncology programs. The facility also houses the Austin Travel Clinic, where would-be world wanderers can receive the necessary shots and health information for travel to any part of the world.

Round Rock

ROUND ROCK MEDICAL CENTER
2400 Round Rock Ave.
(512) 341-1000
www.stdavids.com
Following a major $28 million expansion, this acute-care hospital serves the southern Williamson County area. Part of the St. David's Healthcare Partnership, the hospital has a 24-hour emergency room, family birthing center, medical-surgical unit, intensive-care unit, cardiopulmonary services center, plus an outpatient surgery facility.

i Hospice Austin, (512) 342-4700, www.hospiceaustin.org, serves both Travis and Williamson Counties, covering the Austin and Round Rock metropolitan area. Hospice offers medical, spiritual, and bereavement care for terminally ill patients and their families on an outpatient basis. Payment is on an ability-to-pay basis.

PUBLIC HEALTH SERVICES

The Austin/Travis County Health and Human Services Department, (512) 329-5959, is a joint city and county tax supported service agency that oversees the operation of 13 community clinics in the city of Austin and the surrounding area. The agency also oversees immunization outreach programs that are held in local shopping malls. The clinics offer maternity care, well-child check-ups, dental services at some locations, and tests and treatment for tuberculosis, sexually transmitted diseases, and HIV. The Women, Infant and Children's Nutrition program, commonly known as the WIC program, is also administered by the health department. Fees are charged according to the ability of the patient to pay, but the agency says no one is turned away. Call (512) 972-4242 in Austin for locations (www.ci.austin .tx.us/health).

Community Clinics

PEOPLE'S COMMUNITY CLINIC
2909 North I-35
(512) 478-8924
www.pcclinic.org
Payment is on a sliding scale at this community clinic. No one is refused treatment. The clinic offers adult outpatient and pediatric medical care, free immunizations, family-planning and prenatal services, treatment of sexually transmitted diseases, and women's health services. The clinic's website is an excellent guide to resources for the needy.

SETON MCCARTHY COMMUNITY HEALTH CENTER
2811 East Second St.
(512) 323-4930
www.seton.net

The Seton network provides medical care and social services for residents in the East Austin area. No one is turned away, and fees are charged on a sliding scale. The center is named for the much-loved Bishop McCarthy, now retired.

SETON KOZMETSKY COMMUNITY HEALTH CENTER

3706 South First St.
(512) 323-4940
www.seton.net
The center provides similar services to those at the network's East Austin location, listed previously, including medical care and social services on a sliding-fee scale. No one is turned away.

VOLUNTEER HEALTH CARE CLINIC

4215 Medical Pkwy.
(512) 459-4939
This clinic serves patients who are not eligible for city or county support, Medicare, or Medicaid, and do not have their own insurance. The clinic treats only minor illness. Donations are welcome, but no one is turned away.

Round Rock

ROUND ROCK HEALTH CLINIC

2120 North Mays St., Suite 430
(512) 255-5120
www.lscctx.org/locations
/round-rock-health-clinic
Round Rock Health Clinic is now a part of Lone Star Circle of Care. Medicaid and Medicare patients are accepted at this outpatient clinic that offers well-child checkups, prenatal care, and family medicine.

WILLIAMSON COUNTY AND CITIES HEALTH DISTRICT CLINIC

100 West Third St.
(512) 943-3600
www.wcchd.org
Williamson County and cities in the area fund local public health clinics that provide medical services on a sliding-fee scale. Screenings for diabetes and blood pressure tests for seniors are among the services provided. The clinics also offer prenatal care, well-child checkups, and testing and counseling for tuberculosis, sexually transmitted diseases, and HIV.

Cedar Park

WILLIAMSON COUNTY AND CITIES HEALTH DISTRICT CLINIC

350 Discovery Blvd.
(512) 260-4240
www.wcchd.org
The clinic offers medical services on a sliding-fee scale, plus diabetes and blood pressure screenings for seniors and prenatal and well-child services. Counseling for those diagnosed with tuberculosis, sexually transmitted diseases, and HIV also is available.

AIDS SERVICES

The Austin area has an extensive network of services and programs to assist and support people with HIV and AIDS. For a complete listing of the services, call the AIDS information line, (512) 458-AIDS, or contact AIDS Services of Austin (www.asaustin.org).

AIDS SERVICES OF AUSTIN

P.O. Box 4874, Austin 78765
(512) 458-AIDS (2437)
www.asaustin.org
A clearinghouse for AIDS information in Central Texas, this agency serves HIV-positive

individuals and their families. The agency also provides information on AIDS network services like the Animal Companions program, a volunteer group that provides grooming, veterinary care, in-home care, and a food bank for the pets of AIDS patients.

COMMUNITY AIDS RESOURCE & EDUCATION (CARE)
1631 East Second St., Building E
(512) 804-3650
www.integralcare.org
CARE provides legal referrals, counseling, transportation, screening, and other services for HIV-positive individuals.

DENTAL CLINIC
3000 Medical Arts St.
(512) 479-6633
Dental care for HIV and AIDS patients is offered on a sliding scale by this Central Austin clinic.

Additional AIDS resources include the following:

- Austin/Travis County Health Department, HIV Services, (512) 708-3500
- Austin Area HIV Planning Council, (512) 974-2615, www.ci.austin.tx.us/health
- David Powell Clinic (Austin–Travis County Health Department HIV clinic), (512) 978-9100
- Interfaith Care Alliance (AIDS care teams), (512) 477-3213
- National Aids Hot Line, (800) 342-AIDS
- People's Community Clinic (see above), (512) 478-8942
- Pediatric AIDS League, (512) 892-4776
- Project REACH (HIV education for people of color), (512) 476-4610
- Project Transitions (hospice, assisted living, and supportive housing), (512) 454-8646

- Texas Department of Health, HIV Division, (512) 490-2505
- Waterloo Counseling Center, (512) 444-9922

SUPPORT SERVICES

There is an extensive web of support groups in the Austin area for those with medical, psychological, or family problems. The Austin Area Mental Health Association, (512) 454-3706, operates a clearinghouse to connect individuals to support groups. The listings maintained by the association are not limited to mental health care groups; they include information on medical recovery support groups and substance-abuse groups. The Texas Department of State Health Services website offers a community search tool at www.dshs.state.tx.us/mental health.shtm.

MENTAL HEALTH SERVICES

The Austin area has a wide array of mental health agencies and support services. The Austin area office of the Mental Health Association, (512-454-3706, www.mhatexas.org), offers information and referral services. Following is a sampling of the major agencies and service groups.

THE ARC OF THE CAPITAL AREA
2818 San Gabriel St.
(512) 476-7044
www.arcofthecapitalarea.org
The Arc offers support services for families with developmentally disabled members. Those programs include the following: Pilot Parent, providing support groups and other assistance for families of children with disabilities such as spina bifida, autism, cerebral palsy, or mental retardation; Project Chance,

Emergency Numbers

Emergency police, fire, and EMS Services in the Austin area	911
Police, nonemergency	311
Poison Center	(800) POISON-1
Crisis Intervention/Suicide Hot Line	(512) 472-HELP (4357)
	or TTY (512) 703-1395
Social Services Referral Hot Line operated by 211 or United Way	(512) 323-1899
Travis County Sheriff's Mental Health Unit	(512) 473-9734
Alcoholics Anonymous	(512) 444-0071,
	(512) 441-3369 (Spanish)
Safe Place for victims of rape, sexual abuse, and domestic violence	(512) 267-SAFE
Williamson County Crisis Center	(800) 460-SAFE

working with developmentally disabled juveniles and adults who have been involved with the criminal justice program; Community Advocacy Services, matching volunteers one on one with developmentally disabled adults living in the community or at Austin State School; and Community Living Assistance and Support Services, helping many individuals who might be forced by their disabilities to live in institutional settings.

AUSTIN CHILD GUIDANCE CENTER
810 West Forty-fifth St.
(512) 451-2242
www.austinchildguidance.org
Individual, family, and group therapy are offered at the center, which also provides counseling and testing services, child-abuse services, and parenting classes. Fees are charged on a sliding-scale basis.

AUSTIN RECOVERY CENTER INC.
8402 Cross Park Dr.
(512) 697-8600
www.austinrecovery.org
The center operates a detoxification unit, plus outpatient and inpatient care for chemically dependent adults and teens.

AUSTIN STATE HOSPITAL
4110 Guadalupe St.
(512) 452-0381
www.dshs.state.tx.us
The hospital is under the auspices of the Texas Department of State Health Services, which includes seven other state hospitals around Texas. The Austin facility serves the 37-county Central Texas area. Approximately 300 teens and adults receive care at the hospital.

AUSTIN-TRAVIS COUNTY INTEGRAL CARE CENTER
1430 Collier St.
(512) 447-4141
www.integralcare.org

The center operates a 24-hour hot line, (512) 472-HELP, in addition to emergency psychiatric services and programs for mental illness, mental retardation, and substance abuse. Other services include psychiatric case management, vocational and educational services, diagnosis and evaluation, infant-parent training, child-abuse services, and homeless services. Fees are determined by the individual's ability to pay.

AUSTIN WOMEN'S ADDICTION REFERRAL AND EDUCATION CENTER (AWARE)
2015 South I-35, Suite 110
(512) 326-1222
www.ywcaaustin.org

This YWCA program offers chemical-dependency counseling, assessment, education, information, and referral.

PEOPLE'S COMMUNITY CLINIC
2909 North I-35
(512) 478-4939
www.pcclinic.org

This community clinic (see above) also provides mental health services and links to other community services.

ST. DAVID'S PAVILION
1025 East Thirty-second St.
(512) 867-5800
www.stdavids.com

This clinic, part of the Columbia St. David's Healthcare Network, provides both in- and outpatient care for men, women, and chil-

dren. The pavilion has a special program for those with eating disorders.

Pet Emergencies

Austin is a pet-friendly city, but accidents do happen to our treasured pets. Here are several important numbers to keep handy:

- ASPCA Animal Poison Control Center, toll-free (888) 426-4435
- Austin Animal Cruelty, (512) 974-5750 or 311
- Animal Control or report abuse and roadside animal sales, (512) 972-6060
- 24-hour animal emergency hospitals:
- Animal Emergency Hospital of Austin, 4106 North Lamar Blvd., (512) 459-4336
- Emergency Animal Clinic of Northwest Austin, 12034 Research Blvd., (512) 331-6121
- Emergency Animal Clinic of Northwest Austin, Southwest Branch, 4544 South Lamar, Suite 760, (512) 899-0955

IMMEDIATE-CARE FACILITIES

In the trade they are sometimes called "doc-in-a-box," and immediate-care facilities are springing up in shopping centers and near busy intersections throughout the area. They provide nonemergency, outpatient care for weekend gardeners with battered green thumbs, Sun jocks, and visitors who slip and fall while getting into the Austin spirit. Call ahead for hours and specific locations, and check your insurance before you check in.

South

AUSTIN IMMEDIATE CARE
5000 West Slaughter Lane, Building 6, Suite 100
(512) 282-2273
www.austinimmediatecare.com

PRO MED MEDICAL CARE CENTER
3801 South Lamar Blvd.
(512) 447-9661
www.promedaustin.com

TEXAS URGENT CARE
2100 West William Cannon Dr.
(512) 326-2243
www.texasurgentcare.com

Southwest

NEXT CARE
6001 West William Cannon Dr., Suite 302
(888) 381-4858
www.nextcare.com

West

AUSTIN REGIONAL URGENT CARE CLINIC
6835 Austin Center Blvd.
(512) 346-6611
www.austinregionalclinic.com

BEE CAVES URGENT CARE
11614 FM 224
(512) 263-3911

Northwest

PRO MED MEDICAL CARE CENTER
13831 North Hwy. 183
(512) 335-6260
www.promedaustin.com

North

PRO MED MEDICAL CARE CENTER
2000 West Anderson Lane
(512) 459-4367
www.promedaustin.com

ST. DAVID'S MEDICENTER
810 West Braker Lane
(512) 339-8114
www.stdavids.com

ALTERNATIVE MEDICINE

Austin is a hotbed of alternative therapies and wellness programs, and some practitioners of traditional medicine also include aspects of holistic healing in their own treatments. The area's hospitals offer wellness programs, plus several fitness centers formulate wellness programs for clients (see the Parks & Recreation chapter). There are consultants who work with employers to develop wellness and exercise programs for employees or individuals. All manner of therapies are available, including Chinese, homeopathic, ayurvedic, and Taoist tai chi. Check the Yellow Pages for alternative therapies—the acupuncture listings also include herbal and nutritional therapies.

Another good resource are the bulletin boards at local health food stores. The large outdoor bulletin board at the Whole Foods Market, Sixth Street and Lamar Boulevard, features a variety of alternative therapy providers. (See the Shopping chapter for information.)

Mark Blumenthal runs a nonprofit organization, headquartered in Austin, called the American Botanical Council. The council produces a magazine, *HerbalGram*, that focuses on herbal research and federal regulation of supplements. The council can be contacted at P.O. Box 201660, Austin, TX 78720, or (512) 331-8868, www.herbalgram.org.

A WORD ABOUT ALLERGIES

Allergies. Sooner or later you're gonna get 'em. At least that is what the experts predict for many newcomers to Austin. The abundance of flora has its downside for Central Texas residents. In the winter months—Dec, Jan, and Feb—the junipers in the Hill Country produce pollen that sets off the "cedar fever" season—the trees are colloquially known as cedars, but they are in fact junipers. Some opine that the purple haze produced by the pollen prompted Austin to be dubbed the City of the Violet Crown. Most sufferers are too busy sniffling and wiping their watery eyes to notice the violet glow.

In spring the live oak and elm pollens bring on misery for some, then in summer there are grasses and, of course, year-round attacks by mold spores and animal dander. Not everyone succumbs, but so many do that the local television stations broadcast allergy counts on their daily newscasts. In a classic case of market supply and demand, allergists do a booming business in Austin.

HIGHER EDUCATION

Back in the 1920s and 1930s, Austin's leaders billed the city as "The Athens of the West," both in tribute to, and promotion of, the element of culture bestowed by the area's colleges and universities. While we dropped that lofty title decades ago, Austin's distinction as an eminent educational center of the South remains. our institutes of higher education add luster to the jewel that is Austin. For its sheer size and importance in the economic development of Austin, the University of Texas stands in a class by itself. But Austin's other fine colleges and universities are vitally linked to this city in countless ways as well. The symbiosis that exists between the Austin community and its various institutes of higher education is one of the defining characteristics of the region.

One need only walk through the campuses of our institutes to get a feel for Austin's educational traditions. The sprawling UT campus with its giant shade trees, sculptures, fountains, mammoth buildings, and the 27-story UT Tower, which has become as much an Austin landmark as a UT symbol, are enough to inspire a certain reverence. The Gothic Revival–style Main Building on the St. Edward's University campus stands as a stately landmark in South Austin, while Huston-Tillotson University's elevated site overlooking downtown from the east is a living legacy to Austin's education of African Americans during Reconstruction and ever since. Austin Community College's many modern campuses around central Texas serve as a reminder that there's always room for more centers of learning here. Texas State University south of us in San Marcos and Southwestern University north in Georgetown frame Austin with educational foundations dating back more than a century.

COLLEGES & UNIVERSITIES

Here, listed by size, are the colleges and universities that enrich our city.

UNIVERSITY OF TEXAS AT AUSTIN
Twenty-fourth and Guadalupe Streets
(512) 475-7348
www.utexas.edu
The 40 acres! This fond nickname for the University of Texas at Austin (UT) dates back to 1839, when city planners set aside a 40-acre plot called College Hill to be used for an institute of higher learning. UT didn't come along for another 44 years—and almost didn't come to Austin at all. The University officially opened on that 40-acre site on September 15, 1883. Today the University of Texas at Austin's main campus alone sits on more than 350 acres, while the university operates major research facilities on 915 additional acres around the city. UT owns the Marine Science Institute at Port Aransas, the McDonald Observatory near Fort Davis,

the Winedale Historical Center near Round Top, the Bee Cave Research Center west of Austin, and writer J. Frank Dobie's ranch in Paisano. To top it off, the University of Texas at Austin is the flagship of the UT System's 15 campuses spread throughout the state. It's the city's largest employer, with 21,000 faculty and staff. And, with an enrollment of about 50,000 undergraduate and graduate students, it is one of the nation's largest universities.

UT faculty members have won scores of prestigious awards, honors, and medals—Nobel Prizes, Pulitzer Prizes, the National Medal of Science, and the National Medal of Technology—and have been named to distinguished societies, institutes, and academies across the nation. Many alumni have gone on to leave their mark, both on Austin and on the world. Lady Bird Johnson, Walter Cronkite, Bill Moyers, Lloyd Bentsen, and former First Lady Laura Bush all attended UT. The university's academic programs and professional schools often rank among the top programs and schools in the country.

i Texas Box Office, (512) 477-6060 (charge-by-phone), www.texas boxoffice.com, is the place to go if you want tickets to UT athletics, performing arts, or any upcoming event at UT's Erwin Center. The box office also handles tickets for other Central Texas events.

The university, made up of 17 colleges and schools, the Graduate School, and Continuing and Innovative Education, offers more than 100 undergraduate degree programs and 170 graduate programs. Exceptional facilities abound, including the fifth-largest academic library system in North America, with more than 8 million volumes in 17 facilities (see the chapter on The Literary Scene).

i The wacky "Hi, How Are You" frog mural on The Drag at Twenty-first and Guadalupe Streets—a beloved symbol of Austin "weirdness"—was created by Austin singer-songwriter and artist Daniel Johnston in 1983. A feature-length documentary about him, *The Devil and Daniel Johnston,* premiered at the Sundance Film Festival in 2005.

UT is one of the reasons why so many people around the country get dreamy-eyed just hearing the name Austin. Before the high-tech industry came along to rocket Austin's name into the stratosphere, before the music scene crystallized to give Austin such a hip reputation, before big business discovered us, before the legions of filmmakers and tourists arrived, there was UT. While UT can't take credit for all the excitement surrounding Austin today, its contributions are enormous. Along with state government, the University of Texas has provided the foundation for much of what Austin has become. UT is noted for graduating so many students who've fallen in love with Austin's natural beauty and tolerant atmosphere that they can't bear to leave.

It's no wonder UT students and the public at large get along so well. Not only do these scholars, some of the nation's brightest, bring a palpable energy to this city (and make valuable contributions to its social consciousness—and conscience), having one of the nation's largest universities at our doorstep gives Austinites incredible opportunities for cultural and educational enhancement, for cutting-edge knowledge in an extraordinary range of professional fields—and for just plain fun. A stroll down The Drag, the part of Guadalupe Street that runs alongside UT, will have anyone feeling like a college student in minutes. This strip, with its bookstores, restaurants, coffeehouses, shops, and markets, is the melting pot of UT and the city.

One place on campus notorious for overcrowding is Darrel K Royal–Texas Memorial Stadium on a football Sat. Texas Longhorns games are often the hottest ticket in town as the university and the city turn out to support their beloved, 4-time national championship team. Football isn't the only game in town, however. Many other Longhorns teams draw big crowds, including the UT women's basketball team. UT puts great emphasis on sports and goes all out to recruit some of the nation's top athletes. As a result, Longhorns teams, men's and women's, have won more Big 12 Conference championships than any other college or university. In accordance with tradition, the UT Tower glows orange many a night celebrating major UT athletic victories. In addition to intercollegiate sports, UT hosts an active recreational sports program, which attracts about 80 percent of the student body.

For both students and members of the general public interested in culture and entertainment, UT offers an enormous range of options. Texas Performing Arts' public performance spaces and backup facilities, including the Bass Concert Hall and the Bates Recital Hall, rank among the top 5 on any American campus. The Frank C. Erwin Jr. Special Events Center hosts more than 250 annual events. The Jack S. Blanton Museum of Art has an extensive permanent collection, and the Texas Memorial Museum holds

extensive teaching and research collections and an exhibition space that includes the original Goddess of Liberty statue from atop the State Capitol. Of course UT also is home to the Lyndon Baines Johnson Library and Museum (see the Attractions and The Arts chapters).

Like our other area colleges and universities, UT pays special attention to the continuing education of Austin's adult community and other nontraditional students. UT's University Extension offers a huge selection of evening classes at UT facilities as well as online. The program allows students to earn college credits, but it does not grant degrees. Admission to UT is not required to enroll.

For detailed information on touring UT, check out our Attractions chapter. Information on UT athletics can be found in the Spectator Sports chapter.

AUSTIN COMMUNITY COLLEGE
5930 Middle Fiskville Rd.
(512) 223-4222
www.austincc.edu

Austin Community College, which celebrated its 38th birthday in 2010, is the baby in the neighborhood when it comes to Austin's institutions of higher learning, most of which were born in the 1800s. Perhaps that's why we call it "junior" college. In fact, this public 2-year community college is far from junior in size and in importance to the Austin area. ACC's enrollment has grown to more than 40,000 students on 8 campuses and various education centers in and around Austin, while thousands more take noncredit courses at ACC campuses and at various distance learning sites around the region.

The college is the second-largest institute of higher learning in the Austin area, after the

University of Texas. That is certainly welcome news to those who fought to establish ACC back in the 1960s when, according to the prevailing conventional wisdom, Austin didn't need another college, what with UT and all the city's other fine colleges and universities. In fact, earlier efforts to establish a community college failed twice. At least some of ACC's success can be attributed to its achievement in taking higher education directly to the people it serves. The college's main campuses dot the Austin map from Oak Hill in the south to Round Rock in the north, to the racially mixed, working-class area of East Austin. Each of these campuses demonstrates a strong commitment to provide education to all of Austin's residents.

Today, ACC offers 2-year associate degrees and one-year certificates, and has more than 230 programs. Students who graduate with an associate of arts or associate of science degree are prepared to transfer to a 4-year college or university. The 2-year associate of applied science degree prepares students to enter the local job market or transfer to select universities. For students studying for one-year certificates, ACC is a technical or vocational school, offering courses in such subjects as building construction, automotive technology, financial management, office administration, child development, surgical technology, and electronic technology. As Austin's demand for high-tech workers skyrockets, ACC has established itself as one of the major learning centers focused on filling those jobs. It has invested in both technical infrastructure and in designing programs and courses of study aimed at preparing students for high-tech positions.

TEXAS STATE UNIVERSITY–SAN MARCOS
601 University Dr., San Marcos
(512) 245-2111
www.txstate.edu

Texas State University–San Marcos is the area's third-largest institution of higher education, with more than 30,000 students. More than half its students commute from outside San Marcos, including many from the Austin area.

Texas State—the alma mater of President Lyndon Johnson—gets national recognition in several areas: The Association of Teacher Educators has called it one of the top 3 teacher education programs in the country; the Association of American Geographers consistently ranks its geography department the best in the nation. And some faculty members in geography, speech communication, business, mathematics, and mass communication have been recognized as national leaders in their fields. Texas State is also proud of its record in recruiting ethnic minorities, which now make up 35 percent of the student body. The university, in fact, is among the top 20 producers of Hispanic undergraduate degrees in the country. Additionally, the university receives accolades for its enormous fund-raising efforts and steady increases in endowments.

Texas State's geography department was the first to offer a doctoral program in 1996, and today the university offers 9 Ph.D. programs as well as 81 master's programs. In addition to its well-respected teaching program, the university is known for its business school. The university offers 97 undergraduate majors in education, applied arts, business, fine arts and communication, health professions, liberal arts, and science. Texas State also operates the Round Rock

Higher Education Center, often simply called Texas State-Round Rock, just north of Austin.

Among the university's collections is the Southwestern Writers Collection, which includes J. Frank Dobie properties (see the chapter on The Literary Scene) as well as an extensive archive of written material that captures the literary and artistic spirit of the American Southwest. The Lonesome Dove archives in this collection include props and memorabilia from the film set of Texan Larry McMurtry's epic story about cattle driving.

Texas State first opened its doors in 1903 as a teacher training college called Southwest Texas State Normal School. Through the years it became a normal college, teachers college, and then college. TS became a university in 1969. Located on 457 acres and surrounded by magnificent cypress and pecan trees, the campus sits on the banks of the San Marcos River on the edge of the Texas Hill Country. TS athletes, the Bobcats, compete at the NCAA Division I level in both men's and women's sports. The university also offers a wide range of programs for talented students in dance, band, choir, jazz, symphony orchestra, musical theater, and opera.

i According to the 2010 Census, 38.7 percent of Austinites have college degrees. That puts Austin in 6th place among America's most educated cities. Austin was the only city in Texas to make the top 10. Take that Houston and Dallas!

ST. EDWARD'S UNIVERSITY
3001 South Congress Ave.
(512) 448-8400
www.stedwards.edu

A private Roman Catholic liberal arts university that celebrated its 125th anniversary in 2010, St. Edward's offers undergraduate and graduate degrees to more than 5,000 students from across the United States and abroad.

Located in South Austin on 180 acres of rolling hills, the university was founded in 1885 as a college but got its start 12 years earlier when it opened as a school with just 3 farm boys enrolled the first year. As the school grew and began boarding students, Austin residents started referring to St. Edward's as the Catholic Farm due to the fact that it fed its faculty and staff by raising beef, grain, vegetables, and fruit on its own land. The Main Building, the imposing Gothic Revival–style building made of Texas white limestone, was dedicated in 1889—a grand structure for sure in the early Southwest. Rebuilt after a fire destroyed it in 1903, the Main Building was designated a Texas Historic Landmark in 1973.

Today, St. Edward's confers undergraduate degrees in more than 50 areas of study in 5 pre-professional programs, as well as 11 master's degrees in business administration, counseling, human services, computer information sciences, liberal arts, and others. The undergraduate curriculum has been recognized by the Carnegie Foundation as among the most rigorous in the nation.

In addition to awarding degrees, the university is recognized for its tradition of producing graduates with strong values, both through required course work in ethics, philosophy, or religious studies and through its community outreach programs. It also gets high marks for its adult education program and for its efforts on behalf of Hispanic students, who make up 26 percent of the student body. The university is home to the fine performance space Mary Moody Northern Theatre, the hub

St. Edward's Theater Arts program, one of the only pre-professional undergraduate programs of its kind in the country.

i The Texas Tuition Promise Fund gives parents and grandparents the opportunity to pay today's prices for a future college student's tuition at Texas's 2- and 4-year public institutions, though the investment can also be used at private and out-of-state schools. The fund allows investors to buy tuition in one lump sum or make regular payments. Visit www.texas tuitionpromisefund.com for details.

SOUTHWESTERN UNIVERSITY
1001 East University Ave.,
Georgetown
(512) 863-6511, (800) 252-3166
www.southwestern.edu
"Chartered as the state's first university in 1840, until the 1970s it was doing the conventional thing, providing the B.A. union card for its graduates' first jobs. Then with the catalysts of the new president's vision and the generosity of 3 Texas foundations, it was born again as a place to prepare for the 21st century." So writes Loren Pope in the book, *Colleges That Change Lives*. This book, subtitled *40 Schools You Should Know About Even If You're Not a Straight-A Student,* is one of several guides to colleges and universities that have taken note of Southwestern University in recent years. Called one of the best sleepers in the nation and one of the buried treasures among the nation's liberal arts colleges, Southwestern University may not remain one of Texas's hidden assets much longer.

Located 28 miles north of Austin in the seat of Williamson County government and even closer to our northern neighbors in Round Rock and Pflugerville, Southwestern University is a private Methodist 4-year institute of higher learning that reflects the conservative values of Georgetown itself. Enrollment hovers around 1,300, a figure the university considers ideal.

Southwestern sits on a 100-acre campus filled with trees and dotted with beautiful Texas limestone buildings constructed in the stately Richardsonian Romanesque–style. The university also owns 525 more acres plus a 75-acre golf course. Southwestern has 26 academic departments offering 40 majors and more than 35 minors.

CONCORDIA UNIVERSITY–TEXAS
11400 Concordia University Dr.
(512) 313-3000
www.concordia.edu
For more than 80 years, Concordia University sat on a relatively small 23-acre site on overcrowded and noisy I-35 in central Austin. That all changed in 2008, when Concordia moved to a 389-acre campus and nature preserve in northwest Austin.

Concordia Lutheran College graduated to university status in 1995 when it became a member of the Concordia University System that spans the country. Founded as Concordia Academy in 1926 by pioneers who had Wendish and German ethnic backgrounds, the school originally trained young men for ministry in the Lutheran Church. Women were admitted for the first time in 1955, and in 1979 Concordia implemented a 4-year liberal arts program for undergraduates. Today, Concordia has about 2,100 students and offers 18 undergraduate majors in 4 colleges: business, education, liberal arts, and sciences. It also offers master's degree programs in education and business administration. The university, which is owned and maintained by the Lutheran Church–Missouri Synod, has strong ties to the system's other universities and seminaries. Students can transfer easily between schools and take classes offered at other campuses via the Concordia University Education Network, which uses video technology to transmit and receive courses. In 2010, *US News & World Report* magazine named Austin's Concordia University to its list of best regional colleges in the West.

Lutherans make up less than half of the 1,250-member student body at Concordia, which also attracts Roman Catholics, Baptists, and students from other Christian and non-Christian denominations.

Concordia has made great strides in serving the educational needs of Austin's working adults by offering evening classes and televised courses under its adult degree program. This centrally located university also opens its doors to the public for an extensive range of cultural and academic events, including art exhibits, lectures, theater, and music performances.

HUSTON-TILLOTSON UNIVERSITY
900 Chicon St.
(512) 505-3028
www.htu.edu

Huston-Tillotson University brings much more to Austin than merely its distinctions as the city's oldest institution of higher education and its only historically black college.

In East Austin on 23 acres of rolling hills that overlook downtown, Huston-Tillotson is a center of cultural and community involvement for Austin's East-side neighborhoods and one of Austin's largest minority businesses. The university is known locally for its participation in a number of cooperative relationships with the Austin Independent School District, the City of Austin, Austin Community College, and local business and community organizations.

This private 4-year undergraduate university, affiliated with the United Methodist Church, the United Church of Christ, and the United Negro College Fund, offers bachelor's degrees to about 900 students from a variety of cultural and ethnic backgrounds. Within the college's 6 divisions—business, natural sciences, social sciences, the humanities, education, and science and technology—students can major in many areas of study, including the college's notable programs of chemistry, teacher preparations, sociology, and biology.

Huston-Tillotson University dates back to the 1870s, and one of its former buildings, Allen Hall, was, according to the college, the first building in Texas or anywhere west of the Mississippi constructed for the higher education of black students. Tillotson College was established by Congregationalists in 1875 (although it didn't open to students until 1881), and Samuel Huston College was founded by Methodists a year later. The two colleges merged in October 1952 to become the present-day Huston-Tillotson University, which changed its name from Huston-Tillotson College in 2005.

While the campus has modernized over the past century and a quarter, two of its historic buildings remain as splendid landmarks and fine examples of turn-of-the-20th-century architecture. The Evans Industrial Building, built ca. 1912, was completely renovated in 1984 and designated as a Texas Historical Site. The Old Administration Building, completed in 1914, is one of the few remaining examples of the Modified Prairie Style popularized by Frank Lloyd Wright. This now-restored building was entered in the National Register of Historic Places in 1993.

SCHOOLS & CHILD CARE

Austin is a forward-looking, great place to live. Add those qualities to the city's worldwide reputation as a technology hub and you'll begin to see why the Austin area has experienced a huge population surge over the past quarter century. Likewise, all of the Capitol City area's 10 school districts have experienced growing pains, due either directly to new businesses locating in the districts, to employees searching for suitable housing nearby, or to families fleeing the big city for the more peaceful suburbs. In recent years bulging school districts passed bond issues to build, enlarge, and improve schools at a pace never before witnessed. Some smaller districts have seen their student enrollment more than double, just in the last decade.

Texas as a whole faces considerable challenges in its huge public school system, especially amid the current recession. State leaders from both political parties have focused on improving the schools and, in response to lawsuits from poor school districts, changed the financing system. Business leaders also have played an important role in pressing for educational reforms, recognizing the need for a well-educated 21st-century workforce.

Accountability is a watchword of the educational system in Texas, and testing has become a vital tool. Although there are complaints that schools "teach to the test" or that too much weight is given to the results, parents and teachers generally support the rigorous testing regimen. Under a mandate from the State Legislature, the Texas Education Agency (TEA) evaluates public schools and school districts annually based on test scores and dropout rates. The school ratings, "Academically Unacceptable," "Academically Acceptable," "Recognized" or "Exemplary," are posted on the TEA's website at www.tea.state.tx.us. To access the ratings for an individual school, click the "Find how my school is doing?" link in the right-hand column.

SCHOOL FUNDING

One of the biggest issues facing the state's school system today is funding. In 1993—after 9 years of court cases, public debate, and failed constitutional amendments—the Texas legislature passed a school finance-reform measure that included the so-called share-the-wealth provision. The plan, dubbed "Robin Hood" by critics, requires the state's wealthiest school districts to share their property taxes with poorer districts. The Eanes school district, for example, has consistently been classified a "rich" school district and has contributed to the pool. In the past few years, however, other districts in Central Texas, including Round Rock, Pflugerville, and Lago Vista, have also reached property tax levels that put them into the wealthy category. Surprisingly, the Austin Independent

School District also falls into this group—even though more than 60 percent of its students come from low-income families.

i Educators, school teachers, and librarians get a 10 percent discount off all purchases at Texas-based Half Price Books. Free Educator's Discount Cards are available at any one of the chain's six stores in the Austin area.

Area school district leaders agree that the plan has served poorer districts well. They argue, however, that the state's ever-growing reliance on local property taxes to pay for public education will not solve the basic problem: not enough state money being dedicated to the Texas school system. At the same time, individual schools' costs are growing in Central Texas as enrollments soar and they struggle to meet mandates from Washington. Revenues from the state lottery that go toward public education have not alleviated the pressure on school budgets, and the legislature is forced time and again to revisit the issue of school finance reform.

SCHOOLS

All the school districts in the Austin area operate special schools and/or programs for both physically and mentally handicapped students and those with behavioral or emotional problems.

Students who require more academic challenge are provided a number of opportunities, including honors programs, advanced-placement classes, programs for talented and gifted youth, and, in some cases, magnet schools. The region's many Spanish-speaking students are offered bilingual classes or so-called ESL classes, where they study English as a second language.

The school year varies slightly in Central Texas but generally runs from mid-Aug to the third week in May, for a total of 176 school days. Children entering Austin-area schools must be 5 years old by September 1 to enroll in kindergarten. Texas also requires that all children receive immunizations to attend school.

Public School Districts

AUSTIN INDEPENDENT SCHOOL DISTRICT
Carruth Administration Center
1111 West Sixth St.
(512) 414-1700
www.austinisd.org
The Austin Independent School District puts great emphasis on providing high-quality education for children of all races, economic levels, and English-speaking proficiencies. The district offers a solid core curriculum that stresses math, science, reading, and writing as well as special opportunities for a full range of students, from academically superior to those with learning difficulties.

AISD provides educational opportunities for about 84,000 students at 120 schools and special campuses. The district's commitment to children is evidenced by the number of national honors and rankings it has received in recent years. Austin has achieved a higher than average number of National Merit Scholars and has outperformed other Texas schoolchildren on the Scholastic Aptitude Test (SAT). Nearly 63 percent of the district's students are listed as economically disadvantaged, and 29 percent have limited English proficiency. The student population at individual schools within this huge district reflects the ethnic and economic makeup of the residents themselves. So within AISD some schools have high concentrations of upper-income families while other schools have a higher concentration of economically disadvantaged families. AISD is proud of its record of regularly increasing enrollment of minority and economically disadvantaged students in honors programs and advanced-placement classes. But in a large urban district, the challenge to continue producing top-quality graduates is staggering. TEA rates AISD "Academically Acceptable," although 32 of its schools are "Exemplary" and 36 are "Recognized."

i The University Interscholastic League (UIL), founded by the University of Texas a century ago, is among the nation's premier athletic, academic, and music competitions for school children. Its events draw thousands of competitors to Austin each year. The program is so expansive that one of every two Texas seniors has participated in a UIL event by the time he or she graduates.

DEL VALLE INDEPENDENT SCHOOL DISTRICT
5301 Ross Rd., Del Valle
(512) 386-3000
http://delvalle.tx.schoolwebpages.com
Once a region primarily of farms and ranches, the Del Valle Independent School District witnessed major changes when high-tech industries and Austin's new international airport moved into the area. The district, located in rapidly growing Southeast Austin and Travis County, serves the urban communities of Montopolis, Frontier Valley, Sunridge Park, and Pleasant Valley as well as the rural communities of Garfield, Creedmoor, Mustang Ridge, Elroy, Pilot Knob, Webberville, and Hornsby Bend.

Del Valle ISD's 10,000 students—almost double the number from a decade ago—are spread out on 7 elementary campuses, 3 middle schools, 1 high school, and an alternative learning center. More than 80 percent of the district's students are listed as economically disadvantaged, and 30 percent have limited English proficiency. Yet the district as a whole is rated "Recognized" by the TEA. Del Valle offers an excellent range of courses from preschool through high school for students of all abilities and talents. Bilingual and English as a Second Language classes are in place throughout the district. Del Valle enjoys strong support from the area's business and technology community, which provides scholarships, grants, and awards.

DRIPPING SPRINGS INDEPENDENT SCHOOL DISTRICT
510 West Mercer St., Dripping Springs
(512) 858-3000
www.dsisd.txed.net
Located 19 miles west of Austin in Hays County, the Dripping Springs Independent School District saw explosive growth as a result of the 1990s economic boom in the Austin area. This small district of just 5 schools has doubled in size in recent years to more than 4,300 students. The suburban district always receives good ratings from the state, most recently it was considered "Recognized," and students taking Scholastic Aptitude Tests score among the highest in an area that already beats the national average. The district sets high standards for its students and provides advanced placement and gifted and talented programs to its academically outstanding students. The needs of mentally and physically handicapped students are addressed within the schools themselves, with the assistance and

guidance of the Hays County Co-op. To deal with the problem of overcapacity, the district has improved and expanded existing schools and built a new intermediate school. Ten percent of the district's students are listed as economically disadvantaged and 4 percent have limited English proficiency.

EANES INDEPENDENT SCHOOL DISTRICT
South Don Rogers Administration Building,
601 Camp Craft Rd.
(512) 329-3600
www.eanes.k12.tx.us
Considered one of the finest school districts in Texas, the Eanes Independent School District has earned excellent ratings from the state. Eanes students taking the Scholastic Aptitude Test consistently score well above the national average. This district has about 7,500 students at 6 elementary schools, 2 middle schools, and one high school. The district is the largest in the state to have all schools and the district itself named "Exemplary" by the Texas Education Agency. Seven of its 9 schools, including Westlake High School, are US Blue Ribbon Schools.

Eanes is one of the wealthiest school districts in Texas, and 2.5 percent of its students are listed as economically disadvantaged, while 2 percent have limited English proficiency. Eanes enjoys the benefits of having strong support from parents and the business community. In addition to its outstanding academic programs, the district is well known for its athletic programs for both boys and girls; the district has racked up state championships in sport after sport, including golf, football, girls basketball, and girls swimming. The district encompasses 31.2 square miles

in West Austin and in the municipalities of Rollingwood and West Lake Hills.

LAGO VISTA INDEPENDENT SCHOOL DISTRICT
8039 Bar-K, Lago Vista
(512) 267-8300
www.lagovistaisd.net
The smallest school district in the Capital City region, the Lago Vista Independent School District averages about 1,200 students in its 3 schools. It makes for small class sizes—and excellent schools. The district covers 35 square miles on north Lake Travis and serves the communities of Lago Vista, Point Venture, and South Jonestown Hills. Although its communities are known primarily for resort and retirement living, the district is changing as more and more families with children move into the area, many to take advantage of the high-quality education the district provides.

The district emphasizes college preparatory programs and lifelong sports. Schools provide a number of learning opportunities for children of all learning abilities, however, including special education and English as a Second Language. Students needing more challenge and enrichment are offered a gifted and talented program as well as a number of advanced placement and honors classes. Nearly 25 percent of the district's students are economically disadvantaged, compared with 59 percent statewide, while 5 percent have limited English proficiency. Lago Vista ISD, like most others in this region, is growing. The district receives strong community support.

LAKE TRAVIS INDEPENDENT SCHOOL DISTRICT
3322 RR 620 South
(512) 533-6000
www.ltisdschools.org

The Lake Travis Independent School District, one of the smallest in this region with 9 schools and about 6,500 students, is located west/northwest of Austin along Lake Travis's southwest shore. The district serves many nearby communities, including Apache Shores, Bee Cave, Briarcliff, Homestead, Hudson Bend, Lake Pointe, Lakeway, The Hills, and Vineyard Bay. Once largely comprising resorts and retirement communities, the district is seeing its profile change as more families move into the area. The Lake Travis ISD, with a TEA rating of "Academically Acceptable," offers challenging educational opportunities at all levels and provides classes and programs for both academically superior students and those requiring special help. Lake Travis High School is proud of its reputation for providing rigorous academic programs for high school students, who are required to earn credits in core subjects as well as foreign language, technology, fine arts, physical education, and health.

In addition to its overall good rating, several schools within the district have received top marks from the state. High school students taking the national Scholastic Aptitude Test have scored higher than the national average. The district also produces a steady number of National Merit Scholars annually. The district has 12.7 of its students listed as economically disadvantaged and 5 percent with limited English proficiency.

LEANDER INDEPENDENT SCHOOL DISTRICT
401 South West St., Leander
(512) 943-5000
www.leanderisd.org
The Leander Independent School District is northwest of Austin in Williamson and Travis Counties and educates students from the communities of Leander, Cedar Park, and a part of Austin. With about 30,000 students, Leander is now the third-largest district in this 10-district region. This district, which covers 200 square miles, much of it still undeveloped, is in another fast-growing area of Central Texas. Leander is building schools to keep up with huge enrollment increases and now has 23 elementary schools, 7 middle schools, and 5 high schools.

Leander, which is a "Recognized" TEA district, was among the pioneers in the state to develop an educational program aimed at better preparing high school students for college or the workforce by requiring them to take classes in a specific discipline. Leander ISD provides strong core curriculum classes and, for those requiring more challenge, an honors program. The average SAT score in the district is above the state and national average. Twenty percent of the district's children are listed as economically disadvantaged, and 5 percent lack English proficiency.

MANOR INDEPENDENT SCHOOL DISTRICT
10335 US 290 East, Manor
(512) 278-4000
www.manorisd.net
This small district in Northeast Austin and Travis County doubled in enrollment from 1993 to 2003, and it has almost doubled again since then, to nearly 7,000 students. One of the poorest districts in the state, 75 percent of its students are listed as economically disadvantaged and 29 percent have limited English proficiency. Yet it has made strides since the high-tech boom of the 1990s and TEA considers it "Academically Acceptable." Manor is home to Applied Materials, the world's largest maker of computer-chip

manufacturing equipment, and Samsung's semiconductor factory. Together the companies represent thousands of jobs and major tax revenue.

What's happening in Manor demonstrates the benefits of having dynamic businesses that lend their support to schools. Among its many contributions, Applied Materials donated money to develop an up-to-date physics lab at Manor High School. Samsung and Applied Materials have worked with Austin Community College to develop a curriculum in the district to train students interested in the technology field. Manor has been working to improve its ratings and the SAT scores in the district. The district has 7 elementary schools, 2 middle schools, and 3 high schools, including Manor New Tech, one of the country's innovative educational models that stresses project-based learning with an emphasis on math, science and technology.

PFLUGERVILLE INDEPENDENT SCHOOL DISTRICT
1401 West Pecan, Pflugerville
(512) 594-0000
www.pflugervilleisd.net
Located in Northeast Travis County, close to several of the area's largest high-tech industries, the Pflugerville Independent School District has seen its enrollment more than double over the past decade to nearly 22,000 students today. That enrollment makes Pflugerville the fourth-largest district in the region. While the major high-tech companies are not within the jurisdiction of the Pflugerville school system, residential communities are springing up throughout the district to provide homes for families moving into the area to be close to jobs in Round Rock and Austin. As a result, the district has backed an aggressive expansion

campaign over the past several years that led to the construction of several new schools. Today the district comprises 3 high schools, 5 middle schools, an alternative learning center, and 18 elementary schools. High school students who desire can choose from among 9 vocational programs, or they can choose from among advanced placement courses and honors classes. The district, with a TEA "Academically Acceptable" rating, lists 19 percent of its students as economically disadvantaged and 5 percent with limited English proficiency.

ROUND ROCK INDEPENDENT SCHOOL DISTRICT
1311 Round Rock Ave., Round Rock
(512) 464-5000
www.roundrockisd.org
The Round Rock Independent School District, just north of Austin in northern Travis and Williamson Counties, is a focal point of community involvement. Like several other districts in this area, Round Rock ISD has a fine reputation for offering excellent educational opportunities, and it is rated "Recognized" by TEA. The huge district has 31 elementary schools, 10 middle schools, 5 high schools, and an alternative learning center. Twenty-five percent of its students are economically disadvantaged and 8 percent lack English proficiency.

Round Rock, the second-largest school district in this area with more than 42,000 students, spans nearly 110 square miles in southwest Williamson County and northwest Travis County. Only the Austin school district has more students. Like some other districts in this area, Round Rock has experienced severe growing pains, and the district is increasing enrollment by about 1,000 students per year. The district's Round Rock

Stadium, a $20.5 million, 11,000-seat football and soccer complex, is easily among the finest in the country.

PRIVATE SCHOOLS

Whether you're looking for a parochial school, alternative learning, a college-preparatory program, or a school that focuses on the visual and performing arts, the Austin area probably has a private school that fits the bill. If the city falls short in any category, it would be in the scarcity of high-quality boarding schools similar to those found in larger cities, especially in the East. Only St. Stephen's Episcopal School, an excellent educational institution, provides room and board for high school students. Most of the private schools in the area are coeducational.

In Austin many parents opt for private schools to round out their children's religious education, although the demand for all types of private schools is growing rapidly. In response, several schools in the Austin area have added grade levels a year at a time or expanded existing facilities, although the pressure for space keeps mounting. Many schools have extensive waiting lists and require admissions tests and/or interviews. Some schools do not accept students based on a first-come, first-served system, choosing instead to accept students who meet their requirements. Some schools offer before- and after-school care and/or extracurricular activities; parents should check with the school if those extras are important.

Central

CONCORDIA HIGH SCHOOL
3407 Red River St.
(512) 248-2547
www.concordiaacademy.org

A Lutheran school, Concordia Academy opened in the fall of 2002 as a 9th grade and added a grade level each year until it became a full senior high school by 2005. Affiliated with the Lutheran Church Missouri Synod, the school is on the grounds of St. Paul Lutheran School, an elementary and middle school. Concordia offers a college-preparatory program that, in addition to the core subjects, includes religion, Spanish, art, choir, band, and athletics. Enrollment is about 100 students. The school is not affiliated with Austin's Concordia University.

THE GIRLS' SCHOOL OF AUSTIN
2007 McCall Rd.
(512) 478-7827
www.thegirlsschool.org

As its name implies, this is an all-girls' school that was founded on the philosophy that the male-based educational model does not fit the way girls learn. Since its opening in the Tarrytown neighborhood in 2002, the Girls' School has grown to more than 100 students from kindergarten through 8th grade. The school offers all the core classes, as well as computer studies, public speaking, and a Writers' Workshop. Its mission "is to inspire girls to achieve personal excellence and go on to lead distinguished and fulfilling lives." The school is a member of the National Coalition of Girls' Schools.

HYDE PARK BAPTIST SCHOOLS
3901 Speedway
(512) 465-8331
www.hpbs.org

Hyde Park Baptist Schools offer a Christ-centered educational program to more than 800 students on 2 campuses. The Speedway campus is for students from kindergarten through middle school; while the new Hyde Park High

School is in northwest Austin at 11400 North Mopac Expressway. Hyde Park is a college-preparatory, honors system that stresses educational achievement. The schools aim to produce Christian individuals who are responsible, productive members of society. Hyde Park, established in 1968, is accredited by the Southern Association of Colleges and Schools. In addition to daily Bible classes, the teachings of Christ are integrated daily into the basic curriculum. Additionally, students can choose from among three foreign languages: Latin, French, and Spanish. All elementary students are included in the schools' Excel program for gifted and talented youth. The school offers state-of-the-art computer labs for all students, a wide range of extracurricular sports activities, and more than a dozen other after-school activities. The nondenominational school is sponsored by the Hyde Park Baptist Church.

KIRBY HALL SCHOOL
306 West Twenty-ninth St.
(512) 474-1770
www.kirbyhallschool.org
One of Austin's most academically superior schools, Kirby Hall is an accredited college-preparatory school for students from pre-K through 12th grade. One hundred percent of Kirby Hall graduates go on to college. Students rank 3 to 4 years above the national average on tests such as the Iowa Test of Basic Skills. In a historic brick building near the University of Texas campus, Kirby Hall is situated to allow students to walk to the university to audit classes and, with testing, achieve college credit. All the school's core curriculum classes for high school students are advanced placement classes, and many students graduate from Kirby Hall with college credit hours. This school is an independent, nondenominational Christian school for bright students who want

to excel. It has no facilities for children with learning disabilities or for students with discipline problems. Entrance exams and uniforms are required. About 180 boys and girls attend Kirby Hall in classes that average 14 students in size.

i Gov. Elisha M. Pease signed the bill establishing the Texas public school system on January 31, 1854. The school census that year recorded 65,463 students. The state spent 62 cents per child.

ST. AUSTIN'S SCHOOL
1911 San Antonio St.
(512) 477-3751
www.staustinschool.org
This Catholic parish school was established in 1917 and today educates more than 250 students from pre-kindergarten through 8th grade. Daily religious instruction is an integral part of the curriculum at all grades, and students are prepared for the sacraments of Holy Communion, Reconciliation, and Confirmation. For students in kindergarten and first grade, teachers use a modified Montessori approach stressing basic skills and concepts, designed to encourage students to progress at their own pace. The middle school program reinforces basic skills and emphasizes higher-order thinking skills. In addition to a strong core curriculum at all levels, students study Spanish, computers, art, music, health, and physical education. The music program for students in kindergarten through fifth grade is integrated with religious instruction through preparation for weekly Masses at St. Austin's Church. St. Austin's was the city's first private school to be named a National Blue Ribbon School.

SRI ATMANANDA MEMORIAL SCHOOL
4100 Red River St.
(512) 451-7044
www.samschool.org
The learning approach used at the Sri Atmananda Memorial School was developed in southern India and brought to Austin by the school's director, Patty Henderson. She had placed her 5-year-old son in the Indian school while the family was there on business and was impressed with the results. Students at Sri Atmananda are not assigned a classroom or a teacher but instead are allowed to select their own area of interest from among the many labs available to them: math-geography, computer, art, science, and others. All subject matter is thoroughly integrated, and teachers present material and offer structured activities, especially for older students. Children do not receive grades for their work, although the learning material presented is appropriate for each student's abilities. This small school, which allows only 15 students per grade, offers classes for children from kindergarten through 12th grade. Sri Atmananda is the only school outside India to use this method, and several of the school's teachers have received their training in that country.

South Central

PARKSIDE COMMUNITY SCHOOL
1701 Toomey Rd.
(512) 472-2559
www.parksidecommunityschool.org
About 150 students attend this Montessori school for children ages 3 through 12. Parkside was established in 1991 and focuses on the teaching methods developed by Dr. Maria Montessori in Italy. The program allows children to express their maximum creativity and to work at their own pace under the guidance of the classroom teacher. The classrooms encompass an age span of 3 years, which the school says allows the young students to learn from their older peers and the older students to reinforce their knowledge by helping the younger ones. The core classes of language arts, math, science, and social studies are covered in all classrooms along with art, drama, sewing, and others areas of study. Parkside also has a campus in Wimberly, Texas, for students ages 3 to 14.

ST. IGNATIUS, MARTYR CATHOLIC SCHOOL
120 West Oltorf St.
(512) 442-8547
www.st-ignatius.org/school
For students in pre-kindergarten through 8th grade, St. Ignatius provides a strong Christian education that includes daily scriptural readings and reflection. Children gather at Liturgy to listen to God's word and to learn to apply it to their daily life. Additionally, St. Ignatius offers a strong core curriculum that includes literature and the language arts, science, math, physical education, and the fine arts. Upper-level students are introduced to hands-on learning in the science lab and on computers. The math program includes pre-algebra and algebra for 7th and 8th graders. Students receive instruction in preparation to receive the Sacraments of Holy Eucharist and Confirmation in second grade and Reconciliation in fourth grade. The school demands parent involvement and requires parents to spend a minimum of 20 hours each year in service to the school, either at the school or at any event sponsored by the Parent Teacher Organization. St. Ignatius is accredited by the Texas Catholic Conference Department of Education.

North Central

PARAGON PREP
2001 West Koenig Lane
(512) 459-5040
www.paragonprep.com
Weekly academic competitions, cooperative projects, and an emphasis on technology are just a few of the aspects of this college-preparatory school for middle school students. Founded in 1997, Paragon Prep seeks bright, motivated students who are aiming for higher education. The independent school for students in 6th, 7th, and 8th grades uses renowned educational material, including the Chicago Math Series curriculum and the Junior Great Books program. Paragon calls itself "Internet intensive" and provides Internet classes that emphasize research and multimedia projects. The curriculum is designed so that students returning to public school for senior high will be exceptionally prepared. Paragon expects both student and parental commitments to excellence and offers in exchange a dynamic, fun, and stimulating environment. The school aims to produce students who are well rounded, concerned for others, and knowledgeable about democratic and entrepreneurial principles. Admission is selective, based on student testing and interviews with the student and parents.

REDEEMER LUTHERAN SCHOOL
1500 West Anderson Lane
(512) 451-6478
www.redeemerschool.net
Redeemer Lutheran School is Austin's largest Lutheran school and one of the largest of its kind in the country, with a program that encompasses preschool through 8th grade. Founded in 1954, the school aims to share the Christian faith by assisting parents in providing opportunities for spiritual, intellectual, physical, emotional, and social growth for children in a Christ-centered environment. The school follows the Texas Essential Knowledge and Skills curriculum program found in most public schools but incorporates Christ in the daily education process. Although a Lutheran school, children of all faiths are welcome to attend the school. In addition to the basic core curriculum, Spanish and physical education, Redeemer Lutheran has a School of Performing Arts, which is open to all ages as well as the public. Computers labs give students daily access to computer technology and to the Internet. The school also has an active extracurricular sports program The school is affiliated with the Lutheran Church–Missouri Synod and accredited by the Lutheran School Accreditation Commission.

ST. LOUIS CATHOLIC SCHOOL
7601 Burnet Rd.
(512) 454-0384
www.st-louis.org/school
This school, located on the 20-acre campus of St. Louis parish, was established in 1956 and today provides religious and secular education to more than 470 students from preschool through 8th grade. The school's well-rounded curriculum includes daily religion classes as well as language arts, math, science, health, computers, social studies, music, physical education, Spanish, and the arts. Children attend Mass weekly and are given weekly sacramental preparation to supplement the program at St. Louis parish. The school provides a stimulating and progressive academic program integrated with Catholic values and traditions. Extracurricular activities include liturgical and bell choirs, team sports, cheerleading, student council,

and altar servers. St. Louis School admits students of all religious, racial, and ethnic backgrounds. The school, affiliated with the Catholic schools of the Diocese of Austin, is accredited by the Southern Association of Colleges and Schools and the Texas Catholic Conference Education Department.

North

BRENTWOOD CHRISTIAN SCHOOL
11908 North Lamar Blvd.
(512) 835-5983
www.brentwoodchristian.org
About 720 students attend Brentwood Christian School, a pre-kindergarten through 12th grade college-preparatory school. The school provides a Christ-centered academic environment that gives high school students a choice of degrees to pursue: standard, advanced, or honors advanced. Brentwood students score above the 90th percentile compared with students nationwide on national achievement tests. The school has an extensive extracurricular sports program for boys and girls. Established in 1963, Brentwood welcomes students from all religious, ethnic, and national backgrounds if they are seeking a solid, Christian education. The school is affiliated with the Brentwood Oaks Church of Christ and is accredited by the National Christian Schools Association. Entrance exams are required.

South

STRICKLAND CHRISTIAN SCHOOL
7415 Manchaca Rd.
(512) 447-1447
www.stricklandschool.com
First graders at Strickland Christian School use the King James Version of the Bible as their basic reader. This religiously independent, nondenominational school was established in 1961 and today provides what it calls a "quality, affordable private school education" for students from pre-kindergarten through 8th grade. The school strives to provide academic excellence and a Christian foundation. The school, developed by Texan Corine Strickland, was a leader in teaching children to read phonetically, starting in preschool, and still emphasizes developing strong readers. Its core curriculum also includes writing, spelling, and math. Children also take classes in science, social studies, and physical education.

East

AUSTIN PEACE ACADEMY
5110 Manor Rd., Austin, TX 78723
(512) 926 1737
www.apacademy.org
Founded by members of Austin's Muslim community, the Peace Academy offers the full range of core classes such as math, science, history, etc., but the challenging curriculum also includes Islamic studies and the Arabic language. The East Austin school, which has more than 150 students in pre-kindergarten through high school, aims to help students preserve their Islamic identity, heritage, and practices. The school also boasts a state-of-the-art computer lab, language lab, and small class sizes designed to meet the needs of each student. Peace Academy is accredited by the Southern Association of Colleges and Schools. In 2009 the high school placed second in the highly competitive Texas Math League competition, beating out a number of prestigious high schools around Austin and the state.

West

AUSTIN CITY ACADEMY
13550 US 290 West
(512) 301-0471
www.austincityacademy.org

This pre-K to 12th grade Christian school takes biblically based learning a step further by stressing the arts as well as academics and God. Beginning in 2nd grade every student has the opportunity to receive both vocal and instrumental instruction during the school day, while all students take core classes based on A Beka, Bob Jones, and other Christian materials. The nondenominational school, founded in 2002, is located about 16 miles west of downtown Austin near Dripping Springs. Small classes with a 1 to 10 teacher/student ratio allow for customized instruction. As a member of the Texas Association of Private and Parochial Schools (TAPPS), the City Academy plans to participate in TAPPS fine arts, vocal and instrumental competitions.

REGENTS SCHOOL OF AUSTIN
3230 Travis Country Circle
(512) 899-8095
www.regents-austin.com

Serving about 800 K–12 students, the Regents School is a nondenominational Christian school that integrates a college-preparatory liberal-arts program with a strong Christian education. The school looks for students who are college bound and want to be challenged. Students begin the study of Latin in 3rd grade, which the school says helps them better understand English, science, and history. Students also study language arts, history, geography, math, logic, Spanish, and the arts. The Regents School of Austin opened in 1992 and is a founding member of the Association of Christian and Classical Schools. Admissions tests and interviews are required.

ST. ANDREW'S EPISCOPAL SCHOOL
5901 Southwest Pkwy.—Upper School
(512) 299-9700
www.sasaustin.org

St. Andrew's was established in 1952, making it one of the area's oldest and best-known parochial schools. St. Andrew's serves about 750 students grades 1 through 12 on two campuses and offers a strong college-preparatory program. Along with a challenging core curriculum, the school offers fine arts, foreign languages, and physical education. Admission tests and interviews are required. Entrance is determined through an "applicant pool" instead of by date of application.

ST. MICHAEL'S CATHOLIC ACADEMY
3000 Barton Creek Blvd.
(512) 328-2323
www.smca.com

St. Michael's Catholic Academy offers a rigorous academic environment for about 400 college-bound students. The school, established in 1984 and located on 50 acres in Southwest Austin, challenges students to reach their full potential and helps them achieve that goal by offering a wide range of courses. Students desiring more academic challenge can pursue an Advanced Academic Diploma with Honors, which requires the completion of 10 semester hours of honors courses in addition to writing an honors thesis. The school's success in producing top-quality graduates is reflected in the number of students accepted to the nation's leading colleges and universities, in the amount of scholarships and awards seniors receive, and in the number of National Merit Scholars the school produces. The admissions process is competitive. The school is dedicated to serving a diverse student body and to that end offers a financial-aid program that allows students of all economic backgrounds the opportunity to attend. The school, which is owned and governed by a board of trustees, is accredited by the Texas Catholic Conference Education Department. The school recently added a 24,600-square-foot Campus Center featuring classrooms dedicated to the performing and visual arts as well as the state-of-the-art Gloria Delgado Performing Arts Theatre, which seats nearly 360.

ST. STEPHEN'S EPISCOPAL SCHOOL
6500 St. Stephen's Dr.
(512) 327-1213
www.sstx.org
Austin's only boarding school for high school students, St. Stephen's offers day classes for coed students in 6th through 12th grades. St. Stephen's is among Austin's most academically superior schools. It regularly produces National Merit Scholars, its seniors score well above the national average on Scholastic Aptitude Test scores, and graduates are accepted to the world's most elite colleges and universities. The school stresses Christian and community values but welcomes students from all cultures, backgrounds, and religions. In fact, it was the first integrated boarding school in the South. Its range of academic offerings is outstanding and class sizes are small, both factors in its popularity. Additionally, St. Stephen's offers "Special Academies" in theater, soccer, and tennis, while its Devil's Canyon Wilderness Program takes students on outdoor adventures throughout North America. Admission is competitive and requires interviews, tests, and recommendations. On 428 acres, St. Stephen's has about 630 students, including 70 from 20 different countries. The on-campus observatory features the largest refracting telescope in Central Texas. St. Stephen's was established in 1950 and is affiliated with the National Association of Independent Schools and the Southern Association of Episcopal Schools.

TRINITY EPISCOPAL SCHOOL
3901 Bee Cave Rd.
(512) 472-9525
www.trinitykids.com
About 400 students from kindergarten through 8th grade attend this young, modern campus in the upscale Westlake Hills area. The school aims to provide an intellectually challenging and spiritually nurturing experience for its students, and combines an advanced core curriculum with visual and performing arts, foreign language, physical education, and technology classes. Among its innovative programs is the Think Tank, in which all students, including kindergarteners, spend time each week working on projects that develop creative and critical-thinking skills. A member of the Austin Inter-Parochial League, Trinity offers its students the opportunity to play competitive football, basketball, volleyball, and other sports. The school has a strong Episcopal identity, and all students attend chapel each day. Among the newest buildings on campus is the Trinity Center for Arts & Athletics, site of, among other activities, the school's annual Broadway-style musical. The school is accredited by the Southwestern Association of Episcopal Schools.

Northwest

AUSTIN INTERNATIONAL SCHOOL
12001 Oak Knoll Rd.
(512) 331-7806
www.austinape.org

Founded in 2001, the Austin International School aims to provide a quality French-American curriculum in a multicultural environment to students of all nationalities. Subjects are taught by native speakers in both French and English. Spanish also is taught at all grade levels. The French curriculum closely follows guidelines set by the French Ministry of National Education. The school offers classes to students age 3 through 5th grade. The school also offers a Summer Language Immersion Camp for children ages 3 to 12. The school is a local nonprofit association formed in response to demand by Austin's Francophone community.

AUSTIN JEWISH ACADEMY
7300 Hart Lane
(512) 735-8350
www.austinjewishacademy.org

The only Jewish school in the Central Texas area, the Austin Jewish Academy opened in fall 1997 and now provides a superior education to children from kindergarten through 8th grade. The students at the independent school are motivated, creative self-starters who can work within varying degrees of structure. A strong Jewish education is part of the school's curriculum, but the school does not embrace any particular arm of Judaism or require that students be Jewish. Students study Hebrew daily and also take classes in Jewish history, prayer, Bible, and the study of Israel. The school also offers a sound core curriculum that includes language arts, math, and science as well as social studies, Spanish, art, music, physical education, geography, and world cultures. Judaic and secular studies are highly integrated. Strong parental involvement is one of the academy's greatest attributes. The school, accredited through the Southern Association of Colleges, is located on the 40-acre campus of the Dell Jewish Community Center.

AUSTIN SCHOOL FOR THE PERFORMING AND VISUAL ARTS
5700 North Pace Bend Rd., Spicewood
(512) 773-3398
www.theaustinschool.org

With the opening of the Austin School for the Performing and Visual Arts (ASPVA) in the fall of 2007, the Central Texas area got its first private educational institution for students in 6th through 12th grades who want to emphasize their artistic studies in the areas of dance, music, voice, visual arts, and theater arts. The school, situated on a 450-acre campus on Lake Travis, about 35 miles northwest of downtown Austin, also provides a core curriculum in the language arts, history, math, sciences, geography, and, of course, the fine arts. Its curriculum is in line with Texas Assessment of Knowledge and Skills (TAKS) requirements, so students should be able to move from ASPVA into "regular" schools without missing a beat. An audition is required in the application process, and acceptance is based on "artistic promise," among other things. The school, which works collaboratively with Texas Tech University to provide an accredited curriculum, offers a full-day academic and fine arts curriculum as well as a half-day fine arts program.

HILL COUNTRY CHRISTIAN SCHOOL OF AUSTIN
12124 RR 620 North
(512) 331-7036
www.hccsa.org

Founded in 1996, Hill Country Christian School in North Austin provides a Christian and classical education to children from kindergarten through the 12th grade. The school's educational philosophy is linked to the belief that Jesus Christ is the true foundation of all knowledge and learning. The nondenominational school, affiliated with Hill Country Bible Church, is a college-preparatory institution that also features a Music Conservatory, offering classes in instruments and voice. Teachings from the Bible are integrated into the school's basic curriculum, which also includes language arts, math, science, history, art, and physical education. The Bible also is taught as a separate lesson or course, depending on the grade level. Students in the upper grades can participate in the school's extracurricular sports program. The school is accredited through the Association of Christian Schools International.

ST. THERESA'S CATHOLIC SCHOOL
4311 Small Dr.
(512) 451-7105
www.st-theresa.org
Four-year-olds through 8th graders attend this Catholic school in Northwest Austin. On the campus of St. Theresa's Catholic Church, the school offers a full, academically challenging curriculum designed to allow its 290 students to reach their full potential. St. Theresa's students score on average in the 90th percentile on national achievement tests. St. Theresa's also provides enrichment opportunities for each course of study. In addition to daily religion classes, lessons from the Bible are integrated throughout the basic core subjects. Specially trained instructors provide classes in library skills, physical education, and computer training. Students begin using computers in preschool, with a program that reinforces reading skills, and continue their technology training through middle school on the school's classroom computers and in two Internet-connected computer labs. St. Theresa's offers what it

calls "mastery learning," which couples a well-trained faculty with the use of advanced technology and delivery systems.

Southwest

AUSTIN MONTESSORI SCHOOL
5006 Sunset Trail
(512) 892-0253
www.austinmontessori.org
The Austin Montessori School, with 3 campuses around Austin, provides a Montessori education to students from 18 months to 15 years, depending on the location. The classic Montessori classroom design displays all learning materials on shelves and allows students to act on their own initiative in order to maximize independent learning and exploration. The Montessori approach is hands-on. Children work individually and in small groups and participate in whole-class activities. Teachers, known as guides, are trained to recognize a child's particular developmental stage and offer the appropriate learning materials in social studies, math, reading, writing, art, and music as the child becomes ready to use them. Ethics, social skills, and practical life are emphasized, as the school focuses on developing the whole child. The Austin Montessori School, first established in 1967, is considered a model for the Montessori approach, and has hosted teachers-in-training from all over the world. The school is accredited by Association Montessori Internationale. There is a waiting list.

AUSTIN WALDORF SCHOOL
8700 South View Rd.
(512) 288-5942
www.austinwaldorf.org
The Austin Waldorf School offers an educational program to nearly 400 students from kindergarten through the 12th grade on 19

acres in the Oak Hill area of Austin. Waldorf schools, also known worldwide as Steiner schools, are based on the educational philosophy of Dr. Rudolf Steiner, an educator, artist, and philosopher who devised a method of instruction based on the idea that children pass through distinct developmental stages. The program is designed to engage each child's innate creativity and builds on a strong academic foundation by integrating art, instrumental music, song, stories, and crafts into the daily curriculum. The independent school teaches according to the phases of child development, offering lessons at each stage that are designed to nurture a child's imagination. Mastery of the academic disciplines is of utmost importance at the Waldorf School, where students are introduced to all major fields of human endeavor through the study of mathematics, sciences, and language arts. Students are given the opportunity to explore all aspects of a subject matter and, with the guidance of their specially trained teacher, write and illustrate their own textbooks for each lesson.

CHILD CARE

For parents, few decisions arouse more angst than determining who will care for their preschool-age child while they're at work. As Austin grows, that concern intensifies as more and more parents compete for existing high-quality care. Area child care referral agencies insist that excellent care can be found, especially since more emphasis is placed these days on professional care, as opposed to just babysitting. Finding high-quality child care for infants seems to be the most difficult, according to the referral agencies. In fact, they say that people who are even thinking about having a child need to get on waiting lists at accredited child care

i Austin's trailblazing Institute for Child Care Excellence, has provided top-tier training, scholarships, and other assistance to hundreds of child care providers and managers, with the goal of increasing the quality and quantity of trained child care professionals in the Central Texas area. The Institute got its start with funding from the Michael & Susan Dell Family Foundation.

centers. Parents often do not plan ahead for infant care, believing that because infants sleep so often, care shouldn't be difficult to find or cost too much. However, because state regulations require a higher ratio of providers to infants in licensed facilities than any other age group—4 to 1—it's often not profitable for a center to provide care for the very young, so they don't.

Finding care for toddlers is not as difficult, although in the fastest growing areas, especially in North Austin, Round Rock, and Cedar Park, the challenge to locate high-quality care increases. Child care in downtown Austin, with its high concentration of state office workers, also seems to be increasingly limited. Although after-school programs are offered at most schools in the capital area's 10 school districts and at many private schools, waiting lists can be long, so it's important to register early.

Another option is to have a child picked up by an after-school-care provider. Again, it's important to plan ahead, as these also tend to fill up in some areas.

Choosing a day care provider gets somewhat easier for parents once they know what to look for in a facility. The Texas Department of Protective and Regulatory Services (PRS), which oversees day care providers, lists 3 categories of service: licensed, registered, and listed. The agency's website, www.tdprs .state.tx.us, also offers histories of violations at facilities in Texas. Facilities that care for 13 or more children are considered day care centers and must be licensed by the state. Registered facilities are home care centers that accept 4 to 12 children. The standards vary somewhat for these two categories, although they both are subject to unannounced inspections by the PRS. In 1997 the Texas Legislature created the last category: listed. According to the regulations, persons who care for 1 to 3 children in their home must be listed by PRS and are subject to the same records investigations as other providers. These homes, however, are not inspected unless there is a report of child abuse or neglect.

Finding reliable and affordable child care, for regular daily care, occasional drop-in care, or in-home sitters, can be one of the first tasks a family faces on arrival in Austin. Some neighborhood associations provide residents with lists of babysitters in their areas, while parents in other areas have formed babysitting co-ops, in which parents take turns at sitting responsibilities. Be sure to check with your neighborhood association for information.

Several referral agencies around town can help by offering experienced guidance in the child care search and by providing parents with lists of providers from their databases. Following are some of the sitter services and referral agencies for child care that can help get you off to a good start.

KID SPACE
13376 Research Blvd.
(512) 918-2562
www.kidspacetexas.com

This center in the Galleria Oaks shopping center in Northwest Austin (and its other facility at 1401 South I-35, Round Rock, 512-244-7774) accept children ages 1 to 12 for drop-in child care. Kid Space offers plenty of entertainment for children of all ages. They are open daily at 8:30 a.m. and offer service until 12:30 a.m. on Fri and Sat nights. Only the Round Rock location is open on Sun. It's a good idea to make a reservation as the centers have a legal limit on the number of children they can serve, but that can usually be done the day the service is required. Also call to find out about immunization requirements.

MOM'S BEST FRIEND
1101 Capital of Texas Hwy. South,
Building H, Suite 200
(512) 346-2229
www.momsbestfriend.com

This popular business for the busy parent provides both sitters and nannies. Mom's Best Friend (MBF) can arrange for sitters to come to your home, hotel, or even your office for the amount of time you need. References and previous employers have been checked for all sitters, and a criminal background check has been conducted on all nannies. Clients looking for a certain age group in a sitter can, with enough advance notice, make a special request from among the staff, which ranges in age from mid-20s to mid-60s. MBF also has specialists who care for newborns, preemies, and babies with special needs. Separate housekeeping and household staffing services can also be arranged.

STEPPING STONE SCHOOLS
17 locations around Central Texas
1910 Justin Lane
(512) 459-0258
www.steppingstoneschool.com

Consistently voted "Best Child Care" by readers of *Austin Family* magazine, the Stepping Stone School offers early-childhood education and an "enhancement" program for school-age kids. The schools offer a progressive curriculum and accept children from 6 weeks to 11 years. The locally owned business has been growing in Austin since 1979. Check the website or call the administrative office, listed above, for a location near your home or work.

WORKFORCE SOLUTIONS
6505 Airport Blvd., Suite 101-C
(512) 597-7191
www.wfscapitalarea.com
A private, publicly funded nonprofit organization, Workforce Solutions provides child care subsidies for eligible families in Travis County, in addition to its many other efforts on behalf of the Austin workforce. It also trains child care providers and allows area providers to join a 300-strong network of providers who receive referrals from the program. The website contains a link to the organization's child care services.

HOMESCHOOLING

Homeschools might as well have been called "underground schools" back in the 1970s and early 1980s because so many parents who chose to educate their own children guarded their secret as if they'd committed a crime. Indeed, many were prosecuted for failing to comply with compulsory attendance laws. A lot has changed. Today homeschooling is not only legal in all 50 states but the governor of Texas also recognized the value of homeschooling by proclaiming a Home Education Week. In Austin parents can attend an annual book

fair and convention for homeschoolers. The watershed occurred in 1987 when parents won a class-action suit against the state, which stripped the Texas Education Agency of its authority over homeschools. The Texas Supreme Court upheld the decision in 1994. Now attitudes toward homeschools in Texas are among the most liberal in the country. Here the state asks only that parents pursue a course of study that includes math, reading, spelling, grammar, and a course in good citizenship. The curriculum, however, does not have to be filed with any government agency. An educational approach that was once largely the domain of Christian fundamentalists has spread to families of all kinds, and for many reasons. Certainly, many parents want to emphasize their children's religious education. Some choose to homeschool because they fear their children will be exposed to violence or the wrong influences in traditional schools. Others opt for homeschooling to give their children more flexibility to pursue outside interests. Many aim to ensure that their children achieve academic excellence.

The Texas Home School Coalition, based in Lubbock, is a nonprofit organization that supports parents in their efforts to educate their children at home. The organization operates a database of homeschool support groups around the state, where parents can go to get information about available curriculums for homeschools or about anything else they wish to know about educating their own children. Since 2001 the coalition has sponsored an annual state convention and family conference for homeschool families. For further information on homeschooling, contact the coalition at P.O. Box 6747, Lubbock, TX 79493, (806) 744-4441, www.thsc.org.

MEDIA

Austin's long and rich media history goes as far back as the Capitol City itself. The *Austin City Gazette*, a 4-page weekly, made its debut on October 30, 1839, the same year that Austin became the capital of the Republic of Texas. Published by Samuel Whiting, a journalist from Houston, the *City Gazette* carried local, national, and foreign news; letters to the editor; editorials; and an occasional work of fiction. By the time the *City Gazette* folded in 1842 (some say due to the threat of invasion from Mexico), the frontier town of Austin had other publications to take its place. Austinites, it seemed, were eager for news, although getting it to this remote outpost was never easy—and definitely not quick. During the Civil War, one local publisher debuted his one-page bulletin, the *Texas Almanac Extra*, which he rushed into print 3 times a week after waiting for Pony Express riders to hustle in with the latest editions of the Houston and Galveston newspapers.

Decades later, during the Depression of the 1930s, the dean of American television journalism, Walter Cronkite, got his start in Austin. "My first appearance before a microphone was during the college years at Austin," he writes in his book, *A Reporter's Life*. Cronkite admits that his daily sports report on Austin radio station KNOW consisted of scores he memorized from a Western Union sports ticker at a Sixth Street tobacco shop while pretending to read the newspaper. "Once out of sight of the smoke shop, I ran at breakneck speed back to the studio and typed out my daily sports intelligence before it fled my memory," Cronkite said. He then moved on to work in print journalism in Austin, covering Texas politics. "It was a vast and diverse state, and the fight for dominance and privilege in Austin was never ending," wrote Cronkite.

The Austin media landscape has changed a mite since Cronkite's days here. Today's residents are bombarded with choices over what publications to read, where to land on the radio dial for programming that serves their needs, and which television news program to select. Austin also has about as eclectic a selection of local social media websites and online periodicals as one is likely to find in any city this size. Without a doubt, one of the pleasures of living in Austin, one of the qualities that define this city, is the abundance and diversity of reading material out there. It's not all award-winning stuff, but much of it is—and some of it deserves to be.

PRINT MEDIA

The list you'll find below represents a cross section of publications that make up the bedrock of the Austin print media. If your special interests lie elsewhere—in theater, business, technology, religion, public radio, or politics—take a look around; you're likely to find some publication that speaks to you. While these publications continue to print and distribute physical copies, most have Internet versions to varying degrees as well. Some require a subscription in order to access the entire online publication.

Newspapers

AUSTIN AMERICAN-STATESMAN
305 South Congress Ave.
(512) 445-3500
www.statesman.com
As Austin's only daily newspaper, the *Austin American-Statesman* is in the unenviable position of trying to satisfy all the news demands of a complex society. Although it hasn't always succeeded, the paper has to be commended for its constant efforts to find a formula—both in print and online—that works.

One big change is the *Statesman's* weekly entertainment section. Formerly called XLent, the print section and its online version are now Austin360 (www.Austin360 .com). This product, which appears Thurs, is designed to capture young-at-heart readers who want a viewpoint besides the *Chronicle's* (see listing below) for arts and entertainment news, reviews, and features. The *Statesman* also is working to expand readership of what it calls "niche products," including its online Spanish-language publication *Ahora Si* and its smaller regional publications such as the *Cedar Park Citizen* and others.

The *Statesman's* main section features the top stories of the day, editorials, letters to the editor, and international news. Other sections include Metro & State, Sports, and Life & Style. As with most online publications these days, the blogosphere is alive and well at the *Statesman*, so you'll find a wide assortment of blogs by the paper's reporters, columnists, and other staff, including the popular humor columnist John Kelso. The *Statesman* focuses on coverage of Austin and Central Texas, including local and state government, politics, business, breaking news, art and leisure, and, of course, UT and high school sports.

Amid declining revenues for print newspapers across the country, *Statesman* owner Cox Enterprises shocked the media world in 2008 when it announced a plan to sell the paper, even though it turned a profit. Cox took the *Statesman* off the market a year later, reportedly because no one would meet the asking price. However, the industry in general, along with the *Statesman*, continues to face the double whammy of the economic recession and the era of New Media. In 2009 Managing Editor Debbie Hoitt published a column titled, "Survival of the Newspaper? We're Working on it."

AUSTIN BUSINESS JOURNAL
111 Congress Ave., Suite 750
(512) 494-2500
www.austin.bizjournals.com
Published on Fri—although the online edition is updated continuously—the *Austin Business Journal* is the only newspaper in the area dedicated to business news and information. Founded locally in 1980, the tabloid-format newspaper covers developments affecting the growth of the region and monitors the progress of new businesses coming to the area. For example, it created a link on its website to all its coverage of efforts to open a $180 million Formula One racetrack in the area by 2012. The *Business Journal* also promotes networking by publishing a listing of weekly events and meetings of interest to the business community.

Of special interest to many business-people and newcomers are the *Journal's* annual guides and directories, most notably the *Book of Lists*. This massive volume, issued in Dec, provides information on more than 1,500 companies of interest to the business community. The print version of the *Business Journal* is available for delivery or it can be purchased at newsstands around the area.

AUSTIN CHRONICLE
4000 North I-35
(512) 454-5766
www.austinchronicle.com
It's hard to plan an evening out on the town without first picking up a copy of the *Austin Chronicle*. The *Chronicle* stresses coverage of music, entertainment, and the arts but also provides a vital alternative voice on local political and environmental issues. The *Chronicle*, a big, fat, free publication distributed Thurs around the greater Austin area—and also readily available online—was founded by six local entrepreneurs, several of whom had worked on UT's student newspaper, the *Daily Texan*. Celebrating its 30th anniversary in 2011, the newspaper began treating readers to blasts from the past a full year in advance, publishing vintage ads as well as online versions of earlier editions—including Vol 1, No. 1 from September 4, 1981.

Although at times a little rough around the edges, the *Chronicle* easily disappears from newsstands within a couple of days of publication. Editor Louis Black, one of the original godfathers (as the founders like to call themselves), and his staff are a dynamic voice on the issue of long-range city planning.

But let's not forget the *Chronicle*'s main focus: Entertainment, with a capital E! Movie reviews, book reviews, record reviews, features on the fascinating figures that keep Austin interesting, art, theater and film listings, cartoons, and some insightful columns (blogs) on everything from architecture to zydeco cram this 100-page-plus periodical. Of course the *Chronicle* knows the Austin club scene. You get the feeling that these writers don't just cover their beats, they live them.

i The much-anticipated results in Sept of the *Austin Chronicle*'s "Best of Austin" Readers' Poll and Critics Picks highlight the best the city has to offer in dozens of categories, including arts and entertainment, dining, shopping, politics, high-tech, and so much more. *Chronicle* readers also chose winners for the Austin Music Awards, which honor the best of the best in ceremonies held in March.

DAILY TEXAN
(512) 471-4591
www.dailytexanonline.com
This award-winning student newspaper of the University of Texas is published Mon through Fri when school is in session. It covers mainly campus news, but when the university is one of the largest in the nation, that's a big job. *The Daily Texan* is among the most recognized student newspapers in the country, and many of its graduates have gone on to win Pulitzer prizes with professional publications. *The Daily Texan* also provides some interesting local, state, and national news. Copies are distributed free in bright orange boxes on campus and at various locations around the downtown area.

Magazines

AUSTIN FAMILY
P.O. Box 7559, Austin 78683
(512) 733-0038
www.austinfamily.com
This free magazine, published monthly and available at about 500 distribution points

throughout the greater Austin area, is an excellent resource for parents looking for news and information about summer camps, child care, schools, family-friendly events, and much more.

AUSTIN MONTHLY
11612 Bee Caves Rd., Suite 2-125
(512) 263-9133
www.austinmonthly.com
Started as a free publication in 1992 and dedicated to the positive aspects of city life, *Austin Monthly* has gone decidedly upscale. Now a slick full-color magazine, it is sold by subscription and at local newsstands around the region. Yet it remains true to its origins. Good features on the region's interesting characters and on the events that make Austin such a happening city are combined with pictorial spreads, restaurant reviews, an events calendar, and much more.

AUSTIN WOMAN
1213 West Forty-ninth St.
(512) 328-2421
www.austinwomanmagazine.com
This well-established free magazine celebrates all things female—and we don't mean with the confusing mix of cookie recipes and diet plans that seem to dominate many national women's magazines. Excellent profiles of the women who are leading Austin in business, politics, the arts, environmental, and social activism, and more appear in each monthly issue. In addition, the periodical covers topics of interest to both sexes. AW, available at about 800 locations throughout the Central Texas area, is honest journalism.

TEXAS HIGHWAYS
150 East Riverside Dr.
(512) 486-5858, (800) 839-4997
www.texashighways.com

Stunning color photographs and in-depth articles that celebrate the glory of Texas abound in this monthly magazine, published in Austin by the Texas Department of Transportation. This is the official travel magazine of Texas and provides current and accurate information on travel destinations throughout the state. It is a beautiful publication. *Texas Highways* started as an in-house publication of the Department of Transportation but has been exclusively a travel magazine since May 1974. The magazine clearly stresses protection of the environment and of the state's cultural heritage and has won awards from such organizations as the San Antonio Conservation Society, the Texas Historical Commission, and the International Regional Magazines Association.

TEXAS HILL COUNTRY MAGAZINE
714 Fourth St., Suite 102, Blanco, Texas 78606
(830) 833-0429
www.hillcountrymagazine.com
The more Austin expands, the more the interest grows in seeking Hill Country escapes. This magazine, published quarterly, is an excellent guide to all things Hill Country, from features about the colorful people, places and things that make the Hill Country so unique, to information about upcoming events. The advertisements also are worth a look, as they tout local restaurants, shops, resorts, lodgings and other businesses that might appeal to visitors—or those thinking of moving to the area.

TEXAS MONTHLY
701 Brazos St.
(512) 320-6900
www.texasmonthly.com
Winner of numerous National Magazine Awards, *Texas Monthly* is the state's showcase

magazine. And it's published in Austin. This full-color glossy magazine offers lengthy news and feature articles and spicy true-crime stories of interest to its affluent, well-educated readers. It also provides frequently updated reviews of selected restaurants in Texas's major cities. Its regular column "Around the State" is a city-by-city guide to choice entertainment. The annual Bum Steer Awards, published in the Jan issue, take an irreverent look at the people and situations in Texas that the editors believe have been particularly weird or foolish over the past year; it's perennially one of the magazine's best-selling issues. The Best and Worst Legislators is another popular cover feature that comes out every other July (as the Texas Legislature meets biennially). Look also for the annual Top Twenty issue, which lists the magazine's choice of the 20 most influential Texans of the year. Publisher Mike Levy, who started the magazine when he was 26 years old, has found a formula that satisfies the majority of *Texas Monthly*'s readers.

TEXAS MUSIC
P.O. Box 50273, Austin 78763
(512) 638-8900
www.txmusic.com
This juicy, well-designed quarterly, available by subscription and at newsstands, gets high marks for covering the Texas music scene. Insightful articles about contemporary bands and songwriters around the state combine with some interesting features on the state's long and varied history of music and music makers. Reviews of current CD releases and colorful photographs flesh out this glossy publication. There's also a great calendar of music-related events around Texas.

TEXAS OBSERVER
307 West Seventh St.
(512) 477-0746
www.texasobserver.org
Former *Daily Texan* writer Ronnie Dugger debuted the *Texas Observer* in 1954. Within 6 months the *Observer* established itself as a new voice in Texas media, becoming the first to report on lynchings in East Texas. For half a century this small biweekly magazine has struggled for survival while breaking the silence on story after story dealing with society's underdogs, the liberal movement, and Democratic causes. Dugger, who owned the paper until turning it over to the nonprofit Texas Democracy Foundation in 1994, called his magazine *A Journal of Free Voices,* and wrote in the *Observer's* mission statement, "never will we overlook or misrepresent the truth to serve the interests of the powerful." Today the small Austin staff that runs the magazine and the freelance writers from around the state who contribute articles continue to bring to light liberal/progressive issues not treated in the mainstream media.

TEXAS PARKS & WILDLIFE
4200 Smith School Rd., Building D
(800) 937-9393
www.tpwmagazine.com
This visually enticing, well-written monthly highlights Texas's great outdoors. Published since 1942 by the Texas Parks and Wildlife Department in Austin and distributed all over the state, *Texas Parks & Wildlife* is a great source of information for newcomers and residents alike who love the open air.

In & Around Austin

CEDAR PARK CITIZEN
305 South Bell Blvd., Cedar Park
(512) 267-4449
www.cedarparkcitizen.com
One of the newer area publications in the Cox Newspapers lineup, the *Citizen* was established in 2008 to serve readers in the Cedar Park area north of Austin. A weekly paper distributed free in the area, it's published on Thurs. The *Citizen* focuses on city government, local business, leisure, the Leander school district, and sports. With two top minor league teams—basketball's Austin Toros and hockey's Texas Stars—now playing at the new Cedar Park Center, the paper covers much more than just school sports.

HILL COUNTRY NEWS
103 Woods Lane, Cedar Park
(512) 259-4449
Published on Wed and Fri, *Hill Country News* focuses on community news, business, and features in Cedar Park and northwest Austin. On Wed *Hill Country News* is a free publication available in Cedar Park. Also published on Wed, *Hill Country News Northwest* is aimed at the Northwest Austin area.

LAKE TRAVIS VIEW
2300 Lohmans Spur, Suite 186
(512) 263-1100
www.laketravisview.com
Even if you don't live in the Lake Travis area, don't miss the *View* in Apr when it publishes the annual "Lake Travis Summer Guide," a special section that details fun things to do at the lake, including camping, recreational activities, and dining. The rest of the year, the *View* focuses on local government, the Lake Travis Independent School District,

and on community news along Lake Travis's sprawling south shore.

OAK HILL GAZETTE
7200 US 71 West
(512) 301-0123
www.oakhillgazette.com
Residents of the Oak Hill region in south Austin have a wonderful local newspaper that covers just about everything there is to know in their growing neighborhood. News and sports from the local schools; columns from the district's county, state, and federal government leaders; a column aimed at senior citizens and another on lifestyle combine, of course, with area news and business coverage to make a fine neighborhood publication. Published by the Oak Hill husband-and-wife team of Will Atkins and Penny Levers, the *Gazette* has been in business since 1995. It's published on Fri and is available by subscription or at newsstands in the area.

PFLUGERVILLE PFLAG
200 West Main St., Pflugerville
(512) 251-2220
Pfinding the *Pflag* isn't too hard in Pflugerville, the pfine community with the pfunny name. The *Pflag, another Cox publication,* is Pflugerville's pflourishing weekly newspaper. Published Thurs, it includes features of interest to local readers as well as community and business news about the town and the surrounding areas of Travis and Williamson Counties.

ROUND ROCK LEADER
105 South Blair St., Round Rock
(512) 255-5827
www.rrleader.com

Established in 1877, just a few years after the city of Round Rock itself was formed, the *Leader* has grown significantly from the 4-page, hand-set publication of the early days. The paper emphasizes community and school news, covers local and Williamson County politics, and also keeps readers informed of the city's meteoric growth.

WEST AUSTIN NEWS
5407 Parkcrest Dr.
(512) 459-5474
www.westaustinnews.com
Serving the neighborhoods of West Austin, Northwest Austin, Rollingwood, and West Lake Hills, *West Austin News* focuses on community, society, and school news. The weekly newspaper, published on Thurs, was started by local owner and publisher Bart Stephens in 1986. The paper publishes an annual sports guide in the fall and a shopping guide at Christmastime as well as biannual sections on Healthy Living and Home and Garden. In an effort to "Keep Austin Weird" (see the History chapter), newsroom execs say, the *News* sponsors an annual Art Car Parade in Apr. Artists from all over Texas decorate their cars and show them off during the parade. The Art Car Ball precedes the event.

WESTLAKE PICAYUNE
3103 Bee Caves Rd.
(512) 327-2990
www.westlakepicayune.com
Serving the Westbank area just west of downtown Austin, the weekly *Picayune* covers community and local government news and the Eanes Independent School District as well as local arts and entertainment. Founded in 1976, the newspaper focuses on the cities of Rollingwood and West Lake

Hill, and also serves readers in surrounding communities. The *Picayune* is one of several area weeklies owned by Cox Enterprises, Inc., the Atlanta-based company that owns the *Austin American-Statesman*.

Ethnic Publications

AHORA SI!
305 South Congress Ave.
(512) 445-3822
www.ahorasi.com
This online Spanish-language (with some English) periodical is one of the *Austin American-Statesman*'s niche products targeting specific audiences in the area, and it's published at the Statesman's headquarters on South Congress. The well-received *Ahora Si* makes liberal use of the Associated Press's Spanish-language newswire for state and world news, but also publishes many staff-written stories and Spanish translations of Statesman articles of interest to the Hispanic community in and around Austin. The coverage is comprehensive and in addition to news includes arts and entertainment, immigration issues, sports, business and finance, life and style, and a variety of staffers' blogs.

ARRIBA ART & BUSINESS NEWS
1009 East Cesar Chavez St.
(512) 479-6397
Austin's oldest newspaper for the Mexican-American community, *Arriba* was founded in 1980. This 8- to 12-page tabloid, distributed free biweekly, is written in English and Spanish, highlights community and business news, and goes to great lengths to cover the Hispanic cultural scene. In addition to regular features on Hispanic artists, it publishes listings of gallery shows, museum exhibitions, and other events of interest to the community.

EL MUNDO
2112 East Cesar Chavez St.
(512) 476-8636
www.elmundonewspaper.com
A well-established weekly publication for the area's Spanish-speaking population, *El Mundo* includes local, national, and international news and features, as well as sports and entertainment of interest to the Hispanic community. Locally owned and operated, the newspaper is a strong advocate for area Hispanics and does not shy away from taking issue with the mainstream press over its coverage of the community. The paper is published Thurs and is sold in area newsstands.

EL NORTE
1823 Fort View Rd.
(512) 448-1023
This Spanish-language monthly newspaper provides information relevant to Austin's Hispanic population, including changes in US immigration policy, news on Hispanic and community leaders, community support organizations, and activities within the area's Catholic churches. The newspaper is distributed throughout the Austin area. Journalist Gloria Montelongo Aguilar and her husband, Miguel, started *El Norte* in 1996 in the back room of their home with two used computers and a printer bought at a pawn shop.

NOKOA THE OBSERVER
P.O. Box 1141, Austin 78767
(512) 215-8447
www.nokoanewspaper.com
Working out of his home, publisher, poet, and political activist Akwasi Evans debuted *NOKOA* in 1987 with the goal of creating a newspaper that reflected the interests and views of progressive political activists of all ethnicities. For more than two decades, the free weekly paper has championed the rights of African Americans, Hispanics, Anglos, Asians, Native Americans, women, gays, lesbians, and the disabled communities. Evans calls the publication "a true progressive paper with an unabashed African-American perspective." The paper, published Thurs, covers Austin city government and the Texas Legislature when it is in session, as well as local, regional, national, and international news. The website contains the weekly edition.

VILLAGER NEWSPAPER
1223-A Rosewood Ave.
(512) 476-0082
www.theaustinvillager.com
This free weekly newspaper focuses on news of interest to Austin's African-American community. Owner T. L. Wyatt has been publishing the *Villager* since 1973 as a voice of advocacy with a focus on the positive events in the African-American community. Wyatt calls the *Villager* "the good news newspaper." The paper prints articles not often found in the mainstream press and analyzes news and events that pertain to its readers. Wyatt's weekly editorial column, "Rappin," appears on the front page. Newspapers are available on Fri at distribution points in East, South, and Central Austin. The *Villager* is one of the few family-run newspapers around Austin to have upgraded to a successful electronic version.

Yearly Guides

AUSTIN RELOCATION GUIDE
210 Barton Springs Rd.
(512) 478-9383
www.austin-chamber.org
Published by the Greater Austin Chamber of Commerce, this annual guide provides information on housing, attractions, newcomer information, business, shopping and dining, arts and culture, retirement living, and other areas of interest to the recently arrived. It's sold online or at the chamber offices.

TEXAS STATE TRAVEL GUIDE
150 East Riverside Dr.
(800) 888-8-TEX
www.traveltex.com
Published in Austin by the Texas Department of Transportation's Travel and Information Division, this hefty guide of nearly 300 pages features highlights of tourist attractions throughout the state. Seven special sections summarize attractions around Texas's major cities, including Austin and the Central Texas area. Among the guide's many attributes are listings and descriptions of nearly 150 Texas lakes. The guide also lists national and state forests as well as state parks. The publication is free and can be requested at the toll-free number above or ordered online. It can also be found at the Capitol Information Center on the grounds of the State Capitol. The guide's online version has even more features, allowing you to map out and share a Texas travel itinerary.

TELEVISION

Austin's television industry provides a strong and vital link among residents of Central Texas. Live local news broadcasts relay information and flash the latest images of events and newsmakers around the Texas heartland and the world beyond. In times of tragedy and triumph, no other news medium rivals the awesome power of live television. None but television allows the faces and the voices of the participants themselves to illustrate the immediate events as a story unfolds.

i The *Statesman* has teamed up with Austin's highly praised, location-based social media startup Gowalla. Among the benefits for tourists and newcomers is a series of tours around town, such as the "Austin Margarita Tour," with locations to visit. To get started, you just friend Austin360 on Gowalla (http://gowalla.com).

Local Stations

KTBC, Fox, channel 7 (Time Warner cable (TW) 2)
KVUE, ABC, channel 24 (TW 3)
KXAN, NBC, channel 36 (TW 4)
KEYE, CBS, channel 42 (TW 5)
KNVA, CW affiliated, channel 54 (TW 12)
KLRU, PBS, channel 18 and 20 (TW 9 and 20)
KAKW, Univision, channel 62 (TW 13)
Time Warner's News 8 Austin (TW 8)

Cable/Satellite Providers

Time Warner Cable, (512) 485-5555, (800) 418-8848
Grande Communications, (512) 220-4600
DirecTV, (888) 777-2454
AT&T, (800) 288-2020

RADIO

Alternative
KROX 101.5 FM (Rock)

Christian/Gospel
KFIT 1060 AM (Gospel)
KNLE 88.1 FM (Contemporary)
KLGO 98.5 FM/WORD 99.3 FM (Talk)
KQJZ 92.1 FM ("Positive" music)
Spirit 105.9 FM (Contemporary)

College Radio
KTSW 89.9 FM (Alternative)
KVRX 91.7 FM (Eclectic; 7 p.m. to 9 a.m. weekdays, 10 p.m. to 9 a.m. weekends)

Community
KOOP 91.7 (Community operated, eclectic; 9 a.m. to 7 p.m. weekdays, 9 a.m. to 10 p.m. weekends)

Contemporary Hits
KAMX (Mix-947) 94.7 FM (Rock, alternative)
KGSR 93.3.1 FM (Local bands, blues, jazz, folk, reggae, rock, interviews, live studio performances)
KHFI (Kiss) 96.7 FM (Top 40)
KBPA (Bob) 103.5 FM (Eclectic, pop)

Country
KASE 100.7 FM (Country)
KVET 98.1 FM (Country, Texas music)
US-105 105.5 FM (Country)

News/Sports/Talk
ESPN Austin 104.9 FM and 1530 AM (Sports, Dallas Cowboys)
KLBJ 590 AM (Talk, news, good local news)
KVET 1300 AM (24-hour sports, UT sports)
KXBT 98.9 FM (News, talk)

Public Radio/Listener Supported
KUT 90.5 FM (Eclectic, local bands, NPR)
KMFA 89.5 FM (Classical)

Rock 'n' Roll/Oldies
KXXS 92.5 FM (Oldies)
KKMJ 95.5 FM (Soft rock)
KLBJ 93.7 FM (Rock 'n' roll)

Spanish/Tejano
KLQB 104.3 FM (Mexican ranchero)
KWNX 1260 AM (ESPN sports, talk in Spanish)
KTXZ 1560 AM (Tejano, salsa, merengue, Spanish rock)

Urban/Rhythmic/Jazz
KPEZ 102.3 FM (R&B, hip-hop)
KAZI 88.7 (R&B, hip-hop, jazz, reggae, blues)

INDEX

A

accommodations, 44
Ace Mart Restaurant
    Supply Co., 157
Adams House, 61
Adult Protective Services,
    Adult Abuse and
    Financial Exploitation
    Hot Line, 377
Ahora Si!, 427
AIDS services, 390
AIDS Services of
    Austin, 390
air charters, 37
airports, 35
Alamo Draft House Lake
    Creek, 124
Alamo Draft House
    South, 124
Alamo Draft House
    Village, 124
AlamoRITZ, 124
Allen's Boots, 154
Aloft Austin at the
    Domain, 58
alternative medicine, 394
Alzheimer's
    Association, 377
Amelia Bullock Relocation
    Services, 376
American Association
    of Retired Persons
    (AARP), 376
American Red Cross,
    319, 385
Amtrak, 37
Anderson Coffee
    Company, 157
Andiamo, 101

Anna's Toy Depot, 175
Annual Austin Rugby
    Tournament, 226
Annual Bluebonnet
    Festival, 226
annual events, 224
Annual Shakespeare
    Festival, 227
antiques, 146
Antone's, 133
Antone's Record Shop, 142
apartments, 373
Apple Bar, 106
Aquarelle Restaurant
    Français, 70
Aquarena Center, 210
Arboretum, 146
Arc of the Capital Area, 391
Area Agency on Aging of
    the Capital Area, 376
Arkansas Bend, 287
Arkie's Grill, 101
Armadillo Christmas
    Bazaar, 239
Armadillo RV, 305
Armadillo Sport, 175
Armstrong, Lance, 336
*Arriba Art & Business
    News*, 427
Art City Austin, 227
art galleries, 264
Arthouse at the Jones
    Center, 259
Art in Public Places, 267
art museums, 259
Art on 5th, 264
arts, 243
arts & crafts, 149
arts organizations, 267

Artz Rib House, 86
Asahi Imports, 162
Aspire Adventures, 312
Asti Trattoria, 70
Atlantic Aviation Services,
    Inc., 36
Atomic Cafe, 121
Atomic City, 167
attractions, 177
Aussie's Bar and Grill, 315
Aussie's Volleybar and
    Grill, 110
Austin Acoustical cafe, 133
*Austin American-
    Statesman*, 422
Austin Aqua Fun, 317
Austin Aquatics Office, 320
Austin Astronomical
    Society Tours, 204
Austin-Bergstrom
    International Airport, 35
Austin Books, 274
Austin Business Journal, 422
Austin Cab, 40
Austin Canoe & Kayak, 317
Austin, capital, 16
Austin Carriage, 206
Austin Carriage Tour, 42
Austin Celtic Festival, 238
Austin Chamber Music
    Festival, 233
Austin Child Guidance
    Center, 392
Austin Children's
    Museum, 210
Austin Chronicle, 423
Austin Chronicle Hot Sauce
    Festival, 234
Austin City Academy, 414